User-Centric Cybersecurity Implications for Sustainable Digital Transformation

Saqib Saeed
Imam Abdulrahman Bin Faisal University, Saudi Arabia

Shahzaib Tahir
National University of Sciences and Technology, Pakistan

IGI Global
Scientific Publishing
Publishing Tomorrow's Research Today

Published in the United States of America by
IGI Global Scientific Publishing
701 East Chocolate Avenue
Hershey, PA, 17033, USA
Tel: 717-533-8845
Fax: 717-533-7115
Website: https://www.igi-global.com E-mail: cust@igi-global.com

Library of Congress Cataloging-in-Publication Data

Names: Saeed, Saqib, 1980- editor | Tahir, Shahzaib, 1991- editor
Title: User-centric cybersecurity implications for sustainable digital transformation / edited by Saqib Saeed, Shahzaib Tahir.
Description: Hershey, PA : IGI Global Scientific Publishing, [2026] | Includes bibliographical references and index. | Summary: "User and organizational cybersecurity risks play a crucial role in shaping the success and sustainability of digital transformation initiatives. By addressing cybersecurity concerns effectively, organizations can build trust, enhance data protection, and mitigate risks associated with digital transformation initiatives, thereby maximizing the benefits of these digital initiatives. Additionally, digital transformation often involves the adoption of new technologies and processes, including cloud computing, Internet of Things (IoT), and big data analytics, which have additional technical cybersecurity risks. Such concerns about cybersecurity risks can undermine trust in these technologies. Users may be hesitant to embrace digital transformation initiatives if they perceive them as risky. Similarly, organizations may be reluctant to fully commit to digital transformation if they fear the potential consequences of cyber-attacks. Therefore, it is very important that user, organizational and technological risks are appropriately dealt to adopt sustainable digital transformation. Effective digital transformation requires a proactive approach to cybersecurity that integrates security considerations into every stage of the transformation process, from planning and design to implementation and maintenance. Organizations must prioritize cybersecurity by implementing robust security controls, conducting regular risk assessments, and fostering a culture of security awareness among employees. This book aims to strengthen the body of knowledge by providing case studies and concepts related to user, organizational and technical implications to achieve sustainable digital transformation"-- Provided by publisher.
Identifiers: LCCN 2025013681 (print) | LCCN 2025013682 (ebook) | ISBN 9798337331713 h/c | ISBN 9798337331720 s/c | ISBN 9798337331737 ebook
Subjects: LCSH: Technological innovations--Social aspects | Computer security--Technological innovations | Data privacy--Social aspects | Computer networks--Security measures
Classification: LCC T173.2 .U74 2026 (print) | LCC T173.2 (ebook)
LC record available at https://lccn.loc.gov/2025013681
LC ebook record available at https://lccn.loc.gov/2025013682

British Cataloguing in Publication Data
A Cataloguing in Publication record for this book is available from the British Library.

Table of Contents

Detailed Table of Contents

As users adopt new technologies that offer greater convenience, the incidence of cyber-attacks has been increasing dramatically, resulting in losses for the government on all fronts. This literature review highlights the significance of being aware of both well-known vulnerabilities and new cyber threats to ensure that the computer systems used by the government are safe from hackers and other malicious actors who may try to steal or harm sensitive information. The research community has made significant efforts in this area, but there is still a need for further progress. Our work provides insights into how to protect important electronic government from cyber-attacks in the era of digital transformation within a robust cybersecurity framework. The proposed framework for secure e-government adoption can be used to assess the cybersecurity readiness of government sectors undergoing digital transformation. By evaluating key components, we can ensure that security measures are effective and continuously improved.

While geographical boundaries are not recognized on the Internet, network service providers are driven through internet protocols. The revelations by whistleblowers have shaken the world of a free Internet and have raised concerns about data security. Recent developments in Russian Internet (RUnet) and the Great Firewall of China (GFW) advocate Internet sovereignty as a means to protect sensitive information from foreign surveillance. This paper critically surveys the approaches adopted by nations, evaluates the enacted legislation, and categorizes their actions within the theoretical framework proposed by Mueller, known as the Mueller framework The impact of these actions has also been analyzed along with an overview of cybersecurity measures taken by a few other countries. In this study, we present a conceptual framework aimed at elucidating the implementation of internet control measures, emphasizing the accomplishments and challenges encountered by modern nations in this endeavor.

Information Security Awareness (ISA) is a crucial component in strengthening cybersecurity resilience at both individual and organizational levels. As cyber threats continue to evolve, a lack of security awareness among users remains a significant risk factor, often leading to security breaches, data leaks, and financial losses. We will explores the role of ISA in fostering a security-conscious culture, highlighting effective training programs, awareness campaigns, and behavior-driven security strategies. It examines psychological and cognitive factors influencing security behavior, emphasizing the importance of continuous education and engagement. By integrating ISA into cybersecurity policies and digital transformation initiatives, organizations can proactively mitigate risks, improve compliance with regulatory frameworks, and build a sustainable, security-aware digital environment.

faced by individuals and organizations, including asymmetries in data control, cyber vulnerabilities, and systemic governance failures. The chapter provides a comprehensive overview of global regulatory frameworks such as the GDPR, CCPA, and emerging policies in the Global South, highlighting both progress and persistent compliance gaps. Emphasis is placed on best practices risk assessments, employee training, incident response, and data minimization as well as the role of cutting-edge technologies like AI, blockchain, and encryption in strengthening data protection. Ultimately, the chapter underscores the necessity of cultivating a security-oriented culture that embeds privacy into organizational ethos, urging a shift from reactive compliance to proactive responsibility in managing digital trust.

Cyber security plays a vital role in providing security in digital world. It provides security for systems, networks, data and confidential of all the online activities from different cyber threats. It may be classified into three types' network security, information security and application security. It has become part of our daily applications. Among all the applications providing security and privacy for social media applications has becoming greater importance. Cyber Security uses various strategies for providing security and privacy for social media applications. Cryptography and Network Security are considered as a backbone strategies of cyber security which ensure that sensitive data is been secured in a scalable interconnected networks and plays a key role in enhancing the security of social media applications. In this paper the concepts of cyber security, cryptography and network security-architecture, working process, protocols and algorithms and impact of cyber security on social media applications are considered.

This chapter examines the critical challenge of balancing usability and security in digital system design. As organizations increasingly rely on digital platforms, the tension between creating user-friendly interfaces and ensuring robust security measures has become more pronounced. By exploring human-centered design principles, behavioral insights, and adaptive technologies, the chapter highlights strategies for integrating security seamlessly into user workflows without sacrificing ease of use. Drawing on interdisciplinary research, case studies, and best practices, the chapter emphasizes the importance of transparency, user trust, and iterative design. It concludes by proposing a framework for developing systems that not only protect privacy but also enhance user experience, offering a roadmap for sustainable and secure digital transformations.

In an age of sustainable digital transformation, usability integrity between user experience (UX) and cybersecurity is crucial to building trust, improving commitment, and ensuring long-term digital resilience. This chapter examines the intersections of these domains and argues that effective cybersecurity needs to be seamlessly integrated into an intuitive and accessible user interface. Poor Users find out how friendly can undermine security protocols and how user-focused designs can improve compliance without compromising. By expanding case studies, current industry practices, and academic findings, this chapter shows that promoting a safe but user-friendly environment essential to digital sustainability is possible. This chapter also covers design principles and strategic frameworks that integrate security conditions needed to integrate smooth user interaction and pave the way for an ethically responsible, technically robust digital ecosystem.

Preface

Introduction

In today's digital era, cybersecurity is no longer a peripheral concern—it lies at the heart of sustainable digital transformation. As digital technologies evolve and expand into every sector of society, the security of users and organizations becomes increasingly critical in determining whether digital transformation efforts can thrive or falter. With digital adoption accelerating, from cloud computing and Internet of Things (IoT) to big data analytics, organizations and users are both confronted with new vulnerabilities. These vulnerabilities, if left unaddressed, not only pose technical threats but also erode trust and deter engagement with new digital ecosystems.

This book emerges from the recognition that sustainable digital transformation is impossible without a comprehensive understanding of the user-centric, organizational, and technological implications of cybersecurity. Without effective security practices and a culture of cybersecurity, the promise of digital transformation may be overshadowed by fear and resistance. Organizations may hesitate to invest, and users may be reluctant to adopt digital platforms if risks are not clearly mitigated.

Our intention with this edited volume is to illuminate these risks—offering a holistic perspective that spans users, organizations, and technology. The collection of chapters herein presents a blend of conceptual frameworks and real-world case studies. These diverse contributions reflect the multifaceted nature of cybersecurity in digital transformation, addressing not only technical concerns but also socio-cultural, economic, and policy-related challenges.

Throughout this book, contributors explore proactive cybersecurity strategies, offering practical insights on how to embed security considerations into the complete lifecycle of digital initiatives—from planning and design to implementation and governance. By emphasizing the importance of continuous risk assessment, robust control mechanisms, and organizational cultures, we aim to foster sustainable and resilient digital ecosystems.

This volume is intended to serve as a resource for students, academics, policymakers, and digital transformation practitioners alike. Whether the reader is designing secure digital infrastructures, shaping cybersecurity policy, or simply seeking to understand the nuanced interplay between cybersecurity and digital change, this book offers guidance rooted in contemporary research and practice.

We hope that *User-Centric Cybersecurity Implications for Sustainable Digital Transformation* will stimulate further dialogue and innovation in the field and serve as a foundational reference in the ongoing journey toward secure, inclusive, and sustainable digital futures.

Organization of the Book

In assembling this volume, we sought to highlight the critical intersection of cybersecurity and sustainable digital transformation from user-centric, organizational, and technological perspectives. The chapters in this collection address a wide range of challenges, strategies, and frameworks that are vital to building secure and resilient digital ecosystems. Each contribution brings unique insights, case studies, or conceptual models designed to guide policymakers, researchers, and practitioners in navigating the evolving cybersecurity landscape. The following chapter summaries reflect the diverse themes explored throughout the book.

Chapter 1: Digital Transformation and Cybersecurity

This chapter lays the foundation for the book by examining how digital transformation—through technologies like cloud computing, blockchain, and 5G—has introduced both unprecedented opportunities and heightened cybersecurity vulnerabilities. As businesses increasingly adopt AI-powered tools, IoT, and automation, securing these digital infrastructures becomes essential. The authors discuss emerging strategies such as Zero Trust Architecture, AI-driven threat intelligence, and post-quantum cryptography to secure data systems and ensure resilience in an evolving threat environment.

Chapter 2: Digital Transformation and Cybersecurity Challenges for Electronic Government

Focusing on the public sector, this chapter highlights the vulnerabilities faced by governments undergoing digital transformation. Through a literature review authors have proposed a cybersecurity readiness framework, that emphasizes the importance of proactive threat awareness and resilience planning. The framework assists in assessing and enhancing the security of e-government systems, particularly in the face of escalating cyber threats and increasing public dependency on digital governance.

Chapter 3: Leveraging Internet Sovereignty for Digital Supremacy

This chapter explores the concept of internet sovereignty as a national response to foreign surveillance and global cybersecurity threats. Through a critical analysis of policies and technical implementations in countries such as Russia and China, and framed by Mueller's theoretical model, the authors demonstrate how state-controlled internet ecosystems are reshaping global cybersecurity. The chapter also evaluates legislative efforts and security frameworks employed by various nations striving to assert control over their digital domains.

Chapter 4: Information Security Awareness

User awareness remains a cornerstone of cybersecurity strategy. This chapter delves into the psychological and behavioral aspects of Information Security Awareness, exploring how targeted training, awareness campaigns, and organizational policies contribute to cultivating a culture of security. By linking Information security awareness initiatives to regulatory compliance and digital transformation efforts, the chapter advocates for sustained user education to proactively mitigate risks and support long-term digital resilience.

Chapter 5: Personal Data Privacy and Security at Individual and Organizational Levels

Addressing the dual responsibility of individuals and organizations, this chapter explores practical strategies for safeguarding personal data in a digitally connected world. With threats ranging from identity theft to cyberattacks, the authors underscore the necessity of robust practices such as multi factor authentication, encryption, and privacy-enhancing tools. The chapter reinforces the importance of digital hygiene and individual vigilance in preserving privacy and protecting organizational assets.

Chapter 6: Social Media Privacy and Security—Stacking and Boosting for Misinformation Detection

This chapter introduces a cutting-edge ensemble model that combines machine learning and deep learning techniques to detect misinformation while preserving user anonymity. Leveraging real-world datasets and natural language processing for feature extraction, the framework aims to bolster social media security. The discussion extends to ethical considerations surrounding automation and the tension between privacy and surveillance, ultimately advocating for technologies that restore trust in online information environments.

Chapter 7: The Privacy Paradox—Navigating Security Challenges in Social Platforms

With social media acting as a double-edged sword for digital communication, this chapter explores the complex privacy and security risks associated with these platforms. Highlighting issues such as data mining, tracking, and identity theft, the chapter proposes solutions including blockchain authentication and automated malware detection. It also underscores the role of ethical design and digital literacy in countering misinformation and fostering safe online interactions.

Chapter 8: Navigating the Digital Labyrinth: Personal Data Privacy and Security at Individual and Organizational Levels

This chapter expands on the multifaceted challenges of personal data protection across sectors. Drawing from global regulations such as GDPR and CCPA, it evaluates the effectiveness of compliance frameworks and highlights emerging challenges in the Global South. Emphasizing a shift from reactive to proactive data stewardship, the authors present best practices in risk management, encryption, and cultural change that embed privacy into organizational culture.

Chapter 9: Cybersecurity Strategies for Enhancing the Privacy and Security of Social Media Applications

Focusing specifically on social media applications, this chapter explores the foundational role of cybersecurity strategies—including cryptography and network security—in protecting sensitive user data. It provides a comprehensive overview of architecture, protocols, and algorithms that enable secure digital interactions, demonstrating how these technologies collectively fortify social platforms against evolving threats.

Chapter 10: Balancing Usability and Security: Enhancing User Experience Without Compromising Privacy

Striking a balance between usability and security is a longstanding challenge in digital system design. This chapter proposes a framework that integrates user-centric design principles with adaptive security measures. Drawing on interdisciplinary research and practical case studies, the authors showcase how transparency, trust, and iterative design can deliver systems that are both secure and user-friendly, thus supporting sustainable digital innovation.

Chapter 11: Aligning User Experience and Usability with Cybersecurity for Sustainable Digital Transformation

Building on the theme of usability, this chapter explores the convergence of user experience and cybersecurity. Poorly designed user interfaces can undermine even the best security protocols, whereas thoughtful, intuitive design can promote compliance and engagement. The authors present industry examples, design strategies, and policy recommendations that align user experience with robust cybersecurity, ensuring both accessibility and protection in the digital age.

Together, these chapters form a cohesive and timely exploration of cybersecurity's pivotal role in sustainable digital transformation. Through a blend of technical depth, user-centered insights, and policy considerations, this book offers a roadmap for creating secure, inclusive, and resilient digital futures.

Conclusion

As we bring this volume to a close, we reaffirm the central thesis that sustainable digital transformation cannot be achieved without placing cybersecurity at its core. The contributions in this book collectively underscore that cybersecurity is not merely a technical challenge, but a multidimensional imperative that encompasses users, organizations, and technological systems. In an increasingly digitized world, the protection of data, the integrity of digital infrastructures, and the cultivation of user trust must be woven into the fabric of every digital initiative.

From the evolving threats faced by governments and private enterprises to the personal vulnerabilities encountered by individual users, each chapter has highlighted the pressing need for a holistic, user-centric approach to cybersecurity. The case studies, conceptual frameworks, and practical strategies presented throughout this book demonstrate that proactive security practices—when aligned with human-centered design, ethical policy, and technological innovation—can ensure both resilience and inclusivity.

We hope that this collection serves as a vital resource for scholars, practitioners, policymakers, and students seeking to understand and shape the future of secure digital transformation. As digital ecosystems continue to expand and evolve, the imperative to design with security in mind, educate with awareness, and govern with accountability must remain steadfast.

By fostering dialogue, advancing knowledge, and promoting best practices, this book invites ongoing collaboration across disciplines and sectors to realize the full potential of digital transformation—sustainably, securely, and ethically.

Acknowledgment

Dr. Saqib Saeed would like to thank Saudi Aramco Cybersecurity chair, Imam Abdulrahman Bin Faisal University for their support in completing this book.

Chapter 1
Digital Transformation and Cybersecurity

Sudarshan V. Seshanna
https://orcid.org/0009-0001-1607-4157
CMS Business School, Jain University, India

G. Gopalakrishnan
https://orcid.org/0009-0006-0674-9217
Sri Balaji University, India

Nilesh Anute
https://orcid.org/0000-0001-6599-813X
Sri Balaji University, India

K. Deepthi Reddy
https://orcid.org/0009-0009-7981-5571
CVR College of Engineering, India

Mohit Sharma
https://orcid.org/0009-0007-2280-8077
Maharshi Dayanand University, Rohtak, India

P. Selvakumar
https://orcid.org/0000-0002-3650-4548
Department of Science and Humanities, Nehru Institute of Technology, Coimbatore, India

T. C. Manjunath
https://orcid.org/0000-0003-2545-9160
Rajarajeswari College of Engineering, India

ABSTRACT

Digital transformation is revolutionizing industries by integrating advanced technologies such as cloud computing, blockchain, and 5G connectivity. While transformation drives efficiency and scalability, cybersecurity risks vulnerabilities. The rapid adoption of digital solutions susceptible to vulnerabilities, and AI-powered cyber threats. As businesses migrate to cloud environments, implement IoT ecosystems, and leverage AI-driven automation, securing these digital infrastructures becomes a critical priority. This paper explores the interconnection between digital transformation and cybersecurity, highlighting key challenges, and mitigating risks. Zero Trust Architecture (ZTA), AI-driven threat intelligence, endpoint security, and regulatory compliance frameworks are shaping the future of cybersecurity are

DOI: 10.4018/979-8-3373-3171-3.ch001

adopting multi-factor authentication (MFA) evolution necessitating the development of post-quantum cryptography (PQC) to future-proof data security.

INTRODUCTION TO DIGITAL TRANSFORMATION: THE CHANGING LANDSCAPE OF BUSINESS AND TECHNOLOGY

Traditional industries such as banking, healthcare, retail, and manufacturing are undergoing profound changes, adopting automation, AI-driven insights, and personalized digital services to stay competitive. E-commerce platforms, for instance, leverage AI-powered recommendation engines, chatbots, and seamless payment integrations to enhance customer engagement and drive sales. Similarly, smart factories powered by IoT and machine learning are revolutionizing supply chain management, predictive maintenance, and production efficiency. Significant the shift towards a data-driven economy. Organizations are increasingly relying on them to make informed decisions, improve customer relationships, and identify new market opportunities. Cloud computing enables businesses to scale rapidly, providing collaboration tools, and secure data. Furthermore, the rise of remote work and hybrid workplaces pushed organizations to adopt digital solutions such as virtual collaboration platforms, cybersecurity enhancements, and AI-driven automation to ensure business continuity. However, digital transformation also presents significant challenges. Cybersecurity, regulatory compliance, and workforce upskilling ensure a smooth transition to digital-first operations. Many companies struggle with legacy system modernization, resistance to change, and the complexities of integrating digital technologies into existing workflows. Additionally, as AI and automation continue to evolve, ethical considerations surrounding job displacement, and AI usage have become central topics of discussion.

THE IMPORTANCE OF CYBERSECURITY IN DIGITAL TRANSFORMATION: PROTECTING AGAINST EMERGING THREATS

As organizations embrace digital transformation, integrating cybersecurity has become a critical concern. Digital transformation enhances efficiency, scalability, and customer engagement, but cybercriminals Cyber ransomware, insider threats, and AI-driven cybercrime have increased in complexity, making robust cybersecurity frameworks essential Cybersecurity digital transformation is not merely a priority. Organizations must embed security into their digital ecosystems "security by design" to minimize risks. With the rapid shift to cloud-based infrastructures and remote work, Companies must implement encryption, systems to safeguard digital assets (Saeed et al, 2023). Cybersecurity is the rise of sophisticated cyberattacks targeting critical business functions. Cybercriminals are leveraging AI and automation to launch highly coordinated attacks, exploiting vulnerabilities in cloud environments, IoT devices, and third-party applications. Ransomware attacks, for example, have become more frequent and destructive, with cybercriminals demanding millions in ransom payments to restore access to encrypted data. Additionally, supply chain attacks—where hackers infiltrate trusted vendors or service providers—pose significant risks to organizations that rely on third-party software and cloud platforms (Möller D P F., et al, 2023). Data privacy is another crucial aspect of cybersecurity in digital transformation. With global regulations CCPA, PIPL, strong encryption standards, and access controls. Reputational damage, and loss of consumer trust. The increasing adoption of big data analytics and AI-powered decision-making further raises concerns about data integrity, bias, and ethical use of personal information.

To combat emerging cyber threats, proactive cybersecurity and rapid capabilities. Cyber resilience should be a core part of digital transformation efforts, ensuring that businesses can cyberattack with minimal disruption. Implementing cybersecurity automation, behavioral analytics, and organizations. Another important aspect of cybersecurity in digital transformation is weak password practices. Organizations must invest in phishing simulations, and security to empower and prevent it. The future of cybersecurity in digital transformation will be quantum, blockchain-driven cybersecurity, and next-generation encryption techniques (Mijwil et al, 2023). While these innovations present new opportunities for strengthening cybersecurity, they also introduce new risks that organizations must prepare(Mahadev Madgule, et al. 2023). Quantum computing, for instance, cryptographic solutions. Similarly, while blockchain technology offers enhanced security for digital transactions, it is. Critical shaping cybersecurity policies, and fostering international collaboration to combat cybercrime. Cybersecurity threats are borderless, and a global effort is required to tackle cyber threats effectively (Jimmy, 2021). Initiatives such as public-private partnerships, threat intelligence sharing, and cybersecurity regulations will help create a safer digital environment for businesses and consumers.

THE INTERSECTION OF DIGITAL TRANSFORMATION AND CYBERSECURITY: A COMPLEX RELATIONSHIP

The relationship between digital transformation and cybersecurity is both intricate and interdependent. Cloud environments introduce new attack surfaces, requiring organizations to adopt zero-trust security models, continuous monitoring, and AI-driven threat detection (Mendhurwar S., et al, 2021). Organizations' stringent CCPA and China's PIPL protect personal misuse. Failing to integrate cybersecurity into digital initiatives regulatory. The Role of Cybersecurity in Enabling Digital Transformation: While introduces new risks, cybersecurity is not just about defense—it also enables and accelerates digital transformation. By integrating security by design and default, organizations can build resilient, scalable, and future-proof systems. Cybersecurity AI-powered fraud blockchain-based secure transactions allow businesses to innovate while maintaining trust and data integrity (Saini K., et al, 2024). Legacy System Vulnerabilities – Many companies undergoing digital transformation still rely on outdated IT infrastructure that lacks modern security features, making integration with new technologies difficult and insecure.However, those who prioritize cybersecurity as a fundamental enabler of transformation can achieve faster innovation, greater resilience, and sustained competitive advantage (Nkongolo M., et al, 2023).

THE CHALLENGES OF DIGITAL TRANSFORMATION: CLOUD COMPUTING, IOT, AND BIG DATA

Driving innovation, efficiency, and competitiveness. However, its adoption is not without challenges, particularly in areas These technologies revolutionized operations by enabling scalability, automation, real-time analytics, and enhanced connectivity, but they also present complex security, privacy, compliance, and integration hurdles. Organizations must address these challenges to fully leverage digital transformation without compromising operational integrity, data security, and regulatory compliance. Cloud Computing Challenges in Digital Transformation: has become the backbone allowing organizations to migrate workloads, store vast amounts of data, and access computing resources on demand. However, cloud adoption presents significant challenges, including Security and Data Privacy Risks – organizations' critical concerns over misconfigurations become major. A lack of proper access controls, weak encryption practices, and insider threats can expose sensitive information to cybercriminals. Regulatory Compliance and Data Sovereignty – Different regions enforce China's PIPL), requiring businesses to comply with data residency laws and ensure cross-border data transfers meet legal standards (Devara J S M., et al, 2024). Organizations using global cloud providers must navigate complex compliance landscapes to avoid penalties(Sreenivasulu A., et al. 2022). Multi-Cloud and Hybrid Cloud Complexity – Many businesses use multiple cloud providers or a mix of on-premises and cloud solutions, leading to interoperability issues, inconsistent security policies, and vendor lock-in. Managing diverse environments requires robust cloud governance, standardized security frameworks, and seamless data integration strategies. Cybersecurity Risks and Vulnerabilities – strong prime cyberattacks. Device Management and Scalability – Organizations deploying thousands or millions of IoT devices struggle with device authentication, firmware updates, and network compatibility (Sandhu A K., et al, 2021).

Big Data Challenges in Digital Transformation: Big providing businesses actionable insights, predictive analytics, and enhanced decision-making capabilities. However, handling big data effectively presents several challenges: Data Privacy and Compliance – Organizations collecting and processing large volumes of personal data must adhere to strict privacy laws such as GDPR, HIPAA, and CPRA. Ensuring consent management, secure storage, and anonymization techniques legal violations. Real-Time Analytics and Processing Speed – Traditional databases struggle to process high-speed, high-volume data streams from IoT, financial transactions, and social media analytics (Tran-Dang H., et al, 2021). Organizations must adopt distributed computing, in-memory processing, and AI-driven data analysis to extract insights in real-time. Standardization and Interoperability in IoT – Encouraging industry-wide IoT standards, secure firmware updates, and AI-powered automation to improve device management and security. Advanced Data Governance and AI-powered analytics – checks, AI-driven lakes, real-time monitoring big processing. AI and Automation for Cybersecurity – Using AI-driven behavioral analytics, security orchestration automation, and automated compliance audits to detect and mitigate cyber threats (Rani et al, 2023).

CYBERSECURITY CHALLENGES IN DIGITAL TRANSFORMATION: THREATS, VULNERABILITIES, AND RISKS

Digital transformation has revolutionized industries by integrating into operations. However, as organizations embrace these technologies, they also face evolving cybersecurity threats, vulnerabilities, and risks. Digital transformation expands the attack surface, increases regulatory compliance complexity, and introduces new security gaps that cybercriminals exploit. Without a robust cybersecurity strategy, businesses risk data. Ransomware attacks have surged as businesses migrate to the cloud and remote work environments. Attackers encrypt critical data, demand ransom payments in cryptocurrency, and threaten to leak sensitive corporate or customer information (Benjamin L B., et al, 2024). High-profile ransomware attacks (e.g., Colonial Pipeline, Kaseya, and WannaCry) highlight the devastating impact on business continuity and supply chains. AI-Driven Cyberattacks and Deepfake Threats: AI enables automated malware generation, adaptive phishing campaigns, and deepfake-based fraud, making cyber threats harder to detect (Stewart H., et al, 2023). Vulnerabilities in Digital Transformation: Weak Links in Security Frameworks:

Cybersecurity vulnerabilities emerge when businesses rush digital transformation initiatives without integrating strong security measures. Key vulnerabilities include: Cloud Security Gaps and Data Exposure Cloud misconfigurations lead to exposed databases, unsecured storage buckets, and weak access controls. Unencrypted data, weak API security, and improper cloud identity management create risks for sensitive information. Organizations should adopt zero-trust security models and encryption protocols.

IoT Device Insecurities: IoT devices often lack firmware updates, strong authentication, and encryption, to cyberattacks. Botnet Mirai and Mozi, exploit IoT weaknesses to launch massive DDoS attacks. Cybersecurity risks in digital transformation extend beyond technical vulnerabilities, affecting compliance, business operations, and brand reputation. End-to-end encryption and Data Protection – strong for cloud, transfers, and IoT networks. Security by Design and Default – Embed security in software development, cloud architecture, and digital infrastructure from the ground up. Continuous Security Awareness Training – Educate employees on phishing prevention, data handling best practices, and incident response protocols (Möller D P F., et al, 2023). Multi-factor authentication (MFA) and Identity Management – with MFA, biometric verification, and privileged access controls. Incident Response and Cyber Resilience Planning – Develop rapid response plans, cyber drills, and disaster recovery strategies to handle attacks efficiently. Conclusion: Cybersecurity remains one of the most significant challenges in digital transformation, with threats, vulnerabilities, and risks evolving at an unprecedented rate. Businesses must recognize that digital innovation cannot come at the expense of security—instead, cybersecurity must be embedded into digital transformation strategies from the start.

THE HUMAN FACTOR IN DIGITAL TRANSFORMATION AND CYBERSECURITY: THE ROLE OF EMPLOYEES AND END-USERS

As organizations undergo digital transformation, employees and end-users are cybersecurity. While advanced drive digital evolution, human behavior remains a significant factor in cybersecurity risks and defenses. Cybercriminals often target individuals through phishing attacks, social engineering, credential theft, and insider threats, making employees the first line of defense—or posture. Addressing human-related cybersecurity awareness training, behavioral analytics, access control mechanisms, and a strong cybersecurity culture. The Human Factor: A Key Cybersecurity Challenge in Digital Transformation: Despite advancements in cybersecurity tools, cyber vendors, and customers frequently unknowingly compromise security by: Falling for Social Engineering Attacks – Cybercriminals through phishing emails, phone scams, and deepfake impersonation attacks (Pollini et al, 2022). Using Weak or Reused Passwords – Many employee's credentials credential stuffing attacks. Neglecting Software Updates – Delayed patching of vulnerabilities in applications, IoT devices, and endpoints exposes systems to cyber threats. Employees are both a risk factor and a crucial defense mechanism in digital transformation. Cybersecurity is not solely an IT responsibility—every employee plays a role in protecting organizational assets. Key areas where employees impact cybersecurity include: Security Awareness and Training Programs: Safeguarding login credentials with strong passwords and multi-factor authentication (MFA) (Hakimi et al, 2024). Following best practices for secure remote work and device management. Gamification and real-world phishing simulations can enhance training effectiveness. Implementing a Zero-Trust Security Model: Employees should operate within meaning: automatically identity is required for every access request. Least privilege principles minimize unauthorized data exposure. Insider Threats: Malicious and Negligent Behavior: Insider threats can be malicious (intentional sabotage or data theft) or negligent (accidental data breaches, poor security practices). Implementing user behavior analytics (UBA) can help detect unauthorized access and files.

Endpoint Security and Remote Work Challenges: With the shift to remote and hybrid work, unsecured creates risks. Organizations must enforce: Secure VPN usage and encrypted communication for remote employees. Strict mobile management (MDM) policies. Weak passwords and poor authentication methods remain a major issue in cybersecurity. Organizations should: Implement biometric authentication and password-less login options. Promote the use of password managers to encourage strong password hygiene. Privacy Awareness and Data Protection for End-Users: End-users often unknowingly share personal and financial data online, making them targets for identity theft and fraud (Tikanmäki I., et al, 2024). Organizations must: Educate users about phishing, fake websites, and online scams. Provide clear privacy policies and data protection controls. Offer opt-in consent mechanisms for data collection and limit unnecessary data storage. A strong cybersecurity culture goes beyond policies and technologies—it requires active participation from employees, end-users, and leadership teams. Testing incident response plans ensures rapid containment and mitigation of security breaches (Oladipo et al, 2024). biggest challenges during digital transformation. While technological advancements enhance security, employees, and end-users remain the primary targets for cyber threats. Organizations must recognize that cybersecurity is a shared responsibility, requiring education, awareness, and proactive measures from all stakeholders(Ramakrishnan et al. 2022). By fostering a security-conscious workforce, implementing zero-trust frameworks, enforcing access controls, and promoting user-friendly cybersecurity measures, businesses can reduce vulnerabilities, enhance digital security, and build resilience against cyber threats depends only on the security mindset vigilance of people—the ultimate guardians of cybersecurity.

CYBERSECURITY STRATEGIES FOR DIGITAL TRANSFORMATION: A FRAMEWORK FOR SUCCESS

Introduction: undergoing rapid stay competitive, and integrating advanced and blockchain into operations. Technological and vulnerabilities. A modern cybersecurity strategy must incorporate a multi-layered approach, combining technical controls, risk management policies, regulatory compliance, and employee awareness programs (Yeoh et al, 2022). This framework provides a structured approach to integrating cybersecurity into digital transformation initiatives and embedded technological adoption. Another critical aspect of cybersecurity in digital workloads is they must adopt cloud-native security solutions such as, and security strategies should include data encryption, ISO 27001, and GDPR. Established organizations clarify security responsibilities and ensure comprehensive protection of cloud-hosted assets. Vital cybersecurity by threat intelligence, incident response, and anomaly detection. AI-driven security analytics zero-day, and improve threat hunting capabilities. However, cybercriminals are also leveraging AI for sophisticated attacks, by integrating AI-powered cybersecurity solutions. With devices in healthcare, manufacturing, and cities, securing IoT ecosystems has become a major challenge. IoT devices often have weak security configurations, making them prime targets for cyberattacks. Implementing strong authentication, network segmentation, and continuous monitoring can help mitigate IoT security risks (Ghobakhloo M., et al, 2021). Organizations should adopt Security by Design principles, ensuring that security measures are embedded into IoT devices from the development phase.

Compliance strategies for digital transformation. Security global and industry-specific regulations Cybersecurity Framework. Compliance ensures that organizations follow risk management and incident response. To successfully implement cybersecurity strategies for digital transformation, organizations must adopt a risk-based approach (AlDaajeh et al, 2022). This involves conducting regular risk assessments, identifying critical assets, evaluating threat landscapes, investment frameworks such as NIST, and the methodologies assessing and mitigating risks. Strengthening industries. Governments, businesses, and cybersecurity communities must work together to exchange share develop coordinated mechanisms. Public-private partnerships, industry alliances, and threat intelligence platforms (TIPs) play a crucial role in collective cyber defense efforts. In conclusion, as organizations embrace digital transformation, cybersecurity must be at the core of their strategic initiatives (Yeoh et al, 2023). A robust cybersecurity framework ensures that digital transformation efforts are resilient, regulatory enhancing cloud security, leveraging AI-driven threat intelligence, securing IoT ecosystems, ensuring regulatory compliance, promoting cybersecurity awareness, and implementing a risk-based security strategy, strong future cybersecurity in digital transformation will require continuous innovation, adaptive security strategies, and a proactive mindset Organizations that prioritize cybersecurity as a fundamental pillar of digital transformation will be well-positioned for an interconnected world.

IDENTITY AND ACCESS MANAGEMENT (IAM) IN DIGITAL TRANSFORMATION: BEST PRACTICES

In the era of digital transformation, and entity applications, cloud computing, IoT, artificial intelligence (AI), and other emerging technologies, managing digital identities securely is more complex than ever. Threats. Must implement robust IAM strategies to safeguard their digital assets while enabling seamless and secure access for employees, partners, customers, and devices. IAM critical mitigating risks unauthorized access, insider threats, credential theft, and compliance violations. A well-implemented IAM framework enhances operational efficiency, supports regulatory compliance, and improves user experience by streamlining authentication and authorization processes. This article explores best practices for implementing IAM in digital transformation, ensuring organizations can maintain security, compliance, and business agility (Singh et al, 2023). Implement a Zero Trust Security Model: devices and applications should be inherently trusted, by organizations. Under Zero Trust, IAM enables implementing: Least Privilege (LPAC) only permissions. Micro-segmentation limits lateral movement within the network by restricting access to only required resources. By integrating IAM with Zero Trust principles, significantly. Adopt Single Sign-On (SSO) for Seamless User Experience: Single Sign-On (SSO) enhances both security and repeatedly entering credentials. SSO, and improves productivity. However, to maximize security, SSO should be combined with other IAM controls such as MFA, risk-based authentication, and session timeouts. Organizations should implement secure SSO solutions that support modern authentication protocols to ensure secure access across cloud, on-premises, and hybrid environments (Anderson J., et al, 2022).

Strengthen Identity Governance and Administration (IGA): Ensure that management processes align with compliance, security, and business policies. Effective IGA strategies include: Automated user provisioning and de-provisioning to grant and revoke access rights in real-time. Access reviews and certification to periodically validate user access rights and remove excessive privileges. IGA helps organizations enforce strong identity lifecycle management and violations. Secure API and Machine Identity Management: With microservices, API security becomes a critical IAM component. Organizations must: Use OAuth 2.0 and API gateways to authenticate and authorize API access. Implement certificate-based authentication to secure machine-to-machine communications. Continuously monitor API traffic for anomalies and unauthorized access attempts. Additionally, machine identities, including IoT devices, bots, and automated scripts, should be securely managed using Public Key Infrastructure (PKI), digital certificates, and cryptographic keys to prevent unauthorized access (Ghadge N., et al, 2024). Enable Risk-Based and Adaptive Authentication: Static authentication mechanisms are often insufficient to prevent sophisticated cyberattacks. Risk-based authentication (RBA) and adaptive authentication IAM systems can analyze factors such as User behavior patterns (e.g., login location, and device usage). Unusual access times or high-risk geolocations. Known threat intelligence data. Based on these risk factors, the system can enforce additional authentication steps or restrict access to reduce security risks. Ensure Compliance with Regulatory Standards: Organizations must align IAM practices with industry regulations such as the General Data Protection Regulation (GDPR) – user consent management. Health Insurance Portability and Accountability Act (HIPAA) – Secure access controls. Payment Card Industry Data Security Standard (PCI DSS) – Protecting payment transactions and customer identities (Kumar K., et al, 2024).

DATA PROTECTION AND ENCRYPTION IN DIGITAL TRANSFORMATION: STRATEGIES FOR SECURE DATA MANAGEMENT

In an era defined by digital transformation, organizations. As increasing leverage, However, this shift also brings significant cybersecurity challenges, and regulatory compliance pressures intensify. Adopt and encryption strategies maintain trust, and ensure compliance with evolving laws. Data protection is no longer just an IT concern; it is a critical business priority that affects financial stability, reputation, and regulatory standing. A well-defined data security framework includes encryption, backup recovery, secure sharing, and compliance measures. Encryption, in particular, data prevention By modern techniques, strong policies, and advanced mechanisms, security digital assets throughout the transformation journey. This article explores encryption in digital transformation, providing insights into how secure data management. Understanding Data Protection in Digital Transformation: Data protection encompasses the procedures to secure digital assets from corruption, and loss. The primary objectives of data protection strategies include: Digital transformation amplifies need-centric security, as organizations store, process, and transfer massive amounts of information across cloud platforms, mobile devices, and distributed systems (Díaz et al, 2021). Data in Use Encryption – Encrypting data during processing, ensuring it remains protected even while being accessed or modified. Encryption protocols such as Transport Layer Security (TLS) provide strong security measures to prevent data compromise (Gupta I., 2022).

Data Masking and Tokenization for Enhanced Privacy: masking and tokenization provide advanced methods for securing sensitive information. Data Masking – Replaces original data with obfuscated values while maintaining its usability for testing, analytics, and training. Tokenization – Replaces sensitive data with non-sensitive placeholders (tokens), ensuring that the actual data remains secure in a separate environment. These techniques are particularly valuable for securing and ensuring privacy. Implementing Secure Backup and Data Recovery Strategies: Digital transformation increases reliance on cloud-based storage and distributed systems, making backup and disaster recovery (DR) strategies essential. Organizations must ensure that backups are: Encrypted to prevent unauthorized access to backup data. Stored across multiple locations to mitigate risks of data loss from cyberattacks or disasters. Regularly tested to confirm backup integrity and quick recovery in case of incidents (Timan T., et al, 2021). Ransomware attacks have made immutable and air-gapped backups critical, ensuring that attackers cannot modify or delete backup copies. Enhancing Data Security with AI and Automation: are revolutionizing data protection by enabling anomaly monitoring, mechanisms. Key-driven security features include: Behavioral analytics to detect suspicious data access patterns. Automated incident response to mitigate breaches quickly. Threat intelligence integration for proactive risk assessment. AI-powered transfers enforcing security policies. Educating Employees and Building a Security Culture: Organizations must: Train employees on data security best practices such as recognizing and securing passwords. Implement security awareness programs and protection. Enforce policies for secure data handling and sharing across teams and third parties. Ensures active participation in protecting organizational data (Julakanti S R., et al, 2025).

EMERGING TECHNOLOGIES IN DIGITAL TRANSFORMATION: ARTIFICIAL INTELLIGENCE, MACHINE LEARNING, AND BLOCKCHAIN

Digital transformation is revolutionizing industries by integrating advanced technologies into business processes, enhancing efficiency, security, and innovation. Among the most impactful technologies driving this transformation is Blockchain. The way organizations, offer new opportunities for automation, cybersecurity, and improved transparency. In a fast-evolving landscape, adopting AI, ML, and blockchain has become a strategic imperative. AI and ML enable organizations to harness data and detect security threats in real-time. Blockchain provides immutable, solutions for transactions, identity management, and supply chain integrity. Together, these technologies form the backbone of modern digital transformation strategies, driving innovation across finance, healthcare, manufacturing, retail, and government sectors. This article explores how AI, ML, and blockchain contribute to digital transformation and their key use cases. Artificial Intelligence (AI) in Digital Transformation: What is AI? including enables machines to analyze and execute complex tasks with minimal human intervention (Chowdhury R H., et al, 2024). Key AI Applications in Digital Transformation: AI-driven automation automates repetitive business invoice processing support. Enhance customer engagement by providing real-time responses and personalized interactions. AI-powered chatbots enhance engagement across digital platforms. Challenges of AI Implementation: Ethical AI issues, including bias in algorithms and decision-making transparency (Hussain A A., et al, 2021). Integration challenges with existing IT infrastructure. Organizations must adopt ethical AI frameworks, robust data governance policies, and continuous model improvements to maximize AI's potential. Machine Learning (ML) in Digital Transformation: What is Machine Learning? The Subset enables ML processes, making them essential for digital transformation. Key ML Applications in Digital Transformation: Fraud Detection and Risk Management ML analyzes transaction data to detect anomalies, reducing fraud in banking, insurance, and e-commerce. Financial institutions use ML-driven models to assess credit risk and investment opportunities.

ML in Healthcare

ML-powered predictive analytics helps hospitals optimize patient care and resource allocation. Cybersecurity and Threat Intelligence: ML enhances intrusion detection systems (IDS) by identifying suspicious network behavior. AI-driven security analytics predict and prevent cyberattacks. Challenges of ML Implementation: Data quality and availability affect ML model accuracy. Model interpretability issues create concerns about decision transparency. Computational resource constraints require scalable infrastructure for ML training and deployment. Organizations should adopt data governance best practices, explainable AI models, and scalable cloud-based ML solutions to overcome these challenges. Blockchain in Digital Transformation: What is Blockchain? Decentralized and Unlike traditional centralized systems, immutability, by eliminating intermediaries and enabling peer-to-peer transactions. Key Blockchain Applications in Digital Transformation: Secure Transactions and Financial Services: Blockchain enhances the security of digital transactions, reducing fraud in banking, cryptocurrency exchanges, and online payments (Siddiqui Z

A., et al, 2022). Supply Chain Transparency and Traceability Blockchain ensure end-to-end visibility in logistics, food safety, and pharmaceuticals. Product origins, improving trust and compliance. Identity Management and Digital Credentials: Blockchain-powered decentralized identity (DID) solutions eliminate the need for centralized identity providers. Governments and enterprises use blockchain for secure identity verification, digital passports, and voting systems. Healthcare Data Security: Blockchain ensures secure and interoperable health records, enabling patient data sharing while maintaining privacy. Medical research organizations use blockchain to maintain tamper-proof clinical trial data. Blockchain in Cybersecurity: Blockchain prevents data tampering and unauthorized access by creating an immutable record of transactions. Decentralized authentication solutions credential theft. Challenges of Blockchain Implementation: Scalability issues due to high transaction processing times. Regulatory uncertainty and legal challenges in different industries. Interoperability limitations between blockchain networks. Organizations should focus on hybrid blockchain models, regulatory compliance strategies, and interoperability solutions to address these challenges (Ahmed et al, 2022).

CYBERSECURITY IMPLICATIONS OF EMERGING TECHNOLOGIES: OPPORTUNITIES AND CHALLENGES

As organizations rapidly embrace Quantum Computing, the cybersecurity landscape is undergoing significant transformations. These advanced technologies offer tremendous opportunities for enhancing security measures, automating threat detection, and improving data protection. However, risks, vulnerabilities, and that cybercriminals can exploit. Cybersecurity no longer matters as simple network protection; it is adaptive, multilayered mitigates threats, and safeguards sensitive data. Created a complex environment where while powered security solutions blockchain's decentralized nature offers promising advancements, challenges such as AI-driven cyberattacks, IoT security loopholes, and potential pose significant. This article examines the cybersecurity emerging technologies, highlighting the impact on security frameworks and providing insights into best practices for mitigating risks. Cybersecurity Opportunities Created by Emerging Technologies: Emerging technologies have introduced innovative ways to strengthen cybersecurity defenses and enhance threat detection capabilities (Jimmy, 2021). Organizations can leverage these advancements to improve security posture and mitigate cyber risks effectively. -driven cybersecurity platforms gather global threat intelligence to proactively address potential security risks. Blockchain for Enhanced Security and Data Integrity: Blockchain's decentralized and immutable nature enhances cybersecurity by securing transactions, preventing data tampering, and ensuring secure identity management.

Key advantages include: Decentralized Authentication: identity providers, and identity theft. Secure Transactions: Prevents fraud and unauthorized modifications in financial transactions and supply chains. Smart Contracts: Automates and secures agreements, reducing reliance on third-party intermediaries. IoT Security Enhancements: As IoT devices become more integrated into daily operations, securing them is critical (Lewallen J., et al, 2021). Emerging cybersecurity solutions for IoT include: AI-Driven Intrusion Detection Systems (IDS): Protect IoT networks from cyber threats by identifying and blocking malicious activities.

Cybersecurity Challenges Posed by Emerging Technologies

Despite their benefits, emerging technologies present new attack surfaces, security vulnerabilities, and ethical concerns. Cybercriminals are leveraging these technologies for more sophisticated attacks, requiring organizations to adopt proactive cybersecurity strategies. AI and ML-Based Cyberattacks: While AI and ML enhance security, cybercriminals are also using these technologies to develop AI-powered malware, deepfake scams, and automated phishing attacks. Key risks include: AI-generated phishing Attacks: Attackers use AI to create highly convincing phishing emails, making social engineering attacks more effective. Adversarial AI Attacks: Cybercriminals manipulate AI models by feeding them malicious data, causing incorrect threat assessments. Deepfake Cyber Threats: AI-generated deepfake content can impersonate executives, leading to financial fraud or reputational damage (Nafrees A C M., et al, 2021). Blockchain Security Risks: Although blockchain is known for its security benefits, vulnerabilities exist, including Private Key Theft: Losing access to private keys results in irreversible loss of digital assets. Organizations must start preparing for post-quantum cryptography to mitigate the risks associated with future quantum attacks. Best Practices for Securing Emerging Technologies: To address these cybersecurity challenges, organizations proactive, security modern frameworks best practices. Implement AI-Powered Cybersecurity Solutions: Deploy AI-driven threat intelligence platforms. Use behavioral analytics to prevent AI-powered cyberattacks. Strengthen Blockchain Security Measures: Implement secure smart contract auditing to identify and fix vulnerabilities. Use multi-signature authentication for enhanced blockchain security. Store private keys securely using hardware security modules (HSMs). Enhance IoT Security Protocols: Adopt Zero Trust Architecture to continuously verify IoT devices (Ige et al, 2024). Use firmware security updates and patch management to address vulnerabilities. Implement strong authentication mechanisms for IoT devices. Prepare for Quantum-Resistant Cryptography: Begin transitioning to encryption. Develop hybrid encryption models that combine classical and quantum-resistant security. Integrating this cybersecurity maximizes the benefits of emerging technologies while mitigating risks. Conclusion: Emerging technologies present both opportunities and challenges in cybersecurity.

THE ROLE OF ARTIFICIAL INTELLIGENCE AND MACHINE LEARNING IN CYBERSECURITY: ENHANCING THREAT DETECTION AND RESPONSE

Cybersecurity threats have evolved in complexity and scale, making traditional security approaches insufficient to combat modern cyber risks. Cybersecurity, enabling predict cyberattacks, or malicious activities, and enhance security measures faster and more efficiently than human analysts. Driven attacks, deepfake impersonations, and automated malware. In response, security teams must embrace AI and ML-powered solutions This article explores how to enhance by improving and automating incident response, strengthening behavioral analytics, and mitigating cyber risks. AI and ML in Cybersecurity: A Game-Changer: are reshaping strategies by transforming how threats are detected, analyzed, and neutralized. These technologies enable proactive security approaches, allowing organizations to predict and prevent cyberattacks before they occur. How AI and ML Enhance Cybersecurity: AI and ML introduce automation, intelligence, and adaptability into cybersecurity (Rizvi M., et al, 2023). Their key contributions include: Real-Time Threat Detection: AI-powered security systems analyze massive datasets to identify threats faster than traditional methods. AI-powered across all endpoints. Features include: AI-based malware Detection: Identifies and blocks ransomware, trojans, and fileless malware before they execute. Automated Threat Containment: AI isolates compromised devices, preventing lateral movement across networks. AI for Email Security and Phishing Prevention: Phishing remains one of the most effective cyberattack vectors (Manoharan A., et al, 2023). AI-driven email security solutions detect: Spear-phishing attacks by analyzing sender behavior and message content. Business Email Compromise (BEC) scams that impersonate executives or employees. Deepfake attacks that use AI-generated audio/video to deceive organizations. AI-powered Natural Language Processing (NLP) analyzes email patterns to detect phishing attempts with high accuracy. Machine Learning in Cybersecurity: Strengthening Predictive Analytics: Predicting Cyber Threats Before They Happen: Machine learning models analyze historical attack data and detect early indicators of cyber threats. Predictive analytics helps organizations: Identify attack patterns before cybercriminals exploit vulnerabilities. Assess security risks based on network activity, system behavior, and threat intelligence feeds. Prioritize security alerts, reducing the workload of security teams.

ML in Behavioral Analytics and Insider Threat Detection

Traditional security models struggle to detect insider threats, but ML-based systems excel in: Detecting anomalies in user behavior (e.g., unauthorized data access, unusual login times). Preventing privilege misuse by monitoring access patterns. Identifying compromised credentials through behavioral deviations. ML for Automated Threat Hunting: Security analysts often spend hours manually investigating threats. ML-powered threat-hunting solutions: Automate data correlation across logs, network traffic, and endpoint activity. Identify hidden attack vectors, reducing investigation time. Provide AI-driven recommendations for security teams to act upon. AI in Cyber Incident Response and Mitigation: Automated Threat Response with AI-Powered Security Orchestration: Security teams often face alert fatigue due to overwhelming security events solutions: Reduce incident response times, allowing teams to focus on critical threats. Coordinate across multiple security tools, ensuring a unified defense strategy. AI in Threat Intelligence and Risk Management: AI-driven Threat Intelligence Platforms (TIPs) analyze: Dark web activities, identifying potential data breaches and cybercrime trends (Vaddadi S A., et al, 2023). Threat actor behaviors, predicting attack strategies used by cybercriminals. Risk scores for vulnerabilities, helping organizations prioritize patch management. AI-powered risk management tools reduce attack surfaces and strengthen overall cybersecurity resilience. Challenges and Risks of AI in Cybersecurity: AI-Powered Cyberattacks: leveraging for: Automated phishing campaigns that generate highly convincing scam emails. AI-powered malware that evades detection by altering code dynamically. Deepfake attacks are used for fraud, misinformation, and identity theft. Bias in AI Security Models: False positives or negatives in threat detection. Discriminatory security policies that unfairly impact certain users. Adversarial AI attacks, where attackers manipulate models by injecting misleading data. Conclusion: AI and ML have revolutionized cybersecurity, providing prediction, and cyber From behavioral analytics to incident and predictive cybersecurity, these technologies enhance security efficiency and resilience. However, AI-powered cyberattacks and ethical concerns highlight the need for responsible AI adoption, bias mitigation, and continuous monitoring. As cyber threats evolve, will pivotal securing digital ecosystems, robust defense mechanisms, and protecting critical assets and ML strategies, organizations' adversaries build a more resilient digital future.

CASE STUDY: DIGITAL TRANSFORMATION AND CYBERSECURITY IN THE FINANCIAL SERVICES INDUSTRY

Financial services massive digital As banks, insurance companies, and investment firms shift towards and enable real-time financial transactions, cybersecurity has become a critical challenge. With increased cyber threats, prevent fraud, and ensure regulatory compliance. This case study examines how digital transformation has impacted cybersecurity highlighting strategies, and best practices adopted by a leading global financial institution. Financial firms can leverage cybersecurity frameworks, AI-driven threat intelligence, and regulatory compliance measures to build a secure and resilient digital infrastructure. The Digital Transformation Journey in Financial Services: Overview of Digital Adoption in Banking and Finance: have embraced digital transformation to Key initiatives including Mobile and Internet Banking: Enabling seamless digital transactions and remote financial management. Cloud-Based Core Banking Systems: Migrating from legacy systems to cloud-based platforms for improved scalability and security (Adewumi et al, 2024). Blockchain for Secure Transactions: Implementing distributed ledger technology for secure and transparent transactions. While digital innovation offers significant benefits, it also expands the attack surface, exposing financial institutions to cyber insider threats. Case Study: Global Financial Institution's Digital Transformation Strategy: A leading multinational bank initiated a large-scale Key objective included: Transitioning to cloud-based infrastructure for secure data management. Exploiting vulnerabilities in Open Banking APIs to access sensitive data (Kafi M A., et al, 2023). Data Privacy and Compliance Challenges: Regulatory frameworks CCPA, PCI-DSS, and Basel III require financial institutions to implement strict security controls. Challenges include: Ensuring end-to-end encryption of sensitive financial transactions. Securing customer data against breaches. Multi-jurisdictional laws. Cybersecurity Strategies Implemented: To address cybersecurity risks, the global financial institution implemented a multi-layered security approach, integrating advanced AI-driven cybersecurity solutions, zero-trust security models, and cloud-native security frameworks. AI-Driven Threat Detection and Response: Identify fraudulent transactions using machine learning algorithms. Automate incident response, reducing human intervention. AI-driven threat intelligence platforms provide real-time threat analysis, helping the institution anticipate cyberattacks before they occur.

Zero Trust Security Model

To mitigate insider threats and unauthorized access, the bank implemented a Zero Trust Architecture (ZTA) based on: Continuous authentication and strict access controls. Least privilege access, ensuring employees can only access necessary data. Micro-segmentation, preventing lateral movement of attackers. Cloud Security Framework: The transition to cloud-based banking required robust cloud security strategies: Multi-Factor Authentication (MFA) for secure login. Data encryption at rest and in transit encryption. Regular penetration testing and vulnerability assessments. Blockchain for Secure Transactions: To enhance transaction security, the institution integrated blockchain technology to: Prevent transaction fraud through decentralized ledger mechanisms. Enable transparent and immutable financial records. Reduce third-party risks in cross-border payments. Blockchain significantly improved trust and security in financial transactions(Aragani et al. 2025). Cybersecurity Incident: Ransomware Attack and Response: Incident Overview: Despite robust security measures, the bank faced a ransomware attack targeting its core banking infrastructure (Johri A., et al, 2023). Adhering to GDPR, PCI-DSS, and ISO 27001 strengthens security posture. Incident Response Preparedness: Cybersecurity. Cloud Security Frameworks: Implementing cloud-native security ensures scalability and resilience. Best Practices for Financial Cybersecurity: To strengthen cybersecurity in financial services, organizations should: Adopt AI-driven security solutions for automated threat detection. Implement multi-layered authentication (MFA, biometrics, behavioral analytics) (Hassan et al, 2024). Encrypt financial transactions using end-to-end encryption and blockchain. Regularly conduct cybersecurity audits and penetration testing. Educate employees and customers on cybersecurity awareness. Conclusion: Digital transformation has reshaped the financial services industry, enhancing customer experience and operational efficiency. However, the adoption of cloud services, and AI-driven technologies. By implementing AI-powered cybersecurity, Zero Trust security models, blockchain, and cloud security frameworks, financial institutions can proactively detect cyber threats, secure customer data, and ensure regulatory compliance. The case study demonstrates that cyber resilience is crucial for digital financial ecosystems. As cyber threats continue to evolve, financial institutions' innovation maintains a secure digital future.

BEST PRACTICES FOR CYBERSECURITY IN DIGITAL TRANSFORMATION: LESSONS FROM SUCCESSFUL ORGANIZATIONS

Digital transformation has revolutionized businesses across industries, enabling greater efficiency, innovation, and customer engagement. However, as organizations adopt, they also face a rapidly evolving cybersecurity landscape. Cyber data breaches and insiders have become more sophisticated, targeting enterprises undergoing digital transformation. Successful organizations recognize that cybersecurity must be integrated into digital transformation strategies from the outset. Cybersecurity an imperative to protect customer trust, ensure regulatory compliance, and safeguard critical assets. This article explores the best cybersecurity practices for digital transformation, drawing insights from organizations that have successfully secured their digital ecosystems. A global technology company undergoing a large-scale digital transformation adopted a security-first mindset. Key cybersecurity measures included: Implementing Zero Trust Architecture (ZTA) to secure remote access. Deploying AI-driven threat detection systems. Encrypting data using end-to-end encryption to protect sensitive information. This proactive security strategy enabled the company to scale digital operations securely, reducing cyber incidents by 40% in one year. Best Cybersecurity Practices in Digital Transformation: Organizations that successfully navigate cybersecurity challenges follow key best practices to protect their digital assets while enabling innovation (Mızrak F., et al, 2023). Implementing a Zero Trust Security Model Architecture (ZTA) is a fundamental strategy in digital transformation that assumes no entity—internal or external—can be trusted by default. Successful companies implement the least Privilege Access: Limiting access to data and applications jobs. Micro-Segmentation: Dividing networks of cyber threats. AI-Powered Threat Detection and Response: Leading use of machine learning for real-time cybersecurity monitoring, enabling: Predictive Threat Intelligence: Identifying potential cyberattacks before they occur. Behavioral Analytics: Detecting insider threats and unauthorized access by analyzing user activity(Debnath et al. 2025). For example, a financial services firm implemented AI-driven threat intelligence, reducing fraud by 35% and improving detection accuracy by 60%. Cloud Security and Data Protection Strategies: Cloud adoption but it requires misconfigurations.

Successful organizations implement: Continuous Cloud Security Posture Management (CSPM) to detect vulnerabilities in cloud configurations. Endpoint Security and Secure Remote Work: With hybrid environments, companies must secure IoT systems. Leading enterprises: Endpoint Detection and Response (EDR) to devices and threats. Virtual Private Networks (VPN) and Secure Access Service Edge (SASE) to protect remote connections. Mobile Device Management (MDM) on employees. A global healthcare provider adopted a zero-trust remote work policy, reducing ransomware attacks by 50% within a year. Strengthening Supply Chain Security: Supply chain vulnerabilities are a major cybersecurity risk in digital transformation. Best practices include: Third-Party Risk Assessments: Evaluating the cybersecurity posture of vendors and partners. Secure Software Development Life Cycle (SDLC): Implementing security testing in DevOps pipelines. Software Bill of Materials (SBOM): Tracking open-source (Safitra et al, 2023). A Fortune 500 Company's Response to a Ransomware Attack: A leading manufacturing company suffered a ransomware attack that disrupted operations. Key cybersecurity lessons included: Proactive Cyber Resilience: Implementing AI-driven ransomware detection prevented further spread. Backup and Disaster Recovery: A cloud-based backup strategy enabled rapid data restoration.. Regulatory Evolution and Global Compliance Stronger cross-border cybersecurity regulations to ensure data protection. Conclusion: Successful digital transformation requires a cybersecurity-first approach. Organizations must integrate Zero Trust security, AI-driven threat intelligence, cloud security frameworks, and endpoint protection to safeguard digital ecosystems. Lessons from leading enterprises show that proactive risk management, strong compliance frameworks, and continuous security innovation are key to cybersecurity resilience. As cyber threats evolve, companies' cybersecurity will gain ensuring business continuity, regulatory compliance, and long-term success.

CYBERSECURITY METRICS AND MONITORING IN DIGITAL TRANSFORMATION: MEASURING SUCCESS AND IDENTIFYING AREAS FOR IMPROVEMENT

As organizations undergo digital transformation, cybersecurity becomes a critical enabler of business success. The adoption has expanded the attack surface, making continuous cybersecurity monitoring and performance measurement essential. Businesses need robust cybersecurity to assess security. Demonstrating ROI on cybersecurity tools and processes. Without proper security metrics and monitoring, organizations may fail to detect breaches, misallocate resources, or remain non-compliant with industry regulations (Chaudhary et al, 2022). Case Study: A Financial Institution's Metric-Driven Security Strategy: A leading multinational bank faced increasing cyber threats as it expanded its cloud banking and mobile payment services. To strengthen its security posture, the bank: Implemented a Security Operations Center (SOC) with real-time monitoring dashboards. Used AI-driven behavioral analytics to detect anomalies in financial transactions. By adopting a data-driven approach, the bank improved threat detection efficiency by 50% and reduced fraud-related losses by 35% within a year. Key Cybersecurity Metrics for Digital Transformation: Threat Detection and Incident Response Metrics: Measuring how quickly an organization detects and responds to cyber threats is essential. Key metrics include: Mean Time to Respond (MTTR): required to contain and mitigate threats. Incident Closure Rate: security set timeframe(Shende et al. 2025). False Positive Rate: The number that turns out to be non-threat (high rates indicate inefficiencies). Risk Management and Compliance Metrics: Organizations must track compliance with security frameworks and identify potential risk areas. Risk-Based Vulnerability Management: Percentage of high-risk vulnerabilities patched within SLA timelines (Aldoseri et al, 2024). Regulatory Compliance Score: Adherence to cybersecurity laws (e.g., ISO 27001, GDPR, HIPAA). Data Loss Prevention (DLP) Incidents: The number of unauthorized data exfiltration attempts. Security Awareness

Training Completion Rate: Employee participation in cybersecurity programs. A healthcare company used compliance metrics to improve HIPAA readiness, reducing compliance violations by 40% within two years.

Implementing Effective Cybersecurity Monitoring Strategies

Real-Time Security Monitoring with SIEM and XDR: solutions monitoring. They provide: Centralized security log collection and analysis. Real-time alerts on suspicious activities. Threat correlation using AI and machine learning. For example, a government agency deployed SIEM to detect insider threats, reducing unauthorized data access incidents by 30%. AI-Driven Threat Intelligence and Behavioral Analytics: Modern organizations use AI-powered cybersecurity tools to analyze patterns and predict threats before they occur. User and Entity Behavior Analytics (UEBA) detects unusual activities. Machine learning algorithms identify zero-day vulnerabilities. Organizations implement: Endpoint Detection and Response (EDR) solutions to monitor device activity (Almeida F., et al, 2023). Secure Access Service Edge (SASE) for secure remote connectivityIntegrating cybersecurity workflows with Developers for secure software development (Olanrewaju O I K., et al, 2024). As quantum computing evolves, new metrics will measure the resilience of encryption algorithms against quantum threats. Conclusion: cybersecurity is not just a defensive strategy—it is a business enabler. Organizations that adopt data-driven cybersecurity metrics and real-time monitoring tools gain a competitive advantage by improving threat detection, compliance, and security resilience. By leveraging AI-driven analytics, Zero Trust security, cloud security frameworks, and automated response mechanisms, businesses can measure cybersecurity success and continuously improve their cyber the organizations that prioritize continuous cybersecurity monitoring and proactive risk management will be best positioned for long-term digital success and security resilience.

THE FUTURE OF DIGITAL TRANSFORMATION AND CYBERSECURITY

Reshaping industries, economies, and societies, driven by innovations in 5G connectivity. As businesses embrace digital-first strategies, cybersecurity has become an essential pillar of success, ensuring data protection, regulatory compliance, and business continuity. However, as organizations accelerate their digital initiatives, they also face increasingly sophisticated cyber threats, including ransomware attacks, supply chain vulnerabilities, and AI-powered cybercrime. Digital transformation is how effectively businesses cybersecurity into their innovation strategies(Johri et al. 2025). The Expanding Cyber Threat Landscape: As digital ecosystems grow; organizations face more complex and persistent cyber threats. Key findings include: Cybercrime is becoming more sophisticated: AI-powered attacks, deepfake fraud, and ransomware-as-a-service (RaaS) have increased. Cloud security remains a critical concern: 90% of organizations experience cloud misconfiguration vulnerabilities, leading to data breaches. Supply chain security is a growing challenge: Attackers target third-party vendors to infiltrate enterprise networks (Judijanto L., et al, 2023). Zero Trust Security is Becoming the Industry Standard: To counteract evolving cyber threats, organizations are shifting to a Zero Trust Architecture (ZTA). Findings show: that 80% of enterprises plan to adopt Zero Trust by 2026. Organizations recognize cybersecurity as a strategic business priority rather than an IT expense: Global cybersecurity spending is expected to exceed $300 billion by 2026 (Ghelani D., et al, 2022). Self-healing networks using AI to detect and fix vulnerabilities in real time.

Stronger cloud security controls to prevent unauthorized access and data leaks (Kumar S., et al, 2022). The Growing Role of Cybersecurity in Business Strategy: Cybersecurity will become a core business function, influencing: Corporate mergers and acquisitions (M&A), with security audits becoming a key factor. Brand reputation and customer trust, as businesses prioritize transparent security practices. CISO (Chief Information Security Officer) roles expanding, gaining board-level influence. Preparing for the Future: Key Recommendations: Proactive Cybersecurity Investment: Organizations must invest in advanced security solutions, including AI-driven threat intelligence platforms. Zero Trust and multi-factor authentication (MFA). Post-quantum cryptography and next-generation encryption standards. Strengthening Cyber Resilience and Incident Response: Businesses should develop robust cyber resilience frameworks by: Conducting regular cybersecurity audits and penetration testing. Implementing automated security incident response to reduce downtime. Enhancing employee cybersecurity awareness training to prevent social engineering attacks. Regulatory Compliance and Risk Management: Organizations must stay ahead of evolving cybersecurity regulations by: Regularly updating compliance policies to align with GDPR, NIS2, and SEC requirements. Developing cross-border data security strategies to comply with international laws. Conducting third-party risk assessments for supply chain security (Dash et al, 2022). In the years ahead, automation, and quantum-safe security will redefine cybersecurity strategies, helping organizations build resilient, future-proof digital ecosystems. Businesses that prioritize cybersecurity as a core pillar of digital transformation will be the ones that lead innovation, growth, and long-term success.

CONCLUSION

Digital transformation has become a cornerstone of modern business strategy, driving innovation, efficiency, and scalability through big data analytics, and 5G connectivity. However, as organizations embrace digital technologies, they are also exposed to an evolving cybersecurity threat landscape that includes ransomware, phishing attacks, insider threats, supply chain vulnerabilities, and AI-powered cybercrime. The interdependence of digital transformation and cybersecurity highlights resilient, strategy that aligns with an organization's long-term growth and operational goals. A fundamental shift toward Zero Trust Security, AI-driven cybersecurity, and regulatory compliance is shaping the future of digital security. Businesses are increasingly prioritizing as they strive to strengthen cyber resilience. The rapid expansion of cloud environments and remote workforces necessitates a data-centric security model, where encryption, identity, and access management (IAM), are integral frameworks. The only concern that directly impacts corporate reputation, regulatory standing, customer trust, and financial stability. Governments and regulatory bodies worldwide have introduced stringent GDPR, NIS2, CCPA, and the SEC Cybersecurity Disclosure Rule, to enhance data protection and cyber resilience. Businesses must implement risk-based cybersecurity frameworks, and adopt threat intelligence-driven security operations. Landscape further quantum computing, AI-powered autonomous security systems, blockchain for secure transactions, and decentralized identity management. And next-generation encryption standards will increase. The future of digital transformation and cybersecurity will be defined by automation, predictive analytics, and AI-driven threat intelligence, to prevent, and mitigate cyber. To successfully navigate the evolving digital and security ecosystem, organizations must embrace a security-first approach, where cybersecurity is embedded into every stage of digital transformation. This requires collaborative efforts between IT teams, executives, regulatory bodies, and cybersecurity professionals to create a secure, innovative, and resilient digital future. By integrating advanced cybersecurity technologies, fostering a strong security culture, and continuously adapting to emerging threats, businesses can achieve a sustainable digital transformation era of rapid technological advancements, only those organizations that prioritize cybersecurity as a strategic enabler of innovation will thrive in the digital economy.

REFERENCES

Adewumi, A., Ewim, S. E., & Sam-Bulya, N. J. (2024). Advancing business performance through data-driven process automation: A case study of digital transformation in the banking sector. *International Journal of Business and Management*. Advance online publication. DOI: 10.5296/ijbm.v12i1.23456

Ahmed, I., Zhang, Y., Jeon, G., & Lin, W. (2022). A blockchain-and artificial intelligence-enabled smart IoT framework for sustainable city. *Journal of Intelligent Information Systems*, *60*(2), 267–279. DOI: 10.1007/s10844-021-00691-9

AlDaajeh, S., Saleous, H., Alrabaee, S., & Barka, E. (2022). The role of national cybersecurity strategies on the improvement of cybersecurity education. *Computers & Electrical Engineering*, *102*, 108134. DOI: 10.1016/j.compeleceng.2022.108134

Aldoseri, A., Al-Khalifa, K. N., & Hamouda, A. M. (2024). Methodological approach to assessing the current state of organizations for AI-Based digital transformation. *Applied System Innovation*, *7*(2), 31. DOI: 10.3390/asi7010014

Almeida, F. (2023). Challenges in the digital transformation of ports. *Businesses*, *3*(2), 147–157. DOI: 10.3390/businesses3040034

Anderson, J. (2022). *The Role of Identity and Access Management (IAM) in Securing Cloud Workloads*. ResearchGate.

Aragani, V. M., Anumolu, V. R., & Selvakumar, P. (2025). Democratization in the Age of Algorithms: Navigating Opportunities and Challenges. In Wongmahesak, K., Wekke, I., Seftyono, C., & Nurdin, N. (Eds.), *Democracy and Democratization in the Age of AI* (pp. 39–56). IGI Global Scientific Publishing., DOI: 10.4018/979-8-3693-8749-8.ch003

Bellantuono, N., Nuzzi, A., Pontrandolfo, P., & Scozzi, B. (2021). Digital transformation models for the I4.0 transition: Lessons from the change management literature. *Sustainability (Basel)*, *13*(11), 6231. DOI: 10.3390/su132312941

Benjamin, L. B., & Adegbola, A. E. (2024). Digital transformation in SMEs: Identifying cybersecurity risks and developing effective mitigation strategies. *Global Journal of Management and Business Research*, *14*(2), 1–11.

Chaudhary, S., Gkioulos, V., & Katsikas, S. (2022). Developing metrics to assess the effectiveness of cybersecurity awareness program. *Journal of Cybersecurity*, 2(2), 147–157. DOI: 10.1093/cybsec/tyac006

Chowdhury, R. H. (2024). The evolution of business operations: Unleashing the potential of Artificial Intelligence, Machine Learning, and Blockchain. *World Journal of Advanced Research and Reviews*, *10*(2), 1–13. DOI: 10.30574/wjarr.2024.10.2.0930

Dash, B., Ansari, M. F., Sharma, P., & Ali, A. (2022). Threats and opportunities with AI-based cyber security intrusion detection: A review. *International Journal of Artificial Intelligence and Cybernetics*, *4*(2), 1–15. DOI: 10.5121/ijsea.2022.13502

Debnath, P., Deshmukh, S. M., Laroia, M., Selvakumar, P., Manjunath, T. C., & Bhattacharya, S. (2025). Challenges Faced by Countries in Renewable Energy Adoption. In Özsungur, F., Chaychi Semsari, M., & Küçük Bayraktar, H. (Eds.), *Geopolitical Landscapes of Renewable Energy and Urban Growth* (pp. 295–320). IGI Global Scientific Publishing., DOI: 10.4018/979-8-3693-8814-3.ch010

Devara, J. S. M. (2024). Cloud, Ai, And Digital Transformation: A Winning Combination. *International Journal Of Computer Engineering And Technology*, *13*(2), 1–9.

Díaz, A., Guerra, L., & Díaz, E. (2021). *"Digital transformation impact in security and privacy." Advances in Defense and Security*. Springer.

Ghadge, N. (2024). Use of blockchain technology to strengthen identity and access management (IAM). *International Journal of Information Technology : an Official Journal of Bharati Vidyapeeth's Institute of Computer Applications and Management*, *16*(1), 1–15.

Ghelani, D. (2022). "Cyber security, cyber threats, implications and future perspectives: A Review." *Authorea Preprints*. Doi: DOI: 10.22541/au.166385207.73483369/v1

Ghobakhloo, M., & Iranmanesh, M. (2021). Digital transformation success under Industry 4.0: A strategic guideline for manufacturing SMEs. *Journal of Manufacturing Technology Management*, *32*(6), 1045–1066. DOI: 10.1108/JMTM-11-2020-0455

Gupta, I., Singh, A. K., Lee, C. N., & Buyya, R. (2022). Secure data storage and sharing techniques for data protection in cloud environments: A systematic review, analysis, and future directions. *IEEE Access : Practical Innovations, Open Solutions*, *10*, 53111–53135. DOI: 10.1109/ACCESS.2022.3188110

Hakimi M, Quchi M M, Fazil A W, (2024). "Human factors in cybersecurity: an in depth analysis of user centric studies." Jurnal Informatika Indonesia (JIM-ID), 7(1), 1-12.

Hassan, A. O., Ewuga, S. K., & Abdul, A. A. (2024). "Cybersecurity in banking: a global perspective with a focus on Nigerian practices." Science & IT Conference, 1-12. Doi: DOI: 10.2139/ssrn.4079155

Hussain, A. A., & Al-Turjman, F. (2021). Artificial intelligence and blockchain: A review. *Journal of Telecommunications Technologies, 19*(2), 123–135. DOI: 10.33118/jtt.2021.169730.1032

Ige A B, Kupa E, Ilori O, (2024). "Best practices in cybersecurity for green building management systems: Protecting sustainable infrastructure from cyber threats." Journal of Science and Research Archive. Doi: .DOI: 10.48165/JSRA.2024.12423

Jimmy, F. (2021). *Emerging threats: The latest cybersecurity risks and the role of artificial intelligence in enhancing cybersecurity defenses.* Valley International Journal Digital Library., DOI: 10.47028/valley.ijdl.2021.02.001

Johri, A., & Kumar, S. (2023). Exploring customer awareness towards their cyber security in the Kingdom of Saudi Arabia: A study in the era of banking digital transformation. *Human Behavior and Emerging Technologies, 5*(2), 147–157. DOI: 10.1155/2023/2103442

Johri, S., Selvakumar, P., Satyanarayana, P., Das, A., Gupta, S., & Bhattacharya, S. (2025). Urbanization and Energy: The Nexus of Global Challenges. In Özsungur, F., Chaychi Semsari, M., & Küçük Bayraktar, H. (Eds.), *Geopolitical Landscapes of Renewable Energy and Urban Growth* (pp. 453–478). IGI Global Scientific Publishing., DOI: 10.4018/979-8-3693-8814-3.ch016

Jonas, D., Yusuf, N. A., & Zahra, A. R. A. (2023). *Enhancing security frameworks with artificial intelligence in cybersecurity.* International Transactions on Computer and Information Security., DOI: 10.33050/itee.v2i1.428

Judijanto, L., & Hindarto, D. (2023). Edge of enterprise architecture in addressing cyber security threats and business risks. *Journal of Information and Computational Science, 18*(1), 1–12. DOI: 10.33073/jics.v18i1.1849

Julakanti, S. R. KiranmayeeSattiraju NS, (2025). "Data Protection through Governance Frameworks." arXiv preprint arXiv, 1-12. Doi: /arXiv.2302.03985.DOI: 10.48550

Kafi, M. A., & Akter, N. (2023). Securing financial information in the digital realm: Case studies in cybersecurity for accounting data protection. *American Journal of Trade and Policy, 4*(2), 1–12. DOI: 10.18034/ajtp.v10i1.659

Kechagias, E. P., Chatzistelios, G., Papadopoulos, G. A., & Apostolou, P. (2022). Digital transformation of the maritime industry: A cybersecurity systemic approach. *International Journal of Critical Infrastructure Protection, 37*, 100454. DOI: 10.1016/j.ijcip.2022.100526

Kumar, K., & Zolkipli, M. F. (2024). A Review on Identity and Access Management (IAM) for Digital Environment Security. *Borneo International Journal, 7*(1), 1–12.

Kumar, S., & Mallipeddi, R. R. (2022). Impact of cybersecurity on operations and supply chain management: Emerging trends and future research directions. *Production and Operations Management, 31*(4), 1470–1485. DOI: 10.1111/poms.13859

Lewallen, J. (2021). Emerging technologies and problem definition uncertainty: The case of cybersecurity. *Regulation & Governance, 15*(2), 267–279. DOI: 10.1111/rego.12341

Mahadev Madgule, N. (2023). Vinayaka, Yeshwant M. Sonkhaskar, Dhiren Ramanbhai Patel, R. Karthikeyan, P. Selvakumar,(2023). Mechanical properties and microstructure of activated TIG welded similar joints of Inconel alloys by desirability approaches. *Materials Today: Proceedings, 77*, 528–533. DOI: 10.1016/j.matpr.2022.12.250

Manoharan A, Sarker M, (2023). "Revolutionizing Cybersecurity: Unleashing the Power of Artificial Intelligence and Machine Learning for Next-Generation Threat Detection." Doi: .DOI: 10.56726/ijais/2023.123456

Mendhurwar, S., & Mishra, R. (2021). Integration of social and IoT technologies: Architectural framework for digital transformation and cyber security challenges. *Enterprise Information Systems, 15*(4), 432–451. DOI: 10.1080/17517575.2019.1600041

Mijwil, M., Filali, Y., Aljanabi, M., & Bounabi, M. (2023). The purpose of cybersecurity governance in the digital transformation of public services and protecting the digital environment. *Journal of Cybersecurity*, 1–12. DOI: 10.1093/cybsec/tyac018

Mızrak, F. (2023). Integrating cybersecurity risk management into strategic management: A comprehensive literature review. *Research Journal of Business and Management, 10*(2), 1–15. DOI: 10.17261/Pressacademia.2023.1807

Möller, D. P. F. (2023). *"Cybersecurity in digital transformation." Guide to Cybersecurity in Digital Transformation: Trends*. Springer., DOI: 10.1007/978-3-031-26845-8

Nafrees, A. C. M., Sujah, A. M. A., & Mansoor, C. (2021). Smart Cities: Emerging technologies and Potential solutions to the Cyber security threads. *Computer Technologies and Information Security, 1-5*, 220–228. Advance online publication. DOI: 10.1109/ICEECCOT52851.2021.9707994

Nkongolo, M. (2023). "Navigating the complex nexus: cybersecurity in political landscapes." arXiv preprint arXiv:2308.08005.

Oladipo, J. O., Okoye, C. C., & Elufioye, O. A. (2024). Human factors in cybersecurity: Navigating the fintech landscape. *Journal of Science and Research, 10*(2), 1–13.

Olanrewaju, O. I. K., & Daramola, G. O. (2024). Transforming business models with ESG integration: A strategic framework for financial professionals. *World Journal of Advanced Research and Reviews*, *11*(2), 1–13. DOI: 10.30574/wjarr.2024.11.2.0930

Pollini, A., Callari, T. C., Tedeschi, A., Ruscio, D., Save, L., Chiarugi, F., & Guerri, D. (2022). Leveraging human factors in cybersecurity: An integrated methodological approach. *Cognition Technology and Work*, *24*(2), 267–279. DOI: 10.1007/s10111-021-00683-y PMID: 34149309

Ramakrishnan, T., Mohan Gift, M. D., Chitradevi, S., Jegan, R., & Subha Hency Jose, P. Nagaraja, Rajneesh Sharma H.N., Selvakumar P., Sintayehu Mekuria Hailegiorgis, (2022). "Study of Numerous Resins Used in Polymer Matrix Composite Materials", Advances in Materials Science and Engineering, vol. 2022, Article ID 1088926, 8 pages, 2022. DOI: 10.1155/2022/1088926

Rani S, Bhambri P, Kataria A, Khang A, Sivaraman A K, (2023). "Big Data, Cloud Computing and IoT: Tools and Applications."

Rizvi, M. (2023). Enhancing cybersecurity: The power of artificial intelligence in threat detection and prevention. *Journal of Advanced Engineering Research and Science*, *10*(2), 1–9. DOI: 10.22161/ijaers.105.8

Saeed, S., Altamimi, S. A., Alkayyal, N. A., Alshehri, E., & Alabbad, D. A. (2023). Digital transformation and cybersecurity challenges for businesses resilience: Issues and recommendations. *Sensors (Basel)*, *23*(3), 1–15. DOI: 10.3390/s23156666 PMID: 37571451

Safitra, M. F., Lubis, M., & Fakhrurroja, H. (2023). Counterattacking cyber threats: A framework for the future of cybersecurity. *Sustainability (Basel)*, *15*(11), 8351. DOI: 10.3390/su151813369

Saini, K., & Sehrawat, P. (2024). "Cybersecurity in Digital Transformation: Challenges and Solutions." *2024 Second International Conference*, 1-5. DOI: 10.1109/ICACCTech65084.2024.00079

Sandhu, A. K. (2021). Big data with cloud computing: Discussions and challenges. *Big Data Mining and Analytics*, *4*(2), 123–135. DOI: 10.26599/BDMA.2021.9020005

Shende, A. D., Tekade, S. A., Deshmukh, A. A., Tembhurkar, S. P., & Selvakumar, P. (2025). Water Quality Monitoring and Control With AI. In Ruiz-Vanoye, J., & Díaz-Parra, O. (Eds.), *Smart Water Technology for Sustainable Management in Modern Cities* (pp. 51–80). IGI Global Scientific Publishing., DOI: 10.4018/979-8-3693-8074-1.ch003

Siddiqui, Z. A., & Haroon, M. (2022). *"Application of artificial intelligence and machine learning in blockchain technology." Artificial Intelligence and Machine Learning for Blockchain*. Elsevier., DOI: 10.1016/B978-0-323-85575-5.00001-6

Singh, C., Thakkar, R., & Warraich, J. (2023). IAM identity Access Management—Importance in maintaining security systems within organizations. *European Journal of Engineering and Technology*, *11*(2), 1–12. DOI: 10.24018/ejeng.2023.8.4.3074

Sontan, A. D., & Samuel, S. V. (2024). The intersection of Artificial Intelligence and cybersecurity: Challenges and opportunities. *World Journal of Advanced Research and Reviews*, *12*(2), 1–13.

Sreenivasulu, A., & Manimozhi, T. Satheesh kumar P., Selvakumar P. and Singh P., (2022). "The Model of Smart Sensing Device For Sensitive Nanoclusters Modification in Sensing Properties," 2022 2nd International Conference on Advance Computing and Innovative Technologies in Engineering (ICACITE), Greater Noida, India, 2022, pp. 1043-1047, DOI: 10.1109/ICACITE53722.2022.9823846

Stewart, H. (2023). Digital transformation security challenges. *Journal of Computer Information Systems*, *63*(2), 234–241. DOI: 10.1080/08874417.2021.1877063

Tikanmäki, I., & Ruoslahti, H. (2024). Insights on Human Factors Enhancing Cybersecurity. *Information & Security*, *56*(2), 145–158.

Timan T, Mann Z, (2021). "Data protection in the era of artificial intelligence: trends, existing solutions and recommendations for privacy-preserving technologies." The Elements of Big Data Value: Foundations of, 1-15. Doi: .DOI: 10.1007/978-3-030-86835-8_1

Tran-Dang, H., & Kim, D. S. (2021). The physical internet in the era of digital transformation: Perspectives and open issues. *IEEE Access : Practical Innovations, Open Solutions*, *9*, 111537–111548. DOI: 10.1109/ACCESS.2021.3131562

Vaddadi, S. A., & Vallabhaneni, R. (2023). *Utilizing AI and machine learning in cybersecurity for sustainable development through enhanced threat detection and mitigation*. International Journal of Sustainable Development and Green Economics., DOI: 10.4018/IJSDGG.2023.010205

Wang, S., Asif, M., Shahzad, M. F., & Ashfaq, M. (2024). Data privacy and cybersecurity challenges in the digital transformation of the banking sector. *Computers & Security*, *124*, 103134. DOI: 10.1016/j.cose.2024.104051

Yeoh, W., Liu, M., Shore, M., & Jiang, F. (2023). Zero trust cybersecurity: Critical success factors and A maturity assessment framework. *Computers & Security*, *124*, 103159. DOI: 10.1016/j.cose.2023.103412

Yeoh, W., Wang, S., Popovič, A., & Chowdhury, N. H. (2022). A systematic synthesis of critical success factors for cybersecurity. *Computers & Security*, *122*, 102744. DOI: 10.1016/j.cose.2022.102724

Chapter 2
Digital Transformation and Cybersecurity Challenges for Electronic Government

Hina Gull
https://orcid.org/0000-0002-6685-5189
Imam Abdulrahman Bin Faisal University, Dammam, Saudi Arabia

Bashaier Abdulatif Al-Hamad
https://orcid.org/0009-0005-0823-4025
Imam Abdulrahman Bin Faisal University, Dammam, Saudi Arabia

Noor Al-Dossary
Imam Abdulrahman Bin Faisal University, Dammam, Saudi Arabia

Hayfa Al-Muhaisen
Imam Abdulrahman Bin Faisal University, Dammam, Saudi Arabia

Madeeha Saqib
https://orcid.org/0000-0003-4856-8095
Imam Abdulrahman Bin Faisal University, Dammam, Saudi Arabia

Sardar Zafar Iqbal
Imam Abdulrahman Bin Faisal University, Dammam, Saudi Arabia

ABSTRACT

As users adopt new technologies that offer greater convenience, the incidence of cyber-attacks has been increasing dramatically, resulting in losses for the government on all fronts. This literature review highlights the significance of being aware of both well-known vulnerabilities and new cyber threats to ensure that the computer systems used by the government are safe from hackers and other malicious actors who may try to steal or harm sensitive information. The research community has made significant efforts in this area, but there is still a need for further progress. Our work provides insights into how to protect important electronic government from cyber-attacks in the era of digital transformation within a robust cybersecu-

DOI: 10.4018/979-8-3373-3171-3.ch002

rity framework. The proposed framework for secure e-government adoption can be used to assess the cybersecurity readiness of government sectors undergoing digital transformation. By evaluating key components, we can ensure that security measures are effective and continuously improved.

INTRODUCTION

E-government is an enabler for governments to provide public services, however adoption of e-government is quite challenging, (Moşteanu, 2020; Totonchi, 2023). The technologies are advancing at a rapid rate and advanced technologies such as artificial intelligence and blockchain can transform the citizen engagement, (Bokhari & Myeong, 2023; Al-Beshar & Kumar, 2022; Phadke, Medrano, & Ustymenko, 2022; Gaur, Ujjan, & Hussain, 2022). Governments worldwide are exploring how technology can be leveraged to improve public service delivery and citizen engagement; however, impact of digital divide is also present in e-government sector, (Lněnička & Máchová, 2022). Covid-19 pandemic has further highlighted the importance of provision of electronic services to citizens, (Wilson, 2020). Extensive research has highlighted both the potential and challenges associated with e-government, (Twizeyimana & Andersson, 2019). Cybersecurity of e-government systems has become a critical challenge in e-government adoption and resilience, (Shah, 2022; Saeed et al., 2023). Since governments rely heavily on information technology to provide services and store sensitive information, making it crucial to protect these systems from cyber threats, (Shah et al., 2022; Shah, Wassan, & Usmani, 2022). Extensive mobile usage by general public has also increased the opportunities for delivering digital services to the citizens and usable mobile applications can improve the delivery of public services, (Saeed, 2024).

Strong cybersecurity measures are essential to safeguard government networks, prevent unauthorized access, and maintain the privacy and integrity of citizen data, (Elisa et al., 2023). By implementing robust encryption, (Ihtesham et al., 2023), multi-factor authentication, (Dubey, Saquib, & Dwivedi, 2015), conducting regular security audits, (Aslam et al., 2022), and providing comprehensive cybersecurity trainings (Alshaikh et al., 2019) governments can enhance their cybersecurity defenses. Furthermore, cyber threat agility and capacity building can improve organizational cybersecurity response capabilities, (Naseer et al., 2023; Saeed et al., 2023). Prioritizing cybersecurity in e-government builds trust for stakeholders, ensures operational efficiency, and protects the digital assets, (Mijwil et al., 2023). Citizen engagement to foster secure practices is another challenging aspect where education and training of users can help, (Ahangama, 2023).

Cyberattacks have the potential to breach the integrity, confidentiality, and privacy of information, (Meltzer, 2020). The impact of these attacks on e-government systems can be substantial. Recent digital transformation initiatives have highlighted the cybersecurity implications for organizations, which require robust organizational measures, (Mendhurwar & Mishra, 2021). Sustaining trustworthy e-government infrastructures require huge collaboration among stakeholders ranging from policy makers, technological personnel and citizens (Svärd, 2017) and many case studies in different geographical regions such as Estonia, (Espinosa & Pinto, 2025), Germany, (Jarvers & Schachtner, 2024), Netherland, (Raju, Hannani, & Perumal, 2025), Thailand, (Nookhao & Kiattisin, 2023), Singapore, (Abdou, 2021), Saudi Arabia, (Saeed, 2023; Gull et al., 2022), Pakistan, (Saeed, 2023), Greece, (Maglaras et al., 2020), China, (Mao & Zhu, 2023), and BRICS (Brazil, Russia, India, China, and South Africa) member countries (Ovchinnikova & Upadhyay, 2023) highlighted cybersecurity challenges.

In this paper, we have conducted a detailed literature review to document how digital transformation has changed government services and the implications of cybersecurity. We have proposed a framework for further enhancing the cybersecurity of e-government sectors undergoing digital transformation. By evaluating the key components such as policy and governance, cyber threat intelligence, Security Compliance and Auditing, Incident Response and Reporting, Awareness and Training and Technological Infrastructure security. The findings of this study will assist practitioners, researchers, and government agencies in comprehending the current state of the art in this field and serve as a basis for further research.

Rest of the paper is structured as follows: Section 2 discusses the methodology adopted to conduct this study, Section 3, extensively discusses different literature contributions and is followed by discussion, and a conclusion in Section 4 and Section 5 respectively.

MATERIALS AND METHODS

To extract primary studies, we utilized the Google Scholar database, as shown in Figure 1. We applied five specific keywords in our search criteria. These keywords were carefully selected to help us locate research articles that were relevant to our topic. Our search terms included (Cyber Threat) AND (Electronic Government), (Digital Transformation Cybersecurity) AND (Government), (Digital Technology in Government) AND (Cyber Attack), (Electronic Government and Cybersecurity) and (Cybersecurity) AND (Public Sector Cybersecurity). For each term, we selected top 20 results that were published between the years 2019 and 2025. Out of these 100 papers there were 14 duplicate papers which were removed. To narrow down our search results, we established the inclusion criteria that the selected paper must focus on cybersecurity and digital transformation in government organizations. Furthermore, we implemented the following exclusion criteria for our search results:• The paper is not published in a scientific conference or journal.

- The paper is only focusing on cybersecurity or digital transformation.
- The paper is a review paper.

Figure 1. Systematic literature review details

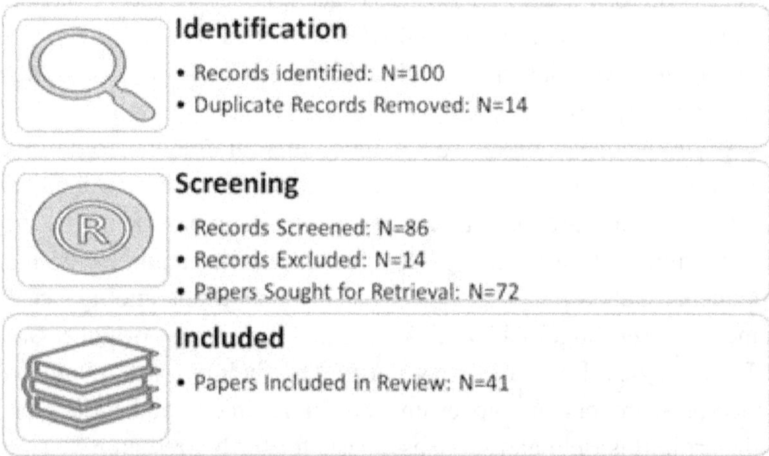

We verified all Google Scholar search results to ensure that they met these criteria. The process of identifying the studies that we extracted involved a quality assessment stage, which began with a quick scan of the title. We then confirmed that these papers were related and relevant to our research, and subsequently assessed the accuracy of the information included in these studies. In Figure 1, we present the total number of articles that were accepted after going through these stages of review. Our final analysis consisted of forty-one papers.

RESULTS

According to Issabayeva, Yesseniyazova, and Grega (2019), one of the most unique and important components of enhancing public procurement processes is electronic public procurement. The authors have examined the main features of the Kazakh e-procurement portal to evaluate it from a national and comparative standpoint and to offer recommendations for cybersecurity improvement in digital transformation. According to the findings, standardized practices, trained personnel, funding and provision of licensed software can secure the public electronic procurement process.

In another study Lubua and Pretorius (2019), carried out an empirical study in Africa to support public sector organizations to comply with security standards of ISO 27001 in enhancing their functional cybersecurity policy. The empirical study was carried out in fifteen companies and authors developed a cybersecurity framework. Data security, network services and Internet governance, physical security, policy administrative concerns, incident response, reporting and usage of company-owned devices, and monitoring were listed as seven key themes for this framework.

In another empirical study, Maharaj and Munyoka (2019) measured the user behavior with the use of e-government systems in Zambia and Zimbabwe to improve the usage. The study used a survey and data was collected from 489 respondents and data highlighted that government authorities need to improve user uncertainties associated with e-government. The empirical data reported a negative relationship in perceived risk and perceived security and trust whereas perceived privacy, trust, and security positively related with user behavior. The results highlighting improved usage of e-government portals require higher cybersecurity controls to foster user trust on the systems.

According to Norris et al. (2019), there has been an increasing number of cyberattacks at the Grass Roots government organizations. It has been identified that the American local governments are vulnerable to such attacks and there has been a major requirement for high levels of security for managing the cyber threats and attacks. The cyberattacks are required to be evaluated by the governments as they eventually practice cybersecurity not effectively. The most distinctive issue that has been highlighted by the authors is that most of these agencies are unaware of the factor that they lack major preparedness for cybersecurity aspects and as a result, they do not have information about the breaching of the information systems. Major recommendations are also made to the local governments for improving the existing practices so that the existing challenges are reduced. The local governments should implement stronger password practices, regular updates of software with the involvement of multi-factor authentication within every account as well as encryption of the most confidential data.

As per Oni et al. (2019), the Nigerian e-government is vulnerable to several challenges and risks related to cybersecurity. The main reason is that the governmental agencies have been using various information and communication technologies so that the overall quality of the governance is enhanced. The authors identified several negative implications of cyberattacks on the implementation of e-government in Nigeria. One such implication is the loss of confidential data. The data gathered has been evaluated with the Routine Activity theory. Data breaches have been increased by government agencies that could bring confidential information and hacktivism should be managed.

Mawgoud et al. (2019) have mentioned that there has been an increasing threat of cyber-attacks and risks in the MENA or Middle Eastern and North African regions. It has been identified for the last few years, the hackers have been focusing on several governmental high-valued sectors such as oil and gas. However, the ICT sector has been vulnerable to the enhancing cybersecurity issues or threats that should be reduced and managed over time. The authors have identified different cybersecurity threats in the MENA region. The most common threats identified in this particular region include DDoS or distributed denial of service attacks, data breaches, ransomware attacks, phishing scams and many more. As a result, several agencies in both private and government sectors have been impacted and become victims of such attacks. To reduce the negative impacts of these issues and risks, the authors have proposed various countermeasures that should be followed by the governments for protecting and maintaining business continuity.

According to Chatfield and Reddick (2019), Internet of Things has been extremely significant in the current technological world. The main reason is that various IoT-enabled capabilities have been bringing digital transformation for government would be included. It is also noted that there are a few challenges identified in the management of IoT cybersecurity as well as systematic use for the US government. The authors have implemented a framework for the overall performance of the IoT-based smart government and the need for technological research on policies would be addressed. A case study analysis for digital technology has been conducted for understanding the significance of IoT cybersecurity policy as well as the major usage of the technology in different application domains for the US federal government. As per the results of the analysis, it is identified that a few agencies would be forward-thinking or strategic for funding and partnering with every sub-national government so that IoT use is promoted.

According to Warkentin and Orgeron (2020), the implementation of blockchain technology can be termed effective for enhancing security, governance as well as regulatory aspects for the public sector agencies or government. The security triad (confidentiality, integrity and accessibility) have been responsible for ensuring the efficiency is enhanced for the respective technology. The authors have identified different benefits that are identified from the non-reputability of distributed ledgers and public managers should consider the technology for blockchain for security aspects so that operations are transformed. It has been noted that the technology often makes it quite difficult for the users to change records accordingly. The overall confidentiality, accuracy and availability of the data would be ensured so that a major plan would be considered for maximum disaster recovery. Hash functions would be used so that data integrity would be verified and data is not corrupted or modified. As a result, the confidential data would be protected and managed over time.

Yarovoy et al. (2020) have stated that a country's financial as well as information security is dependent on the implementation of the e-government. It has been identified that the digital economy has been based on the overall information as well as communication and different digital technologies so that a positive effect would be placed on the business, economy and society to improve the existing procedures or operations. The authors have identified various threats that are often associated with the electronic governance system in global countries so that information security is enhanced. The E-Government Development Index has been considered for different indicators related to such development so that every key public policy trend is identified and managed accordingly. The authors have considered different countries such as the UK, France, Japan, Denmark, Singapore and many more. The results identify different trends such as interoperability, equity and inclusiveness, open standards and many more. As a result, technological sustainability will be increased and there will be maximum information security.

According to Al-Zahrani (2020), a major integration of the information system success model would be effective with different cybersecurity factors. Such integration is required for a successful and effective implementation of the e-government in the Kingdom of Saudi Arabia. The main benefits of this specific integration include considering a positive influence on the overall users' satisfaction with different e-government services. The author has identified that the DeLone and McLean information systems success model can act as the framework that can easily assess the overall success factors of the information systems. The model is responsible for considering different technical aspects of any system with a major effect on users as well as the company. A quantitative method has been used with the structural equation modelling and technology acceptance model. It has been identified that different e-government services of the KSA would be impacted positively for better effectiveness and usage of the model.

According to Hoffman and Cseh (2020), there have been several challenges related to cybersecurity issues in the Hungarian municipalities. These challenges are mainly related to electronic administration, cybersecurity as well as municipalities in the country. It has been noted that the digitalization of the public administration comprises significant relations with different security issues or complexities. A vital reason that has been identified for such issues is that the economic power or financial condition of the Hungarian municipalities is weaker as compared to other countries. It is required to be focused on the overall development of the horizontally integrated electronic administration that should be prioritized. The authors have also identified that the major attacks on security aspects of the e-governance system could take place in various aspects such as hacking, network security issues, malware, virus attacks, damage to the critical databases and many more. The authors ensured that different solutions should be implemented for reducing the impacts of these challenges in the Hungarian municipalities.

Maglaras et al. (2020) have highlighted the overall cybersecurity progress in Greece from the successful creation as well as the implementation of the National Cybersecurity Authority in the country as the nationwide coordination and even policy-making unit. Cybersecurity plays a vital role in the distinctive era of digital transformation in Greece. It even refers to the aspect that there would be a critical requirement for several robust security measures since the companies in the country have adopted new and improved digital technologies rapidly. These technologies majorly involve IoT services, big data and cloud computing that should be managed and prioritized accordingly. As a result, major protection from such attacks would be required so that cybersecurity would be a major part of the most successful digital transformation strategies. The authors have also stated that the implemented structured efforts have been responsible for gaining the highest rank or position for the prestigious index for the country within 160 countries.

According to Popkova and Gulzat (2020), it has been identified that there is a major contradiction between the digital economy for public well-being and cyber threats. The authors have considered the logical interlink of different social consequences of the digitalized economy as well as its major consequences for improved cybersecurity. A systematic monitoring of the economy would be required to be prioritized for ensuring that the digital economy can be managed so that there would be a chance to improve public well-being. As a result, major cyber risks would be reduced and managed. An interdependence between the cybersecurity index and human development index is determined and to complete the experiment, the authors have used correlation and regression analyses. The authors have been successful in proving that the major social consequences of the digital economy can be analyzed and identified for cybersecurity so that the technical components can be checked and focused.

According to Renaud et al. (2020), cybersecurity responsibilities should be prioritized and considered for the overall assessment of different intervention approaches that are successfully adopted by China and the Five Eyes countries, which include Australia, New Zealand, Canada, the United Kingdom and the United States. The respective governments could eventually intervene to a major or lower extent for reducing the impacts of different risks faced. It has been noted that these governments could adopt a hands-off approach or maximal intervention approach that would be responsible for ensuring that the cybersecurity aspects are focused on. The cyber risks are managed and it could be done with the successful establishment of different cybersecurity policies as well as guidelines. Such an intervention would even ensure that the respective citizens of these countries are successful in considering cyberattacks individually and there would be a major aspect in considering responsibilities for different cybersecurity actions for various stakeholders.

Norris et al. (2021) have mentioned that cybersecurity should be managed and maintained at the American grassroot government organizations. The main reason is that such security aspects are required to be prioritized so that any kind of discrepancy or issue is eradicated over time. The authors have collected the data from the first nationwide survey from grassroots and local governments within the United States so that cyberattacks are reduced. Since the US local governments have been facing frequent cyberattacks, it is evident that there should be a major responsibility for securing information assets. For managing cybersecurity threats, local governments should conduct sufficient risk management evaluations and due diligence on the third-party vendors for having specific accessibility to confidential information so that a proper interaction with government systems would be identified. The authors have identified that local governments are required to arrange different policies and strategies for managing the cybersecurity risks and the existing issues would be resolved.

Mishra, Alowaidi, and Sharma (2021) have stated that there is a major impact of different security policies and standards on the overall credibility of the electronic government. Several cyber-attackers have the intention of stealing the user information that could be sold over the dark web. As a result, it could eventually damage the overall brand image of different companies as well as create an exploitation of any e-commerce website. Different companies such as NIST and ISO-based standards for the overall security and safety of the information systems so that data breaches would be avoided. It has been identified that the research would be dealing with the effect of different policies and standards on the credibility and performance of the electronic government. The authors have used meta-analysis qualitative analysis. An open-sourcing scanning tool, called OWSZAP has been used for the quantitative data analysis and it has been noted that there should be a proper adoption of different factors related to the e-government as well as its potential barriers.

According to Aminah and Saksono (2021), the Indonesian government is required to consider the pros and cons of digital transformation. It has been identified that the Industrial Revolution 4.0 and 5.0 have been responsible for using different technologies such as big data, the IoT, robotic technologies and even artificial intelligence so that the existing social challenges and technological problems are resolved over time. However, it has been identified that the respective government would be facing challenges in improving the public services as well as government administrations. The current development of electronic government would be analyzed and considered so that maximum efficiency would be gained. A major transformation would be required so that the negative impacts are reduced. Several barriers have been identified for the e-government including lack of data integration, limited ICT competence, insufficient regulations for encouraging and guiding e-government and many more. The transformation would enhance the existing operations of the Indonesian government.

As per Atkins and Lawson (2021), an improved framework is required to be implemented so that the overall success as well as failure aspects of cybersecurity policy can be checked and managed for critical infrastructure. The overall vulnerabilities related to critical infrastructure would be managed for the financial networks, pipelines and the power grid so that cyberattacks would be reduced. There could be sectoral partnerships with the private operators for critical infrastructure so that there would be an involving regulation degree. The authors have interviewed more than 40 senior private sector managers. Two major predictors of policy success can be considered that include regulatory pressure over firms and the nature of the cyber risks for the operations of firms. The findings reveal that there are major implications for public administration for regulatory ramifications as well as civilian cybersecurity aspects in different policy domains.

Masombuka, Grobler, and Duvenage (2021) have highlighted that the cybersecurity, as well as local government aspects, should be prioritized in every sector so that the existing challenges and issues are resolved and maximum efficiency is gained. The South African government has been selected to understand the current concern. The main reason is that the African government often lacks digital resources and economic strength. As a result, a proper change or improvement is required to be considered so that the existing cyberattacks or threats are managed. The most common challenges identified by the authors include lack of adequate resources, inadequate training that is provided to the employees, lack of documented governance policies as well as cybersecurity procedures and better equipment. National security would be protected with the involvement of cybersecurity aspects for the African government and data management would be enhanced for the critical infrastructure and confidential citizen data.

According to Smith, Dhillon, and Carter (2021), an updated cybersecurity policy should be developed for the successful implementation of the Internet of Things. Different user values would be considered and prioritized for the public policy. The authors have identified that various IoT user values would be converted and elicited into different objectives that would be bringing major security issues for the usage of the Internet of Things. Moreover, group and individual-based utility functions should be evaluated that would demonstrate preferences for IoT user policy accordingly. It has been identified that the public administrators would be developing public policies for managing the increasing complexities or issues related to the technological adoption. The lack of policy direction would be common and the management is often unable to understand the user values that are associated with cybersecurity accordingly. Moreover, the lack of clarity in developing IoT public policies should also be managed so that the stakeholder aspects are understood and a better approach is identified.

Kassen (2022) has explored the usage of blockchain technology to improve information processing in e-government systems. The findings highlighted that city management activities can be improved by fostering public trust and transparency in blockchain based technologies. Another study (Chodakowska, Kańduła, & Przybylska, 2022) explored the local government sector in Poland and highlighted that although majority of local governments have developed security policies but they are not implemented accordingly. Furthermore, it was also reported that government organization lack agility and awareness to respond to cyber-attacks. Therefore, appropriate policies, cybersecurity awareness, auditing and training are key enablers to make local government sector cybersecurity resilient.

In another study (Luo & Choi, 2022) authors have looked into the government involvement in improving the cybersecurity practices in e-commerce sector. The study looked into the impact of penalties imposed by government to improve cybersecurity measures and found it counterproductive. The findings highlighted that those extreme positions of applying stricter penalties or not taking any action are adopted by government sector. In another study Schaberreiter et al. (2022) developed a cybersecurity response mechanism to support local governments in responding to cyber-attacks. The system was able to analyze data sources and autonomously adopt mitigation strategies in line with the situation.

Elsafty and Yehia (2023) believe that Egypt's political leaders have embraced the digital transformation movement, which began in government agencies such as the traffic department, civil registry, and real estate center. Several ministries are making every effort to implement digital transformation. Digital transformation in the public sector refers to the automation of governmental operations, including providing more convenient and enhanced client experience, implementing laws that permit employees to work from home, and modernizing and streamlining procedures to save both time and money. One fundamental factor that might have either a beneficial or detrimental effect is employee conduct; a positive impact will result in faster transformation and more services so that upper management can fulfill its goals. A self-administered questionnaire was given to Egyptian public sector government officials. The analysis's findings supported the link between a number of variables such as financial assets, IT system accessibility, workplace culture, collaboration among civil society, the private sector, the government, and institutions of higher education, employee skills, leadership selection, diverse management and the adoption of digital transformation in the Egyptian government.

Elisa et al. (2023) believe that Blockchain technology enables the development of distributed platforms that are highly secure, safeguard privacy, and do not rely on third parties to manage transactions. The immutable and verifiable storing of both new and old data in a sealed compartment of blocks (a ledger) scattered throughout the network is made possible by blockchain technology. This study suggests a structure for a blockchain-based decentralized e-government peer-to-peer (p2p) system that can guarantee security of information and privacy while also boosting public sector trust. A theoretical and qualitative study of the system's security and privacy implications is also provided, along with a prototype of the suggested system. One of the drawbacks of current e-government systems is the incompatibility between government divisions, which the suggested solution may be able to resolve. The active future task is to construct such a framework and then further investigate its full potential in a real setting, as current work is restricted to the design and conceptual level.

Shandler and Gomez (2023) makes the case that more subtle societal hazards, such a decline in public confidence in the government, are the main danger posed by cyberattacks. They gather and examine survey data immediately following a ransomware assault on a hospital in Düsseldorf. It has been shown that being vulnerable to cyberattacks considerably reduces public trust in the affected sectors of society. Cyberattacks cause a sharp decline in trust among citizens by taking advantage of specific aspects of cyberspace that are closely related to issues of public confidence. They also pinpoint the psychological process such as anger that causes this effect. The trust of the public is increased by attitudes of rage brought on by being exposed to cyberattacks, but it is decreased by the stronger emotion of fear. Because the public may believe that the federal government is unable to protect against potential hazards. They also discussed how growing cyberthreats can lead to significant societal unrest and erode confidence in democratic institutions, as well as what exactly qualifies as exposure to the latest round of cyberattacks

Jha and Jha (2024) investigated the incorporation of artificial intelligence (AI) into cybersecurity for e-governance, with an emphasis on its main findings, contributions, difficulties, and potential future directions. Enhanced threat identification, and response, including scaling abilities are given by AI-powered cybersecurity solutions, which enhance the protection of confidential data and vital infrastructure in the realm of digital government. According to them, machine learning algorithms can recognize trends that point to criminal activity, adjust to changing threat environments, and strengthen governance systems' defenses against intrusions. Routine cybersecurity jobs are automated by AI technology, which streamlines processes and shortens responses. Additionally, they provide scalability to accommodate evolving security settings and the expanding requirements of e-governance systems. To guarantee the responsible and efficient use of AI technology, ethical issues like responsibility, accountability, and fairness as well as problems with algorithm prejudices, confidentiality of data, and the cybersecurity skills gap must be resolved. Moreover, to ensure adherence to data protection laws and stop unwanted access or exploitation, data privacy and security are crucial. To protect personal data and maintain citizen privacy, strong data governance regulations, encryption techniques, and access controls are required.

Al Hawamleh (2024) have highlighted that in an effort to increase effectiveness, accessibility, and citizen-centricity, the Kingdom of Saudi Arabia (KSA) has accepted digital transformation and electronic government services. However, the nation still has to deal with issues like changing security threats. Their study examines the complicated nature of cybersecurity procedures and how they affect the efficacy and caliber of e-government services. The culture of the organization, technological infrastructure, compliance with norms and laws, employee knowledge and understanding, and financial investment in cybersecurity are the five main elements that were examined. The study collected data from 320 participants using a quantitative approach. After eliminating unsuitable or incomplete replies from 285 completed questionnaires, the researcher used partial least squares structural equation modeling to examine the final data set. The results demonstrate that the implementation of strong cybersecurity practices is highly influenced by the investment of money in cybersecurity, staff knowledge and training, and compliance with cybersecurity rules. It is less clear how business atmosphere and cybersecurity procedures relate to one another. The study shows that cybersecurity practices and the quality of e-government services are strongly positively correlated, emphasizing the importance of security in promoting user happiness and public trust as well as in satisfying the changing demands of both enterprises and citizens.

Dev and Saha (2024) examined the connection between the number of women in the workforce and the level of cybersecurity proficiency of countries, as well as the moderation effect of e-government growth. Using secondary archive data for 149 nations, the authors performed fixed-effects regression. Additionally, the authors used clustering techniques to divide the group of countries into four cybersecurity maturity levels: unprepared, reactive, anticipatory, and innovative. They then examined the effects of their interest factors on each category. Findings indicate that national cybersecurity maturity is positively impacted by female labor force involvement, and that the growth of e-government positively moderates this link, allowing women to be empowered. Additionally, they argued that the gender equality in the cybersecurity industry can be advanced by e-government growth, which can help foster an atmosphere that is more encouraging for women to pursue and thrive in cybersecurity-related occupations. Their study emphasizes the moderating effect of e-government development on the association between female labor force participation and a country's cybersecurity maturity for empirical research scholars. They anticipate that this finding will stimulate more investigation into this connection. They also give managers and policymakers with information to help them create future plans and national regulations that foster the development of cybersecurity.

Gaie and Karpuk (2024) highlighted that in the information age, digital platforms offer a great deal of opportunity to address societal demands, particularly ones met by the government. However, e-administration must stay up to date with technology advancements in order to achieve the technical requirements intended for government services and provide them effectively. Because digital services can change drastically and quickly, the government must continuously track, analyze, and, if needed, adjust to these developments. The growth of public e-services and the efficient functioning of electronic administration are hampered by various legislative barriers, particularly in the cutthroat market for information society services. Management agencies must operate within the bounds of the law and in accordance with it, especially in the digital marketplace, which necessitates a high degree of mobility. In contrast to the government, which lacks this liberty and is only able to conduct legally mandated actions, they must simultaneously adapt to the constantly shifting demands of the players in the market and the freedom of decision that exists there.

Ramadhani, Suyitno, and Suryantoro, 2024) have highlighted that because the system gathers, stores, and processes publicly available personal data, privacy concerns become the main topic of discussion when it comes to or e-government. Through e-Government organizations (EGOs), government stakeholders and general public can access transparent, efficient, and effective public services over the Internet. Existing government-related websites need to be analyzed and appraised as quickly as possible in order to minimize the probable harm caused by cyberattack. In their study, the Web Security Testing Guide (WSTG) is examined as a method for evaluating the security of information technology. As a result of this study's release, an ITSA technique is now available. To lessen the number of flaws, present in all government information systems, ITSA, a public service, offers vulnerability assessments, advice, and suggestions on information security.

Raza (2024) highlighted that e-government nowadays face many concerns in providing services to citizens. The two main issues in this respect are data privacy and cyber security. E-Government requires information security best practices in order to implement good governance. Data must be safeguarded against online threats. Both national and international frameworks ought to be used to address e-governance issues. Existing legislation must be implemented, and efforts are being made to address the cyber security issue. The study also highlighted that a cyberspace is an extensive interrelationship between many sectors, including software, services, and people-to-people interactions, and it is facilitated by the global dispersion of networks and electronic devices. In this context, the Indian government has developed a framework to examine it. They also have introduced a National e-Government Plan to create an atmosphere that encourages electronic government. This could prove to be an economical approach to implementing government services across the nation's multiple industries. The Indian government also has a plan for governance that makes use of privacy and cyber security standards. They have launched a National Cyber Alert System which is an early warning and response system for malicious activity. Additionally, it has established a procedure for exchanging information with foreign authorities. Numerous security training sessions have been held to enhance skills and competency. Among these trainings are domain-specific courses that use network and system secure administration and cyber forensics.

Putro, Sensuse, and Wibowo (2024) created a framework for protecting critical information in smart government as a substitute for popular cybersecurity frameworks in Indonesia. The methodology employed adheres to the predicting malfunctions in socio-technical systems approach, created especially to anticipate any problems in the old socio-technical system, to guarantee the authenticity of the data. The primary data gathering methods in this study were observation and a systematic literature review. The fuzzy Delphi method (FDM) was used for expert validation and theme analysis. The objectives, interdependency, functions, risk management, resources, and governance are some of the components that make up the suggested Critical Information infrastructure (CII) protection structure. There are twenty elements and forty-one variables for each of those aspects. In smart governance, especially in government administration services, this framework may serve as an alternate set of guidelines for CII protection.

A study by Serohina et al. (2024) looks at the crucial connection between the implementation of cyber security in the local government system and its role as an aspect of national security. Its objective is to assess the global experience of guaranteeing cyber security in the administration of local self-governments in Poland, Ukraine, and Germany. The study compares the systems of local self-government organizations in the chosen nations and shows how much faith is placed in local administrations in Poland, Germany, and Ukraine. It was determined that the development of a sufficient cybersecurity system is necessary. According to the study's findings, not every examined nation has the Local self-government organizations' duty to guarantee cyber security at the level of regulation. Based on this the recognition of the necessity to develop and create a sufficient cyber security system becomes evident. Given the ongoing rise in the quantity and severity of cyberthreats, all subjects of authority must share responsibility for ensuring cyber security.

Alhanatleh et al. (2024) sought to determine the degree of public utility of using mobile financial services from the viewpoint of "citizens in the government context in Jordan" by connecting knowledge about cybersecurity and its predecessors. The quantitative method has been altered to meet the needs of this investigation. Data was gathered using a method of convenience sampling based on 550 Jordanians who completed an e-survey. According to the findings, knowledge about cybersecurity and economic system forecasts significantly influence the use of financial services systems and the value that comes from doing so. All hypotheses are accepted at less than P<0.001. Furthermore, a key strategy for evaluating the effectiveness of government agencies, particularly those in the financial services sector, is to combine cybersecurity knowledge with public value theory. According to them, these findings can be applied to the development of financial services and to the needs of Jordanians. They are of the opinion that in order to secure the future viability of microfinance services, it is vital to provide widely accepted factors that determine the value of microfinance service use among Jordanians.

Hilowle et al. (2024) focuses on human-centric cybersecurity (HCCS) and examines the difficulties in implementing National Digital Identity Systems (NDIDs) in Australia. It looks at adoption hurdles such lack of confidence, privacy issues, security risks, and insufficient cybersecurity knowledge. Many Australians hesitate to use NDIDs because of worries about identity theft, data breaches, and inadequate verification. They also worry about how data is stored because of clear privacy policy. Moreover, the successful use of NDIDs by underprivileged communities is hindered by low digital literacy and language hurdles. As a result, they recommend implementing multiple factor authentication and human centric cybersecurity strategies in order to improve user protection.

Schneider (2025) investigates cybersecurity and digital government initiatives. The research aims to underscore the need for incorporating strong cybersecurity measures into digital government structures to tackle rising threats, ensure service trustworthiness, and build public trust. The study utilizes a qualitative analysis of case studies from European countries, including Estonia, Finland, and the Netherlands, known for their sophisticated digital security and e-governance plans. The research shows that effective digital governments incorporate adaptable cybersecurity methods, collaborative administrative protocols, and cutting-edge technologies such as artificial intelligence and blockchain. These strategies reduce risks, strengthen data security, and foster public confidence.

Alam et al. (2025) offer a thorough comprehension of the psychological and technical factors affecting citizen involvement in e-governance systems in Bangladesh, with consequences for policy formulation and forthcoming investigations. This study uses a cross-sectional research design to explore how citizens in Bangladesh relate to cybersecurity strategies. This research examines how citizens view estimated danger intensity on various aspects of cybersecurity, including technical security attributes, user-friendly security measures, and the effectiveness of security systems. The investigation reveals that Risk Assessment is vital for establishing Technical Security Attributes, User-Friendly Security, and Benevolence.

Makatur, Gultom, and Wadjidi (2025) believe that the public's digitization may motivate governmental services and business actors to adhere to trends, demonstrating the growing number of internet-connected parties. Government-owned businesses (BUMN) and the Indonesian government sector are still creating public services that contribute to digitization. National infrastructure may become vulnerable due to the growth of the digital world. The Six-Ware Cyber Security Framework (SWCSF) and the idea of an Electronic-Based Government System (SPBE) can help reduce this. This paper's goal is to evaluate the efficacy of the SPBE and SWCSF principles, which have been applied by a number of Indonesian government organizations. Results showed that the SPBE assessment approach is inadequate for comprehensively assessing the ICT system in the contemporary digitalization period, as it does not examine the cybersecurity system. However, SWCSF measuring model serves to assess an agency's preparation for cybersecurity.

Espinosa and Pino (2025) investigate how e-govt promotes economic development and transition in Estonia. With the goal of improving health and productivity, e-govt uses IT in the public sector as part of its development strategy. Drawing on Weberian bureaucracy, it highlights two key institutions: secure property rights and governance rules that give transparency, trust, and security (TTS) top priority. These groups offer a comprehensive evaluation of e-govt benefits. The study outlines strategies for optimizing these advantages, makes recommendations for the ultimate application of e-govt, and points out areas that require more research in developing countries.

Based on the findings of the systematic literature review, it is evident that digital transformation in electronic government presents challenges in terms of cybersecurity, (Moşteanu, 2020; Gull et al., 2023; Saeed, 2025). As government systems adopt new technologies, the frequency of cyber-attacks increases, highlighting the need for a sophisticated and comprehensive secure E-government Adoption framework. The framework covers many important aspects of information security that are critical for securing e-government systems and services. By implementing measures across multiple domains, from technical controls to policy and processes, the framework aims to establish a robust security posture. Traditional security measures are no longer adequate in addressing the complex nature of cyber threats. Therefore, it is important to develop a well-designed framework, particularly for government sectors undergoing digital transformation, (Issabayeva, Yesseniyazova, & Grega, 2019; Chatfield & Reddick, 2019; Saeed, 2025). Based on the analysis of relevant research, we propose an E-government Adoption framework to enhance the cyber threat response capabilities of E-government. The architecture of the security framework is presented in Figure 2. The framework consists of six key components policy and governance, cyber threat intelligence, Security Compliance and Auditing, Incident Response and Reporting, Awareness and Training and Technological Infrastructure security.

Figure 2. Framework for secure e-government adoption

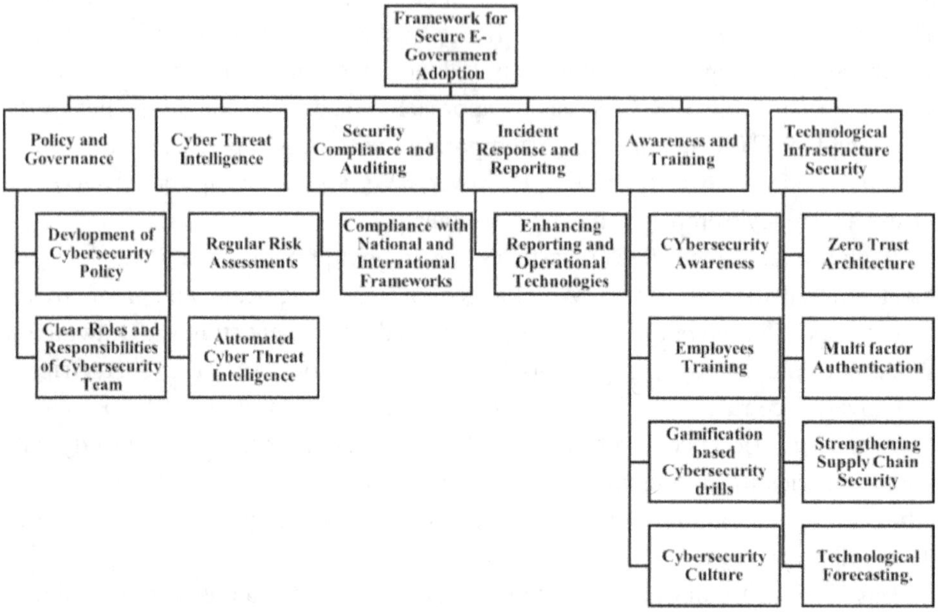

At Governance, robust governance structure is crucial for establishing accountability and responsibility for cybersecurity within an organization, (Lubua & Pretorious; Yarovoy et al., 2020; Maglaras et al., 2020). It plays a critical role in defining roles and responsibilities, establishing policies and procedures, and ensuring proper oversight of cybersecurity initiatives. Effective governance ensures that cybersecurity is prioritized at all levels of the organization and foster trust in the e-government, (Warkentin & Orgeron, 2020; Jha & Jha, 2024; Putro, Sensuse, & Wibowo, 2024).

At Risk Management, it's important to adopt comprehensive risk management frameworks that encompass risk assessment, vulnerability identification, risk mitigation, and continuous monitoring and evaluation to effectively manage cybersecurity risks and protect organizations and individuals from cyber-attacks, (Ramadhani, Suyitno, & Suryantoro, 2024; Alam et al., 2025). By prioritizing cybersecurity at all levels and proactively managing risks, government organizations can minimize the likelihood and impact of cyber-attacks.

At Compliance, adhering to regulatory requirements and industry standards is essential for maintaining a secure e-government environment, (Warkentin & Orgeron, 2020; Atkins & Saksono, 2021). Given that encompass adherence to relevant laws, regulations, and guidelines pertaining to cybersecurity. Compliance measures help government organizations stay updated with best practices and maintain a strong security posture.

At Incident Response, rapid and effective response to cybersecurity incidents is crucial for minimizing damage and restoring normal operations as suggested in literature, (Lubua & Pretorious, 2019). Government must establish the development and implementation of robust incident response plans that incorporate comprehensive procedures for incident detection, containment, eradication, and recovery.

At Awareness and Training, building a culture of cybersecurity awareness and training in preventing cyberattacks, protecting sensitive data, and fostering a culture of cybersecurity within organizations and the broader society as proposed in earlier literature, (Masombuka, Grobler, & Duvenage, 2021; Chodakowska, Kańduła, & Przybylska, 2022; Al-Hawamleh, 2024). By the implementation of awareness and training programs that target different audiences, including individuals, employees, government officials, and law enforcement personnel. Furthermore, data usage policies should be published and any change to these policies should be communicated to end users. Security alerts and error messages should be appropriately designed to provide user cues in completing the tasks. Advanced security mechanisms for user authentication should be implemented. Furthermore, security controls should be designed keeping in view citizens with audio and visual impairments for inclusive usage of e-government services. Human-centric security is. a paradigm that advocates for aligning the design of cybersecurity controls of software artifacts with end-user needs and behavior to improve the cybersecurity resilience of software systems, (Shah, 2022; Luo & Choi, 2022). The adoption of user user-centric design process enables organizations to design software systems aligned with the user needs as well as designing usable security and privacy controls, (Saeed, 2024). User-centric design allows for intuitive security controls which can help users to use the system securely. Furthermore, it reduces the cognitive load on end users allowing them user-friendly controls to protect themselves against phishing and other scams. It has also been discussed in literature that the awareness and education about cybersecurity threats can improve user resilience, so appropriate security warnings and guidelines integrated into system features can minimize the probability of cybersecurity attacks. Additionally, user behavior and diversity of technical skills also need to be considered when designing inclusive and usable security controls. Another important aspect of user-centric security is transparent data usage by software systems to develop trust with end users.

Since technology is the backbone of secure e-government infrastructure so e-government initiatives need to have the ability of technological forecasting to integrate advanced technologies in their business processes, (Warkentin & Orgeron, 2020. Additionally, expertise in secure technology deployment and management are also critical to ensure business continuity of e-government operations. Integration of modern technologies such as zero trust architecture, (Rebouças Filho, 2025), quantum cryptography, (Subramani & Svn, 2025), multi factor authentication should be enabled to secure the infrastructure. Another aspect is to improve supply chain security by ensuring the infrastructure of third parties is also secured so that vulnerabilities from third party infrastructures is also controlled, (Żurawski et al., 2025). As a result of these collective strategies cybersecurity resilience can be achieved to improve end user trust and foster successful technology adoption, (Saeed et al., 2024; Saeed et al., 2024).

CONCLUSIONS AND FUTURE DIRECTIONS

The impact of digital transformation and the challenges of cybersecurity on electronic government are examined in this comprehensive systematic literature review. The research highlights the growing occurrence of cyber-attacks and the importance of protecting government computer systems from hackers. It emphasizes the critical intersection of digital transformation, e-government, and cybersecurity, illustrating how technological advancements bring benefits to government services but also expose them to increasing cyber threats. The findings underscore the urgent need to strengthen cybersecurity measures in government sectors amidst the rapid pace of digital transformation. In conclusion, the literature review advocates for the development and adoption of a robust framework specifically tailored for secure e-government. This framework integrates governance, risk management, compliance, incident response, and awareness and training programs as essential pillars to enhance the cybersecurity posture of government sectors in the era of digital transformation. Governments must prioritize cybersecurity to protect sensitive information and maintain public trust. Continuous research and development in cybersecurity are crucial to stay ahead of emerging threats and adapt to evolving technologies in the realm of e-government. As part of future work, impact of emerging technologies such as machine learning, blockchain, internet of things, 6G connectivity and edge computing needs to be explored in the context of e-government effectiveness. The associated cybersecurity implications and user trust on e-governments can be an interesting domain. Furthermore, case studies and best practices in adopting zero trust architectures, quantum cryptography and cybersecurity compliance frameworks can strengthen the e-government literature and enable knowledge exchange in government policy makers from north to south. Another interesting domain for future research is to study complex interplay in ethical aspects, citizen privacy, and digital surveillance by governments. Additionally, cybersecurity operation technologies, cyber threat intelligence, recovery strategies to deal with cyber terrorism and warfare is another interesting future area.

AUTHOR CONTRIBUTIONS

"Conceptualization, S.S., H.G. and M.S..; methodology, H.G. and S.S.; data curation, B.A.; N.A.; H.A.; writing—original draft preparation, S.S.; S.Z.I.; B.A.; N.A.; H.A.; M.S.; writing—review and editing, S.S.; S.Z.I.; H.G.; supervision, S.S. All authors have read and agreed to the published version of the manuscript

REFERENCES

Abdou, A. M. (2021). Good governance and COVID-19: The digital bureaucracy to response the pandemic (Singapore as a model). *Journal of Public Affairs*, *21*(4), e2656. DOI: 10.1002/pa.2656 PMID: 34230813

Ahangama, S. (2023). Relating social media diffusion, Education level and cybersecurity protection mechanisms to e-participation initiatives: Insights from a cross-country analysis. *Information Systems Frontiers*, *25*(5), 1–17. DOI: 10.1007/s10796-023-10385-7 PMID: 37361893

Al-Besher, A., & Kumar, K. (2022). Use of artificial intelligence to enhance e-government services. *Measurement. Sensors*, *24*, 100484. DOI: 10.1016/j.measen.2022.100484

Al-Hawamleh, A. M. (2024). Investigating the multifaceted dynamics of cybersecurity practices and their impact on the quality of e-government services: Evidence from the KSA. Digital Policy. *Regulation & Governance*, *26*(3), 317–336. DOI: 10.1108/DPRG-11-2023-0168

Al-Zahrani, M. (2020). Integrating IS success model with cybersecurity factors for e-government implementation in the Kingdom of Saudi Arabia. *International Journal of Electrical and Computer Engineering*, *10*(5), 4937–4955. DOI: 10.11591/ijece.v10i5.pp4937-4955

Alam, M. S., Ahmed, S., Dhali, M., & Alam, S. S. (2025). Citizens' engagement with cybersecurity measures in Bangladesh: A cross-sectional study. *International Journal of Information Security*, *24*(1), 4. DOI: 10.1007/s10207-024-00918-9

Alhanatleh, H., Khaddam, A., Abudabaseh, F., Alghizzawi, M., & Alzghoul, A. (2024). Enhancing the public value of mobile fintech services through cybersecurity awareness antecedents: A novel framework in Jordan. *Investment Management & Financial Innovations*, *21*(1), 417–430. DOI: 10.21511/imfi.21(1).2024.32

Alshaikh, M., Naseer, H., Ahmad, A., & Maynard, S. B. (2019). Toward sustainable behaviour change: an approach for cyber security education training and awareness.

Aminah, S., & Saksono, H. (2021). Digital transformation of the government: A case study in Indonesia. Jurnal Komunikasi. *Malaysian Journal of Communication*, *37*(2), 272–288.

Aslam, M., Abbasi, M. A. K., & Khalid, T. (2022). Getting Smarter about Smart Cities: Improving Data Security and Privacy through Compliance. *Sensors (Basel)*, *22*(23), 9338. DOI: 10.3390/s22239338 PMID: 36502039

Atkins, S., & Lawson, C. (2021). An improvised patchwork: Success and failure in cybersecurity policy for critical infrastructure. *Public Administration Review*, *81*(5), 847–861. DOI: 10.1111/puar.13322

Bokhari, S. A. A., & Myeong, S. (2023). The influence of artificial intelligence on e-Governance and cybersecurity in smart cities: A stakeholder's perspective. *IEEE Access : Practical Innovations, Open Solutions*, *11*, 69783–69797. DOI: 10.1109/ACCESS.2023.3293480

Chatfield, A. T., & Reddick, C. G. (2019). A framework for Internet of Things-enabled smart government: A case of IoT cybersecurity policies and use cases in US federal government. *Government Information Quarterly*, *36*(2), 346–357. DOI: 10.1016/j.giq.2018.09.007

Chodakowska, A., Kańduła, S., & Przybylska, J. (2022). Cybersecurity in the Local Government Sector in Poland: More Work Needs to be Done: More work needs to be done. Lex localis-journal of local self-government, 20(1), 161-192.

Dev, M., & Saha, D. (2024). Does e-government development moderate the impact of female labor participation on national cybersecurity maturity? An empirical investigation. *Information and Computer Security*, *32*(1), 74–92. DOI: 10.1108/ICS-03-2023-0042

Dubey, A., Saquib, Z., & Dwivedi, S. (2015, October). Electronic authentication for e-Government services—A survey. In 10th IET System Safety and Cyber-Security Conference 2015 (pp. 1-5). IET.

Elisa, N., Yang, L., Chao, F., & Cao, Y. (2023). A framework of blockchain-based secure and privacy-preserving E-government system. *Wireless Networks*, *29*(3), 1005–1015. DOI: 10.1007/s11276-018-1883-0

Elisa, N., Yang, L., Chao, F., Naik, N., & Boongoen, T. (2023). A Secure and Privacy-Preserving E-Government Framework Using Blockchain and Artificial Immunity. *IEEE Access : Practical Innovations, Open Solutions, 11*, 8773–8789. DOI: 10.1109/ACCESS.2023.3239814

Elsafty, A., & Yehia, A. (2023). Digital Transformation Challenges for Government Sector. *Business and Management Studies, 9*(1), 11. DOI: 10.11114/bms.v9i1.6160

Espinosa, V. I., & Pino, A. (2025). E-Government as a development strategy: The case of Estonia. *International Journal of Public Administration, 48*(2), 86–99. DOI: 10.1080/01900692.2024.2316128

Gaie, C., & Karpiuk, M. (2024). The Provision of e-Services by Public Administration Bodies and Their Cybersecurity. In *Transforming Public Services—Combining Data and Algorithms to Fulfil Citizen's Expectations* (pp. 175–188). Springer Nature Switzerland. DOI: 10.1007/978-3-031-55575-6_7

Gaur, L., Ujjan, R. M. A., & Hussain, M. (2022). The Influence of Deep Learning in Detecting Cyber Attacks on E-Government Applications. In *Cybersecurity Measures for E-Government Frameworks* (pp. 107–122). IGI Global. DOI: 10.4018/978-1-7998-9624-1.ch007

Gull, H., Alabbad, D. A., Saqib, M., Iqbal, S. Z., Nasir, T., Saeed, S., & Almuhaideb, A. M. (2023). E-commerce and cybersecurity challenges: Recent advances and future trends. Handbook of Research on Cybersecurity Issues and Challenges for Business and FinTech Applications, 91-111.

Gull, H., Saeed, S., Iqbal, S. Z., Bamarouf, Y. A., Alqahtani, M. A., Alabbad, D. A., Saqib, M., Al Qahtani, S. H., & Alamer, A. (2022). An empirical study of mobile commerce and customers security perception in Saudi Arabia. *Electronics (Basel), 11*(3), 293. DOI: 10.3390/electronics11030293

Hilowle, M., Yeoh, W., Grobler, M., Pye, G., & Jiang, F. (2024). Leveraging Human-Centric Cybersecurity to Improve Usage of National Digital Identity Systems in Australia. *Computer, 57*(7), 87–98. DOI: 10.1109/MC.2024.3395523

Hoffman, I., & Cseh, K. B. (2020). E-administration, cybersecurity and municipalities–the challenges of cybersecurity issues for the municipalities in Hungary. *Cybersecurity and Law, 2*(2), 199–211. DOI: 10.35467/cal/133999

Ihtesham, M., Tahir, S., Tahir, H., Hasan, A., Sultan, A., Saeed, S., & Rana, O. (2023). Privacy preserving and serverless homomorphic-based searchable encryption as a service (SEaaS). *IEEE Access : Practical Innovations, Open Solutions, 11*, 115204–115218. DOI: 10.1109/ACCESS.2023.3324817

Issabayeva, S., Yesseniyazova, B., & Grega, M. (2019). Electronic Public Procurement: Process and Cybersecurity Issues. *NISPAcee Journal of Public Administration and Policy*, *12*(2), 61–79. DOI: 10.2478/nispa-2019-0014

Jarvers, S., & Schachtner, C. (2024). Linking smart city projects to the internal e-government projects of municipalities in Germany: synergies and challenges. In *Proceedings of the Central and Eastern European eDem and eGov Days 2024* (pp. 61-69). DOI: 10.1145/3670243.3670261

Jha, R. K., & Jha, M. (2024). Optimizing E-Government Cybersecurity through Artificial Intelligence Integration. *Journal of Trends in Computer Science and Smart Technology*, *6*(1), 67–87. DOI: 10.36548/jtcsst.2024.1.005

Kassen, M. (2022). Blockchain and e-government innovation: Automation of public information processes. *Information Systems*, *103*, 101862. DOI: 10.1016/j.is.2021.101862

Lněnička, M., & Máchová, R. (2022). A theoretical framework to evaluate ICT disparities and digital divides: Challenges and implications for e-government development. *Review of Economic Perspectives*, *22*(1), 25–51. DOI: 10.2478/revecp-2022-0002

Lubua, E. W., & Pretorius, P. D. (2019, Jul). Cyber-security policy framework and procedural compliance in public organisations. In *Proceedings of the International Conference on Industrial Engineering and Operations Management* (pp. 1-13).

Luo, S., & Choi, T. M. (2022). E-commerce supply chains with considerations of cyber-security: Should governments play a role? *Production and Operations Management*, *31*(5), 2107–2126. DOI: 10.1111/poms.13666

Maglaras, L., Drivas, G., Chouliaras, N., Boiten, E., Lambrinoudakis, C., & Ioannidis, S. (2020, Nov). Cybersecurity in the Era of digital transformation: the case of Greece. In *2020 International Conference on Internet of Things and Intelligent Applications (ITIA)* (pp. 1-5). IEEE. DOI: 10.1109/ITIA50152.2020.9312297

Maharaj, M. S., & Munyoka, W. (2019). Privacy, security, trust, risk and optimism bias in e-government use: The case of two Southern African Development Community countries. *South African Journal of Information Management*, *21*(1), 1–9.

Makatur, M. Y., Gultom, R. A., Wadjidi, A. F., & Dinisfusya'ban, D. (2025). Analysis of Electronic-Based Government Systems (SPBE) Using the Six-Ware Cyber Security Framework (SWCSF) in West Sumatra Province. *Formosa Journal of Multidisciplinary Research*, *4*(2), 899–912. DOI: 10.55927/fjmr.v4i2.67

Mao, Z., & Zhu, Y. (2023). Tension between the safe flow of government data across organizational boundaries and fragmentations in secure collaboration: The Chinese e-government. *Aslib Journal of Information Management.*

Masombuka, M., Grobler, M., & Duvenage, P. (2021, June). Cybersecurity and local Government: Imperative, Challenges and Priorities. In ECCWS 2021 20th European Conference on Cyber Warfare and Security (p. 285). Academic Conferences Inter Ltd.

Mawgoud, A. A., Taha, M. H. N., Khalifa, N. E. M., & Loey, M. (2019, October). Cyber security risks in MENA region: threats, challenges and countermeasures. In *International conference on advanced intelligent systems and informatics* (pp. 912-921). Cham: Springer International Publishing.

Meltzer, J. P. (2020). Cybersecurity, digital trade, and data flows: Re-thinking a role for international trade rules. Global Economy & Development WP, 132.

Mendhurwar, S., & Mishra, R. (2021). Integration of social and IoT technologies: Architectural framework for digital transformation and cyber security challenges. *Enterprise Information Systems, 15*(4), 565–584. DOI: 10.1080/17517575.2019.1600041

Mijwil, M., Filali, Y., Aljanabi, M., Bounabi, M., & Al-Shahwani, H. (2023). The Purpose of Cybersecurity Governance in the Digital Transformation of Public Services and Protecting the Digital Environment. Mesopotamian journal of cybersecurity, 2023, 1-6.

Mishra, S., Alowaidi, M. A., & Sharma, S. K. (2021). Impact of security standards and policies on the credibility of e-government. *Journal of Ambient Intelligence and Humanized Computing*, 1–12. DOI: 10.1007/s12652-020-02767-5

Moşteanu, N. R. (2020). Challenges for organizational structure and design as a result of digitalization and cybersecurity. *The Business & Management Review, 11*(1), 278–286. DOI: 10.24052/BMR/V11NU01/ART-29

Naseer, A., Naseer, H., Ahmad, A., Maynard, S. B., & Siddiqui, A. M. (2023). Moving towards agile cybersecurity incident response: A case study exploring the enabling role of big data analytics-embedded dynamic capabilities. *Computers & Security, 135*, 103525. DOI: 10.1016/j.cose.2023.103525

Nookhao, S., & Kiattisin, S. (2023). Achieving a successful e-government: Determinants of behavioral intention from Thai citizens' perspective. *Heliyon, 9*(8), e18944. DOI: 10.1016/j.heliyon.2023.e18944 PMID: 37588601

Norris, D. F., Mateczun, L., Joshi, A., & Finin, T. (2019). Cyberattacks at the grass roots: American local governments and the need for high levels of cybersecurity. *Public Administration Review, 79*(6), 895–904. DOI: 10.1111/puar.13028

Norris, D. F., Mateczun, L., Joshi, A., & Finin, T. (2021). Managing cybersecurity at the grassroots: Evidence from the first nationwide survey of local government cybersecurity. *Journal of Urban Affairs*, *43*(8), 1173–1195. DOI: 10.1080/07352166.2020.1727295

Oni, S., Berepubo, K. A., Oni, A. A., & Joshua, S. (2019, Apr). E-government and the challenge of cybercrime in Nigeria. In 2019 Sixth International Conference on eDemocracy & eGovernment (ICEDEG) (pp. 137-142). IEEE.

Ovchinnikova, O., & Upadhyay, N. K. (2023). The Level of Cybersecurity of the BRICS Member Countries in International Ratings: Prospects for Cooperation. *BRICS Law Journal*, *10*(1), 7–34. DOI: 10.21684/2412-2343-2023-10-1-7-34

Phadke, A., Medrano, F. A., & Ustymenko, S. (2022, Feb). Applications of Blockchain in E-government. In *2022 International Symposium on Electrical, Electronics and Information Engineering (ISEEIE)* (pp. 157-164). IEEE. DOI: 10.1109/ISEEIE55684.2022.00035

Popkova, E. G., & Gulzat, K. (2020). Contradiction of the digital economy: public well-being vs. cyber threats. In Digital Economy: Complexity and Variety vs. Rationality 9 (pp. 112-124). Springer International Publishing.

Putro, P. A. W., Sensuse, D. I., & Wibowo, W. S. S. (2024). Framework for critical information infrastructure protection in smart government: A case study in Indonesia. *Information and Computer Security*, *32*(1), 112–129. DOI: 10.1108/ICS-03-2023-0031

Raju, V., Hannani, A., & Perumal, K. (2025). The Impact of Organizational Challenges and Technical Challenges on the Implementation of E-government Military Institutions in Netherlands. Spectrum Bizsctech Journal, 1(1).

Ramadhani, E. H., Suyitno, D., & Suryantoro, S. (2024, Feb). Information technology security assessment (ITSA) methodology for web-based E-government. In AIP Conference Proceedings (Vol. 2838, No. 1). AIP Publishing.

Raza, M. A.Md. Asaad Raza. (2024). Cyber Security and Data Privacy in the Era of E-Governance. *Social Science Journal for Advanced Research*, *4*(1), 5–9. DOI: 10.54741/ssjar.4.1.2

Rebouças Filho, W. L. (2025). The Role of Zero Trust Architecture in Modern Cybersecurity: Integration with IAM and Emerging Technologies. *Brazilian Journal of Development*, *11*(1), e76836–e76836. DOI: 10.34117/bjdv11n1-060

Renaud, K., Orgeron, C., Warkentin, M., & French, P. E. (2020). Cyber security responsibilization: An evaluation of the intervention approaches adopted by the Five Eyes countries and China. *Public Administration Review, 80*(4), 577–589. DOI: 10.1111/puar.13210

Saeed, S. (2023). Digital Workplaces and Information Security Behavior of Business Employees: An Empirical Study of Saudi Arabia. *Sustainability (Basel), 15*(7), 6019. DOI: 10.3390/su15076019

Saeed, S. (2023). A customer-centric view of E-commerce security and privacy. *Applied Sciences (Basel, Switzerland), 13*(2), 1020. DOI: 10.3390/app13021020

Saeed, S. (2024). Usable Privacy and Security in Mobile Applications: Perception of Mobile End Users in Saudi Arabia. *Big Data and Cognitive Computing*, *8*(11), 162. DOI: 10.3390/bdcc8110162

Saeed, S. (2025). Digital Transformation in Governmental Public Service Provision and Usable Security Perception in Saudi Arabia. *Information (Basel), 16*(3), 247. DOI: 10.3390/info16030247

Saeed, S., Altamimi, S. A., Alkayyal, N. A., Alshehri, E., & Alabbad, D. A. (2023). Digital transformation and cybersecurity challenges for businesses resilience: Issues and recommendations. *Sensors (Basel), 23*(15), 6666. DOI: 10.3390/s23156666 PMID: 37571451

Saeed, S., Azizi, N., Tahir, S., Ahmad, M., & Almuhaideb, A. M. (Eds.). (2024). Strengthening Industrial Cybersecurity to Protect Business Intelligence. IGI Global. 5. DOI: 10.4018/979-8-3693-0839-4

Saeed, S., Gull, H., Aldossary, M. M., Altamimi, A. F., Alshahrani, M. S., Saqib, M., ... & Almuhaideb, A. M. (2024). Digital Transformation in Energy Sector: Cybersecurity Challenges and Implications. Information, 15(12), 764. 4.

Saeed, S., Suayyid, S. A., Al-Ghamdi, M. S., Al-Muhaisen, H., & Almuhaideb, A. M. (2023). A Systematic Literature Review on Cyber Threat Intelligence for Organizational Cybersecurity Resilience. *Sensors (Basel), 23*(16), 7273. DOI: 10.3390/s23167273 PMID: 37631808

Schaberreiter, T., Röning, J., Quirchmayr, G., Kupfersberger, V., Wills, C., Bregonzio, M., & Spyros, A. (2022). A cybersecurity situational awareness and information-sharing solution for local public administrations based on advanced big data analysis: the CS-AWARE project. In *Challenges in Cybersecurity and privacy-the European research landscape* (pp. 149–180). River Publishers. DOI: 10.1201/9781003337492-8

Schneider, G. B. C. (2025). The Importance of Cybersecurity in Digital Government Implementations. *COGNITIONIS Scientific Journal*, *8*(1), e585–e585. DOI: 10.38087/2595.8801.585

Serohina, S., Harashchuk, I., Murtishcheva, A., Poproshaieva, O., & Fomina, S. (2024). International Experience in Ensuring Cybersecurity in Local Self-Government Management as a Component of the National Security of Ukraine. *Pakistan Journal of Criminology*, *16*(2).

Shah, I. A. (2022). Cybersecurity Issues and Challenges for E-Government During COVID-19: A Review. Cybersecurity Measures for E-Government Frameworks, 187-222.

Shah, I. A., Habeeb, R. A. A., Rajper, S., & Laraib, A. (2022). The Influence of Cybersecurity Attacks on E-Governance. In *Cybersecurity Measures for E-Government Frameworks* (pp. 77–95). IGI Global. DOI: 10.4018/978-1-7998-9624-1.ch005

Shah, I. A., Wassan, S., & Usmani, M. H. (2022). E-Government Security and Privacy Issues: Challenges and Preventive Approaches. In Cybersecurity Measures for E-Government Frameworks (pp. 61-76). IGI Global.

Shandler, R., & Gomez, M. A. (2023). The hidden threat of cyber-attacks–undermining public confidence in government. *Journal of Information Technology & Politics*, *20*(4), 359–374. DOI: 10.1080/19331681.2022.2112796

Smith, K. J., Dhillon, G., & Carter, L. (2021). User values and the development of a cybersecurity public policy for the IoT. *International Journal of Information Management*, *56*, 102123. DOI: 10.1016/j.ijinfomgt.2020.102123

Subramani, S., & Svn, S. K. (2025). Review of security methods based on classical cryptography and quantum cryptography. *Cybernetics and Systems*, *56*(3), 302–320. DOI: 10.1080/01969722.2023.2166261

Svärd, P. (2017). *Enterprise content management, records management and information culture amidst e-government development*. Chandos Publishing.

Totonchi, A. (2023). E-government Challenges in Developing Countries: Development of Iraqi e-government. *Journal of Computing Research and Innovation*, *8*(2), 200–214.

Twizeyimana, J. D., & Andersson, A. (2019). The public value of E-Government–A literature review. *Government Information Quarterly*, *36*(2), 167–178. DOI: 10.1016/j.giq.2019.01.001

Warkentin, M., & Orgeron, C. (2020). Using the security triad to assess blockchain technology in public sector applications. *International Journal of Information Management*, *52*, 102090. DOI: 10.1016/j.ijinfomgt.2020.102090

Wilson, S. (2020). The pandemic, the acceleration of digital transformation and the impact on cyber security. *Computer Fraud & Security*, *2020*(12), 13–15. DOI: 10.1016/S1361-3723(20)30128-7

Yarovoy, T. S., Kozyrieva, O. V., Bielska, T. V., Zhuk, I. I., & Mokhova, I. L. (2020). The E-government development in ensuring the country financial and information security. Financial and credit activity problems of theory and practice, 2(33), 268-275.

Żurawski, S., Ciekanowski, Z., Pauliuchuk, Y., & Ratter, E. (2025). The Impact of Supply Chain Security Management on the Functioning of Modern Organizations. *European Research Studies*, *28*(1), 44–56. DOI: 10.35808/ersj/3889

Chapter 3
Leveraging Internet Sovereignty for Digital Supremacy

Bilal Ahmed
https://orcid.org/0009-0006-8664-7463
National University of Sciences and Technology, Pakistan

Wajahat Sultan
https://orcid.org/0009-0007-6271-7268
National University of Sciences and Technology, Pakistan

Imran Rashid
https://orcid.org/0000-0001-8958-672X
National University of Sciences and Technology, Pakistan

Sehrish Ferdous
https://orcid.org/0009-0004-6495-9939
National University of Modern Languages, Pakistan

Shahzaib Tahir
https://orcid.org/0000-0003-4737-0191
National University of Sciences and Technology, Pakistan

Saqib Saeed
https://orcid.org/0000-0001-7136-3480
Imam Abdulrahman Bin Faisal University, Saudi Arabia

Faisal Amjad
National University of Sciences and Technology, Pakistan

ABSTRACT

While geographical boundaries are not recognized on the Internet, network service providers are driven through internet protocols. The revelations by whistleblowers have shaken the world of a free Internet and have raised concerns about data security. Recent developments in Russian Internet (RUnet) and the Great Firewall of China (GFW) advocate Internet sovereignty as a means to protect sensitive information from foreign surveillance. This paper critically surveys the approaches adopted

DOI: 10.4018/979-8-3373-3171-3.ch003

by nations, evaluates the enacted legislation, and categorizes their actions within the theoretical framework proposed by Mueller, known as the Mueller framework The impact of these actions has also been analyzed along with an overview of cybersecurity measures taken by a few other countries. In this study, we present a conceptual framework aimed at elucidating the implementation of internet control measures, emphasizing the accomplishments and challenges encountered by modern nations in this endeavor.

INTRODUCTION

The Internet was primarily created for information exchange without anyone predicting that it would become as powerful as it is today. It can change social orders, trigger insurgencies, and overthrow rulers by mobilizing protests (Breuer, 2012). The notion that the Internet knows no borders is widely accepted as a fact. However, the capability and political will to establish borders on the Internet have gradually matured among nations. There is a growing significance of internet sovereignty frameworks within contemporary geopolitical landscapes. Understanding the achievements and limitations of such frameworks is essential for informing policy decisions and ensuring the effective management of digital ecosystems. By exploring these frameworks, we aim to contribute to the discourse surrounding internet governance and cybersecurity, addressing critical concerns in an increasingly interconnected world.

The Internet is a common asset among countries and a communication medium with profound social and political impacts. Countries have a significant stake in ensuring that social values are upheld and political stability is maintained. Nations are expected to comply with global standards, including respecting the autonomy of other states in their geographical and domestic matters (Sanjay, 2017). Despite global ethical considerations, nations continue to engage in conflicts supported by propaganda, as discussed by Fielding and Cobain (2011). The conflict between the United States and China over 5G technology, commonly referred to as the "US-China Tech War" is a recent example. The U.S. government, like several other nations, including China, exercises caution when adopting foreign technology for critical communication infrastructure, primarily due to concerns regarding espionage backdoors and data security vulnerabilities. This cautious stance is particularly evident concerning 5G networks, given their pivotal role in enabling advanced technologies such as autonomous vehicles and the Internet of Things. For instance, Vodafone Group's discovery and subsequent rectification of backdoors in Huawei equipment contributed to a climate of uncertainty regarding Huawei's credibility (Bloomberg, 2023). Additionally, rumors regarding a potential ban on the use of iPhones by

Chinese government officials attracted considerable media attention, resulting in a financial setback of approximately USD 200 Billion for Apple (Goodkind, 2023). Although these rumors were later clarified by the Chinese government, it is notable that China has expressed ongoing concerns regarding security incidents associated with iPhones (Zhang & Judd, 2023).

The revelation of surveillance activities by the National Security Agency (NSA) of the United States in 2013 sparked a heated debate regarding Internet governance. In response to the substantial influence of foreign governments in conducting surveillance and to assert its sovereignty in technical and cyber domains, United States National Telecommunication and Information Administration (NTIA) declared its intention to transfer control of key internet domain name functions to the global multi-stakeholder community (NTIA, 2014; Maurer et al., 2015). According to revelations by Edward Snowden, NSA engages in various forms of surveillance activities, including intercepting deliveries, collecting email address books and IM buddy lists, and tracking individuals' locations. The agency can remotely access a phone's microphone and camera, crack most encryption protocols, and record all phone calls made in a country. Additionally, Steele (2014) also reveals that NSA intercepts selected computer shipments and installs malware for surveillance purposes. The technical community maintaining the Internet infrastructure has already warned against Internet fragmentation on national grounds and advocated for multi-stakeholder management of the Internet globally (ICANN, 2013). These stakeholders may include state governments, the private sector, civil society, and academia. Castro (2013) mentioned that Internet sovereignty and data localization efforts in the wake of the Snowden revelations may cost the US cloud computing industry up to USD 35 Billion as they lose credibility in the eyes of Asian and European clients. Reuters (2014) reported that the European Union (EU) has also considered establishing a Europe-only network named Schengen Cloud. Moreover, the General Data Protection Regulation (GDPR) imposes heavy fines for infringements of the regulation by data processors in the EU (EU, 2016) and gives rights to data owners to confirm the purpose and occasion of processing their data. Recently, many cities around the globe have announced their planned transition to smart cities and deployment of smart city technologies. Their dependence on Information and Communication Technologies (ICT) will generate massive amounts of data, including personal data critical for the privacy of citizens. Moreover, businesses are also transforming digitally, and the security of this data will be a major consideration for the administrations of these cities (Aslam et al., 2022, Saeed et al., 2021). This chapter offers a comprehensive examination of international legislative frameworks governing internet usage. An illustration of global dependency on the internet is depicted in Figure 1.

Figure 1. Global dependency on the internet

Contributions

The primary contributions of this study are:-

- Discussion on the concept of Internet sovereignty through the lens of Snowden's revelations, its impact as perceived by the technical community and other states, and an in- depth analysis of the Internet Sovereignty frameworks implemented by contemporary countries.
- Categorization of the measures taken by Russia and China within the framework proposed by Mueller and presentation of guidelines for policymakers to evaluate the potential outcomes associated with cybersecurity policies by highlighting the impact of these measures.
- Review of cybersecurity measures implemented by different countries, exploring the legal, technical, and organizational dimensions as well as their global cybersecurity index and Internet penetration rate.

Organization

The paper is organized as follows: Section II sheds light on Global actions for Cyber Resilience and Related Work. Section III outlines the internet sovereignty frameworks by Contemporary Countries. Section IV analyzes these frameworks within the context of the Mueller Framework of Internet Fragmentation. Section V assesses the impact of the measures implemented by Russia and China, detailing both achievements and setbacks. Section VI discusses the two models for achieving internet sovereignty. Finally, Section VII concludes the paper.

GLOBAL ACTIONS FOR CYBER RESILIENCE AND RELATED WORK

Previous studies have explored the measures taken by Russia and China to assert control over their domestic Internet ecosystems and achieve digital sovereignty. Epifanova (2020) discusses how Russia's "Sovereign Internet Law" aims to give Russian authorities more centralized powers over the Internet within Russia's borders. Stadnik (2019b) discusses four components of Russia's policy towards Internet governance and Russian focus on an Internet kill switch. Researchers in Wilson (2022) discuss how Russia's chances for genuine independence in digital sovereignty are uncertain due to technical dependence. However, a robust legal framework and a plethora of regulations have been introduced to chart out Russia's future digital sovereignty (Epifanova & Dietrich, 2022). Authors in Segal (2020) argue that China is aiming to increase its grip on information, cybersecurity, technological autonomy, and global impact through its pursuit of cyber sovereignty. As a consequence of these endeavors, the Internet is expected to become more restricted and less liberal.

Researchers in Mckune and Ahmed (2018) explore how cyber sovereignty has been conceptualized and operationalized by various states, including China and Russia, and the challenges it poses to the liberal international order. Budnitsky and Jia (2018) explores China and Russia's use of digital media to construct a narrative of a joint cyber alliance that seeks to challenge the Western-led Internet governance model. Studies have also identified various policies and strategies employed by the two countries, including censorship, surveillance, and technical controls. Some researchers have also highlighted the implications of these measures for freedom of expression, privacy, and the global governance of the Internet (Mok, 2022). However, previous studies have not compared the measures taken by Russia and China in attaining Internet sovereignty, examined their impact, analyzed their grouping under the Meuller Framework, nor compared them with cybersecurity measures taken by other countries.

Certain countries have also enacted laws to safeguard personal data privacy and regulate its cross-border transfer. For instance, Australia passed the Personally Controlled Electronic Health Record Act (PCEHR), which restricts the transfer of health records outside Australia (Government, 2014a). Brazil passed the marco civil da Internet law, which ensures civil rights in the use of the Internet (Government, 2014b). Canada has the Personal Information Protection and Electronic Documents Act (PIPEDA), which does not restrict the transfer of personal data outside Canada but imposes conditional exclusions (Government, 2019a). The British Columbia Freedom of Information and Protection of Privacy Act mandates that public bodies store personal information in Canada, with few exceptions (Commissioner, 2004). The Chinese information security technology guidelines for personal information protection within public and commercial services information systems prohibit the transfer of personal data abroad without the consent of the data subject or approval from the legal authority (Cai & Chen, 2022). France has promoted local data centre infrastructure, also known as "le cloud souverain," and has made direct investments in cloud computing firms (Onetrust, 2021). Germany is working on cybersecurity solutions known as "IT security made in Germany" (Teletrust, 2019). The Indian National Security Council proposed a policy that mandates all email service providers to host servers in India (Thomas, 2014). Indonesia's electronic information and transaction law mandates that data centres and disaster recovery centres be located inside Indonesia (Robinson et al., 2012). The Malaysian Personal Data Protection Act (PDPA) mandates that data about Malaysian nationals be stored inside Malaysia (Government, 2010). The South Korean Personal Information Protection Act mandates the consent of data subjects before providing data overseas (Government, 2011). Similarly, Vietnam's "Management provision and use of Internet services and information content online law" imposes a ban on the use of the Internet for criticizing the government (Government, 2013).

A brief comparison of cybersecurity measures taken by contemporary countries has been made considering the most significant aspects. These include legal measures taken by the country, its status of compliance by the cyber laws, the presence of Computer Emergency Response Teams (CERTS), enactment of National standards for cyber security compliance, presence of cyber policy and national roadmap, presence of a sponsoring agency leading the national cyber security efforts and national benchmarks for cyber security hygiene (UN, 2019; ITU, 2019c, 2019b, 2019a). The presence or absence of these measures is indicated in Table 1 using ✓ and & ✗, respectively. Henceforth, our attention will be directed towards a detailed examination of the strategies implemented by two prominent contemporary nations, namely Russia and China, in their pursuit of internet sovereignty. These countries have enacted comprehensive measures aimed at exerting control over the internet landscape, thereby warranting a closer analysis of their respective approaches and methodologies.

Table 1. Cybersecurity measures taken by other countries

Country	Legislation	Compliance	CERT	Standards	Certification	Policy	Roadmap	Lead Agency	National Benchmark	CS Index	Internet Pen %age
France	√	√	√	√	√	√	X	√	√	97.6	86
Russia	√	√	√	√	√	√	√	√	√	98.06	90.87
Australia	√	√	√	√	√	√	√	√	√	97.5	96
China	√	√	√	√	√	√	√	√	√	92.53	75.6
Brazil	√	√	√	√	√	√	X	X	√	96.6	81
Canada	√	√	√	√	X	√	√	√	X	97.7	93
India	√	√	√	√	X	√	√	√	√	97.5	46
Indonesia	√	√	√		X	X	X	√	X	94.9	62
South Korea	√	√	√	√	√	√	√	√	√	98.5	98
Malaysia	√	√	√	√	√	√	√	√	√	98.1	97
Germany	√	√	√	√	√	√	X	√	√	97.4	91
Vietnam	√	√	√	X	X	X	X	√	X	94.6	74

INTERNET SOVEREIGNTY MODELS

The evolution of internet sovereignty measures has seen a distinct trajectory, characterized by a concerted effort to assert national control over cyberspace. This journey begins with the recognition of the internet as a strategic domain, prompting the formulation of comprehensive frameworks aimed at safeguarding national interests. These frameworks encompass various aspects, including legal regulations, technological developments, and geopolitical strategies, all aimed at ensuring greater autonomy and security in the digital realm. Figure 2 illustrates the factors contributing to internet sovereignty.

National Strategies of Russia

Russian government aims at dividing the Internet into national segments dubbed as RUnet. RUnet is the title given to Country Code Top Level Domain (TLD) .RU, which was previously referred to as .SU for the Soviet Union. .SU is still functional, and around 100,000 domain names are still registered with .SU (Netim, 2015). Later it was used for referring to a geographically defined network space in state control. Russian lawmakers and government agencies have been working on various legislations to secure and stabilize the Internet in Russian territory, independent from the global Internet and external interference (Stadnik, 2019b). Work on this legislation is in progress with different levels of success.

Figure 2. Factors contributing to internet sovereignty

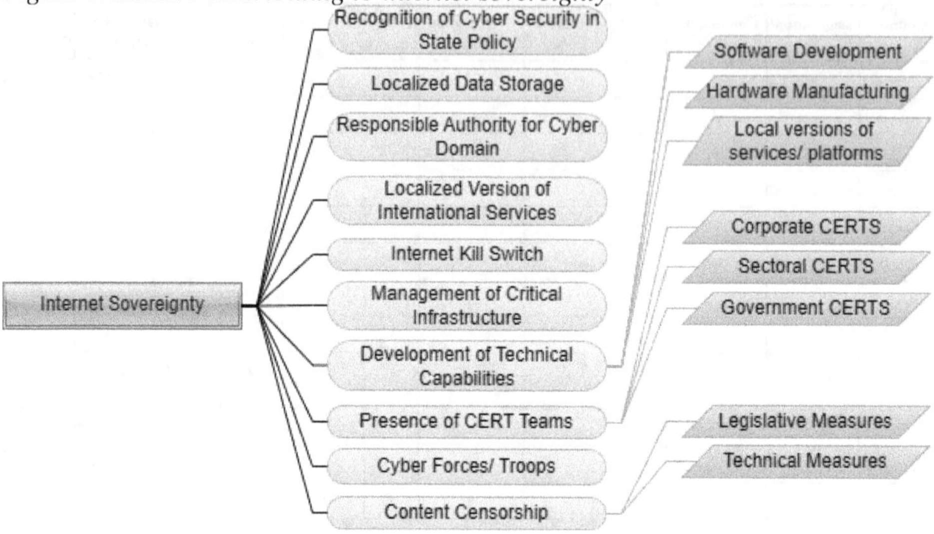

Re-Framing Cybersecurity

The Russian doctrine on information security was approved by the Russian president in 2016 (Kremlin, 2016a). It defines information security as a "state of protection of individuals, society, and the state from internal and external information threats." Russian doctrine reframes cybersecurity as a national security issue in the information domain by treating threats to information security as threats to national interest (Kremlin, 2016b).

Recruitment of Cyber Troops

The framework titled *Conceptual Views on the Activity of Armed Forces in the Information Space* was developed in 2011 by the Ministry of Defence of the Russian Federation (NATO, 2011). In 2017, it was formally recognized that Russia possesses Information Operations troops. According to the Russian cybersecurity firm Zecurion, Russia was among the top five countries in 2017 in spending on cyber operations and in the number of cyber troops (Kolomychenko, 2017). Although the capabilities of Russian troops are not disclosed, their primary purpose is to repel cyberattacks.

Russian CERTs

Russia has raised several CERTs that provide services in different domains. Many of these CERTs were members of the Forum of Incident Response and Security Teams (FIRST). However, their membership status has been suspended by FIRST (FIRST, 2024). Details of Russian CERTs are as follows:

- **RU-CERT.** It responds to all users within Russian territory. It also assists in contacting LEAs (RuCert, 2024).
- **CERT-GIB.** This cert provides emergency responses to all clients round the clock in cases of network intrusion, online frauds, DoS/DDoS, malware, and phishing attacks. CERT-GIB is a leading Russian cybersecurity firm with expertise in Advanced Persistent Threats (APTs). It collaborates with all Russian TLDs and collaborates with anti-cybercrime agencies worldwide. CERT-GIB is a member of the FIRST and an official partner of OIC-CERT and APCERT (Group-ib, 2024).
- **GOV-CERT.** It is a cybersecurity and incident response team for the Russian government. It coordinates with LEAs, local and state authorities to deal with computer incidents in state networks. It focuses on incidents of malware, botnets, DoS/DDoS, and unauthorized access (Gov-cert, 2024).
- **Fin CERT.** This cert is part of the Directorate of Security & Protection of the Bank of Russia. It coordinates information exchange between LEAs and financial institutions, analyzes attacks on these institutions, and issues protection guidelines (FinCERT, 2024).
- **BI.ZONE CERT.** Bi.Zone is a digital risk management company that offers security solutions and services to businesses and organizations worldwide (Bi.Zone, 2024).
- **IN4 CERT.** In4security is a digital threat protection company that offers security solutions and services to businesses and organizations worldwide. It specializes in Financial Institutions, Commercial organizations and Industrial organizations (In4-CERT, 2024).
- **ISL CSIRT.** Information Security Lab (ISL) is a commercial Incident Response Provider for Russian clients. They offer services to banks, retail, industrial, and other non-governmental entities. In addition to incident response, they also provide services in fraud monitoring, threat management, and anti-phishing domains (ISL-CERT, 2024).
- **Jet CERT.** Jet Infosystems is a Russian company providing services in IT sector. In the domain of Cyber Security, they provide security monitoring and incident response services. Their clients belong to the finance, commercial, and SCADA sector (Jet-CERT, 2024).

- **RTS CERT.** Rostelecom-Solar is a Russian company providing cyberattack countermeasures services to clients. They also provide emergency incident response services. Their clients include government entities and small to large organizations (RTS-CERT, 2024).

Role of Non-State Actors in Russia's Internet Sovereignty

State institutions in Russia have primarily led the nation's approach towards internet sovereignty. However, non-state actors (private cybersecurity firms), while operating independently, play a role in the cyberspace of state, at times supporting and extending the state's capacity.

Kaspersky Labs, a globally renowned cybersecurity firm known for its Antivirus solutions, is known to be closely aligned with the Russian state's cybersecurity ambitions. The firm is operating globally however, it has been scrutinized for its linkage to FSB and has been banned from selling its products in the U.S. It is claimed that Kaspersky antivirus could be used by the Russian government for surveillance of Americans, although the claims have been denied by Kaspersky (Lyngaas, 2024). The U.S. later imposed sanctions on several Kaspersky executives, citing their potential affiliation with Russian military intelligence (Reuters, 2024).

Another well-known firm, Group-IB, is famous for its cybersecurity products and services globally. In 2023, Russian authorities detained Ilya Sachkov, chief executive and co-founder of Group-IB, on treason charges and sentenced him to 14 years in prison. The company is one of the biggest in Russia, and it moved its headquarters to Singapore in 2018, after the U.S. government accused Moscow of meddling in U.S. presidential elections (Whittaker, 2021; Group-IB, 2023).

Killnet hacktivist group is recognized as a pro-Russian threat actor. It was involved in conducting DDoS attacks against Ukraine and other countries supporting Ukraine. The group has also claimed to have attacked government networks in the West, including the European parliament (Avertium, 2023; Rousi, 2022).

Telegram is deeply linked with Russia while having a huge footprint globally. It has been used as a platform by anti-government movements. A 2018 failed ban and continued use suggest deliberate tolerance and potentially strategic co-option by the state. During the Ukrainian war, Telegram has been used to promote the Russian narrative. Such an arrangement positions Telegram as a non-state actor supporting both the state-aligned narrative and dissent (Seddon, 2020; Bergengruen, 2022).

The situation highlights the sensitive and precarious nature of the relationship between the Russian government and cybersecurity firms.

Establishment of GOSSOPKA & Coordination of Threat Intelligence

Federal Security Service (FSB) to take necessary steps to create a system named GOSSOPKA for the detection and prevention of consequences of cyberattacks (RGRU, 2013). This initiative aimed to develop a capability for threat forecasting and act as a point of interaction for all stakeholders in the information security domain. It also monitors the state of security for Critical Information Infrastructure (CII). The first centres under GOSSOPKA emerged in 2015 in government organizations (Stadnik, 2019b). In 2017, the Russian parliament passed the FZ-187 Law. It defined GOSSOPKA as; geographically distributed centres comprising a system where information about cyberattacks is shared. These centres were mandatory to be established in all private and public entities owning CII. The law defined CII objects and established a registry for them (Government, 2017b). Criminal liabilities were also included in the law for actions against CII as an amendment to the Criminal Code of Russia. Unauthorized access to data at CII is liable to a maximum of six years imprisonment and a fine of up to one million rubles (Sukharenko, 2019). Figure 3 shows the territorial structure of GOSSOPKA centres (Borisov, 2015). In 2018 several legislations were passed for the establishment of the National Coordination Centre for Computer Incidents (NCCCI), a listing of information required to be shared with GOSSOPKA (Epifanova & Dietrich, 2022) and regulating information exchange among CII entities (OneTrust, 2018). NCCCI was mandated to deal with all international interactions for incident response with the authority of refusing the information sharing if deemed harmful to Russian National Security (Stadnik, 2019b).

IT Made in Russia

In 2015, a government decree imposed a ban on foreign software for state use. In compliance, a Register of Russian software is maintained having more than five thousand records (TAdvisor, 2022b). Only the software listed in the register is preferred for procurement by government entities.

Figure 3. Structure of GOSSOPKA centres

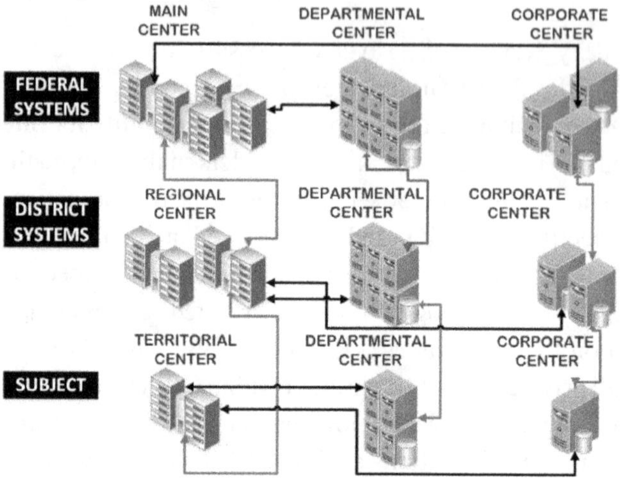

Internet Kill Switch

In 2014 Russian Ministry of Communications conducted a cyber exercise to assess the security and stability of the national segment of the Internet and the degree of its connectivity with the global Internet (Government, 2014c). The post-exercise report in 2015 suggested more legal and technical measures. Among legal measures, it suggested more state regulations, stricter control over operators, and a traffic monitoring system. Technical measures include reserving root DNS servers and a duplicate registry of IP addresses. These measures were recommended to cater for an event of external Internet shutdown (Golitsyna & Sergina, 2015).

In 2017, another cyber exercise was conducted to test the security and stability of the Russian Internet. The Russian Government is always concerned with the threat of an external shutdown of the Internet. Hence, both exercises were conducted to test the resilience of RUnet. The exercises concluded that RUnet is vulnerable to external attacks (Government, 2017a). In 2019, the Ministry of Communication passed a law under which Roskomnadzor would be allowed to unplug the Runet from the global Internet under three types of threats, including threats to the integrity, resilience, and network security of RUnet (Government, 2019c). Between June 15 and July 15, 2021, a series of exercises were conducted to ensure the sustainable, secure, and comprehensive operation of the Russian segment of the Internet in the event of physical disconnection from the global Internet (Chebakova & Balashova, 2021).

Content Censorship

In 2012, amendments to the Information Protection law mandated that operators limit access to illicit content on the Internet. A register comprising domain names, network addresses, and Internet resources containing illicit content was established. Upon the discovery of a website containing prohibited content, Roskomnadzor would issue a notification requesting the removal of said content. Failure to comply with the notification within three days would result in the site being added to the register of prohibited content (Anna et al., 2017). The role of Roskomnadzor has been pivotal in enabling the Russian government to assert greater control over the Internet in Russia. This has been achieved through various measures such as managing an extensive blocklist containing over 1.2 million URLs and issuing censorship orders to major companies, including Facebook, Instagram, TikTok, Twitter, Google Search, YouTube, and Pinterest (Sherman, 2022).

In 2015, a system known as Revizor was implemented to monitor and ensure operators' compliance with regulations about prohibited content registration. Operators found in violation of these regulations were subject to significant financial penalties (Anna et al., 2017). In 2019, a system was proposed for creating a safer Internet environment for children under the state-sponsored program titled "Digital Economy". This system was implemented in the year 2020. It is designed to restrict access to web content to only those websites that have been pre-approved and placed on a whitelist. To gain access to uncensored content, users are required to make an explicit request to their Internet service provider (Zykov, 2017).

Localized Data Storage and Processing

In 2016, the Russian government passed the law FZ-242, which requires companies to store and process data related to Russian citizens within the country's borders. This legislation also mandates that hosting and storage services must be relocated to Russia. Failure to comply with these regulations may result in a fine or even blockage, as noted in Stadnik (2019b).

Management of Critical Internet Resources

The Russian government is keen on protecting RUnet from external shutdowns (Luxmoore, 2019). State law on the Security of CII went into effect on January 1st, 2018. This law covers the government, defence industries, finance, energy, and nuclear sectors. It requires these critical systems to be connected to GOSSOPKA (Rbc.ru, 2017).

Discussions about an independent national segment of the Internet have been going on in Russia since 2016. The Ministry of Communications introduced a bill in 2016 that describes the elements of critical infrastructure. Subsequently, several amendments were issued in 2016 and 2017, adding details about critical infrastructure, including Internet Exchange Points (IXPs), TLD registries, IP addresses, and autonomous system numbers. In 2018, a new Bill was introduced, which required operators to route traffic through traffic exchange points listed in a special registry. It also established a national DNS. The bill also mandated operators to install special means for the protection of their networks (Stadnik, 2019b). This new law was signed in May 2019 (Government, 2019b). On March 30, 2022, an executive order was issued regarding measures to ensure the technological independence and security of CII of the Russian Federation. This order stipulates that to maintain technological independence and security, customers must obtain prior approval from federal agencies before acquiring foreign software and hardware for use in sectors classified as CII (Krelmlin, 2022).

National Strategies of China

The Chinese concept of "Internet Sovereignty" is based on two principles: the absence of unauthorized influence in the country's information space and the shift of Internet management to an international body (Schia & Gjesvik, 2017). In the Chinese community, unauthorized influence in the information space is seen as a threat to stability, and the Internet is viewed as a facilitator of multiple avenues of information exchange without state control. The potential use of social media platforms and the Internet for activities like civil disobedience and mass protests is viewed as a significant concern. However, there has never been an incident of mass agitation staged with the help of social media in China (Diamond, 2015). During the peak of the Arab Spring in 2011, China imposed censorship control over terms like Jasmine in an effort to deal with calls for the Jasmine Revolution, and the police force was physically employed to deal with protests (Ramzy, 2011). The issue of international management of the Internet is based on the general sentiment that cyberspace is America-centric, which is evident based on Snowden's revelations of the PRISM surveillance program (Greenwal & MacAskill, 2013). Although there is no unified policy document for Chinese cyberspace, this study reviews open-source data about Chinese policies.

Cybersecurity in State Security Policy

The Chinese government considers Internet sovereignty to be critical for the maintenance of its core values and views telecommunications resources as a matter of high politics intertwined with national security and stability (Pitt et al., 1996). The government has commissioned numerous projects including the GFW and the Great Cannon (GC), to reinforce its nationalist sentiments and to control the flow of information and data on the Internet.

Chinese Cyber Troops

China has established dedicated cyber troops for both civil and military domains. Within the civil sphere, there are cyber specialists employed in various organizations, including some ministries. Meanwhile, the People's Liberation Army (PLA) has its own Military Network Warfare forces responsible for conducting offensive and defensive cyber operations (Tiezzi, 2015). According to Kolomychenko (2017), China ranks as the second-largest country in terms of spending on cyber troops and the largest in terms of the number of personnel involved. In 2015, China introduced a new domain within the PLA with the raising of the Strategic Support Force (SSF). It has the same status as the PLA's land, air, and naval forces. The SSF looks after war efforts in the information sphere encompassing space, cyber, and electromagnetic domains (Kania & Costello, 2018).

Cyber Militias and Hacktivist Units

There are numerous active cyber groups in Chinese cyberspace other than PLA cyber units. Cyber militias comprise IT experts, IT firms, domain experts, hackers, foreign language speakers, etc. They participate in military exercises but are not managed directly by PLA (Stevens, 2016). One of the most prominent groups is Red Hacker Alliance with around eighty thousand members. Such groups operate in parallel to the government and do not like to be under serious government control (Reud, 2016).

Chinese CERTS

Several Chinese CERTS are functional in multiple domains. All of them are members of FIRST less Qi An Xin CERT. Out of these CERTS, Five CERTS are looking after their corporate clients. These CERTS include Huawei Product Security Incident Response Team (Huawei PSIRT), ZTE Product Security Incident Response Team (ZTE PSIRT), Dahua Product Security Incident Response Team (Dahua

PSIRT), China Mobile CERT (CM-CERT) and Alibaba Security Response Centre (ASRC) (Huawei-PSIRT, 2024; ZTE-PSIRT, 2024; Dahua-PSIRT, 2024; Alibaba, 2024). Other CERTS are as under:

- **National Computer Network Emergency Response Technical Team/ Coordination Centre of China (CNCERT-CC).** CNCERT-CC is a non-profit, non-government cybersecurity technical centre. It coordinates China's cybersecurity emergency response community. It acts as the national CERT of China and guards CII. It also manages GFW (CNCERT, 2024).
- **Eversec.** Hengan Jiaxin Technology is a network security provider to the telecom operators, the government, and the corporate sector (Eversec, 2024).
- **HSRC.** Hikvision runs a private cybersecurity centre providing support in recognized cybersecurity standards (Hikvision, 2024).
- **Qi An Xin CERT.** Qi An Xin Group is a cybersecurity firm providing services to the government, finance, energy, and telecom sectors. The group specializes in big data (QiAnXin, 2024).
- **Data Star Observatory.** Data Star Observatory provides digital asset threat management and operations services, asset threat monitoring, analysis, and vulnerability life cycle management services (Datastar, 2024).

Role of Non-State Actors in China's Internet Sovereignty

The Chinese approach towards incorporating state resources and non-state actors is unique and synergised. Private corporations and academic institutions are working in liaison with the government. Technology giants like Huawei and ZTE have a major role in advancing the Chinese digital influence globally. However, the U.S. have banned equipment from these companies, citing national security concerns, potential data breaches and espionage (BBC News, 2022). A NATO report analysed China's cybersecurity strategy, highlighting that the Chinese government is in close collaboration with the private sector and private citizens for conducting cyber operations and aiming to acquire technological secrets from the West and extend geopolitical influence (SC World, 2016).

The Cybersecurity Law of 2017 makes it mandatory for the network operators, including private firms, to manage the security of their infrastructure and data. The law compels private entities to align themselves with the state-governed policies on cybersecurity. The move will ensure that non-state actors are also integrated into the state's strategy for securing cyberspace. The law states the imposition of fines in case of lapses, and it will ensure that non-state actors also contribute to the maintenance and upkeep of internet sovereignty (DigiChina, 2018).

GFW

Figure 4. Simplified decision flow of the Great Firewall

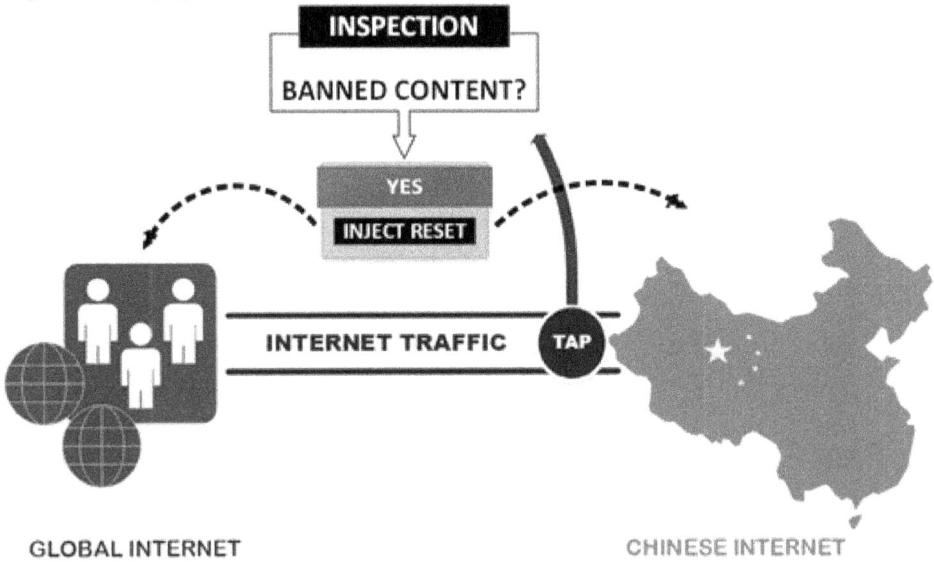

The GFW was established in 1990 and is managed by CNCERT-CC under the Ministry of Industry and Information Technology (MIIT). Various government institutions are responsible for censorship policies and decisions. These include the central propaganda department, the State Council Information Office (SCIO), and the Public Information Network security supervision department of the Ministry of Public Security (MPS). The hardware used in GFW is domestically produced by Sugon and Huawei. Three international gateways are in Beijing, Shanghai, and Guangzhou, and the bulk of the filtering hardware is located at border routers. Some hardware has also been placed internally, which indicates surveillance of domestic traffic (Shen, 2014). Moreover, several laws regulate the flow of web data. The simplified decision flow of GFW is illustrated in Figure 4 (Marczak et al., 2015).

Blocked websites and web resources are classified as foreign social media platforms, foreign news sites, file-sharing services, overseas Chinese portal sites and discussion forums, dissident/pro-democracy/human rights sites, circumvention, and anonymity tools, sites associated with Falun Gong, and pornography and gambling (Perunicic, 2023). The domestic network is monitored with the help of human censors, the internet police force, hired bloggers, and even regional Internet shutdowns. International network traffic is managed through IP blocking, DNS manipulation, URL filtering, and keyword filtering (Shen, 2014).

GC

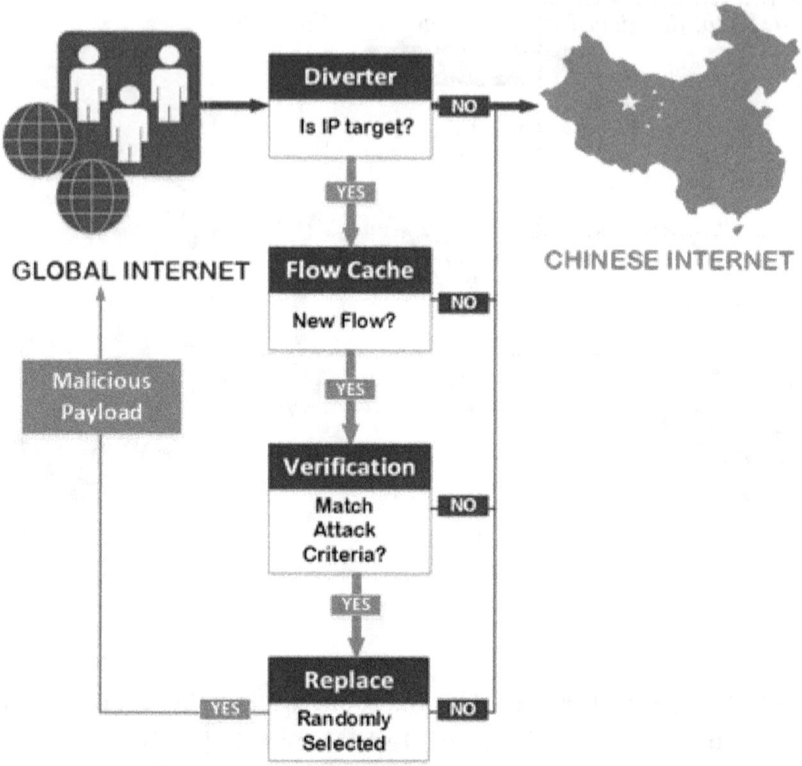

The GC was commissioned in 2015 as an active tool employed for DDoS attacks. It works by redirecting intercepted web traffic to target websites, allowing authorities to intercept traffic flowing from outside of China towards Chinese websites, inject malicious code, and use this traffic as intended, just like a Man-in-the-Middle attack (Perlroth, 2015). The malicious code makes a non-suspecting Internet user a participant in the DDoS attack. Although the GC is separate from the GFW, researchers have found it collocated with the GFW. The decision flow of the GC is illustrated in Figure 5 (Marczak et al., 2015).

Social Management Strategy

The Chinese government has utilized the Internet as a tool for implementing social management in a manner that is not directly invasive. This has been accomplished through a combination of technical, legal, and regulatory measures, which instil a fear of legal consequences in Internet users and promote desired behaviour. Such measures help to maintain social stability in Chinese society and protect it from the negative effects of global Internet use (Pieke, 2017).

Content Localization

The Cybersecurity Law of China requires companies operating in China with an established network to store information inside China. The law came into effect on June 1st, 2017, and applies to CII operators including operators in communications, information services, energy, finance, and public services (LawBlog, 2018).

Cross-Border Data Transfer Control

The measures for security assessment for cross-border transfer of personal information (draft) were issued by the Cyberspace Administration of China (CAC) on June 13th, 2019. The measures regulate operators and cross-border receivers of data through secure data transfer contracts. The measures also deal with the application and approval apparatus for cross-border data transfer (Ning et al., 2019). Authorities may demand the seizure of cross-border data transfer under the following conditions (Hunton, 2019):-

- Data breach suffered by the "operator" of the cross-border receiver.
- Unsustainable protection of rights and interests by data subjects.
- Operator or cross-border receiver's inability to protect data.

Chinese Version of Online Platforms/Services

Another strategy of China has been to block the global platforms/services and replicate them in-house. Popular platforms are listed in Table 2.

Table 2. Chinese versions of online services

Chinese Service	Global Service	Category
Baidu	Google	Search engine
QQ	MSN messenger	Instant messaging
Weibo	Twitter	Social network
Zhihu	Quora	Social network
Taobao	Amazon	Online shopping
Youku	Youtube	Video

continued on following page

Table 2. Continued

Chinese Service	Global Service	Category
Pan.baidu	Dropbox	Online storage
QQ music	Spotify	Online music
Dian ping	Groupon	Lifestyle
Baidu maps	Google maps	Navigation
Gaode maps	Google maps	Navigation

ANALYSIS OF FRAMEWORKS

This study reviews the state of affairs in the domain of Internet governance and highlights the efforts of the two most advanced and developed cyber powers after the US. Both Russia and China have their reasons and concerns regarding the unmatched dominance of the US in the global infrastructure of the Internet and its potential usage by US authorities to spy on these countries. We analyse the approaches taken by both of these countries under the Mueller framework of "Internet Fragmentation". Accordingly, the efforts by states to establish ultimate authority over respective national segments of cyberspace are examined, and methods to achieve alignment are explained. These methods include national securitisation, territorialization of information flows, and alignment of critical Internet resources (Mueller, 2017).

1. **National Securitization**. It involves securing the national information frontier. It consists of four parts. The first part is the recognition of cybersecurity as a national security issue. The second part involves the nationalization of threat intelligence and the creation of a central threat picture. The third one focuses on promoting and adopting national ICT. The fourth part entails the development of a kill switch. Details on National Securitization measures can be found in Table 3.
2. **Territorialization of Information Flows**. It encompasses the steps taken for content filtering and data localization. Both Russia and China have taken measures for the implementation of content censorship policies and the localization of data within national boundaries. Details are available in Table 4.
3. **Alignment of Critical Internet Resources**. It involves identifying and managing critical infrastructure. It is also focused on the security of these assets through legislation and law enforcement. Both Russia and China have taken measures in this direction, including the creation of dedicated organizations and particular laws for the protection of CII assets. Additional details are provided in Table 5.

This section assesses the overall effectiveness of the measures taken by Russia and China under the umbrella of Internet sovereignty frameworks.

Cataloging Threats

Russian Approach

Cataloging of Potential Threats in the Information Security Doctrine of the Russian Federation. In December 2016, Russia enforced the information security doctrine, which identifies potential threats (Kremlin, 2016b). These threats include the illegal cross-border flow of data, the employment of ICT to influence the minds of the populace, the use of foreign IT equipment (hardware and software), the exposure of critical infrastructure to threats, and the irregular control over critical Internet resources and their distribution. Cataloging these threats enabled lawmakers to focus on addressing them. The developments against these cataloged threats are discussed here:

- ***Illegal cross-border flow of data***: Law FZ-242 was adopted on July 4th, 2014. It enforces local data policy, requiring operators to ensure that any data collection or processing is done within Russia and nullifying any illegal content sharing across borders (Stanford, 2014).
- ***Employment of ICT to influence public opinion:*** Amendments to the law on information protection were passed in 2012. These additions require operators to restrict Internet access to prohibited content cataloged in a national registry (Anna et al., 2017).
- ***Foreign IT equipment (Hardware and Software):*** A government decree was passed in 2015 that imposed a ban on foreign software for state use (TAdvisor, 2022b).
- ***Exposure of critical infrastructure to threats:*** The security of CII law went into effect in January 2018 (RBC.ru, 2017).
- ***Irregular control and distribution of resources:*** Law FZ-187 passed in 2017 defines CII objects and their owners and establishes a registry for CII objects (Government, 2017b).

Russia added information security as part of the Russian national security strategy published in December 2015 (Government, 2015). It enabled lawmakers to focus on information security. The information security doctrine of the Russian Federation was enforced in December 2016 (Coalson, 2016).

Chinese Approach

Unauthorized Influence in INFORMATION SPACE and Unrest in Society. Unauthorized influence in the information space and unrest in society are seen as interrelated phenomena in China. China has successfully curtailed both through a blend of technical, legal, and regulatory measures. These measures isolate local Internet users from the global Internet, preventing the possibility of foreign influence and instilling a change of conduct in Internet users due to the fear of litigation (Pieke, 2017).

Table 3. National securitisation

Country	Cataloguing of threats	Cyber Troops	Threat Intelligence	CERTs	National Technologies	Internet Kill Switch
Russia	• A range of potential threats was catalogued (Kremlin, 2016b). • Addition of threats in Russian doctrinal documents (Kremlin, 2016b). • Inclusion of cybersecurity as part of the national security domain (Kremlin, 2016b).	• Russia is the fifth-largest spender on cyber troops (Kolomychenko, 2017). • Russia has the fifth-largest number of cyber troops (Kolomychenko, 2017).	• Creation of GOSSOPKA to provide a wholesome picture (RGRU, 2013). • Establishment of NCCCI for dealing with international incident response (Epifanova & Dietrich, 2022).	• Russia has nine active CERTs. • CERTs deal with LEAs, general cyber threats, government networks, finance, and industry. • Two Russian CERTs are members of FIRST (FIRST, 2024).	• Banning foreign software for official use in Russia (TAdvisor, 2022b). • Laws implemented for the transition to local software (TAdvisor, 2022b).	• A law passed in 2019 for • unplugging RUnet (Anna et al., 2017). • Sovereign RUNet tested in July 2021 (Chebakova and Balashova, 2021).
China	• Unauthorized influence in the information space and unrest in society are seen as threats (Schia and Gjesvik, 2017).	• China is the second-largest spender on cyber troops (Kolomychenko, 2017). • The largest number of cyber troops (Kolomychenko, 2017). • Presence of cyber militias and hacktivist units (Reud, 2016).	• Establishment of CNCERT-CC as the National CERT of China, which coordinates with other stakeholders (CNCERT, 2024). • Foundation of China National Vulnerability Database (CNVD), Anti Network-Virus Alliance of China (ANVA), and China Cyber Threat Governance Alliance (CCTGA) (CNCERT, 2024).	• China has ten active CERTs. • All are members of FIRST (FIRST, 2024).	• Local development of software and hardware as part of the government vision (Quishi, 2017).	• Speculations about China having a kill switch but never acknowledged (WebproNews, 2012).

Table 4. Territorialization of information flows

Country	Content Censorship	Data Localization
Russia	• A registry created for prohibited content (Anna et al., 2017). • Roskomnadzor was made responsible for adding names to the registry (Anna et al., 2017). • The Revizor system checks operators' compliance (Anna et al., 2017). • The digital economy program aims to create a safer Internet environment for children (Zykov, 2017).	• The law mandates local storage and processing of data (Stadnik, 2019b). • Hosting and storage services are required to be shifted to servers in Russia (Stadnik, 2019b).
China	• The GFW (Shen, 2014). • The GC (Perlroth, 2015).	• Establishment of local data centres (LawBlog, 2018). • Law for cross-border data transfer control (Hunton, 2019).

Table 5. Alignment of critical Internet resources

Country	**Measures Taken**
Russia	• Creation of GOSSOPKA (RGRU, 2013). • Law on the security of CII (Rbc.ru, 2017). • Creation of a registry for CII (Stadnik, 2019b).
China	• Operations security for CII under cybersecurity law (Creemers et al., 2018).

Cyber Troops

Russian Approach

Fifth Largest Spender on Cyber Troops. Russia has earned a reputable stature as a cyber power in recent times. The cyberattacks against Ukraine in 2015 and 2016 that caused a huge power outage and affected critical infrastructure are attributed to Russia (CFR, 2023). Furthermore, in 2017, the NotPetya ransomware inflicted a huge financial loss on Ukraine. The US, UK, Canada, and Australia all attribute NotPetya to Russia. Hence, Russia's cyber posture is considered offensive (Popescu & Secrieru, 2018). The 2016 US elections are said to have been manipulated by Russia. Although no evidence of Russia's direct involvement and tampering was found (Ward, 2019), the Federal Bureau of Investigation (FBI) is currently seeking eleven Russian military intelligence officers for interference in the 2016 US elections (FBI, 2023). In February 2022, satellite Internet services in Ukraine were disrupted during the Russian invasion of Ukraine. The attack on satellite Internet services has been attributed to Russia by both the UK and EU (Pearson & Bing, 2022).

Chinese Approach

Second-Largest Spender on Cyber Troops. China houses the largest number of cyber troops and is a formidable cyber power. China is attributed with several significant data breaches, including the 2007 Lockheed Martin breach, which gave away details about the F35 fighter (Nasaw, 2009). Similarly, the 2013 breach gave away designs of the advanced Patriot missile, "THAAD," and Aegis ballistic-missile defence system (Nakashima, 2013). A security breach in 2018 resulted in the exposure of data about advanced naval projects of the US Navy (LaGrone, 2018).

Threat Intelligence

Russian Approach

Creation of GOSSOPKA. The creation of GOSSOPKA and its deployment in 2015 marked a significant development in Russian cyber defence. It has NCCCI within the FSB for the management of cyber defence. Our study identifies that legislation concerning GOSSOPKA initially struggled to get through the State Duma due to the huge costs involved and the lack of trained staff. Despite these issues, it laid the foundations for well-coordinated cybersecurity operations, incorporating state, government, and corporate sectors. By 2016, GOSSOPKA was in place with ten state organizations. Two response centres were established in Rostec and the Central Bank of Russia. Rostec is a "state-owned" corporate holding comprising around seven hundred enterprises, most of which are related to defence and civil industries (Rostec, 2024). It is worth noting that Rostec analyses thousands of security events each month. However, by 2020 (four years after the creation of GOSSOPKA), only 30 percent of the enterprises in the defence industries were able to be connected to Rostec's cyber defence system. One of the reasons for this delay is said to be the lack of qualified staff (Petrov, 2016).

The Russian military has been accused of obtaining electronic components for a research institute owned by the FSB (Meshcheryakov, 2013). The equipment was used to study cyber-attack scenarios and develop responses. In addition, imported software is required to be certified for any bugs or vulnerabilities. These procurements cost thousands of dollars annually but are never used by research institutes. The lack of technical staff is often filled by hiring contracted cybersecurity experts (Baranovskaya, 2017).

The government of Russia credited GOSSOPKA for successfully dealing with fifty million cyberattacks in 2016. One example of such an attack is the "WannaCry virus," which targets telecommunications and government sectors. However, according to the government, no critical infrastructure suffered damage in these attacks (Chernenko, 2019). In 2018, the day of the election of the Russian President witnessed a rise in cyberattacks involving 20,000 attack sources. These sources were stopped and dealt with by NCCCI, which later took over the role of GovCERT as part of the FSB (Mskagency, 2018). In 2019, the Russian government announced that it thwarted a cyber attack against the Russian power grid by the US; however, no further details were given (Reuters, 2019).

Chinese Approach

Establishment of CNCERT. CNCERT is an essential coordinating point for cybersecurity response. The CNCERT-CC website presents details about reporting an event, its acceptance, handling, and feedback. CNCERT also operates a 24/7 helpline and publishes weekly and monthly reports on malicious programs, DDoS attacks, and other security events it has managed. Additionally, CNCERT collaborates internationally with organizations such as the Asia Pacific Emergency Organization (APCERT) in cyber drills. Hence, from the status of its updated reports, international collaboration, and 24/7 helpline, one can assume that CNCERT-CC has been working optimally to fulfill its purpose.

According to a 2014 report by CNCERT, it successfully managed fifty-six thousand seventy-two incidents out of fifty-six thousand one hundred and eighty and took down seven hundred and forty-four large-scale botnet attacks. Most of these attacks originated from three locations, including the US (CNCERT, 2014). In 2019, a CNCERT report indicated that large-scale cyberattacks originated from the US and affected millions of Chinese computers (Lindsey, 2019). Weekly reports of CNCERT cover key findings, including infected computers, backdoored websites, phishing websites, and zero-day vulnerabilities cataloged by the CNVD.

CERTS

Russian Approach

Russian - CERTS. In contrast to private sector CERTS, Russian public CERTS do not operate 24/7. The only public CERT that operates around the clock is FinCERT, especially structured for the financial sector. Hence, public CERT websites do not present updated data; for example, RU-CERT is a member of FIRST, but it has only an eight-hour working time. At one time, there was only a single report on their website regarding a phishing attack that occurred in 2017. Although Russia has established all these CERTS, their efficacy is ambivalent.

Chinese Approach

Chinese - CERTS. All the Chinese CERTs are members of FIRST, with CNCERT/CC being the official CERT of China. Out of these, five CERTS serve their parent company's customers concerning product and service vulnerabilities. Eversec, Dauha, HSRC, and Qi An Xin are private cybersecurity companies. These companies maintain websites with updated security advisories, best practices, publications, and newsletters. CNCERT-CC also maintains a website with updated reports on a weekly and monthly basis. Chinese CERTs have demonstrated strong capabilities and have continued to expand their portfolio and expertise.

ROLE OF NON-STATE ACTORS IN INTERNET SOVEREIGNTY

Russian Approach

State Tolerated Proxy Ecosystem

In Russia, cybersecurity firms like Kaspersky, Group-IB and hacktivist groups like Killnet have a significant presence inside and outside Russia. There is no official obligation to align themselves with the state's narrative and strategy in cyberspace. They are expected to be independently aligned with the state's ambitions. Kaspersky and Killnet act independently, where Kaspersky faced a ban in U.S. on allegations of spying for the Russian government, and Killnet was involved in cyber operations against Western entities. On the contrary, Group-IB was never alleged as such, and their Chief Executive was imprisoned on charges of espionage, suggesting a state-tolerated proxy ecosystem without any official law to dictate adhering to state policy.

Chinese Approach

Integrated Role of Non-State Actors

Private technology firms are integrated and involved in national internet governance. Through a fusion of civil and military resources, the line between civil and military cyber operations is blurred. The legislation enforces compliance by technology firms while fostering a culture of innovation and technical breakthroughs. The rise of Huawei and ZTE, while being banned in the U.S. is testimony to the implementation of this strategy.

National Technologies

Russian Approach

Banning Foreign Software. Foreign software was banned for use in state organizations and municipal departments in 2016. The national registry of domestically produced software has been maintained since then, and it has more than five thousand seven hundred entries. One issue with this arrangement is the availability of a category titled "Russian commercial organization with foreign persons in the chain of ownership." Another issue is the challenge of shifting to domestic software when an organization has a license for foreign software, and local software is not efficient or user-friendly. Moreover, switching to domestically produced alternatives is not possible in a short span of time (Stadnik, 2019b).

In December 2018, Russian authorities requested the removal of foreign-origin software from the national registry within 6 months (Zhukova, 2018; TAdvisor, 2022a). In April 2021, a new law was passed requiring smartphones, tablets, smart televisions, laptops, and PCs to be pre-installed with Russian-origin software (Reuters, 2021). Accordingly, a registry of domestic software is maintained. However, efforts are still in progress to remove foreign-origin software from the national registry and to remove software that does not comply with regulations. Another issue faced by Russia is the lack of ICT hardware development industries. A lot of work is yet to be done in the field of software and hardware ICT technologies. There are no notable Russian companies, except Kaspersky, that have a significant presence in the field of cybersecurity.

Chinese Approach

Local Development of Software and Hardware. Foreign technology is seen as a threat to China, and the government is sensitive to it. Local technology companies have been able to provide potent hardware and IT services. However, a significant portion of this technology originates from the US and Europe. It is almost an unquestioned fact that foreign systems are bugged to steal Chinese secrets. For this reason, strict controls have been imposed on foreign investors.

The Chinese fifteen-year plan calls for a ban on acquiring core technologies that have an impact on the national economy and national security from abroad (Reud, 2016). China has also announced a five-year tax break for chip makers and software developers (Shidong, 2019) to achieve the goals of the Made in China 2025 strategy (Kania, 2019). Chinese companies are among the top equipment vendors in the world, and China is aiming to spearhead the race for 5G. Nine out of the top twenty technology firms are in China. Out of thirty-five thousand seven hundred and forty-four Chinese software firms, more than a dozen are valued at more than USD 1 Billion (Ross, 2021). These stats reflect the success story of China in the local development of ICT technologies.

Content Censorship

Russian Approach

Registry for Prohibited Content. After the establishment of a prohibited content registry, a law was passed in Russia in 2018, making it mandatory to connect to this system for automatic filtering by service providers. Violators would face a financial penalty (Stadnik, 2019b). By October 2018, most Internet companies had connected their servers to the system. One notable incident occurred when Google did not comply and was fined USD 7,500. The company quietly paid the fine. Later, Google complied by removing the banned content from its search engine (Boletskaya, 2019). It has also been observed that, since the hostilities between Russia and Ukraine in February 2022, there has been a surge in content censorship. This has affected various social media and news platforms, including Instagram, Facebook, Twitter, and BBC News (Migliano & Woodhams, 2023).

The control over Internet content has gradually matured under Russian authorities, with practical applications seen since Russia's operations against Ukraine in February 2022. More than 4,300 URLs have been blocked, which include notable social media platforms, online services, news platforms, and human rights watchdogs, mainly due to hosting content related to the military conflict.

Digital Economy Program. The Russian government announced plans to implement the digital economy program by 2020. As part of this program, the League of Internet Security compiled a white list of more than one million entries. However, experts argue that white lists may not be effective unless the content is independently verified and prohibited content is actively blocked. Social media administrators also bear the responsibility of removing illegal and prohibited content to protect vulnerable users, particularly children (Zykov, 2017). Reports also suggest that the implementation of the digital economy program faces delays due to recurrent amendments, budget cuts, and a shortage of qualified personnel in the related fields (Sitalieva et al., 2022).

Chinese Approach

GFW/GC. Commissioned in 1990, the GFW has been the world's largest Internet censorship system. The stability in China and public acceptance of the Chinese Communist Party are attributed to the effectiveness of GFW. Other blocked websites and services include those that contain any information about civil unrest, either currently or in the past. The stringent censorship policies have significant effects on businesses. Chinese Internet users have to rely on Virtual Private Networks (VPNs) to access foreign websites (Tang, 2016).

GFW detects and drops data packets related to popular VPN traffic patterns. It employs deep packet inspection and machine learning techniques. Only a few commercial VPNs can operate to facilitate foreign business operations. The Tor browser also struggles against the GFW algorithm (Tor, 2019).

The GC also has a significant impact. It is presumed that higher authorities are taken into the loop before launching an attack, as targeting a foreign website may result in potential backlash. In one such attack by GC against Greatfire.org, Baidu's international traffic was redirected. Such actions could prove costly for the reputation of the website and may result in litigation outside China.

Data Localization

Russian Approach

Law for Local Storage of Data and Processing. The aforementioned law was passed in 2016, requiring the local storage and processing of data, and the shifting of personal data inside Russia instead of abroad. However, LinkedIn refused to shift its servers, which contained the data of Russian citizens. As a result, it was the first company to be registered as a violator of personal data rights and was blocked by Roskomnadzor (Tang, 2016). Facebook and Twitter also failed to comply with Russian law and subsequently faced criminal proceedings, resulting in a fine of four million rubles each in 2020 (Sivetc, 2021; Browne, 2019). In contrast, other technology giants such as Uber, Microsoft, Lenovo, Samsung, PayPal, eBay, and AliExpress opted to use special cloud services instead of physically shifting their servers to Russia to comply with the FZ-242 law (Stadnik, 2019b). Meanwhile, Google, Apple, Alibaba, Viber, and Booking.com shifted their servers to Russia (Newton, 2018; Ewdn, 2019).

According to estimates, around 2.5 million companies are affected by the law. Non-compliant firms will face repeated fines and ultimately a ban (Sivetc, 2021). The law is expected to lead to a capacity crunch in the data centre industry and high credit charges for financing (DCD, 2015). However, the development of new data centres is good news for Russian software engineers, as it creates new jobs (Hopping, 2019). Despite the capacity crunch and high credit charges faced by firms, it appears that most of them have complied with the law, as to date, only one company has been banned for non-compliance.

Chinese Approach

Establishment of Local Data Centers. The Chinese cybersecurity law mandates the creation of local data centres not only for personal data but also for important data that concerns CII. The law is believed to be ambiguous in some parts, but still, it is solving the purpose (Wei, 2018). In compliance with Chinese cybersecurity law, Apple established its first data centre in China in 2021 (Swinhoe, 2021). Additionally, Amazon, Microsoft, and IBM have a footprint in China through local cloud service partners. However, the data centre market will suffer in developed cities due to the shortage of space and infrastructure availability (DataEconomy, 2019). In contrast, data centres in the central, western, and northeastern parts of China are only half used despite incentives announced by the government (DataEconomy, 2018).

The National Development and Reform Commission (NDRC), the country's economic planner, officially launched the Eastern Data and Western Computing project in February 2022. The primary goal of the plan is to boost data centres in China's economically deprived, yet energy-rich western regions. The plan aims to take part of the data processing workload currently handled predominantly in eastern facilities, where energy costs are higher (ERCHI & MIN, 2022). The availability of data centre infrastructure shuns the fear of overcapacity amid the new Chinese law. However, ambiguous definitions of terminologies will be a problem in compliance and may cause undue litigation. For example, the definition of "important data" is not specific and will be at the discretion of authorities. Moreover, any new firm coming to China will have to understand the possibility of scrutiny of its data by Chinese authorities. During the first two years of this law, 11,000 arrests were made, and Japanese companies' facilities in China were raided by local authorities, demonstrating the will of the Chinese government in its enforcement (Kodama, 2018).

Cross-Border Data Transfer Control. The cross-border data transfer control law, which will give China significant control over the flow of data from the Chinese mainland, was drafted in June 2019 and implemented in September 2022. Under this law, companies are required to submit a self-assessment report to the CAC that includes information on the intended recipients of the data to be shared. The CAC will then conduct a comprehensive security review, which may take up to forty-five working days to complete. However, there is a lack of guidance on how to prepare for compliance with this law. For instance, there is no guidance on measuring the risk factor, which is a crucial component to be mentioned in the self-assessment report. Similarly, there is no clarity among cybersecurity experts about the specific details to be included in the report regarding security protocols and vulnerabilities (Shen, 2022). Despite the potential benefits of the Cross-Border Data Transfer Control Act, there are serious concerns regarding the lack of information on compliance requirements. The lack of detailed instructions on how to measure risk factors, as well as the particular facts that must be included in the self-assessment report, raises concerns about the law's effectiveness and openness. To ensure the law's successful implementation and to foster trust among overseas partners, the Chinese government must provide more guidance and clarity on compliance requirements.

Alignment of Critical Internet Resources

Russian Approach

Law on the Security of CII. Russian lawmakers have pursued multiple laws regarding the security of CII, first in 2016 and then in 2017. However, objections from the telecom sector and budget constraints hindered their adoption (Stadnik, 2019b). A new bill was introduced in 2018, which was signed by President Putin in May 2019 after making its way through the legislative process. Despite debates during its adoption, many ambiguities were left unaddressed (Stadnik, 2019a).

Reports suggest that companies owning CII objects are not complying with the FSB's requirement to inform the NCCCI about cyber incidents before sharing them with international IT firms (TAdvisor, 2019). Article seven of the law mandates entities, including those not perceiving themselves as CII subjects, to submit categorization results to the federal executive body. While this grants the authority an active role in the process, it does not impose a full obligation for categorization, leading to both benefits and drawbacks. The provision streamlines the categorization process but also gives the authority greater power compared to the entities involved.

The implementation of the law also faces the problem of distinguishing information infrastructure objects, which is complicated by interconnected computer systems and networks. Consequently, the issue of defining the boundaries of information infrastructure in this context remains a challenge (Polyakova et al., 2021). The Russian government has shown a strong commitment to safeguarding RUnet, the national segment of the Internet, against external shutdowns, as evidenced by their efforts to enhance CII security. However, several challenges are hampering the effectiveness of the GOSSOPKA initiative and the establishment of a registry for CII objects. These challenges include incomplete registration of objects, inadequate information sharing from telecom operators and financial institutions, a low completion rate in the categorization process, and the absence of a defined timeframe for categorization. These factors undermine efforts to define CII and its owners and hinder the progress of creating a comprehensive registry of CII objects.

Chinese Approach

Operations Security for CII Under Cybersecurity Law. Chinese cybersecurity law has a dedicated section for the security of critical infrastructure. It was implemented in September 2021. The implementation of the cybersecurity law in China imposes stricter data security requirements and increased government oversight on companies designated as CII operators. The regulations provide detailed guidelines for the responsibilities of CII operators and regulatory departments, along with specified penalties for security violations. A hierarchical reporting system is also established, which mandates CII operators to report anomalies to regulatory departments. These anomalies will then be reported to central government bodies (Huld, 2021). However, the regulations lack clarity regarding the scope of businesses classified as CII, leaving certain companies uncertain about their regulatory obligations. In short, the government has taken a comprehensive approach, incorporating all stakeholders to mitigate potential issues in the future. They have addressed all possible concerns and established a sustainable and future-proof cybersecurity review system. With its complex intermeshed strategies, regulations, and standards, the Chinese approach is considered even more comprehensive than that of the US or EU (Sacks, 2019).

Internet Kill Switch

Russian Approach

Internet Isolation Bill - Law Passed in 2019. The law for unplugging RUnet, signed by President Putin in May 2019, was enforced in November 2019. Russia cites threats to the stable functioning of the national segment of the Internet as the main reason for this law. However, critics differ from the Russian government's stance regarding the Internet Corporation for Assigned Names and Numbers (ICANN). They argue that ICANN is an international body, and cutting out Russian domains on the order of the US government could lead to a loss of credibility forever. Moreover, this action may also result in the reemergence of regional networks similar to those seen in the 1990s.

The law also authorizes Roskomnadzor to take control of communication networks in case of a threat. However, neither the operators nor Roskomnadzor were able to prevent network crashes. Thirty bylaws were also required to be drafted before November 2019 to fill in the missing details (Stadnik, 2019a). According to estimates, an Internet shutdown in Russia would cause a loss of 3.47 million dollars per hour (Carmichael, 2019). Russia has already tested a scenario where it isolated the Russian segment of the Internet from the global Internet. However, some speculations suggest that unplugging the Internet will raise concerns for the business community and service providers. Some web pages and services operating in Russia might face trouble operating normally if their data or resources depend on foreign domains/sources. Moreover, people in other countries may also face issues if their traffic is routed through Russia. In March 2022, Ukraine requested ICANN to disconnect Russia from the Internet as a punishment for aggression against Ukraine (Xinhua, 2023). The request was denied, but it supported the Russian narrative of the possibility of the use of the Internet by Western countries against Russia. In December 2024, Roskomnadzor tested its sovereign internet capabilities in regions with ethnic minorities, including Dagestan, Chechnya, and Ingushetia, from December 6 to 7, 2024. These tests involved restricting access to foreign websites and applications such as Google, YouTube, WhatsApp, and Telegram, even bypassing virtual private networks (VPNs). Roskomnadzor confirmed that the tests were aimed at assessing the functionality of "key replacement infrastructure" in case of deliberate disconnection from the global Internet. This aligns with the Kremlin's broader strategy to control the information space during periods of potential unrest in unstable regions (ISW, 2024).

Roskomnadzor also warned foreign hosting providers like AWS and GoDaddy of potential bans due to noncompliance with Russian censorship laws, further pressuring Russians to adopt domestic hosting and social media platforms under Kremlin control. These actions follow significant investments of approximately 59 Billion rubles into restricting internet traffic and reinforcing the Kremlin's technical capabilities. The initiative underscores Russia's efforts to tighten internet governance and assert digital sovereignty (ISW, 2024).

Chinese Approach

Internet Kill Switch - Speculations?. China is said to have passed a security law that gives the government the power to control access to the Internet. The law requires companies to use Chinese technology exclusively and help create an Internet kill switch (Endtime, 2015). However, the Chinese government has never officially acknowledged the existence of an Internet kill switch. Although the Internet shutdown in 2012 is attributed to the Chinese Internet kill switch, it has never been confirmed (Branigan, 2012). Moreover, the Great Firewall is already used for filtering, and access to many foreign websites is blocked. The GC also has the potential to restrict access to unwanted foreign websites, but the open discussion of an Internet kill switch has never been found in any Chinese literature or domestic websites. In the case that China shuts down the Internet, it will face a loss of 179.04 million dollars per hour (Carmichael, 2019).

DISCUSSION

The analysis of internet sovereignty measures undertaken by nations studied in this research reveals two distinct models emerging from their approaches: the first model, exemplified by China, emphasizes stringent control over online content and infrastructure. China, for instance, has erected a national firewall, imposed bans on foreign apps deemed politically sensitive, and actively promoted indigenous products since the early stages of internet development. This approach prioritizes national security and ideological stability, gradually building up internet control mechanisms over time. On the other hand, a different model, observed in Russia, initially embraced foreign technologies but gradually exerted sovereignty by developing indigenous alternatives and tightening regulations. Russia, for example, initially relied on foreign technologies but gradually shifted towards promoting indigenous platforms and imposing stricter regulations. This approach balances regulatory oversight with efforts to foster innovation and economic growth, encouraging entrepreneurship and international collaboration.

Moreover, Russia has demonstrated how internet sovereignty can extend into the kinetic domain, particularly evident during the Russia-Ukraine conflict. By exerting control over online narratives and censoring dissenting voices, Russia effectively shaped the information landscape, both domestically and internationally. This control over information dissemination enabled Russia to influence public opinion, sow discord among adversaries, and justify its military actions. Additionally, Russia's ability to disrupt communication channels and infrastructure in Ukraine underscored the significance of internet sovereignty in modern warfare. This example highlights the multifaceted nature of internet sovereignty and its implications beyond cyberspace, emphasizing its strategic importance in geopolitical conflicts.

International IMPLICATIONS of Internet Sovereignty Measures

The pursuit of Internet Sovereignty by Russia and China has impacted their diplomatic interaction worldwide. Their state-centric policies and strict cyberspace governance are in sharp contrast to the multistakeholder model advocated by the U.S. and the European Union. This significant diversion in policy has led to friction in global policy platforms such as the International Telecommunication Union (ITU) and ICANN. Russia's development towards establishing RUnet and disconnecting itself from the global internet has been perceived as a step towards Internet Balkanization. These moves are criticized as threats to the open and global model of the internet. Likewise, the Great Firewall of China and Cross-Border Data Transfer Controls have triggered regulatory pushbacks from the trading counterparts. The implementation of Cybersecurity Law 2017 and Cross-Border Data Transfer

Regulations 2022 has affected foreign companies operating in China, by having an impact on data flow and bilateral digital agreements. In addition, the state's control over technology firms like Huawei has prompted national security concerns across Western markets concerning Huawei's Global 5G deployments. Several markets have banned Huawei and ZTE. The trend has set a snowball effect, and recently, a ban on multiple applications owned by a Chinese-origin company ByteDance, was announced by the U.S. government (Yang & Couts, 2025).

Policies Adopted by Other Countries

While Russia and China have taken stringent legislative measures to achieve holistic state control and cyberspace sovereignty. Other countries have taken varied approaches. The EU has increasingly expressed concern regarding dependence on imported technologies, and it aims to curtail this dependency to improve its security posture (Fahey, 2024). The term Digital Sovereignty is discussed in debates within the EU, and requirements of digital sovereignty have been incorporated in laws being drafted, such as the Cybersecurity Certification Scheme for Cloud Services, which obligates service providers to prove the effectiveness of their cyber defences. Enactment of GDPR is a paradigm shift in the realm of Cybersecurity for EU. It has an impact across the geographical boundaries, where data of EU citizens is processed. This obligation has prompted other countries to revisit their cybersecurity legislations (Propp 2023). In contrast to the EU, the U.S. has relied upon domain-specific regulations. A comprehensive data protection legislation is absent, and a dynamic environment has flourished where different sectors adhere to disparate rules, fulfilling varying standards (Propp 2023). Facebook, a U.S.-based technology giant, faced complex challenges while aligning with GDPR. They had to reassess their data processing procedures to comply with the GDPR's requirements (Cook, 2021). The U.S. itself doesn't use the term sovereignty but refers to cyberspace in security terms. It has the maximum number of global internet assets available within its borders, including root servers. Nigeria in 2021banned platform X (formerly Twitter) in 2021 after the platform deleted Nigerian President's tweets (Princewill & Busari, 2021). Uganda ordered a complete shutdown of the internet in 2021 after Facebook deleted pro-government accounts before elections (Kafeero, 2021). Zimbabwe contained protests in 2019 by shutting down the internet in the country (Al Jazeera, 2019).

South Asian nations, India and Pakistan, have repeatedly used internet closures to manage public protests, discontent and politically motivated violence (Shah, 2021; Wagner, 2018).

Russia and China may be among the first states who openly adopt the model of sovereignty in the digital realm. Other states took the idea, and we have witnessed the proliferation of internet sovereignty models across the globe. Today, the pursuit of internet sovereignty is not limited only to Russia and China. Other countries, regardless of their geopolitical standing, have demonstrated their resolve to assert sovereignty in their cyberspace. As countries develop their digital infrastructure, there will be an increased exposure to cybersecurity threats across financial, health, government, business and industrial sectors (Saeed, 2025; Saeed, 2024; Saeed et al, 2023). Another important sector that merits cybersecurity legislation and investment by developing countries in the energy sector. As the drivers of the economy, the implications of digital transformation in the oil and gas, electricity and renewable energy sectors are crucial and legislations to protect these assets are expected to increase in the developing world (Saeed et al., 2024a; Saeed et al., 2024b). We may witness more robust measures to secure internet sovereignty in their respective geographical boundaries.

CONCLUSION

In conclusion, the pursuit of internet sovereignty by certain nations has profoundly impacted individual freedoms, national security, digital advancement, and financial aspects. The implementation of stringent censorship mechanisms and extensive data control restricts information flow and limits individuals' ability to express themselves and engage in open discourse. This control fosters self-censorship, suppresses dissent, and undermines privacy rights and personal freedoms. However, from a national security perspective, these measures have bolstered the state's ability to safeguard its digital infrastructure against external threats. The establishment of national cyber forces and comprehensive cybersecurity laws demonstrates a commitment to protecting CII. However, the centralization of internet control, including mechanisms like internet kill switches, raises concerns about potential abuse of power and restrictions on civil liberties.

We have also witnessed that digital advancement has been influenced by the promotion of indigenous technologies and the regulation of foreign technology within national borders, aiming to achieve technological autonomy and enhance digital self-reliance. While this drives innovation within national boundaries, it limits the exchange of ideas and technologies globally, potentially hindering overall technological progress. Financially, the development of local technologies and infrastructure can stimulate domestic economic growth and reduce reliance on foreign entities. However, restrictions on cross-border data flows and requirements for foreign companies to comply with local regulations can deter international investment and collaboration, affecting the global digital economy. In summary, the drive for internet sovereignty presents a complex interplay between enhancing national security and digital independence while posing challenges to individual freedoms and global digital cooperation. Balancing these aspects requires careful consideration and international dialogue to ensure that the pursuit of sovereignty does not come at the expense of fundamental human rights and global technological advancement.

REFERENCES

Al Jazeera. (2019, January 18). *Zimbabwe imposes internet shutdown amid crackdown on protests.* https://www.aljazeera.com/news/2019/1/18/zimbabwe-imposes-internet-shutdown-amid-crackdown-on-protests

Alibaba. (2024). *Alibaba security response centre.* https://www.alibabacloud.com/en/product/mss?_p_lc=1&spm=a3c0i.11071746.3212395230.25.54b75db90d9icB

Aslam, M., Khan Abbasi, M. A., Khalid, T., Shan, R. U., Ullah, S., Ahmad, T., Saeed, S., Alabbad, D. A., & Ahmad, R. (2022). Getting smarter about smart cities: Improving data security and privacy through compliance. *Sensors (Basel)*, *22*(23), 9338. https://doi.org/10.3390/s22239338

Avertium. (2023, July 18). *An update on the pro-Russia threat actor, Killnet.* https://www.avertium.com/resources/threat-reports/an-update-on-pro-russia-threat-actor-killnet

Baranovskaya, S. (2017, July 19). *Moscow's cyber-defence: How the Russian government plans to protect the country from the coming cyberwar. Meduza.* https://meduza.io/en/feature/2017/07/19/moscow-s-cyber-defense

BBC News. (2022, November 26). *US bans sale of Huawei, ZTE tech amid security fears.* https://www.bbc.com/news/world-us-canada-63764450

Bergengruen, V. (2022, March 10). *How Telegram became the digital battlefield in Russia's invasion of Ukraine.* TIME. https://time.com/6158437/telegram-russia-ukraine-information-war/

Branigan, T. (2012, April 12). *China's internet users temporarily blocked from foreign websites.* The Guardian. https://www.theguardian.com/world/2012/apr/12/china-internet-users-foreign-websites

Breuer, A. (2012). *The role of social media in mobilizing political protest: Evidence from the Tunisian revolution. SSRN.* https://papers.ssrn.com/sol3/papers.cfm?abstract_id=2179030

Browne, R. (2019, January 21). *Russia reportedly opens civil proceedings against Facebook, Twitter.* CNBC. https://www.cnbc.com/2019/01/21/russia-reportedly-opens-civil-proceedings-against-facebook-twitter.html

Budnitsky, S., & Jia, L. (2018). Branding Internet sovereignty: Digital media and the Chinese–Russian cyberalliance. *European Journal of Cultural Studies*, *21*(5), 594–613. https://doi.org/10.1177/1367549417751151

Cai, C., & Chen, Y. (2022). China's personal information protection law: A systematic and contextualized approach to understanding data protection. *International Data Privacy Law*, *12*(2), 75–88. https://doi.org/10.1093/idpl/ipac006

Carmichael, C. (2019, November 12). *The cost of shutting down the internet. Website Builder Expert*. https://www.websitebuilderexpert.com/blog/cost-of-shutting-down-the-internet/

Castro, D. (2013). *How much will Prism cost the US cloud computing industry?* The Information Technology & Innovation Foundation. https://itif.org/publications/2013/08/05/how-much-will-prism-cost-us-cloud-computing-industry/

Chernenko, E. (2019). Cyber security in EU–Russia relations. In Fernandes, S., Leonard, M., & Krastev, I. (Eds.), *The Routledge handbook of EU–Russia relations* (pp. 240–248). Routledge. https://www.taylorfrancis.com/chapters/edit/10.4324/9781351006262-20/cyber-security-eu-russia-relations-elena-chernenko

CNCERT. (2014). *China's cybersecurity landscape from the perspective of CNCERT/CC*. https://conference.apnic.net/data/39/chinathreatlandscapecncert_1425425126.pdf

Coalson, R. (2016, December 6). *New Kremlin information-security doctrine raises internet-freedom concerns. Radio Free Europe/Radio Liberty*. https://www.rferl.org/a/russia-information-security-internet-freedom-concerns/28159130.html

Cook, M. M. (2021). Bringing down big data: A call for federal data privacy legislation. *Oklahoma Law Review*, *74*(4), 733–762. https://digitalcommons.law.ou.edu/olr/vol74/iss4/8/

Council on Foreign Relations. (2023). *Cyber operations tracker*. https://www.cfr.org/cyber-operations/

Creemers, R., Triolo, P., & Webster, G. (2018). *Section 2: Operations security for critical information infrastructure - Cybersecurity law of the People's Republic of China*. In DigiChina (Trans.). https://digichina.stanford.edu/work/translation-cybersecurity-law-of-the-peoples-republic-of-china-effective-june-1-2017/

Cyberspace Administration of China (CAC). (2023, July 1). *General Secretary Xi Jinping's introduction to important ideology regarding China as a cyber powerhouse: Chapter 5: Building a durable national cybersecurity barrier*. https://interpret.csis.org/translations/general-secretary-xi-jinpings-introduction-to-important-ideology-regarding-china-as-a-cyber-powerhouse-chapter-5-building-a-durable-national-cybersecurity-barrier/

Dahua-PSIRT. (2024). *Dahua PSIRT*. https://www.dahuasecurity.com/ceen/aboutUs/trustedCenter/trustworthy

Datastar. (2024). *Data Star Observatory*. https://pitchbook.com/profiles/company/438955-21#overview

DCD. (2015). *Data moves to mother Russia*. https://www.datacenterdynamics.com/en/analysis/data-moves-to-mother-russia/

Diamond, L. (2015). Liberation technology 1. In *In Search of Democracy* (pp. 132–146). Routledge. https://doi.org/10.4324/9781315685175

DigiChina. (2018, June 29). *Translation: Cybersecurity law of the People's Republic of China (effective June 1, 2017)*. https://digichina.stanford.edu/work/translation-cybersecurity-law-of-the-peoples-republic-of-china-effective-june-1-2017/

Epifanova, A. (2020). *Deciphering Russia's sovereign internet law*. DGAP. https://dgap.org/en/research/publications/deciphering-russias-sovereign-internet-law

Epifanova, A., & Dietrich, P. (2022). *Russia's quest for digital sovereignty: Ambitions, realities, and its place in the world*. https://www.ssoar.info/ssoar/handle/document/77994

Erchi, Z., & Min, C. (2022). *Five things to know about China's mega east-west data centre plan*. Nikkei Asia. https://asia.nikkei.com/spotlight/caixin/five-things-to-know-about-china-s-mega-east-west-data-center-plan

EU. (2016). *General Data Protection Regulation*. https://gdpr-info.eu/

Eversec. (2024). *Eversec – Hengan Jiaxin (Beijing) Technology Co. Ltd.* https://eversec.com.cn/about/

Ewdn. (2019). *Apple provides details on compliance with Russian data-localization law*. https://www.intellinews.com/apple-provides-details-on-compliance-with-russian-data-localization-law-156416/

Fahey, E. (2024). The evolution of EU–US cybersecurity law and policy: On drivers of convergence. *Journal of European Integration*, *46*(7), 1073–1088. https://doi.org/10.1080/07036337.2024.2411240

FBI. (2023). *Russian interference in 2016 U.S. elections*. https://www.fbi.gov/wanted/cyber/russian-interference-in-2016-u-s-elections

Fielding, N., & Cobain, I. (2011, March 17). *Revealed: US spy operation that manipulates social media*. The Guardian. https://www.theguardian.com/technology/2011/mar/17/us-spy-operation-social-networks

FIRST. (2024). *Forum of Incident Response and Security Teams (FIRST)*. https://www.first.org/

Golitsyna, A., & Sergina, E. (2015). *Report on the sovereignty of the Russian internet*. Freedom House. https://freedomhouse.org/sites/default/files/FOTN%20 2016%20Russia.pdf

Goodkind, N. (2023, September 7). *Apple lost 200 billion dollars in two days after reports of iPhone ban in China*. CNN Business. https://edition.cnn.com/2023/09/07/investing/apple-stock-iphone-china-ban/index.html

Group-IB. (2023, July 26). Statement on the conviction of Ilya Sachkov. *Group-IB*. https://www.group-ib.com/media-center/press-releases/statement-on-the-conviction-of-ilya-sachkov/

Group-IB. (2024). *CERT GIB*. https://www.group-ib.com/services/cert/

Hikvision. (2024). *Hikvision Cyber Security Centre*. https://us-legacy.hikvision.com/en/support-resources/cybersecurity-center-0

Hopping, C. (2019). *Huawei moves into Russian cloud market with third-party data centre support*. https://russoft.org/news/english-huawei-moves-into-russian-cloud-market-with-third-party-data-centre-support/

Huawei-PSIRT. (2024). *Huawei Product Security Incident Response Team*. https://www.huawei.com/en/psirt

Hunton. (2019). *China issues draft regulation on cross-border transfer of personal information*. https://www.hunton.com/privacy-and-information-security-law/china-issues-draft-regulation-on-cross-border-transfer-of-personal-information

In4-CERT. (2024). *In4-CERT*. https://www.first.org/members/teams/infosecurity_incident_response_team-in4-cert

Internet Corporation for Assigned Names and Numbers. (2013, October 7). *Montevideo statement on the future of internet cooperation*. https://www.icann.org/en/announcements/details/montevideo-statement-on-the-future-of-internet-cooperation-7-10-2013-en

ISL-CERT. (2024). *ISL-CERT*. https://www.ransomware.live/csirt/RU

ISW. (2024, December 7). *Russian offensive campaign assessment*. https://understandingwar.org/backgrounder/russian-offensive-campaign-assessment-august-4-2025

ITU. (2019a). *Global cybersecurity index.* https://www.itu.int/en/ITU-D/Cybersecurity/Pages/Global-Cybersecurity-Index.aspx

ITU. (2019b). *Global cybersecurity index & cyber wellness profiles.* https://www.itu.int/pub/D-STR-SECU-2015

ITU. (2019c). *ITU statistics.* https://www.itu.int/en/ITU-D/Statistics/pages/stat/default.aspx

Jet-CERT. (2024). *Jet-CERT.* https://www.ransomware.live/csirt/RU

Kafeero, S. (2021). Uganda cuts off internet ahead of election polls opening. *Quartz Africa.* Retrieved from https://qz.com/africa/1957137/uganda-cuts-off-internet-ahead-of-election-polls-opening

Kania, E. (2019, February). *Made in China 2025, explained.* The Diplomat. https://thediplomat.com/2019/02/made-in-china-2025-explained/

Kania, E. B., & Costello, J. K. (2018). The strategic support force and the future of Chinese information operations. *The Cyber Defence Review, 3*(1), 105–122. https://cyberdefensereview.army.mil/CDR-Content/Articles/Article-View/Article/1589125/the-strategic-support-force-and-the-future-of-chinese-information-operations/

Kodama, S. (2018, November 28). *China's strict new cybersecurity law ensnares Japanese companies.* Nikkei Asia. https://asia.nikkei.com/business/business-trends/china-s-strict-new-cybersecurity-law-ensnares-japanese-companies

Kolomychenko, M. (2017). *Introduced cyber military. Kommersant.* https://www.kommersant.ru/doc/3187320

LaGrone, S. (2018, June 8). *China has stolen vast amounts of navy submarine, missile data in multiple breaches from contractor's servers.* USNI News. https://news.usni.org/2018/06/08/china-stolen-vast-amounts-navy-submarine-missile-data-multiple-breaches-contractors-servers

Lindsey, N. (2019). *New CNCERT report shows most cyber attacks on China originate from the United States.* CPO Magazine. https://www.cpomagazine.com/cyber-security/new-cncert-report-shows-most-cyber-attacks-on-china-originate-from-united-states/

Luxmoore, M. (2019, May 20). *'Wholeness, resilience, and security': Russia clarifies threats to sovereign Internet.* Radio Free Europe/Radio Liberty. https://www.rferl.org/a/wholeness-resilience-security-russia-clarifies-threats-to-sovereign-internet-/29961306.html

Lyngaas, S. (2024, July 15). *US bans Russian cybersecurity firm Kaspersky Lab over espionage fears*. CNN. https://edition.cnn.com/2024/07/15/tech/russian-firm-kaspersky-lab-ban/index.html

Marczak, B., Weaver, N., Dalek, J., Ensafi, R., Fifield, D., McKune, S., Rey, A., Scott-Railton, J., Deibert, R., & Paxson, V. (2015). An analysis of China's "Great Cannon." In *5th USENIX Workshop on Free and Open Communications on the Internet (FOCI 15)*. https://www.usenix.org/conference/foci15/workshop-program/presentation/marczak

McKune, S., & Ahmed, S. (2018). The contestation and shaping of cyber norms through China's internet sovereignty agenda. *International Journal of Communication, 12*, 22. https://ijoc.org/index.php/ijoc/article/viewFile/8540/2461

Mok, C. (2022, February 17). *China and Russia want to rule the global internet*. The Diplomat. https://thediplomat.com/2022/02/china-and-russia-want-to-rule-the-global-internet/

Mueller, M. (2017). *Will the Internet fragment?: Sovereignty, globalization, and cyberspace*. Wiley. https://www.wiley.com/en-it/Will+the+Internet+Fragment%3F%3A+Sovereignty%2C+Globalization+and+Cyberspace-p-9781509501229

Nasaw, D. (2009, April 21). *Hackers breach defences of Joint Strike Fighter jet program*. The Guardian. https://www.theguardian.com/world/2009/apr/21/hackers-us-fighter-jet-strike

Netim. (2015). *SU domain name*. https://www.netim.com/en/domain-name/su-domain

Newton, M. (2018, October 15). *Russian data localization: Enriching security and the economy*. The Henry M. Jackson School of International Studies. https://jsis.washington.edu/news/russian-data-localization-enriching-security-economy/

Ning, S., Han, W., Yuanshan, L., & Xuezi, D. (2019). *Development of PRC regulations on cross-border data transfer*. King & Wood Mallesons. https://www.kwm.com/cn/en/insights/latest-thinking/development-of-prc-regulations-on-cross-border-data-transfer.html

NTIA. (2014). *NTIA announces intent to transition key internet domain name functions*. https://www.ntia.gov/press-release/2014/ntia-announces-intent-transition-key-internet-domain-name-functions

Pearson, J., & Bing, C. (2022, May 10). *The cyber war between Ukraine and Russia: An overview*. Reuters. https://www.reuters.com/world/europe/factbox-the-cyber-war-between-ukraine-russia-2022-05-10/

Perlroth, N. (2015, April 10). *China is said to use powerful new weapon to censor internet*. The New York Times. https://www.nytimes.com/2015/04/11/technology/china-is-said-to-use-powerful-new-weapon-to-censor-internet.html

Pieke, F. N. (2017). The Communist Party and social management in China. In *Critical Readings on Communist Party of China* (pp. 998–1018). BRILL. https://journals.sagepub.com/doi/abs/10.1177/0920203x12442864

Pitt, D. C., Levine, N., & Yan, X. (1996). Touching stones to cross the river: Evolving telecommunication policy priorities in contemporary China. *Journal of Contemporary China*, *5*(13), 347–365. https://doi.org/10.1080/10670569608724259

Polyakova, E., Filonova, O., Chelovechkova, A., & Zmyzgova, T. (2021). Condition and prospects of legal regulation of the security of critical information infrastructure in Russia and in foreign countries. *SHS Web of Conferences, 93*, 02014. https://doi.org/10.1051/shsconf/20219302014

Popescu, N., & Secrieru, S. (Eds.). (2018). *Hacks, leaks and disruptions: Russian cyber strategies*. Institute for Security Studies, European Union. https://www.iss.europa.eu/publications/chaillot-papers/hacks-leaks-and-disruptions-russian-cyber-strategies

Princewill, N., & Busari, S. (2021, June 4). *Nigeria suspends Twitter's operations*. CNN. https://edition.cnn.com/2021/06/04/africa/nigeria-suspends-twitter-operations-intl/index.html

Propp, K. (2023). A US perspective on negotiating with the European Union. In Fahey, E. (Ed.), *Routledge International Handbook on Transatlantic Relations* (pp. 38–51). Routledge., https://doi.org/10.1080/07036337.2024.2411240

QiAnXin. (2024). *Qi An Xin CERT*. https://en.qianxin.com/

Ramzy, A. (2011, February 28). *State stamps out small 'Jasmine' protests in China*. TIME. https://time.com/archive/6954716/state-stamps-out-small-jasmine-protests-in-china/

Reuters. (2014). *U.S. knocks plans for European communication network*. https://www.reuters.com/article/technology/u-s-knocks-plans-for-european-communication-network-idUSDEEA34043/

Reuters. (2019, June 17). *Russia thwarts U.S. cyber attacks on its infrastructure*. https://www.reuters.com/article/world/russia-thwarts-us-cyber-attacks-on-its-infrastructure-news-agencies-idUSKCN1TI1U6/

Reuters. (2021, March 10). *Russian law requires smart devices to come pre-installed with domestic software*. https://www.reuters.com/article/technology/russian-law-requires-smart-devices-to-come-pre-installed-with-domestic-software-idUSKBN2BO4P2/

RGRU. (2013). *Decree of the president of the Russian Federation of January 15, 2013, N 31S, Moscow*. https://www.prlib.ru/en/section/681611#:~:text=818,Moscow%2C%202016

Robinson, S., Sakurayuki, B., & Dawborn, D. (2012). *Law no. 11 of 2008 on electronic information and transactions*. https://www.flevin.com/id/lgso/translations/JICA%20Mirror/english/4846_UU_11_2008_e.html

Rostec. (2024). *Rostec*. https://rostec.ru/en/

RTS-CERT. (2024). *RTS-CERT*. https://www.ransomware.live/csirt/RU

RuCert. (2024). *RuCert*. https://www.ransomware.live/csirt/RU

Sacks, S. (2019). *China's emerging cyber governance system*. Center for Strategic and International Studies. https://www.csis.org/programs/strategic-technologies-program/resources/china-cyber-outlook/chinas-emerging-cyber

Saeed, S., Altamimi, S. A., Alkayyal, N. A., Alshehri, E., & Alabbad, D. A. (2023). Digital transformation and cybersecurity challenges for business resilience: Issues and recommendations. *Sensors (Basel)*, *23*(15), 6666. https://doi.org/10.3390/s23156666

Saeed, S., Azizi, N., Tahir, S., Ahmad, M., & Almuhaideb, A. M. (Eds.). (2024). *Strengthening industrial cybersecurity to protect business intelligence*. IGI Global. https://doi.org/10.4018/978-1-6684-8868-2

Saeed, S., Bolívar, M. P. R., & Thurasamy, R. (2021). *Pandemic, lockdown, and digital transformation*. Springer International Publishing. https://link.springer.com/book/10.1007/978-3-030-86274-9

Saeed, S., Gull, H., Aldossary, M. M., Altamimi, A. F., Alshahrani, M. S., Saqib, M., & Almuhaideb, A. M. (2024). Digital transformation in energy sector: Cybersecurity challenges and implications. *Information (Basel)*, *15*(12), 764. https://doi.org/10.3390/info15120764

Schia, N., & Gjesvik, L. (2017). *China's cyber sovereignty* (Policy brief). ResearchGate. https://www.researchgate.net/publication/315784625_China's_cyber_sovereignty_Policy_Brief

Seddon, M. (2020). *Telegram becomes a digital battleground in Russia's war on Ukraine*. Financial Times. https://www.ft.com/content/b1e76905-29f2-4ac0-99e0-7af07cef280d

Segal, A. (2020). *China's vision for cyber sovereignty and the global governance of cyberspace: An emerging China-centric order*. In *China's Vision for a New World Order in Practice*. https://www.nbr.org/publication/chinas-vision-for-cyber-sovereignty-and-the-global-governance-of-cyberspace/.

Shah, N. (2021). Digital infrastructure, liminality, and world-making via Asia|(dis) information blackouts: Politics and practices of internet shutdowns. *International Journal of Communication*, *15*, 17. https://www.researchgate.net/publication/354149995_Digital_Infrastructure_Liminality_and_World-Making_Via_Asia_The_Infrastructural_Politics_of_Liminality_Introduction

Shen, F. (2014). *Great Firewall of China*. https://www.researchgate.net/profile/Fei_Shen6/publication/281030754_Great_Firewall_of_China/links/55d1ba4f08aee5504f68ed36/Great-Firewall-of-China.pdf

Sherman, J. (2022). *Russia's internet censor is also a surveillance machine*. Council on Foreign Relations. https://www.cfr.org/blog/russias-internet-censor-also-surveillance-machine

Shidong, Z. (2019, March 20). *China offers five-year tax breaks to chip makers, software developers to bolster industry as trade war stretches to tech*. South China Morning Post. https://www.scmp.com/business/article/3011377/china-offers-five-year-tax-breaks-chip-makers-software-developers-bolster

Sitalieva, A., Homyakova, V., Zheleznov, M., & Shorokhov, K. (2022). Analysis of the national program "Digital Economy of the Russian Federation". *SSRN*. https://ssrn.com/abstract=4256387

Sivetc, L. (2021). Controlling free expression "by infrastructure" in the Russian internet: The consequences of Runet sovereignization. *First Monday*, *26*(3). https://firstmonday.org/ojs/index.php/fm/article/view/11698

Stadnik, I. (2019a). *A closer look at the "sovereign Runet" law*. Internet Governance Project. https://www.internetgovernance.org/2019/05/16/a-closer-look-at-the-sovereign-runet-law/

Stadnik, I. (2019b). *Internet governance in Russia: Sovereign basics for independent Runet*. https://www.researchgate.net/publication/334663215_Internet_Governance_in_Russia_-_Sovereign_Basics_for_Independent_Runet

Steele, C. (2014). *The 10 most disturbing Snowden revelations*. PCMag. https://www.pcmag.com/news/the-10-most-disturbing-snowden-revelations

Stevens, T. (2016). Breaching protocol: The threat of cyber espionage. *Jane's Intelligence Review*, *22*(3), 8–13. https://pure.royalholloway.ac.uk/en/publications/breaching-protocol-the-threat-of-cyberespionage

Sukharenko, A. (2019). *Russian ICT security policy and cybercrime*. PONARS Eurasia. https://www.ponarseurasia.org/wp-content/uploads/attachments/Pepm601_Sukharenko_July2019_4-2.pdf

Swinhoe, D. (2021). *Apple officially opens data centre in China*. DataCenter Dynamics. https://www.datacenterdynamics.com/en/news/apple-officially-opens-data-center-in-china/

TAdvisor. (2019). *Law "about security of critical information infrastructure of the Russian Federation"*. https://tadviser.com/index.php/Article:Critical_Information_Infrastructure_of_Russia#:~:text=Critical%20Information%20Infrastructure%20(CII)%20is,related%20to%20CII%20in%20Russia

TAdvisor. (2022a). *The Ministry of Digital Industry is preparing a mechanism to counter the sale of rights to Russian software abroad*. https://tadviser.com/index.php/Article:Import_substitution_of_software_in_the_public_sector

TAdvisor. (2022b). *Register of Russian programs*. https://tadviser.com/index.php/Article:The_register_of_Russian_software_requires_a_large_upgrade._Russian_Railways_proposes_to_make_it_an_analogue_of_VDNKh

Tang, C. (2016). *In-depth analysis: Great Firewall of China* [Class paper]. Tufts University, COMP 116. https://www.cs.tufts.edu/comp/116/archive/fall2016/ctang.pdf

Teletrust. (2019). *IT security made in Germany*. https://www.teletrust.de/en/itsmig/

Thomas, T. K. (2014, November 13). *National security council proposes 3-pronged plan to protect internet users*. The Hindu Business Line. https://www.thehindubusinessline.com/info-tech/National-Security-Council-proposes-3-pronged-plan-to-protect-Internet-users/article20727012.ece

Tiezzi, S. (2015, March 4). *China finally admits to hacking*. The Diplomat. https://thediplomat.com/2015/03/china-finally-admits-to-hacking/

Tor. (2019). *Tor: Pluggable transports*. https://2019.www.torproject.org/docs/pluggable-transports

UN. (2019). *Social indicators*. https://unstats.un.org/sdgs/report/2019/The-Sustainable-Development-Goals-Report-2019.pdf

Wagner, B. (2018). Understanding internet shutdowns: A case study from Pakistan. *International Journal of Communication, 12*(1), 22. https://ijoc.org/index.php/ijoc/article/view/8545

Ward, A. (2019, July 25). *New Senate Intelligence report shows "extensive" Russia 2016 election interference*. Vox. https://www.vox.com/2019/7/25/8930616/senate-intelligence-report-russia-50-states

Wei, Y. (2018, October 11). *Chinese data localization law: Comprehensive but ambiguous*. University of Washington JSIS News. https://jsis.washington.edu/news/chinese-data-localization-law-comprehensive-ambiguous/

Whittaker, Z. (2021, September 29). *Russian authorities arrest cybersecurity giant Group-IB's CEO on treason charges*. TechCrunch. https://techcrunch.com/2021/09/29/russian-authorities-arrest-cybersecurity-giant-group-ibs-ceo-on-treason-charges/

Wilson, J. (2022). *Digital sovereignty on paper: Russia's ambitious laws conflict with its tech dependence*. Wilson Center. https://www.wilsoncenter.org/blog-post/digital-sovereignty-paper-russias-ambitious-laws-conflict-its-tech-dependence

World, S. C. (2016, September 29). *New NATO report claims China's cyber-space influence continues to grow*. https://www.scworld.com/news/new-nato-report-claims-chinas-cyber-space-influence-continues-to-grow

Xinhua. (2023, January 23). *China spending on research and development hits 3 trillion yuan in 2022*. https://english.news.cn/20230123/3c445a4108a24f1b9da0b19c472ca5d4/c.html#:~:text=23%20(Xinhua)%20%2D%2D%20China's%20total,Bureau%20of%20Statistics%20(NBS)

Yang, Z., & Couts, A. (2025, April 25). *A US TikTok ban could wipe out other ByteDance apps too*. Wired. https://www.wired.com/story/bytedance-tiktok-ban-lemon8-capcut-gauthai-app-stores/

Zhang, M., & Judd, D. (2023, September 13). *China says it hasn't issued any ban on Apple's iPhone*. CNN Business. https://edition.cnn.com/2023/09/13/tech/china-denies-iphone-ban-intl-hnk/

Zone, Bi. (2024). *Bi.Zone*. https://bi.zone

ZTE-PSIRT. (2024). *ZTE PSIRT*. https://www.zte.com.cn/global/about/trust-center/ztepsirt.html

Chapter 4
Information Security Awareness

Binastya Anggara Sekti
https://orcid.org/0000-0001-5489-4888
Universitas Esa Unggul, Indonesia

ABSTRACT

Information Security Awareness (ISA) is a crucial component in strengthening cybersecurity resilience at both individual and organizational levels. As cyber threats continue to evolve, a lack of security awareness among users remains a significant risk factor, often leading to security breaches, data leaks, and financial losses. We will explores the role of ISA in fostering a security-conscious culture, highlighting effective training programs, awareness campaigns, and behavior-driven security strategies. It examines psychological and cognitive factors influencing security behavior, emphasizing the importance of continuous education and engagement. By integrating ISA into cybersecurity policies and digital transformation initiatives, organizations can proactively mitigate risks, improve compliance with regulatory frameworks, and build a sustainable, security-aware digital environment.

INTRODUCTION

Information Security

The definition of information security has various opinions and I will try to share some definitions of information security according to several sources/experts. Information security is a form of effort made to secure information that is a high-value asset from threats that may arise at any time. Thus, information security has a role in indirectly ensuring business continuity, reducing risks, and optimizing

DOI: 10.4018/979-8-3373-3171-3.ch004

profits. The more company information that is managed, the greater the risk of damage or loss of information. Based on the factors of increasing the number and impact of information security breaches, it has been found that there is a significant relationship between information security breaches and the risk of stock price falls (Garg et al., 2025). According to the ISO/IEC 17799:2005 standard on information security management, information security is an efforts in protecting information from various threats that come to ensure business sustainability, minimize risks, and increase investment and business opportunities (Iskandar et al., 2021).

The definition of information is a set of data that has been processed so that it has a meaning that is indispensable in decision-making. In all business organizations, information is a valuable asset because it is indispensable in the organization's operations, executing its business strategy, and creating a competitive advantage. Accurate and timely information enables management to make better decisions, improve operational efficiency, and optimize resources. In today's digital era, data and information are the main keys in various business sectors, such as the services, finance, health, manufacturing, and government sectors. Therefore, information protection is crucial in protecting data and information from data leaks, information manipulation, or other cyber threats that can harm the organization.

Every organization or company has different types of information that support operations and decision-making. Individual information security behaviors will be able to pose a risk to the security of their organization's information (Grill et al., 2025). Some of the main types of information contained within a company include:

- Operational Information, which is all data related to daily business processes, such as sales transactions, inventory, and production schedules.
- Financial Information, i.e. financial statements, accounting journals, and records of outgoing and incoming money transactions are all necessary for financial analysis and business planning.
- Human Resources Information, namely employee data, organizational structure, employee attendance records, and performance evaluations used to manage human resources.
- Strategic Information, which is data used by top-level management to conduct strategic planning, such as market trend analysis and competitor analysis.
- Customer Information, i.e. customer data that includes customer identity, transaction history, and feedback that is also necessary to improve customer satisfaction.
- Legal and Compliance Information, i.e. company regulatory documents, employee employment contracts, and company policy statements in accordance with government regulations.

Internal and External Threats

Threats to information can come from internal or external. Some of the main types of threats to information include:

- Cyber Attacks, cyber-attacks that often occur are attacks from outside such as phishing, malware, ransomware, and DDoS. All of these types of attacks aim to steal or corrupt information from low to high levels of damage.
- Insider Threats, which are threats that come from within the organization, either intentional (fraud, sabotage) or unintentional (human error, negligence). Organizations should also remain vigilant against these insider attacks.
- Data Theft, which is an unauthorized act that aims to steal sensitive data, for example the theft of customer data, financial data, and others.
- Information Leakage, i.e. data that is accidentally shared or leaked to unauthorized parties.
- IT Infrastructure Disruptions, i.e. system failures, attacks on the network, or power outages that cause loss of access to important information.

Information corruption can occur due to a variety of factors, both due to cyberattacks and technical errors. Some forms of information corruption include:

- Data Corruption – Data that is corrupted or unreadable due to malware, software errors, or hardware failures.
- Data Manipulation – Unauthorized data changes, often by parties intent on fraud or sabotage.
- Data Loss – Loss of important information due to accidental deletion, system failure, or cyberattack.
- Unauthorized Access – Data used by unauthorized parties, either due to weak access controls or credential theft.
- Information Delay or Inaccessibility – A system or network disruption that causes information to be inaccessible in a timely manner.

To protect information from various threats, organizations may implement appropriate information security standards. Some of the widely used standards include:

- ISO/IEC 27001 – An international standard for information security management that contains policies, procedures, and technical controls.
- NIST Cybersecurity Framework – A guide to assist organizations in managing information security risks that has been developed by the National Institute of Standards and Technology (NIST).

- COBIT (Objective Control for Information and Related Technologies) – A framework on IT governance provided to organizations in managing information security risks well.
- PCI DSS (Payment Card Industry Data Security Standard) – Which is a security standard applied in the financial industry for digital payment activities in order to protect data for each cardholder.
- GDPR (General Data Protection Regulation) – A data protection regulation used by European Union countries that governs how organizations collect, store, and process personal data.

The purpose of implementing this information security standard is to assist organizations in identifying, preventing, and responding to various possible threats to data and information and ensuring compliance with applicable regulations. As cyber threats increase in every organization, investment in information security cannot be ignored. Continuous digital transformation will increase the vulnerability of systems to cyberattacks, which can disrupt operations and lead to catastrophic consequences (Arunthavanathan et al., 2025).

CIA Triad

Information security is a proactive effort to protect data from unauthorized access, use, recording, inspection, disclosure, disruption, alteration, or destruction. The information security aspect usually relates to three essential principles known as the CIA Triad (Confidentiality, Integrity, and Availability) (Abushark et al., 2025; Albinali et al., 2025; Lallie et al., 2025; Mabunda, 2025):

1. Confidentiality, that is ensuring that access to information is limited to authorized individuals only. Information protection ensures that only authorized parties can access certain data. Another definition of confidentiality includes measures taken to prevent access by unauthorized individuals or entities..
2. Integrity, that is to guarantee that the data remains correct and not modified by unauthorized parties. Information protection ensures the integrity of data and avoids damage or other threats that can cause changes to the original information. Another definition of integrity is ensuring that the data remains intact, accurate, and has not been altered by unauthorized parties.
3. Availability, that is guaranteeing that the data is always accessible to the appropriate individual when needed. Data protection ensures that users can obtain information at any time without hindrance and not in an unhelpful form. The user in this context could be an individual, or a computer system that has permission

to obtain the information. Accessibility ensures that users have opportunities and avenues to access information.

The three fundamental components that include confidentiality, integrity, and availability (CIA) form the foundation of the designed security initiative. These three components are interrelated in the framework of understanding data protection.

Type of Information Security

Information security can be obtained in several ways done simultaneously or in combination with each other. The strategies of information security each have a focus and are built with specific objectives as needed. Below examples of information security:

- Physical security is information security that focuses on strategies to secure individuals to protect physical assets in the workplace from a variety of threats that include unauthorized access, fire hazards, and natural disasters.
- Personal security is information security that focuses on personnel activity. Usually interrelated with the scope of physical security.
- Operational security is information security that discusses how an organization's strategy is to secure the organization's ability to operate without interruption.
- Communication security is information security that aims to secure communication media, communication technology and what is still in it. As well as the ability to leverage media and communication technology to achieve organizational goals.
- Network security is information security that focuses on how to secure network equipment, organizational data, networks and their contents, as well as the ability to use the network to fulfill the organization's data communication function.

Each type of information security contributes to the overall information protection program. Therefore, information security is tasked with safeguarding system data and the tools used to store and transmit it.

Cyber Security

Network security involves a set of policies and procedures that aim to protect and monitor illegal access, misuse, or denial that may occur at any time on a computer network system. In the principle of network security, data access within the network is governed through authorizations managed by network administrators. Users are provided with or select an ID as well as a password or other authentication details that allow them to access information and applications based on the access rights granted to them. Network security involves different types of computer networks, both public and private, that are used for daily activities; conduct transactions and communications between businesses, government agencies and individuals. These networks can be private, such as those within a company, as well as other networks that may be accessible to the public. Network security plays an important role in organizations, companies, and other types of institutions. This includes methods for protecting the network, as well as maintaining and supervising the activities carried out. One of the most common and easy ways to protect network resources is to set up a unique username and proper password.

Why is cyber security a crucial problem? The expense of resolving a cybercrime can be quite expensive, and it can take months for the other party to detect it, depending on the type of attack. An example of cybercrime is APTs (advanced persistent threats) that utilize persistent hacking methods to gain access to computer systems and can survive in them for months before being detected. Cyber security is a very important key issue. New rules and reporting requirements make cyber risks difficult to overcome. The Board will continue to seek assurances from management that their approach to cyber risk will reduce the likelihood of an attack and reduce the financial and operational impact. Having a solid Cyber Security approach is crucial in protecting against cyber-related failures and errors, as well as malicious attacks. Therefore, it is crucial to implement appropriate cyber security measures to safeguard your organization.

What is the impact of a cyberattack? Digital attacks can cause major disruption and can destroy even the most powerful organizations. Affected organizations will experience a loss of assets, reputation, and revenue, as well as face sanctions and recovery costs. Cyber Security Elements are a solid foundation for cybersecurity depending on a well-planned strategy, which includes:

- Software security. In software security as it happens on the web, weaknesses in security features in web applications are often a common target for hackers. This happens because apps are increasingly becoming an important part of an organization.
- Infrastructure security. The infrastructure security process focuses on protecting the functionality and integrity of the network and company's proprietary data.
- Platform security. Platform protection serves to maintain the company's core operations by monitoring critical data and resources related to the system to find weaknesses.

With the emergence of increasingly complex cyber threats, maintaining cybersecurity is a job that needs special attention. Given the huge impact of successful Cyber attacks, cybercriminals are becoming more proficient in their strategies, thus making cyber threats a constant occurrence. Here are some of the most common types of cyber attacks and threats.

- Virus. A virus is a series of malicious code that is inserted into a computer without the user's permission. It is able to duplicate itself and spread itself to other devices by attaching it to different computer files.
- Worm. Worms have similarities with viruses in terms of their ability to reproduce, but they don't need to be attached to an application. They actively look for loopholes and report any loopholes they manage to find to the creator.
- Trojan. Trojan is a form of malicious software that disguises itself as legitimate applications, such as antivirus programs, yet carries out harmful actions once launched.
- Spyware/adware. Spyware/adware can be installed on your system without you realizing it when you open attachment files, access malicious links, or download malicious applications. After installation, it will monitor your computer activity and collect personal data.
- Malware. Malware refers to a general term used to describe any file or software designed to damage a computer system; and includes Trojans, social engineering techniques, worms, viruses, and spyware.
- Phishing. A method that has been around for a long time but is still widely practiced, phishing is a form of social engineering that attempts to trick individuals into revealing personal or confidential information. Sometimes it is difficult to distinguish it from legitimate and unauthorized communications, these scams can result in significant losses for an organization.
- Social Engineering. This social engineering comes in many forms of engineering that go beyond phishing, but it has the same purpose: it is used to deceive and manipulate targets in order to obtain information or gain access to their devices. This is done by tricking users into clicking on malicious links or gaining physical access to the computer through deception.
- DDoS. DDoS (Distributed Denial-of-Service) attacks attempt to disrupt the normal flow of internet traffic and disable websites by piling up processes on systems, servers, or networks with a number of requests that exceed their capacity..
- Ransomware. The fastest-growing type of cyberattack, ransomware is a category of malware that demands payment after locking the victim's files, thus blocking access. Please note that paying the ransom does not guarantee the recovery of encrypted data.

- SQL injection. A SQL injection attack occurs when an attacker injects malicious code into a server that leverages SQL. SQL injection will succeed only if the application software has a security hole. When a SQL attack is successful, the server will be forced to grant access or modify the data.
- MITM. A MITM (Man-in-the-Middle)attack occurs when a hacker places themselves in the middle of communication between a client (device) and a server. MITM attacks often occur when someone accesses an unsecured public Wi-Fi network. An attacker can be between the visitor's device and the network. As a result, users will unknowingly send information through the hacker.
- Weaknesses on websites and networks. Cybercriminals are constantly trying to find new loopholes in systems, networks, or applications that can be exploited. This is done through an automated attack and can affect anyone anywhere.

Strategies in Dealing with Cyber Attacks

A way to protect against Cybersecurity attacks. The most powerful approach to mitigating and mitigating the impact of cyberattacks is to create a solid foundation on which to grow your Cybersecurity Technology stack. Service providers often tell their clients that the applications they offer are 100% compatible and will work seamlessly with their existing IT infrastructure, and in many cases, this is true. However, problems start to arise as we try to add IT security solutions from different vendors—even though the details of configuration settings vary, technology gaps will always exist.

Compliance with information security protocols. Compliance means acting in accordance with the provisions that have been approved by the authorities, the environment, the community, and others. For example, driving within the permitted speed limit is a form of compliance, or a rule that states that only one handbag is allowed on board. DVD players designed and manufactured in accordance with the technical criteria for discs are considered to have met the established standards. Compliance can also refer to the implementation of a number of regulations or guidelines so that an organization can operate legally. The implementation of these measures to achieve compliance may require several criteria. IT compliance refers to the application and management of information technology in accordance with the norms that apply in a certain environment or organization. Therefore, it is wrong to assume that IT Compliance is only related to technological elements. IT Policy Compliance can be defined as a complete ecosystem that includes:

- Strategic objectives of the organization.

- Training and awareness of Computer users.
- Policies at the top level.
- Security Procedures and standards.
- IT Configuration settings.
- Control over technology.
- Continuous monitoring.
- Internal and External Auditors.
- Business risk assessment.

Overall, compliance is related to individuals, procedures, and technology. Many organizations are more technology-focused and end up failing in audits due to a lack of attention to the human and process aspects. Some examples of government and industry regulations that have an impact on IT compliance policies for example:

- COBIT (Control Objectives for Information and Related IT).
- NIST (National Institute of Standards and Technology) standards.
- ISO 27001 (International Standards Organization 27001).
- ITIL (Information Technology Infrastructure Library.
- PCI DSS (Payment Card Industry Data Security Standard).
- CIP (NERC Critical Infrastructure Protection) standards.
- FFIEC (Federal Financial Institution Examination Council) Information Security Book.
- SCAP (Security Content Automation Protocol).

In compliance assessment, the main focus is on the conformity of all activities with applicable policies, regulations, norms, and laws. On the other hand, propriety leads to leadership honor in decision-making. A violation of propriety does not necessarily mean a violation of compliance. In addition, compliance serves to assess whether the audited entity has followed certain procedures, standards, and regulations set by the competent authority. The purpose of this is to evaluate whether the audit is carried out in accordance with the relevant requirements, provisions, and laws.

As already explained, there are two main points of view regarding compliance with regulations, namely instrumental and normative. The instrumental point of view shows that individuals act on self-interest and accept changes in behavior. Meanwhile, the normative point of view is related to moral values and is contrary to personal interests. A person tends to obey laws that are considered legitimate and in harmony with the norms they hold. Normative commitment based on morality means obedience to the law because the law is considered a must, while normative commitment that comes from legitimacy shows compliance with the rules because the party who makes the law has the authority to establish the law. In modern organizations, the existence of a system is the core that moves the wheels of the organization so that it can run in accordance with the vision and mission proclaimed. A system can be defined as a set of rules, rules, and even a culture within an organization that provides instructions and directions for action and behavior for the members of the organization.

The effectiveness of regulations in an organizational system is also inseparable from the factor of obedience or compliance of each member of the organization to the existing rules. Kelman distinguishes the quality of obedience or obedience to rules into three types:

1. Compliance occurs when individuals follow a rule simply because they are worried about the consequences it will bring.
2. Compliance in the form of identification occurs when a person follows the rules simply because they are afraid that their good relationship with others will be disrupted.
3. Obedience through internalization is when individuals follow the rules because they fully believe that they have important meaning both materially and spiritually, in accordance with the values they hold.

Relevant Rules and Standards

Regulations are less effective if the level of compliance only revolves around compliance or identification. On the other hand, if the level of compliance reaches internalization, it means that the quality of regulatory effectiveness is very high, so that the system runs in accordance with existing rules without emphasizing strict control functions. Compliance with regulations, norms, and guidelines is essential in maintaining the bank's image, so that it can meet the expectations of customers, the industry, and society as a whole. Banks that neglect their compliance functions and responsibilities will immediately experience what is referred to as compliance risk, which is described by Basel. The Banking Supervision Committee identifies these risks as legal consequences or sanctions, as well as potential financial or material losses and damage to the bank's reputation due to violations of laws, regulations, and policies related to organizational norms that constitute the bank's internal guidelines. In Indonesia, Bank Indonesia (BI) explained that compliance risk is a risk that arises due to banks' non-compliance with applicable laws and regulations, including Syariah principles for Islamic commercial banks and Islamic business units.

Compliance Standard:

- GLBA for financial services
- HIPAA for healthcare

- ISO 17799
- Sarbanes-Oxley for public companies
- PCI DSS for Card holder data
- COBIT for IT Governance
- NIST, ISO 27001, BSI Standard, FISMA, FERPA, etc

ISO 17799 is an international standard that contains guidance on information security management. This standard was originally published by the International Organization for Standardization (ISO) which was developed from the British Standard BS 7799. ISO 17799 was first published in 2000 and was later updated and further developed as part of the ISO/IEC 27000 series of standards, specifically ISO/IEC 27002. ISO 17799 is a standard that is a framework for technical policies, procedures, and controls to manage and protect an organization's information assets from various security threats such as unauthorized access, data theft, cyberattacks, and information loss. ISO 17799 has contents:

- 10 items of Control Clauses
- 36 items of Control Objectives
- 127 items of Securiy Controls

Ten items of control clauses include:

a. Description of company security policy
b. Description of system development and system maintenance
c. Description of access control system
d. Description of operation management and communication
e. Description of physical security and environment security
f. Description of compliance
g. Description of personnel guard
h. Description of information security
i. Description of business continuity
j. Description of asset control

Security Policy is a policy created by a company to maintain business continuity by securing and maintaining the security and integrity of all important company data. Security policies are very necessary for companies because there are many non-technical things that need to be regulated, such as the use of a password together in completing work. The use of password sharing is a form of non-compliance or violation in information security. To prevent unwanted things from happening, it is necessary to collect data on password holders. In realizing information security, there must be regulations issued by top management or directors to be implemented by all departments.

Security Policy covers various aspects consists:

- The description of information security infrastructure
- The description of information security policy

The implementation of an access control system is a way to regulate users in accessing information on the system according to their access rights. This access control is carried out for users on the local computer network as well as users who access it from the internet. The aspects that govern control are included in the following procedures:

- Procedures for controlling access to the system.
- Procedures for setting up access rights.
- Procedures for user liability.
- Procedures for network security settings
- Procedures for operating system security settings
- Procedures for setting up application access security.
- Procedures for user monitoring.
- Procedures for remote access activity.

Good operations management will create the protection of information system infrastructure and ensure the availability of documented system procedures to avoid errors in operations. The management of the operation consists of several aspects:

- Procedures in operation.
- System planning and operation.
- System protection from malicious software.
- Internal regulations
- Computer network system settings.
- Handling of the media.
- Data and information exchange arrangements.

System development and maintenance, guarantees that the operating system as well as the newly implemented application can work together effectively through a verification and validation process before being deployed to the actual environment. Actions in the development and maintenance of existing systems include several aspects:

- Aspect of Security requirements of the system.
- Aspect of Security in the application system.
- Aspect of Cryptographic control
- Aspect of Security of system files
- Aspect of Security in development and support process.

Physical and Environmental Security discusses protection from the physical and environmental perspective of a network, in order to avoid loss or damage to data that can be caused by environmental factors, such as natural disasters and data theft that occurs on storage devices or other information places. Matters to be discussed include:

- Secure Areas
- Equipment security
- General Control

Compliance; is ensuring that security policies have been implemented in accordance with existing regulations, following contract requirements and conducting regular system inspections. Good compliance with the company's expectations is:

- Compliance with legal requirements and provisions
- Implementation of security and compliance policies at the technical scope.
- Implementation of the audit system

Personnel Security, which is to reduce the possibility of human error, or minimize human error in manipulating information during activities on the system. Security awareness training is very important for everyone to be able to protect information and data in their respective work areas. Personnel Security includes several aspects:

- Safety at work.
- Information Security Awareness Training.
- Steps in dealing with incidents in the event of a system security breach.

Security Organization; aims to regulate security in an organization and maintain the integrity of information systems during operations, including information control involving third parties (outsourcing). These security aspects are:

- Security control of third-party access
- Security control for vendor or outsourcing

Asset classification and control can provide protection to all the company's assets based on the desired level of protection. Some aspects in Asset protection are:

- Information Classification.
- Accountability for Assets.

Business Continuity Management prepares to address risks that may arise in business activities that could lead to “major failures” or major failure risks, as well as “disasters” or unforeseen incidents. Therefore, it is very important to make arrangements and management for the continuity of business processes, taking into account several aspects of information security.

The management aspect in business continuity aims to realize information system security in preventing damage to avoid corrective actions due to system damage. The ISO 17799 standard has regulated this matter, and the existence of a good and structured management framework will improve the performance of the information security system. The assets and aspects assessed in ISO 17799 are

- Information assets
- Software assets
- Physical assets
- Services

ISO-17799 is not a:

- A rule or stipulation issued by the government. A technical standard or standard based on the orientation of the product/technology.
- A methodology for evaluating equipment (tools) such as general criteria (CC/ISO 15408), which is agreed upon for specific functions or guarantees contained in specially manufactured equipment.
- The section called “Generally Accepted System Security Principles” or “GASSP” is a component of a set of best practices in the implementation of security systems.
- It is one of the five points contained in the “IT Security Management Guidelines” or GMITS/ISO-13335, which offers a conceptual structure for IT security management.
- A system that facilitates security certification (at this time, only BS 7799-2 and national variations provide certification procedures).
- ISO 17799 does not establish obligations related to risk assessment methods. Choose according to the needs of the organization.

Advantages of applying ISO-17799. The main advantage of BS7799/ISO17799 relates to public trust. Just like ISO 9000 which reflects quality assurance.

- This standard is a sign of trust in the entire security of the company.
- Centralized policy and procedure management.
- Ensure appropriate information services.
- Reduce management costs,
- Complete documentation of any changes/revisions.
- A method for determining targets and proposing improvements.

A company that implements ISO 17799 will have a tool to measure, organize and control information that is critical to the operations of their systems. In turn, this can drive customer trust, efficiency and effectiveness. Terms and Definitions in ISO-17799:

- ISO - ISO is a private organization that issues standard operating guidelines to ensure the quality of a service.
- Information Security - is an overview of 3 important aspects of information security which include confidentiality, integrity and availability
- Risk Assessment – estimating possible threats due to weak information system security and information availability processes that can cause disruptions.
- Risk Management is a step to recognize, monitor, reduce, or remove security threats that can impact information systems, with reasonable expenditure.
- ISMS (Information Systems Management System) is a system that regulates information security in an organization by providing a structured method for managing sensitive data to be protected. It involves employees, procedures, and information systems.
- In accordance with ISO/IEC 27001:2022, the term information security is defined as an effort to protect information from various threats with the aim of maintaining business continuity, reducing risks, and increasing business opportunities through the implementation of appropriate security controls (Culot, Nassimbeni, Podrecca, & Sartor, 2021). In addition, in some academic literature, information security is defined as "a systematic effort to protect data and information systems from internal and external attacks to ensure operational continuity and user trust" (Luh et al., 2025). Information security includes various aspects such as cybersecurity, physical security, access policies, data encryption, risk management, and legal compliance. The domains of information security are ICT security, physical security, legal security, and personal-organizational security (Pietras, 2019). Figure 1 is an illustration of the information security.

Figure 1. Information security

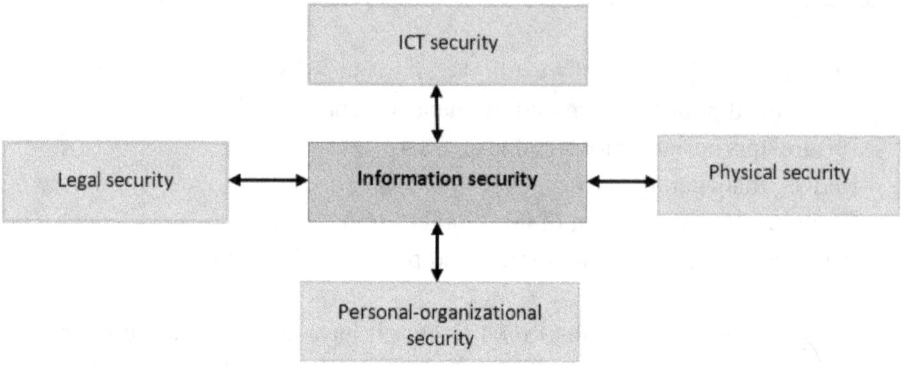

Awareness of information security is related to the understanding that every person and institution must have about the possible dangers associated with digital activities as well as approaches to mitigate those risks. Understanding information has become crucial in today's digital world, where cyber threats are increasingly complex and spreading. The majority of cyberattacks exploit human weaknesses, so having an educated and alert user is critical to an organization's security posture..

The importance of understanding information security has been emphasized through the latest data. An international survey conducted on Cybersecurity Awareness Month showed that nearly half of workers have experienced a cyberattack or fraud, with 45% reporting a personal data breach. However, only 23% of affected organizations then implemented cybersecurity training programs, confirming significant shortcomings in the preventive measures taken (2024, n.d.).

The goal of the security awareness training initiative is to bridge this gap by educating staff on possible threats and the appropriate way to respond. Such programs seek to reduce the potential for breaches by creating a mindset that focuses on information security in the workplace, thus placing employees as the first barricades against cyberattacks. By making information security awareness a vital part of a cybersecurity plan, and educating individuals about potential threats and how to respond to them, organizations can significantly reduce the risk of cyber incidents and strengthen their overall security posture.

THE IMPORTANCE OF INFORMATION SECURITY AWARENESS

Information security awareness is the understanding and proactive attitude of individuals and organizations in protecting information assets from various cyber threats. In today's digital age, where data is a valuable commodity, increasing awareness of information security is critical to preventing adverse incidents. Security awareness plays a critical role in reducing cybersecurity risks. Organizations that invest in security training and awareness programs are more resilient against cyber threats. Key benefits include:

- Reduction in Human Error: Many security incidents occur due to lack of awareness, such as falling for phishing scams or using weak passwords.
- Enhanced Incident Response: Educated employees and users can recognize and report potential security threats, minimizing the damage.
- Regulatory Compliance: Many industries require security awareness training as part of regulatory frameworks (e.g., GDPR, HIPAA, ISO 27001).
- Improved Organizational Security Culture: Awareness fosters a proactive security mindset, encouraging best practices among employees.

The Impact of Human Error on Information Security

Many information security incidents occur as a result of human error, such as the use of weak passwords or ignorance of phishing threats. An IBM study showed that nearly 60% of security incidents stem from internal errors, whether intentional or unintentional. Table 1 is an example of human error that led to a security incident.

Table 1. Examples of human error that cause security incidents

Types of Human Error	Example Incident	Impact
Weak password usage	Employees use a password "123456" or date of birth	Unauthorized access to corporate systems
Not understanding about phishing	Employees click on phishing links	Malware infection on the company's internal computer network
Share access with unauthorized parties	Employees share login credentials	Sensitive data leaks

Benefits of Increasing Information Security Awareness

Increasing information security awareness to individuals and groups has several main benefits, namely:

- Digital Asset Protection: By understanding cyber threats, individuals and organizations can adopt proactive measures to protect their digital assets.
- Reduced Risk of Data Leakage: High awareness can prevent reckless actions that could potentially lead to data leaks.
- Improved Organizational Reputation: Organizations that rarely experience security incidents tend to have a better reputation in the eyes of customers and business partners.

Strategies to Increase Information Security Awareness

The following are some strategies that can be applied to increase information security awareness including:

- Regular Training: Organize regular cybersecurity training programs for employees.
- Simulated Attacks: Simulated phishing attacks to test and increase employee vigilance.
- Awareness Campaign: Hold an internal campaign that emphasizes the importance of implementing awareness about information security.

As new and evolving technologies are rapidly adopted by organizations, often without the integration of cybersecurity protection, information systems become increasingly vulnerable to various cyber threats. There are 3 main components related to information security vulnerability awareness, namely vulnerability assessment, information system security control assessment, and knowledge of the scope of the organization's cyber threats. Figure 2 shows the information security vulnerability awareness component (Mejias, Greer, Greer, Shepherd, & Reyes, 2025).

Figure 2. Information security vulnerability awareness component

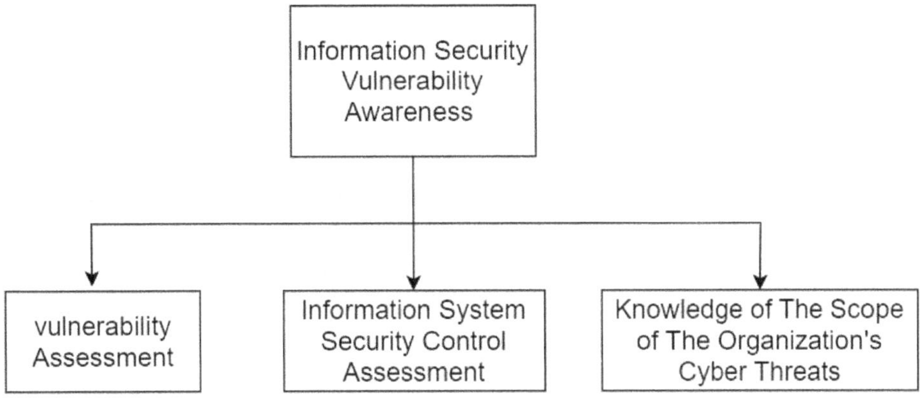

Information security awareness is crucial in protecting data and systems from cyber threats. By increasing understanding and awareness of potential threats, individuals and organizations can minimize risk and maintain the integrity and availability of information.

COMMON CYBER THREATS AND RISKS

Anyone cannot protect oneself from unknown threats and let alone threats that are taken for granted. Therefore, it is advisable to be familiar with all potential threats that can arise at any time in an organization. These threats can seriously harm the organization and its customers (Abergos & Medjek, 2024; Amft et al., 2023; Chang et al., 2022; Daah et al., 2024; Ghayoomi et al., 2021; González-Granadillo et al., 2021; Hale et al., 2021; Malatji et al., 2022; Padmaja et al., 2021; Radoglou-Grammatikis et al., 2021; Tawalbeh et al., 2020; Wilner et al., 2021).

In the zero-trust (ZT) model, every user, device, or network traffic is assumed to be untrusted before it is proven to be true. It's important to verify and authenticate each user and device, and limit access to resources. New authentication credentials and access rights are granted once user identity, device health, location, and behavior are deemed appropriate. Access monitoring is constantly evaluated and updated whenever there are changes in user properties, locations, and behaviors (Azad et al., 2024). Attacks in the form of real-time threat intelligence also need to be watched out, where currently there are more and more smart devices so that there is an increase in security risks due to Man-in-the-Middle attacks carried out by cybercriminals by manipulating data that is crossing between devices (Kandasamy et al., 2025).

An indispensable factor of the proper functioning of ICT systems in safe conditions is the identification of proper threats. It is precisely the identification of threats that makes it possible to determine the scale of complexity of the security problems analyzed as well as to indicate the main causes of system failures. Identifying threats that exist within a company and pointing out their occurrence may concern unintentional threats, but also threats that are carried out in a deliberate way, for example, by humans. Examples of human-caused threats include, among others: theft, unauthorized disclosure, alteration, destruction, and data loss. No one is perfect, so it is only possible to reduce human error to a certain degree. A few decades ago, ensuring the right level of information security was not as difficult a task as it is today. Pietras (2019) defines a threat as: "possible potential ICT system breaches" namely (Pietras, 2019):

- Cultural
- Technological
- Ecological
- Economic
- Existential
- Political
- Informational

Information security threats are primarily driven by the rapid advancement of technology. Organizations must adapt to these evolving threats with suitable information security measures. While technological progress can help mitigate existing threats, it does not eliminate them entirely; instead, it may make them easier to manage. However, it also introduces new challenges. The graphical representation of the distribution of threats is illustrated in Figure 3.

Figure 3. The factor of informational threats in a developing company

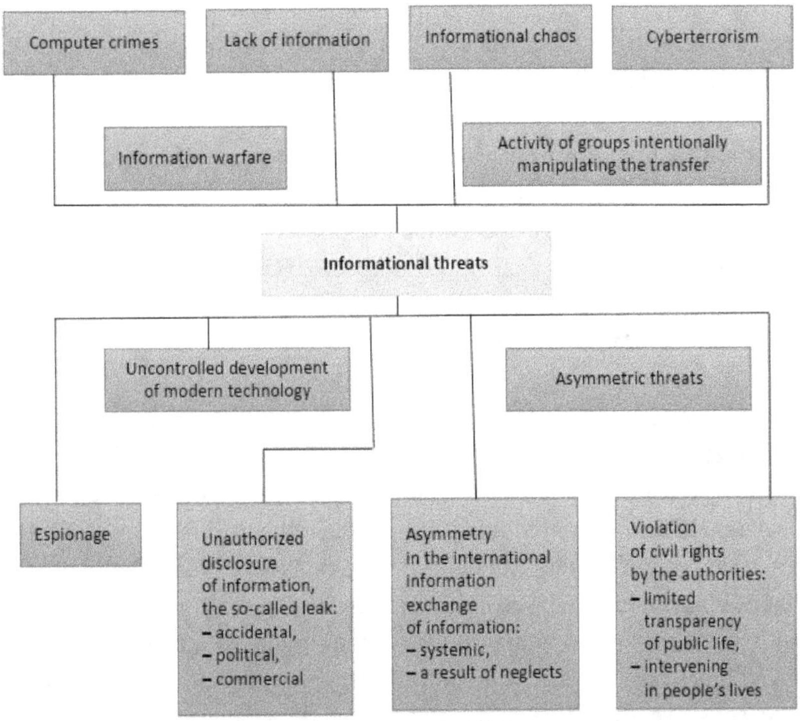

Understanding the cyber threats that are common will help users and organizations better prepare for attacks. Frequent threats include:

Phishing Attacks

All phishing attacks are any form of fraudulent attempt that aims to obtain sensitive information such as usernames, user ids, passwords, and credit card information (Al Ihsan et al., 2024; Berdik et al., 2021; Culot et al., 2021; Ferrag et al., 2020; Li & Liu, 2021; Lobe et al., 2020; Misra et al., 2022; Ogbanufe et al., 2023; Tran et al., 2024; Tully et al., 2020; Vasudev et al., 2023; Yang et al., 2020). In Indonesia, phishing attacks increased significantly, with 26,675 reports in the first quarter of 2023 compared to 6,106 in the fourth quarter of 2022 (Goodstats.id, 2023).

Social Engineering

Social engineering is the psychological manipulation of a person to take action or reveal confidential information. These social engineering activities can use the victim's ignorance to gain unauthorized access. Cybercriminals can make huge profits with these unauthorized ways. In an attempt to gain financial gain, phisher uses social engineering or fake websites to trick awakened victims into providing personal information such as credit card numbers, bank passwords or other sensitive information (Ariffin, Iqbal, Yusoff, & Zulkefli, 2025).

Malware and Ransomware

Malware is often malicious software designed to damage, infiltrate, or misuse computer systems and networks without the user's knowledge. One of the most destructive types of malware is ransomware. Malicious software that encrypts the victim's data will be considered inaccessible and redeemed in money (usually cryptocurrency) as a condition for the decryption key. Not only can these attacks cause significant financial losses based on operational bottlenecks and recovery costs, but they can also damage an organization's reputation due to a loss of trust from customers and business partners. Ransomware is a type of malware that is often used to encrypt sensitive users' files and networks and demands large ransoms to decrypt them. The advent of modern technologies such as artificial intelligence today such as ransomware as a service (RaaS) makes it challenging for novice attackers to carry out ransomware attacks and victimize deceived individuals and organizations, often demanding ransoms of millions and billions (Kritika, 2025).

Malicious Insider

A Malicious Insider comes from an employee or individual who has legitimate access rights to an organization's systems but misuses his or her access rights—either intentionally or unintentionally—resulting in an information security breach. These unauthorized actions are such as data theft, system sabotage, or omissions such as clicking on malicious phishing links. One of the biggest challenges in dealing with insider threats is the difficulty in detecting the perpetrators, because they already have legitimate authority and access rights, so their suspicious activities often escape the conventional security system. The impact can be devastating, ranging from leaks of sensitive information to severe system damage, which can ultimately threaten an organization's operations and reputation.

Weak Passwords

Examples of weak and easy-to-guess passwords such as "123456", "password", "birth date" and " child's name" if used by employees will significantly increase the level of the security risk of information unauthorized access to the system, hackers can easily guess passwords or break into through brute-force attacks or social engineering techniques. The decision to use the same password for multiple accounts also increases the risk of data leakage, as one password can unlock access to several other services. Therefore, it is urgent to encourage each employee to create a unique and hard-to-guess password for each account, with a combination of letters and numbers and special symbols. The implementation of two-factor authentication (2FA) is also recommended to be able to significantly improve information security against unauthorized access. Another example of a security breach is the use of passwords that are easy to remember and rarely make password changes (Kollar & Katona, 2024).

Public Wi-Fi Risks

Using a public Wi-Fi network is highly discouraged from performing important transactions. Free public Wi-Fi, which is easy to find in hotels, restaurants, airports, or other public places, can open loopholes and be used by attackers to access and steal sensitive data sent or received over those networks. While public networks are often poorly encrypted or have minimal protection, cybercriminals can easily carry out man-in-the-middle (MitM) attacks to intercept important information such as user IDs, passwords, or other financial information. Therefore, every user is advised to be very careful in working using public network facilities and should avoid making important transactions, especially financial transactions. The use of a Virtual Private Network (VPN) is highly recommended because it can encrypt data traffic, hide IP addresses, and protect users' privacy from potential cyber threats. MitM attacks allow cybercriminals to intercept and manipulate communication streams between devices, often remaining undetected (Kandasamy & Roseline, 2025). Table 2 shows the common cyber threats and their impact. Ongoing education and training are essential to reduce the risks associated with these threats.

Table 2. Summary of common cyber threats and their impact

Threat	Description	Main Impact
Phishing	Fraud to obtain sensitive information	Identity theft, financial losses
Social Engineering	Manipulation of individuals to reveal confidential information	Unauthorized access, data leaks
Malware/ Ransomware	Malicious software that corrupts or encrypts data	Data loss, financial loss
Insider Threats	Abuse of access by individuals with authority	Data leaks, system crashes
Weak Passwords	Use of easy-to-guess passwords	Unauthorized access to the account
Public Wi-Fi Risks	Data exposure when using an unsecured Wi-Fi network	Pencurian data, serangan man-in-the-middle

BEST PRACTICES FOR SECURITY AWARENESS

Efforts to raise awareness of information security are a key step for organizations and all employees to protect their digital assets. Here are some best practices that can be implemented:

Implementation of Security Training Program

It is essential to receive daily cybersecurity training for employees and users. This training should cover topics such as cyber threat implementation, corporate security guidelines, and incident response procedures. According to an article from SHI, understanding the starting point is the first step in building an effective security awareness program. To ensure maximum effectiveness, your cybersecurity training program should include the following elements:

Cyber Threat Recognition

Employees must be educated to have an understanding of the dangers and various types of threats in cyberspace, such as phishing, social engineering, malware, ransomware, and threats from within. Conducting case studies and simulated attacks will help every employee improve their detection capabilities and deal with these threats.

Security Policy and Compliance

The training provided should cover the organization's security policies, including acceptable use (AUP) policies, data handling protocols, and access control measures. After training, employees should be knowledgeable about the laws and regulations on information security on ISO 27001, GDPR, and HIPAA, as well as ensure compliance with industry standards.

Incident Response Procedures

Employees should be provided with an understanding of how to respond to various security incidents, how to report suspicious activity, handle data breach cases that may arise, and follow escalation protocols. A quick and effective response can minimize damage and prevent further exploitation.

Training Methods and Delivery Approaches:

In-Person Workshops and Seminars

- Interactive sessions led by security experts
- Hands-on exercises and role-playing scenarios
- Open discussions on security challenges

Online Learning Platforms

- Self-paced courses with quizzes and certification
- Video tutorials explaining security best practices
- AI-driven adaptive learning for personalized training

Gamification and Interactive Exercises

- Cybersecurity escape rooms
- Security awareness leaderboards
- Real-time attack simulations

Continuous Training and Reinforcement. Information security training needs to be carried out regularly and continuously. Organizations should conduct refresher courses regularly, provide security tips through newsletters, and integrate security reminders into daily workflows.

Use of Strong Authentication Mechanisms

Encourage every employee to implement multi-factor authentication (MFA) which aims to be able to significantly improve security. MFA requires more than one form of verification, such as passwords and codes sent to mobile devices, to access the system. According to the EC-Council, MFA is one of the best practices in security awareness training.

Secure Password Management

Implementing secure and unpredictable password management is an important step in inhibiting and preventing unauthorized access to information systems. Each employee needs to change their passwords to be more complex and unique to each account they have, as well as password management to store credentials securely, which can significantly reduce the risk of data leakage caused by weak or easily guessed passwords by unauthorized persons. According to the EC-Council, secure password management is an important part of security awareness training because it can help users understand the importance of maintaining the confidentiality of their digital identity.

Recognizing and Avoiding Phishing Attacks

The ability for users to identify and avoid phishing attacks is essential to prevent data damage or loss. Training on understanding suspicious emails such as emails coming from unknown senders, requests for confidential information, suspicious links, etc. The meter must be part of the information security training program. Training mentors should explain that effective training for security awareness can significantly reduce phishing attacks and improve each employee's ability to respond to various cyber incidents.

Regularly Update Software and Systems

Ensuring that all application software and systems are regularly updated with the latest security patches, the implementation of the latest security patches is an important thing to do in order to close vulnerabilities that can be exploited by threat actors. Software updates include not only the operating system, but also other applications, and the hardware related to those applications. According to the EC-Council, regular system updates are the best and safest way to conduct security awareness training materials, as many cyberattacks succeed as a result of systems that have not updated their security features and still contain old security holes.

Restricting Access to Sensitive Information

Restricting access to sensitive information by implementing role-based access controls (RBACs) helps in the potential for data misuse by minimal, light, and unauthorized parties. Only those who are allowed according to the role must have access to certain data to maintain the minimum principle of privilege. PCI Security Standards – Council emphasizes that access restrictions are part of the best practices of the training program for security awareness.

Promoting Safe Remote Work Practices

With the development of a remote work model such as work from anywhere (WFA), it is important for organizations to equip their employees with the knowledge and tools they need to keep information secure when working outside the office. Practices such as protecting your home network, using a VPN for a secure connection, and understanding potential security threats in a remote work environment should be part of security awareness training training. The EC-Council states that the promotion of safe remote work practices is an important element of security awareness training, given the increased risk of inadequately protected remote access. Table 3 shows Best Practices for Security Awareness.

Table 3. Best practices for security awareness

Best Practices	Description
Implementation of Security Training Program	Conduct regular cybersecurity training sessions for employees and users.
Use of Strong Authentication Mechanisms	Promote using multi-competency authentication (MFA) to improve security.
Secure Password Management	Promote to use the complex passwords using password manager generation.
Recognizing and Avoiding Phishing Attacks	Teach users how to identify suspicious emails and report them.
Update Software and Systems in regular basis	Implement security patches to mitigate vulnerabilities.
Restricting Access to Sensitive Information	Apply role-based access controls (RBAC) to prevent ilegal access.
Promoting Safe Remote Work Practices	Secure home networks, use VPNs, and educate users about remote security threats.

By implementing these measures, every employee can increase information security awareness and protect the organization's digital assets from various cyber threats.

MEASURING THE EFFECTIVENESS OF SECURITY AWARENESS PROGRAMS

Measuring the effectiveness of information security awareness programs is critical for organizations that have successfully improved employee behavior and knowledge in cyber threats. Here are the most commonly used methods:

Simulated Phishing Test

Phishing simulation tests involve sending fake phishing-emails to employees to assess their ability to recognize and report phishing attempts. This method can help identify weaknesses in areas that require additional security awareness and training. According to Proofpoint, phishing simulations can test security guidelines and practices, increase employee awareness and reduce vulnerability to attacks.

Security Audits and Assessments

Audit and safety assessments are used to assess compliance with designated guidelines and security practices. This process involves investigating employee behavior related to IT infrastructure, security policies, and information security. According to the National Institute of Standards and Technology (NIST), measuring success is an important but challenging aspect of security awareness programs, with many organizations not measuring the effectiveness of the program

User Feedback and Surveys

Gathering feedback from employees through specific assessment activities and interviews can provide insight into the effectiveness of training programs and areas for security awareness that need to be improved. According to articles on online CSOs, surveys, interviews, short quizzes, exams, audits, there are several common assessment methods that allow you to measure your progress.

Metrik Respons Insiden

By analyzing how employees respond to real security threats, you can provide an indication of the effectiveness of the program for security warm-ups. You can assess employees' willingness to handle security incidents to assess metrics such as response time, procedural compliance, and response outcomes. According to NIST, the goal of the program to raise awareness of organizational safety is to have a positive impact on employee safety behavior. Table 4 shows how to measure the effectiveness of a security awareness program.

Table 4. Methods for security awareness program measurement

Method	Description
Simulated Phishing Test	Simulated sending fake emails to employees to assess employees' ability to recognize and report phishing.
Security Assessments	Conduct compliance checks on security policies and practices through audit of IT infrastructure and employee behavior.
User Feedback and Surveys	Gather an understanding of each employee on the effectiveness of the training program and to identify areas that need improvement.
Incident Response Metrics	Analyze employee performance in responding to real security threats to assess program readiness and effectiveness.

By implementing these methods, organizations can effectively assess and improve their security awareness programs, ensuring that employees are prepared for cyber threats and minimizing risks to information assets.

CONCLUSION

Awareness of information protection is a key element of an effective cyber-security plan. With digital threats increasing in both complexity and number, it's important to create a culture that supports proactive security so that individuals and organizations can safeguard sensitive data and critical infrastructure. The increased reliance on digital technology has enlarged the areas that can be attacked, making security awareness an important factor in reducing risk. Some of the things that can be concluded are:

- Increased awareness of information security. Improving understanding of cyber threats and best practices is crucial to reducing vulnerabilities related to humans. Research shows that human error is the dominant cause of security breaches, with phishing attacks and weak authentication methods being common entry points for hackers. By integrating security awareness into the culture of the organization, the likelihood of a successful cyberattack can be significantly reduced.
- Training and workshops on information security. Security training programs that include real-world situations, such as simulated phishing tests as well as interactive modules, have proven to be effective in improving users' ability to detect and deal with threats. Regular training sessions, the implementation of

two-factor authentication, the implementation of strong password policies, and the practice of safe browsing are key components of an effective awareness program..

- Organizational and individual responsibilities. While organizations need to implement robust security policies and provide ongoing training, individuals also have a vital role to play in safeguarding their digital assets, both personal and professional. Adopting good security practices, reporting suspicious actions, and staying up-to-date on the latest threats contributes to a shared defensive strategy in the face of cyber risks.
- Continuous improvement of information security awareness. Measuring the success of a security awareness program is essential for continuous improvement. Organizations need to use key performance indicators such as the level of vulnerability to phishing, the level of compliance with policies, and the effectiveness of the response to incidents to assess the impact of the initiatives they are implementing.

Future Directions in Security Awareness. As cybersecurity threats become more sophisticated, the future of security awareness will likely incorporate emerging technologies such as artificial intelligence (AI)-driven security training, behavior analytics, and personalized learning experiences. Additionally, regulatory frameworks are expected to evolve, mandating more rigorous security awareness initiatives across industries. By integrating security awareness into everyday digital practices, individuals and organizations can strengthen their cybersecurity posture, reduce the risk of breaches, and foster a safer digital ecosystem. Moving forward, a commitment to ongoing education, policy enforcement, and technological advancements will be vital in addressing the ever-changing cybersecurity landscape.

REFERENCES

Abergos, V. J., & Medjek, F. (2024). A Risk Assessment Analysis to Enhance the Security of OT WAN with SD-WAN. *Journal of Cybersecurity and Privacy*, *4*(4), 910–937. DOI: 10.3390/jcp4040042

Abushark, Y. B., Hassan, S., & Khan, A. I. (2025). Optimized Adaboost Support Vector Machine-Based Encryption for Securing IoT-Cloud Healthcare Data. *Sensors (Basel)*, *25*(3), 731. DOI: 10.3390/s25030731 PMID: 39943369

Al Ihsan, R., & Sekti, B. A. (2024). Pentingnya Keamanan Data Dalam Era Digital: Refleksi Terhadap Serangan Hacker Pada Pusat Data Nasional Indonesia. *Prosiding SISFOTEK*, *8*(1), 7–11.

Albinali, H., & Azzedin, F. (2025). Replay attacks in RPL-based Internet of Things: Comparative and empirical study. *Computer Networks*, *257*, 110996. DOI: 10.1016/j.comnet.2024.110996

Amft, S., Höltervennhoff, S., Huaman, N., Krause, A., Simko, L., Acar, Y., & Fahl, S. (2023). "We've Disabled MFA for You": An Evaluation of the Security and Usability of Multi-Factor Authentication Recovery Deployments. In *CCS 2023 - Proceedings of the 2023 ACM SIGSAC Conference on Computer and Communications Security* (pp. 3138–3152). DOI: 10.1145/3576915.3623180

Ariffin, N. H. M., Iqbal, M. I. M., Yusoff, M., & Zulkefli, N. A. M. (2025). A Study on the Best Classification Method for an Intelligent Phishing Website Detection System. *Journal of Advanced Research in Applied Sciences and Engineering Technology*, *48*(2), 197–210. DOI: 10.37934/araset.48.2.197210

Arunthavanathan, R., Khan, F., Sajid, Z., Amin, M. T., Kota, K. R., & Kumar, S. (2025). Are the processing facilities safe and secured against cyber threats? *Reliability Engineering & System Safety*, *260*, 111011. DOI: 10.1016/j.ress.2025.111011

Azad, M. A., Abdullah, S., Arshad, J., Lallie, H., & Ahmed, Y. H. (2024). Verify and trust: A multidimensional survey of zero-trust security in the age of IoT. *Internet of Things : Engineering Cyber Physical Human Systems*, *27*, 101227. DOI: 10.1016/j.iot.2024.101227

Berdik, D., Otoum, S., Schmidt, N., Porter, D., & Jararweh, Y. (2021). A Survey on Blockchain for Information Systems Management and Security. *Information Processing & Management*, *58*(1), 102397. DOI: 10.1016/j.ipm.2020.102397

Chang, V., Golightly, L., Modesti, P., Xu, Q. A., Doan, L. M. T., Hall, K., Boddu, S., & Kobusińska, A. (2022). A Survey on Intrusion Detection Systems for Fog and Cloud Computing. *Future Internet, 14*(3), 89. DOI: 10.3390/fi14030089

Culot, G., Nassimbeni, G., Podrecca, M., & Sartor, M. (2021). The ISO/IEC 27001 information security management standard: Literature review and theory-based research agenda. *The TQM Journal, 33*(7), 76–105. DOI: 10.1108/TQM-09-2020-0202

Daah, C., Qureshi, A., Awan, I., & Konur, S. (2024). Enhancing Zero Trust Models in the Financial Industry through Blockchain Integration: A Proposed Framework. *Electronics (Basel), 13*(5), 865. DOI: 10.3390/electronics13050865

Ferrag, M. A., Maglaras, L., Moschoyiannis, S., & Janicke, H. (2020). Deep learning for cyber security intrusion detection: Approaches, datasets, and comparative study. *Journal of Information Security and Applications, 50*, 102419. DOI: 10.1016/j.jisa.2019.102419

Garg, M., Wang, T., & Wilkin, C. L. (2025). Impact of reporting information security breaches, accounting quality, and the opportunistic disclosure of good news and bad news. *International Journal of Accounting Information Systems, 56*, 100729. DOI: 10.1016/j.accinf.2025.100729

Ghayoomi, H., Laskey, K., Miller-Hooks, E., Hooks, C., & Tariverdi, M. (2021). Assessing resilience of hospitals to cyberattack. *Digital Health, 7*, 20552076211059366. DOI: 10.1177/20552076211059366 PMID: 34868621

González-Granadillo, G., González-Zarzosa, S., & Diaz, R. (2021). Security information and event management (SIEM): Analysis, trends, and usage in critical infrastructures. *Sensors (Basel), 21*(14), 4759. DOI: 10.3390/s21144759 PMID: 34300500

Goodstats.id. (2023). Serangan Phishing di Indonesia Terus Meningkat. https://goodstats.id/article/serangan-phishing-di-indonesia-terus-meningkat-ini-statistiknya-U8VdY

Grill, M., Sommestad, T., Karlzén, H., & Pousette, A. (2025). Training for improved information security culture: A longitudinal randomized controlled trial. *Information and Computer Security*. Advance online publication. DOI: 10.1108/ICS-08-2024-0189

Hale, B., van Bossuyt, D. L., Papakonstantinou, N., & O'Halloran, B. (2021). A zero-trust methodology for security of complex systems with machine learning components. In *Proceedings of the ASME Design Engineering Technical Conference* (Vol. 2). DOI: 10.1115/DETC2021-70442

Iskandar, O., Yusuf, B., Mahmudjon, S., Azizbek, X., & Javohir, I. (2021). Analysis of existing standards for information security assessment. In *International Conference on Information Science and Communications Technologies: Applications, Trends and Opportunities, ICISCT 2021*. DOI: 10.1109/ICISCT52966.2021.9670428

Kandasamy, V., & Roseline, A. A. (2025). Harnessing advanced hybrid deep learning model for real-time detection and prevention of man-in-the-middle cyber attacks. *Scientific Reports*, *15*(1), 1697. DOI: 10.1038/s41598-025-85547-5 PMID: 39799192

Kollar, A. M., & Katona, J. (2024). Enhancing Password Security: Analyzing Password Management Practices Among IT Students. In *CANDO-EPE 2024 - Proceedings: IEEE 7th International Conference and Workshop Obuda on Electrical and Power Engineering* (pp. 59–64). DOI: 10.1109/CANDO-EPE65072.2024.10772755

Kritika, E. (2025). A comprehensive literature review on ransomware detection using deep learning. *Cyber Security and Applications*, *3*, 100078. DOI: 10.1016/j.csa.2024.100078

Lallie, H. S., Thompson, A., Titis, E., & Stephens, P. (2025). Analysing Cyber Attacks and Cyber Security Vulnerabilities in the University Sector. *Computers*, *14*(2), 49. DOI: 10.3390/computers14020049

Li, Y., & Liu, Q. (2021). A comprehensive review study of cyber-attacks and cyber security; Emerging trends and recent developments. *Energy Reports*, *7*, 8176–8186. DOI: 10.1016/j.egyr.2021.08.126

Lobe, B., Morgan, D., & Hoffman, K. A. (2020). Qualitative Data Collection in an Era of Social Distancing. *International Journal of Qualitative Methods*, *19*, 1609406920937875. DOI: 10.1177/1609406920937875

Luh, R., Eresheim, S., Tavolato, P., Petelin, T., Gmeiner, S., Holzinger, A., & Schrittwieser, S. (2025). Gamifying information security: Adversarial risk exploration for IT/OT infrastructures. *Computers & Security*, *151*, 104287. DOI: 10.1016/j.cose.2024.104287

Mabunda, S. (2025). The South African and Senegalese Legislative Response to Malware-Facilitated Cybercrime. In *Advances in Information Security* (Vol. 91, pp. 233–249). DOI: 10.1007/978-3-031-66245-4_10

Malatji, M., Marnewick, A. L., & Von Solms, S. (2022). Cybersecurity capabilities for critical infrastructure resilience. *Information and Computer Security*, *30*(2), 255–279. DOI: 10.1108/ICS-06-2021-0091

Mejias, R. J., Greer, J. J., Greer, G. C., Shepherd, M. M., & Reyes, R. Y. (2025). A model for information security vulnerability awareness. *Computers & Security, 151*, 104305. DOI: 10.1016/j.cose.2024.104305

Misra, N. N., Dixit, Y., Al-Mallahi, A., Bhullar, M. S., Upadhyay, R., & Martynenko, A. (2022). IoT, Big Data, and Artificial Intelligence in Agriculture and Food Industry. *IEEE Internet of Things Journal, 9*(9), 6305–6324. DOI: 10.1109/JIOT.2020.2998584

2024. N. Y. P. (n.d.). Nearly half of employed people have fallen victim to cyberattack or scam. https://nypost.com/2024/09/26/lifestyle/nearly-half-of-employed-people-have-fallen-victim-to-cyberattack-or-scam/

Padmaja, K., & Seshadri, R. (2021). Analytics on real time security attacks in healthcare, retail and banking applications in the cloud. *Evolutionary Intelligence, 14*(2), 595–605. DOI: 10.1007/s12065-019-00337-z

Pietras, E. (2019). Information security–its essence and threats. *Scientific Journal of the Military University of Land Forces, 51*(1), (191), 25–34.

Radoglou-Grammatikis, P., Sarigiannidis, P., Iturbe, E., Rios, E., Martinez, S., Sarigiannidis, A., Eftathopoulos, G., Spyridis, Y., Sesis, A., Vakakis, N., Tzovaras, D., Kafetzakis, E., Giannoulakis, I., Tzifas, M., Giannakoulias, A., Angelopoulos, M., & Ramos, F. (2021). SPEAR SIEM: A Security Information and Event Management system for the Smart Grid. *Computer Networks, 193*, 108008. DOI: 10.1016/j.comnet.2021.108008

Tawalbeh, L., Muheidat, F., Tawalbeh, M., & Quwaider, M. (2020). IoT privacy and security: Challenges and solutions. *Applied Sciences (Basel, Switzerland), 10*(12), 4102. DOI: 10.3390/app10124102

Tully, J., Selzer, J., Phillips, J. P., O'Connor, P., & Dameff, C. (2020). Healthcare Challenges in the Era of Cybersecurity. *Health Security, 18*(3), 228–231. DOI: 10.1089/hs.2019.0123 PMID: 32559153

Van Tran, D., Van Nguyen, P., Nguyen, A. T. C., Vrontis, D., & Dinh, P. U. (2024). Exploring the influence of government social media on cybersecurity compliance: Employee attitudes, motivation and behaviors. *Journal of Asia Business Studies, 18*(1), 204–223. DOI: 10.1108/JABS-09-2023-0343

Vasudev, R., Harini, N., & Neethu, M. R. (2023). Multi-Factor Authentication System With ID Card Credentials For Secure Transactions. In *2023 14th International Conference on Computing Communication and Networking Technologies, ICCCNT 2023*. DOI: 10.1109/ICCCNT56998.2023.10308252

Wilner, A. S., Luce, H., Ouellet, E., Williams, O., & Costa, N. (2021). From public health to cyber hygiene: Cybersecurity and Canada's healthcare sector. *International Journal (Toronto, Ont.)*, *76*(4), 522–543. DOI: 10.1177/00207020211067946

Yang, P., Xiong, N., & Ren, J. (2020). Data Security and Privacy Protection for Cloud Storage: A Survey. *IEEE Access : Practical Innovations, Open Solutions*, *8*, 131723–131740. DOI: 10.1109/ACCESS.2020.3009876

ADDITIONAL READING

Ogbanufe, O. M., & Baham, C. (2023). Using Multi-Factor Authentication for Online Account Security: Examining the Influence of Anticipated Regret. *Information Systems Frontiers*, *25*(2), 897–916. DOI: 10.1007/s10796-022-10278-1

Chapter 5
Personal Data Privacy and Security at Individual and Organizational Levels

Jasbir Kaur
GNIMS Business School, India

Shiney Chib
https://orcid.org/0000-0001-7648-9963
Datta Meghe Institute of Management Studies, India

Guru Basava Aradhya S.
https://orcid.org/0000-0002-3335-2681
Dayananda Sagar Business Academy, India

Prashant Bhavarlal Chordiya
https://orcid.org/0009-0005-6227-2583
Savitribai Phule Pune University, India

Nilesh Anute
https://orcid.org/0000-0001-6599-813X
Sri Balaji University, India

P. Selvakumar
https://orcid.org/0000-0002-3650-4548
Department of Science and Humanities, Nehru Institute of Technology, Coimbatore, India

Manjunath T. C.
https://orcid.org/0000-0003-2545-9160
Rajarajeswari College of Engineering, India

ABSTRACT

In the digital era, personal data is critical to both individuals and organizations. With increasing reliance on digital platforms, the being collected, processed, and stored has reached unprecedented levels. However, this expansion has also led to significant security threats, data breaches, identity theft, and cyberattacks, impacting personal privacy and organizational integrity. This paper explores the essential aspects of addressing individual organizations in safeguarding sensitive information. At the individual level, maintaining data security involves adopting strong cybersecurity practices, including password management, multi-factor authentication (MFA), en-

DOI: 10.4018/979-8-3373-3171-3.ch005

cryption, safe browsing habits, and awareness of phishing attacks. Individuals must exercise caution when sharing personal information online, use privacy-enhancing tools such as VPNs, encrypted messaging services, and ad blockers, and remain vigilant against evolving cyber threats.

INTRODUCTION TO PERSONAL DATA PRIVACY AND SECURITY

Era, Personal Critical Individuals, and Governments Worldwide

Widespread internet usage, and connected devices amount being generated, collected, and stored. Often includes sensitive browsing history and even real-time location tracking. While data collection has enabled many conveniences and advancements, it has also created significant risks, making it paramount. Primary data and security have become a growing concern due to the increasing frequency of cyberattacks and data breaches. High-profile breaches affecting major corporations, financial institutions, healthcare providers, and government agencies have exposed millions of Hackers and cybercriminals to exploit vulnerabilities in digital systems, often using sophisticated techniques personal and corporate the consequences are losses, and ramifications for organizations, as well as emotional distress and financial hardship for individuals. Beyond cyberattacks, concerns over data privacy have intensified due to the growing influence of tech giants and digital platforms that analytics, and artificial intelligence development. Apple was scrutinized for its data collection practices, raising ethical and legal consent, transparency, and personal information being monetized. Many consumers are unaware of how much data they are sharing when using online services, mobile applications, and smart devices, leading to an increased demand for greater control over personal information. Governments and regulatory bodies have responded to these concerns by introducing stringent data protection laws and regulations. Setting while rights data. And increase transparency in data handling practices. Other countries have followed suit, implementing or strengthening data protection laws to hold organizations accountable for safeguarding user information. However, enforcement remains a challenge, and companies often struggle to comply with varying regulations across different jurisdictions.

As privacy concerns continue to rise, businesses are increasingly investing in cybersecurity measures to protect customer and company data. Are commonly used to mitigate risks. Additionally, organizations are adopting privacy-by-design principles, and integrating security measures Despite these efforts, cybersecurity is essential for employees and users alike. Further complicated landscape privacy. AI-powered systems rely on massive datasets to improve performance, but bias, discrimination, and misuse. For example, debated Governments and organizations must responsibly use. Another growing concern is interconnected smart home appliances to wearable health monitors, which collect and transmit data continuously. While these technologies enhance convenience and efficiency, they also present as encryption making IoT devices easy targets for cybercriminals, leading to potential breaches and unauthorized access to personal data. Protecting and security(Sugumaran K. M, D., et al. 2024). Practicing good cybersecurity habits, and strong, emails, helps Additionally, individuals familiarize themselves with online services, and mobile apps to share. As must strategies regulations designed to protect personal privacy will involve more advanced security measures, increased user control over data, and greater collaboration between governments, businesses, and technology experts to establish ethical standards. While complete privacy may never be achievable in an interconnected world, prioritizing transparency, accountability, and security can help mitigate risks and ensure a safer digital environment for everyone(Vijayakumar G, et al. 2024).Ultimately, personal data privacy and security are no longer optional concerns but essential aspects of modern life. Whether for individuals safeguarding their digital footprint or businesses ensuring compliance with regulations, protecting sensitive information must remain a top priority. By staying informed and proactive, society age maintaining trust increasingly data-driven.

THE EVOLUTION OF DATA PROTECTION REGULATIONS: FROM GDPR TO CCPA AND BEYOND

The rapid digitalization of the modern world of technology, communication, and commerce, has also raised critical businesses and government processes, storer comprehensive regulations Over the years, regulatory frameworks have evolved to address these concerns, with landmark legislations such as new global Beyond these, several developed shaping a complex and evolving landscape policies worldwide. The Pre-GDPR Era: The Foundations of Data Protection: Before the introduction of GDPR, various countries had already implemented data protection laws, though they often lacked consistency, enforceability, and broad applicability. One of the earliest efforts to address data privacy an was which established foundational privacy principles such as notice, choice, access, and security. (1981) Another milestone, is a legal treaty (Fakeyede et al, 2023). The adopted 1995, laid the groundwork for privacy rights but lacked uniformity across member states. Similarly, in the U.S., data protection laws were sectoral, (1996) (1999) However, these early regulations struggled to keep pace with the rise of the internet, e-commerce, and online collection practices. The General Data Protection Regulation (GDPR): A Global Benchmark: stronger, more approach to introducing stricter rules, enhanced user rights, and severe penalties for non-compliance. Some of its key provisions include: Stronger Consent Requirements: informed, before collecting their data. Expanded Individual Rights: GDPR introduced the "right to be forgotten," and access and rectification. Data Breach Notifications: Companies must report data breaches to authorities' discovery. The impact of GDPR extended far beyond Europe. Many global companies revised to comply making their principles a de facto global standard. The regulation also inspired other nations to strengthen their own. The California Consumer Privacy Act (CCPA): The U.S. Response to GDPR: traditionally followed fragmented different governing different industries (Oye E., et al, 2022).

Beyond GDPR and CCPA

Emerging Data Protection Regulations Worldwide

Following GDPR and CCPA, many other nations and regions have enacted or updated there: Brazil's General Data Protection Law (LGPD) (2020): Inspired by GDPR, LGPD introduces strict data processing rules and requires businesses to appoint a Data Protection Officer (DPO).

China's Personal Information Protection Law (PIPL) (2021): PIPL is stringent on data collection, cross-border transfers, and corporate responsibilities, resembling GDPR's principles.

India's Digital Personal Data Protection Act (DPDP) (2023): A long-awaited law that regulates data collection, processing, and consent requirements, aligning with global privacy standards (Voss , 2021).

Canada's Consumer Privacy Protection Act (CPPA) (Proposed): Expected to replace Canada's existing privacy framework, enhancing transparency and user control. Additionally, took expanded by adding stricter rules on data minimization, sensitive data processing, and establishing a dedicated enforcement agency.

The Future of Data Protection

Trends and Challenges

So do the complexities surrounding data privacy. Some key trends shaping the future of data protection include: Artificial Intelligence and Privacy: AI-driven analytics, facial recognition, and algorithmic decision-making bias, unauthorized data use.

Cross-Border Data Transfers: Businesses face challenges complying with different national laws governing data transfers, leading to frameworks like Framework. Future regulations may include data sovereignty laws, stricter biometrics regulations, and increased consumer control over automated profiling. Federal U.S. Data Privacy Law: Discussions continue around a unified federal privacy law that could establish national standards, reducing reliance on state-specific laws like CCPA and CPRA (Pazhohan, 2023). The evolution of data protection regulations reflects society's growing awareness of privacy rights and the risks posed by unchecked data collection(Mahadev Madgule, et al. 2023). From GDPR's global influence to CCPA's impact on U.S. policy, privacy laws continue to be new While businesses must navigate an increasingly complex regulatory environment, consumers stand to benefit from greater transparency, control, and security over their data. Moving forward, governments, organizations, and individuals must work together on privacy ensuring a secure ethical digital future for all.

THE IMPACT OF DATA BREACHES ON INDIVIDUALS AND ORGANIZATIONS

Serious, Affecting Millions of Individuals and Organizations Worldwide

Institutions Infrastructure, Online Continues to Grow

However, this dependency also exposes them to cyberattacks, hacking incidents, insider threats, and accidental leaks, leading to devastating consequences. Regulatory penalties, and organizations, may suffer from identity theft, fraud, emotional distress, and long-term financial difficulties. Over the past decade, have highlighted the vulnerabilities in cybersecurity urgently stronger.

Understanding Data Breaches

How They Occur

A data breach occurs when unauthorized parties gain access to confidential information stored in a database, network, or cloud system (Schlackl et al, 2022). These breaches can be caused by various factors, including Cyberattacks and Hacking: Malicious actors exploit system vulnerabilities using phishing, malware, ransomware, and brute force attacks.

Insider Threats

Unintentionally leak due to negligence malicious intent. Third-Party Vulnerabilities: Many breaches occur due to weak security in vendors or service providers with access to sensitive data. Human Error: Poor password management, misconfigured security settings, and accidental data exposure contribute to many breaches(Sreenivasulu et al. 2022).

Recent High-Profile Data Breaches and Their Impact

Several major underscored severities of the issue, affecting both individuals and organizations on a massive scale. Equifax Data Breach (2017): significant data birthdates, addresses. Was attributed vulnerabilities in Equifax's web application. The consequences were severe: Equifax faced lawsuits and regulatory penalties, resulting in a $700 million settlement with U.S. regulators. were exposed credit (Bachura et al, 2022). The Company suffered long-term reputational damage, leading to a loss of consumer trust.

Facebook (Meta) Data Breaches (2019, 2021): Facebook has faced multiple data breaches, including a 2019 incident where 540 million user records were exposed due to misconfigured cloud storage. Another 2021 leak compromised email. The impact included: Increased cases of phishing attacks and spam calls targeting exposed users. Heightened scrutiny over Facebook's data privacy policies and handling of user data. Global €265 fine by Irish Data Protection Commission.

Marriott International Data Breach (2018-2020): Suffered a massive affecting 500 million guests in 2018, followed by another breach in 2020 impacting 5.2 million people. Hackers gained access to reservation history. The consequences were: customer Marriott's guest. Exposure of high-profile individuals' travel details, increases risks of corporate espionage.

Colonial Pipeline Ransomware Attack (2021): Carried out by the Darkside cybercriminal group, one of the pipelines the U.S. disrupted causing the company to end up paying off its systems. The attack highlighted: The financial operational impact of ransomware attacks.

T-Mobile Data Breach (2021, 2023): Has experienced multiple breaches, with the 2021 incident exposing 50 customers, details. Another 2023 affected 37 million customers due to an API vulnerability (Almulihi et al, 2022). The aftermath included: Regulatory fines and class-action lawsuits, with T-Mobile agreeing to a $350 million settlement in 2022. Increased risk of identity theft for affected individuals.

Damage to T-Mobile's

The Consequences of Data Breaches

Impact on Individuals: For individuals, data breaches are severe: Identity Theft and Fraud: Exposed data can be used in activities. Financial Losses: monetary due to unauthorized transactions and fraudulent activities. Privacy Violations: Personal conversations, browsing history, and health records can be exposed, leading to embarrassment or blackmail. Phishing and Scams: use it for targeted phishing attacks.

Impact on Organizations: For businesses and institutions, data breaches lead to significant financial and operational consequences: Companies can face hefty fines under laws like GDPR and CCPA (Ramakrishnan et al. 2022). Loss of consumer trust affects brand loyalty and market value.

Operational Disruptions: Cyberattacks like ransomware can halt operations, resulting in massive financial losses.

UNDERSTANDING PERSONAL DATA: WHAT IS IT, AND WHY IS IT VALUABLE?

World, Personal Commodities, Driving Economies, Shaping Industries, and Influencing Global Policies

From continuously, analyzed, by businesses, governments, and cybercriminals alike. Understanding what personal data is, why it holds immense value, and how it can be protected seeking to navigate the complexities of digital privacy security. What is Personal Data? Identifies or encompasses a wide range of data types, including Basic Identifiers and Sensitive Personal Data: Social Security numbers, and passport details. Financial Information: Health Records: genetic data.

Online Activity

IP addresses, Location Data: GPS tracking, geotags from photos, and mobile device locations.

Behavioral and Preference Data: Shopping habits, social media activity, and streaming preferences (Birch et al, 2021). Under laws is classified based on its sensitivity, with stricter protections applied to highly.

Why is Personal Data Valuable?

Personal "new oil" because of its immense economic and strategic value. Organizations leverage personal data for various purposes, including Business and Marketing: Companies collect user data to understand consumer behavior, personalize advertising, and improve customer experiences. Online retailers, for example, use browsing history and purchase patterns to recommend products tailored to individual preferences. Social media platforms analyze user engagement to deliver targeted advertisements, generating billions in revenue.

Artificial Intelligence and Big Data Analytics

(AI) models rely on personal improvement algorithms, enhance automation, and develop new technologies. Facial recognition systems, speech assistants, and recommendation engines all depend on personal data for training and optimization. Government and Law Enforcement: Governments collect personal data for identity verification, national security, and public services (Guay R., et al, 2022). Tax records, census data, and biometric passports help authorities manage populations and enforce regulations.

How Can Personal Data Be Protected?

Given the increasing threats to personal must Here are key strategies to protect personal data:

Strengthen Passwords and Use Multi-Factor Authentication (MFA)

Weak to enhance security:

Be Cautious with Social Media and Online Sharing

Oversharing personal information on social media increases the risk of identity theft. To minimize exposure: Limit the amount of personal data shared publicly. Adjust privacy settings to restrict access to personal profiles. Be wary of phishing messages and fake friend requests that attempt to steal information.

Use Secure Networks and Encrypted Communication

- VPN browsing networks. Ensure websites use HTTPS encryption before entering sensitive information. Avoid accessing financial accounts or entering passwords on untrusted networks.
- Regularly Update Software and Security Patches: Outdated operating are vulnerable to cyberattacks (Jörke et al, 2023).

Best practices include:

- Regularly updating operating systems, browsers, and applications.
- Enabling automatic security updates to protect against newly discovered threats.
- Installing reputable antivirus and anti-malware software.

Monitor Financial and Online Accounts: Cybercriminals often exploit stolen data months or years after a breach.

To stay ahead: account to detect unauthorized. Freeze credit reports if identity theft is suspected.

Understand and Exercise Privacy Rights

Rise more CCPA, and other privacy laws: stored companies. Collection third-party sharing. From company databases. Report violations to regulatory authorities if data is mishandled. Educate Yourself and Stay Informed: Cyber threats and privacy laws are constantly evolving. Staying informed helps individuals and businesses remain vigilant: Follow cybersecurity news and updates from organizations like. Take online courses on privacy awareness and digital security. Read apps and websites.

The Future of Personal Data Protection

As technology advances, the importance of personal protection will only grow. Future trends include: Stronger Privacy Regulations: Countries are introducing stricter data protection laws, requiring companies to be more transparent and accountable (Verma A., et al, 2024).

INDIVIDUAL RIGHTS AND RESPONSIBILITIES: DATA PROTECTION, CONSENT, AND ACCESS

Digital interactions shape life, and storage, central to modern economies, governance, and daily communication. While businesses and governments benefit from access to personal data, individuals have fundamental rights that protect their privacy and control over their information. These rights are enshrined in other important consent, access, and security data. At the same time, individuals bear certain responsibilities in safeguarding their data, making informed decisions, and understanding how their digital footprint affects their privacy.

Understanding Individual Rights in Data Protection

Modern data protection laws are designed for information. The following key rights are outlined in various global regulations, including GDPR, CCPA, and other regional frameworks:

Right to Be Informed

Processed, stored, shared. Privacy policies detailing: Whether the data is shared with third parties. Many countries require businesses to disclose their data practices to users, rather than hiding critical information in complex legal terms (Di Minin et al, 2021).

Right to Consent and Withdraw Consent

A fundamental Under GDPR similar regulations, explicit and informed: Consent must be freely given, without coercion. Users should be able to opt in rather than being automatically included in data collection. There must be a clear mechanism. For example, websites must provide users with clear options to accept or reject cookies, and social media platforms must allow users to modify privacy settings regarding data collection and targeted advertising.

Right to Access and Portability

Stored and copies of their Under GDPR's users: Obtain (e.g., switching one cloud storage provider to another without losing files). This right promotes data ownership, preventing companies from unfairly restricting access to user-generated data.

Right to Rectification

If an individual's incorrect This is particularly important in: Financial records, where errors could affect credit scores. Medical records, where incorrect data could impact treatment (Gray et al, 2021). Employment records, where inaccuracies could lead to misrepresentation. Timely corrections data accuracy is maintained.

Right to Object to Data Processing

Users data specific: (e.g., receiving unsolicited emails or phone calls). Automated decision-making (e.g., AI-driven credit scoring or job application filtering). Profiling based on personal data may lead to discrimination. Organizations exercise this right and stop processing their data upon request.

Right to Lodge Complaints and Seek Redress

- Authority (DPA). Misuse personal. Request compensation damages caused by data breaches or privacy violations. Individual Responsibilities in Data Protection: While regulations grant individuals significant rights, they also bear responsibilities for ensuring their privacy and security. Some key responsibilities include:
- Managing Privacy Settings: Individuals should actively: Email accounts and cloud storage services. Mobile applications and smart devices. For example, limiting location tracking and third-party data sharing can reduce exposure to unnecessary data collection (Liang et al, 2022).
- Being Cautious with Data Sharing: Many cyber threats arise from oversharing personal information online.

To minimize risk,

- Avoid sharing on public platforms. When filling out online forms that request unnecessary personal data.
- Verify the legitimacy of websites and applications before providing information.
- Use Strong Passwords and Security Measures
- Use unique, complex (MFA) whenever updating passwords to avoid easily guessed information (e.g., birthdates, common words).
- Recognizing and Avoiding Scams: Phishing and social engineering attacks exploit individuals' lack of awareness. To stay safe: suspicious Verify requests for personal information by contacting companies directly. Stay informed about common cyber threats and investment fraud.
- Keeping Devices and Software Updated: Regular updates help protect against malware and security vulnerabilities. Individuals should: Enable automatic software updates. Install security patches for operating systems and applications.
- Use reliable antivirus and anti-malware software. Exercising Caution with Public Wi-Fi: Public making personal data interception.

Best practices include: Using a VPN (Virtual Private Network) when avoiding online shopping networks. Disabling automatic connections to prevent unintentional exposure (Wylde et al, 2022).

The Future of Individual Data Rights and Responsibilities

As technology advances, new challenges in data protection continue to emerge.

BEST PRACTICES FOR PERSONAL DATA SECURITY: PASSWORD MANAGEMENT, ENCRYPTION, AND MORE

In an increasingly digital world, protecting personal data is more critical than ever. From social media accounts and banking details to private emails and confidential documents, personal information is constantly at cyberattacks, using various methods, including social engineering, to steal sensitive data. To mitigate these threats, individuals must adopt strong cybersecurity practices, including password management, encryption, secure browsing, and proactive monitoring. This guide explores personal offering practical steps for your identity and privacy.

Strong Password Management: The First Line of Defense

Passwords are the most common method of authentication, yet they are also the weakest link in cybersecurity. Weak or reused passwords make it easier for hackers to gain and data breaches.

Best Practices for Password Security:

- Use Strong and Unique Passwords at least 12–16 characters long. A mix of uppercase and lowercase letters, numbers, and special characters. Not based on guessed (Omotunde H., et al, 2023). Example of a strong password: J8d#6!2pX@Y$3zK.
- Enable Multi-Factor Authentication (MFA): password (OTP): verification (fingerprint or facial recognition). An authentication app (e.g., Google Authenticator, Authy). Even if a hacker obtains MFA they gain too.
- Use a Password Manager: stores auto-fills differently, ensuring that each account has a unique and strong password. Popular password managers include: Bitwarden, 1Password, LastPass, and Dashlane.
- Avoid Common Password Mistakes: Do not reuse if others become vulnerable. Do not share passwords with anyone, even trusted friends or family.

Encryption: Protecting Data from Unauthorized Access: This protects users, intercepted (Abid et al, 2022). Use a VPN (Virtual Private Network): personal hackers, especially on public Wi-Fi networks. Some reputable VPN services include: NordVPN, ExpressVPN, and ProtonVPN.

Safe Browsing Practices

Avoiding Phishing and Malware: Recognizing and Avoiding Phishing Attacks

Signs of phishing include: Emails or messages with urgent requests (e.g., "Your account will be locked unless you act now!"). Links to suspicious websites with misspelled domains (e.g., "amaz0n.com" instead of "amazon.com"). Attachments that request you to enter passwords or download unknown files.

How to Stay Safe Online

Website before entering sensitive data. Use ad blocker anti-phishing browser extensions, such as uBlock Origin or Privacy Badger. Keep browsers updated to patch security vulnerabilities (Kaur et al, 2022).

Secure Cloud Storage and Backups: Why Backups Are Essential

Backing up data ensures that important files can be restored in case of: Ransomware attacks, where hackers encrypt files and demand payment. Device failure or accidental deletion.

Best Practices for Secure Backups

Use encrypted external hard drives for offline backups. Store data on reliable cloud services with strong security measures. Enable automatic backups to prevent data loss. Recommended cloud backup services: Back blaze iDrive Google Drive (with two-factor authentication enabled)

Protecting Personal Data on Mobile Devices

Smartphones prime cyberattacks.

How to Secure Mobile Devices

Enable screen lock with a strong password, PIN, or biometric authentication. Be cautious with app permissions—only grant access to necessary features. Use anti-theft tools.

Monitoring and Responding to Data Breaches

Check if Your Data Has Been Compromised Use tools (https://haveibeenpwned.com/) email or password leaked (Chhetri et al, 2022).

ORGANIZATIONAL RESPONSIBILITIES: DATA PROTECTION BY DESIGN AND DEFAULT

In today's digital economy, data protection is a fundamental responsibility. Regulatory frameworks like organizations strong individuals' A critical principle embedded in these regulations is Data Protection which privacy operations transparency, and compliance are core components of business operations, risks, and regulatory penalties. The article explores outlining organizational responsibilities, and key implementation compliance while maintaining trust with customers and stakeholders.

Understanding Data Protection by Design and Default: What is Data Protection by Design?

Refers to integrating privacy and security principles into an organization's systems, processes, and technologies from the very beginning. Instead of applying privacy controls reactively, organizations must embed security measures into product development, IT infrastructure, and operational policies (Cavoukian, 2021). CCPA and CPRA mandate similar principles, requiring businesses to limit data collection and provide greater transparency in handling personal information. Other privacy laws, such as Brazil's LGPD, Canada's PIPEDA, and India's DPDP Act, align with these principles, reinforcing global expectations for responsible data management.

Organizational Responsibilities in Implementing Data Protection by Design and Default

Minimizing Data Collection and Processing

Organizations must ensure that they collect only the data that is strictly necessary for their business operations. This involves: Conducting projects or processing and Implementing data minimization strategies to limit unnecessary data collection. Pseudonymized whenever possible.

Ensuring Secure Data Storage and Access Controls

Organizations must securely store personal data and or process Key security measures include: transmission. Employees. Embedding Privacy in Software and Systems: Organizations developing websites, applications, and digital services must incorporate privacy-enhancing technologies from the outset. This includes: Designing systems that automatically delete outdated user data instead of retaining it indefinitely (Haque A K M B., et al, 2021). Offering privacy-focused default settings that protect users rather than requiring them to opt-in for better security. Implementing).

Case Studies: Organizations Implementing Data Protection by Design and Default

Case Study 1: Apple's Privacy-Focused Approach

Apple has set a high standard for privacy by integrating Data Protection by Design into its products. Examples include: App Tracking Transparency (ATT): Which requires user consent before apps can track their data. End-to-end encryption: Applied to iMessage and FaceTime, conversations. On-device processing: Minimizes data sent to Apple's servers, reducing privacy risks (Yeung K., et al, 2022).

Case Study 2: Google's Privacy Enhancements

Google has implemented various Data Protection by Default measures, such as: Auto-deleting user data after 18 months (by default) for new accounts. Giving users control over ad personalization and data collection settings. Providing transparency tools like "My Activity," where users can review and delete their stored data.

The Consequences of Non-Compliance

Implement protection by Design and Default faces significant risks, including Legal Penalties and Fines: GDPR, CCPA, and other privacy laws can result in hefty fines. GDPR violations can lead to fines of annual. CCPA to $7,500. Global regulators are increasingly imposing penalties for data privacy failures.

Data Breaches and Reputational Damage

Organizations that fail to implement strong security measures often suffer high-profile data breaches. Consequences include:

1. Loss of customer trust, leading to decreased revenue.
2. Legal actions and lawsuits from affected users.
3. Operational disruptions due to cybersecurity incidents (Andrew J., et al, 2021).

DATA GOVERNANCE AND RISK MANAGEMENT: STRATEGIES FOR PROTECTING SENSITIVE DATA

In an era where data governance and risk management have become and compliance must ensure that sensitive data—ranging from and is properly managed, secured, and protected from breaches, leaks, and misuse. Effective data governance frameworks not only regulate CCPA, but also cyber threats, and operational inefficiencies. This article explores the key principles essential for protecting across industries.

Understanding Data Governance and Risk Management: What is Data Governance?

Processes, standards, and technologies ensure disposed of securely, ethically, and efficiently. It establishes who is responsible for data, how it is accessed, and how it is protected (Viljoen, 2021). A strong data governance framework ensures that data integrity: is consistent. Data security: Sensitive is protected against cyber threats. Data transparency: Employees understand how data is used and managed.

What is Risk Management in Data Protection? Sensitive data.

This includes:

- Cybersecurity risks (hacking, malware, phishing, ransomware).

- Insider threats (employees misusing or mishandling data).
- Operational risks (loss due to system failures or human errors).

A well-defined risk management strategy helps organizations minimize the likelihood.

Key Principles of Effective Data Governance

To build a data governance framework, organizations must focus on the following core principles:

Data Classification and Sensitivity Levels

Not all data carries the same level of risk. Such as

- Public data (low risk): Marketing materials, and public reports.
- Internal data (moderate risk): Internal communications, operational data.
- Confidential data (high risk): Employee records, financial statements.
- Restricted data (critical risk): Personal customer information (PII), trade secrets, and medical records. By categorizing data properly, implement risk levels.

Data Ownership and Accountability

Every piece of data within an organization should have an assigned data owner or steward responsible for its:

- Security (implementing proper access controls).
- Compliance (ensuring data handling aligns with regulatory requirements) (Calder A., et al, 2024).

Developing an Incident Response Plan (IRP)

- No security system is 100% breach-proof. Ensures the organization's impact of a data breach. Key elements include:
- Immediate detection and containment (blocking malicious activity).
- Notification protocols (alerting affected individuals and regulatory bodies).
- Post-incident review to strengthen security measures.

- Employee Training and Awareness Programs: Data organizations conduct: Regular cybersecurity training on phishing, malware, and data handling. Simulated cyberattack exercises to test employee readiness.

Strict Data-Handling Policies to Prevent Accidental Data Exposure.

- Third-Party Risk Management: cloud providers, and contractors that handle sensitive data (Arigbabu et al, 2024). To reduce third-party risks: Conduct vendor security assessments before sharing data. Require strong data protection agreements (DPAs) with vendors. Monitor third-party access and enforce regular security audits.
- Regulatory Compliance and Best Practices: protection avoids penalties.
- Key Data Protection Regulations: GDPR (Europe): Requires organizations to implement strong security controls and provide users with data access rights.
- CCPA/CPRA (California): Grants consumers control over their data. HIPAA (U.S.): Protects healthcare data privacy and security. PCI-DSS: transactions.
- Best Practices for Ensuring Compliance: Implement privacy by design (integrate security into products and services from the start).
- Conduct regular compliance audits to identify gaps (Shahid et al, 2022).

INCIDENT RESPONSE AND BREACH NOTIFICATION

Introduction

Digital cybersecurity incidents for organizations of all sizes. Whether caused by malicious cyberattacks, insider threats, or system vulnerabilities, security breaches are devastating and legal liabilities. Well-structured and breach notifications contain threats, HIPAA, and PCI-DSS. This article outlines best practices for incident response and breach notification, covering preparation, detection, containment, communication, remediation, and compliance to help organizations effectively manage security incidents.

Understanding Incident Response and Breach Notification: What is Incident Response?

Systematic management, recover from The goal is to structure (IRP) quickly and efficiently threats.

What is Breach Notification?

Breach notification refers to the legal and ethical obligation to inform affected parties when a security incident results in the compromise of sensitive data (Verstraete M., et al, 2021). Regulatory frameworks like GDPR, CCPA, and HIPAA customers, within specified timeframes after detecting a breach.

Containment

- Best practices include:
- Isolating affected systems (disconnect compromised devices from the network).
- Disabling compromised accounts to prevent unauthorized access.
- Blocking domains.
- Applying patches and updates to vulnerable systems (Shinde N., et al, 2021).

Best Practices for Breach Notification

Breach notify the customer and comply with legal obligations.

Compliance with Data Protection Regulations

Organizations must adhere to legal breach notification requirements, including GDPR (EU) – Requires notification within 72 hours of detecting a breach affecting EU citizens. CCPA (California) – Mandates timely disclosure to affected consumers and regulators. HIPAA (U.S.) – Requires notification within 60 days for healthcare data breaches. PCI-DSS – Requires immediate action for breaches involving credit card information. Key Steps in Breach Notification: Assess the Impact: Determine what data was compromised and how many individuals were affected (Althobaiti et al, 2021).

Identify Legal Obligations

Regulatory Adherence: **Prepare an Incident Report**. Document breach details, including the cause, timeline, and containment measures.

Notify Affected Individuals

Provide clear, concise information on what happened, potential risks, and recommended actions.

Communicate with Regulators

Submit required reports to data protection authorities.

Engage with the Media (If Necessary)

Issue a transparent statement to manage public relations and minimize reputational damage.

Craft an Effective Breach Notification Message

A well-crafted breach notification should include:

- A clear explanation of what happened.
- The type of data compromised (e.g., names, credit card details, passwords).
- The potential risks to affected individuals.
- Steps taken by the organization to address the breach.
- Advice for affected individuals, such as password changes or fraud monitoring (Staves et al, 2022).

EMERGING TRENDS IN DATA PROTECTION: BLOCKCHAIN, AI, AND IOT

Introduction

The rapid volume and complexity of data are growing at an unprecedented rate. Like blockchain, organizations face new new in privacy, and security. These are crucial data protection strategies, offering innovative solutions for securing sensitive information and ensuring global cyberattacks. This article explores how blockchain, AI, and IoT are transforming data protection, highlighting their benefits, and challenges.

Blockchain for Data Protection: What is Blockchain?

Securely and transparently nodes. Leveraged for protection, identity management, and secure transactions.

How Blockchain Enhances Data Security: Decentralization

Unlike centralized databases that can be targeted by hackers, blockchain stores data across a network of nodes, reducing points Encryption and Cryptographic Hashing: Blockchain employs strong.

Smart Contracts:

Automated self-executing contracts enhance security by enforcing rules and conditions without intermediaries, reducing human error and fraud risks.

Use Cases of Blockchain in Data Protection

Healthcare

Storage of electronic health records (EHRs) while ensuring patient privacy and compliance with HIPAA (Alharbi et al., 2022). AI-driven fraud detection and risk assessment in banking and credit transactions. AI-powered patient data anonymization and HIPAA-compliant privacy controls.

Enterprise Security

AI-enhanced firewalls and intrusion detection systems (IDS) for corporate networks.

Cloud Security

AI-based security monitoring for cloud environments to detect misconfigurations and vulnerabilities.

Challenges of AI in Data Protection

Bias and Ethical Concerns

AI models can unintentionally discriminate if trained on biased datasets, leading to ethical issues in data privacy.

Adversarial Attacks

Cybercriminals can manipulate AI algorithms using poisoned data to bypass security systems.

Data Privacy Risks

AI requires large amounts.

The Internet of Things (IoT) and Data Security: What is IoT?

A connected collect, process, and transmit over includes smart home industrial healthcare autonomous vehicles. While IoT enhances convenience introduces cybersecurity.

How IoT Affects Data Protection

Increased Attack Surface

Cybercriminals to exploit.

Weak Authentication and Default Passwords

Many credentials, making them targets for hacking.

Lack of Encryption

Some IoT devices transmit data in plain text, exposing sensitive information to eavesdropping.

Supply Chain Risks

Vulnerabilities in third-party IoT components can compromise entire networks (Hemamalini et al, 2024).

Best Practices for IoT Data Security

Strong Authentication

(MFA) unique passwords for IoT devices.

Firmware and Software Updates

Regularly update IoT firmware.

Network Segmentation

Isolate IoT devices from critical business systems to limit potential breaches.

IoT Security Standards

Follow industry frameworks like NIST's IoT cybersecurity guidelines.

Use Cases of IoT Security

Smart Cities

Securing connected infrastructure, including traffic systems and surveillance cameras.

Healthcare IoT

Protecting medical devices like pacemakers and remote monitoring systems.

Industrial IoT (IIoT)

Preventing cyber threats in manufacturing, logistics, and energy sectors.

Challenges of IoT in Data Protection

Device Heterogeneity

A lack of standardization across IoT devices makes security implementation difficult.

Data Overload

IoT generates massive volumes of data, requiring robust storage and security solutions.

Regulatory Compliance

Many IoT manufacturers do not fully comply with data protection laws, leading to security risks (Nair M M., et al, 2023).

THE ROLE OF ARTIFICIAL INTELLIGENCE IN DATA PROTECTION

Introduction

Modern vast expansion collection, storage, and processing has heightened Organizations across industries dealing with increasingly sophisticated cyber threats, regulatory compliance requirements, and the challenges of managing vast amounts of sensitive information. To address these issues, powerful tool data protection, automated security responses, and enhanced privacy controls. However, while AI presents significant opportunities for strengthening cybersecurity measures, it also introduces ethical, legal, and technical challenges. AI-driven security systems must be carefully implemented to prevent bias, privacy violations, and adversarial attacks that could compromise data protection rather than enhance it (Murdoch, 2021). This article explores AI in protection, cybersecurity, and privacy management, examining how AI-driven solutions are while addressing key concerns that arise from its adoption. Isolate compromised systems immediately upon detecting a breach. Block malicious IP addresses and domains before they infiltrate networks. Initiate forensic investigations to assess the scope and impact of security incidents. Automate software patching and vulnerability management to reduce exposure: Federated Learning – without exposing sensitive information (Aldoseri et al, 2023).

Challenges

Risks and Limitations of AI in Data Protection

While offers substantial benefits and risks organizations: Bias and Ethical Concerns in AI Models: AI models can inadvertently discriminate if trained on biased datasets, leading to ethical concerns in data protection. Biased algorithms can disproportionately flag certain user groups as security risks. AI-driven surveillance systems may violate privacy rights if improperly deployed. Automated decision-making in security protocols can result in false accusations or unfair access restrictions. To mitigate bias, organizations must ensure representative fairness and transparency.

Adversarial Attacks on AI Security Systems

Cybercriminals can manipulate AI-driven security solutions using adversarial machine learning techniques, such as Poisoning AI models with misleading data to bypass detection systems. Generating adversarial examples (e.g., modifying malware signatures to evade AI-based antivirus programs) (Aung Y Y M., et al, 2021).

Comply with global data protection regulations by embedding privacy safeguards into AI systems.

Lack of Explainability and Transparency ("Black Box" AI)

Many AI-driven cybersecurity solutions "black boxes,": verify driven security decisions. Hinder accountability. Erode users. To overcome challenges, organizations should prioritize Explainable AI (XAI), ensuring that security professionals and auditors can understand how AI models reach their conclusions (Bécue et al, 2021).

QUANTUM COMPUTING AND DATA PROTECTION

Introduction

Digital, quantum computing is emerging as both an opportunity and a challenge for data protection. Binary use of that capability allows complex calculations exponentially even available today. While quantum computing holds tremendous potential for scientific research, optimization problems, and artificial intelligence, serious modern data, encryption, and cybersecurity. Many encryption (Elliptic Curve Cryptography), Diffie-Hellman, break encryption standards within seconds. Given the implications for data privacy, cybersecurity, and regulatory compliance, organizations and governments post-security era. The article explores the vulnerabilities it exposes and the strategies required for encryption cybersecurity threats.

The Impact of Quantum Computing on Data Protection: How Quantum Computing Threatens Encryption

Modern techniques within timeframe (Abdikhakimov, 2024). Massive Decryption Capabilities: Sensitive data, including banking transactions, healthcare records, government secrets, and personal communications, could be decrypted once quantum computing reaches maturity. "Harvest Now, Decrypt Later" Attacks: Cybercriminals or state actors might steal encrypted data today, storing it for future decryption when quantum computers become powerful enough (Jowarder R A., et al, 2024).

Threat to Blockchain and Cryptocurrencies

Blockchain technology, which relies on cryptographic hash functions and digital signatures, could be compromised by quantum attacks.

Preparing for the Post-Quantum Era: Strategies for Future-Proofing Data Protection

Transitioning to Quantum-Resistant Cryptography (Post-Quantum Cryptography – PQC): counteract threats, organizations which involve developing encryption even presence computers. Uses quantum entanglement and Heisenberg's Uncertainty Principle to detect eavesdropping attempts (Malina et al, 2021). Ensures that any interception of data destroys the quantum state, alerting users to security breaches. Is already being tested in secure military and government communications. Leading organizations and governments are investing in QKD to secure sensitive communications against future quantum threats.

Hybrid Cryptographic Approaches

Since the transition to full quantum-resistant encryption will take time, a hybrid cryptographic approach can provide security in the interim. This involves: Combining classical cryptographic methods with PQC algorithms to ensure backward compatibility. Implementing stronger symmetric encryption (e.g., AES-256) to mitigate potential vulnerabilities. Using hardware modules (HSMs) layers.

Developing Quantum-Resistant Security Standards

Governments and cybersecurity agencies must collaborate to: Establish new regulatory frameworks for quantum-resistant encryption. Encourage global adoption of PQC standards across industries (How M L., et al, 2023). To prepare for the quantum era, businesses should: Stay informed about NIST's post-quantum cryptography standards. Begin testing and implementing PQC algorithms in critical systems. Invest in communications. Adopt hybrid approaches to transition smoothly. Collaborate with cybersecurity experts to develop quantum-resistant security policies. While quantum computing's full potential is still years away, the risks to data protection are imminent. Organizations that act now to embrace quantum-resistant security measures safeguard sensitivity, ensuring compliance resilience in the face of the quantum revolution.

THE IMPORTANCE OF PERSONAL DATA PRIVACY AND SECURITY IN THE DIGITAL AGE

Introduction

Landscape, personal commodities. As individuals interact with digital platforms—whether through social media, online banking, e-commerce, or cloud-based services—an immense amount includes sensitive details such as financial transactions, health records, location history, biometric data, and online behaviors. While this digital transformation offers unparalleled convenience, connectivity, and innovation, it also exposes individuals to privacy risks, cyber threats, identity theft, and mass surveillance (Rawas, 2024). Customer insights and behavioral analytics to improve user experience. AI and machine learning algorithms predictive decision-making. However, this monetization personally raises a lack of transparency in how personal: User consent issues, where individuals unknowingly agree to extensive data tracking. Potential misuse or sale of personal data without individuals' knowledge. ProHigh-profile cyberattacks have exposed intimate user data, leading to public backlash and lawsuits (Paul et al, 2023). California Consumer Privacy Act (CCPA) (United States): Provides greater control Allows users to opt out of sales request data deletion. Requires businesses to disclose how they collect and use personal data.

Other Global Regulations

China's Personal Information Protection Law (PIPL)

Introduces and rules.

Brazil's LGPD (Lei Geral de Proteção de Dados)

To enhance privacy rights for Brazilian citizens.

India's Digital Personal Data Protection Act (DPDP)

Strengthens protection rules for companies handling Indian citizens' data. As regulatory scrutiny increases, businesses must adapt by implementing protection.

Best Practices for Personal Data Privacy and Security

Both must enhance data security and minimize privacy risks.

Best Practices for Individuals

Use Strong, Unique Passwords and Multi-Factor Authentication (MFA)

Enable two-factor authentication (2FA) for sensitive accounts.

Limit Data Sharing and Adjust Privacy Settings

Review and modify social media and app permissions to restrict data access. Be cautious when sharing personal information online (e.g., location data, birthdate) (Gawer, 2022). Challenges and Innovations so do the challenges and innovations in data privacy (Wan et al, 2024). Key future trends include:

- AI and Machine Learning in Data Protection – for anomaly analysis.
- Decentralized Identity and Blockchain-Based Privacy Solutions – Reducing reliance on centralized databases vulnerable to breaches.
- Quantum-Resistant Encryption – Preparing for quantum computing threats to encryption. While these advancements offer enhanced security mechanisms, the ongoing battle between cybercriminals, regulators, and technology companies will shape the future of data privacy.

RECOMMENDATIONS FOR INDIVIDUALS AND ORGANIZATIONS

Introduction

Personal data has become a necessity rather than a choice. With the growing reliance on digital platforms for banking, shopping, communication, and professional activities, both individuals and. Cybercriminals continue to exploit vulnerabilities in weak passwords, unsecured networks, outdated software, and phishing tactics, leading to massive data leaks and financial fraud.

- Create at least 12–16 characters long (Tursunbayeva et al, 2022).
- Enable Multi-Factor Authentication (MFA): or biometric authentication where possible.
- Prefer hardware security keys or authentication apps like Google Authenticator instead of SMS-based 2FA.

- Limit Personal Data Sharing: Minimize sharing of location, birth date, and financial details on social media.
- Review app and website permissions—deny unnecessary data access.
- Use Privacy-Focused Browsers and Search Engines: Prefer Brave, Firefox, or DuckDuckGo instead of data-tracking browsers.
- Block trackers with extensions like uBlock Origin or Privacy Badger (Ma, 2021).
- Encrypt Sensitive Files and Communications: Encrypt important files using BitLocker, VeraCrypt, or File Vault.
- Recognizing and Preventing Cyber Threats: Avoid Phishing and Social Engineering Attacks: Don't click on suspicious emails or links—verify sender authenticity. Be cautious of urgent requests for financial or personal information.

Secure Data with Encryption and Access Controls

Implement Zero Trust Security Framework

Verify every user device before granting access. Require continuous authentication using behavioral analysis and MFA.

Enhancing Employee Security Awareness and Training

Regular Cybersecurity Training for Employees

Conduct mandatory security awareness programs. Train employees on identifying phishing emails and social engineering tactics.

Implement Strong Internal Security Policies

Require password rotation and MFA for employee accounts. Restrict USB usage and external device connections on company networks (Rachmad, 2024).

Conduct Regular Security Audits and Penetration Testing

Perform annual assessments. Use simulated cyberattacks and strengthen defenses.

Securing Cloud and Third-Party Services

Adopt Secure Cloud Storage and Backup Policies

Store sensitive data in encrypted cloud environments. Implement regular automated backups to prevent data loss. Establish an incident response team (IRT). Define containment, recovery, and communication strategies.

Ensure Compliance with Breach Notification Laws

Report breaches within 72 hours (per GDPR requirements). Notify affected users promptly and provide mitigation guidance.

Regularly Test Data Recovery and Disaster Preparedness

Conduct cyberattack simulation drills. Ensure backups are tested and retrievable during crises (Kickbusch et al, 2021).

Future Considerations

Adapting to Emerging Cybersecurity Threats

AI-powered threat detection can identify anomalies and prevent attacks in real-time. Automated security tools reduce reliance on manual threat analysis.

EPILOGUE: THE FUTURE OF PERSONAL DATA PRIVACY AND SECURITY—CHALLENGES, OPPORTUNITIES, AND RESPONSIBILITIES

Meanwhile, policymakers must continue refining data protection laws innovations. This epilogue explores the challenges, opportunities, and responsibilities that will shape the future of personnel highlighting what made a safer digital world for all (Liu et al, 2022). The rise of big data analytics, facial recognition, and AI-powered surveillance raises serious concerns: Companies use behavioral tracking and profiling to influence consumer decisions. Governments implement mass surveillance programs in the name of national security, sometimes infringing on personal privacy rights. AI algorithms discrimination and privacy violations. Balancing data-driven innovation with ethical considerations in coming years. Lack of Global Standardization in Privacy Regulations: While regulations like GDPR (EU), CCPA (California), PIPL

(China), and LGPD (Brazil) have improved data protection laws, the lack of a universal data privacy framework creates inconsistencies: Cross-border data transfers remain complex and legally challenging (Admass et al, 2024). More people are recognizing the importance of digital privacy: Privacy-focused movements like "The Right to Be Forgotten" are gaining traction. Consumers are demanding more transparency from companies about data usage. Governments are responding with stronger enforcement of privacy laws. As awareness grows, individuals will demand pushing business policymakers toward better standards (Prodinger B., et al, 2023). Promote global cooperation on cybersecurity and data privacy standards (VanLeeuwen et al, 2021). Rising cyber threats, AI surveillance, lack of global regulation. Opportunities: AI-driven security, privacy-enhancing tech, blockchain solutions. Responsibilities: Individuals must protect their data, businesses must enforce security policies, and governments must refine privacy laws. By embracing innovation, responsibility, and data future where privacy security is not sacrificed for convenience, ensuring a trusted and resilient digital ecosystem for generations to come.

CONCLUSION

Personal have required a collective effort from individuals, organizations, and governments. Digital platforms, blockchain, personally collected, processed. While these technological advancements offer unprecedented convenience and efficiency, they also expose individuals and businesses to cyber espionage and financial fraud. Both individuals and security to protect sensitive information. At the individual level, users must take ownership of their digital privacy by implementing password managers, encrypted communication channels, and privacy-enhancing tools like VPNs and secure browsers. The rise of phishing attacks, ransomware, and AI-driven social engineering necessitates greater vigilance and education on cybersecurity best practices. Additionally, as data protection regulations CCPA, and PIPL greater control information, people must exercise their rights by managing consent preferences, restricting unnecessary data sharing, and understanding how their data is used by companies. Raising awareness of privacy is to digital vulnerabilities. At the organizational level, businesses and institutions must ensure the privacy components of their systems and operations. Robust cybersecurity strategies, including advanced encryption methods, zero-trust security models, AI-driven threat detection, and continuous vulnerability assessments, are essential to safeguarding customer and employee data. Organizations are global and regional to prevent legal reputational consequences. Cybersecurity awareness training for employees, incident response planning, and third-party vendor risk management are key measures in reducing the likelihood of breaches. Additionally, ethical considerations surrounding data collection, processing, and AI-driven decision-making must be prioritized to maintain public trust. Despite growing efforts to enhance cybersecurity, emerging threats such as quantum computing, deepfake fraud, and large-scale AI-powered attacks pose new challenges. The lack of a unified global privacy framework further complicates cross-border data transfers and regulatory compliance. Governments must step up by enforcing stricter data protection regulations, promoting international cooperation, investing in cybersecurity research, and developing quantum-resistant encryption standards to prepare for future risks. The ethical implications of mass surveillance, biometric data collection, and AI-driven profiling must also be addressed through transparent policies and legal safeguards to protect individual rights and prevent data exploitation. personal privacy and how effectively individuals, organizations, and policymakers collaborate to create a secure digital ecosystem. A multi-stakeholder approach is necessary, where individuals exercise greater control over their data, businesses integrate privacy-first strategies into their operations, and governments establish stronger legal frameworks and cybersecurity initiatives. By fostering a privacy-conscious digital culture, leveraging cutting-edge security technologies, and advocating for ethical data governance, we technological personal data protection. conclusion, personal data security interconnected. The responsibility lies with everyone—individuals must stay informed and take proactive security measures, organizations must build secure systems and comply with regulations, and governments must create robust policies to enforce privacy rights. Only through collective action, technological advancements, and continuous vigilance can we ensure a trusted, privacy-centric digital future that safeguards sensitive data while enabling innovation and progress.

REFERENCES

Abdikhakimov I, (2024). "Preparing for a Quantum Future: Strategies for Strengthening International Data Privacy in the Face of Evolving Technologies". International Journal of Law and Policy.

Abid, A., Cheikhrouhou, S., Kallel, S., & Jmaiel, M. (2022). NovidChain: Blockchain-based privacy-preserving platform for COVID-19 test/vaccine certificates. *Software, Practice & Experience*, *52*(12), 2551–2566. DOI: 10.1002/spe.2983 PMID: 34226768

Admass W S, Munaye Y Y, Diro A A, (2024). "Cyber security: State of the art, challenges and future directions". Cyber Security and Applications, 1-18. Doi: .DOI: 10.1016/j.csap.2023.100101

Aldoseri, A., Al-Khalifa, K. N., & Hamouda, A. M. (2023). Re-thinking data strategy and integration for artificial intelligence: Concepts, opportunities, and challenges. *Applied Sciences (Basel, Switzerland)*, *13*(11), 1–24. DOI: 10.3390/app13127082

Alharbi, S., Attiah, A., & Alghazzawi, D. (2022). Integrating blockchain with artificial intelligence to secure IoT networks: Future trends. *Sustainability (Basel)*, *14*(11), 1–18. DOI: 10.3390/su142316002

Almulihi, A. H., Alassery, F., Khan, A. I., & Shukla, S. (2022). Analyzing the Implications of Healthcare Data Breaches through Computational Technique. *Automation & Soft Computing*, *11*(2), 1–12. DOI: 10.32604/iasc.2022.023460

Althobaiti, K., Jenkins, A. D. G., & Vaniea, K. (2021). A case study of phishing incident response in an educational organization. *Proceedings of the ACM on Human-Computer Interaction*, *5*(1), 1–27. DOI: 10.1145/3476079

Andrew, J., & Baker, M. (2021). The general data protection regulation in the age of surveillance capitalism. *Journal of Business Ethics*, *168*(2), 257–272. DOI: 10.1007/s10551-019-04239-z

Arigbabu A T, Olaniyi O O, Adigwe C S, (2024). "Data governance in AI-enabled healthcare systems: A case of the project nightingale". Asian Journal of Business Ethics.

Aung, Y. Y. M., Wong, D. C. S., & Ting, D. S. W. (2021). The promise of artificial intelligence: A review of the opportunities and challenges of artificial intelligence in healthcare. *British Medical Bulletin*, *139*(1), 55–66. DOI: 10.1093/bmb/ldab016 PMID: 34405854

Bachura, E., Valecha, R., & Rao, H. R. (2022). The OPM data breach: An investigation of shared emotional reactions on Twitter. *Management Information Systems Quarterly*, *46*(2), 1–15. DOI: 10.25300/MISQ/2022/15596

Bécue, A., Praça, I., & Gama, J. (2021). Artificial intelligence, cyber-threats and Industry 4.0: Challenges and opportunities. *Artificial Intelligence Review*, *54*(2), 1517–1543. DOI: 10.1007/s10462-020-09942-2

Birch, K., Cochrane, D. T., & Ward, C. (2021). Data as asset? The measurement, governance, and valuation of digital personal data by Big Tech. *Big Data & Society*, *8*(1), 1–16. DOI: 10.1177/20539517211017308

Calder A, Watkins S, (2024). "IT governance: an international guide to data security and ISO 27001/ISO 27002".

Cavoukian, A. (2021). *Privacy by design: The seven foundational principles*. IAPP Resource Center.

Chhetri, T. R., Kurteva, A., DeLong, R. J., Hilscher, R., Korte, K., & Fensel, A. (2022). Data protection by design tool for automated GDPR compliance verification based on semantically modeled informed consent. *Sensors (Basel)*, *22*(11), 1–25. DOI: 10.3390/s22072763 PMID: 35408377

Di Minin, E., Fink, C., Hausmann, A., Kremer, J., & Kulkarni, R. (2021). How to address data privacy concerns when using social media data in conservation science. *Conservation Biology*, *35*(4), 1074–1084. DOI: 10.1111/cobi.13708 PMID: 33749044

Fakeyede, O. G., Okeleke, P. A., & Hassan, A. O. (2023). Navigating data privacy through IT audits: GDPR, CCPA, and beyond. *Journal of Research*, *12*(3), 1–15. DOI: 10.1016/j.jr.2023.02.001

Gawer, A. (2022). Digital platforms and ecosystems: Remarks on the dominant organizational forms of the digital age. *Innovation (North Sydney, N.S.W.)*, *25*(1), 1–15. DOI: 10.1080/14479338.2021.1965888

Gray, C. M., Santos, C., Bielova, N., & Toth, M. (2021). "Dark patterns and the legal requirements of consent banners: An interaction criticism perspective". *Proceedings of the 2021 CHI Conference on Human Factors in Computing Systems*. DOI: 10.1145/3411764.3445779

Guay, R., & Birch, K. (2022). A comparative analysis of data governance: Socio-technical imaginaries of digital personal data in the USA and EU (2008–2016). *Big Data & Society*, *9*(2), 20539517221112925. DOI: 10.1177/20539517221112925

Haque, A. K. M. B., Islam, A. K. M. N., Hyrynsalmi, S., Naqvi, B., & Smolander, K. (2021). GDPR compliant blockchains–a systematic literature review. *IEEE Access : Practical Innovations, Open Solutions*, *9*, 129494–129514. DOI: 10.1109/ACCESS.2021.3069877

Hemamalini, V., Mishra, A. K., & Tyagi, A. K. (2024). Artificial intelligence–blockchain-enabled–internet of things-based cloud applications for next-generation society. *Journal of Software (Malden, MA)*. DOI: 10.1002/smr.2406

How, M. L., & Cheah, S. M. (2023). Business Renaissance: Opportunities and challenges at the dawn of the Quantum Computing Era. *Businesses*, *3*(2), 1–18. DOI: 10.3390/businesses3040036

Jörke, M., Sefidgar, Y. S., Massachi, T., & Suh, J. (2023). "Pearl: A technology probe for machine-assisted reflection on personal data". *Proceedings of the 28th*. DOI: 10.1145/3581641.3584054

Jowarder, R. A., & Jahan, S. (2024). *Quantum computing in cyber security: Emerging threats, mitigation strategies, and future implications for data protection*. World Journal of Advanced Engineering and Technology.

Kaur, J., Hazrati Fard, S. M., Amiri-Zarandi, M., & Dara, R. (2022). Protecting farmers' data privacy and confidentiality: Recommendations and considerations. *Frontiers in Sustainable Food Systems*, *6*, 1–12. DOI: 10.3389/fsufs.2022.903230

Kickbusch, I., Piselli, D., Agrawal, A., Balicer, R., & Banner, O. (2021). "The Lancet and Financial Times Commission on governing health futures 2030: growing up in a digital world". The Lancet, 398(10298), 473-492. DOI: 10.1016/S0140-6736(21)00756-9

Liang, W., Yang, Y., Yang, C., Hu, Y., & Xie, S. (2022). PDPChain: A consortium blockchain-based privacy protection scheme for personal data. *IEEE Transactions on Industrial Informatics*, *18*(10), 7341–7350. DOI: 10.1109/TII.2022.3141409

Liu, X., Ahmad, S. F., Anser, M. K., Ke, J., Irshad, M., Ul-Haq, J., & Abbas, S. (2022). Cyber security threats: A never-ending challenge for e-commerce. *Frontiers in Psychology*, *2*, 1–12. DOI: 10.3389/fpsyg.2022.927398 PMID: 36337532

Ma, C. (2021). Smart city and cyber-security; technologies used, leading challenges and future recommendations. *Energy Reports*, *7*, 3359–3367. DOI: 10.1016/j.egyr.2021.08.124

Mahadev Madgule, N. (2023). Vinayaka, Yeshwant M. Sonkhaskar, Dhiren Ramanbhai Patel, R. Karthikeyan, P. Selvakumar,(2023). Mechanical properties and microstructure of activated TIG welded similar joints of Inconel alloys by desirability approaches. *Materials Today: Proceedings*, *77*, 528–533. DOI: 10.1016/j.matpr.2022.12.250

Malina, L., Dzurenda, P., Ricci, S., & Hajny, J. (2021). Post-quantum era privacy protection for intelligent infrastructures. *IEEE Transactions on Industrial Informatics*, *17*(4), 2556–2565. DOI: 10.1109/TII.2020.3031478

Mayer, P., Zou, Y., Schaub, F., & Aviv, A. J. (2021). ""Now I'm a bit {angry:}" Individuals' Awareness, Perception, and Responses to Data Breaches that Affected Them". 30th USENIX Security Symposium.DOI: 10.5555/3477114.3477123

Murdoch, B. (2021). Privacy and artificial intelligence: Challenges for protecting health information in a new era. *BMC Medical Ethics*, *22*(1), 1–11. DOI: 10.1186/s12910-021-00687-3 PMID: 34525993

Nair M M, Tyagi A K, (2023). "AI, IoT, blockchain, and cloud computing: The necessity of the future". Distributed Computing to Blockchain, 1-12. .DOI: 10.1016/B978-0-323-99243-5.00001-5

Omotunde, H., & Ahmed, M. (2023). A comprehensive review of security measures in database systems: Assessing authentication, access control, and beyond. *Mesopotamian Journal of CyberSecurity*, *4*(1), 1–20.

Oye, E., & Mitchell, N. (2022). "Future of Data Privacy Regulations Beyond CCPA". ResearchGate. DOI: 10.13140/RG.2.2.36055.75684

Paul, M., Maglaras, L., Ferrag, M. A., & Almomani, I. (2023). Digitization of healthcare sector: A study on privacy and security concerns. *ICT Express*, *9*(1), 1–12. DOI: 10.1016/j.icte.2023.02.007

Pazhohan, H. (2023). *Global Data Protection Standards: A Comparative Analysis of GDPR and Other International Privacy Laws*. Legal Studies in Digital Age., DOI: 10.5206/lsda.2023.1.1

Prodinger B, Neuhofer B, (2023). "Never-ending tourism: Tourism experience scenarios for 2030". ENTER22 e-Tourism Conference, 1-12.

Rachmad Y E, (2024). "The Future of Influencer Marketing: Evolution of Consumer Behavior in the Digital World".

Rajawat A S, Bedi P, Goyal S B, Shaw R N, (2022). "AI and blockchain for healthcare data security in smart cities". AI and IoT for Smart City, 1-12. .DOI: 10.1007/978-981-19-0743-1_1

Ramakrishnan, T., Mohan Gift, M. D., Chitradevi, S., Jegan, R., & Subha Hency Jose, P. Nagaraja, Rajneesh Sharma H.N., Selvakumar P., Sintayehu Mekuria Hailegiorgis, (2022). "Study of Numerous Resins Used in Polymer Matrix Composite Materials", Advances in Materials Science and Engineering, vol. 2022, Article ID 1088926, 8 pages. DOI: 10.1155/2022/1088926

Rawas, S. (2024). ChatGPT: Empowering lifelong learning in the digital age of higher education. *Education and Information Technologies*, *29*(6), 6895–6908. DOI: 10.1007/s10639-023-12114-8

Schlackl, F., Link, N., & Hoehle, H. (2022). Antecedents and consequences of data breaches: A systematic review. *Information & Management*, *59*(3), 1–18. DOI: 10.1016/j.im.2022.103638

Selvakumar, P., Palanisamy, S. K., Cinthaikinian, S., Palanisamy, V., Mariappan, R., & Selvakumar, P. K. (2024). Biosensors and its diverse applications in healthcare systems. *Zeitschrift für Physikalische Chemie*, *2024*. DOI: 10.1515/zpch-2023-0406

Shahid, J., Ahmad, R., Kiani, A. K., Ahmad, T., Saeed, S., & Almuhaideb, A. M. (2022). Data protection and privacy of the internet of healthcare things (IoHTs). *Applied Sciences (Basel, Switzerland)*, *12*(11), 1–24. DOI: 10.3390/app12041927 PMID: 36330151

Shinde, N., & Kulkarni, P. (2021). Cyber incident response and planning: A flexible approach. *Computer Fraud & Security*, *2021*(1), 10–14. DOI: 10.1016/S1361-3723(21)00009-9

Sreenivasulu, A., & Manimozhi, T. Satheesh kumar P., Selvakumar P. and Singh P.,(2022). "The Model of Smart Sensing Device For Sensitive Nanoclusters Modification in Sensing Properties," 2022 2nd International Conference on Advance Computing and Innovative Technologies in Engineering (ICACITE), pp. 1043-1047, DOI: 10.1109/ICACITE53722.2022.9823846

Staves, A., Anderson, T., Balderstone, H., Green, B., Gouglidis, A., & Hutchison, D. (2022). A cyber incident response and recovery framework to support operators of industrial control systems. *International Journal of Critical Infrastructure Protection*, *37*, 100454. DOI: 10.1016/j.ijcip.2021.100505

Sugumaran, K. M. D., Pandiyarajan V., Y. B S, Selvakumar P. and M. S, (2024). "Analysis of Electromyography Signals for Control of Mechanical Prosthesis using Machine Learning Techniques," 2024 2nd International Conference on Intelligent Data Communication Technologies and Internet of Things (IDCIoT), pp. 1059-1067, DOI: 10.1109/IDCIoT59759.2024.10467707

Tursunbayeva, A., Pagliari, C., Di Lauro, S., & Antonelli, G. (2022). The ethics of people analytics: Risks, opportunities and recommendations. *Personnel Review*, *51*(5), 1423–1443. DOI: 10.1108/PR-12-2019-0680

VanLeeuwen, C. A., Veletsianos, G., Johnson, N., & Belikov, O. (2021). Never-ending repetitiveness, sadness, loss, and "juggling with a blindfold on:" Lived experiences of Canadian college and university faculty members during the COVID-19 pandemic. *British Journal of Educational Technology*, *52*(4), 1431–1446. DOI: 10.1111/bjet.13065 PMID: 34230673

Verma, A., & Gurtoo, A. (2024). *Evaluating global data policies around non-personal data on social and public good.* Digital Policy, Regulation and Governance., DOI: 10.1108/DPRG-03-2023-0044

Verstraete, M., & Zarsky, T. (2021). Optimizing breach notification. *U. Ill. L. Rev.*, *2021*(3), 551–604.

Vijayakumar, G., Rajkumar, M., Rajiv Chandar, N., Selvakumar, P., & Duraisamy, R. (2024). Muniyandi Rajkumar, Rajiv Chandar N, Selvakumar P and Ramesh Duraisamy, (2024). Environmentally friendly TDS removal from waste water by electrochemical ion exchange batch-type recirculation (EIR) technique. *Environmental Science. Water Research & Technology*, *10*(4), 826–835. DOI: 10.1039/D3EW00793F

Viljoen, S. (2021). A relational theory of data governance. *The Yale Law Journal*, *130*(6), 1314–1344. DOI: 10.2307/26796823

Voss, W. G. (2021). "The CCPA and the GDPR are not the same: why you should understand both". CPI Antitrust Chronicle. DOI: 10.2139/ssrn.3912121

Wan, S., Lin, H., Gan, W., & Chen, J. (2024). Web3: The next internet revolution. *IEEE Internet of Things Journal*, *11*(2), 1–14. DOI: 10.1109/JIOT.2023.3235512

Wylde, V., Rawindaran, N., Lawrence, J., Balasubramanian, R., Prakash, E., Jayal, A., Khan, I., Hewage, C., & Platts, J. (2022). Cybersecurity, data privacy and blockchain: A review. *SN Computer Science*, *3*(2), 1–14. DOI: 10.1007/s42979-022-01020-4 PMID: 35036930

Yeung, K., & Bygrave, L. A. (2022). Demystifying the modernized European data protection regime: Cross-disciplinary insights from legal and regulatory governance scholarship. *Regulation & Governance*, *16*(2), 257–275. DOI: 10.1111/rego.12401

Chapter 6

Social Media Privacy and Security: Stacking and Boosting for Misinformation Detection

Sanaa Ashiq
https://orcid.org/0009-0008-0070-9403
National University of Modern Languages, Rawalpindi, Pakistan

Sehrish Ferdous
https://orcid.org/0009-0004-6495-9939
National University of Modern Languages, Rawalpindi, Pakistan

Muhammad Adnan
https://orcid.org/0009-0004-2537-0398
National University of Computer and Emerging Sciences (FAST), Islamabad, Pakistan

Wajahat Sultan
https://orcid.org/0009-0007-6271-7268
National University of Sciences and Technology, Pakistan

Hasan Tahir
https://orcid.org/0000-0002-0966-0721
National University of Sciences and Technology, Pakistan

Bilal Ahmed
https://orcid.org/0009-0006-8664-7463
National University of Sciences and Technology, Pakistan

Qamar Yasmeen
Niazi Medical and Dental College, Sargodha, Pakistan

Madeeha Saqib
https://orcid.org/0000-0003-4856-8095
Imam Abdulrahman Bin Faisal University, Dammam, Saudi Arabia

ABSTRACT

Despite being a modern means of communication, social media is one of the biggest risks to privacy and security because of the misinformation that it perpetuates. This chapter proposes a new ensemble model that uses stacking and boosting techniques

DOI: 10.4018/979-8-3373-3171-3.ch006

for misinformation detection with identity protection. The developed framework combines machine learning and deep learning algorithms to improve detection accuracy while reducing the threat of fake news, identity fraud, and cyber terrorism. The chapter covers the implementation of natural language processing for feature extraction and model evaluation with real life datasets containing misinformation. It also addresses the policy and ethical consequences of automating misinformation detection from the perspective of safety, privacy, and freedom of speech. The resulting system encourages safety in a digital space by increasing privacy and surveillance of information among individuals and organizations, thus fostering trust in online content.

INTRODUCTION

Cybersecurity and privacy are key challenges of digital age and this chapter introduces the background, motivation, and significance of detecting misinformation in terms of social media privacy and security (Saeed, 2023, Saeed 2023a, Saeed, 2025). In the contemporary digital age, the internet has become the main medium whereby people receive news and information. Social media applications like Facebook, Twitter, Instagram, and YouTube have been central to this evolution. With increasingly busy lifestyles, consumers rely on online news and social media for quick and convenient sources of information. These websites are no longer limited to informal communication; instead, they play vital functions in areas like education, healthcare, business, and politics. For example, platforms like Facebook and Twitter are widely visited for numerous reasons like consumption of information, entertainment, e-commerce, and exchange of opinions (Ledford, 2020).

Despite the communication platforms, there are some other platforms to be popularly used as alternative search engines. For a lot of users, it is easier to navigate trending news or content of specific topics using social media instead of traditional search engines (Monti et al., 2019). Due to this, people are becoming more concerned about whether the information shared on social media is true and reliable. Misinformation simply defined as a false, misleading, or manipulated content, which can be spread either by mistake or on purpose. Sometimes misinformation can be spread on purpose to harm someone's reputation, influence elections, make money, or mislead the public (Garcia et al., 2020), (Brummette et al., 2018). Others might spread false information without knowing it, because of their personal opinions, lack of knowledge, or strong beliefs. The famous example is the 2016 US presidential election, where false information was shared on purpose to influence voters and change public opinion (Hakak et al., 2021).

The distribution or spreading of disinformation particularly on social media may include serious threats to individual consumers, communities, and organizations. Made up or false information also have a critical impact like changing public opinion, modification of economic behavior, and how people react in crisis conditions. For example, fake news has been known to impact stock markets, confuse health decisions, and mislead people during emergencies. (Hakak et al., 2021). Misinformation often causes confusion that results in taking attention away from true information, and changes the people perception by distracting them from fact-based content. Identifying this kind of false content is not easy as it needs smart, flexible, and powerful tools or analytical models to detect and handle it. Social media websites are famous for the real-time spread of both correct and incorrect information. Although fact-checking facilities exist, they tend to be resource-intensive, domain-specific, and fall behind the sheer amount of content produced on a daily basis (Napoli, 2018). Therefore, there is an increasing demand for intelligent, responsive, and scalable automated misinformation detection systems.

Additionally, the social media environment introduces an extra layer of complexity. Short-form texts, slang, emojis, abbreviations, and multilingually complicate traditional NLP pipelines. Misinformation can also be in multimedia form, e.g., images or video with misleading text, adding further complexity to detection. Changing consumption patterns for news are also driving rising threats of misinformation. Social media is a cheaper, more accessible, and interactive option in contrast with traditional sources like television or the newspaper. The audience is able to respond, comment, and share within peer groups instantly. According to a Pew Research Center report, the proportion of U.S. adults that use social media to get news increased from 49% in 2012 to 62% in 2016. Consequently, social media now surpasses television as the main source of news for many but with less editorial power and greater opportunities for exposure. to misinformation (Social media 'outstrips TV, 2022). The challenge is that most content-based misinformation detection techniques are limited. Proper interpretation typically requires domain knowledge, context knowledge, and socio-political knowledge considering which even the best-of-breed AI models cannot fully replicate. To overcome this, the study of misinformation detection has progressed to include three main categories: content-based, social context-based, and propagation-based methods (Shu et al. 2017), (Zhou & Zafarani, 2018).

- Content-based approaches depend on linguistic characteristics including vocabulary use, sentence structure, and writing style. These approaches try to recognize deceptive writing patterns based on lexical, syntactic, and stylistic indicators (Afroz et al., 2012; Rubin et al., 2016; Rashkin et al., 2017; Potthast et al., 2017; P´erez-Rosas et al., 2017). However, upon dealing with advanced disinformation that include credible content or include multilingual context, then they fail.

- The methods specifically based on Social context will use metadata including profiles of users, their past activity and friend connections. This will also include the way people interact with posts for example shares, likes, and retweet to verify whether the uploaded content is genuine or fake (Shu et al., 2018; Long, 2017; Shu et al., 2017; Shu et al., 2019; Ruchansky et al., 2017, Tacchini et al., 2017). Despite the usefulness of these methods, there are still some ethical concerns regarding protection and tracking of user's personal data.
- Similarly, the methods based on Propagation context mainly aims at how misinformation spreads on social media platforms. It has been observed in recent studies that the misinformation is distributed quite differently like a virus and reaching numerous people at once as compared to actual news (Kucharski, 2016). Such propagation methods observe that how information will spread on various platforms by using different models and making them less dependent on language as well as difficult for attackers to mislead (Vosoughi et al., 2018).

Due to the limitation of each method, the chapter recommended the use of hybrid model that combines the various techniques such as ensemble models with boosting and stacking. By combining, these techniques can help detect misinformation much better.

Chapter Contributions

This chapter makes several significant contributions toward addressing the growing threat of misinformation on social media platforms while promoting privacy and security:

- Suggests a stacking and boosting hybrid ensemble-based approach with ML and DL for improved misinformation detection.
- Applies NLP for extracting features, with feature selection and dimensionality reduction to process intricate social media data.
- Confirmed on the two real-world datasets, demonstrating improved accuracy and reduced error compared to current methods.
- Mentions ethical concerns such as privacy, identity protection, and freedom of speech in automated detection.
- Seeks to make online environments safer, enable fake news monitoring and assist in making informed choices.

Chapter Organization

The Chapter is organized in the following way: Section II contains the preliminary studies and related work. Section III represents various machine learning techniques which are available to process the misinformation detection. The Section IV outlines the details of the Proposed Model, Lastly, Section V concludes the chapter and describes the future research directions.

PRELIMINARY STUDIES AND RELATED WORK

Misinformation Detection by Using Machine Learning and Deep Learning Methods

In their study, (Oshkaw et al., 2018) described the challenges regarding misinformation detection and performed a detailed review on previous studies that uses machine learning techniques for this purpose. Their focus is particularly on identifying the relationship between misinformation detection with existing natural language processing (NLP) tasks. Moreover, the researchers tested their model with dataset containing claims, full articles, and social media posts and evaluated the performance of the proposed model by using accuracy as their evaluation metric. As the suggested model does not provide any technique to reduce the size as well as complexity of data that can affect the performance of model. A machine learning approach was proposed by (Lakshmanarao et al., 2019) for detecting misinformation. The four different models were tested by authors. Upon comparing these models, Random Forest outperforms with highest accuracy but, Support Vector Machine provided the lowest accuracy results. The results were evaluated by confusion matrix and accuracy as evaluation metric.

Misinformation Detection by Using Knowledge-based and Content-based Techniques

A multimodal method for detecting misinformation was proposed by (Kumari and Ekbal, 2021) that includes information in the form of text as well as images. This includes the combination of different techniques such as CNN with RNN and many others. The model was tested on datasets like Twitter and Weibo. Though the attained results give better performance as compared to existing methods in terms of precision, recall, and F1-score. Their study has a limitation of not including any video and audio material during the detection of misinformation.

A model was introduced by (Alkhodair et al., 2020) specifically to detect the rumors mainly in news breaking events. A recurrent neural network was used in model along with other techniques such as word embedding techniques. Experiments on real world datasets and PHEME indicates that the performance of model is better than existing approaches in precision, recall, and F1-score. But main focus of model was on breaking news, so it has been observed that this may not work well for detection of misinformation in long term stories of news.

A model utilizing the bidirectional long short-term memory (BiLSTM) was proposed by (Hamed et al. 2023) for fake news detection. The model involves the features from sentiment analysis from the news headlines as well as the emotion analysis from the various comments of users. The model was trained and tested on the Fakeddit dataset that include both the news headlines and user comments. By the involvement of sentiment and emotion features as well as the content feature of the news, the recommended model gives a high detection rate of 96.77% as evaluated by the area under the ROC Curve. This surpasses other cutting-edge research and emphasizes the importance of news sentiment analysis and comment emotion analysis in enhancing misinformation detection efficiency. The article (Seddari et al., 2022) proposes a hybrid system for misinformation detection that merges linguistic and knowledge-based approaches. The system uses two categories of features: linguistic features, such as title, word count, reading ease, lexical diversity, and sentiment, and a new category of fact-verification-based features. The system only uses eight features, which is less than the usage in other methods. Evaluation on a dataset of misinformation reveals that the integration of linguistic and fact-verification features performs with a higher accuracy of 94.4% versus using only linguistic features (89.4% accuracy) or fact-verification features (81.2% accuracy).

The objective of the present research work (Iparraguirre-Villanueva et al., 2013) is to analyze the emotions (positive, negative, and neutral) tweeted by people using the hashtag Monkeypox. A hybrid model combining CNN and LSTM was used to make accurate predictions in order to understand the way people view this disease. The model was tested on a complete dataset related to monkeypox and achieved a prediction accuracy of 83%. The study by (Mohbey et al., 2022) focuses on understanding the opinion of people about monkeypox disease using a hybrid model that uses CNN along with LSTM. With this architecture that involves CNN and LSTM, the proposed model achieved the high prediction accuracy of 94% on monkeypox tweet dataset. Moreover, the remaining evaluation measures such as accuracy, recall, and F1-score were used to measure the performance of models in a time and resource effective way. The hybrid approach gives better result upon comparing with traditional machine learning methods.

MACHINE LEARNING MODELS AND TECHNIQUES USED FOR MISINFORMATION DETECTION

This section focuses on providing a better and advance understanding of the recommended research model by describing initial experiments. This is initiated by introducing various classifiers that has been used im the study to attain more accurate results. The classifiers include Support Vector Machine (SVM), Decision Tree, Random Forest, Naive Bayes, and Logistic Regression. These were used to analyze how well the proposed solution works.

Classifiers

A classifier is defined as a tool of machine learning to be used in data science for sorting data into various categories. This can be done by learning from labeled data meaning that the data has already the correct answers. Such as, in different tasks like classification of image or text, the classifier is trained using images and texts which are pre-labeled. Once the classifier is trained, it can take new, unlabeled data and correctly predict which category it belongs to.

Support Vector Machine (SVM)

The SVM is a popular and efficient machine learning algorithm known for its accuracy and speed. It is based on statistical learning theory with SVM and regression, and represents all data objects in an n-dimensional space, where each dimension corresponds to an attribute value. The classification of data is then performed by plotting a line or finding a hyperplane to separate the classes. Boosting algorithms are used to convert weak learners into stronger ones ("Pizzagate conspiracy theory - Wikipedia", 2022). In this, each data point is represented as a point in a high-dimensional space, with each feature corresponding to a particular coordinate. The algorithm then finds the hyper plane that maximally separates the two classes in this space. Figure 1 shows Support Vector Machine.

Figure 1. Support vector machine

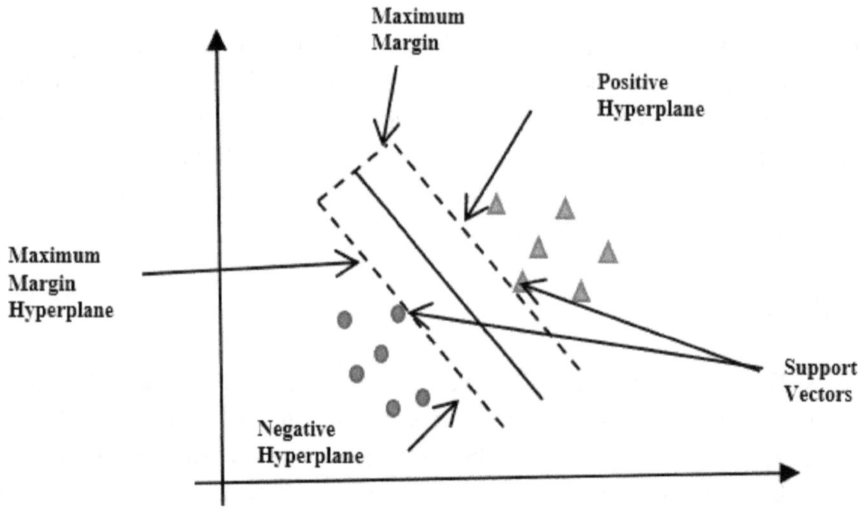

Decision Tree (DT)

This is a decision-making tool that represents possible outcomes in the form of a tree-like graph. It consists of conditional statements used to classify data based on numerical and categorical variables. It is a key classifier in machine learning and can be used to create at least two homogeneous datasets on which decision analysis can be performed using independent variables. DT is sometimes referred to as Classification and Regression Tree" (CART) in certain contexts, but it is commonly known as a decision tree.

The classification or regression methods in decision trees are represented as a tree structure. These structures consist of exhaustive and exclusive if/then rules, which are learned one at a time through training data. As each rule is learned, the tuples covered by it are successively removed until a terminated condition is achieved. The process of building decision trees uses a top down divide and conquer strategy, where everything is categorized. The top attributes of the tree are identified based on their impact, using the concept of information gain. Overfitting can occur when there are too many branches, resulting in noise and anomalies. To mitigate this, pre-pruning and post-pruning methods can be used. However, decision trees have poor performance on unseen data." Figure 2 shows DT.

Figure 2. Decision tree

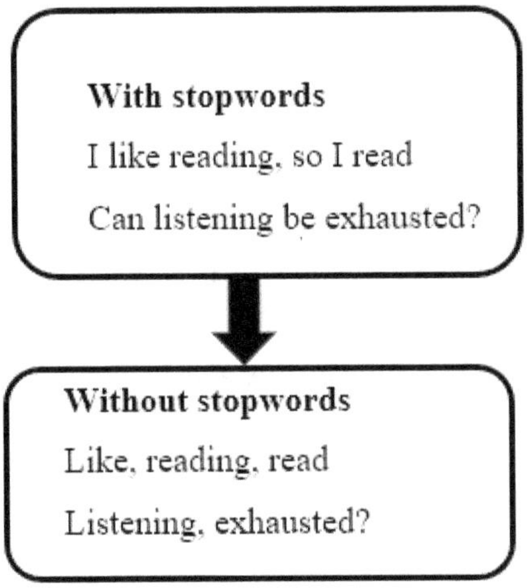

Random Forest (RF)

This is an ensemble learning method utilized for regression as well as classification problems. It involves a group of decision trees, where each tree contributes to the classification process. RF is an efficient and effective approach, widely used in various applications. To address the challenge of overfitting in decision trees, a technique is utilized where multiple simpler decision trees are constructed during the training phase. During the classification phase, a majority vote is conducted to determine the final classification outcome. This approach aids in mitigating the overfitting problem associated with decision trees.

To build the random forest, a general technique is applied that bags individual trees and replaces them with others from the training set, and each tree is grown without pruning. (Random Forest", Corporate Finance Institute, 2022). Figure 3 predicts RF.

Figure 3. Random forest

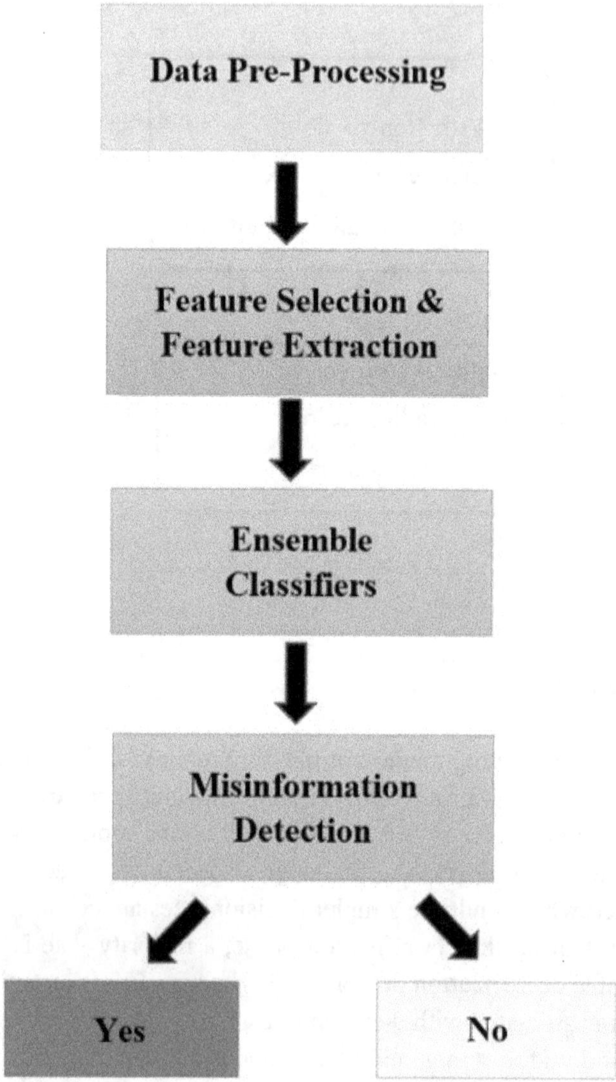

Naive Bayes (NB)

The NB classifier is a straightforward classification technique that is highly suitable for handling large datasets. It predicts the class of an unknown object by leveraging Bayes' Theorem, which assumes that the presence of a particular feature is independent of the presence of any other feature. Due to its simplicity and effectiveness, the NB classifier is widely utilized in machine learning as a versatile tool for problem-solving classification tasks (Naïve Bayes Algorithm", Medium, 2022).

This is a Bayes theorem-based classifier relying on probabilistic principles. Assuming a condition of independence between features, the Naive Bayes classifier applies Bayes' theorem for classifying, seeking to obtain the maximum posterior probability. Through the use of some assumptions in the Bayes theorem, this method practically minimizes computational expenses connected with the process of classification. Equation 1 depicts NB formula.

$$P(HE) = \frac{P(EH)*P(H)}{P(E)} \tag{1}$$

Above,

- P(H,E) is the posterior probability of class (c, target) given predictor (x, attributes).
- P(H) is the prior probability of class.
- P(E,H) is the likelihood which is the probability of predictor given class.
- P(E) is the prior probability of predictor.

Logistic Regression (LR)

Logistic Regression (LR) is a statistical technique commonly employed for binary classification tasks, where a set of independent variables is involved. It facilitates the establishment of a relationship between the dependent and independent variables by fitting the data into the logit function. LR is a linear method used for prediction and learning purposes in the statistics and ma chine learning communities (Logistic Regression in Machine Learning, Medium, 2022). The LR model produces a continuous output in the form of a function. Unlike Logistic Likelihood (LL), LR values are non-discrete. Since, this technique is limited to only binary classification problems therefore if there is a problem that has more than two classes, then for this purpose another classification approach such as Linear Discriminant Analysis (LDA) is used.

LDA is useful technique for identifying the patterns and making data simpler by reducing the size and complexity. It works by finding a combination of features that can separate and classify data into more than two groups or classes. Figure 4 shows LR.

Figure 4. Logistic regression

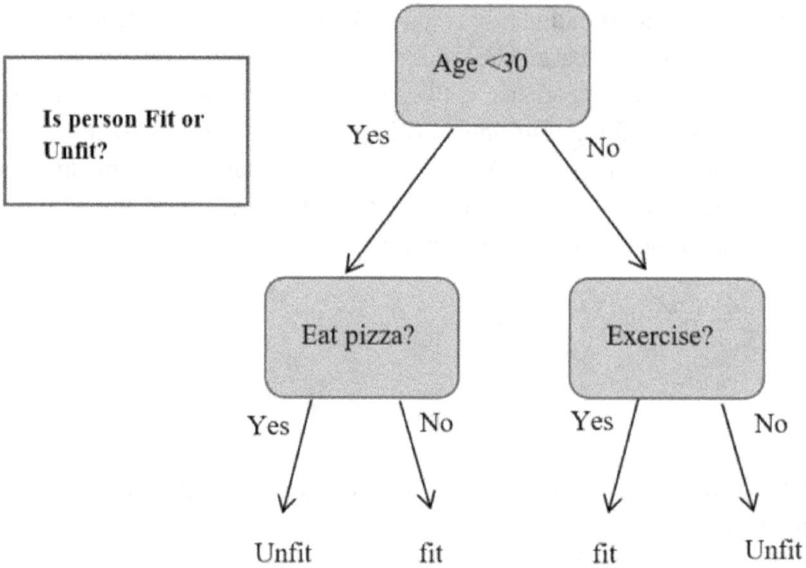

Gradient Boosting Regression

This is an ensemble model that utilizes boosting technique to learn from mistakes and improve performance. Unlike other methods that update the weights of data points, gradient boosting learns directly from residual errors. This approach is a more advanced version of Adaboosting and is sometimes referred to as gradient tree boosting.

Convolution Neural Network (CNN)

This is an exceptional type of architecture in Artificial Neural Networks (ANN). It is widely used for intricate pattern recognition tasks driven by images, thanks to its precise and uncomplicated structure that makes it easier to work with ANNs. ANNs are based on the way our biological nervous system, particularly the human brain, operates, and consist of numerous interconnected computational nodes. The structure is shown in the Figure 1.5 (Understanding of Convolutional Neural Network (CNN) — Deep Learning", Medium, 2022.)."

The process starts by loading the input into the input layer, represented as a multidimensional vector. This input is then propagated through the hidden layers.

The hidden layers make decisions based on the output from the previous layer and assess the impact of stochastic changes within themselves on the final output, thus facilitating the learning process. When multiple hidden layers are sequentially stacked, it is referred to as deep learning. According to Figure 5, CNNs are composed of three fundamental layers: an input layer, a hidden layer, and an output layer.

This foundational structure can be extended to accommodate any desired number of inputs. They belong to the category of multi-layer feedforward Artificial Neural Networks (ANNs) and feature self-optimizing neurons that receive input and execute diverse operations. The collective network produces a solitary perceptual score function, which involves converting raw image vectors into a final output of class scores. The ultimate layer generates output by building upon the output of the preceding layer.

Figure 5. Convolutional neural network

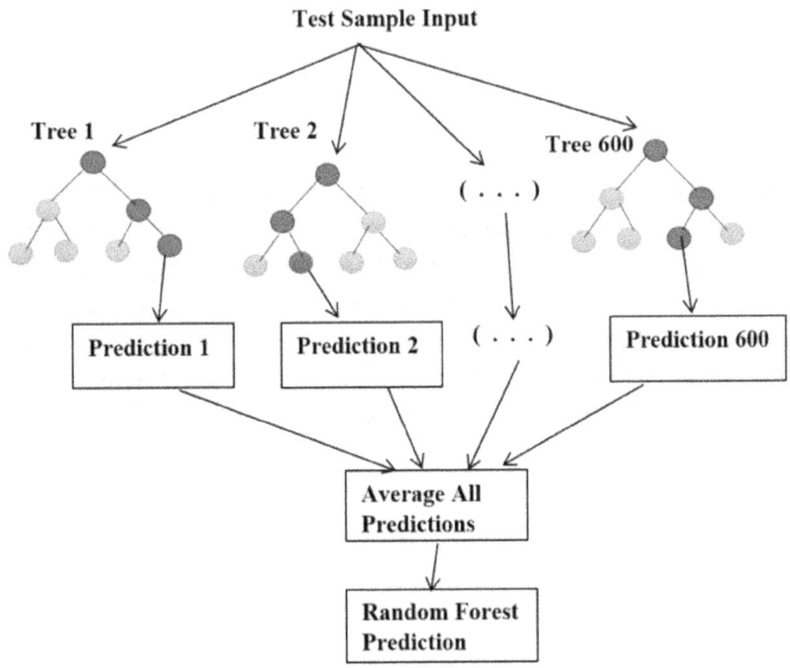

Long-Short Term Memory

Figure 6. Long short term memory

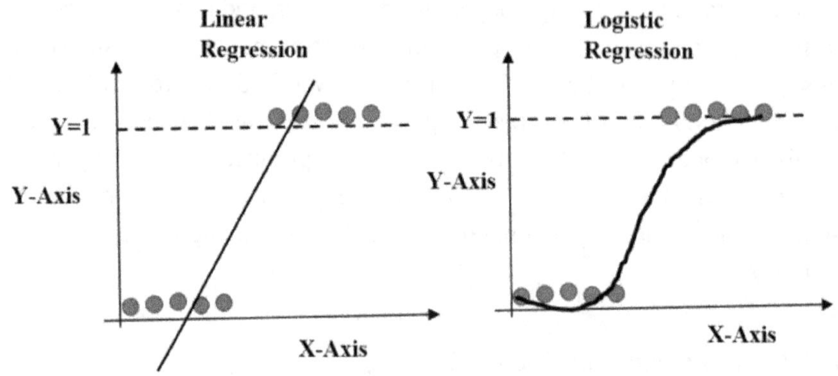

Long-Short Term Memory (LSTM) is a type of recurrent neural network that is good at storing memory over a period of time. LSTM (Long Short-Term Memory) is better than regular recurrent neural networks (RNNs) especially in remembering the complex patterns over time. Just like traditional neural networks, LSTM can have multiple layers of hidden units. When the data moves through each layer, then useful information is kept, while unimportant information is filtered out within special units called cells. Figure 6 shows the structure of an LSTM.

Recurrent Neural Network

Figure 7. Re-current neural network

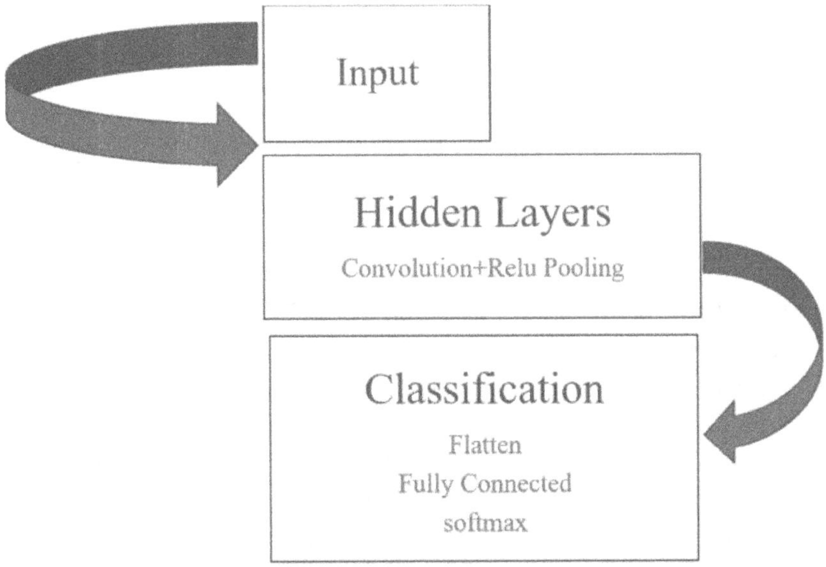

Recurrent Neural Networks (RNNs) have been around since the 1980s. They are not new like many other deep learning methods, but their use has grown with recent advances in computing power and data availability. RNNs can remember the vital information of the input that it is given because of their internal memory and are very accurate in predicting the next sequence. Consequently, RNNs are extremely popular to handle sequential data, such as speech, time series, text, financial data, video, audio, weather, and other many areas. This feature enables RNNs to gain a rich knowledge of the sequence as well as its contextual in formation, beyond the capabilities of other algorithms. In Figure 7 illustrates the architecture of RNNs.

Ensemble Technique

In order to improve the performance of our work, some ensemble techniques are applied to build the ensemble classifier. Weighted sampling is used to merge both machine learning classifiers. In order to apply this technique, a weight column is appended to the data frame, and an initial value is given to each record. Using equation 2, initial weight is calculated.

$$Weight\ (xi) = \frac{1}{n} \tag{2}$$

For each data point, the weight (xi) in the training set D1 will be calculated with the use of Equation 6. A base classifier is trained on this dataset where it makes the predictions. It has been observed that the few predictions are correct and others are incorrect. The incorrectly predicted datapoints are then identified from D1. The weights of these data points are updated in the next round of training. In Det et al. (2018), algorithm is provided to update these weights. Misclassification rate is computed as:

$$Total\ error = \frac{Total\ weight}{Weight\ (xi)\ x\ number\ of\ misclassified\ instances} \tag{3}$$

In order to find the weight (xi), Equation 2 can be helpful for every instance in the training set D1. predictions were made on the base classifier with same training set D1. This can be done by correctly classifying these instances while misclassifying the remaining. Then the weights of misclassified instances can be updated by weight adjustment process which has been mentioned in in Det et al. (2018). Thus, to identify about how often the classifier made mistakes, then a Total Error is computed. This is the sum of the initial weights of the misclassified instances in D1 and the Total Weight is actually the sum of initial weights of all instances in the dataset. Each instance has an initial weight called Weight (xi). The actual number of records specifically that are misclassified means that how many instances the base classifier got wrong. By using Equation 4, a Stage value, is computed that determine how much influence a prediction should have.

$$Stage = Instage = ln\frac{1 - Total\ error}{Total\ error} \tag{4}$$

The weight prediction is computed with the help of equation 1.4, that includes taking of the natural logarithm (ln). These weighted predictions are then used to update the weights for every instance which can be is achieved by providing higher value or weight to misclassified instances and lesser value or weight to correctly classified instances by equation 5. This equation actually calculates the updated weights from the weight predictions and finally the original weights are assigned to every instance.

$$Updated\ Weight\ (xi) = \exp(Stage) \tag{5}$$

The misclassification rate is computed by using equation 3. The stage value, can also give the weight of any prediction and is attained with equation 4. The new weight of each instance is identified using equation 5, and new data is represented as d2. Weighted sampling is applied to d2, and the most weighted instances are assigned with more probability for classification in the subsequent iteration. The new data is then forwarded to the subsequent classifier, and the process continues until the required accuracy level is attained. The ensemble technique flowchart is depicted in Figure 8.

Figure 8. Flowchart of ensembles technique

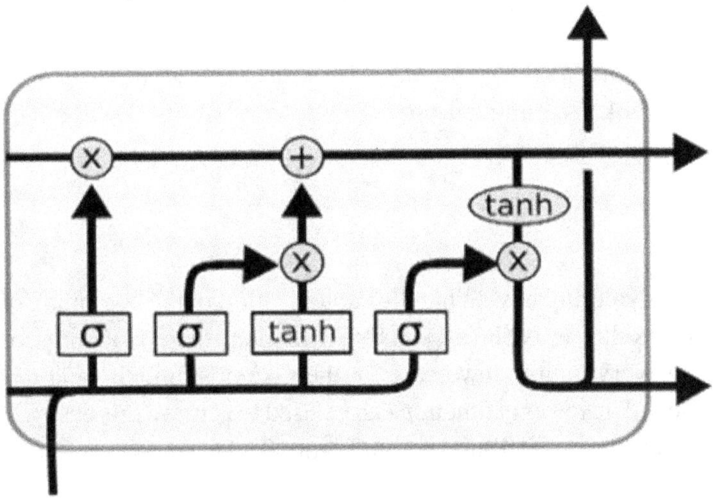

Natural Language Processing

The dataset index contains various errors that need to be corrected and re moved to obtain accurate results. Before connecting the classifiers to the dataset, it is transformed and organized into a proper format. The dataset mainly comprises the English language, and therefore, natural language processing (NLP) techniques are applied to extract only the English words, which enhances the accuracy of the results. Text transformation and con version of binaries are also performed on the dataset to facilitate data preprocessing. Several preprocessing techniques are applied to the dataset, which are detailed below.

Tokenization

Tokenization is a text preprocessing technique that involves dividing the given text data into several pieces or tokens, and it may also remove certain special characters like apostrophes, commas, and periods. Typically, tokens are formed based on spaces, and the tokenization of a sentence based on spaces results in multiple tokens. For instance, if we consider the sentence “Never give up”, it can be divided into three tokens- “Never”, ”give”, and ”up”. This process is known as Word Tokenization, where each token corresponds to a word. Similarly, tokens can be either characters or sub words. For example, let us consider “smarter”:

- Character tokens: s-m-a-r-t-e-r
- Subword tokens: smart-er

Lowercase

If you are wondering how to handle capitalization in the beginning of sentences or proper nouns during NLP tasks and text mining, there is a common approach of converting everything to lowercase for the sake of simplicity and maintaining a consistent flow. The lower () function can be used to achieve this easily. The process of how to lowercase text is illustrated in Figure 9.

Figure 9. Lowercase technique

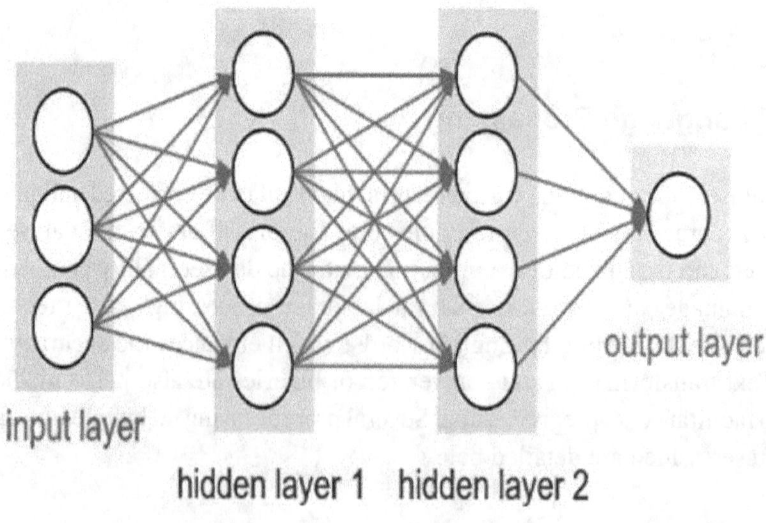

Remove Punctuation

Another commonly used text preprocessing technique is removing punctuation from the text data. This is done to standardize the text and treat words with or without punctuations in the same way. Punctuation symbols such as !"()*+,-./:;¡=¿?@ are removed from the text. Stop words are words that are very common across all documents in a corpus and do not provide much value in distinguishing documents from each other. Examples of stop words are "but", "for", "is", "are", "am". Removing these stop words can improve the accuracy and efficiency of text analysis. In Figure 10, the working of stop word technique is shown.

Figure 10. Stopword technique

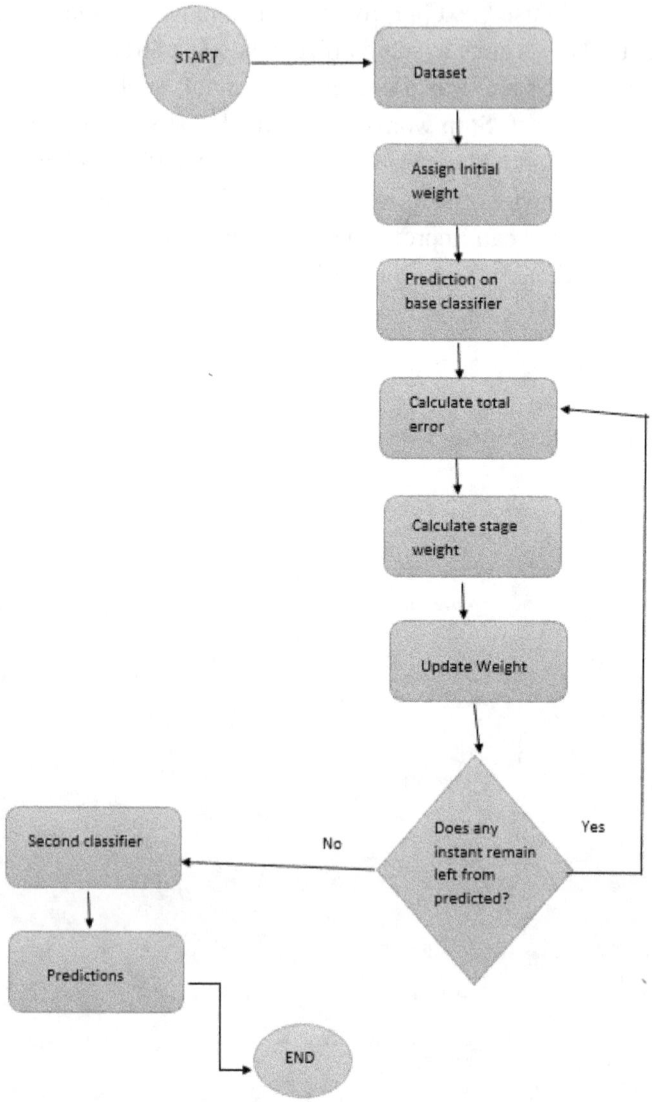

Lemmatization

Lemmatization is a technique used to group various forms of a word together to their base or root form, which holds the same meaning. This process is similar to stemming but results in words that have a meaningful dictionary definition. Morphological analysis involves identifying the appropriate base form or lemma of each word. To illustrate, words such as "operate", "operation", and "operating" can all be reduced to their common root "operate" through stemming or lemmatization.

Features Extraction

Feature extraction is a procedure that involves converting raw data into numeric features that can be analyzed while retaining the essential information from the initial dataset. This approach is more effective than directly applying machine learning algorithms to raw data. Various techniques are employed for feature extraction, as outlined below.

CountVectorizer

It is a process of extracting unique words from a text and creating a list of them. After that it calculates the frequency of each word across the whole corpus of documents to show their respective occurrence rates. It is commonly used in computing word occurrences in a specific text.

$$Vectorizer = Count\ Vectorizer(analyzer='word'n\ gram\ range = (1,1)) \quad (6)$$

TF-IDF Vectorizer

TF-IDF is used to determine the frequency and relevance of a particular word in a specific document. The calculation can be done using the formula given below.

$$tfidf(t,d,D) = tf(t,d)\,.\,idf(t,D) \quad (7)$$

- **TF (Term frequency)** is the frequency of appearance of a word in a document. It can be calculated in various ways, such as by simply counting how many times a word appears in the document. There are also ways to normalize the frequency over factors such as the length of the document or the raw frequency of the most common word in the document.
- **IDF (The inverse document frequency)** of a word is the word's frequency of occurrence within a group of documents. It indicates how frequently or infrequently a word occurs in the entire document collection. The value nearer 0 indicates that the word occurs more frequently. This is calculated by dividing the total document number by the frequency of documents with the word and then taking the logarithm of this. IDF value of a word is proportional to its least frequency and use in most documents. The more frequent a word

appears and occurs in most documents, the nearer its IDF value is to 0. The less frequent a word appears and occurs in fewer documents, the nearer its IDF value is to 1.

Word2Vec

Word2Vec is a common method in some NLP models with a feature of transforming words into vectors. It can be done by a two-layer neural network that processes text data. The text corpus is given as input to the network and a set of vectors is obtained as output. With training on a vast dataset, Word2Vec can accurately deduce the meaning of a word based on how it appears in the text, establishing semantic relationships between words in the corpus. For instance, words such as "King" and "Queen" would share analogous vector representations. By doing algebraic manipulations on these word representations, an estimate of the similarity between words can be obtained. For example, if one were to subtract the 2-dimensional embedding vector of "man" from the 2-dimensional embedding vector of "king" and add the 2-dimensional embedding vector of "woman", one would obtain a vector very close to the embedding vector of "queen".

Glove

GloVe (Global Vectors) is an unsupervised word-embedding model that produces dense word vector representations from word co-occurrence in the large textual data. The words are embedded in a dense vector space, where distance between words is equal to the semantic similarity of the words. Therefore similar words will be located close to one another. GloVe stands out for its ability to better capture semantic and context relations than other conventional word representation techniques such as TF-IDF, one-hot encoding and Bag-of-Words. These word representations have gone a long way in enhancing the performance of machine learning as well as deep learning models, particularly in use cases such as neural machine translation.

Bag-of-Words (BOW)

A BOW representation is a form of textual data representation that presents the frequency of words in a document. It ignores their sequential position or grammatical complexity. It is also known as a "bag" of words because it does not pay attention to any hint of the specific order or shape of the words. This model is only concerned with the fact that it has seen familiar words or not in the document, but not their spatial or positional placement.

Feature Selection Technique

Feature selection is an important technique that is used to reduce the number of input variables utilized in creating a predictive model. The primary objective is to decrease the computational burden of modeling and, in some cases, enhance the model's performance by choosing only the most pertinent features. There are several commonly employed techniques for feature selection.

Chi-Square

The aim of this method is to choose features that have a strong association with the response variable. If two features are independent, the observed count will be similar to the expected count, resulting in a less Chi-Square value. Thus, a greater Chi-Square value suggests that the assumption of independence is incorrect. The formula used to calculate Chi-Square value is provided below:

$$x^2 = \frac{(O_i - E_i)^2}{E_i} \tag{8}$$

Principal Component Analysis

In Principal Component Analysis (PCA), a method for feature selection in volves identifying a subset of variables that preserves a significant amount of information from the complete dataset. The information retained is quantified by calculating the percentage of consensus using generalized Procrustes analysis.

Information Gain

IG or Information Gain is a method employed to calculate the reduction in entropy or surprise in partitioning a dataset according to one particular value of a random variable. The formula for the calculation of Information Gain is given below.

$$IG = \frac{Count\ (Group1)}{Count(\ dataset)*Entropy\ (Group1)} + \frac{Count\ (Group2)}{Count(\ dataset)*Entropy\ (Group2)} \tag{9}$$

Document Frequency

This is an easy but useful measure of feature selection for text categorization. It measures the frequency of documents within a corpus that contain a given feature, which may be a word, phrase, n-gram, or derived feature.

Some of these works utilized statistical and machine learning (ML) approaches to detect misinformation and were also part of Human-Computer Interaction (HCI) since they extended the knowledge about how people use and accept information (Buntain & Golbeck, 2017; Dey et al., 2018; Aydin et al., 2018). Ahmed et al. enhanced identification by extracting language features such as n-grams and training diverse ML models like SVM, Logistic Regression, and Decision Trees. While initial models held promise, performance deteriorated in the long run, prompting researchers to include user behavior and social media trends for stronger results (Jin et al., 2017). Wang (2017) presented a hybrid method of CNN and BiLSTM to examine text data along with metadata such as speaker and political leaning, performing well on political datasets.

Later attempts concentrate on ensemble models that use both ML and deep learning. Experiments utilized Kaggle datasets, using NLP methods such as stemming and tokenization, with feature extraction software like TF-IDF, GloVe, and Word2Vec. These features were given as inputs to classifiers such as SVM, Random Forest, CNN, and LSTM, and they indicated that ensemble approaches, particularly SVM and Random Forest-based models, performed very well. Better performance was noted when content-based features were combined with knowledge-based factors. The models were tested on standard metrics on public datasets, validating the efficacy of ensemble methods in detecting fake news.

The emergence of social media and online news sites has altered the way people consume and exchange information (Ahlers, 2006), with sites such as Facebook responsible for as much as 70% of traffic to news sites (Wong, 2016). Yet this development has also created an opportunity for nefarious actors to use these sites to disseminate disinformation for financial gain, shape public opinion, and manipulate social narratives (Lazer, 2018; Garcia et al., 2020). Techniques for identifying misinformation have traditionally been split into content-based, social context-based and propagation-based methods (Shu et al., 2017; Zhou & Zafarani, 2018), the most common of which is content-based. They are based on linguistic features and stylistic patterns (Afroz et al., 2012), whereas statistical classification utilizing n-gram features were utilized by Ahmed et al. (2017) in machine learning. Even though earlier approaches were limited, feature optimization and ensemble modeling have yielded better outcomes. Riedel et al. (2017) aimed at headline-article body stance detection with a slight improvement. Based on their study, the current research introduces a hybrid approach incorporating feature extraction and ensemble learning that works more effectively in identifying false news.

The recent monkey-pox outbreak has also had implications for public health, with 1,964 cases reported in Peru as of September 2022. Social media platforms like Twitter have also become important channels to follow individuals' sentiment, with individuals posting right as well as wrong information in different formats—emphasizing the importance of effective misinformation detection mechanisms into the future.

PROPOSED MODEL FOR MISINFORMATION DETECTION

Since cybersecurity has assisted in securing information and promoting privacy across various fields so misinformation detection in social media also received considerable attention (Iqbal et al., 2022, Saeed et al., 2023, Gull et al, 2023). This section explores the work methodology of the Misinformation detection proposed model, which will detect misinformation available in social media networks. The model proposed here integrates feature selection and feature extraction methods with ensemble classifiers using machine learning and deep learning. There are several methods utilized to extract features, and then feature selection is applied to decrease the vector space. The Support Vector Machine (SVM) and Random Forest (RF) based ensembles classifier is proposed to obtain substantial performance in identifying fake news. SVM is selected as one of the base classifiers because it can handle various forms of data, including unstructured and semi-structured data. RF is, on the other hand, selected as a second classifier since it can handle noisy data. Hence, an ensembles technique is applied to merge these two classifiers to obtain the best result.

This work suggests the Misinformation Detector model, which is an ML/DL ensemble classifier comprising various regression model combinations. The model employs diverse Natural Language Processing (NLP) methods for preprocessing on chosen datasets. The proposed work is divided into three parts. In the first part, Misinformation Detector employs 5 types of preprocessing techniques (Tokenization, Stemming, Stop Words, Remove Punctuation, Lowercase, and Lemmatization) using an NLP tool on the selected dataset. In the second part, fractal features are extracted, and relevant features are selected using Word2Vec, Count Vectorizer, TF-IDF, Bag of Words, and Glove techniques, and Chi-Square technique, respectively. In the final part, ensemble classifiers are utilized for binary classification of news as misinformation or real based on the resultant feature. The model diagram of the model is shown in Figure 11.

Figure 11. Proposed model for misinformation detection

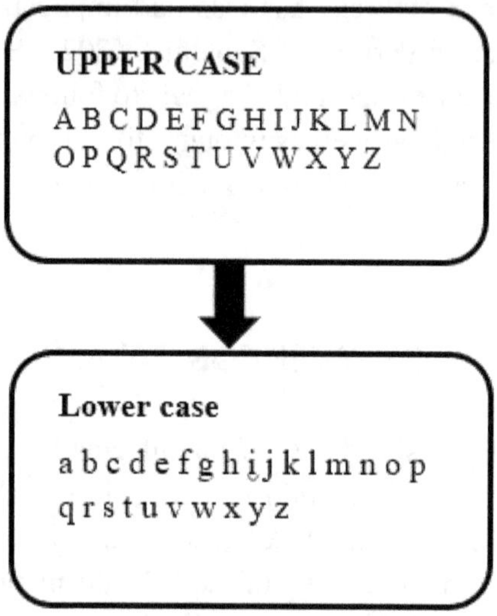

The data utilized in the study was sourced from public repositories, as discussed earlier. Data preprocessing started with the application of natural language processing on the dataset to extract English words only. This was for the purpose of increasing accuracy by removing noise and incoherencies from the data.

The dataset was then converted to text and binary format for easy preprocessing. Then, the dataset was divided into sentences and tokenized into separate words. Stop words were discarded, and punctuation like commas and colons were also removed. Stemming and lemmatization were done on the dataset. Word stemming is a critical part of preprocessing since it normalizes words/tokens to a common form by bringing derived words back to their root or stem. Porter's stemming algorithm, a well-known popular one, was utilized to strip the text of suffixes like "ing," "es," and "ers." Lemmatization, however, yields the reduced word with some meaning in the dictionary. Having done preprocessing on the dataset, different feature extraction methods were employed. The text was converted to vectors with the help of a Count Vectorizer, taking the frequency of every word throughout the entire text into account. TF-IDF, in contrast, measured each word's frequency in a document by taking the frequency of each word and dividing it by the document's word count.

After the feature extraction process, various feature selection techniques were utilized in this study. Not all features are equally significant in developing an accurate statistical model, as some play a more critical role in improving model accuracy and prediction. Therefore, two feature selection techniques, including chi-square and PCA, were employed to reduce the feature space and select the most relevant features. The selected features were then passed to the base classifiers, which news. The classifiers output 0 or 1, which indicates true news by 0 and misinformation by 1.

The misclassified instances were marked and their weights were updated and passed to the resultant classifiers as a training set. The resultant classifiers identified whether the news is authentic (true or misinformation) or not from the test dataset. Stacking method of machine learning is a method where a number of base classifiers are used to provide predictions, and finally, these predictions are amalgamated with a meta-classifier.

The concept behind this method is to enhance the model's accuracy by taking advantage of the strengths of various base classifiers. In the stacking method, we generally employ five or more distinct base classifiers, each with its own parameters and hyperparameters. These classifiers can be of different kinds such as decision trees, support vector machines, or neural networks. The meta-classifier can be any machine-learning model such as logistic regression or a neural network and it accepts the ensemble of predictions from the base classifiers and provides a final prediction.

The meta-classifier is then trained on the validation set, and its accuracy is evaluated on an independent test set. In an attempt to combine sentiment analysis, the proposed model can utilize natural language processing (NLP) techniques to identify sentiment features from the news article text, such as sentiment polarity, subjectivity, and emotion intensity. The inclusion of sentiment analysis in the proposed model for detecting misinformation could improve its performance by providing more information on the emotional tone of the news item, which could be beneficial to improve distinguishing between fact and misinformation.

CONCLUSION

The final section of this chapter encapsulates the key findings of the study and offers suggestions for future research. Each paragraph in this section maps onto particular sections of this chapter, establishing relevant connections between the research aims, methods, outcomes, and wider implications in the field of social media privacy and security.

In Section I, the chapter began with an elaborated introduction to the envisaged work, which revolves around the detection of misinformation in text-based data posted on social media platforms. The section defined the increasing issue of misinformation, especially in the era of the internet, when user-generated content can quickly sway public opinion and shape societal behavior. The chapter focused on the urgent necessity for strong detection mechanisms as part of an overall attempt to protect both personal privacy and community digital security. The rationale for the research stemmed from actual real-world events in which spreading misinformation has resulted in negative societal and political consequences. In addition, the chapter defined precise goals to fill research gaps in existing studies. A comprehensive problem statement was made, summarizing the challenges of differentiating between fact-based content and malicious or incorrect information. The contribution of this work was then clearly outlined, with a strong focus on how it extends existing literature while presenting novel angles for consideration. A critical review of existing methodologies and systems demonstrated the limitations and shortcomings that still prevail in the field, hence justifying the need for an innovative solution. The Research Methodology section laid out a structured, phased approach that highlights the systematic planning and execution of this study, providing a replicable framework for future researchers. The importance of this work resonates beyond academia, offering substantial value to industry practitioners, policymakers, and technology developers seeking to enhance content verification systems on social media platforms.

Section II presents the preliminary studies and related work. Section III presented various machine learning and deep learning models and techniques, which can the process of misinformation detection over the social networking sites. Section IV explored the technical background and the real-world operations of the model that was put forward. The architecture of the model, its sequential steps, data processing methods, feature selection methods, and classification procedures were elaborated upon in detail. In particular, the performance analysis proved that the given model not only achieved but also exceeded the standards that other efforts had established. All the evaluation metrics like precision, recall, F1-score, and accuracy proved the model's excellence in reliability, robustness, and scalability. That means the system is capable of effectively detecting and countering misinformation, hence playing a crucial role in maintaining the integrity of social media platforms. They imply a clear way ahead for deploying such technologies as part of broader digital systems, especially those run by social networking behemoths and government agencies fighting fake news and cyber-disinformation.

Looking ahead, some suggestions for future research and development from this chapter are apparent. First, although the model presented here has solid performance in text-based misinformation identification, subsequent work can extend its capability by including multimodal sources like images, videos, and memes, which are equally common purveyors of misleading information. Second, the changing nature of misinformation, such as shifting language use, slang, and context-aware semantics, requires that learning systems adapt using potentially continuous learning and reinforcement learning paradigms. Third, ethical and legal issues must remain uppermost. With more autonomous detection systems, their application should be balanced against respect for user privacy, freedom of expression, and transparency in algorithmic decision-making. Moreover, cross-disciplinary teamwork comprised of ideas in computer science, psychology, communication studies, and legal frameworks will be crucial in creating holistic solutions that are both technologically efficacious and socially responsible. Therefore, in summary, this chapter adds to the increasing literature committed to addressing social media privacy and security challenges. By introducing a new, high-performance misinformation detection model and placing it in the broader framework of digital trust and user safety, the research highlights both the imperative and the viability of resolving these challenges. As digital platforms, continue to shape every aspect of our lives, the importance of reliable, ethical, and efficient mechanisms to ensure the credibility of online content becomes paramount. This chapter, thus, is a stepping-stone towards the creation of safer, more accountable, and more informed online communities.

REFERENCES

Adiba, F. I., Islam, T., Kaiser, M. S., Mahmud, M., & Rahman, M. A. (2020). Effect of corpora on classification of fake news using Naive Bayes classifier. *International Journal of Automation.*

Afroz, S., Brennan, M., & Greenstadt, R. (2012). Detecting hoaxes, frauds, and deception in writing style online. In *2012 IEEE Symposium on Security and Privacy* (pp. 461–475). IEEE. DOI: 10.1109/SP.2012.34

Ahlers, D. (2006). News consumption and the new electronic media. *The Harvard International Journal of Press/Politics, 11*(1), 29–52. DOI: 10.1177/1081180X05284317

Ajao, O., Bhowmik, D., & Zargari, S. (2018). Fake news identification on Twitter with hybrid CNN and RNN models. In *Proceedings of the 9th International Conference on Social Media and Society*, Copenhagen, Denmark (pp. 226–230). DOI: 10.1145/3217804.3217917

Alkhodair, S. A., Ding, S. H. H., Fung, B. C. M., & Liu, J. (2020). Detecting breaking news rumors of emerging topics in social media. *Information Processing & Management, 57*(2), 102018. DOI: 10.1016/j.ipm.2019.02.016

Antonakaki, D., Fragopoulou, P., & Ioannidis, S. (2021). A survey of Twitter research: Data model, graph structure, sentiment analysis and attacks. *Expert Systems with Applications, 164*, 114006. DOI: 10.1016/j.eswa.2020.114006

Asr, F. T., & Taboada, M. (2019). Misinfotext: A collection of news articles, with false and true labels.

Aydin, I., Sevi, M., & Salur, M. U. (2018). Detection of fake Twitter accounts with machine learning algorithms. In *2018 International Conference on Artificial Intelligence and Data Processing (IDAP)* (pp. 1–4). DOI: 10.1109/IDAP.2018.8620830

Bharadwaj, P., & Shao, Z. (2019). Misinformation detection with semantic features and text mining. *International Journal of Natural Language Computing, 8*(3), 17–22. DOI: 10.5121/ijnlc.2019.8302

Brummette, J., DiStaso, M., Vafeiadis, M., & Messner, M. (2018). Read all about it: The politicization of 'fake news' on Twitter. *Journalism & Mass Communication Quarterly, 95*(2), 497–517. DOI: 10.1177/1077699018769906

Buntain, C., & Golbeck, J. (2017). Automatically identifying fake news in popular Twitter threads. In *2017 IEEE International Conference on Smart Cloud (SmartCloud)* (pp. 208–215). New York, NY. DOI: 10.1109/SmartCloud.2017.40

Chen, T., Li, X., Yin, H., & Zhang, J. (2018). Call attention to rumors: Deep attention-based recurrent neural networks for early rumor detection. In *Lecture Notes in Computer Science* (pp. 40–52). Springer.

Chowdhary, K. (2020). Natural language processing. In *Fundamentals of Artificial Intelligence* (pp. 603–649). Springer. DOI: 10.1007/978-81-322-3972-7_19

Conroy, N. K., Rubin, V. L., & Chen, Y. (2015). Automatic deception detection: Methods for finding fake news. *Proceedings of the Association for Information Science and Technology*, *52*(1), 1–4. DOI: 10.1002/pra2.2015.145052010082

Da Silva, C. D., Vieira, F., & Garcia, R. (2019). Can machines learn to detect fake news? A survey focused on social media. In *Proceedings of the 52nd Hawaii International Conference on System Sciences*. DOI: 10.24251/HICSS.2019.332

de Souza, J. V., Gomes, J., de Souza Filho, F. M., de Oliveira Julio, A. M., & de Souza, J. F. (2020). A systematic mapping on automatic classification of fake news in social media. *Social Network Analysis and Mining*, *10*(1), 48. DOI: 10.1007/s13278-020-00659-2

Dey, A., Rafi, R. Z., Parash, S. H., Arko, S. K., & Chakrabarty, A. (2018). Fake news pattern recognition using linguistic analysis. In *2018 Joint 7th International Conference on Informatics, Electronics & Vision (ICIEV)* and *2nd International Conference on Imaging, Vision & Pattern Recognition (icIVPR)* (pp. 305–309). DOI: 10.1109/ICIEV.2018.8641018

García, A., Gómez García, S., Sanz Prieto, G., Moreno Guerrero, M., & Jiménez, A. J. (2020). The impact of the term misinformation on the scientific community: Scientific performance and mapping in Web of Science. *Social Sciences*, *9*(5), 1–18.

García, A., Gómez García, S., Sanz Prieto, G., Moreno Guerrero, M., & Jiménez, A. J. (2020). The impact of term fake news on the scientific community: Scientific performance and mapping in Web of Science. *Social Sciences*, *9*(5).

Girgis, S., & Amer, E. (2022, May). A proposed ensemble voting model for misinformation detection. In *2022 2nd International Mobile, Intelligent, and Ubiquitous Computing Conference (MIUCC)* (pp. 316–322). IEEE.

Granik, M., & Mesyura, V. (2017). Misinformation detection using naive Bayes classifier. In *2017 IEEE First Ukraine Conference on Electrical and Computer Engineering (UKRCON)*, Kiev. DOI: 10.1109/UKRCON.2017.8100379

Gull, H., Alabbad, D. A., Saqib, M., Iqbal, S. Z., Nasir, T., Saeed, S., & Almuhaideb, A. M. (2023). E-commerce and cybersecurity challenges: Recent advances and future trends. Handbook of Research on Cybersecurity Issues and Challenges for Business and FinTech Applications, 91-111.

Hakak, S., Alazab, M., Khan, S., Gadekallu, T. R., Maddikunta, P. K. R., & Khan, W. Z. (2021). An ensemble machine learning approach through effective feature extraction to classify fake news. *Future Generation Computer Systems*, *117*, 47–58. DOI: 10.1016/j.future.2020.11.022

Hamed, S. K., Ab Aziz, M. J., & Yaakub, M. R. (2023). Misinformation detection model on social media by leveraging sentiment analysis of news content and emotion analysis of users' comments. *Sensors (Basel)*, *23*(4), 1748. DOI: 10.3390/s23041748 PMID: 36850346

Hua, J., & Shaw, R. (2020). Coronavirus (COVID-19) "infodemic" and emerging issues through a data lens: The case of China. *International Journal of Environmental Research and Public Health*, *17*(7), 2309. DOI: 10.3390/ijerph17072309 PMID: 32235433

Iparraguirre-Villanueva, O., Alvarez-Risco, A., Herrera Salazar, J. L., Beltozar-Clemente, S., Zapata-Paulini, J., Yáñez, J. A., & Cabanillas-Carbonell, M. (2023). The public health contribution of sentiment analysis of Monkeypox tweets to detect polarities using the CNN-LSTM model. *Vaccines*, *11*(2), 312. DOI: 10.3390/vaccines11020312 PMID: 36851190

Iqbal, Y., Tahir, S., Tahir, H., Khan, F., Saeed, S., Almuhaideb, A. M., & Syed, A. M. (2022). A novel homomorphic approach for preserving privacy of patient data in telemedicine. *Sensors (Basel)*, *22*(12), 4432. DOI: 10.3390/s22124432 PMID: 35746213

Jain, V., Kaliyar, R. K., Goswami, A., Narang, P., & Sharma, Y. (2021). AENeT: An attention-enabled neural architecture for misinformation detection using contextual features. *Neural Computing & Applications*, *34*(1), 1–12. PMID: 34305326

Jin, Z., Cao, J., Zhang, Y., Zhou, J., & Tian, Q. (2017). Novel visual and statistical image features for microblogs news verification. *IEEE Transactions on Multimedia*, *19*(3), 598–608. DOI: 10.1109/TMM.2016.2617078

Kaggle. (2022). *Datasets*. https://www.kaggle.com/datasets

Kaliyar, R. K., Goswami, A., & Narang, P. (2021). DeepFakE: Improving misinformation detection using tensor decomposition-based deep neural network. *The Journal of Supercomputing*, *77*(2), 1015–1037. DOI: 10.1007/s11227-020-03294-y

Karimi, H., & Tang, J. (2019). Learning hierarchical discourse-level structure for misinformation detection. In *Proceedings of the 2019 Conference of the North American Chapter of the Association for Computational Linguistics*, Minneapolis, Minnesota.

Kaur, S., Kumar, P., & Kumaraguru, P. (2020). Automating misinformation detection system using multi-level voting model. *Soft Computing*, *24*(12), 9049–9069. DOI: 10.1007/s00500-019-04436-y

Klyuev, V. (2018). Fake news filtering: Semantic approaches. In *2018 7th International Conference on Reliability, Infocom Technologies and Optimization (Trends and Future Directions) (ICRITO)*, Noida, India.

Kucharski, A. (2016). Post-truth: Study epidemiology of fake news. *Nature*, *540*(7634), 525. DOI: 10.1038/540525a PMID: 30905947

Kumari, R., & Ekbal, A. (2021). AMFB: Attention based multimodal Factorized Bilinear Pooling for multimodal misinformation detection. *Expert Systems with Applications*, *184*, 115412. DOI: 10.1016/j.eswa.2021.115412

Lakshmanarao, A., Swathi, Y., & Kiran, T. S. R. (2019). An efficient misinformation detection system using machine learning. *International Journal of Innovative Technology and Exploring Engineering*, *8*(10), 3125–3129. DOI: 10.35940/ijitee.J9453.0881019

Lazer, D. M. J., Baum, M. A., Benkler, Y., Berinsky, A. J., Greenhill, K. M., Menczer, F., Metzger, M. J., Nyhan, B., Pennycook, G., Rothschild, D., Schudson, M., Sloman, S. A., Sunstein, C. R., Thorson, E. A., Watts, D. J., & Zittrain, J. L. (2018). The science of fake news. *Science*, *359*(6380), 1094–1096. DOI: 10.1126/science.aao2998 PMID: 29590025

Ledford, H. (2020). How Facebook, Twitter and other data troves are revolutionizing social science. *Nature*, *582*(7812), 328–330. DOI: 10.1038/d41586-020-01747-1 PMID: 32555492

Long, Y. (2017). *Misinformation detection through multi-perspective speaker profiles*. Association for Computational Linguistics.

Mahabub, A. (2020). A robust technique of misinformation detection using ensemble voting classifier and comparison with other classifiers. *SN Applied Sciences*, *2*(4), 525. DOI: 10.1007/s42452-020-2326-y

Mohbey, K. K., Meena, G., Kumar, S., & Lokesh, K. (2022). A CNN-LSTM-based hybrid deep learning approach to detect sentiment polarities on Monkeypox tweets. *arXiv preprint arXiv:2208.12019.*

Monti, F., Frasca, F., Eynard, D., Mannion, D., & Bronstein, M. M. (2019). Misinformation detection on social media using geometric deep learning. *arXiv preprint arXiv:1902.06673*.

Napoli, P. M. (2018). What if more speech is no longer the solution? First Amendment theory meets misinformation and the filter bubble. *Federal Communications Law Journal*, *70*, 55–104.

Naresh, A., & Krishna, P. V. (2021). An efficient approach for sentiment analysis using machine learning algorithm. *Evolutionary Intelligence*, *14*(2), 725–731. DOI: 10.1007/s12065-020-00429-1

Oshikawa, R., Qian, J., & Wang, W. Y. (2018). A survey on Natural Language Processing for misinformation detection. *arXiv preprint arXiv:1811.00770*.

Pérez-Rosas, V., Kleinberg, B., Lefevre, A., & Mihalcea, R. (2017). Automatic detection of fake news. *arXiv preprint arXiv:1708.07104*.

Potthast, M., Kiesel, J., Reinartz, K., Bevendorff, J., & Stein, B. (2017). A stylometric inquiry into hyperpartisan and fake news. *arXiv preprint arXiv:1702.05638*.

Ramos, J. (2003). Using tf-idf to determine word relevance in document queries. In *Proceedings of the First Instructional Conference on Machine Learning* (Vol. 242, pp. 29–48).

Rashkin, H., Choi, E., Jang, J. Y., Volkova, S., & Choi, Y. (2017). Truth of varying shades: Analyzing language in misinformation and political fact-checking. In *Proceedings of the 2017 Conference on Empirical Methods in Natural Language Processing* (pp. 2931–2937). DOI: 10.18653/v1/D17-1317

Riedel, B., Augenstein, I., Spithourakis, G. P., & Riedel, S. (2017). A simple but tough-to-beat baseline for the Fake News Challenge stance detection task. *arXiv [cs.CL]*.

Robb, A. (2017). Anatomy of a fake news scandal. *Rolling Stone (San Francisco, Calif.)*, *1301*, 28–33.

Ruchansky, N., Seo, S., & Liu, Y. (2017). CSI: A hybrid deep model for misinformation detection. *arXiv preprint arXiv:1703.00956*, 797–806.

Sabeeh, V., Zohdy, M., & Bashaireh, R. A. (2019). Enhancing the misinformation detection by applying effective feature selection based on semantic sources. In *International Conference on Computational Science and Computational Intelligence (CSCI)* (pp. 1365–1370).

Saeed, S. (2023). Digital workplaces and information security behavior of business employees: An empirical study of Saudi Arabia. *Sustainability (Basel), 15*(7), 6019. DOI: 10.3390/su15076019

Saeed, S. (2023a). A customer-centric view of E-commerce security and privacy. *Applied Sciences (Basel, Switzerland), 13*(2), 1020. DOI: 10.3390/app13021020

Saeed, S. (2025). Digital Transformation in Governmental Public Service Provision and Usable Security Perception in Saudi Arabia. *Information (Basel), 16*(3), 247. DOI: 10.3390/info16030247

Saeed, S., Suayyid, S. A., Al-Ghamdi, M. S., Al-Muhaisen, H., & Almuhaideb, A. M. (2023). A systematic literature review on cyber threat intelligence for organizational cybersecurity resilience. *Sensors (Basel), 23*(16), 7273. DOI: 10.3390/s23167273 PMID: 37631808

Sahoo, S. R., & Gupta, B. B. (2021). Multiple features based approach for automatic misinformation detection on social networks using deep learning. *Applied Soft Computing, 100*, 106983. DOI: 10.1016/j.asoc.2020.106983

Samadi, M., Mousavian, M., & Momtazi, S. (2021). Deep contextualized text representation and learning for misinformation detection. *Information Processing & Management, 58*(6), 102723. DOI: 10.1016/j.ipm.2021.102723

Samani, F. S., Zhang, H., & Stadler, R. (2019). Efficient learning on high-dimensional operational data. In *2019 15th International Conference on Network and Service Management (CNSM)*, Halifax, NS, Canada (pp. 1–9). DOI: 10.23919/CNSM46954.2019.9012741

Sawan, A., & Thaher, T. (2021, Oct). Sentiment analysis model for fake news identification in Arabic tweets. In *2021 IEEE 15th International Conference on Application of Information and Communication Technologies (AICT)* (pp. 1–6). IEEE. DOI: 10.1109/AICT52784.2021.9620509

Seddari, N., Derhab, A., Belaoued, M., Halboob, W., Al-Muhtadi, J., & Bouras, A. (2022). A hybrid linguistic and knowledge-based analysis approach for misinformation detection on social media. *IEEE Access : Practical Innovations, Open Solutions, 10*, 62097–62109. DOI: 10.1109/ACCESS.2022.3181184

Shu, K., Bernard, H. R., & Liu, H. (2019). Studying fake news via network analysis: Detection and mitigation. In *Lecture Notes in Social Networks* (pp. 43–65). Springer.

Shu, K., Sliva, A., Wang, S., Tang, J., & Liu, H. (2017). Misinformation detection on social media: A data mining perspective. *SIGKDD Explorations, 19*(1), 22–36. DOI: 10.1145/3137597.3137600

Shu, K., Wang, S., & Liu, H. (2017). Beyond news contents: The role of social context for misinformation detection. *arXiv preprint arXiv:1710.08998*, 312–320.

Shu, K., Wang, S., & Liu, H. (2018). Understanding user profiles on social media for misinformation detection. In *2018 IEEE Conference on Multimedia Information Processing and Retrieval (MIPR)* (pp. 430–435). IEEE. DOI: 10.1109/MIPR.2018.00092

Singh, V., Dasgupta, R., Sonagra, D., Raman, K., & Ghosh, I. (2017). Automated misinformation detection using linguistic analysis and machine learning. In *International Conference on Social Computing, Behavioral-Cultural Modeling, Prediction and Behavior Representation.*

Soll, J. (2016). The long and brutal history of fake news. *Politico Magazine, 18*(12).

Tacchini, E., Ballarin, G., Della Vedova, M. L., Moret, S., & de Alfaro, L. (2017). Some like it hoax: Automated misinformation detection in social networks. *arXiv preprint arXiv:1704.07506.*

Thota, A., Tilak, P., Ahluwalia, S., & Lohia, N. (2018). Misinformation detection: A deep learning approach. *SMU Data Science Review*, 1(3).

Vedova, D., Tacchini, M. L., Moret, E., Ballarin, S., Dipierro, G., & De Alfaro, M. (2018). *Automatic online misinformation detection combining content and social signals.*

Vosoughi, S., Roy, D., & Aral, S. (2018). The spread of true and false news online. *Science*, *359*(6380), 1146–1151. DOI: 10.1126/science.aap9559 PMID: 29590045

Wang, W. Y. (2017). Liar, liar pants on fire: A new benchmark dataset for misinformation detection.

Wong, J. (2016). *Almost all the traffic to fake news sites is from Facebook, new data show*. The Medium.

Yu, L., Zhao, Y., & Chin, W. S. (2019). Extracting typhoon disaster information from VGI based on machine learning. *Journal of Marine Science and Engineering*, 7(9), 318. DOI: 10.3390/jmse7090318

Zhang, C., Gupta, A., Kauten, C., Deokar, A. V., & Qin, X. (2019). Detecting fake news for reducing misinformation risks using analytics approaches. *European Journal of Operational Research*, *279*(3), 1036–1052. DOI: 10.1016/j.ejor.2019.06.022

Zhou, X., & Zafarani, R. (2018). A survey of fake news: Fundamental theories, detection methods, and opportunities. *arXiv preprint arXiv:1812.00315*, 1–40.

Chapter 7
The Privacy Paradox:
Navigating Security Challenges in Social Platforms

S. Aarthi
https://orcid.org/0009-0006-9064-2091
Marwadi University, Rajkot, India

Ravikumar R. N.
https://orcid.org/0009-0009-3705-1681
Marwadi University, Rajkot, India

Valisher Sapayev Odilbek Uglu
Mamun University, Khiva, Uzbekistan

Abduvali Sottarov
Termez University of Economics and Service, Termez, Uzbekistan

Anand Singh
Marwadi University, Rajkot, India

ABSTRACT

Social media has transformed digital communication by enabling global, instant connectivity. However, this accessibility has introduced significant privacy and security risks. The exposure of personal data, coupled with data breaches, cyber-attacks, misinformation, and identity theft, has made users increasingly vulnerable. As social media platforms act as central digital controllers, sustainable ecosystems must integrate strong security and privacy measures. This chapter evaluates core privacy and security concerns, highlighting major risks and vulnerabilities. It explores threats such as data mining, tracking, and inter-organizational data sharing. Solutions include blockchain-based authentication, AI-driven malware detection, and

DOI: 10.4018/979-8-3373-3171-3.ch007

privacy-enhancing technologies (PETs). Emphasizing ethical practices and digital literacy, the chapter blends expert views and regulatory frameworks to improve trust. The findings guide policymakers and educators in building safer, resilient digital platforms that support sustainable digital transformation.

INTRODUCTION

In the digital age, social media altered information, communication, and interaction. Current social media platforms like Facebook, Twitter, Instagram, and LinkedIn must combine worldwide users for rapid communications and business networking. Technology poses major privacy problems since it poses several security dangers to consumers. Sharing sensitive information prolongs the privacy paradox, putting user privacy at risk. Users demand privacy yet risk their data via weak security. Online risk-taking is caused by unverified accounts, weak passwords, and privacy violations. Social media firms earn from user tracking data's personalized recommendations. Due to phishing, fake news, and government surveillance, internet security threats have increased. Cyberattacks may access social media users' databases even if they lack information security (Jafari & Shaghaghi, 2023). Worldwide user account data breaches have increased. Cybercriminals employ AI data mining to tweak news and exploit user data to spread disinformation. User-facing systems must offer privacy-protecting security and secure features. Globally, the GDPR safeguards data like CCPA. Blockchain authentication with PETs and AI enhances security plan noncompliance. Scientific web security mechanisms for social media networks protect user skills and ethics. Companies and users may better comprehend privacy paradox concerns and design secure digital solutions.

Overview of Social Media's Role in Modern Communication

Social media has changed personal and business communication, making it essential for digital survival. Facebook, Twitter, Instagram, LinkedIn, and TikTok started global social media's instant connection age. Social media impacts public discourse, social engagement, and business-personal connections. Best of all, social media allows urgent real-time worldwide contacts. Global internet communities share ideas and life experiences. Unfiltered social media live broadcasts and text, picture, and video communications generate cross-cultural and time-regional interactions. Improved social media communication has boosted cooperation, customer interactions, market data, and brand visibility. Social media facilitates global communication. Individuals, news organizations, and private reporters update social media quickly. Unstructured social media distribution gives customers global events and real-time updates throughout development (Bright et al., 2021). Fast information transmission spreads misinformation, public opinion manipulation, and fake news. Social media is crucial for industry-wide marketing. Social media advertising helps brands find and interact with desirable audiences. New marketing uses prominent influencers to influence buyers. Social media lets companies rapidly acquire client input on goods and services to enhance delivery. Essential social media teaching tools boost activist and emergency response. Students and teachers use LinkedIn and YouTube. Better education and professional training via learning and forums. Campaigners and organizations utilize social media to educate and improve policy. Disaster and epidemic relief are communicated via social media. Personalization algorithms complicate data monitoring and value transactions. Customers lose more data than ever to phishing, hacking, and identity theft. Social media is used to link people in modern digital communication (Mohamed et al., 2024). To ensure safe communication, privacy measures are required.

Figure 1. Social media connectivity

Figure 1 illustrates the global exchange of digital communication across platforms such as Facebook, Twitter, Instagram, LinkedIn, and TikTok, highlighting user interaction through laptops and mobile devices.

The Privacy Paradox: Convenience vs. Security Concerns

Online consumers provide personal data to fulfil this privacy demand despite security dangers. People want rapid social media access yet worry about privacy. People use social media regularly nowadays. Profiles disclose sensitive information such location data, photos, and occupational titles beyond people's initial estimates about how it will affect their public accessibility. Free network users agree to computer-targeted advertising data collection. By gathering personal data, the company customizes basic user-friendly services. Users don't know how much data social media networks gather, creating a privacy dilemma. Most users disregard the vast business data collected from their personal data (Hakimi et al., 2024). Complex privacy agreements with unfamiliar material make people uninformed of privacy risks. Users choose speedy personalized communications over privacy services because they prioritize speed above security. Psychological online behavior threatens privacy. Science suggests most people misunderstand online data privacy. Online users risk information leak by assuming their activities are safe. Personal information is provided for social activity validation comments. The privacy paradox causes data security threats. Phishing, identity theft, and social engineering using user data may earn. Professional security breaches occur when millions of individuals lose their personal data due to inadequate protection.

Since social networking services exchange data with third-party advertisers, users contest their privacy rights. Collaboration is essential to resolve privacy issues. Digital security procedures must be learned to protect data online in secure digital spaces. Social media firms require simple privacy regulations, solid security, and user-friendly privacy changes. GDPR and CCPA need company data protection. Social media users must pick between privacy and service options. Despite its benefits, social media users must be private. To attain digital privacy, learn security standards and forcibly apply enhanced security processes and ethical data management (Quinn & Epstein, 2018).

Importance of Addressing Cybersecurity in Digital Transformation

Security is the top operational concern in the digital age since it protects all security components and allows sustainable technology deployment. Each enterprise uses digital technology for business, healthcare, education, and government. Excellence in integration provides new hacker entry points and solutions. Since digital systems need user data, privacy is essential. Digital transformation helps organizations defend against cyberattacks. Cloud computing systems with AI and IoT devices have security risks that harm companies and consumers. Internet fraudsters use ransomware to steal rights and security holes to damage businesses.

Defending against advanced cybersecurity threats including data breaches, malicious code attacks, and phishing requires new methods. The largest danger is social media users sharing institutional and personal data. Through social engineering, attackers may steal personal data for identity theft, money fraud, and system penetration. Unauthentic account data advances system refinement and weakens public security and trust. Security infrastructure should be the first priority in digital transformation project development. AI-based threat detection, end-to-end encryption, and multimodal authentication improve cybersecurity. Global digital systems require GDPR and ISO 27001-compliant cybersecurity frameworks to protect user data (Yerby et al., 2019). To prevent operational attacks, all government entities must give basic cybersecurity training. Organizations must train users and staff in threat detection and security incident response. Governments and authorities must enforce data protection restrictions. Only cyber security needs drive digital organization development. On protected networks, consumers may see digital security innovation to combat unknown cyber threats. Security-enabled digital strategies enhance application trust across corporate, government, and individual users.

Theoretical Framework for Privacy and Security in Social Media

A clear understanding of user behavior, risk perception, and data-sharing decisions in social media platforms requires a strong theoretical foundation. The following frameworks provide conceptual lenses to analyze the dynamics of privacy, motivation, and information disclosure in online environments:

Privacy Calculus Theory

This theory holds that people weigh the positive and negative sides of sharing their details before making any decision. Sometimes, users on social media still share sensitive data, thinking it is worth the risk for the benefits they receive. This explains why the privacy paradox occurs: people say they are worried about privacy, but their actions usually reveal personal information.

Protection Motivation Theory (PMT)

The concept of Protection Motivation Theory (PMT), which was postulated first in health psychology can provide a good framework to study the choices that users make in respect to taking privacy preserving behavior, especially on online platforms such as social media. According to PMT there are four key cognitive processes that affect protective behavior, which include perceived severity (severity of the threat e.g. data theft), perceived vulnerability (you might be a target), response efficacy (the likelihood that a certain protective measure e.g. enable two-factor authentication will work) and self-efficacy (that you can take that defensive action). On a social media environment, PMT can be used to understand why some users would apply proactive measures such as changing privacy settings or the amount of information shared, whereas others fail to take such precautionary measures. As in an example, a user who thinks that the likelihood of identity theft is high and knows how to prevent it through 2FA and is confident about using it, will be willing to act. Accordingly, the PMT offers an organized manner of interpreting personal differences in decision-making made regarding privacy.

Communication Privacy Management (CPM) Theory

Communication Privacy Management Theory, developed by Sandra Petronio, emphasizes that individuals believe they own their private information and have the right to control it through privacy boundaries. On social media, users manage these boundaries by deciding what, when, and with whom to share information. However, once information is shared, co-ownership is created (e.g., friends tagging photos), which often leads to boundary turbulence when others violate perceived privacy norms. CPM helps explain conflicts and trust issues when social media platforms or third parties breach user expectations of control. These theories collectively guide the analysis of user behavior and platform responsibility in managing digital privacy (Yang et al., 2023). They serve as a conceptual backbone for evaluating privacy risks, decision-making, and policy interventions discussed throughout this chapter.

EVOLUTION OF SOCIAL MEDIA AND PRIVACY CONCERNS

Digital relationship forming across all internet-based entities, including individual contacts with organizations and governmental bodies, transformed due to social media technology. In 2002, Friendster opened, followed by Myspace in 2003, which allowed users to create profile pages for their connections. Following Facebook's 2004 breakthrough, Twitter started in 2006 and Instagram in 2010 to provide real-time content sharing and automatic audience matching. The market got social media platforms with extraordinary commercial outcomes that made them important for daily usage.

Social media's growth made consumers increasingly concerned about privacy and data security. Unknowingly sharing personal information without comprehending the ramifications led consumers to ignore privacy concerns in the beginning.

Large user data was used to adapt ads and increase platform interactions on these extended platforms. User permission and personal data ownership required ethical operations, yet also raised problems regarding data collecting. Uncontrolled data gathering systems produced severe privacy problems that were revealed thereafter. Facebook's crisis revealed weak data safeguards and political meddling that cost billions in stock market losses (2018). Multiple LinkedIn and Twitter account information theft events occur because these security breaches highlight platform security flaws.(Wardhono et al., 2018)

To regulate company privacy data processing, many government agencies produced the 2018 General Data Protection Regulation (GDPR) and the California Consumer Privacy Act (CCPA). Digital hazards and AI surveillance and misleading methods generate privacy issues. Technological innovation and privacy protection are the contemporary challenges. Modern social media development demands user-focused privacy rules, moral artificial intelligence standards, and cybersecurity technologies to protect digital security. Technological innovation and privacy protection are the contemporary challenges. Modern social media development demands user-focused privacy rules, moral artificial intelligence standards, and cybersecurity technologies to protect digital security.

Growth of Digital Communication and Social Platforms

Technology combined Internet access with mobile networks and social network software from decades ago to boost digital communication. After email was introduced, internet users relied on increasingly advanced social media platforms to communicate digital information until instant messaging. Digital communication technology originated from 1990s internet-based technological development. Real-time text messaging was available on ICQ (1996), AOL Instant Messenger (1997), and MSN Messenger (1999). In 2003, Friendster and Myspace launched, while LinkedIn expanded a year later. Profiles and social networking become popular elements of social media platforms.

Facebook revolutionary digital communication tools enabled consumers to tailor their interactions in 2004. Facebook changed social media by integrating account authentication, newsfeed organizing, and user data monitoring. Twitter and Facebook competed in 2006, but Instagram started in 2010, Snapchat in 2011, and TikTok in 2016. The global rise of social media led to three digital modifications of picture sharing mechanisms and user participation systems. Modern communication technologies advanced with streaming capabilities, allowing worldwide video calls and multimedia material. Social media networks allowed corporations and celebrities to execute audience-engaging promotions, increasing brand awareness. All major social media apps delivered political movements, emergency systems, and government messaging (Hermansyah et al., 2023).

New users faced significant privacy and safety hazards due to their increased internet access during digital service onboarding. Social platform services' substantial data storage caused an ethical issue that put gathered data at risk of security breaches. The world's biggest technology issue was data breaches, identity assaults, and disinformation. Blockchain-connected AI chatbot systems may construct metaverse initiatives for digital communication progress. To enhance ethical security operations and management technologies, many security systems must work together.

Major Events in the Development of Social Media Privacy Guidelines

The massive rise in social media users raised privacy and ethical issues that made data security harder for organizations. Technology businesses globally needed common reporting procedures after receiving public authority privacy rules in newly implemented privacy legislation. The US Children's Online Privacy Protection Act requires parents to monitor preteen-targeted social media networks (Chen, 2018). Effective management of any social media sites launched after 2000 requires the 1998 COPPA laws.

GDPR evolved from the EU's 2018 universal data protection legislation. The GDPR setup step requires business operations to specify data collecting and storage processes. Users acquired consent rights under GDPR, and businesses may delete and move data via data disclosures. GDPR's worldwide privacy framework imposes severe legal penalties on non-compliant firms. In 2020, the California Consumer Privacy Act (CCPA) became federal legislation to provide users protection and control over their personal data. Users might seek access to their data records and opt out of data sharing and erasure under CCPA. New regulations forced other states to pass identical legislation, resulting in federal data protection rules.

Facebook-Cambridge Analytica's 2018 hack took millions of users' personal data for political ad marketing. Facebook worked with Twitter to improve privacy measures and user privacy settings after the data theft raised considerable concerns. The 2021 Personal Information Protection Law (PIPL) in China regulates corporate data gathering and international data exchange like GDPR. LGPD was Brazil's domestic privacy legislation, whereas India's Data Protection Bill followed international standards. New privacy measures on social media sites strive to comply with government regulations. End-to-end encryption, two-factor authentication, and AI content monitoring systems secure platforms. Given that technology precautions currently exist, several experts doubt they can stop contemporary cyberattacks. Research shows three ways AI governance systems will interact with biometric data protection and cross-border data exchange rules. Digital privacy protection demands adaptive solutions since contemporary technology users need safe operating systems for worldwide interactions.

Figure 2. Timeline of social media launches, breaches, and regulations

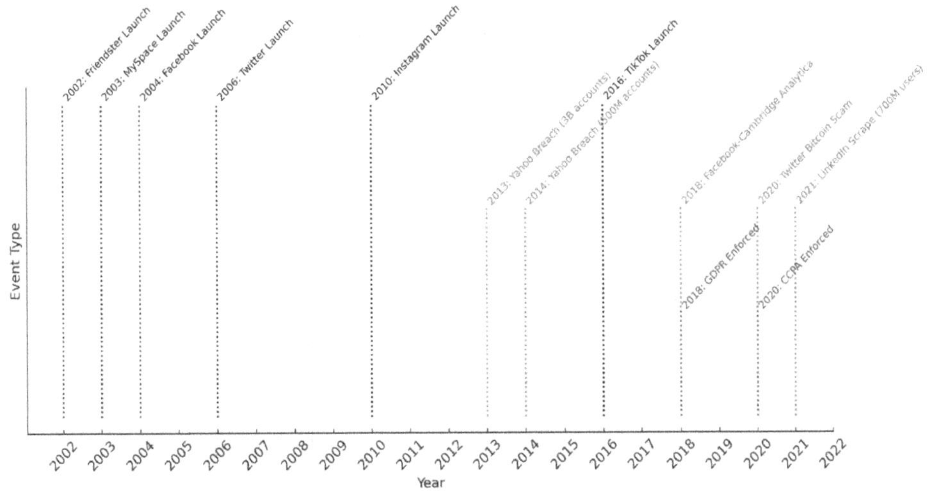

Figure 2 illustrates the growth of key social media platforms alongside major privacy and regulation events. Starting with Friendster in 2002, the timeline shows ongoing security issues, including LinkedIn's recent data scraping incident. The introduction of GDPR (2018) and CCPA (2020) highlights that privacy laws often follow major breaches. This underscores the need for strong security and unified privacy standards in the digital era.

Case Studies on Historical Privacy Breaches

Millions of user accounts on social media platforms fell victim to account thefts and falsification strategies and fraud because of security vulnerabilities together with unethical practices and cyberattacks. The five major historic compromises of privacy throughout world history drove both cybersecurity development and data protection laws together with their enforcement measures

Facebook-Cambridge Analytica Scandal (2018)

Scandal involving Facebook Cambridge Analytica in 2018 was one of the most dramatic turning points in the worldwide debate on data privacy and ethical access to personal information. The scandal got its start when it was found that a British political consulting Company called Cambridge Analytica was irrevocably misusing the personal information belonging to more than 87 million Facebook users and had done so without direct permission. This data was mined in an unsuspected personality assessment tool produced by a third-party researcher that not only gathered information of people who installed the tool but also the friends of those people via Facebook. Feeding the data collected allowed the subsequent creation of psychographic profiles that were then used in political campaigns such as the 2016 U.S. presidential election and the Brexit referendum. The scandal revealed serious imperfections of Facebook data-sharing processes and put the whole world in concern of user privacy, data safety, and the possible control over the democratic system using the targeted political advertisements. It caused a wave of public indignation, numerous governmental investigations, and even a congressional hearing with Mark Zuckerberg, CEO of Facebook, being one of the witnesses. The aftermath consisted in Facebook paying huge fines and getting a dent in its reputation as well as having to better enforce its privacy policies. This event has become a milestone in the movement towards more secure data-protection policies like the EU-based General Data Protection Regulation (GDPR) and has led to the rise of more people knowing of their rights to digital privacy.

Yahoo Data Breaches (2013-2014)

Yahoo data breaches in 2013 and 2014 were regarded as one of the biggest data breaches in history affecting the accounts of billions of customers and causing severe inefficiencies in data protection strategies employed by the company. The hack of 2013 exposed data of 3 billion user accounts and the one in 2014 500 million of them. The data that was stolen included names, email addresses, telephone numbers, dates of birth and hashed passwords as well as security questions and answers in a few cases. What was even more unnerving, is that Yahoo took its time in revealing the issue: news of the 2014 hack was not published until 2016, when Verizon Communications adopted Yahoo in its workplace. The two breaches had a strong negative effect on the reputation of Yahoo and caused the company to lose $350 million in the form of a decreased price of the company during its sale to Verizon. More so, U.S. Securities and Exchange Commission (SEC) has looked into the manner in which Yahoo has treated and reported the breaches accusing the company of not exercising their transparency appropriately at the right time.

These caused a demand on intensified security on cyberspace, improved detection structures, and more responsibility over the processing of data. They also sensitized the people on the dangers of using reused passwords, unserviceable encryption, and poor incident response plans. Yahoo case is still a warning of the long-term financial and reputation outcome of the data breach.

LinkedIn Data Breach (2021)

In 2021, LinkedIn was involved in a major data leak where personal data of around 700 million users, nearly 90 percent of all users, were posted on a hacker site that has been listed with a sale price. The leaked information involved complete names, email addresses, phone numbers, geolocation data, job titles, LinkedIn profile URLs, and other professional stuff. The scale and nature of the data leak were quite alarming though the breach did not concern passwords or other financial information. Encroachment on LinkedIn happened not because of direct security vulnerability in the systems but was based on the use by malicious parties of the public API interface through which they scraped data in breach of the LinkedIn terms of service. As confirmed by LinkedIn, private data had been accessed but this is only information that is publicly visible although there is a possibility of risk with this form of data collection in large quantities. The incursion fuelled the threats of phishing attacks, identity thefts and social engineering. As a countermeasure, LinkedIn recommended users to change security settings and consider using more secure authentication methods of protection by using two-factor authentication.

Twitter Bitcoin Scam (2020)

The Twitter Bitcoin trick of 2020 was a well-known cybersecurity event that revealed flaws in the management of social media and the internal system of access to sections. On July 15, 2020, a variety of high-profile Twitter accounts got in possession of the hackers, including Elon Musk, Barack Obama, Bill Gates, Jeff Bezos and Apple. The accounts were used to tweet a false message suggesting that any payments in Bitcoin to a given address would be doubled. The fraud was a success since within no time, the hackers found their way through to collect more than 100,000 Bitcoins among unsuspecting users. It was found that the attackers had accessed internal administrative tools of Twitter by socially engineering of some few employees. This would allow them to change the passwords of accounts and circumvent security measures. The incident was a vivid reminder on the importance of securing internal systems and training of employees when they are exposed to social engineering tricks. Twitter reacted by locking verified accounts until they could carry out a security overhaul. The incident highlighted the long-term implications of short-term impediments to platforms affecting world influence.

MAJOR PRIVACY AND SECURITY CHALLENGES IN SOCIAL PLATFORMS

The worldwide adoption of digital humanity due to social media created an entire active transformation while user data mining alongside security vulnerabilities and regulatory requirements resulted in multiple privacy and security threats for platform users(Jafari & Shaghaghi, 2023). The subsequent segment introduces vital problems together with their main concerns:

Table 1. Key privacy and security challenges in social media platforms

Challenge Area	Description
Data Privacy and User Consent	Platforms collect extensive user data via location tracking and preferences, often using complex and unclear privacy policies to obtain consent.
Cyber Threats and Data Breaches	Core systems of platforms are targeted by cyberattacks, as seen in the Yahoo breach affecting billions, including Facebook and LinkedIn users.
Misinformation and Fake Accounts	Algorithms rapidly spread misinformation and deepfakes, often aided by bot accounts, threatening digital trust and political stability.
Identity Theft and Impersonation	Attackers use stolen data for identity theft and fraud, tricking users into revealing sensitive info via social engineering and impersonation.
Third-Party Data Sharing & Surveillance	Platforms share user data with advertisers, brokers, and governments; unregulated AI leads to biased profiling and discriminatory outcomes.
Lack of Strong Global Regulations	While GDPR and CCPA offer protection, enforcement varies. A unified approach with blockchain, ethical AI, and user education is needed for comprehensive digital safety.

Table 1 highlights major privacy and security challenges in social media, including data privacy, misinformation, identity theft, and third-party surveillance. These issues underscore the urgent need for ethical AI governance and stronger digital protection frameworks.

Data Breaches and Personal Data Exposure

The unauthorized breach of user data permits intruders to access names along with addresses and financial records and passwords and personal communications. The principal data targets for cybercriminals who operate on social media platforms are massive user data repositories (Cain & Imre, 2022).

Causes of Data Breaches

Cybersecurity incidents usually occur due to several weaknesses in a digital structure of an organization. The most common problems that lead to poor security platforms include ineffective encryption mechanism, lack of good access control measures and poor management of passwords. Conceivably, the insiders who have access to sensitive information may be a source of risk as well since they may leak information on purpose or divulge confidential information because of negligence. The other serious threat is third party applications which are not subjected to stringent security tests and compliance procedures and are therefore easy targets to enter into an organization by a cybercriminal. Another equally used method to access the user credentials still involves the use of phishing. Scammers devise misleading messages and false messages so as to divert the user into giving the Login details, many times through some appearing to be genuine, messages or websites. A combination of these susceptibilities poses a highly diverse and dynamic threat environment in which organizations need to be proactive in mitigating by implementing thorough cybersecurity plans and conducting frequent awareness training.

Consequences of Data Breaches

Identity theft usually starts with criminals gaining access to personal information so as to create fraudulent identities to use in committing fraudulent actions in the form of unfair financial transaction and other unscrupulous deals. The consequences of such happenings are far reaching both to the individual person as well as the business. Companies being punished as a result of the breach of their data frequently lose consumers to the extent of losing value in the stock market and trading in the commercial world. Personally, victims of data breach usually experience emotional distress whereby publicity of their personal information causes some sense of victimization and digital insecurity. Regulatory agencies in most parts of the world have put in place tough privacy standards due to the increased significance of data privacy. The GDPR is already enforced by the European law enforcement agencies, and the CCPA was initiated by the authorities in California and has been brought by the global trends towards more stringent policy on data protection. All these developments call on strong data security and compliance.

Notable Social Media Data Breaches

Major data breaches in recent years have highlighted the critical failures of leading tech companies in safeguarding user information. In 2019, Facebook exposed data from approximately 530 million accounts due to inadequate security measures, revealing personal information and eroding user trust. Similarly, LinkedIn suffered a large-scale data scraping incident that compromised information from 700 million users, much of which later appeared on the dark web, posing significant risks for identity theft and phishing attacks. One of the most severe breaches occurred at Yahoo between 2013 and 2014, which remains the largest in history, affecting all 3 billion of its user accounts. These incidents underscore the urgent need for stronger data protection protocols, proactive security strategies, and compliance with international privacy regulations to prevent such widespread exposure of sensitive user data (Arzoglou et al., 2023).

Preventing Data Breaches

The protection of user data storage needs requires professionals to implement encryption technology as their security protocol. The security control MFA serves as an efficient security measure for its ability to protect against unauthorized access. Security audits executed on a regular basis allow systems to discover vulnerabilities so their fixings are applied before major system upgrades. Employee training programs through User Awareness must provide staff members complete understanding about phishing tendencies and scams.

Figure 3. Top social media data breaches and number of affected accounts

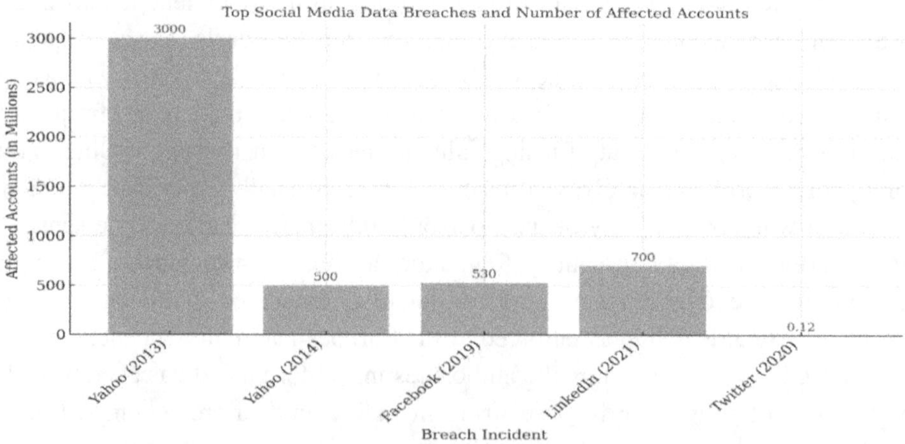

Figure 3 highlights the top social media data breaches by the number of affected accounts. It shows that the Yahoo 2013 breach was the largest, compromising 3 billion accounts, followed by LinkedIn (2021) and Facebook (2019). The chart visually emphasizes the scale of these incidents and underscores the critical need for stronger data protection measures on social platforms.

Cyberattacks, Identity Theft, and Misinformation Campaigns

Different forms of cyberattacks, identity theft and organized rumours often happen on social media nowadays. Hackers achieve these threats by using phishing, deepfakes and algorithms that distribute content for them. The end result is that people's trust in the business declines, its reputation is damaged and users' cyber security gets worse. To control digital risks as they change, it is important to use AI for detecting threats and validating contents.

Table 2. Overview of cybersecurity threats and prevention in social media

Cybersecurity Threats	Prevention in social media
Cyberattacks on social media	• Use of phishing to steal private data • Account hijacking and fake profile spamming • DDoS attacks disrupt platform availability • Social engineering exploits user trust
Identity Theft Through social media	• Creation of fake accounts using harvested profile data • Layered identity scams with false credentials • Use of deepfakes for financial exploitation and blackmail
Misinformation and Fake News	• Algorithms spread misinformation rapidly • False news impacts elections and financial markets • AI-generated deepfakes mislead users with fake videos
Impact of Cyberattacks and Misinformation	• Decline in platform trust due to fake content and scams • Reputational harm to individuals and organizations • Profile exploitation leads to corporate espionage
Preventive Measures	• Real-time AI-based threat detection • Media literacy and verification platforms for users • Content moderation systems reduce spread of false information

Table 2 summarizes key cybersecurity threats on social media, including phishing, deepfakes, and misinformation, along with AI-based detection and moderation strategies to protect users and platforms.

Role of Data Mining, Tracking, and Third-Party Data Sharing

Knowing how data is collected and saved on social media websites is necessary to handle privacy problems. Most social media sites get their user data from cookies and tracking systems that keep an eye on how people browse the web. Operator verifies people's real identities by checking their pictures and behavioural testing allows them to judge what users prefer. People are troubled when they unintentionally share their personal details with analytics and marketing firms, without any reward (T. Li, 2024). Data brokers usually combine user data they have access to in order to assist in targeted advertising. Political power often uses information from social media to monitor people's actions, usually justifying it by saying they need to do so for national security. People not being aware of how their data is used can bring about ethical and legal issues. Users are regularly asked for personal details, but most platforms still use this information for profit without giving people a strong choice to prevent it. Also, there are still issues with both the GDPR and CCPA and the authorities do not enforce them effectively which makes privacy defense harder all over the internet.

Table 3. Comparison of data types mined on social media vs. associated privacy risks

Type of Data Mined	Example	Primary Risk	Potential Impact
Cookies and Trackers	Browsing history, click patterns	Behavioural profiling	Targeted advertising, surveillance
Location Data	GPS tags, check-ins	Geolocation tracking	Physical safety threats, stalking
User Likes and Interests	Page follows, reactions to posts	Preference inference	Political manipulation, ad targeting
Search and Viewing History	Watched videos, search queries	Behavioural prediction	Filter bubbles, misinformation exposure
Uploaded Content (Photos, Posts)	Images, text posts	Facial recognition, content misuse	Deepfakes, identity spoofing
Personal Info (Name, DOB, Phone)	Profile fields	Identity theft	Fraud, impersonation
Friends and Social Graph	Friend list, interactions	Network inference	Third-party targeting, phishing campaigns
Device Metadata	Device type, OS, IP address	Device fingerprinting	Unauthorized tracking, session hijacking

Table 3 summarizes key cybersecurity threats faced by social media platforms, including cyberattacks, identity theft, and misinformation campaigns. It outlines the tactics used by attackers such as phishing, deepfakes, and algorithm-driven misinformation as well as their broader impact on user trust and organizational security. Additionally, the table highlights preventive strategies such as AI-based threat detection, media literacy programs, and modern content moderation systems aimed at minimizing risks and safeguarding digital communities.

AI, CYBERSECURITY, AND PRIVACY PROTECTION

The main use of AI in cybersecurity is to find threats and apply protection to stop breaches and protect the information of people using the internet. Since cyber threats are becoming more serious, AI is being trusted more to find threats instantly by linking to security measures on social media and other digital sites. AI reviews unusual behavior of users or employees by checking a lot of data, regardless of when the business is open or closed. They can monitor the network, identify any failures, report security alerts and prevent suspicious contact from happening (Bright et al., 2021). Also, incorporating machine learning into one cybersecurity framework helps decrease mistakes in detecting untested malware.

AI is vital for organizations because it offers effective privacy protection for their sensitive data and business procedures. The current AI industry focuses on using homomorphic encryption and federated learning to help keep data private during processing. AI also helps with security checks, enabling organizations to determine their own safety precautions based on particular risks. Data management tools powered by AI ensure that all users' personal data is protected during every part of sharing files. Still, AI also creates some problems and ethical questions. If data is handled improperly in the development process, it can open up opportunities for threats and make decisions biased. Ethics in AI-based security systems should be checked all through the development process. Moreover, today's digital security platforms are using blockchain authentication that includes biometric authentication.

AI-Driven Cybersecurity Solutions for Social Media

It has moved from simple threat detection to handle more complicated cybersecurity challenges on social media. Today, platforms rely on artificial intelligence to find out if content is real or fake, trace suspicious user behavior and immediately stop new phishing schemes. Because of advanced AI, it is easier to respond quickly to threats and negative content posted around the world.

Table 4. AI applications in social media cybersecurity

AI Use Case	Platform Example	Threats Mitigated	Techniques Used
Threat Detection & Prevention	Facebook, Instagram	Phishing, malware, unauthorized access	Behavioural analysis, anomaly detection, deep learning
Fake Account & Bot Detection	Twitter, LinkedIn	Spam, disinformation, fake profiles	NLP, facial recognition, user pattern analysis
Automated Security Response	Twitter, Meta	Account takeovers, suspicious messages	AI-powered chatbots, message filtering, user alerts
Deepfake & Misinformation Detection	YouTube, TikTok	Fake news, deepfake videos, manipulated content	Deepfake detection tools, content authenticity models

Table 4 discover how artificial intelligence is used on different social media sites to help cybersecurity. It outlines different purposes of AI which are finding threats, spotting bots and detecting deepfake videos and describes the websites where these techniques are applied. By means of behavioural analysis, NLP and deepfake detection, AI is developing new and effective ways to handle the newest online threats in real-time.

Machine Learning for Threat Detection and Mitigation

ML positively affects cybersecurity by letting systems identify and react to threats on a real-time scale. ML algorithms can also be used to study a large body of data to determine tendencies of malign behavior, which are more effective compared to rule-based systems. The known threats, like phishing or malware, are identified with supervised learning techniques, whereas the unknown threats can be identified through unsupervised learning by anomaly detection in user behavior. Such models keep changing in response to any attack methodologies and hence can be used to respond well to a dynamic threat environment. The threat response can also be automated by ML, which makes the entire process less human reliant, and increases a response rate, hence the overall resiliency of digital environments (Zhu et al., 2024).

ML in Malware and Phishing Detection

The AI-based malware analysis system uses a scanning method to track incoming files and applications for code threat control and pre-execution code destruction prevention. Original AI tools offer immediate phishing website protection by analyzing domain features as well as URL elements and webpage structural details (Quinn & Epstein, 2018). The filtering system of Nvidia analyzes email content through machine learning models which refer to sender reputation information to block potential phishing attacks.

AI-Enhanced Intrusion Detection Systems (IDS)

Network traffic analysis together with ML direction enables IDS to detect cyber security intrusions which are then eliminated. System database analysis uses signature-based detection methods to scan the malware signatures stored within its database. The system achieves security threat detection through its ability to track atypical network patterns thanks to artificial intelligence technology. The real-time identification of prospective cyberattacks through multi-source threat aggregation allows ML-based security operations transformation to build its main benefit.

AI-Driven Incident Response and Risk Mitigation

Automated processes enable an AI system to protect compromised accounts after threats are detected by automated systems. Security systems with integrated ML technology autonomously monitor cybersecurity threats throughout the day regardless of specific times. Organizations obtain automatic defense against immediate cyber threats through real-time security protocols established by their systems. Social media platforms alongside businesses deploy machine learning detection tools to locate security risks after which they activate parallel incident response protocols to minimize cyber threats by improving precise operations (Y. Li & Guo, 2022).

Ethical Considerations in AI for Privacy Protection

Cryptographic systems give effective computer system protection yet raise ethical problems since they establish rigorous surveillance measures and enable decision-making bias from algorithms.

AI and User Privacy Concerns

AI systems' capacity to conduct extensive surveillance leads users to worry about their data since they handle broad data collections yet end up mishandling the information. AI personalization tools create major privacy issues for users because their operation requires them to share all types of personal information to generate complete behavioural profiles. Technology platforms that use AI run security operations which users cannot monitor because their technical decision processes remain undocumented (Gogus & Saygn, 2019).

Ethical AI Practices for Privacy Protection

Placing certain essential steps as standard for AI implementation makes it ethical for organizations. Transparency can be improved using Explainable AI (XAI) to make the way AI makes decisions visibly clear to everyone concerned. User data privacy is improved with encryption, data anonymization and differential privacy as important elements of Privacy-Enhancing Technologies (PETs). Following regulations is very important, so AI security tools should meet the standards set by global privacy laws such as the GDPR, CCPA and the AI Act proposed in the EU. Lastly, using HITL security systems together with AI guarantees there is a good balance between computers and human experts for ethical monitoring. AI-driven cybersecurity systems run at their peak when ethical aspects are handled properly. It calls for using policies against harassment and designing approaches that strengthen trust among people using the internet (Wu, 2019).

BLOCKCHAIN AND PRIVACY-ENHANCING TECHNOLOGIES (PETS) IN SOCIAL MEDIA SECURITY

The combination of Blockchain technology with Privacy-Enhancing Technologies (PETs) powers both improved social media security and enhanced privacy characteristics. Users enjoy privacy protection from social networks by employing blockchain-PETs technology to obtain systems with advanced encryption and self-managed control together with system transparency features.

Figure 4. Integration of blockchain and PETs

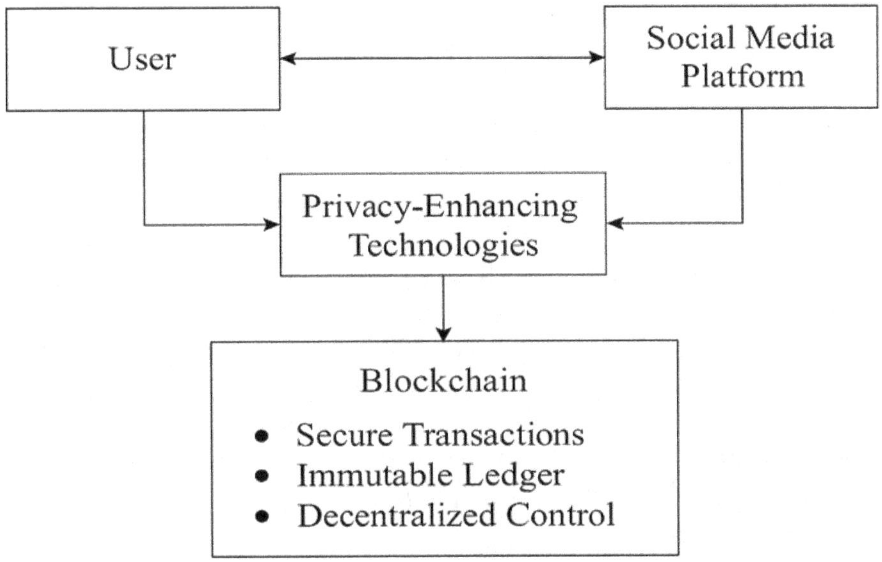

Figure 4 describes Blockchain and Privacy-Enhancing Technologies (PETs) are combined in the diagram to help protect user data in social media. It reveals the way people, social media places, smart devices and a secure blockchain system influence each other. With this architecture, users are more able to manage their own information without having to depend on single authorities.

Benefits of Blockchain in Social Media Security

Blockchain technology can play a very major role in making social media very secure because it allows transparency, data integrity, and privacy of the user. This helps it in that its decentralized architecture removes points of failure, and minimizes the possibility of data being breached or hacked. Blockchain could offer safe verification of identity that shields users against impersonations and counterfeit accounts. It enables individuals to manage their information with the help of smart contracts, implying their consent to sharing. Immutable records also assist in tracking misinformation and malicious material, bringing accountability. All these features create a safer and more reliable social media environment, which is of great concern concerning data manipulation, censorship, and infringing on user privacy.

Limitations and Challenges

Although there is considerable potential, blockchain has a number of limitations and challenges related to it in terms of social media security. One of the issues is scalability since a large number of transactions can congest the network and delay processing rates. Particular blockchain models such as proof-of-work energy consumption raise the concerns about sustainability. The blockchain makes data stored on it irreversible, making content moderation and other aspects of the right to be forgotten more difficult. Also, implementing blockchain within the framework of the current social media sites implies that there would be considerable technical and organizational transformations involved. Mal-standardized regulatory uncertainty is another common obstacle to uptake, and there is a dearth of systems that allow large platforms to implement them easily and cheaply.

Case Studies on Successful Privacy-Enhancing Technologies (PET) Implementations

Various industries achieve data protection and security enhancement by implementing Privacy-Enhancing Technologies (PETs) to fulfil privacy standards. The following part shows real-world deployment of PETs as successful operational examples.

Brave Browser's Use of PETs for Privacy-Preserving Advertising

Chrome The Brave browser combines Privacy-Enhancing Technologies (PETs) to provide the users with a robust level of privacy and security of browsing with taking care of the wide use of targeted advertising being supported. It has on-device ad matching which works by using in-built machine learning tools to show relevant ads without browsing data being sent off the phone. In order to encourage participation, Brave employs blockchain-based Basic Attention Tokens (BATs), which pay users each time they see ads and allow those moving digital marketing to be transparent. It ensures safety against fingerprinting by the browser, which blocks trackers and HTTPS (Gruzd & Hernandez). Consequently, Brave allows browsing that is free of ads, free of trackers and pursues a more ethical approach to advertising, as well as having a strong base of privacy-conscious users.

Google's Federated Learning for AI Model Training

Google created Federated Learning, which is the technology that enhances privacy by training AI models without the need to collect and verify user data at one center. It is critical in the use of apps such as Gboard and Google Assistant. This technology will allow the AI to be trained on the user devices, so that person data never leaves the device. Google engine is only presented with aggregated model updates, leaving user privacy intact. With this decentralized method, AI model fine-tunes its accuracy based on the information of millions of users without revealing personal data. Federated Learning is not only more powerful in predictions but also less prone to sensitive data exposure in health, finance, and individualized AI solutions, as such data is not subjected to unauthorized access and monitoring. The PET system demonstrates through tests that organizations can maintain privacy requirements without compromising their core business operation requirements. The cooperation between Apple and Google enables them to embed privacy tools across their systems which protect user data privacy during AI technology advancements (Oducado et al., 2019). Blockchain systems operated by Brave employ decentralized solutions that let users make private electronic payments through their crypto-secured transactions. User personal data stays secured because PET allows access to digital economy opportunities at the same time.

GLOBAL PRIVACY REGULATIONS AND POLICY FRAMEWORKS

Organizations and governments established privacy-regulated systems after users started to worry about data privacy so they can stop unauthorized data access. Organizations which apply collaborative privacy standards create documentation tools to push social media users to follow ethical conduct standards (Kwok Choon, 2018). Protecting people's data on the internet depends in large part on key worldwide privacy rules. GDPR states that all enterprises must first get user approval for data transfer and are compelled to notify users instantly if a security breach is observed. According to the CCPA, California residents are allowed to control their personal data and refuse the sale of their information to others. In Singapore, online organizations are required by the PDPA to take care of data and ensure strong cybersecurity measures. The Chinese PIPL law sets tough regulations for handling, moving and managing the personal information of individuals entrusted to businesses. Because of these laws, social media platforms are prompted to put in place encryption, privacy protection and ways to match compliance policies. As a result, they support the establishment of worldwide standards for digital privacy and increase the safety and transparency of data.

Overview of GDPR, CCPA, and Other Privacy Laws

Empirix Nordic AB along with its associations must follow privacy regulations to secure user information and maintain ethical guidelines for data collection and processing operations. Major privacy legislation at the global level consists of:

Table 5. Global data privacy regulations comparison

Regulation	Region	Key Provisions	Penalties
GDPR	European Union	Consent-based data processing, right to be forgotten, data portability	Up to €20 million or 4% of global annual turnover
CCPA	California, USA	Right to know, delete, and opt-out of data sale; data transparency	Up to $7,500 per intentional violation
PIPEDA	Canada	Fair information principles, individual access, consent, accountability	Up to CAD $100,000 per violation
LGPD	Brazil	Legal basis for processing, data protection officer, reporting breaches	Up to 2% of revenue in Brazil (max ~R$50M)
PDPA	Singapore	Purpose limitation, data access and correction rights, security safeguards	Up to SGD $1 million
India DPDP (2023)	India	Consent-driven data processing, grievance redressal, cross-border transfer rules	Penalties up to 250 crore for significant breaches

Table 5 outlines key international privacy laws, summarizing their provisions, enforcement regions, and associated penalties, enabling a comparative understanding of the global data protection landscape.

Governmental and Institutional Role in Social Media Security

Social media systems receive their security measures from both governmental authorities and institutional bodies whose primary responsibility entails safeguarding privacy standards and cyber regulations.

Policy Implementation and Regulatory Bodies

Both national and international oversight organizations are central to ensuring privacy standards and cybersecurity regulations are enforced by specifying corrective action through selective oversight and enforcement measures. One of the agencies at the European level is the European Data Protection Board (EDPB). The EDPB oversees the implementation of the GDPR throughout the EU, and it enhances consistency in data protection practices. The Federal Trade Commission (FTC) in the United States is an enforcer of USD privacy laws such as CCPA, fighting against data abuse and unethical action. In the meantime, the Cyberspace Administration (CAC) of China has considerable power within the framework of the Personal Information Protection Law which regulates data exchanges and the work of social networks. Such breaches of data are also investigated by these agencies and fines are imposed which is making organizations consider the factor of privacy-by-design in their systems and operations (Masur, 2023).

Collaboration Between Governments and Tech Companies

Public authorities create security enhancements through their partnerships with social media platforms and technology companies. AI technology should be utilized for developing security tools which identify deepfakes as well as misinformation and cyber dangers. The disclosure of information regarding user data management should be promoted through transparency reports. The enforcement of algorithmic accountability measures should exist to stop bias and discrimination in social media content moderation operations.

Law Enforcement and Cybercrime Prevention

The exploitation of social media platforms leads to cybercrime activities together with spread of misinformation and personal data theft incidents. The establishment of Cybercrime task forces helps both trace and prosecute cybercriminals in their networks. Cross-border data-sharing agreements for international cooperation in digital investigations. AI surveillance oversight and restrictions for social media usage must be established through government-made protecting-user-privacy protocols. Through public funding institutions operate educational programs which teach vital cyber security threats and security policy standards to users (Tian et al., 2022).

Regulatory Challenges

The dynamic digital environment will pose various regulatory issues to businesses, particularly to multinational companies. Different laws on privacy exist in different countries, and hence the multinational companies find it difficult to comply with them, and various laws of different countries conflict. Further, data sovereignty regulations make cross-border data processing tricky, and limit operational flexibility. The existing regulatory systems are not able to provide enough control over new technologies such as AI, blockchain, IoT and leave some of the most important security issues unresolved. Also, implementation systems are generally very feeble and data protection agencies are not well empowered to act as a deterrence to privacy invaders in many areas. Such issues point to the fact that harmonized global standards and more robust regulatory infrastructures are required to make sure that the protection of the data is holistic.

USER-CENTRIC STRATEGIES FOR ENHANCING PRIVACY AND SECURITY

Users need to deploy bottom-up security measures that defend their personal information while ensuring that platforms also take responsibility for safeguarding user data. When processing user data, the Users Controller requires its own encryption system to provide authentication security while automatically restricting data collection. The entire user base of social media platforms requires comprehensive training on recognizing phishing attacks, social engineering assaults, and other data security threats. Every platform member should have access to their own control panel, allowing them to manage data-sharing permissions and control the level of access granted to advertisers (Watney, 2024).

The system achieves higher security levels through Privacy-Enhancing Technologies (PETs), which incorporate anonymous data processing components, decentralized user identity management functions, and zero-knowledge verification mechanisms. Security frameworks that integrate Artificial Intelligence systems can monitor threats in real time while simultaneously detecting unfair or harmful actions and deception attempts. Social media systems must implement GDPR and CCPA privacy requirements to ensure users can easily access information about how their data is processed. By adopting these design strategies, social media platforms can build secure, protected digital networks that foster trust among users.

Figure 5. User strategies to enhance social media privacy

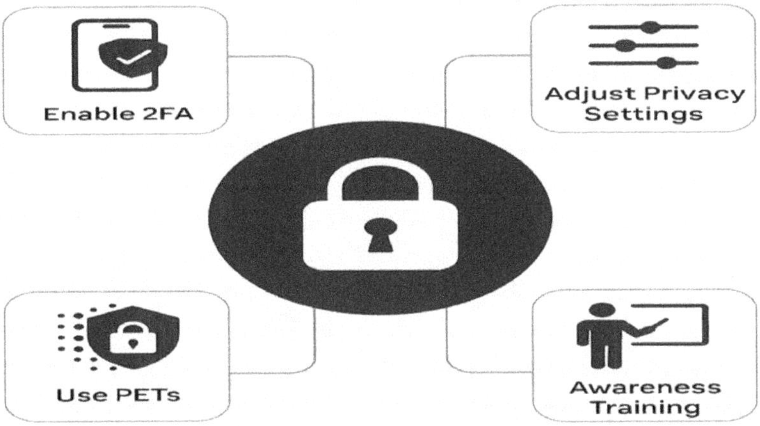

Figure 5 shows how users can apply four useful strategies to increase their privacy on social media. They are, among others, Two-Factor Authentication (2FA), adjusting privacy options, training to be aware and using Privacy-Enhancing Technologies (PETs). All of these guidelines help users be ready to handle their online data and reduce the chances of being exposed to online risks. The central lock stresses that everyone is agreed on the importance of protecting digital identities.

FUTURE DIRECTIONS IN SOCIAL MEDIA PRIVACY AND SECURITY

Modern technology and flexible rules and personal security measures improve social media user privacy security. Since threat monitoring powers AI-based cybersecurity solutions, real-time security threat identification is necessary. Since Blockchain authentication and decentralized identity management remove centralized storage systems, users have improved privacy. New GDPR and CCPA laws improve data privacy and business responsibility. New social media platforms seek to safeguard user data via zero-knowledge proofs, homomorphic encryption, and AI-based anonymization (Beigi & Liu, 2020). Education on digital competences and ethical norms for AI deployments determine data misuses. Privacy-oriented design components safeguard individuals while enabling exposure across platforms and satisfying creative demands on social media sites. Properly constructed structures enable safe world-wide user contact.

Figure 6. Rise of AI and blockchain adoption vs. breach incidents (2010–2023)

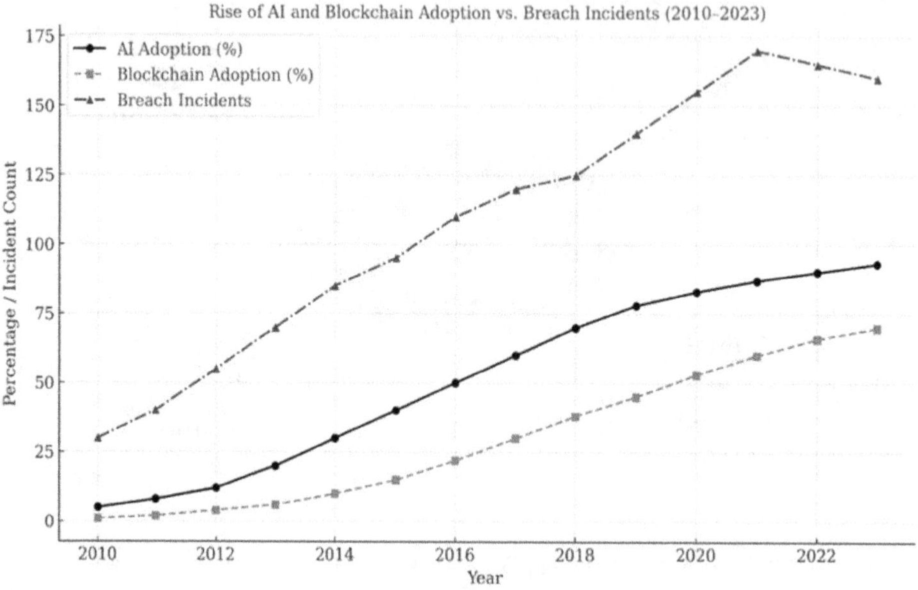

Figure 6 shows a steady increase in AI and blockchain adoption over the years, alongside a fluctuating but overall rising trend in data breach incidents, emphasizing the need for evolving security frameworks.

Emerging Trends in AI and Cybersecurity Solutions

Businesses may construct defensive systems with optimum operational speed by using AI security solutions to discover security flaws early. AI algorithms examine large data sets to find security flaws and automatically identify phishing, malware, and illegal access. Social media networks are better protected against cyberattacks using ML threat pattern detection. Deep learning and NLP help identify deepfakes and social engineering assaults in fake news. Virtual assistants and chatbots enable artificial intelligence to discover security concerns via privacy control management. Automatic cyber threat deactivation is enabled by pre-installed artificial incident response mechanisms. Blockchain systems leverage AI for transaction and identity verification security. Absence of ethical norms in AI production has caused a steady stream of difficulties as it breaches confidentiality requirements and allows systematic prejudice while networks remain at danger of exploiting AI (Zouai et al., 2024).

Ethical and Sustainable Data Practices in Digital Privacy and Security

Because digital technologies are evolving, taking care of personal data need to focus on ethics and sustainability. These laws such as GDPR and CCPA, require companies to get clear approval from users before starting to collect their data. Many governments, for example those in China and India, have introduced privacy legislation that agrees with worldwide regulations. They are designed to bring about global privacy rules involving international data management, rules on surveillance and fair rights for all (Ahmed & Rashid, 2024). Regulators are now introducing rules that do not allow the use of ambiguous, discriminatory or false algorithms in AI. It is important for AI evaluation to guarantee that it is clear, ensure that algorithms are unbiased and prevent discrimination. Partnerships should be developed by national governments with companies and organizations addressing IT issues and privacy, so digital environments can be built that suit all needs.

In the meantime, making digital privacy and security more sustainable has grown very important. Since the demand for data storage increases quickly, it has become necessary to build green data centers to save energy. They rely on renewable resources to cut back on emissions and ensure their digital infrastructure is safe. In addition, ethical use of AI calls for using established data formats and simple cryptographic tools that protect data privacy without overloading the system. Besides, people should know how to read data privacy terms, control their information, use technology to protect their privacy and master digital literacy. Together, users and providers should adopt both ethical and sustainable methods so secure digital environments thrive and protect the environment at the same time (Patel et al., 2024).

Summary of High-Impact Data Breaches and Their Regulatory Consequences

The section goes on to summarize the largest breaches seen on social media, describing how they were sized, responded to and how these events led to policy changes. Thanks to these incidents, the need for global privacy laws such as GDPR and CCPA, became clearer. Check the below list to see the outcomes of the breaches and their part in creating today's data governance approaches.

Table 6. Summary of major breaches and their impact

Top 5 Breaches	Accounts Affected	Security Response	Resultant Policy Change
Yahoo (2013–14)	3 billion (2013), 500M (2014)	Delayed disclosure, forced internal security review	Pushed industry toward mandatory breach reporting
Facebook–Cambridge Analytica (2018)	87 million	$5B FTC fine, privacy audits, API restrictions	Sparked GDPR enforcement and CCPA legislation
LinkedIn Scraping (2021)	700 million	API rate limiting, improved bot detection	Renewed focus on ethical scraping & data usage
Twitter Bitcoin Scam (2020)	High-profile accounts	Admin access lockdown, MFA deployment for staff	Introduced internal access control reforms
Facebook Leak (2019)	530 million	Data cache removed, bug patched	Raised awareness on cloud misconfigurations

Table 6 highlights five of the most significant breaches, detailing their scale, how platforms responded, and the subsequent policy or regulatory outcomes they influenced.

CONCLUSION

Although social media developments have greatly influenced people's communication all around the world, they have also brought new security and privacy problems for users and companies. In the last several years, events such as the Yahoo breach for 3 billion and the Cambridge Analytica case for 87 million on Facebook have caused many new regulations to be introduced, like GDPR and CCPA. Tabule X shows that these occurrences increased the focus on security and also drove new developments in data governance. At the same time, using artificial intelligence and blockchain has given platforms the ability to secure their services better and allow users to manage their accounts effectively. Now, AI tools play an important role in handling threats such as recognizing fake profiles, detecting AI-based videos and detecting unusual posts. Additionally, because identity checks on blockchain are decentralized and its ledgers cannot be altered, user data is well secured. Even so, for these technologies to bring real benefits, ethics must be center stage so honesty, equality and responsibility are ensured.

As we proceed, social media ecosystems should always focus on privacy and sustainability. Both governments, providers of technology and users are responsible for supporting global data protection rules, including Privacy-Enhancing Technologies (PETs) and helping to spread awareness of digital matters. Since hackers now use more advanced techniques, the answer is in merging smart rules, responsible

AI and security systems that people use. By cooperating and being alert, we can make sure digital platforms become safe, reliable and trustworthy, protecting user data while allowing valuable online communication.

REFERENCES

Ahmed, L. K., & Rashid, R. D. (2024). Advanced security: The application social media and their security. ITM Web Conf., 64, 1006. DOI: 10.1051/itmconf/20246401006

Arzoglou, E., Kortesniemi, Y., Ruutu, S., & Elo, T. (2023). The role of privacy obstacles in privacy paradox: A system dynamics analysis. *Systems*, *11*(4), 205. DOI: 10.3390/systems11040205

Beigi, G., & Liu, H. (2020). A survey on privacy in social media. *ACM/IMS Transactions on Data Science*, *1*(1), 1–38. DOI: 10.1145/3343038

Bright, L. F., Lim, H. S., & Logan, K. (2021). "Should I Post or Ghost?": Examining how privacy concerns impact social media engagement in US consumers. *Psychology and Marketing*, *38*(10), 1712–1722. DOI: 10.1002/mar.21499

Cain, J. A., & Imre, I. (2022). Everybody wants some: Collection and control of personal information, privacy concerns, and social media use. *New Media & Society*, *24*(12), 2705–2724. DOI: 10.1177/14614448211000327

Chen, H.-T. (2018). Revisiting the privacy paradox on social media with an extended privacy calculus model: The effect of privacy concerns, privacy self-efficacy, and social capital on privacy management. *The American Behavioral Scientist*, *62*(10), 1392–1412. DOI: 10.1177/0002764218792691

Gogus, A., & Saygn, Y. (2019). Privacy perception and information technology utilization of high school students. *Heliyon*, *5*(5), e01614. DOI: 10.1016/j.heliyon.2019.e01614 PMID: 31193323

Gruzd, A., & Hernández-García, Á. (2018). Privacy concerns and self-disclosure in private and public uses of social media. *Cyberpsychology, Behavior, and Social Networking*, *21*(7), 418–428. DOI: 10.1089/cyber.2017.0709 PMID: 29995525

Hakimi, M., Sazish, B., Rastagari, M. A., & Shahidzay, K. (2024). Artificial intelligence for social media safety and security: A systematic literature review. *Smjc*, *1*(1), 10–21. DOI: 10.32996/smjc.2023.1.1.2x

Hermansyah, M., Najib, A., Farida, A., Sacipto, R., & Rintyarna, B. S. (2023). Artificial intelligence and ethics: Building an artificial intelligence system that ensures privacy and social justice. *The International Journal of Science in Society*, *5*(1), 154–168. DOI: 10.54783/ijsoc.v5i1.644

Jafari, M., & Shaghaghi, Z. (2023). Navigating privacy concerns: Social Media users' perspectives on data sharing. *Aitechbesosci, 1*(1), 20–26. DOI: 10.61838/kman.aitech.1.1.4

Kwok Choon, M. J. (2018). Revisiting the privacy paradox on social media: An analysis of privacy practices associated with Facebook and Twitter. *Canadian Journal of Communication, 43*(2), 339–358. DOI: 10.22230/cjc.2018v43n2a3267

Li, T. (2024). Analysis of personal privacy risks and protection countermeasures under the privacy paradox dimension. Transactions on Social Science. *Education and Humanities, 11*, 509–515.

Li, Y., & Guo, H. (2022). Sustainable development of shared mobility in China in relation to the privacy paradox of users. *Journal of Advanced Transportation, 2022*, 1–11. DOI: 10.1155/2022/8538347

Masur, P. K. (2023). Understanding the effects of conceptual and analytical choices on 'finding' the privacy paradox: A specification curve analysis of large-scale survey data. *Information Communication and Society, 26*(3), 584–602. DOI: 10.1080/1369118X.2021.1963460

Mohamed, E. A. S., Osman, M. E., & Mohamed, B. A. (2024). The impact of artificial intelligence on social media content. *Journal of Social Sciences (New York, N. Y.), 20*(1), 12–16. DOI: 10.3844/jssp.2024.12.16

Ni, S. (2023). How do privacy concerns affect consumers' self-disclosure on social media? In Advances in Social Science, Education and Humanities Research (pp. 953–962). Atlantis Press SARL.

Oducado, R. M. F., Sales, M. R., Magarzo, A. J. P., Panes, P. M. A., & Lapastora, J. T. P. (2019). Perceptions and attitude on using social media responsibly: Toward social media literacy in nursing education. *Belitung Nursing Journal, 5*(3), 116–122. DOI: 10.33546/bnj.789

Patel, V., Department of Computer Engineering Silver Oak College of Engineering & Technology, S. O. U. and D. D. J. A., Khara, D. S., & Tivari, G. D. (2024). Examining the integration of responsible AI principles in Social Media Marketing for Digital Health: A theoretical analysis. INTERANTIONAL JOURNAL OF SCIENTIFIC RESEARCH IN ENGINEERING AND, 08(07), 1–13.

Quinn, K., & Epstein, D. (2018, July). #MyPrivacy. *Proceedings of the 9th International Conference on Social and Society.*

Riyanto, Y. E., & Zhang, J. (2020). Diminishing personal information privacy weakens image concerns. *PLoS One*, *15*(4), e0232037. DOI: 10.1371/journal.pone.0232037 PMID: 32339179

Tian, X., Chen, L., & Zhang, X. (2022). The role of privacy fatigue in privacy paradox: A PSM and heterogeneity analysis. *Applied Sciences (Basel, Switzerland)*, *12*(19), 9702. DOI: 10.3390/app12199702

Wardhono, W. S., Priandani, N. D., Ananta, M. T., Brata, K. C., & Tolle, H. (2018). End-to-end privacy protection for Facebook mobile chat based on AES with multi-layered MD5. *Int. J. Interact. Mob. Technol.*, *12*(1), 160. DOI: 10.3991/ijim.v12i1.7472

Watney, M. (2024). Privacy and personal information protection by social media companies in an AI era. *European Conference on Social Media*, 11(1), 266–272. DOI: 10.34190/ecsm.11.1.2089

Wu, P. F. (2019). The privacy paradox in the context of online social networking: A self-identity perspective. *Journal of the Association for Information Science and Technology*, *70*(3), 207–217. DOI: 10.1002/asi.24113

Yang, R., Chen, X., & Fu, S. (2023). Unlocking privacy paradox in social media from a configurational perspective. *Proceedings of the Association for Information Science and Technology*, *60*(1), 1197–1199. DOI: 10.1002/pra2.990

Yerby, J., Koohang, A., & Paliszkiewicz, J. (2019). Social media privacy concerns and risk beliefs. *Online J. Appl. Knowl. Manag.*, *7*(1), 1–13. DOI: 10.36965/OJAKM.2019.7(1)1-13

Zhu, G., Li, F., Yan, Y., & Guenis, H. (2024). Privacy paradox resolution in mHealth: The moderating effect of rationality degree. *Journal of Enterprise Information Management*, *37*(1), 55–75. DOI: 10.1108/JEIM-03-2023-0119

Zouai, M., Naidji, I., Tibermacine, A., & Aloui, A. (2024). The evolution of social media: Implications for privacy and personal data. *STUDIES IN ENGINEERING AND EXACT SCIENCES*, *5*(2), e6074. DOI: 10.54021/seesv5n2-050

Chapter 8
Navigating the Digital Labyrinth:
Personal Data Privacy and Security at Individual and Organizational Levels

Md Mehedi Hasan Emon
https://orcid.org/0000-0002-6224-9552
American International University-Bangladesh, Bangladesh

ABSTRACT

This chapter critically examines the evolving landscape of personal data privacy and security amid rapid digital transformation. It explores the multifaceted challenges faced by individuals and organizations, including asymmetries in data control, cyber vulnerabilities, and systemic governance failures. The chapter provides a comprehensive overview of global regulatory frameworks such as the GDPR, CCPA, and emerging policies in the Global South, highlighting both progress and persistent compliance gaps. Emphasis is placed on best practices risk assessments, employee training, incident response, and data minimization as well as the role of cutting-edge technologies like AI, blockchain, and encryption in strengthening data protection. Ultimately, the chapter underscores the necessity of cultivating a security-oriented culture that embeds privacy into organizational ethos, urging a shift from reactive compliance to proactive responsibility in managing digital trust.

DOI: 10.4018/979-8-3373-3171-3.ch008

INTRODUCTION

As digitalization, that is the interconnection of cities, businesses and peoples for the modern era, becomes more and more prevalent in today's world, the issue centering around personal information is of fundamental importance. The purpose of this chapter is to define the dynamic and complex body of personal data privacy and security as both individual and corporate. The title references the complexity and fluidity of efforts to shelter information in the coming generations of invisible and living political technology, where legal movements adapt to fast-paced technical and social technological movements. The chapter starts with putting emphasis on how urgent the issue is by understanding it through the prism of digital change. Although such digitalization is efficient, convenient and provides, at the same time, the possibility to innovate, it also exposes the individuals and businesses to new risks like identity theft, surveillance, harm to reputation, and legal liability. The contribution of this chapter consists in the critical analysis of four empirical examples and real-world case studies that show that data security breaches do not rely on technical errors only but are also signs of impassable organizational, ethical, and structural deficiencies. In the following sections, the main challenges to both individuals and institutions are addressed: lack of access to information, weak governance frameworks, and human-centric weakness. Next, discourse moves on to discuss the subject of international regulatory frameworks such as the General Data Protection Regulation (GDPR) and the California Consumer Privacy Act (CCPA) in terms of their scope, efficiency, and limitations that arise for companies to remain compliant in distinct jurisdictions. Therefore, the chapter takes care to note that a mere legal compliance is not enough and recommends a set of best practices that seek to increase data privacy using proactive organizational strategies. These encompass personnel training, ongoing risk evaluation, and comprehensive incident response planning. I also make particular emphasis on the future technologies blockchain, encryption protocols, and artificial intelligence—as both future remedies and the causes of new kinds of ethical struggles. The chapter finishes with the discussion that technology and policy must nexus with a general corporate culture of responsibility, mindfulness, and caution. Leadership is needed to be both socially accountable and technologically advanced and ethically aware. This chapter combines theoretical with practical's, painting information security and privacy picture and offers help to academics, policymakers, practitioners, and students hoping to penetrate and deal with challenging data security and privacy circumstances. Instead of proposing specific and seductive solutions, it attempts to offer readers the analytic resources that allow them to wander through the digital labyrinth by means of intelligent resilience and moral posture.

CHALLENGES IN DATA PRIVACY AND SECURITY

Digital technologies revolutionized today's world and brought a new stage of immeasurable connectivity and data occurrence. However, this digital transformation, though full of promise, has also generated a bunch of data privacy and security problems at the individual and organizational levels. With the proliferation of digital platforms and their increasing engagement with digital platforms, the vulnerabilities are proliferated for multifaceted and deeply embedded ones in system, policies and practices. At an individual level, the main issue is that of asymmetry of information between data subjects and data controllers. Most of the average users don't know exactly how personal data is collected, processed, shared and stored. As a result, corporations and digital platforms that mobilize opaque data governance models have an excessive amount of power (Saeed, 2025; Zhang et al., 2022). Although there are an abundance of privacy policies and consent mechanisms, too many are formulated in ways that are obscure to interpret, and which therefore leave users poorly informed and powerless. Additionally, behavioral data (i.e., passively logged cookies, mobile apps and IoT devices) allow increasingly invasive monitoring techniques that most often happen without explicit consent (Pathmabandu et al., 2023). For this reason, people are becoming more and more vulnerable to threats like identity theft, spying, phishing attacks, and data guile. The Cambridge Analytica scandal is one of many telling's cases of how personal data can be weaponized for political and commercial ends (Heawood, 2018). And finally, no matter how harmless it may sound, even actions such as location tracking or voice commands can easily add up to building up into a detailed behavioral dossier containing potential long-term privacy risks. Some users try to prevent these threats using privacy-oriented tools or behavioral means, but those efforts rarely suffice against the advanced surveilling capitalism model (Saeed, 2024; Taufick, 2021). And the challenges are equally, in some cases more, complex at the organizational level. Speed always is given priority over security, in digital transformation because of the sudden need for speed, agility, and innovation. Organizations deployed cloud services, data analytics platforms, artificial intelligence and IoT solutions without considering its security ramifications considerably (Ahmad et al., 2021). These technologies are powerful, but they exponentially increase the surface area to be attacked. A perfect example could be the 2020 Microsoft Power Apps incident that involved more than 38 million data (Sufi & Alsulami, 2021), caused by misconfigured cloud storage.

Figure 1. Spectrum of digital privacy challenges at individual and organizational levels

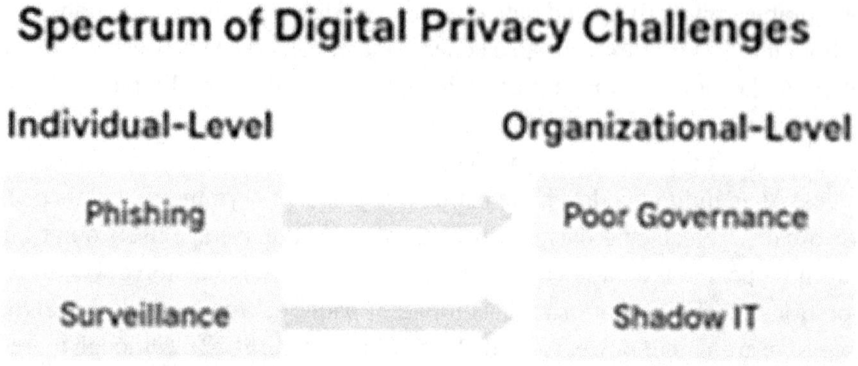

Figure 1 splits digital privacy problems into two main groups, those faced by individuals and those faced by organizations. Over on the left, it shows the dangers people face from phishing, spyware and being watched. The right column identifies problems facing companies, including poor leadership and independent IT solutions within the organization. This relationship is represented by arrows linking the listed categories, to show the increased effects from personal privacy problems in larger institutions. The graphics make it clear how incidents at a lower level can cause problems at a higher one.

The compounding of these issues comes from the fact that legacy systems are relied upon extensively particularly in critical sectors such as healthcare, education and financial services. These were systems-built decades ago and without today's modern notion of cybersecurity threats. It is both technically and financially burdensome to retrofit them with contemporary security measures, with what I will call a patchwork of a loose solutions that rarely reach systemic vulnerabilities (Panakaduwa et al., 2024). Most of the time, small and medium sized enterprises (SMEs) don't have automation in place for regular security audits or do not have the competence of dedicated cybersecurity personnels because of their low budgets (Chidukwani et al., 2022). Data breach consequences have become more severe in size & reach. According to Alkhalil et al., (2021) high profile breaches continue to reveal the personal information of hundreds of millions of people. The point is simply made that no matter how rich a company may be in terms of resources, there is potential for massive lapses in data security. Immediate financial repercussions (i.e., regulatory fines and legal settlements) are also followed by long-term reputational damage and stakeholder's trust loss (Raynor, 2022). What is more, cyber threat landscape is constantly evolving. Ransomware as a service, social engineering, as well as artificial intelligence is becoming too tempting tool for Cybercriminals to exploit system weaknesses. Geopolitical risks also come from state sponsored actor's targeting critical infrastructure and data repository systems to advance their strategic interests (Adeyeri & Abroshan, 2024). In such a volatile environment, risk management walks a fine line, on one side being too risky and on the other too willing for innovation to take place in the market space they are working on.

The human factor is yet another problem that plagues us. You can have the best cybersecurity infrastructure however, there are several acts of employee negligence that have capabilities of compromising that security infrastructure such as falling victim to a phish email or mishandling sensitive information. IBM's Cost of a Data Breach Report 2023 sees 74% of breaches emanating from human error, privilege misuse or compromised credentials (Neelakrishnan, 2024). This is proof of why there must be organizations with a culture that continually trains and educates its employees about cybersecurity. In short, the data privacy and security challenges are far from technical or regulatory; they are social, organizational and ethical. Such systems have limitations that must be addressed as well as the behaviors of the individuals that are inside such systems must be addressed by a multidimensional strategy. But to create digital ecosystems that are secure, equitable, and trustworthy, we first must acknowledge and confront these challenges.

REGULATORY LANDSCAPE

Personal data privacy and security laws across international jurisdictions have undergone significant developments in recent times because individuals have become more aware and multiple major breach incidents have occurred while concerns about surveillance capitalism continue to grow. All jurisdictions have enacted various policies and laws which grant people control of their personal data but must maintain transparent operations by organizations that collect and manage personal data. GDPR serves as the primary regulatory system for data protection since its implementation date of May 25th, 2018. Since its establishment as the broadest data protection policy GDPR established itself as the new standard for privacy discussion through its subjects' data authority reconstruction. Individuals possess fundamental rights under GDPR to get data access along with data correction and data deletion and request data processing restrictions and oppose data utilization (Neelakrishnan, 2024). The framework also forces organizations to maintain fairness and transparency as well as compliance with legal principles (Neelakrishnan, 2024). Under GDPR firms must design data protection as an intrinsic element of their systems and operational development processes from the beginning (Labadie

& Legner, 2023). The GDPR demonstrates extended territorial jurisdiction beyond European borders because it affects both local companies alongside entities marketing to EU citizens and monitoring EU persons no matter the organization's location. The worldwide adoption of GDPR made it an effective global benchmark for data protection operations which forces non-European companies to adjust their data handling systems (Pauletto, 2021).

The data privacy regulations of the United States exist as separate laws across different sectors of the economy. The California Consumer Privacy Act (CCPA) launched its major territorial privacy protection measures through the January 2020 implementation. California citizens through the CCPA enjoy the right to learn about data collection purposes while requesting deletion and remaining unaffected by the sale of their information. CPRA became law in California to enhance data protection through requirements for data minimization and it formed the California Privacy Protection Agency (CPPA) to serve as an independent enforcement body (Shandilya et al., 2024). Multiple American states like Virginia and Colorado plus Connecticut and Utah have prioritized the creation of their own privacy rules which makes compliance efforts complex for businesses extending across borders. A federal privacy law absence in the United States created a fragmented regulatory framework that generates unclear standards which increase the difficulties for enterprises to maintain compliance. According to Shandilya et al., (2024), Various federal privacy laws have been introduced in Congress, but political disagreements have prevented their passage. Multiple countries are now building or have already installed comprehensive data protection legislations across the world. In 2020 Brazil established its General Data Protection Law (LGPD) which features comparable provisions and enforcement scope to the GDPR. The regulations define rules regarding data reduction together with purpose limitation and permission and create the Autoridade Nacional de Proteção de Dados (ANPD) as its governing agency (Bezerra Sales Sarlet & Piñeiro Rodriguez, 2023). After thorough evaluation India passed the Digital Personal Data Protection (DPDP) Act during 2023. As per the DPDP Act individuals receive rights for access, correction, erasure and grievance redressal and data fiduciaries must act to maintain adequate security standards (Malhotra & Malhotra, 2024). The Personal Information Protection and Electronic Documents Act (PIPEDA) currently operates in Canada as the country upgrades privacy regulations toward international standards. The Consumer Privacy Protection Act (CPPA) proposes to provide stronger enforcement powers together with expanded individual rights because the government recognizes modern data protection needs (Farhad, 2024).

Figure 2. Global regulatory frameworks comparison (GDPR, CCPA, LGPD, DPDP, PIPEDA)

Global Regulatory Frameworks Comparison

	GDPR	CCPA	LGPD	DPDP	PIPEDA
Coverage	Individuals in the EU	Residents of California	Individuals in Brazil	Digital personal data of individuals in India	Personal data collected federally
Penalties	Up to €20 million or 4 % of global turnover	Up to $7.500 per violation	Up to 2 % of revenue or 50 million BRL	Up to ₹250 crore	Up to $ 100.000
Consent	Requires opt-in conset	Opt-out with some opt-in requirements	Requires opt-in consent	Allows for deemed consent	Requires implied or express cusen
Cross-Border Data Transfer	Restrictions with sdequacy or safeguards	No specific requirements	Restrictions with safeguards	Allowed if requirements are met	Restrictions with safeguards

Figure 2 compares the important regulations for data protection in the EU, California, Brazil, India and Canada. The chart indicates important points related to what businesses can expect to be covered, the possible penalties, how consent is requested and what data protection rules apply when businesses are in different countries. It points out that GDPR and LGPD need active agreement from individuals and carry big fines, but CCPA takes a less strict and lets users opt out. There are big differences in how international data transfer regulations work. GDPR, LGPD and PIPEDA all require security measures, while DPDP specifies when transfer can be allowed and CCPA imposes no rules.

Efficient data privacy legislation implementation faces multiple barriers even when new progress is observed. The different sets of regulations between nations create major operational obstacles for multinational organizations. International businesses face challenges from different interpretations and enforcement procedures related to compliance dates which escalate their administrative obligations and create legal interpretation difficulties. The diverse interpretations between legal entities regarding fundamental expressions along with words like "consent," "legitimate interest," and "personal data" make it difficult to achieve harmonization goals (Kun, 2025). Enforcement capability faces an important operational obstacle. Data protection authorities (DPAs) across various areas encounter financial limitations together with technical shortages and insufficient staffing to properly conduct complex computer investigations or complicated enforcement procedures. The insufficient funding between parties creates an environment where ethical laws remain ineffective thus specific organizations continue non-compliant operations without proper consequences (Shandilya et al., 2024). The lack of suitable privacy regulations in a particular nation leaves its citizens exposed to harmful data exploitation practices. Technological privacy frameworks in specific African territories along with parts of Southeast Asia and the Middle East do not exist completely or lack robust enforcement capabilities. These jurisdictions do not have adequate legal protection for data collection which allows both domestic and international groups to gather information without notifying or seeking approval from affected data subjects (Calzati, 2022; Emon & Khan, 2025). The world requires international cooperation to create data protection standards which must match different jurisdictions because privacy safeguards are distributed unequally. Different organizations are working to shrink the existing discrepancies between privacy protection methods. Through its membership of more than 130 privacy and data protection authorities the Global Privacy Assembly works to establish better international policy collaboration. The regulator must maintain an ability to adapt since technological progress (especially AI alongside widespread surveillance and biometric identification) continues to develop. Technological advancements render regulatory definitions outdated in addition to outdated procedural requirements that become easily superseded in modern high-tech environments. An active regulatory plan needs to safeguard current privacy expectations while developing predictive capabilities to prevent possible risks that emerge through new ethical problems (Emon & Khan, 2024). The worldwide regulatory response toward data privacy matters has shown great improvement yet the pathway toward complete, fair and executable privacy safeguards remains incomplete. The GDPR along with CCPA serve as vital components protecting individual rights in the digital realm yet substantial operational barriers requiring solutions to defend human dignity across every regulation timeline. Every stakeholder must embrace their responsibility to fight for privacy protection in the digital world both governments and regulators and organizations and civil society groups.

BEST PRACTICES FOR ENHANCING DATA PRIVACY

The present time of extensive data collection and rapid digital progression requires companies to improve data privacy because it represents both a mandatory compliance element and vital organizational integrity and consumer trust factor. Enterprises must shift from their current reactive approaches because the increasing number of cyberattacks as well as enhanced regulatory oversight requires them to use a proactive strategic data privacy model. The core of data privacy needs integration into both company culture alongside technical setup and organizational decision structures. Efficient data privacy management depends on performing complete risk assessments as its cornerstone. Assessments covering the whole data lifespan need to analyze the full process from collection to storage and processing and deletion of essential data assets and potential threats. The National Institute of Standards and Technology (NIST) presents current risk assessment frameworks as an ongoing method to reevaluate privacy threats that stem from evolving threats and changing business operation needs (Beuchelt, 2025). Through regular assessment companies receive the capability to create tailored privacy safeguards which match their risk conditions and degree of digital sophistication. An organization needs employee training and awareness programs to establish their enhancement practices. Progress in technical safeguards has not eliminated human mistakes which remain among the major reasons why data breaches occur (Javaid et al., 2023). Unpunished mistakes including falling for phishing attempts and reusing weak passwords or mishandling crucial data cause the breakdown of sophisticated technical protection systems. The development of privacy-conscious workers constitutes an essential requirement. Every training program must be scheduled with periodic privacy instruction that appears in both initial worker orientation and ongoing employee development and performance evaluations. Building engagement and understanding of essentials happens through simulated phishing tests combined with privacy examinations and true case-study discussions (Dawson, 2020). Training programs need to adapt to individual work responsibilities of employees for maximizing their knowledge application.

The establishment of powerful incident response approaches directly depends on how well employees understand their preparedness role. Fast and coordinated responses to data breaches decrease their detrimental outcomes. All incident response plans require distinct definitions of relevant roles together with legally compliant notification protocols for breaches and forensic tools and result evaluation frameworks (Khan & Hasan Emon, 2024; Staves et al., 2022). Throughout different scenarios organizations need to perform tabletop exercises together with breach simulations to evaluate their procedures and identify areas that need improvement. Predefined communication strategies that combine templates and escalation guidelines must be established in advance to deliver immediate and legally proper messages to regulators and affected parties and media sources. Organizations should base their privacy-focused work on data reduction because it stands as a fundamental principle. Every organization needs to collect data only for specific valid reasons and keep it active for no lengthier than it requires. Through data reduction organizations protect both the volume of compromising information in breaches and adhere to GDPR Article 5(1)(c) requirements. The strategy of purpose limitation aligns with minimization by preventing data collection for one reason from being used beyond established boundaries that align with user expectations or consent agreements (Labadie & Legner, 2023). Data security specialists consider encryption to be the most effective means of safeguarding data reliability and system security. The best encryption practices use AES-256 cryptography to secure data as it rests on storage systems and while moving between locations. Accompanying these measures must be strict access control implementation which grants users access to only their necessary responsibilities. A solid access management approach demands the implementation of RBAC systems along with MFA features and auditing procedures (Wairagade, 2025).

The privacy engineering principle called Privacy by Design (PbD) demands organizations to embed privacy requirements during architectural design and procedural development stages before considering privacy as a supplementary feature. Ann Cavoukian first proposed PbD in the 1990s until the GDPR incorporated it into law. Privacy by Design (PbD) requires developers to weave privacy requirements into all stages of system development as well as acquisition procedures and internal operations practices (Bu et al., 2020). New mobile application developers need to determine which personal data the app requires for processing as well as specify the related processing methods and necessary user-controllable features during application design. Implementing PbD through DPIAs acts as a crucial tool for both Privacy by Design execution and organizational accountability. Transparency has dual importance since it satisfies the law while remaining essential to proper data ethics standards. The system must clearly present to users all the data they collect alongside purposes and periods of storage and all share partners. All notifications seeking permission along with consent forms and cookie banners need to facilitate understanding instead of producing unavailable data disclosures. Research shows that businesses which make their data handling practices accessible to customers achieve higher user trust combined with better customer loyalty based on findings (Aslam et al., 2020; Dehghanpouri et al., 2020; Khan et al., 2024). What makes the approach revelatory is the way it builds its operational framework on Privacy Enhancing Technologies (PETs). Four Privacy Enhancing Technologies (PETs): differential privacy, federated learning and homomorphic encryption, and secure multi-party computation facilitate the data use without explicitly disclosing individual information to be analyzed. Apple and Google both carry out privacy preserving consumption statistics monitoring (throughline differential privacy) that doesn't reveal identity of individuals. A current solution approach for managing data utility against privacy constraints are Privacy-Enhancing Technologies (PETs) (Kaaniche et al., 2020). All organizations must continue to pay proper attention to third party risk management. Cloud services and analytics providers extend data beyond the original business boundaries by also increasing data through software manufacturers. To conclude data processing agreements with their third parties, organizations have to perform extensive privacy practice examinations, but to perform sustained compliance testing, they have to build assessment programs (ISO/IEC 27701, etc.). This has revealed the need for extended privacy coverage across the entire data ecosystem, as organizations fail in covering their 3rd party risks (Quach et al., 2022).

Figure 3. Data privacy risk management framework

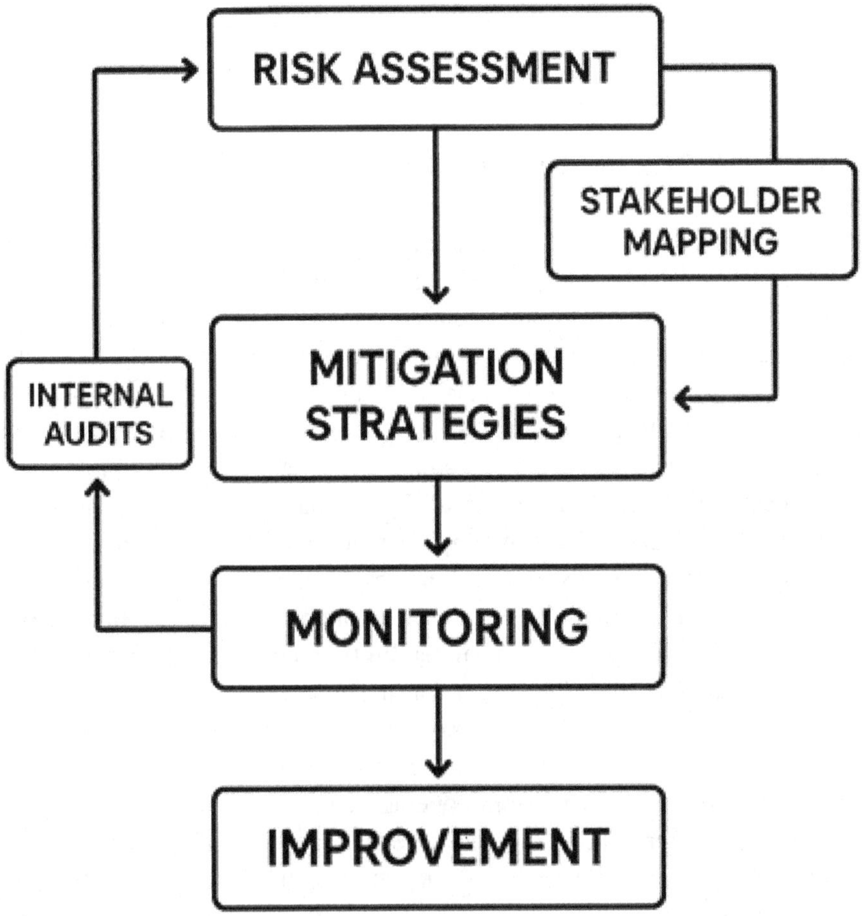

Figure 3, The flowchart pictures the iterative nature of protecting data privacy. The first step is Risk Assessment, which helps formulate what is done to manage risk. After the strategies are subjected to Monitoring, deciding on Improvement actions is based on the findings. The framework relies on Internal Audits to include the information gathered back into deciding on risks and Stakeholder Mapping which ensures all necessary stakeholders are considered in forming a strategy. All components of this framework are designed to keep improving data privacy protections.

To achieve better data privacy, organizations need to keep trying harder to foster their corporate values and technical capabilities, and they must adhere to the laws and maintain the right ethical yardstick. Continuing with the development of digital technology is that privacy strategies need to move away from restraining practices towards substance driven governance. When best practices are applied strategically instead of as minimum requirements, organizations have better control and defense of their regulatory obstacles, protect stakeholder rights and nurture powerful digital trust.

TECHNOLOGICAL INNOVATIONS

An increasing need for modern technological complexity is required to protect personal data and comply with privacy requirements. Today, Enterprises must do two things: they aim to boost their security structures but regard privacy as one of the basics in technical design development. Several modern technological advances that combine blockchain with artificial intelligence and privacy-protecting computational methods have established important solutions to achieve this goal. The vast potential of these technologies cannot be achieved unless their integration is deliberate and ethical and successful governance remains continuous. The attribute that sets blockchain technology apart makes it a leading instrument for maintaining transparent data systems with robust integrity. The core attributes of decentralization and immutability together with tamper-resistance found in Blockchain directly address key points of vulnerability which exist in centralized data management systems (Jin & Xiao, 2022). The healthcare sector together with supply chain management now benefits from blockchain that enables clear audit tracking while protecting critical data through removal of single central authority restrictions. The e-governance system that Estonia operates serves as a perfect illustration of this concept. The Estonian government started using blockchain systems since the mid-2000s to protect both healthcare records and legal documents and legislative information while ensuring traceability and privacy protection (Heckler & Kim, 2022). Keyless Signature Infrastructure (KSI) uses blockchain technology to build trust in digital networks through its robust framework which benefits multiple public and private institutions. Profitable partnerships between Artificial Intelligence (AI) and Machine Learning (ML) systems exist to fight cyber threats as well as halt the exploitation of sensitive data. Automation technology in security systems demonstrates superior abilities to detect abnormal behaviors and patterns which speeds up the identification of dangerous action patterns. Through analyzing vast datasets in real time computers determine sophisticated indicators of compromise which include network lateral movements and irregular standard access patterns (Asiri et al., 2023). The ability of threat detection tools powered by artificial intelligence allows them to automatically gain intelligence and develop advanced capabilities during continuous operations. Machine learning algorithms currently help financial institutions stop suspected fraudulent transactions from getting worse. Such systems combine behavioral biometrics and contextual analysis to detect genuine security threats accurately which produces less false alarm alerts and better client safety (Solano et al., 2021).

Through AI systems financial institutions are developing automated solutions for compliance work as well as GDPR-based data subject management systems which processes requests efficiently. A machine learning system called Automated Data Mapping (ADM) utilizes its capabilities to track personal data through multiple databases which makes the administrative process more efficient for regulatory inspections and risk evaluations. This operational environment allows technology to defend data while simultaneously maintaining compliance with ethical and legal boundary standards for privacy regulations. Modern encryption technology has transformed the way organizations approach the usage of safe data assets. Although encryption provides excellent transmission and storage protection, the analysis of encrypted data becomes a challenge before privacy risks occur. The computational system Homomorphic encryption lets data analysts work directly on encrypted information without having to access its plain text form. Technology's primary applications extend to financial services and medical practices as well as cloud storage operations because it unites protective capabilities with operational flexibility (Yang et al., 2020). External processing occurs under Homomorphic encryption through protected information sharing which preserves confidentiality during operations and computation tasks.

ZKPs enable someone to prove the validity of a fact through verification without revealing any details about the underlying information. Digital identification systems together with safe electoral technology develop through the addition of Zero-Knowledge Proof capabilities. User identification on decentralized frameworks through zero-knowledge proof technology lets people prove their authenticity without exposing their private details to service providers (Zhou et al., 2024). These technologies follow the principles of contemporary privacy rules by promoting data minimization. The innovative approach known as federated learning maintains rapid growth in healthcare research collaboration settings among similar fields. Statistics demonstrate that regular machine learning models require all training data to be located at a central point thus creating privacy problems. Federated learning operates in the exact opposite way of traditional systems by allowing algorithms to move to the data locations instead of moving the data to the algorithms. Different devices or institutions can work together to develop models by keeping their information safely stored on their individual systems. Google uses this technology through worldwide to provide optimized text prediction services that protect user privacy (Rafiq et al., 2022). Medical diagnostic applications represent a notable prospective use of this method because data privacy requirements are critical. These technologies face problems when deployed for practical use. The implementation of complex cryptographic methods like homomorphic encryption and zero-knowledge proofs poses major scalability and computational complexity issues. Several data tools exist in prototype development due to their incompatible performance with time-sensitive data needs (Rafiq et al., 2022). The application of AI in privacy situations requires complete examination of possible bias factors and transparency problems when using automated systems without interpretability.

Standardization and interoperability implementation requires further development to overcome existing procedural obstacles. The continuous development of multiple technologies demands specific engineering together with cross-sectoral relationships to establish single privacy control systems. Standards making organizations ISO and IEEE began work toward establishing privacy-preserving technology standards, but the domain lacks unified benchmarks recognized worldwide (Arshad & Asghar, 2024). All technical barriers fail to diminish the promising path created by uniting powerful data governance standards with developing technologies. By uniting blockchain technology with federated learning a healthcare system becomes able to secure patient data privacy yet achieve broad-based medical research at various locations. A joint implementation of AI anomaly detection together with encrypted data approaches increases protectability of systems while simultaneously increasing perimeter security. Technical innovation stands as a solution that should serve definite purposes instead of serving as its own independent goal. An organization needs to demonstrate a thorough dedication to openness as well as ethical accountability and regulatory compliance. The proper use of these tools leads to unprecedented privacy gain of institutions and allows them to successfully compete and innovate in their digital economy.

CULTIVATING A SECURITY-ORIENTED CULTURE

With the environment becoming digitalized, and all connected, the businesses in all sector types are then to put safety of their organizational resources, and personal information at the top of their strategic organizational objectives. Data privacy and security cannot be seen as something that can be implemented independently of cultural progress of the organization in regard to advancement of technology together with legal structures. This means that every organization will have to ensure that they create an organizational culture that is security oriented in the protection of data. And as for the cultural makeover, it doesn't start and end in IT departments, it must cover the whole organization. Technical systems alone cannot lead to a strong security culture, but rather the organization's belief that security and privacy, as well as other responsibilities for handling data, is an integral part of the organization.

Figure 4. Building a culture of cybersecurity

A circular model in Figure 4 has four areas Leadership, Integration, Training and Incentives connecting around the word "Security-First Culture." All these elements are connected and include executive leadership (Leadership), aligning security throughout the business (Integration), continuous training and awareness efforts (Training) and rewards rewarding secure business practices (Incentives). As a result, employees from all areas become aligned in their security thinking.

Leadership Commitment and Organizational Alignment

To have strong leadership present is paramount in creating a successful security culture. Security policies should be actively promoted by the leaders at executive and senior management level. Data privacy needs total executive awareness because it serves both strategic business purposes and legal and compliance requirements which affect every organizational aspect. Data protection must be considered everyone's responsibility in establishing an effective security culture since it applies to all organizational members including IT specialists along with employees from departments like marketing human resources and legal. Ali et al., (2021) identifies leadership commitment as an essential element which enables proper implementation of best security practices across the entire enterprise. The organization demonstrates its commitment through security project resource allocation and through continuous security-first initiatives promotion. Yet one of the most pivotal functions that leaders play in strengthening security culture stems from their actions which determine workplace conduct standards. Leaders need to demonstrate security-minded conduct as an essential practice. Security procedures must be implemented deeply while managers need to show ongoing responsibility in handling data. Leaders demonstrate exemplary behavior which acts as a powerful motivator because employees observe security procedures through senior executives' actions (Subramaniam et al., 2023). Embedding data privacy into organizational fundamental values enables executives to establish security as a main priority which supersedes other considerations. Organizations need this approach most now because they strive to find equilibrium between data-driven innovation and risk exposure in current economic conditions.

Organizational Integration of Security

Organizations need to bake privacy-by-design techniques along with privacy-by-default standards into every aspect of their operational flow and systems creation and service delivery models. Bu et al., (2020) explains privacy-by-design as an approach that embeds privacy elements in every step of organization operations starting with conception through execution. Forthright data management has gained wide acceptance in multiple market segments, especially among healthcare finance technology and other sectors that handle sensitive information. The incorporation of privacy measures into all development stages of products marks the essence of privacy-by-design before final implementation. Programmers need to integrate privacy and security features in each stage of the software development lifecycle (SDLC) during new application and system creation (Khan et al., 2024). The default privacy setting allows users to control their data collection because it ensures that products only recover the minimum data needed to operate. Besides their regulatory standards, the principles establish trust relationships with client groups such as customers and business partners. To flourish a design-oriented security implementation should be fully acknowledged by all parties as having value to the stakeholders and those stakeholders should have their training leading to master execution (Zavolokina et al., 2024).

The development of organizational security culture is not possible without continuous cooperation from all departments involved. Beyond IT departments or security personnel, the care of privacy and security responsibilities should be extended (Argaw et al., 2020; Khan et al., 2024). These perspectives should be integrated by the decision-making authorities within all departments, starting with marketing and going all the way to product development, legal, and human resources. These departments are vital data points in processing and collection of data. The understanding of data collection consequences for marketing personalization and advertising must exist in marketing teams who then need to follow privacy mandates together with organizational privacy rules. Protected access to employee data must be provided by HR departments to prevent unauthorized entities and security breaches of this sensitive information.

Training and Awareness Programs

Staff knowledge and education serve as the foundation for security-focused cultural development. Data breaches frequently occur because employees make errors in security practices when their awareness of security matters is inadequate. Businesses need to establish complete workforce training programs for teaching proper cyber hygiene methods which must include lessons about phishing threats along with password security and data protection procedures. Security awareness training programs delivered regularly to staff members create a 70% reduction of data breach probabilities (Khando et al., 2021). Organizations need repeated training sessions organized as ongoing procedures for maintaining awareness which adapt to new security challenges. The organization should utilize phishing simulation exercises to test employee responses to social engineering attacks alongside using current examples of security incidents to illustrate breach consequences (Wang et al., 2021). Specialist training programs should be provided to all staff who handle sensitive information or access critical infrastructure components to create proficient risk identifiers. The ability of an organization to create a security culture depends heavily on its capability to maintain employee inclusion in continuous feedback processes. The organization needs to establish feedback systems through which every employee level can notify superiors about weaknesses and suggest security measure improvements while reporting potential risks. An organization promotes responsive security resolutions through open communication channels which drives employee participation in the total security strategy. When employees are involved in decision-making, they develop mutual feelings of stewardship and responsibility which leads to enhanced organizational resistance toward upcoming threats.

Incentivizing Proactive Security Behavior

Employee security practices lead to outstanding security results which must be rewarded through proper internal systems. The practice of rewarding employees through internal systems and public recognition and performance-linked bonuses makes clear the essential nature of data safety and privacy to an organization. The recognition of security-minded employee behaviors by businesses consistently leads to better security measure compliance (Orehek & Petrič, 2021). Such acknowledgment creates new security perspectives that transform regulatory security practices into fundamental organizational goals while protecting its reputation. Developing security accountability within the organization enables staff members to handle their personal activities together with guarding the whole data infrastructure system of the company. Members of the organization participate actively in defending data integrity because security awareness and proactive security practices exist as core cultural standards for all employees. A security-focused culture demands long-term commitment by all personnel running from executive staff to new hires in every company. The ability of organizations to protect their assets depends most heavily on the way employees think and interact because both legal requirements and technological defenses represent fundamental but secondary data protection elements. All this is built on security oriented organizational culture, fueled by dedicated leadership, with effective functional synergy between teams and reoccurring training / rewards for proactive action. This culture is needed by an organization to deal effectively with the growing threats of their complex, digital environment.

INTEGRATING PRINCIPLES FOR HOLISTIC DATA PROTECTION

As digital systems are complex and connected, using both technology and following regulations is needed to protect data privacy. Because digital tools are vital for organizations to operate smoothly, customer service and innovation, they must put a higher emphasis on protecting personal information at the same time. A data protection strategy should bring together policies, advanced tools and the habits of employees (Farhad, 2024). A good data governance structure usually depends on three factors: meeting regulations, using technology and transforming the organization for employees. Accountability is provided by instruments like the GDPR and CCPA which are features of regulatory compliance (Labadie & Legner, 2023; Shandilya et al., 2024). Nonetheless, laws cannot always handle the fast-changing and sometimes uncertain threats in cyber space. It is important to use and review new tech such as AI that detects threats and blockchain that provides bookkeeping, to face growing cyber risks (Demirkan et al., 2020; Han et al., 2023). However, some of the newest technologies are just as vulnerable when placed in organizations lacking the right knowledge or mindsets. Every part of a company must work together to ensure data privacy guidelines are set everywhere. When IT or legal departments handle security and compliance on their own, the results are usually not well coordinated and can leave gaps. Sustainable protection of privacy should include collaboration between IT, compliance, human resources, marketing and the executive team (Imran et al., 2023; Malik et al., 2021). As a result, companies can meet regulations, as well as improve their brand recognition, performance from stakeholders and overall ability to compete in the market. Privacy integration in business processes is now considered a main aspect of ethical digital leadership (Gierlich-Joas et al., 2020).

Cyber threats becoming more advanced stresses the importance of flexible and strong cyber defense. Organizations are required to build ways for institutional learning that convert incidents into opportunities for the company's progress. An organization should have a planned, frequent response process, rather than react to problems only when they occur (Kock et al., 2021). Both technical controls and employee training should be guided by the outcomes of incident studies, user input and intelligence about current threats. Many studies show how people view privacy risks and behave changes based on their faith in institutions, how easy data policies are to understand and how much control they perceive over their personal information (Tan & Saraniemi, 2023). That's why organizations should include behavioral insights into their security plans by creating interventions that support openness, strengthen users and improve digital skills. When training programs include both practical advice and messages about values, they strongly increase a company's resilience (Lu et al., 2023). It is just as important for everyone to develop a feeling of responsibility for doing the right thing. Data projects are now critical elements of our economy and society which means companies must help encourage ethical behavior in the use of data. Among other examples, this covers asking for fair data usage, ensuring fairness in algorithms and joining international talks about digital rights. Involvement in multistakeholder initiatives and policy advise groups increases a company's reputation and helps it better prepare for future challenges. Real data privacy integration is not mainly made up of legal compliances or advanced technology. It features dedication to continually improving practices, teamwork across departments and honest responsibilities. By adopting this method, privacy supports and leads the way to sustainable growth in digital services.

THE ROLE OF STAKEHOLDER ENGAGEMENT IN STRENGTHENING DATA PRIVACY

Strong personal data protection often depends on how engaged various stakeholders are, but this aspect is usually not used to its full potential. The way individuals, organizations, regulators and civil society interact requires everyone to work together so that data privacy is developed through discussion and equally shared responsibility, rather than being only set by regulators. Interacting with different stakeholders in the information ecosystem makes privacy culture both safer and more shared (Ismagilova et al., 2022). From the perspective of an organization, people and groups internal to the company such as employees, executives and board members, as well as people and groups coming from the outside such as customers, suppliers, industry partners, advocacy groups and regulators, are considered stakeholders. All three groups in society are responsible for special concerns, rights and obligations surrounding data privacy. For instance, people typically want to know how their data is handled, but organizations that regulate the sector pay more attention to obeying the law and minimizing widespread risks. To align these viewpoints, groups must keep talking, use flexible systems of governance and manage shared risks (Safitra et al., 2023). Active engagement with stakeholders comes in several different ways. Providing access to reports, involving users in advisory groups, forming ethical data groups and bringing together many organizations to consult is useful for highlighting issues and gaining the public's trust.

User-centric tools, for example, privacy dashboards and consent managers, allow users to decide what happens with their data which strengthens their sense of control online (Pathmabandu et al., 2023). In the same way, working in groups with different teams or choosing departmental champions can support understanding data privacy and bringing it into line with the organization's main targets. Organizations should make sure to respond to the input they get from stakeholders. It includes receiving users' views and showing action by updating policies, making interfaces friendlier or changing the way data is shared with third parties. Acting this way ensures stakeholders that the company is committing to responsible data use. Additionally, stakeholder co-design is commonly seen as a best method in areas such as health care, finance and education where the risks are high. Engaging communities helps data-based systems work better and be widely accepted because they are developed to fit local needs and beliefs. During the COVID-19 pandemic, bringing contact tracing apps to the public required their support and meant that countries who involved citizens from the start and remained honest saw better uptake without breaking public trust (Sideri & Prainsack, 2023). Experts can also assist in creating conditions that help different stakeholders communicate. Modern agencies are choosing teamwork over punishments when it comes to maintaining compliance.

If regulators provide directives, support standalone environments for privacy experiments and organize gatherings with industry groups, organizations can try out innovations as they continue to follow important data privacy rules (Rakova et al., 2021; Wang et al., 2022). There are more advantages to using a stakeholder-centric method for privacy governance than just managing risks. Businesses that involve stakeholders in their privacy plans can drive innovative growth, avoid scandals that harm their image and hold onto a sharp edge over the competition. Because people are becoming more connected online and we see the ethical side of datafication more clearly, only organizations that work together, adapt and lead inclusively can help determine the future of privacy. Community engagement is an element that should be fully included in an organization's strategy, rather than treated as a separate issue. Because trust is easily lost online and truth is hard to come by, it is both the right and necessary thing to engage with stakeholders to build solutions.

CONCLUSION: NAVIGATING PERSONAL DATA PRIVACY AND SECURITY IN THE AGE OF DIGITAL TRANSFORMATION

Where once personal data protections were easily and clearly defined, involving the extraordinary circumstances of modern technological progress, it has become crucial to redefining it sooner rather than later. The rising dependence of businesses and public authorities alongside private people on digital networked systems has triggered substantial growth in both data volume and its sensitivity and data complexity. The transition opens several benefits alongside multiple risks which need an advanced and complex solution. Through a comprehensive analysis the author investigated five fundamental aspects of personal data privacy and security which include user trust breakdown forces and regulatory development and information security practices and technological prospects and organizational cultural aspects. Modern privacy concerns mainly stem from the major power asymmetry between organizations controlling personal data and the subjects whose information they control. People generally remain unacquainted with how their personal data is gathered and processed before it is shared with others. Openness has declined significantly due to complicated data analytics and monitoring technology thus creating conditions of heightened vulnerability between individuals and organizations. Fundamental problems exist in the way privacy data has been designed and deployed because prominent privacy violations along with identity theft incidents continue to occur. Today's high-speed and intense cyber threats exceed the management capabilities of organizational structures that work primarily in healthcare sectors and financial services plus e-commerce companies. This results in problems in security management due to the combination of old technology systems, disparate technology security standards, and insufficient IT skills.

It has undergone a mixed bag of changes across its network from the regulatory environment worldwide. GDPR from the EU, CCPA from California, LGPD from Brazil and Digital Personal Data Protection Act from India together define the data sovereignty and consent regulation along with accountability standard. The legal framework is set by these laws. Yet, digital regulations are more than just regulatory requirements; they are in fact also necessary for the protection of fundamental rights of people in their digital public roles. It is a difficult and irregular path to compliance. Continuous problems faced by the organizations are caused by unevenness of laws that are supported by uneven capabilities of enforcement and territorial disputes as the situation that significantly impacts the organizations that are doing business across borders. Regulatory framework is an unpredictable space that an unpredictable number of institutional operators are operating in. As a partial answer for resolving the current gap between regulatory requirements and day-to-day operations, a complete framework of best practices needs to be created. For example, when it comes to data protection, specific risks should have been evaluated not only for the minimization of data kept but also for encryption features and secure access limitations as well as to name a couple. But just these essential steps are not enough to solve the current situation. The organizations must arrange a permanent improvement approach including up to date incident reaction conventions and digital threat preparing and security arranged item advancement and administration planed. Unlike more common practices, institutional resilience is not carried out through the addition of extra components but based on having awareness programs as its central foundation. Human mistakes continue to be the primary breach trigger, so a staff which combines their combined alertness and knowledge with their commitment to ethical action and works towards preventing the breach remains crucial. Modern technology provides sturdy instruments that provide some security measures in protecting privacy. Three innovative processes, namely homomorphic encryption, blockchain technology and AI threat detection, can make data protection and predictive security possible. Such security tools are reasonably implemented and in so doing organizations enable organizations to move from mandatory compliance to active security benefits. There is no single problem that technological solutions solve. The major problem with any advanced tool is if it is not aligned with the strategic objective of governance structures and ethical framework. Today, the success of practical applications shows that implementation methods, on the contrary, don't work unless they properly integrate platforms.

Fundamental integration of data privacy and security into an organization wide business culture is the most important step. Writing policies and creating firewalls by themselves don't bring security. A security focused organizational culture requires all staff at organizations to understand data stewardship, whether they are finance, Human Resources, marketing, sales, or any other job function. The right handling of data is not just a matter of budget allocation and needs to be initiated and demonstrated by executive level of leadership. Three elements are required for the transformation of organizational culture, among the things one of the requirements are specific feedback methods, teamwork that includes various groups of people and safe practice recognition. Privacy is in fact, the amount to which organizations establish respect for the freedom and dignity of citizens within which they minister. Our collective efforts to keep people's personal data safe must become strong enough for the advancement of digital change. As the system is being modified, the regulatory system becomes more complex, protective mechanisms are more complex and the complications become more complex. The genesis for building a dependable digital future lies in purposefully unifying the elements of policy, practice, technology and cultural bodies. Having this in mind, the most important thing is that our actions show the importance of privacy protection in our current digital society because it is one of the most important human rights.

REFERENCES

Adeyeri, A., & Abroshan, H. (2024). Geopolitical Ramifications of Cybersecurity Threats: State Responses and International Cooperations in the Digital Warfare Era. *Information (Basel), 15*(11), 682. DOI: 10.3390/info15110682

Ahmad, W., Rasool, A., Javed, A. R., Baker, T., & Jalil, Z. (2021). Cyber Security in IoT-Based Cloud Computing: A Comprehensive Survey. *Electronics (Basel), 11*(1), 16. DOI: 10.3390/electronics11010016

Ali, R. F., Dominic, P. D. D., Ali, S. E. A., Rehman, M., & Sohail, A. (2021). Information Security Behavior and Information Security Policy Compliance: A Systematic Literature Review for Identifying the Transformation Process from Noncompliance to Compliance. *Applied Sciences (Basel, Switzerland), 11*(8), 3383. DOI: 10.3390/app11083383

Alkhalil, Z., Hewage, C., Nawaf, L., & Khan, I. (2021). Phishing Attacks: A Recent Comprehensive Study and a New Anatomy. *Frontiers of Computer Science, 3*, 563060. DOI: 10.3389/fcomp.2021.563060

Argaw, S. T., Troncoso-Pastoriza, J. R., Lacey, D., Florin, M.-V., Calcavecchia, F., Anderson, D., Burleson, W., Vogel, J.-M., O'Leary, C., Eshaya-Chauvin, B., & Flahault, A. (2020). Cybersecurity of Hospitals: Discussing the challenges and working towards mitigating the risks. *BMC Medical Informatics and Decision Making, 20*(1), 146. DOI: 10.1186/s12911-020-01161-7 PMID: 32620167

Arshad, R., & Asghar, M. R. (2024). Characterisation and Quantification of User Privacy: Key Challenges, Regulations, and Future Directions. *IEEE Communications Surveys and Tutorials*, 1–1. DOI: 10.1109/COMST.2024.3519861

Asiri, M., Saxena, N., Gjomemo, R., & Burnap, P. (2023). Understanding Indicators of Compromise against Cyber-attacks in Industrial Control Systems: A Security Perspective. *ACM Transactions on Cyber-Physical Systems, 7*(2), 1–33. DOI: 10.1145/3587255

Aslam, W., Hussain, A., Farhat, K., & Arif, I. (2020). Underlying Factors Influencing Consumers' Trust and Loyalty in E-commerce. *Business Perspectives and Research, 8*(2), 186–204. DOI: 10.1177/2278533719887451

Beuchelt, G. (2025). Information Technology Security Management. In *Computer and Information Security Handbook* (pp. 475–508). Elsevier., DOI: 10.1016/B978-0-443-13223-0.00027-8

Bezerra Sales Sarlet, G., & Piñeiro Rodriguez, D. (2023). Alternatives for an adequate structuring of the national data protection authority (ANPD) in its independent profile: Proposals to overcome the technological challenges in the age of digital governance. *International Cybersecurity Law Review*, *4*(2), 197–211. DOI: 10.1365/s43439-023-00081-2 PMID: 36819767

Bu, F., Wang, N., Jiang, B., & Liang, H. (2020). "Privacy by Design" implementation: Information system engineers' perspective. *International Journal of Information Management*, *53*, 102124. DOI: 10.1016/j.ijinfomgt.2020.102124

Calzati, S. (2022). 'Data sovereignty' or 'Data colonialism'? Exploring the Chinese involvement in Africa's ICTs: A document review on Kenya. *Journal of Contemporary African Studies*, *40*(2), 270–285. DOI: 10.1080/02589001.2022.2027351

Chidukwani, A., Zander, S., & Koutsakis, P. (2022). A Survey on the Cyber Security of Small-to-Medium Businesses: Challenges, Research Focus and Recommendations. *IEEE Access : Practical Innovations, Open Solutions*, *10*, 85701–85719. DOI: 10.1109/ACCESS.2022.3197899

Dawson, P. (2020). *Defending Assessment Security in a Digital World*. Routledge., DOI: 10.4324/9780429324178

Dehghanpouri, H., Soltani, Z., & Rostamzadeh, R. (2020). The impact of trust, privacy and quality of service on the success of E-CRM: The mediating role of customer satisfaction. *Journal of Business and Industrial Marketing*, *35*(11), 1831–1847. DOI: 10.1108/JBIM-07-2019-0325

Demirkan, S., Demirkan, I., & McKee, A. (2020). Blockchain technology in the future of business cyber security and accounting. *Journal of Management Analytics*, *7*(2), 189–208. DOI: 10.1080/23270012.2020.1731721

Emon, M. M. H., & Khan, T. (2024). A Systematic Literature Review on Sustainability Integration and Marketing Intelligence in the Era of Artificial Intelligence. *Review of Business and Economics Studies*, *12*(4), 6–28. DOI: 10.26794/2308-944X-2024-12-4-6-28

Emon, M. M. H., & Khan, T. (2025). The mediating role of attitude towards the technology in shaping artificial intelligence usage among professionals. *Telematics and Informatics Reports*, *17*, 100188. DOI: 10.1016/j.teler.2025.100188

Farhad, M. A. (2024). Consumer data protection laws and their impact on business models in the tech industry. *Telecommunications Policy*, *48*(9), 102836. DOI: 10.1016/j.telpol.2024.102836

Gierlich-Joas, M., Hess, T., & Neuburger, R. (2020). More self-organization, more control—Or even both? Inverse transparency as a digital leadership concept. *Business Research, 13*(3), 921–947. DOI: 10.1007/s40685-020-00130-0

Han, H., Shiwakoti, R. K., Jarvis, R., Mordi, C., & Botchie, D. (2023). Accounting and auditing with blockchain technology and artificial Intelligence: A literature review. *International Journal of Accounting Information Systems, 48*, 100598. DOI: 10.1016/j.accinf.2022.100598

Heawood, J. (2018). Pseudo-public political speech: Democratic implications of the Cambridge Analytica scandal. *Information Polity*, *23*(4), 429–434. DOI: 10.3233/IP-180009

Heckler, N., & Kim, Y. (2022). Crypto-Governance: The Ethical Implications of Blockchain in Public Service. *Public Integrity*, *24*(1), 66–81. DOI: 10.1080/10999922.2020.1848106

Imran, R., Alraja, M. N., & Khashab, B. (2023). Sustainable Performance and Green Innovation: Green Human Resources Management and Big Data as Antecedents. *IEEE Transactions on Engineering Management*, *70*(12), 4191–4206. DOI: 10.1109/TEM.2021.3114256

Ismagilova, E., Hughes, L., Rana, N. P., & Dwivedi, Y. K. (2022). Security, Privacy and Risks Within Smart Cities: Literature Review and Development of a Smart City Interaction Framework. *Information Systems Frontiers*, *24*(2), 393–414. DOI: 10.1007/s10796-020-10044-1 PMID: 32837262

Javaid, M., Haleem, A., Singh, R. P., & Suman, R. (2023). Towards insighting cybersecurity for healthcare domains: A comprehensive review of recent practices and trends. *Cyber Security and Applications*, *1*, 100016. DOI: 10.1016/j.csa.2023.100016

Jin, H., & Xiao, J. (2022). Towards trustworthy blockchain systems in the era of "Internet of value": Development, challenges, and future trends. *Science China. Information Sciences*, *65*(5), 153101. DOI: 10.1007/s11432-020-3183-0

Kaaniche, N., Laurent, M., & Belguith, S. (2020). Privacy enhancing technologies for solving the privacy-personalization paradox: Taxonomy and survey. *Journal of Network and Computer Applications*, *171*, 102807. DOI: 10.1016/j.jnca.2020.102807

Khan, R. A., Khan, S. U., Akbar, M. A., & Alzahrani, M. (2024). Security risks of global software development life cycle: Industry practitioner's perspective. *Journal of Software (Malden, MA)*, *36*(3), e2521. DOI: 10.1002/smr.2521

Khan, T., Emon, M. M. H., & Nath, A. (2024). Quantifying the Effects of AI-Driven Inventory Management on Operational Efficiency in Online Retail. *2024 27th International Conference on Computer and Information Technology (ICCIT)*, 2092–2097. DOI: 10.1109/ICCIT64611.2024.11021996

Khan, T., Emon, M. M. H., & Rahman, S. (2024). Marketing Strategy Innovation via AI Adoption: A Study on Bangladeshi SMEs in the Context of Industry 5.0. *2024 6th International Conference on Sustainable Technologies for Industry 5.0 (STI)*, 1–6. DOI: 10.1109/STI64222.2024.10951050

Khan, T., & Hasan Emon, M. M. (2024). Determinants of AI Image Generator Adoption Among Marketing Agencies: The Mediating Effects of Perceived Usefulness. *2024 IEEE 3rd International Conference on Robotics, Automation, Artificial-Intelligence and Internet-of-Things (RAAICON)*, 177–182. DOI: 10.1109/RAAICON64172.2024.10928548

Khando, K., Gao, S., Islam, S. M., & Salman, A. (2021). Enhancing employees information security awareness in private and public organisations: A systematic literature review. *Computers & Security, 106*, 102267. DOI: 10.1016/j.cose.2021.102267

Kock, F., Berbekova, A., & Assaf, A. G. (2021). Understanding and managing the threat of common method bias: Detection, prevention and control. *Tourism Management, 86*, 104330. DOI: 10.1016/j.tourman.2021.104330

Kun, E. (2025). Searching for the appropriate legal basis for personal data processing for cybersecurity purposes under the NIS 2 Directive: Legal obligation and/or legitimate interest? *Computer Law & Security Review, 56*, 106098. DOI: 10.1016/j.clsr.2024.106098

Labadie, C., & Legner, C. (2023). Building data management capabilities to address data protection regulations: Learnings from EU-GDPR. *Journal of Information Technology, 38*(1), 16–44. DOI: 10.1177/02683962221141456

Lu, Y., Zhang, M. M., Yang, M. M., & Wang, Y. (2023). Sustainable human resource management practices, employee resilience, and employee outcomes: Toward common good values. *Human Resource Management, 62*(3), 331–353. DOI: 10.1002/hrm.22153

Malhotra, C., & Malhotra, U. (2024). Putting Interests of Digital Nagriks First: Digital Personal Data Protection (DPDP) Act 2023 of India. *The Indian Journal of Public Administration, 70*(3), 516–531. DOI: 10.1177/00195561241271575

Malik, S. Y., Hayat Mughal, Y., Azam, T., Cao, Y., Wan, Z., Zhu, H., & Thurasamy, R. (2021). Corporate Social Responsibility, Green Human Resources Management, and Sustainable Performance: Is Organizational Citizenship Behavior towards Environment the Missing Link? *Sustainability (Basel)*, *13*(3), 1044. DOI: 10.3390/su13031044

Neelakrishnan, P. (2024). Data Security Fundamental Requirements. In *Autonomous Data Security* (pp. 1–39). Apress., DOI: 10.1007/979-8-8688-0838-8_1

Orehek, Š., & Petrič, G. (2021). A systematic review of scales for measuring information security culture. *Information and Computer Security*, *29*(1), 133–158. DOI: 10.1108/ICS-12-2019-0140

Panakaduwa, C., Coates, P., & Munir, M. (2024). Identifying sustainable retrofit challenges of historical Buildings: A systematic review. *Energy and Building*, *313*, 114226. DOI: 10.1016/j.enbuild.2024.114226

Pathmabandu, C., Grundy, J., Chhetri, M. B., & Baig, Z. (2023). Privacy for IoT: Informed consent management in Smart Buildings. *Future Generation Computer Systems*, *145*, 367–383. DOI: 10.1016/j.future.2023.03.045

Pauletto, C. (2021). Options towards a global standard for the protection of individuals with regard to the processing of personal data. *Computer Law & Security Review*, *40*, 105433. DOI: 10.1016/j.clsr.2020.105433

Quach, S., Thaichon, P., Martin, K. D., Weaven, S., & Palmatier, R. W. (2022). Digital technologies: Tensions in privacy and data. *Journal of the Academy of Marketing Science*, *50*(6), 1299–1323. DOI: 10.1007/s11747-022-00845-y PMID: 35281634

Rafiq, F., Awan, M. J., Yasin, A., Nobanee, H., Zain, A. M., & Bahaj, S. A. (2022). Privacy Prevention of Big Data Applications: A Systematic Literature Review. *SAGE Open*, *12*(2), 21582440221096445. DOI: 10.1177/21582440221096445

Rakova, B., Yang, J., Cramer, H., & Chowdhury, R. (2021). Where Responsible AI meets Reality. *Proceedings of the ACM on Human-Computer Interaction*, *5*(CSCW1), 1–23. DOI: 10.1145/3449081

Raynor, B. (2022). The shadow of sanctions: Reputational risk, financial reintegration, and the political economy of sanctions relief. *European Journal of International Relations*, *28*(3), 696–721. DOI: 10.1177/13540661221100540

Saeed, S. (2024). Usable Privacy and Security in Mobile Applications: Perception of Mobile End Users in Saudi Arabia. *Big Data and Cognitive Computing*, *8*(11), 162. DOI: 10.3390/bdcc8110162

Saeed, S. (2025). Digital Transformation in Governmental Public Service Provision and Usable Security Perception in Saudi Arabia. *Information (Basel)*, *16*(3), 247. DOI: 10.3390/info16030247

Safitra, M. F., Lubis, M., & Fakhrurroja, H. (2023). Counterattacking Cyber Threats: A Framework for the Future of Cybersecurity. *Sustainability (Basel)*, *15*(18), 13369. DOI: 10.3390/su151813369

Shandilya, S. K., Datta, A., Kartik, Y., & Nagar, A. (2024). *Navigating the Regulatory Landscape*., DOI: 10.1007/978-3-031-53290-0_3

Sideri, K., & Prainsack, B. (2023). COVID-19 contact tracing apps and the governance of collective action: Social nudges, deliberation, and solidarity in Europe and beyond. *Policy Studies*, *44*(1), 132–153. DOI: 10.1080/01442872.2022.2130884

Solano, J., Camacho, L., Correa, A., Deiro, C., Vargas, J., & Ochoa, M. (2021). Combining behavioral biometrics and session context analytics to enhance risk-based static authentication in web applications. *International Journal of Information Security*, *20*(2), 181–197. DOI: 10.1007/s10207-020-00510-x

Staves, A., Anderson, T., Balderstone, H., Green, B., Gouglidis, A., & Hutchison, D. (2022). A Cyber Incident Response and Recovery Framework to Support Operators of Industrial Control Systems. *International Journal of Critical Infrastructure Protection*, *37*, 100505. DOI: 10.1016/j.ijcip.2021.100505

Subramaniam, C., Johari, J., Mashi, M. S., & Mohamad, R. (2023). The influence of safety leadership on nurses' safety behavior: The mediating role of safety knowledge and motivation. *Journal of Safety Research*, *84*, 117–128. DOI: 10.1016/j.jsr.2022.10.013 PMID: 36868640

Sufi, F. K., & Alsulami, M. (2021). Automated Multidimensional Analysis of Global Events With Entity Detection, Sentiment Analysis and Anomaly Detection. *IEEE Access : Practical Innovations, Open Solutions*, *9*, 152449–152460. DOI: 10.1109/ACCESS.2021.3127571

Tan, T. M., & Saraniemi, S. (2023). Trust in blockchain-enabled exchanges: Future directions in blockchain marketing. *Journal of the Academy of Marketing Science*, *51*(4), 914–939. DOI: 10.1007/s11747-022-00889-0

Taufick, R. D. (2021). The underdeterrence, underperformance response to privacy, data protection laws. *Technology in Society*, *67*, 101752. DOI: 10.1016/j.techsoc.2021.101752

Wairagade, A. (2025). Role of Identity and Access Management in Corporate Management. In *Corporate Management in the Digital Age* (pp. 397–424). IGI Global., DOI: 10.4018/979-8-3693-8412-1.ch014

Wang, Z., Li, M., Lu, J., & Cheng, X. (2022). Business Innovation based on artificial intelligence and Blockchain technology. *Information Processing & Management, 59*(1), 102759. DOI: 10.1016/j.ipm.2021.102759

Wang, Z., Zhu, H., & Sun, L. (2021). Social Engineering in Cybersecurity: Effect Mechanisms, Human Vulnerabilities and Attack Methods. *IEEE Access : Practical Innovations, Open Solutions, 9*, 11895–11910. DOI: 10.1109/ACCESS.2021.3051633

Yang, P., Xiong, N., & Ren, J. (2020). Data Security and Privacy Protection for Cloud Storage: A Survey. *IEEE Access : Practical Innovations, Open Solutions, 8*, 131723–131740. DOI: 10.1109/ACCESS.2020.3009876

Zavolokina, L., Bauer-Hänsel, I., Hacker, J., & Schwabe, G. (2024). Organizing for value creation in blockchain information systems. *Information and Organization, 34*(3), 100522. DOI: 10.1016/j.infoandorg.2024.100522

Zhang, Q., Sun, X., & Zhang, M. (2022). Data Matters: A Strategic Action Framework for Data Governance. *Information & Management, 59*(4), 103642. DOI: 10.1016/j.im.2022.103642

Zhou, L., Diro, A., Saini, A., Kaisar, S., & Hiep, P. C. (2024). Leveraging zero knowledge proofs for blockchain-based identity sharing: A survey of advancements, challenges and opportunities. *Journal of Information Security and Applications, 80*, 103678. DOI: 10.1016/j.jisa.2023.103678

KEY TERMS AND DEFINITIONS

Artificial Intelligence (AI): Machines that are able to perform tasks such as decision making, pattern recognition, and a host of other functions that humans can currently do that are supported by human intelligence.

Blockchain: A decentralized, immutable digital ledger used to record securely transactions across multiple computers.

Cybersecurity: The process of protecting systems, networks, and data from any unauthorized attack, damage or access.

Data Breach: An event whereby confidential or sensitive resource is accessed or stolen or is disclosed without authorization.

Data Privacy: To exercise individuals' right to regulate how an organization collects, uses, and shares their personal information.

Digital Transformation: Digital technologies integrated into all areas of business altering the way of doing business and the delivery of value.

General Data Protection Regulation (GDPR): A European Union privacy and data protection law that gives individuals a broader set of rights as to their personal data, and imposes new obligations on organization's handling that data.

Privacy-by-Design: A principle that applies data protection and privacy to the ages of systems, products, and services from the start.

Chapter 9
Cyber Security Strategies for Enhancing the Privacy and Security of Social Media Applications

Shaheen Layaq
https://orcid.org/0000-0002-1785-610X
Singareni Collieries Women's Degree and PG College, India

Pakalapati Arpitha
Telangana Social Welfare Residential Degree College for Women, India

Shaik Parvez Ahammad
Kavitha Memorial Degree and PG College, India

ABSTRACT

Cyber security plays a vital role in providing security in digital world. It provides security for systems, networks, data and confidential of all the online activities from different cyber threats. It may be classified into three types' network security, information security and application security. It has become part of our daily applications. Among all the applications providing security and privacy for social media applications has becoming greater importance. Cyber Security uses various strategies for providing security and privacy for social media applications. Cryptography and Network Security are considered as a backbone strategies of cyber security which ensure that sensitive data is been secured in a scalable interconnected networks and plays a key role in enhancing the security of social media applications. In this paper the concepts of cyber security, cryptography and network security- architecture, working process, protocols and algorithms and impact of cyber security on social

DOI: 10.4018/979-8-3373-3171-3.ch009

media applications are considered.

INTRODUCTION

The most important buzz word in today's world is security. The security is needed for people, property and data. Among them the data security is most important and crucial one. Cyber security (CS), (Saeed et al., 2023; Saeed et al., 2024; Saeed et al., 2024; Saeed et al., 2023) plays a vital role in providing security and privacy for digital data. CS provides security for systems, networks and data from different cyber threats. CS not only secures the personal information but also maintains confidential of all the online activities. CS may be classified into three types'

a) **Network security** - It protect computer system and networks from cyber attacks which may include integrity, availability and confidentiality.
b) **Information security** - It deals with personal and private information of individuals which may include authentication, authorization and cryptography.
c) **Application security** - It secure programs and software applications on the system which may include data breaches, code modification and unauthorized access.

CS has become part of our daily applications such as safeguarding online activities, protecting private information, browsing securely, protecting smart devices, securing social media applications and mailing security. Among all the applications providing security and privacy for Social Media Applications (SMA) (Facebook, Twitter, Instagram, LinkedIn, YouTube, Tik Tok, Telegram, Snapchat, so on) has becoming greater importance. CS uses various strategies such as data encryption using cryptography, network security, identity and access management, monitoring and logging, cloud security strategy and compliance and governance for providing security and privacy for social media applications.

Cryptography and Network Security (CNS) are considered as a backbone strategies of cyber security which ensure that sensitive data is been secured in a scalable interconnected networks. The relationship between CS, network security and cryptography can be shown in Figure 1. CS is superset or it consists of network security and cryptography as subset. The SMA requires both CNS and CS for secure communication.

Figure 1. Relationship between cyber security, network security and cryptography

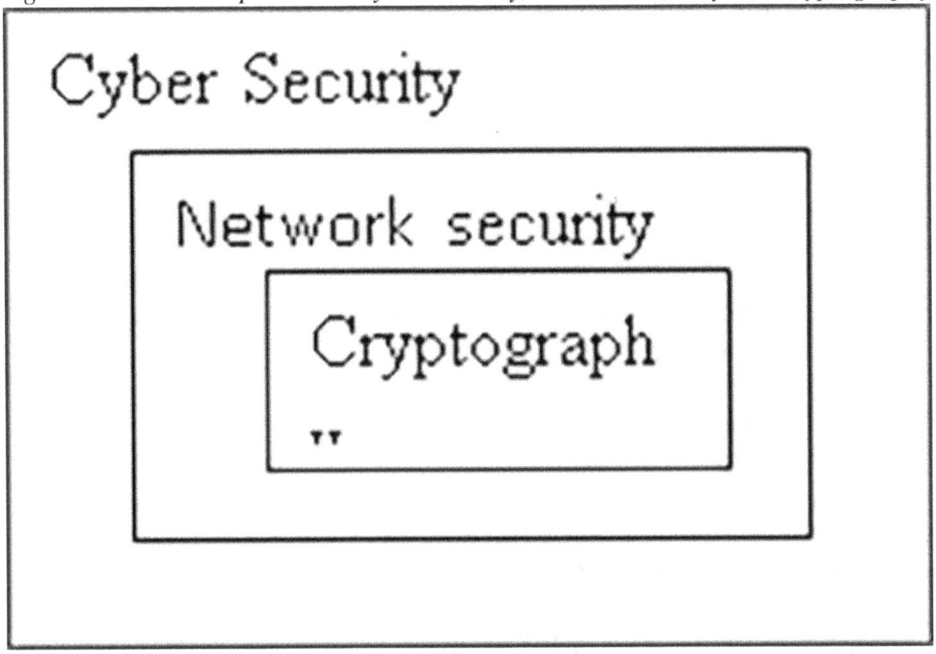

Cryptography uses mathematical encryption protocols and key management to prevent unauthorized access of data. Network security uses measures like firewalls, segmentation of network, data loss prevention, VPN, Email security and intrusion detection systems which protects data and infrastructure from cyber attacks. Cryptography is fundamental and network security is essential strategies of cyber security which are been applied to the social media. So, CS plays a key role in enhancing the security of SMA.

After the COVID-19 pandemic situation most of the people are depending on virtual communications which requires security and trust. As per the record the SMA has been used by 62 percentage of the population, (Data Reportal, 2024). To have secure social media communication it has to relay on CNS and CS protocols.

Cryptography

The cryptography is divided into two words crypto and graphy. "Crypto" is derived from Greek kryptos word which means hidden and "graphy" means writing. The cryptography is the branch of mathematics which aims to encrypt the text into unreadable format (codes) by which the data security is been provided. Cryptography provides security for data, messages, transactions and user identities. The main objectives of cryptography (Stallings, 2011) are given below

1. **Data Confidentiality:** Providing security for the data through using codes.
2. **Data Integrity:** It defines the accuracy of the data.
3. **Non repudiation:** It avoids the refusing the action made by the sending party.
4. **Authentication:** The sending and receiving side can confirm each other.
5. **Access control:** It provide the ability to control and limit access to the application and other users.

Network Security

The Network security (Dittrich, n.d.) provides and protects data security, traffic, network infrastructure, unauthorized access, cyber attacks, misuse, access control, intrusion prevention system and firewalls.

Cryptography and Network Security

The cryptography and network security (Foro Uzan, n.d.) are closely related to each other. Cryptography can be implemented without network security but to implement network security cryptography is required. Cryptography mainly depends on the encryption and decryption techniques, key management and digital signature. Network security depends on techniques like authentication, authorization, data encryption, virtual private network and data intrusion.

The CNS provides many applications like ecommerce, online banking, secure messaging, virtual private network, digital signature encryption, identity verification, protection of password, protection from malware, access control, firewall, block chaining methods(Electronic Code Book Mode, Cipher Block Chaining Mode, Cipher Feedback Mode, output Feedback Mode, Counter mode), SIM card authentication, quantum technology and social media application.

G.J. Simmon's stated that providing security to information is all about preventing attacks. Cryptographic attack is defined as breaking of security measures. It may be classified as cipher text only attack, know plain text attack, side channel attack and chosen plain text attack.CNS attacks are divided into two types namely active attacks and passive attacks.

a) **Active attacks –** It makes few modifications on the data stream. It includes attacks like denial of service (DOS), replay attacks, man in middle attacks, masquerade attacks, message modification attack, spoofing attack and malware attack.
b) **Passive attack –** These attacks are quite opposite to that of active attacks which do not modify the content but it just monitor the actions. It includes traffic analysis, phishing attack, session hijacking, sniffing of packets, internal threats, fraudulent authorizing transaction and eavesdropping.

LITERATURE SURVEY

The many researchers had work on cyber security strategies and security of social media applications. Table 1 which shows the earlier work with its title of the paper, year, advantages and disadvantages.

Applications

Table 1. Earlier work on cyber security strategies and security of social media

S.No	Title	Year	Advantages	Disadvantages
1	The Social Network Dilemma: Safeguarding Privacy and Security in an Online Community (Bikku et al., 2024)	2024	Merge technical measures with policy and educational approaches, adapted to regional contexts.	Highlights a variety of audience, but scope and objectives are not defined clearly and with very little empirical evidence.
2	Cyber security Practices for Social Media Users: A Systematic Literature Review (Herath, Khanna, & Ahmed, 2022)	2022	Shows strong research approaches, wide coverage of threats, and useful demographic findings.	Falls short in Structural details.
3	Privacy Intelligence: A Survey on Image Privacy in Online Social Networks (Liu et al., 2020)	2020	Framework for protecting privacy in image sharing.	Limited focus.
4	Helping Users Tackle Algorithmic Threats on social media: A Multimedia Research Agenda (Weth et al., 2020)	2020	Transparency in algorithms and prototype development.	Related to an early stage problem and not tested in practical scenarios.
5	Social media security and privacy protection concerning youths: "How to be safe, secure and social" (Sundaram & Radha, 2019)	2019	Main concentration on youth and providing immediate guidance.	Minimal technical depth with insufficient assessment.
6	Privacy perception and information technology utilization of high school students (Gogus & Saygin, 2019)	2019	Good survey basic with valuable awareness findings.	Restricted demographic focus and absence of mitigation strategies.

CRYPTOGRAPHY AND NETWORK SECURITY ARCHITECTURE AND ITS WORKING PROCESS

CNS architecture mainly aims at services, mechanisms and attacks. The architecture of cryptography and network security can be present in two ways:

1. Symmetric key architecture of CNS
2. Asymmetric key architecture of CNS

Symmetric Key Architecture of CNS

In this model as, same key is present at sender and the receiver so it is known as symmetric key model. The key is shared by both sender and receiver through a secure channel. This model consists of seven basic elements which are given below.

- **Sender-** Generates the plain text
- **Plain Text-** Human readable format text.
- **Cipher Text-** Human unreadable or understandable format text
- **Symmetric key-**A key which is shared by both sender and receiver and common for encryption and decryption.
- **Encryption Algorithm-**Used to convert the plaintext to the cipher text.
- **Decryption Algorithm-**Used to convert the cipher text to the plaintext.
- **Receiver-** Receiver receives the cipher text.

The detailed process of symmetric key model is explained in Figure 2. At the sender side, the sender generates the plaintext and passes to the encryption algorithm. The encryption algorithm along with symmetric key generates the cipher text which is passed to network (in air). At the Receiver side, the receiver receives the cipher text and passes it to the decryption algorithm. The decryption algorithm along with the symmetric key it generates the plaintext which is understandable by the receiver.

Figure 2. Symmetric key architecture of CNS

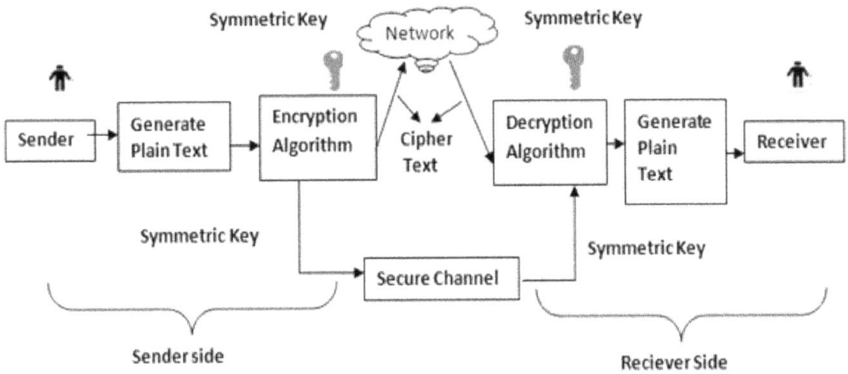

The mathematical representation or working process of generating cipher text from plain text and plain text from cipher text for Symmetric key model of CNS is given below Equations (1) and (2).

$$CT = E_K(PT) \quad (1)$$

$$PT = D_K(CT) \quad (2)$$

Where,
CT: Cipher Text
PT: Plain Text
K: Symmetric key
$E_{K:}$ Encryption using symmetric key
$D_{K:}$ Decryption using symmetric key

Asymmetric Key Architecture of CNS

In this model as, different keys are present at sender and the receiver it is known as asymmetric key model or it is also known as public key encryption technique. The separate key is generated by both sender and receiver. This model consists of seven basic elements which are given below.

- **Sender-** Generates the plain text
- **Plain Text-** Human readable format text.
- **Cipher Text-** Human unreadable or understandable format text

- **Asymmetric key-**public key and a private key is generated by the both sender and the receiver.
- **Encryption Algorithm-**Used to convert the plaintext to the cipher text.
- **Decryption Algorithm-**Used to convert the cipher text to the plaintext.
- **Receiver-** Receiver receives the cipher text.

The detailed process of asymmetric key architecture is explained in Figure 3. At the sender side, the sender generates the plaintext, his own public key and private key. The encryption algorithm is performed using receiver public key (generated and shared by receiver) and cipher text is generated which is passed to network (in air). At the receiver, receiver generates his own public key and private key and the cipher text which is obtained through sender is passes to the decryption algorithm along with his private key and plaintext is generated by which confidentiality is been obtained.

Figure 3. Asymmetric key architecture of CNS

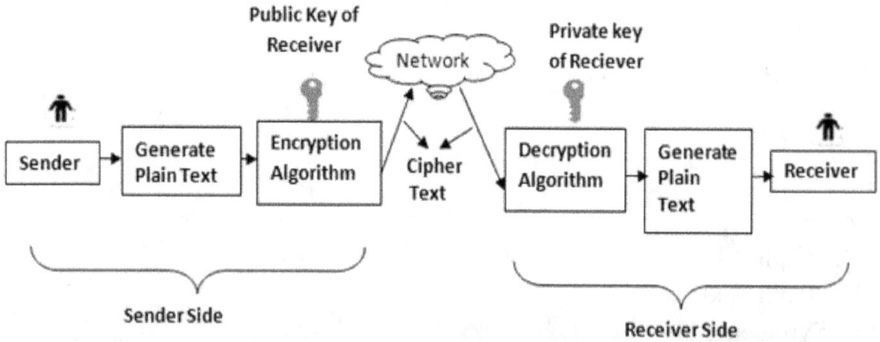

The mathematical representation or working process of generating cipher text from plain text and plain text from cipher text for asymmetric key model of CNS is given below equations (3) and (4).

$$CT = E_{RUK}(PT) \tag{3}$$

$$PT = D_{RVK}(CT) \tag{4}$$

Where,
CT: Cipher Text
PT: Plain Text
E_{RUK}: Encryption using receiver's public key

D_{RVK}: Decryption using receiver's private key

CNS ALGORITHMS

Cryptography uses codes to provide confidentiality for message and that codes are only understandable by the indent users. To generate secure codes secure algorithms are been used. CNS algorithms (Algorithms.com, n.d.) are classified into three types such as Symmetric key algorithms, (Kiran et al., 2016; Tayal et al., 2017), Asymmetric key encryption and Hash Function algorithm.

Symmetric Key Algorithms

It uses single secure key for encrypting and decrypting of the text. This algorithm can further divided into block cipher and stream cipher. In block cipher the data is encrypted as fixed blocks (64 bits or 128 bits). In stream cipher the data is encrypted as one bit or one byte at a time and it also generates a key which is of stream type. The following Table 2. gives detailed list of symmetric algorithms.

Table 2. Symmetric key algorithms

S.No	Algorithm	Type	Description	Attack
1	Simplified Data Encryption Standard (SDES)	Block	It performs encryption on small quantity of data.	Brute force, linear cryptanalysis, Differential cryptanalysis and knowledge of known cipher text and plain text attack.
2	Data Encryption Standard (DES)	Block cipher	It's an older model with 64 bit block and 64 bit key. It has 16 rounds.	Brute force, linear cryptanalysis, Differential cryptanalysis, side channel and Davies attack.
3	Advanced Encryption Standard (AES) (Federal Information Processing Standards, 2001)	Block cipher	It is a most secure and widely used algorithm. It converts readable text to unreadable format. It encrypts the data in the form of 128 bits and keys size of 128 with 10 rounds, 192 bits with 12 rounds or 256 bits with 14 rounds.	Side channel, Brute force, Replay and key management attacks.
4	Triple DES	Block cipher	It uses DES three times with different size of key.	Brute force, differential and linear cryptanalysis, Meet in the middle attack.
5	Rivest Cipher 4 (RC4)	Stream cipher	One byte of data is encrypted along with the stream key and uses XORed operation.	Bar mitzvah attack and bit flipping attack.

continued on following page

Table 2. Continued

S.No	Algorithm	Type	Description	Attack
6	Chacha20	Stream cipher	It uses 256 key and 96 bit nonce. Integrates with poly1305.	Timing, key reuse, key derivation issues, nonce reuse, cipher text oracle attack.
7	Salsa20	Stream cipher	High secure and high speed encryption. Nonce is used to have security. Uses 128 or 256 bit keys.	Key recovery attack, chosen plaintext attack and related cipher text attacks.
8	Trivium	Stream cipher	It uses single secure key for both encryption and decryption.	Cube attack, Differential fault analysis and Brute force attack

Asymmetric Key Algorithm

It is also known as public key cryptosystem. Here private key and public key concept is been used for encryption and decryption. The following Table 3. gives detailed list of Asymmetric algorithms.

Table 3. Asymmetric key algorithm

S.No	Algorithm	Description	Attack
1	Rivest Shamir Adleman (RSA)	It is dependent on two different keys a public key used in encryption and a private key used in decryption.	Plain text attack, chosen cipher, key related and factorization attack.
2	Elliptic Curve Cryptography (ECC)	It has elliptic curves structure. It uses public key in encryption and private key in decryption. Key size and computational efficiency is better than RSA.	Side channel attacks and fault attacks
3	Digital Signature Standard (DSS)	The main purpose of it is for digital signature. Here the sender signs with it private key and verify it with its public key.	Chosen method attack (generic), known message attack and key only attack.
4	ElGamal	It used to encrypt the message and to provide communication. The **discrete logarithms** is been used.	Discrete algorithm, meet in the middle, cross configuration, side channel, chosen cipher text attack and improper implementation

Hash Functions

The concept of key or keys are not used here. A hash code (Mihir et al., 1996) which is of fixed size is generated from the plaintext of any length. The following Table 4. gives detailed list of hash function algorithms.

Table 4. Hash function algorithm

S.No	Algorithm	Description	Attack
1	Secure Hash algorithm256 (SHA256)	It generates 256 bit hash function, for data integrity and digital signature.	Collision attack
2	Message Digest5 (MD5)	It takes a message of fixed size and produces 128 bits of hash value.	Collision attack
3	SHA-1	Not as strong as SHA256.	Collision attack, birthday attack and Man in middle attack.
4	Cyclic Redundancy Check32 (CRC32)	Here stream of data is been considered and 2 bit of CRC is been generated. It identifies the error data.	Known-plaintext attack

IMPACT OF CNS ON SMA

CNS plays a vital role in providing security for SMA. CNS provides benefits like data privacy, security, authentication, user trust, integrity, confidentiality and non repudiation for SMA. The benefits of CNS to SMA are obtained by various techniques. The cryptography provides various techniques to SMA like encryption, digital signature, end to end encryption, authentication, authorization, hashing, transport layer security, public key system and key management.

Whereas network security also provides various techniques to SMA like firewalls, Virtual Private Networks, Intrusion Detection, Intrusion Prevention System, data loss prevention and network segmentation. There are various social media applications like Facebook, Twitter, Instagram, LinkedIn, YouTube, Tik Tok, Telegram, Snapchat, WhatsApp, tiktok, WeChat, so on. Among them ten top SMA are Facebook(FB), YouTube(YT), WhatsApp(WAPP), Instagram(IG), TikTok(TT), WeChat(WC), Telegram(TEL), Facebook Messenger(FBM), Snapchat(SC) and Douyin(DY). Figure 4 shows top ten SMA depending on number of user's (Investopedia.com, n.d.). The each SMA uses various CNS techniques to have secure communication. Table 5. shows top ten SMA and various techniques used by them.

Figure 4. Top ten SMA depending on number of user's

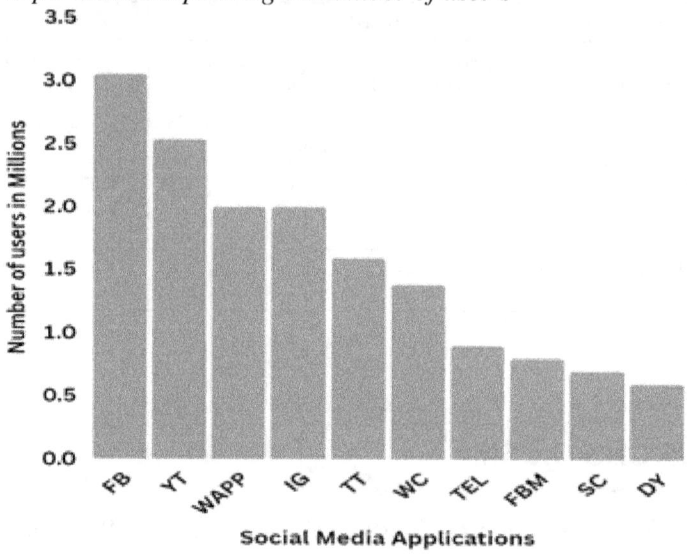

Table 5. SMA and its CNS techniques

S.No.	SMA	Description	CNS Techniques
1	Facebook	It helps to online share and connects with family and friends.	End to End encryption, TLS encryption, hashing, SHA256, HMAC, App secret proofing and Two factor authentication.
2	YouTube	It provides video sharing facility (like share, comment, watch and upload)	Encryption, Digital Signature, HTTPS, Firewalls, IDS, Key Management, Symmetric and Asymmetric encryption and hash function.
3	WhatsApp	It is a free cross platform application using mobile phone.	Signal protocol, asymmetric key cryptography (Curve2519), AES256, HMAC-SHA256, Prekeys, Auditable Key Directory, E2EE and Key transparency.
4	Instagram	It provides free online sharing of photos and videos.	SSL/TLS, hashing, end to end encryption, Two factor authentication.
5	TikTok	It is a short form video platform where users can create his own videos and can share.	HTTPS, Web Sockets, Real Time messaging Protocol, QUIC
6	WeChat	It is a mobile payment, messaging, social characteristics.	MMTLS, AES256, Business layer encryption
7	Telegram	It is instant messaging, cloud based and cross platform.	MTProto, client server and end to end encryption, AES256, RSA208 bits and Diffie Hellman key exchange.

continued on following page

Table 5. Continued

S.No.	SMA	Description	CNS Techniques
8	Facebook Messenger	Standalone app for instant messaging and characteristics of Facebook that allows to send messages, communicate, share photos, video and voice can also be done.	End to end encryption, labyrinth protocol, ECDH, HMAC,SHA256, HKDF,AES, Cipher Block Chaining.
9	Snapchat	It is a visual communication Application used to send videos and photos (snap) and it disappears after seen. It is not meant for chat.	End to end encryption, ECC, AES256, TLS/SSL, IPSec, Kerberos and WPA.
10	Douyin	It is Chinese version SMA TIKTOK. It provides live streaming, short videos and ecommerce facilities.	Encryption, digital signature, key management, TLS/SSL, IPSec, HTTPS and PGP.

THE POSSIBLE CYBER THREATS AND PRIVACY RISK IN SOCIAL MEDIA

By knowing the cyber threats and its privacy risk in social media it plays an important role to safeguard the identity and finance and to have mental well being. The following are the key cyber threats and privacy risk in social media.

1. **Phishing and Spear Phishing:** Phishing is a type of misleading cyber attack where the attackers try to send common emails, direct messages or text messages as if it is been sent from trusted party like banks and so on. By which sensitive information is revealed from the user or some malware is downloaded into system. On other hand spear phishing is more targeted here attacker's attacks in more effective way.

Measures- To overcome this attack always verify the sending party, enable Multi Factor Authentication, use email filters and anti phishing tools, trained yourself and think before responding immediate messages.

2. **Account Hijacking:** If users are using weak passwords or reuse passwords and not using Multi Factor Authentication makes attackers to hijack the account very easily.

Measures - It can be avoided by using strong password, Multi Factor Authentication, keep track of login activity and alerts, keep software updated and use security tools and avoid phishing.

3. **Malware and Ransomware Distribution:** Malware or Ransom ware can unknowingly install into the system by using social media channels harmful links or file attachments.

Measures - From trusted source only software and files must be download, avoid clicking on unknown links and install anti malware tool.

4. **Data leak and Data Mining:** Social Media collects large amount of personal data from user which may leads to many security breaches or data leak and may create problem to normal users.

Measures - limited sharing of personal data, control the permissions and know your rights.

5. **Social Engineering and Pre texting rewrite sentence:** publicly shared data may be misused by cyber attacker. Attackers can use that public information for building trust, to get other or more data and to grant access.

Measures - To avoid it always verify before sharing, training must be provided and enable Multi Factor Authentication.

6. **Doxing and Cyberstalking:** Cyber attackers can misuse the personal details ad can create threats or harassment.

Measures- It can be avoided by using strong password, Multi Factor Authentication, use VPN, monitoring of personal data, antivirus must be used, be alert and block the unnecessary messages.

7. **Cyberbullying and Harassment:** Serious emotional problems (public shaming) can be created.

Measures- Strong security measures, self care, take help, document everything, block or mute.

8. **Disinformation and Deepfakes:** Generating of wrong content using AI and spreading it may damage the reputations.

Measures- By training, making personal information as private, use detection tools.

9. **Fake Accounts and Impersonation Scams:** Attackers creates wrong profiles to draw money from users.

Measures- Verify, secure account, training, report and block unknown accounts.

10. **AI enabled Privacy Threats:** Many AI Tools can be used by attackers for doxing, cyber stalking and to get personal information.

Measures- Think before sharing, tight privacy settings, ongoing awareness, End to End encryption, VPN setups, Multi Factor Authentication and remove metadata.

THE PROPOSED METHODOLOGY FOR CYBER SECURITY ON SOCIAL MEDIA

To create safer social media environment to overcome cyber attacks cyber security is required.

The most important cyber securities on social media are user awareness when using social media, user behavior when using social media, privacy regulations in social media and protective measures for mobile social media.

User Awareness When Using Social Media

To stay secure on social media raising of user awareness plays an important role. The following are few strategies that can be followed to stay secure on social media by user.

- Users must be given training and encourage them to educate them self on posting habits and privacy setting.
- The strong and unique passwords and Multi Factor Authentication must be habituated to add an essential layer of protection.
- Users must rethink and verify before clicking the unknown links and while confirming the requests.
- The devices must maintain safe by using anti malware and antivirus software and some advanced biometric.
- Third party app permissions can also revoke.
- Interactive sessions like workshop, seminars, quizzes and simulations can be conducted.
- Talk openly about online conversation.

User Behavior When Using Social Media

The following effective user behavior can be used to reduce the cyber attack on social media.

- By using strong, unique passwords and by implementing Multi Factor Authentication.
- Regularly check security and privacy settings.
- Put a limit on sharing of personal information.
- Don't click on unknown links.
- Secure devices and network.
- Educate users by interactive sessions like workshop, seminars, quizzes and simulations.
- Habituate to maintain backup data and be prepare for recovery.

Privacy Regulations in Social Media

Privacy laws like GDPR, CCPA, COPPA 2.0 and rising acts globally enable individuals, establish strong and reliable cyber security protocols, defend underserved groups, cultivate trust and cultivate ethical digital ecosystems.

Protective Measures for Mobile Social Media

Mobile social media (Saeed, 2024) provides mobility and convenience but, may also lead to SIM jacking, phishing, impersonation, tracking user location, harassment, surveillance and mental health issues. To overcome it use authenticate and audit Apps, turn off GPS, use mobile security tools, report and block harassment.

CONCLUSION AND FUTURE WORK

As large amount of sensitive data is generated by social media networks the online transactions has to be secured. To have secured connection and communication through social media cryptography and network security and cyber security plays an important role. The cyber security is superset of cryptography and network security. So, in this paper the concepts of cryptography and network security, its process of communications and algorithms are discussed in detailed. The impact of cryptography and network security on social media application was also discussed by considering top ten social media application. The different possible cyber threats and privacy risk in social media with its measures were also considered. Finally, the proposed methodology for cyber security on social media was presented which mainly depends on four measures for secure communications such as user awareness when using social media, user behavior when using social media, privacy regulations in social media and protective measures for mobile social media. By considering four measures the cyber security attacks can be overcome easily and trusted communication system social media application can be establish.

In future work the real time application and its implementation has to be considered with advanced protocols.

REFERENCES

Bellare, M., Canetti, R., Krawczyk, H., & Krawczyk, H. (1996). Hash functions for message authentication. *Advances in Cryptology — CRYPTO '96*, 55–73. DOI: 10.1007/3-540-68697-5_6

Bikku, T., Biyyapu, N. S., Sekhar, J. C., Kumar, M. K., Nokerov, S. M., & Pratap, V. K. (2024). The social network dilemma: Safeguarding privacy and security in an online community. *International Journal of Safety and Security Engineering, 14*(1), 125–133.. DOI: 10.18280/ijsse.140112

Cryptography World. (n.d.). *Algorithms*. https://www.cryptographyworld.com/algo.html

DataReportal. (2024). *Digital 2024: Global overview report*. https://datareportal.com/reports/digital-2024-global-overview-report

Dittrich, D. (n.d.). Network monitoring intrusion detection systems (IDS). University of Washington. http://staff.washington.edu/dittrich/misc/faqs/ids.faq

Forouzan, B. A. (2006). *Data communication and networking* (4th ed.). McGraw-Hill Education.

Gogus, A., & Saygın, Y. (2019). Privacy perception and information technology utilization of high school students. *Heliyon, 5*(9), e02420. DOI: 10.1016/j.heliyon.2019.e01614 PMID: 31193323

Herath, G., Khanna, T. B. G., & Ahmed, M. (2022). Cybersecurity practices for social media users: A systematic literature review. *Journal of Cybersecurity and Privacy, 2*(3), 436–455. DOI: 10.3390/jcp2010001

Investopedia. (n.d.). *Social media*. https://www.investopedia.com/terms/s/social-media.asp

Kiran, J. S., Anusha, M., Kumar, A. V., & Kavya, M. (2016). Cryptography: The science of secure communication. *International Journal of Computer Science and Network Security, 16*(6), 1–6.

Liu, C., Zhu, T., Zhang, J., & Zhou, W. (2020). Privacy intelligence: A survey on image privacy in online social networks. *arXiv*. https://arxiv.org/abs/2007.07906

National Institute of Standards and Technology. (2001, November 26). *Announcing the Advanced Encryption Standard (AES) (FIPS PUB 197)*. U.S. Department of Commerce. https://nvlpubs.nist.gov/nistpubs/FIPS/NIST.FIPS.197.pdf

Saeed, S. (2024). Usable privacy and security in mobile applications: Perception of mobile end users in Saudi Arabia. *Big Data and Cognitive Computing*, *8*(11), 162. DOI: 10.3390/bdcc8110162

Saeed, S., Altamimi, S. A., Alkayyal, N. A., Alshehri, E., & Alabbad, D. A. (2023). Digital transformation and cybersecurity challenges for businesses resilience: Issues and recommendations. *Sensors (Basel)*, *23*(15), 6666. DOI: 10.3390/s23156666 PMID: 37571451

Saeed, S., Azizi, N., Tahir, S., Ahmad, M., & Almuhaideb, A. M. (Eds.). (2024). *Strengthening industrial cybersecurity to protect business intelligence*. IGI Global., DOI: 10.4018/979-8-3693-0839-4

Saeed, S., Gull, H., Aldossary, M. M., Altamimi, A. F., Alshahrani, M. S., Saqib, M., Zafar Iqbal, S., & Almuhaideb, A. M. (2024). Digital transformation in energy sector: Cybersecurity challenges and implications. *Information (Basel)*, *15*(12), 764. DOI: 10.3390/info15120764

Saeed, S., Suayyid, S. A., Al-Ghamdi, M. S., Al-Muhaisen, H., & Almuhaideb, A. M. (2023). A systematic literature review on cyber threat intelligence for organizational cybersecurity resilience. *Sensors (Basel)*, *23*(16), 7273. DOI: 10.3390/s23167273 PMID: 37631808

Stallings, W. (2011). *Cryptography and network security: Principles and practice* (5th ed.). Pearson.

Sundaram, A., & Radha, P. (2019). Social media security and privacy protection concerning youths: "How to be safe, secure and social". *International Journal of Business Innovation and Research*, *18*(4), 453–471. DOI: 10.1504/IJBIR.2019.098761

Tayal, S., Gupta, N., Gupta, P., Goyal, D., & Goyal, M. (2017). A review paper on network security and cryptography. *Advances in Computational Sciences and Technology, 10*(5), 1337–1343. ISSN: 0973-6107

Weth, C. V. D., Abdul, A., Fan, S., & Kankanhalli, M. (2020). Helping users tackle algorithmic threats on social media: A multimedia research agenda. *arXiv*. https://arxiv.org/abs/2012.05701

Chapter 10
Balancing Usability and Security:
Enhancing User Experience Without Compromising Privacy

Md Mehedi Hasan Emon
https://orcid.org/0000-0002-6224-9552
American International University-Bangladesh, Bangladesh

Md. Mazid-Ul-Haque
https://orcid.org/0000-0002-9091-7191
American International University-Bangladesh, Bangladesh

ABSTRACT

This chapter examines the critical challenge of balancing usability and security in digital system design. As organizations increasingly rely on digital platforms, the tension between creating user-friendly interfaces and ensuring robust security measures has become more pronounced. By exploring human-centered design principles, behavioral insights, and adaptive technologies, the chapter highlights strategies for integrating security seamlessly into user workflows without sacrificing ease of use. Drawing on interdisciplinary research, case studies, and best practices, the chapter emphasizes the importance of transparency, user trust, and iterative design. It concludes by proposing a framework for developing systems that not only protect privacy but also enhance user experience, offering a roadmap for sustainable and secure digital transformations.

DOI: 10.4018/979-8-3373-3171-3.ch010

INTRODUCTION

The modern digital ecosystem demands that safe system development combines usability and security without treating them as conflicting elements. Since digital transformation reshapes public services and enterprise activities along with personal communication it has become a central problem in academic literature and practical system development regarding strong cybersecurity maintenance alongside quality user experience. A detailed analysis of how usability interacts with security elements appears in this discussion. The discussion in this chapter evaluates design choices that affect user engagement and system integrity from multiple fields of HCI along with behavioral cybersecurity and risk management. In stark contrast to this view, the author introduces users as an indispensable part of modern cybersecurity infrastructure rather than posing them as security threats to the system. It shows, through evidence-based approaches and through psychological theories and real-case scenario analysis that when the interfaces are poorly designed together with complex authentication protocols, insecure practices and circumvention alongside increased vulnerability appear.

The chapter looks at security solution related burnout and potentially risky tracking systems to understand how users think and act when they are dealing with security solutions. A collection of pragmatic security design examples which successfully marry usable security with the domains of healthcare, financial services and e commerce are presented in this chapter. This proves through practical examples that security systems developed through emotional comprehension and continuous feedback from the users are the most productive ways to approach the design that resolves conflicts between usability and security. This chapter also addresses the need for changeable security models, rather than one-size-fits-all, in favor of models that match human capacity and capabilities. Security systems should be augmented with behavioral design elements as well as clear and accessible security measures, alongside guidelines that could promote privacy protecting innovation. As the chapter demonstrates, acceptance is not a short-term demand that digital transformation can come and go with once it comes to an end sustainability must be acceptable too. We introduce a security paradigm where accessibility and trust are outcomes rather than obstacles to usability in terms of human machine interactions.

THE DUAL IMPERATIVE OF USABILITY AND SECURITY

Users now interact with services, obtain their information and institutional interactions through digital technologies. This transition provided easier connectivity but also revealed a continuous problem that is keeping the central cyber security norms safe and still providing the best user interaction features. So, we have these usability and security debates, and usability and security are often considered to be mutually exclusive things. Digital infrastructure health is deteriorating because the interoperability between usability and security has demonstrably aged and now presents a serious threat to the ongoing viability of digital systems (Brissaud et al., 2022; Fürstenau et al., 2023).

Security measures have historically spent their resources on improving technical strength through encryption methods and access rules yet paid little attention to usability requirements. Theoretical security has led to broad-scale system installation which results in systems that frustrate normal users and remain inaccessible to them. Security breaches as well as identity theft attacks and surveillance dangers endanger users when systems possess excellent usability without sufficient protection measures. Digital system design methodology issues have produced multiple system weaknesses because they combine technical failures with social and technical system limitations that show how human behavior deviates from requirements (Díaz-Rodríguez et al., 2023; Emon & Khan, 2025a).

Understanding Usability and Security in Contemporary Contexts

The understanding of usability in modern times derives from international standards such as ISO 9241-11:2018 which identifies it as the measure of how a system enables its specific users to meet their declared targets effectively and efficiently through satisfaction within an established usage context. User engagement includes psychological dimensions and psychological aspects which extend past interface elements to include learnability and mistake reaction ability and user contentment (Bellos et al., 2025). The concept of security primarily concentrates on upholding information system confidentiality alongside preservation of integrity and availability. The fundamental security pillars have kept their essential role yet how people interact with systems became increasingly vital during modern cybersecurity analysis. User security is dependent on behavior according to researchers who prove that design elements and information density and risk evaluation shape what users do (Emon et al., 2025; Heidari et al., 2022). Security convergence with usability represents a detailed relationship that requires entire system-wide management strategies.

The Myth of the Trade-Off

Multiple empirical studies have continuously disproven the misconception that usability stands in direct opposition to security. Studies in behavioral cybersecurity show users choose weak security measures when security procedures are complex or hard to understand by writing down passwords or using simple password combinations and skipping software updates (Weickert et al., 2023). Users display these behaviors logically because they interact with poorly designed systems which overload them with complex procedures and thinking tasks. Systems which overlook usability requirements during security design will force users to handle extremely complex security tasks without proper instructions and support. Users develop security fatigue which leads them to stop implementing protective measures thus hurting the security targets the system originally aimed to fulfill (Cram et al., 2021). Security mechanisms that match users' expectations and mental models of operations provide better security as well as improved user experience. Biometric authentication and single sign-on systems prove effective in security enhancement because they ease user interaction methods (Shinde et al., 2023). Semantic verification has proven effective for security enhancement because it modifies protection protocols based on user conduct and location-specific conditions (Golightly et al., 2023).

Toward a Unified Design Ethos

The requirement involves bringing together usability with security through deliberate evidence-based design approaches. Human-centered design approaches grounded in HCI study provide an effective organizational structure to integrate usability with security. User involvement during regular design stages allows developers to recognize security-related usability issues that lead to risky user actions before improving protective solutions that maintain practicality (Distler et al., 2021). User assessments regarding security measures receive better comprehension through behavioral frameworks which include the Technology Acceptance Model (TAM) and Protection Motivation Theory (PMT). Security behavior adopted by users depends on four important factors namely perceived usefulness, simplicity, threat awareness, and self-confidence (Khan et al., 2024). Security features which integrate fundamental behavioral design principles result in user-friendly and context-aware solutions that bother users minimally (Khan et al., 2024). Quantifying the Effects of AI-Driven Inventory Management on Operational Efficiency in Online Retail

Figure 1. Human-centered security design model

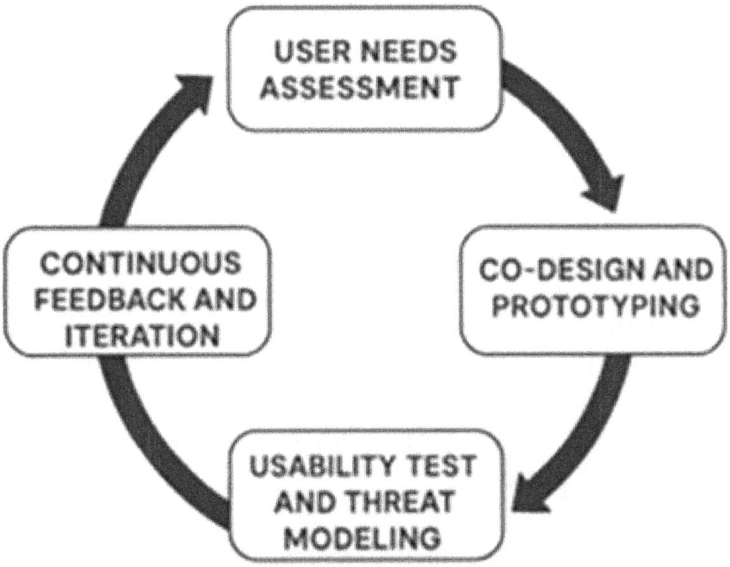

Figure 1 displays a circular flow diagram that shows the Human-Centered Security Design Model. The model takes a form of four iterative and sequential stages in a clockwise loop: User Needs Assessment, Co-Design and Prototyping, Usability Test and Threat Modeling, and Continuous Feedback and Iteration. The stages are represented in a rounded rectangle box with curved arrows that indicate the continuous and cyclic nature of the design process. The layout is placed on a white background showing the simplicity and focus of an iterative process of involving users in the secure development of systems.

HUMAN-CENTERED SECURITY DESIGN: A THEORETICAL AND PRACTICAL IMPERATIVE

Human-centered security design increases in importance because digital threats coupled with complex technological systems are growing in number. Current security vulnerability challenges exceed the limits of firewalls and system hardening combined with cryptographic protocols in the conventional technology-based security framework. Current evidence from research and practice demonstrates without a doubt that security systems need to integrate detailed knowledge about human behavior and cognitive processes (Emon et al., 2024; Habbal et al., 2024). The users have evolved from peripheral to central roles within cybersecurity ecosystems because their operational behaviors together with their routines and system capabilities determine security results. Human security design understands that people do not use systems in optimal ways because they operate under stress while being sidetracked and constrained by their time and surrounded by information overload. Security approaches and technologies which fail to consider user behavior facts usually produce unexpected negative results because users tend to either practice insecure workarounds or discretely avoid security protocols (Saeed, 2025; Tyagi et al., 2022). Multiple research studies have revealed this pattern in healthcare frameworks and corporate information technology platforms due to demanding login requirements that lead users to share passwords or complex password policies that drive erratic storage methods (Bhuiyan et al., 2021).

Theoretical Foundations: Behavioral and Cognitive Perspectives

Human-centered security design holds essential value because it finds support from psychological and Human-Computer Interaction (HCI) theories. The human cognitive system faces restricted working memory capacity because of Cognitive Load Theory (Paas & van Merriënboer, 2020). The limit of cognitive capabilities among users leads to increased error risks whenever they need to remember multiple passwords or make sense of ambiguous security alerts. These security shortcomings stem from poor design choices that ignore human limitation factors rather than from user unprofessionalism.

According to Mental Models Theory (Jaeger & Eckhardt, 2021) users form internal perspectives about system operations which stem from their past interactions or lack of system knowledge to determine their security-related conduct. Users perform dangerous acts while perceiving safety because their mental models about the system differ from its real operational conditions. Users tend to falsely trust browser HTTPS indicators believe these confirm website authenticity thus they overestimate phishing websites that show valid certificates. Protection Motivation Theory (PMT) together with the Technology Acceptance Model (TAM) offer basic models which help explain how users judge security-related behavior usefulness versus their accompanying efforts. According to Ou et al., (2022) within the Protection Motivation Theory people initiate protective actions more frequently if they deem threats serious and prevention solutions both functional and manageable. Users tend to discount security measures when they become too intrusive, so they develop security weariness (Cram et al., 2021).

Designing Security with the User in Mind

Human-oriented security design starts with empathic user analyses which focus on understanding actual working conditions of people. User research becomes extensive through ethnographic studies combined with task-based evaluation for security features (Shibuya et al., 2022). Technical robustness alone does not suffice because designers should ensure both users can use security features accurately while using them consistently and voluntarily. Security nudging offers success as an approach that guides users through interface signals toward better security without imposing any specific actions. Browsers using clear security warning labels and mobile operating systems merging permissions into one area both enhance user capabilities in making secure choices (Jagannath & Jain, 2024; Khan & Hasan Emon, 2024). The decisions made during design do not depend only on technical restrictions because they combine behavioral economics with persuasive design to gently encourage specific behaviors. Security facts together with alternative options become available to users in measured amounts through progressive disclosure that depends on their requirements or risk evaluations. Technological systems should provide timely explanations along with options before presenting multiple rights and configurations to users. The approach improves both mental clarity and the ability of users to understand and practice security procedures (Marabelli et al., 2021). The technology of biometric authentication through fingerprint scanning and face recognition system serves as a specific illustration. Despite operating at an advanced level, the product offers substantial usability benefits. Biometric systems enhance authentication security through password-free authentication procedures that keep processes computationally protected. Its deployment requires intensive monitoring to address privacy concerns and spoofing difficulties along with accessibility problems because such assessments matter for user experiences (Arshad & Asghar, 2024).

From Design to Deployment: Organizational and Policy Implications

The implementation of human-centered security design for practical systems requires both appropriate design methodologies together with organizational dedication and policy coherence. Most security policies receive their origins from senior leadership yet end users and operational staff rarely participate before final decisions. Security policy deficiencies create noncompliance practices that produce tensions among security personnel and frontline workers (Aggarwal & Dhurkari, 2023). The solution requires businesses to establish participatory design methodologies so they can involve users in creating security protocols and technologies together. Participation during system development enables users to better understand as well as accept and follow resulting systems. The current security training programs should evolve beyond basic compliance courses to deliver practical hands-on education about phishing detection as well as access right control in authentic workplace situations (Edwards, 2024). Security frameworks need to implement policies with dynamic security measures. Risk-based authentication represents a possible security solution because it implements dynamic security requirements based on user actions and environment conditions. System protocols adjust based on user roles as well as device choices and physical locations allowing each user to find both safety and comfortability (Ullah et al., 2024).

Figure 2. Organizational integration of human-centered security design

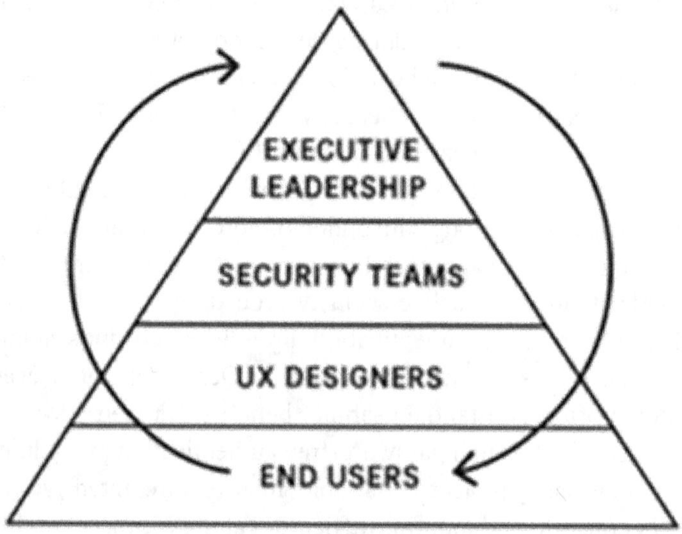

This figure shows an organizational pyramid with four layers that reflect the composition of the human-centered security design integration. The Executive Leadership is at the peak of the pyramid, and it is entrusted with the mandate of providing strategic direction and a security culture. Security Teams are below them, and they build and implement security policies. The next level is that of UX Designers who are concerned with creating easy-to-use and safe user experiences. End Users are at the bottom, and their actions and reactions are essential to determining actual security requirements in the real world. The circling of arrows around the pyramid means that there are on-going cross-functional work and feedback cycles amongst all stakeholders. Figure 2 highlights that successful human-centered security is not restricted to a particular position, but it is a collective task of the company.

CHALLENGES IN BALANCING SECURITY AND USABILITY

The ongoing advancement of cybersecurity technology and academic and professional consciousness has failed to solve the ongoing challenge of finding suitable security-usability equilibrium in digital system design. A longstanding battle exists between security needs and user-friendly requirements reaches its peak in present-day digital interactions because people perform security tasks across numerous devices and platforms daily. The exchanges between users and systems are shaped by implementation constraints together with fundamental psychological and behavioral elements as well as organizational factors (Khan & Emon, 2024; Krishna et al., 2025). A comprehensive solution to resolve this tension must move beyond simple safe-user friendly terms since it requires multiple methodological approaches. User safety demands recognition of the complex relationship between mental strain on users, motivational drive, risk awareness levels and established corporate guidelines.

Authentication Complexity vs. Convenience

Security measures make their most apparent trade-offs during the authentication process. MFA illustrates the security challenge by becoming a widespread authentication practice. MFA technology which employs knowledge and possession, and inherent aspect factors (password and smartphone and biometric data) creates a powerful shield against unauthorized access. The implementation of MFA generates unwanted user friction and reduces adoption through rigid or context-independent execution methods. The research shows that multi-factor authentication (MFA) strengthens security for accounts, yet users view it negatively due to daily frequency of prompts or low-security situations (Zimmermann et al., 2025). Several users deactivate MFA while also using the "remember this device" functionality which negates MFA's effectiveness since they face time restrictions and access difficulties or wish to bypass the security measure. Certain population groups who include elderly people with disabilities encounter MFA as burdensome which contributes to digital service exclusion for these groups (Tsatsou, 2022). A better user-friendly approach to authentication technology called biometric authentication has gained prominence. Without passwords, individuals gain easy access through fingerprint and facial recognition systems which successfully reduce cognitive burden when correctly deployed. Nonetheless, they have hurdles. The integrity of biometric information remains permanent which means users cannot reset it after it gets exposed like passwords. Lack of faith and governance issues in biometric observation together with facial recognition misuse by authoritarian governments create long-lasting ethical conflicts regarding trust and data protection (Emon & Khan, 2025b; Shandilya et al., 2024). Authentication technique design needs to include context-adjustment capabilities to help users make or adjust their choices based on their security needs.

Over-Collection of User Data

The excessive gathering of personal information poses the main concern since companies use personalization and security reasons as their justification. Digital marketing companies together with technology organizations continually pursue surveillance-based business models as part of their operational strategies. The benefit of enhanced security for risk-based authentication or fraud detection via full user profile data collection exists only in theory due to data collection exceeding ethical and necessary measures. The data collection method damages user privacy and creates doubts about services that preach user protection while exploiting user data to generate profits. Regular users often ignore the reality that antivirus programs along with VPNs track their online activities then sell anonymous or fake-anonymous usage statistics to businesses using complicated and tricky permission documents. After GDPR implementation authorities started multiple initiatives that intended to restore control of personal data for end users. User behavior shows acceptance of every request without understanding adversely impacts the fundamental effectiveness of these data protection measures (Emon & Khan, 2025c; Quach et al., 2022). Users lack the ability to manage sophisticated privacy choices or inform their decisions because there is no openness along with real choices and acceptable privacy settings. Such conditions lead to a surveillance environment which abuses security measures for watching users without protecting their freedom to make choices independently.

Security Fatigue

Security fatigue represents the worst obstacle in managing security versus usability because it develops when users lose sensitivity to security procedures from encountering too many vague security alerts and warnings. Cram et al., (2021) explains psychological exhaustion develops through both security system alarms and the mental burden of dealing with password complexity and software updates and protectively monitoring new security threats. The exhaustion triggers different security actions which consist of software update avoidance together with firewall deactivation and password repetition and unrestricted disregard of security alerts. According to Acquisti et al., (2020), many consumers demonstrated a sense of powerlessness toward continual digital dangers as they adopted a view that security breaches will happen regardless. Even the best security framework becomes less effective because of this resignation response. The design issue consists of two interconnected components. Numerous security communications begin with ineffective methods that rely on technical terminologies or fear-based messaging which ends up confusing users instead of providing information. User workflows face disruptive interruptions from security interventions at times that reduce their satisfaction level. Security measures that seem to primarily serve the system instead of users create substantial reduction in user willingness to engage (Ismagilova et al., 2022). Security designers need to abandon their current mindset of enforcing regulatory compliance because users need an empowerment approach that allows them to actively take part. Security education programs during employee onboarding and behavioral risk assessment-based adaptive security mechanisms together with progressive information disclosure affect appropriate times make up a new approach to user-quality assurance (Cheimonidis & Rantos, 2023).

Toward a More Sustainable Balance

The mentioned problems transcend technical repair requirements to expose fundamental conflicts between security infrastructure and human practicalities. Security procedures must transform how organizations treat users from security obstacles to partners who participate in security initiatives. People need investments at three levels: technology development as well as user research about security needs and sociocultural transformation through policy reform. Interdisciplinary collaboration is crucial. Solutions need coordinated development by psychologists alongside designers and data ethics together with legal experts and cybersecurity professionals who will create security solutions suited for real-world application and motivational factors. Security and usability need to merge as core components of good protection because usability represents an indispensable protection factor instead of a secondary addition to security measures. The key to securing users in a digital world lies in the road ahead, one that begins overcoming separation of security from usability to build a secure infrastructure that protects users and their assets.

Based on the order above, the academic section, summarized by the following table, provides the key challenges to balance security and usability:

Table 1. Key challenges to balance security and usability

Challenge	Description	Implications
Authentication Complexity vs. Convenience	Multi-factor authentication (MFA) increases security but may reduce usability when implemented without context sensitivity.	Users may disable MFA or opt for insecure alternatives if usability is poor.
Over-collection of User Data	Excessive and non-transparent data collection, often justified for personalization or security purposes.	Leads to erosion of trust, consent fatigue, and ethical concerns.
Security Fatigue	Users become overwhelmed and apathetic due to frequent security prompts, alerts, or requirements.	Results in desensitization, risky shortcuts, or total disengagement.
Rigid Compliance-Based Models	The security systems are often built on very strict security policies that disregard real user behavior and situation.	Cause user cooperation to be reduced, and it can also result in system circumvention.
Lack of Interdisciplinary Design	Many security designs omit input from behavioral science, HCI, and ethics altogether to the exclusion of technical robustness.	Limit's ability and excludes variety of user needs and use cases, risk profiles.

CASE STUDIES: LESSONS FROM THE FIELD

It is difficult for businesses to achieve it as it involves grasping intricacies of security implementations in real life projects. The focus of these case studies is the importance of well-thought out, user focused methods for engineering secure operating systems for different industrial sectors. These scenarios can teach companies important things about how they manage the usability and security requirements, and visualizations of the scenarios will elicit discussions among the different market stakeholders.

Healthcare: Usability Failures with Dire Consequences

Electronic health records systems were introduced to healthcare with the aim of making patient data management process better and improving clinical services. The U.S. hospital embarked on deploying their new EHR system, which, upon deployment, failed systemically leading to security issues because they did not think of usability aspects. The UI of the system was complicated, and users reported the login process to be confusing, even though technological security attributes showed strength in the system. Healthcare staff who needed to deliver rapid medical services faced major difficulties while trying to obtain medical records during their work (Hielscher et al., 2021). The healthcare staff-initiated workaround sequences which compromised security by giving passwords to colleagues and disabling timeout features to avoid constant re-authentication. Security initiatives which ignore usability create dangerous risks that are plainly demonstrated by this example. The system flaws coupled with complex authentication measures increased the number of data leakage occurrences. The security breach damaged patient privacy protection and decreased healthcare provider digital system trustworthiness. An approach that started with user needs could have constructed security measures without requiring procedure changes to prevent these risks. The study requires clinicians to have sound faith in system usability, so their decisions won't be affected by cognitive overload and workflow interruptions when it comes to security protocol compliance (Kulkarni, 2022). Security strategies require users and operational requirements to be included in their execution processes for successful implementation. Non-observance of protocols leads to patient confidentiality breaches which harm reputation alongside possible catastrophic effects on both confidentiality and institutional image.

Finance: Success through Behavioral Integration

Behavioral integration enables the financial industry to achieve better security results alongside usability implementation in its security solutions. A primary European financial institution had to enhance its authentication procedures while keeping consumer demands reasonable. Finger scanning together with behavioral analysis which included key-tapping speed assessments and mouse tracking analysis formed the basis of this solution. Clients benefited from easily accessible features together with strict security protocols provided by this system. The achievement in this project stemmed from both technological security elements as well as user education methods about system operations. The bank achieved its success by placing consumer education together with transparency at the core of its operations. The security advantages of the system were explained to customers who received simple user-friendly directions to learn new authentication methods. The bank established trust by showcasing its operational methods to users by allowing greater adoption rates because users could understand the extent of convenience versus security trade-offs. Users needed no extra effort because behavioral analytics allowed the system to improve its security automatically (González-Granadillo et al., 2021). The example confirms security systems must incorporate user needs into their creation process because this supports security features as beneficial assets instead of limitations. Security systems become stronger through user behavior integration during system design thus leading to better protocol adherence by users who behave naturally. Financial service companies can obtain optimum security alongside crucial user experience via biometric systems that utilize behavioral analytics.

E-Commerce: Security Through Nudging

The e-commerce sector, where customer engagement and usability are crucial, has successfully balanced usability and security through new behavioral nudging approaches. An eminent e-commerce site aimed to enhance password robustness among its users, who often employed weak, easily decipherable passwords. Instead of forcing users to meet rigorous password criteria that they would refuse to meet, and fire, the platform took a different route: behavioral nudging. The platform used visual feedback systems that provided users feedback about the strength of their passwords in real time as they were entered. The users were not asked to meet any set criteria but enticed to come up with more robust passwords with positive reinforcement in the form of green highlights and friendly suggestions. The resulting impact on the userbase was a dramatic increase in password strength, with absolutely no perceivable adverse impact on shopping cart abandonment rates, which had been a priority to the platform's user experience team (Emon, 2025; Tian, 2025). This is the scenario where behavioral science can do wonders in security design. The software improved password security using straightforward, unobtrusive hints, maintaining user experience. Nudging corresponds with research in behavioral cybersecurity, indicating that users are more inclined to adopt secure habits when directed in a user-friendly manner rather than through explicit coercion (Bonicalzi et al., 2023). This strategy underscores the significance of contextual sensitivity; by acknowledging that users prioritize convenience and the reduction of disturbances, the platform may promote secure behaviors while ensuring a fluid shopping experience.

BEST PRACTICES FOR SECURE AND USABLE SYSTEM DESIGN

Security design alongside user-friendliness proves complex for system developers due to the need for advanced knowledge about technical specifications and human interaction patterns. The development life cycle begins with a unified understanding of security measures and usability since modern approaches reject former techniques which view security as fixed elements while usability remains secondary. Modern system designers and developers together with policymakers need to adopt a complete user-oriented method based on continuous evidence-based development.

Incorporating User Feedback into Security Design

Secure system design relies on user feedback integration as a vital practice which many systems fail to incorporate. The literature recommends multiple user involvement through the stages of requirements collection and prototyping as well as deployment and post-implementation review (Hinderks et al., 2022; Saeed et al., 2013). The mismatch between user activities and personal preferences together with their cognitive framework structures produces reduced security compliance or intentional user workarounds. Users often maintain weak account identifiers to avoid problems caused by ambiguous password reset systems. Security development requires human-centered design frameworks to integrate participatory design with usability testing (Dutta et al., 2024; Khan & Emon, 2025). Engineers who view their users as collaborators instead of obstacles to security can co-develop solutions that maintain technical strength along with relevant suitability. Through user feedback systems organizations become capable of detecting and improving user friction points before extensive system deployment takes place.

Implementing Adaptive Security Measures

Adaptive security brings about a fundamental change in security design methods and execution approaches. The system adapts its behavior through real-time analysis of risks and human activities along with contextual environments instead of using standardized controls for all users across situations (Wang et al., 2024). The authentication standards adopt dynamic modifications through risk-based authentication mechanisms to achieve high security standards and preserve user convenience for authorized users. Users can boost authentication security by incorporating three types of biometric systems such as face detection along with voice analysis and fingerprint authentication. Implementation should occur with both awareness and care. The examination of biometric data accuracy and consent needs continuous research due to privacy concerns across different population segments (North-Samardzic, 2020; Saeed, 2024; Saeed & Amjad, 2013). Security protocols that combine behavioral analytic data and contextual understanding enable the delivery of robust defenses that remain user-friendly. Google uses reCAPTCHA v3 to verify users through behavioral data without interrupting their verification process. The risk assessment method retains user security while respecting their time and attention so that it enhances overall system protection.

Minimizing Cognitive Load

User errors in security-related jobs stem mainly from cognitive overload conditions. Excessive technical terms combined with complex authentication processes alongside ambiguous warning messages cause users to either ignore these elements or make mistakes (Dwivedi et al., 2022). Security designs that operate efficiently free users from excessive mental strain because they present information that is clear and simple while maintaining its relevance. Security options should appear on their own during designated times while jargon needs reduction and security indicators must use simple visual or audio elements. People using computers follow security protocols more effectively when interface designs implement distinct visual organization and contextual explanations (Jaeger & Eckhardt, 2021). Mozilla Firefox displays phishing and malware warnings through direct communications and specific commands that lead to better user adoption of security protocols. The importance of accessibility needs to be understood to its full extent. All security elements must accommodate users with disabilities and support individuals with language restrictions and restricted technical abilities. The ethical requirement to include all stakeholders during system design fortifies security systems against threats.

Figure 3. Reducing cognitive load in security interfaces

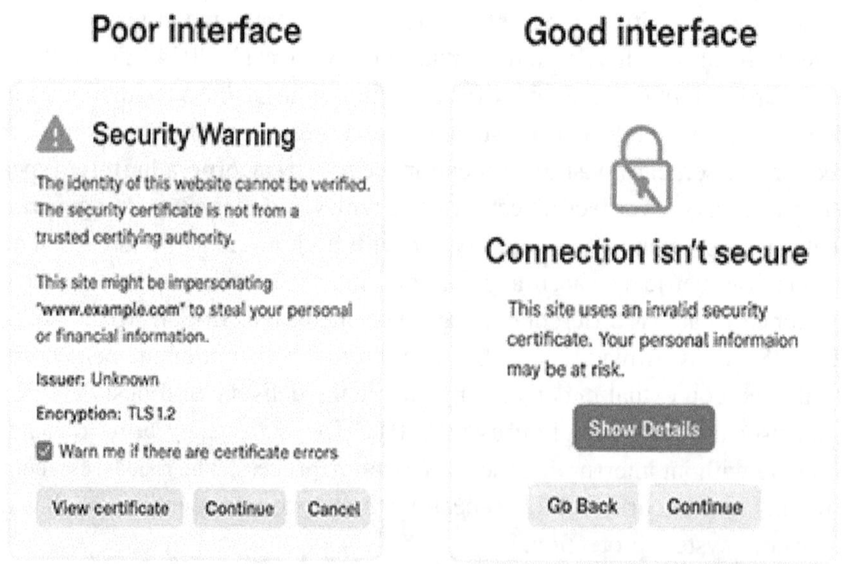

This figure shows a side-by-side comparison of two security interface designs to show how one can minimize the cognitive load on users via careful design. The poor interface on the left panel is overcrowded with technical terms, several warning signs, and unorganized text that might overwhelm the users and obstruct the decision-making process. The right panel has a good interface, with a clean layout, plain language and progressive disclosure. Colors, intelligent icons and other visual indicators enable a user to grasp the security risk at a glance and respond accordingly. Figure 3 emphasizes with simplified and user-centric design, there is enhanced understanding, and willingness to follow the security measures.

Educating Without Overwhelming

User education remains essential but excessive manual delivery of detailed instruction through independent training causes inefficiency. The user experience needs to integrate educational content using "just-in-time" learning principles which deliver minimal and contextualized information increments (Emon & Khan, 2024). A user about to click a doubtful link would benefit more from an unobtrusive and brief overview of security risks and protective steps than from general security training. The concept of security literacy should be treated as both evolving and extending indefinitely. Organizations need to apply microlearning and gamification and customized feedback approaches which sustain user interest in security training. Research shows that initiatives which adopt public health cyber hygiene methods can change user behavior patterns throughout the course of time (Zhang-Kennedy et al., 2016). The fundamental goal stands to build security awareness that will enable users to understand protective measures' rationale while having power to practice security instead of forcing compliance.

Designing for Error Recovery

User interfaces optimized for usability together with knowledgeable users fail to eliminate errors completely. The integration of error recovery design becomes essential for achieving useable security systems. Security systems should predict common user mistakes involving forgotten passwords as well as unintended clicks or accidental logouts then provide clear non-discriminatory solutions for users to resolve these issues. Microsoft makes it safe for users to recover their accounts using an account recovery system that fuses multiple verification channels with predictive prompts, such as "Do you still use this phone number?". Clear guidance should be given to users through the recovery process so that no one is blamed but ensure that security is not compromised by vulnerability that could be exploited by attackers to reset passwords easily. Immediate feedback in place with confirmation dialogs can catch multiple error-preventing errors before they appear. Systems should not only help users through risk evaluation steps, but also allow them to make choices, when necessary, when such irregular operations are noticed by these systems. These design components improve security results while at the same time building end-user trust in the system.

FUTURE DIRECTIONS AND POLICY IMPLICATIONS

The struggle between security and usability has become more of a problem, specifically for professionals and academic researchers as well as government authorities. New security problems are created along with unprecedented benefits from AI and ML, for usability elements were integrated to security design enhancements. Their handling should be approached with active cooperation between several disciplines and under the policy using technology, its ethical effects, and social and legal boundaries.

The Promise of AI and ML for Usable Security

The security model undergoes rapid transformation with artificial intelligence because this technology enables predictive frameworks that adapt and perceive their operational context. Current security structures operate from fixed regulations together with reactive response procedures. Behavioral analytics operating via artificial intelligence provides real-time capabilities to track user behavior combined with environmental signals to discover security threats in advance (Kumar et al., 2024; Sarker, 2023). During late-night hours when a Dhaka-based user tries unsuccessful login from outside their locality an AI system would realize this deviation and prevent the breach before users recognize it. The capabilities of machine learning systems grow stronger through continuous user interaction learning that enables better model development of normal and abnormal behavior patterns independently from rule-based systems. Security enhancement occurs simultaneously with usability improvement because artificial intelligence reduces both false discovery alerts and disruptive user interruptions. A new implement of machine learning technology uses real-time modifications for user interface design from processed personal cognitive processes. Machine-learning algorithms modify the content and tone of security alerts through five different adjustment types which base their changes on user digital experience and mood detection and past reactiveness (V. Kumar et al., 2024). Despite these technological possibilities to combine usability and security harmoniously they still contain risks.

Challenges of Opacity, Bias, and Accountability

The main safety issue with AI security systems stems from their inability to display clear operational logic. Many machine learning models operate as difficult to interpret entities when compared to the easily auditable rule-based systems. This deficiency in explainability erodes user trust and legal accountability. A system that restricts access or marks users as suspicious subjects without presenting any rationale will generate fairness and procedural due process problems (Leerssen, 2023). The training data used to develop AI systems directly corresponds to the biased output produced by those systems. Security applications using skewed training data produce discriminatory results that unify high-risk assessments to specific population segments such as geographically defined regions or demographic groups. Algorithmic decisions implemented in financial sectors and medical facilities carry special concerns about their life-changing effects. Complete thorough audits are essential for security systems as improper implementation without them results in the permanent integration of bias which deepens existing discrimination within security networks (Dordunoo, 2024). The path to identifying accountability becomes harder to track because AI systems work by themselves. Security breaches usually result in human agents being held accountable for the incident, especially developer's administrators and organizational executives. During self-learning situations in which algorithm fails to detect a breach alongside its flawed identification of legitimate users through misclassification, then who bears responsibility? The above issues have evolved from theory to become urgent matters requiring speedy legislative and regulatory action.

Toward Fair and Explainable AI in Security

XAI has emerged as a fundamental solution to overcome hidden algorithm processes. Within security applications, explainability enables users to acquire understandable explanations about security decisions along with guidance to resolve encountered issues. Users blocked from accessing their account because of suspicious behavior should receive specific details about their actions and necessary steps to recompose the situation from the system. The ethical deployment of AI in critical situations requires interpretability (Murikah et al., 2024). External rules should establish institutional regulations which formalize fairness principles when AI plays a role in security systems. The Artificial Intelligence Act developed by the European Union marks a revolutionary movement for such systems. Kreutz & Jahankhani, (2024) defines security-related AI implementations as "high-risk" operations requiring strict transparency measures as well as bias reduction protocols together with ongoing human control systems. Metropolitan nations Singapore and Canada together with other jurisdictions continue developing parallel systems. The worldwide governance structure remains divided into unaligned parts despite efforts to unify it. Firms might carry out regulatory arbitrage through the selection of jurisdictions which have more flexible regulations when there are no standard norms established. It should also serve as platforms for necessary protection establishment and best practice spreading.

Policy Implications: A Multi-Level Agenda

Given these challenges and opportunities, a multi-level policy agenda is in order.

National Regulations: For security applications like Artificial Intelligence, political entities must come up with laws that direct the use of Artificial Intelligence. Mechanisms to illustrate the algorithmic process, the principles of data reduction and detection of algorithmic bias must now be part of the legal frameworks. Regulatory sandboxes can be a way to establish an innovative yet oversight– compliant process for testing new technologies as they develop.

Organizational Governance: AI ethics boards must be set up by institutions comprised by technologists, legal experts and user advocacy representatives. System installations should be evaluated by AI ethics boards within institutions on security aspects and the verification of the AI following institution directives.

Standardization and Certification: The second such organizational goal concerns the requirements on international organizations to create security specifications for AI systems and to establish performance criteria for system explanation and human–centered design. Systems that achieve independent certification have received certification from a compliant system, as these systems are audited by independent certification bodies.

Public Education and Empowerment: As artificial intelligence systems are increasingly working their way into systems that serve the public such as used in workplace logins and banking apps, users need education as to what this means and how to begin to understand automated security decisions. Governmental funds and civil society organizations should come together to promote public awareness of AI technology and promote digital educational initiatives for the public.

Academic-Industry Collaboration: Academia and industry need permanent partnerships to achieve their objectives. The deployment leadership mainly rests with companies, but institutions deliver ethical evaluation and methodological rigor. Institutes for joint research with data-sharing terms along with cross-industry exchange programs help academic and industrial organizations partner for collaboration.

TOWARD A SUSTAINABLE DIGITAL FUTURE

Digital system sustainability together with resilience requires factors beyond technical complexness in our modern digitally connected society. Security and usability now represent a critical moral duty and essential strategic requirement. The old-fashioned view that security improvements collide with usability improvements needs replacement since it does not work for advanced digital infrastructure systems. The digital realm needs a total system which puts users as the focus throughout design phases while developing systems and creating policy frameworks (Volberda et al., 2021).

Redefining the Usability–Security Relationship

Multiple studies now question the common belief that security functions in opposite directions compared to usability. Security design techniques which focus on people show systems can maintain safety without sacrificing usability given enough attention to how users think and behave in their context (Distler et al., 2021). The new security paradigm accepts users as active protectors of system resilience when they receive proper tools alongside necessary knowledge (Safitra et al., 2023). Security and usability merge when users move beyond control methods which remain unchanged and fixed to adjust their security measures in accordance with dynamic user situations. Security responses from these systems become customized through analysis of current data streams and user behavior indicators which match security measures to real-time system environment and activity. The strength of adaptive multi-factor authentication verification process adjusts based on device recognition parameters and geolocation data and user activities within secure systems (Suleski et al., 2023).

Behavioral Design and the Role of Trust

Behavioral economics together with cognitive psychology should be included in future designs of secure systems to establish sustainable digital futures. Users develop security weariness through insufficient system usability because lack of user-friendly security features causes them to become indifferent and uncooperative with security warnings (Di Nocera et al., 2023). Systems must be designed with engineered friction reductions combined with decision-oriented cognitive processes that mirror ordinary human decision patterns when developed for this purpose. The implementation of nudge elements which guide user behavior without restrictions proves to be an effective interface solution for this purpose. Users can improve their security practices through immediate visible password strength indicators and simplified goal-based privacy setting presentations without any enforcement (Gumzej, 2021). These behavioral approaches give better compliance rates and simultaneously help build trust which serves as a fundamental feature of digital sustainability. Systems based on digital technology become trustworthy as users consider the operational effectiveness together with fair practices and clear information along with honest responsiveness. People become more ethically involved with technology through statistical understanding of data utilization and feeling empowered to control their digital presence (Ahmad et al., 2022). The continuous care of trust requires organizations to maintain open communication, uphold data principles and always honor user autonomy.

Design for Inclusion and Accessibility

Digital health requires equal inclusion for its success in the future. Accessibility together with security must exist as an integrated system. Insecure conditions originate from system elements that prove difficult for people with disabilities and elderly users together with people using low bandwidth. The application of inclusive design principles which include voice controls together with alt-text provision and multilingual assistance and simplified navigation supports both ethical requirements and operational success (Michtner & Pinzolits, 2025). Along with its principles the practice of inclusive design brings forward an understanding that each user from any demographic and at any technical level deserves equivalent security protection. Developing digital empowerment instead of digital gaps requires analyzing usability differences because they create a sustainable digital society (Henni et al., 2022).

Institutionalizing Human-Centered Security

Sustainable human-centered security requires organizations to integrate this concept into their institutional culture combined with operational practices. The path to sustainable human-centered security requires organizations to use compliance checklists as starters before creating learning environments along with collaborative program design and continuous improvement cycles. Security requires active participation from the entire organizational structure because all departments starting from IT and extending to legal teams and end-users and developers and designers share the responsibility for system protection (Poehlmann et al., 2021). Cross-functional security task forces together with ethics committees should form part of organizational structures to connect policy outcomes with practical application. KPIs that combine user satisfaction and security metrics should be utilized to demonstrate how usability supports system resilience thus making it central to overall system protection instead of peripheral.

The Role of Public Policy and Global Governance

Symptoms of sustainable digital design appear through national and international regulatory frameworks which influence these activities. The establishment of joint usability and security standards falls under the essential responsibility of governmental entities. The AI Act on the horizon as well as the GDPR from the European Union are two pieces of legislation that require designers to design responsible technology system via requiring transparency, consent protocols and accountability systems (Bukhari & Irfan Zafar, 2025b; Díaz-Rodríguez et al., 2023). Internet Governance Forum joining OECD and World Economic Forum elaborates heritage of interoperable framework with support of ethical innovations in the world. Digital initiatives development relies on the creation of partnerships between civil society organizations on the one hand, and academic and marginalized community stakeholders on the other side to provide services for users not coming from a wealthy and an expert background. In addition to being needed by the technical system, humans should view digital system sustainability as a moral duty that transcends technical or regulatory boundaries (Bukhari & Irfan Zafar, 2025a). With AI tools spreading into other fields like finance and public administration, their mistakes are more dangerous because they have a greater impact on broader groups of people. Anticipatory governance must be able to deal with new risks, as it has a set of core values including dignity to defend in conjunction with equity and democracy.

CONCLUSION

All designers and governments alike and their consumers are continually negotiating a series of conflicts between interface usability and data security in the ever-evolving world of digital systems. This chapter also contains discoveries, showing that implementing both functionalities of security and usability in systems requires complicated methods. In today's world, companies must juggle efforts to make their systems user friendly on one hand and protecting data on the other hand as digital operations have now become part and parcel of all human experiences. What this discussion shows is that usability and security need never be at odds. These components should be seen as built in concert, operating symbiotically when successfully implemented. Systems that cause security to invade users' space, or to create a problem that users must solve to operate the system, will fail because users will simply ignore the problem rather than tolerate the problem. Systems are vulnerable to malicious attacks from attackers in systems which have been designed with a user interface in which convenience is prioritized over security. To achieve balance, researchers must further elaborate knowledge about security requirements, and the behavioral patterns of users, as well as continuously improve the design based on feedback from users. The base foundation of achieving equilibrium is based on human centered design. Applying behavioral research along with shrinking mental strain, and programming in flexibility into security features, software designers can build secure systems that respect user autonomy. Instead, users need to receive teaching resources and decision-making instruments for security, rather than experience mere enforcement-based constraints. They promote transparency and trust to instead build security cultures that help enact user privacy protection rather than security related alienation or encumbrance.

The chapter presented shows that interdisciplinary cooperation becomes a necessary requirement to tackle complex problems inherent in usability and security. The combination of design and psychology, cybersecurity and law, through a joint effort provides an excellent infrastructure to engineer security features secure enough, and efficient and fair enough. Regulatory entity and government collaboration is a necessary and strategic partnership that not only helps support ethical operations but also drive innovation and preserve privacy and security standards of the digital age. While the GDPR and similar rules mark significant progress in this field, additional rules need to exist to deal with the fresh issues posed by developments in new technologies particularly artificial intelligence, raising fresh security and usability difficulties. In the next future, Artificial intelligence combined with the machine learning technology will also affect the security systems through creation of both the advantages as well as difficult circumstances. What this creates is AI security protocols that allow for detailed, situation sensitive defenses, but it also brings to question the ethical nature of algorithm understanding, of the system oversight, of the bias factors involved. Improving the technical sophistication of forward-thinking research must be borne through the development of ethical standards and regulatory mechanisms that will guarantee AI systems are neutral and transparent, and that individuals' privacy exists and is respected. To build such future secure and usable systems, there should be an approach that considers the changing dynamics of technology vis a vis the user requirements for sustainable development. When an organization uses people's first design and develops several expert relationships to design solutions that safety needs to be met while providing users with excellent experiences in privacy preserving frameworks, system development becomes possible. When it comes to digital transformation navigation, the usability and security integration should be a function of the goal, which benefits people and communities while not compromising one over the other. Therefore, aiming for a user centered development path has become a path to building trust and protecting privacy and ethical use of technology.

REFERENCES

Acquisti, A., Brandimarte, L., & Loewenstein, G. (2020). Secrets and Likes: The Drive for Privacy and the Difficulty of Achieving It in the Digital Age. *Journal of Consumer Psychology*, *30*(4), 736–758. DOI: 10.1002/jcpy.1191

Aggarwal, A., & Dhurkari, R. K. (2023). Association between stress and information security policy non-compliance behavior: A meta-analysis. *Computers & Security*, *124*, 102991. DOI: 10.1016/j.cose.2022.102991

Ahmad, K., Maabreh, M., Ghaly, M., Khan, K., Qadir, J., & Al-Fuqaha, A. (2022). Developing future human-centered smart cities: Critical analysis of smart city security, Data management, and Ethical challenges. *Computer Science Review*, *43*, 100452. DOI: 10.1016/j.cosrev.2021.100452

Arshad, R., & Asghar, M. R. (2024). Characterisation and Quantification of User Privacy: Key Challenges, Regulations, and Future Directions. *IEEE Communications Surveys and Tutorials*, •••, 1–1. DOI: 10.1109/COMST.2024.3519861

Bellos, C., Stefanou, K., Tzallas, A., Stergios, G., & Tsipouras, M. (2025). Methods and Approaches for User Engagement and User Experience Analysis Based on Electroencephalography Recordings: A Systematic Review. *Electronics (Basel)*, *14*(2), 251. DOI: 10.3390/electronics14020251

Bhuiyan, M. N., Rahman, M. M., Billah, M. M., & Saha, D. (2021). Internet of Things (IoT): A Review of Its Enabling Technologies in Healthcare Applications, Standards Protocols, Security, and Market Opportunities. *IEEE Internet of Things Journal*, *8*(13), 10474–10498. DOI: 10.1109/JIOT.2021.3062630

Bonicalzi, S., De Caro, M., & Giovanola, B. (2023). Artificial Intelligence and Autonomy: On the Ethical Dimension of Recommender Systems. *Topoi*, *42*(3), 819–832. DOI: 10.1007/s11245-023-09922-5

Brissaud, D., Sakao, T., Riel, A., & Erkoyuncu, J. A. (2022). Designing value-driven solutions: The evolution of industrial product-service systems. *CIRP Annals*, *71*(2), 553–575. DOI: 10.1016/j.cirp.2022.05.006

Bukhari, S. D., & Irfan Zafar. (2025a). *Mass Media and Impact of Fake News on Supply Chains* (S. D. Bukhari & I. Zafar (eds.)). IGI Global. DOI: 10.4018/979-8-3373-2175-2

Bukhari, S. D., & Irfan Zafar. (2025b). *Supply Chain Disruptions and Impact on Global Inflation* (S. D. Bukhari & I. Zafar (eds.)). IGI Global. DOI: 10.4018/979-8-3373-1982-7

Cheimonidis, P., & Rantos, K. (2023). Dynamic Risk Assessment in Cybersecurity: A Systematic Literature Review. *Future Internet, 15*(10), 324. DOI: 10.3390/fi15100324

Cram, W. A., Proudfoot, J. G., & D'Arcy, J. (2021). When enough is enough: Investigating the antecedents and consequences of information security fatigue. *Information Systems Journal, 31*(4), 521–549. DOI: 10.1111/isj.12319

Di Nocera, F., Tempestini, G., & Orsini, M. (2023). Usable Security: A Systematic Literature Review. *Information (Basel), 14*(12), 641. DOI: 10.3390/info14120641

Díaz-Rodríguez, N., Del Ser, J., Coeckelbergh, M., López de Prado, M., Herrera-Viedma, E., & Herrera, F. (2023). Connecting the dots in trustworthy Artificial Intelligence: From AI principles, ethics, and key requirements to responsible AI systems and regulation. *Information Fusion, 99*, 101896. DOI: 10.1016/j.inffus.2023.101896

Distler, V., Fassl, M., Habib, H., Krombholz, K., Lenzini, G., Lallemand, C., Cranor, L. F., & Koenig, V. (2021). A Systematic Literature Review of Empirical Methods and Risk Representation in Usable Privacy and Security Research. *ACM Transactions on Computer-Human Interaction, 28*(6), 1–50. DOI: 10.1145/3469845

Dordunoo, Lord. (2024). (pp. 283–348). Integrating Organizational and Social Network Theories to Mitigate Racial Bias in Facial Recognition Technology. DOI: 10.4018/979-8-3693-8562-3.ch009

Dutta, P. K., Raj, P., Sundaravadivazhagan, B., & Selvan, C. P. (2024). *Artificial Intelligence Solutions for Cyber-Physical Systems.* Auerbach Publications., DOI: 10.1201/9781032694375

Dwivedi, Y. K., Hughes, L., Baabdullah, A. M., Ribeiro-Navarrete, S., Giannakis, M., Al-Debei, M. M., Dennehy, D., Metri, B., Buhalis, D., Cheung, C. M. K., Conboy, K., Doyle, R., Dubey, R., Dutot, V., Felix, R., Goyal, D. P., Gustafsson, A., Hinsch, C., Jebabli, I., & Wamba, S. F. (2022). Metaverse beyond the hype: Multidisciplinary perspectives on emerging challenges, opportunities, and agenda for research, practice and policy. *International Journal of Information Management, 66*, 102542. DOI: 10.1016/j.ijinfomgt.2022.102542

Edwards, D. J. (2024). Security Awareness and Skills Training. In *Critical Security Controls for Effective Cyber Defense* (pp. 405–434). Apress., DOI: 10.1007/979-8-8688-0506-6_14

Emon, M. M. H. (2025). The Mediating Role of Supply Chain Responsiveness in the Relationship Between Key Supply Chain Drivers and Performance: Evidence from the FMCG Industry. *Brazilian Journal of Operations & Production Management, 22*(1), 2580. DOI: 10.14488/BJOPM.2580.2025

Emon, M. M. H., & Khan, T. (2024). Unlocking Sustainability through Supply Chain Visibility: Insights from the Manufacturing Sector of Bangladesh. *Brazilian Journal of Operations & Production Management, 21*(4), 2194. DOI: 10.14488/BJOPM.2194.2024

Emon, M. M. H., & Khan, T. (2025a). The mediating role of attitude towards the technology in shaping artificial intelligence usage among professionals. *Telematics and Informatics Reports, 17*, 100188. DOI: 10.1016/j.teler.2025.100188

Emon, M. M. H., & Khan, T. (2025b). The Role of Traditional Media in Crisis Amplification: How Mainstream Media Magnifies Fake News and Ethical Dilemmas in Supply Chain Crises. In *Mass Media and Impact of Fake News on Supply Chains* (pp. 59–90). IGI Global., DOI: 10.4018/979-8-3373-2175-2.ch003

Emon, M. M. H., & Khan, T. (2025c). The Rise of Circular Supply Chains: Recycling and Closed-Loop Systems Could Mitigate Inflationary Pressures. In *Supply Chain Disruptions and Impact on Global Inflation* (pp. 195–226). IGI Global., DOI: 10.4018/979-8-3373-1982-7.ch008

Emon, M. M. H., Khan, T., Rahman, M. A., Hamid, A. B. A., & Yaakub, N. I. (2025). GreenTech Revolution: Navigating Challenges and Seizing Opportunities. In *AI and Green Technology Applications in Society* (pp. 63–90). IGI Global Scientific Publishing. DOI: 10.4018/979-8-3693-9879-1.ch003

Emon, M. M. H., Khan, T., Rahman, M. A., & Siam, S. A. J. (2024). Factors Influencing the Usage of Artificial Intelligence among Bangladeshi Professionals: Mediating role of Attitude Towards the Technology. *2024 IEEE International Conference on Computing, Applications and Systems (COMPAS)*, 1–7. DOI: 10.1109/COMPAS60761.2024.10796110

Fürstenau, D., Gersch, M., & Schreiter, S. (2023). Digital Therapeutics (DTx). *Business & Information Systems Engineering, 65*(3), 349–360. DOI: 10.1007/s12599-023-00804-z

Golightly, L., Modesti, P., Garcia, R., & Chang, V. (2023). Securing distributed systems: A survey on access control techniques for cloud, blockchain, IoT and SDN. *Cyber Security and Applications, 1*, 100015. DOI: 10.1016/j.csa.2023.100015

González-Granadillo, G., González-Zarzosa, S., & Diaz, R. (2021). Security Information and Event Management (SIEM): Analysis, Trends, and Usage in Critical Infrastructures. *Sensors (Basel), 21*(14), 4759. DOI: 10.3390/s21144759 PMID: 34300500

Gumzej, R. (2021). *Intelligent Logistics Systems for Smart Cities and Communities*. Springer International Publishing., DOI: 10.1007/978-3-030-81203-4

Habbal, A., Ali, M. K., & Abuzaraida, M. A. (2024). Artificial Intelligence Trust, Risk and Security Management (AI TRiSM): Frameworks, applications, challenges and future research directions. *Expert Systems with Applications*, *240*, 122442. DOI: 10.1016/j.eswa.2023.122442

Heidari, A., Navimipour, N. J., & Unal, M. (2022). Applications of ML/DL in the management of smart cities and societies based on new trends in information technologies: A systematic literature review. *Sustainable Cities and Society*, *85*, 104089. DOI: 10.1016/j.scs.2022.104089

Henni, S. H., Maurud, S., Fuglerud, K. S., & Moen, A. (2022). The experiences, needs and barriers of people with impairments related to usability and accessibility of digital health solutions, levels of involvement in the design process and strategies for participatory and universal design: A scoping review. *BMC Public Health*, *22*(1), 35. DOI: 10.1186/s12889-021-12393-1 PMID: 34991540

Hielscher, J., Kluge, A., Menges, U., & Sasse, M. A. (2021). "Taking out the Trash": Why Security Behavior Change requires Intentional Forgetting. *New Security Paradigms Workshop*, 108–122. DOI: 10.1145/3498891.3498902

Hinderks, A., Domínguez Mayo, F. J., Thomaschewski, J., & Escalona, M. J. (2022). Approaches to manage the user experience process in Agile software development: A systematic literature review. *Information and Software Technology*, *150*, 106957. DOI: 10.1016/j.infsof.2022.106957

Ismagilova, E., Hughes, L., Rana, N. P., & Dwivedi, Y. K. (2022). Security, Privacy and Risks Within Smart Cities: Literature Review and Development of a Smart City Interaction Framework. *Information Systems Frontiers*, *24*(2), 393–414. DOI: 10.1007/s10796-020-10044-1 PMID: 32837262

Jaeger, L., & Eckhardt, A. (2021). Eyes wide open: The role of situational information security awareness for security-related behaviour. *Information Systems Journal*, *31*(3), 429–472. DOI: 10.1111/isj.12317

Jagannath, R. O., & Jain, A. K. (2024). Browser-in-the-middle attacks: A comprehensive analysis and countermeasures. *Security and Privacy*, *7*(5), e410. DOI: 10.1002/spy2.410

Khan, T., & Emon, M. M. H. (2024). Exploring the Potential of the Blue Economy: A Systematic Review of Strategies for Enhancing International Business in Bangladesh in the context of Indo-Pacific Region. *Review of Business and Economics Studies, 12*(2), 55–73. DOI: 10.26794/2308-944X-2024-12-2-55-73

Khan, T., & Emon, M. M. H. (2025). Supply chain performance in the age of Industry 4.0: Evidence from manufacturing sector. *Brazilian Journal of Operations & Production Management, 22*(1), 2434. DOI: 10.14488/BJOPM.2434.2025

Khan, T., Emon, M. M. H., & Nath, A. (2024). Quantifying the Effects of AI-Driven Inventory Management on Operational Efficiency in Online Retail. *2024 27th International Conference on Computer and Information Technology (ICCIT)*, 2092–2097. DOI: 10.1109/ICCIT64611.2024.11021996

Khan, T., Emon, M. M. H., & Rahman, S. (2024). Marketing Strategy Innovation via AI Adoption: A Study on Bangladeshi SMEs in the Context of Industry 5.0. *2024 6th International Conference on Sustainable Technologies for Industry 5.0 (STI)*, 1–6. DOI: 10.1109/STI64222.2024.10951050

Khan, T., & Hasan Emon, M. M. (2024). Determinants of AI Image Generator Adoption Among Marketing Agencies: The Mediating Effects of Perceived Usefulness. *2024 IEEE 3rd International Conference on Robotics, Automation, Artificial-Intelligence and Internet-of-Things (RAAICON)*, 177–182. DOI: 10.1109/RAAICON64172.2024.10928548

Kreutz, H., & Jahankhani, H. (2024). *Impact of Artificial Intelligence on Enterprise Information Security Management in the Context of ISO 27001 and 27002: A Tertiary Systematic Review and Comparative Analysis* (pp. 1–34). DOI: 10.1007/978-3-031-52272-7_1

Krishna, B., Krishnan, S., & Sebastian, M. P. (2025). Understanding the process of building institutional trust among digital payment users through national cybersecurity commitment trustworthiness cues: A critical realist perspective. *Information Technology & People, 38*(2), 714–756. DOI: 10.1108/ITP-05-2023-0434

Kulkarni, S. (2022). Expert Systems in Behavioral and Mental Healthcare: Applications of AI in Decision-Making and Consultancy. In *Big Data Analytics and Machine Intelligence in Biomedical and Health Informatics* (pp. 147–186). Wiley. DOI: 10.1002/9781119792376.ch6

Kumar, R., Hamid, A. B. A., Inayah Binti Ya'akub, N., Nyamasvisva, T. E., & Tiwari, R. K. (2024). *AI and Green Technology Applications in Society (R. Kumar, A. B. Abdul Hamid, N. I. Binti Ya'akub* (Nyamasvisva, T. E., & Tiwari, R. K., Eds.). IGI Global., DOI: 10.4018/979-8-3693-9879-1

Kumar, V., Ashraf, A. R., & Nadeem, W. (2024). AI-powered marketing: What, where, and how? *International Journal of Information Management*, *77*, 102783. DOI: 10.1016/j.ijinfomgt.2024.102783

Leerssen, P. (2023). An end to shadow banning? Transparency rights in the Digital Services Act between content moderation and curation. *Computer Law & Security Review*, *48*, 105790. DOI: 10.1016/j.clsr.2023.105790

Marabelli, M., Newell, S., & Handunge, V. (2021). The lifecycle of algorithmic decision-making systems: Organizational choices and ethical challenges. *The Journal of Strategic Information Systems*, *30*(3), 101683. DOI: 10.1016/j.jsis.2021.101683

Michtner, P., & Pinzolits, R. F. J. (2025). Web accessibility gaps in online video platforms: Video services ahead of the European Accessibility Act (EAA). *Universal Access in the Information Society*. Advance online publication. DOI: 10.1007/s10209-025-01219-1

Murikah, W., Nthenge, J. K., & Musyoka, F. M. (2024). Bias and ethics of AI systems applied in auditing - A systematic review. *Scientific African*, *25*, e02281. DOI: 10.1016/j.sciaf.2024.e02281

North-Samardzic, A. (2020). Biometric Technology and Ethics: Beyond Security Applications. *Journal of Business Ethics*, *167*(3), 433–450. DOI: 10.1007/s10551-019-04143-6

Ou, C. X., Zhang, X., Angelopoulos, S., Davison, R. M., & Janse, N. (2022). Security breaches and organization response strategy: Exploring consumers' threat and coping appraisals. *International Journal of Information Management*, *65*, 102498. DOI: 10.1016/j.ijinfomgt.2022.102498

Paas, F., & van Merriënboer, J. J. G. (2020). Cognitive-Load Theory: Methods to Manage Working Memory Load in the Learning of Complex Tasks. *Current Directions in Psychological Science*, *29*(4), 394–398. DOI: 10.1177/0963721420922183

Poehlmann, N., Caramancion, K. M., Tatar, I., Li, Y., Barati, M., & Merz, T. (2021). *The Organizational Cybersecurity Success Factors: An Exhaustive Literature Review* (pp. 377–395). DOI: 10.1007/978-3-030-71017-0_27

Quach, S., Thaichon, P., Martin, K. D., Weaven, S., & Palmatier, R. W. (2022). Digital technologies: Tensions in privacy and data. *Journal of the Academy of Marketing Science*, *50*(6), 1299–1323. DOI: 10.1007/s11747-022-00845-y PMID: 35281634

Saeed, S. (2024). Usable Privacy and Security in Mobile Applications: Perception of Mobile End Users in Saudi Arabia. *Big Data and Cognitive Computing*, *8*(11), 162. DOI: 10.3390/bdcc8110162

Saeed, S. (2025). Digital Transformation in Governmental Public Service Provision and Usable Security Perception in Saudi Arabia. *Information (Basel)*, *16*(3), 247. DOI: 10.3390/info16030247

Saeed, S., & Amjad, A. (2013). Understanding Usability Issues of Pakistani University Websites. *Life Science Journal*, *10*(6s), 479–482. https://www.lifesciencesite.com/lsj/life1006s/073_17605life1006s_479_482.pdf

Saeed, S., Wahab, F., Cheema, S. A., & Ashraf, S. (2013). Role of Usability in E-Government and E-Commerce Portals: An Empirical Study of Pakistan. *Life Science Journal*, *10*(1s), 8–13.

Safitra, M. F., Lubis, M., & Fakhrurroja, H. (2023). Counterattacking Cyber Threats: A Framework for the Future of Cybersecurity. *Sustainability (Basel)*, *15*(18), 13369. DOI: 10.3390/su151813369

Sarker, I. H. (2023). Machine Learning for Intelligent Data Analysis and Automation in Cybersecurity: Current and Future Prospects. *Annals of Data Science*, *10*(6), 1473–1498. DOI: 10.1007/s40745-022-00444-2

Shandilya, S. K., Datta, A., Kartik, Y., & Nagar, A. (2024). *Navigating the Regulatory Landscape*., DOI: 10.1007/978-3-031-53290-0_3

Shibuya, Y., Hamm, A., & Cerratto Pargman, T. (2022). Mapping HCI research methods for studying social media interaction: A systematic literature review. *Computers in Human Behavior*, *129*, 107131. DOI: 10.1016/j.chb.2021.107131

Shinde, R. D., Jathar, K. R., Pardeshi, A. D., & Thorat, S. A. (2023). Graphical Password Authentication Using Decentralized Single-Sign-On. *2023 World Conference on Communication & Computing (WCONF)*, 1–9. DOI: 10.1109/WCONF58270.2023.10235134

Suleski, T., Ahmed, M., Yang, W., & Wang, E. (2023). A review of multi-factor authentication in the Internet of Healthcare Things. *Digital Health*, *9*, 20552076231177144. Advance online publication. DOI: 10.1177/20552076231177144 PMID: 37252257

Tian, X. (2025). Unraveling the dynamics of password manager adoption: A deeper dive into critical factors. *Information and Computer Security*, *33*(1), 117–139. DOI: 10.1108/ICS-09-2023-0156

Tsatsou, P. (2022). Vulnerable people's digital inclusion: Intersectionality patterns and associated lessons. *Information Communication and Society*, *25*(10), 1475–1494. DOI: 10.1080/1369118X.2021.1873402

Tyagi, A. K., Abraham, A., Kaklauskas, A., Sreenath, N., Rekha, G., & Malik, S. (2022). *Security and Privacy-Preserving Techniques in Wireless Robotics*. CRC Press., DOI: 10.1201/9781003156406

Ullah, A., Anwar, S. M., Li, J., Nadeem, L., Mahmood, T., Rehman, A., & Saba, T. (2024). Smart cities: The role of Internet of Things and machine learning in realizing a data-centric smart environment. *Complex & Intelligent Systems*, *10*(1), 1607–1637. DOI: 10.1007/s40747-023-01175-4

Volberda, H. W., Khanagha, S., Baden-Fuller, C., Mihalache, O. R., & Birkinshaw, J. (2021). Strategizing in a digital world: Overcoming cognitive barriers, reconfiguring routines and introducing new organizational forms. *Long Range Planning*, *54*(5), 102110. DOI: 10.1016/j.lrp.2021.102110

Wang, B., Zhou, H., Li, X., Yang, G., Zheng, P., Song, C., Yuan, Y., Wuest, T., Yang, H., & Wang, L. (2024). Human Digital Twin in the context of Industry 5.0. *Robotics and Computer-integrated Manufacturing*, *85*, 102626. DOI: 10.1016/j.rcim.2023.102626

Weickert, T. D., Joinson, A., & Craggs, B. (2023). Is cybersecurity research missing a trick? Integrating insights from the psychology of habit into research and practice. *Computers & Security*, *128*, 103130. DOI: 10.1016/j.cose.2023.103130

Zimmermann, V., Schäfer, S., Dürmuth, M., & Marky, K. (2025). Authenticate as You Go: From Exploring Smart Home Authentication with Daily Objects to Authenticating with Primary Tasks. *ACM Transactions on Computer-Human Interaction*, *32*(2), 1–69. DOI: 10.1145/3702318

KEY TERMS AND DEFINITIONS

Security: This is where the protection of data must include the control of the systems from the unauthorized actions to achieve the following three main principles: confidentiality, integrity, and availability.

User Experience (UX): Functionality and emotion are the combination of things that determine the quality of user's interaction with a system in a way that it will provide them with complete experience while they use it.

Privacy: People must have the authority to decide who will gain access to their private data according to legal and ethical standings for the purpose of receiving, storing and distributing it.

Human-Centered Design (HCD): Human centered design acknowledges the end users by focusing on learning their requirements and then developing interface systems that are usable and correlating to human ability.

Behavioral Cybersecurity: Investigations of the cognitive biases as well as the established habits and social system traits that affect security practices allow security specialists to analyze behavioral effects on cybersecurity.

Adaptive Security: A security system that works in the way of securing less with more obstacles but with a stronger defense system that changes status depending on context value, risk evaluation and user behavior pattern aims to minimize obstacles.

Cognitive Load: Users have to provide mental commitments during harder tasks and it becomes harder when user interfaces, or security protocols or system factors get in the way.

Chapter 11
Aligning User Experience and Usability With Cybersecurity for Sustainable Digital Transformation

Muhammad Usman Tariq
https://orcid.org/0000-0002-7605-3040
Abu Dhabi University, UAE & University College Cork, Ireland

ABSTRACT

In an age of sustainable digital transformation, usability integrity between user experience (UX) and cybersecurity is crucial to building trust, improving commitment, and ensuring long-term digital resilience. This chapter examines the intersections of these domains and argues that effective cybersecurity needs to be seamlessly integrated into an intuitive and accessible user interface. Poor Users find out how friendly can undermine security protocols and how user-focused designs can improve compliance without compromising. By expanding case studies, current industry practices, and academic findings, this chapter shows that promoting a safe but user-friendly environment essential to digital sustainability is possible. This chapter also covers design principles and strategic frameworks that integrate security conditions needed to integrate smooth user interaction and pave the way for an ethically responsible, technically robust digital ecosystem.

DOI: 10.4018/979-8-3373-3171-3.ch011

INTRODUCTION

Digital transformation will change the global economic landscape, governance, healthcare, education, and social interaction. It is a fundamental rethink of digital tools and platforms and the integration of advanced technology to create a fundamental rethink of organizational processes, customer loyalty, and service processing models. This transformation is fueled by the widespread availability of cloud infrastructure, artificial intelligence, machine learning, and the Internet of Things (IoT), among other things. These technologies allow organizations to collect, process, and use large amounts of data in real-time. It allows for a more personalized, efficient, and efficient system. However, this digital shift presents the weaknesses and challenges of the new series, particularly in terms of security and data protection. Organizations become more connected, and with data control, the potential targets of cyber threats are scaled exponentially. From customer-oriented applications to backend servers and interconnected IoT devices, all digital touchpoints provide potential entry points for malicious actors. Therefore, cybersecurity is not just a technical requirement but a strategic need. Without strong protection measures, innovations with automated decision-making, cloud-based cooperation, and seamless data exchange can be used for debt. A safety violation can disrupt the service, damage the trust of the customers, and lead to significant financial and reputational damage. Therefore, digital conversion initiatives must be supported by a proactive, deep, integrated, comprehensive cybersecurity framework adaptable to all digital infrastructure layers. It is where users-friendly work. Whether employees, customers, or partners interact with digital systems regularly, users' experience significantly impacts adoption rates and long-term commitment (Zipperle et al., 2024).

Safe but difficult-to-use systems are often avoided by users who are comfortable with them, inadvertently introducing risks. On the other hand, users are generally friendly but cautious about organizations with known security gaps. The intersection of ease of use and cybersecurity represents the key voltage for digital conversion. The fight against this voltage requires a subtle approach to align technical protection with human-centered design principles. User acceptance is not just the first adoption. It includes lasting commitment, trust, and satisfaction. Users often use digital solutions that are intuitive, accessible, and meet their needs. However, if these systems are not secure, the resulting violations or data abuse can quickly ruin all usability benefits. Suppose the system is bothering you to require long authentication methods, frequent password changes, or non-intuitive navigation for users. In that case, navigation users can oppose or find ways to circumvent security measures. It undermines both user trust and system integrity (Zabalaw et al., 2024). The challenge is, therefore, to create a digital environment where user-friendliness and cybersecurity are seen not as conflicting forces but as complementary aspects of a well-designed system. It is closely related to perceptions of system robustness. A delicate balance is required to maintain consistency. The system must be open enough to enable innovation and interoperability, but sufficient to prevent unauthorized access and operation. User-friendliness contributes to this balance by allowing legitimate users to perform tasks easily without friction. For example, suppose security protocols are seamlessly embedded in the user interface. In that case, this chapter aims to convey a general understanding of how secure systems and user-centric design contribute to the overall success and sustainability of initiatives for digital transformation. It is argued that digital security needs to develop beyond firewalls and encryption to include behavioral, emotional, and experimental aspects of digital interaction. User-friendliness is not a luxury or an afterthought but a key part of digital resilience. This chapter aims to provide readers with a framework for designing secure and user digital systems by examining case studies, theoretical models, and practical applications (Al-Hajri et al., 2024).

The scope of this chapter includes an interdisciplinary investigation of digital transformation through the lens of cybersecurity and the interaction between humans and computers. It is to explain how to build a secure system that does not alienate users based on findings from information systems, design thinking, behavioral psychology, and risk management (Affandi et al., 2025). The most important priorities include authentication mechanisms, user behavior analysis, adaptive security design, and the role of feedback and transparency to drive trust. This chapter also addresses the challenges of implementing safe but usable systems in various contexts, such as healthcare, finance, education, and government, highlighting sector-specific considerations and best practices. In this context, sustainability refers to environmental issues and digital systems' long-term viability and adaptability. A safe or unusable system will fail, regardless of its technical refinement or strategic orientation. Sustainable digital transformation requires a future approach that predicts future threats, adapts to changing user expectations, and develops with technological advances. It includes introducing new concepts such as zero trust architecture, design privacy, and ethical AI (Albarrack, 2024). These concepts emphasize the need to embed security and user-friendliness in the DNA of digital systems rather than treating them as external add-ons or conflicting goals. They are working on a paradigm shift, seen as integral parts of system design and digital innovation. Usability and cybersecurity integration must begin during the planning stage and continue throughout the lifecycle of the digital system. It requires interdisciplinary cooperation between designers, developers, security experts, and end users. User-friendliness also requires continuous evaluation, repetition, and security approval, not static. Both must be continuously refined according to user feedback, threat information, and organizational goals. Through the interaction between user experience and system security, this chapter contributes to a more differentiated and more practical discourse about digital innovation. The true measure of successful digital transformation emphasizes how progressive the system is and how effective and protected it is for those who use it. With this lens, digital transformation is a technical upgrade and a human-directed journey, making it a safer, integrated, and more sustainable digital future.

DEFINING USER EXPERIENCE (UX), USABILITY, AND CYBERSECURITY

Digital transformation is a multifaceted concept that constitutes the integration of digital technologies in all areas of the enterprise, how they work, and how they provide value to their stakeholders. The term is often used when referring to technical upgrades. However, its effectiveness is much deeper, including cultural changes, business model innovation, process communication, and changing customer expectations. At the core, digital transformation is about using digital functions to automate existing tasks, allowing for a new way of thinking and functionality. It requires a redefinition of roles, relationships, and strategies within the organization. Data often leads to a complete reorganization of priorities related to controlled decision-making, agility, and user-centric services. The basic step lets you store, process, and transfer data electronically. For example, paper documents are created to create PDFs and convert vinyl datasets to MP3 files. Digitalization itself does not change business processes or results. It is a technology process with limited strategic effectiveness unless it becomes part of a broader initiative (Alfityani et al., 2024)

Beyond efficiency improvements, create new sources of value. For example, retailers who change completely from the front of a physical store to a digital e-commerce platform will carry out digital conversions. Cybersecurity is not limited to defense against external threats. It also safeguards against internal weaknesses such as employee negligence and system inconsistencies. Cybersecurity must be both a technical and an organizational issue. Not only are you required to have a firewall, encryption, and intrusion detection system, but you also need clear guidelines, user training, and incident response protocols. The effectiveness of cybersecurity depends on how well these technical and human components work (Tariq, 2025). Cybersecurity is becoming more critical in the context of digital conversion. Organizations digitize more aspects of their operations, thus increasing the amount and sensitivity of data they manage accordingly. Potential entry points for cyberattacks will increase the number of devices, platforms, and services connected to the internet. Therefore, cybersecurity must be included in the organization of strategies for digital transformation and treated as a separate or secondary issue. Usability is the fundamental principle of interaction and UX design (human-computer interaction and user experience). It includes factors such as simple learning, speed of tasks, frequency of errors, and user satisfaction. User-friendliness is especially important in digital conversion, as new systems need to be able to succeed. Suppose users find minors or unintended digital tools. In that case, they are unlikely to take over, and the organization's corporate goals will be compromised. Conversely, highly usable systems that minimize user failures can suspend the organization of security risks without robust access control or data validation. However, this perceived dichotomy is increasingly questioned by the idea that ease of use and cybersecurity can and should coexist in harmony. The ambitious area of usage security focuses on designing security features. Security features are not only practical, but they are also simple and intuitive for users who can interact with them (Al-Janabi et al., 2024). Examples are biometric authentication, an adaptive security system that adapts to the user's behavior, and transparent encryption that works in the background without user intervention. The two terms are used frequently but are related to various aspects of system interaction. Usability is a component of UX and focuses on the efficiency and ease of performing tasks for users. Conversely, UX includes users' broader emotional and psychological responses to interacting with the system. It includes aesthetics, trust, satisfaction, and even recognition of joy. The system may be very usable, but it offers a reduced user experience if it is not visually appealing or does not match the value and expectations of the user. In the context of digital conversion, optimizing a UX digital environment includes working well and finding it intuitive, attractive, and reliable.

Trust is another important concept in digital transformation, closely linked to user-friendliness and cybersecurity. Trust affects whether users feel comfortable, especially when dealing with digital systems, particularly those who deal with sensitive personal and financial information. A lack of trust can hamper acceptance and commitment, even if the system is technically safe and functionally efficient. The trust structure requires transparency, consistency, and a proven user privacy and security commitment. It includes clear communication about how data is collected, used, and protected, and how users can provide digital interactions with wise control. Trust is not built overnight but must be cultivated through the organization's consistent ethical behavior (Tariq, 2025). The concept of system integrity is also central to this discussion. System integrity assures that a digital system performs its intended function correctly and consistently without approved operation or failure. Integrity involves both the data's accuracy and the process's proper functioning. Maintaining system integrity is extremely important for digital conversion to ensure that digital services are reliable and that the decision-making process is robust based on digital data (Al-Kfairy et al., 2024). Cyberattacks, software, human errors, or hardware errors can compromise integrity. Therefore, it must be protected by combining technical protection measures, such as test summaries and testing protocols, and organizational practices such as quality assurance and change management. Digital resilience goes beyond our ability to adapt to emerging threats, user needs, and changing environments. Resilient digital systems are not only safe and usable, they are also adaptable and sustainable. Whether it causes a cyber incident, hardware error, or changes to regulatory requirements, it may work effectively with faults in mind. Resilience is increasingly seen as an essential attribute of successful digital transformation, as it reflects the organization's ability to manage risk and ensure the continuity of a volatile digital environment. It concludes that environmental sustainability includes economic and social aspects, reduced energy consumption, and a sustainable digital transformation that ensures digital initiatives are scalable, queued, and integrated. It considers the lifecycle costs of digital systems, the skills required to support them, and the impact on various user groups. Inclusivity is vital to sustainability as it allows all users to access digital services, including those with disabilities, limited digital literacy, or low-bandwidth connectivity. Companies can create digital environments that serve different groups and promote equity by adopting universal design principles and integrated practices. Each of these concepts contributes to a deeper understanding of how companies can control the complexity of digital change. Clearly defining and distinguishing these terms will help users better clarify the challenges and opportunities of digital transformation and design strategies that are innovative, efficient, safe, and sustainable (Ambore, 2024).

Cybersecurity is the area of technical experts focused on protecting assets, systems, and data from unauthorized access or attacks. In contrast, UX was a problem for designers and product managers who were tasked with producing intuitive and engaging user interactions. However, when digital conversions deepened in the sector, these silos became unsustainable. The interdependencies between UX and cybersecurity can now be recognized in almost every digital interaction, from registration to system, online payment activities, and managing data exchange permissions for mobile apps (Asem et al., 2024). A technically robust security system that is difficult to understand and use can be achieved. For example, if a user generates and notifies or changes keywords in a security process, the user can use insecure behavior in a way that is written down or reused on some platforms. Similarly, suppose multi-factor authentication (MFA) is implemented in a way that feels intrusive or time-consuming. In that case, users can decide to disable them or avoid using the entire platform. In these cases, the system could theoretically be safe, but in practice, it is because of low user kindness. Friction-reducing properties like click applications, persistent sessions, and minimal identity testing provide speed and comfort. They can also please users by creating weaknesses. These could be exploited by malicious actors trying to infiltrate a system through meetings, fake identities, or social engineering. Therefore, the goal must be to design systems where UX and cybersecurity strengthen and do not harm each other. This integrated approach requires an overall design philosophy that user friendliness and security are not competing goals but additional columns of reliability. The available security focuses on creating security mechanisms that users can understand, are intuitive, and can enhance. Instead of burdening users with available security protections, an attempt is made to seamlessly embed in user travel. For example, biometric methods such as face recognition and fingerprint scanning provide strong security, but are user-friendly and improving (Azevdeo et al., 2024).

Another example is context-related authentication, which rates system, user behavior, location, and device properties to determine risk levels. Only additional checks are required to see if an abnormality is recognized. These approaches respect the user's time and mental stress and ensure robust protection. Despite these advances, there is a compromise between user friendliness and security. I am frequently convinced that one improvement will inevitably affect the other zero-sum games. But this compromise is more myth than reality. Often, perceptual voltages are based on unimplemented security features rather than inherent incompatibility. For example, systems that require complex passwords every 30 days are technically secure, but can unnecessarily irritate users (Tariq, 2025). In contrast, a system-integrated password manager can maintain high password security restrictions while simplifying the user experience. In such cases, this does not lead to weaker security. Security is often added to the system after core functions and interfaces are designed. This continuous approach can lead to security measures that disrupt user flows. Instead, security considerations must be part of the design process. By including cybersecurity experts in the early design stage, you can coordinate user needs, expectations, and protection goals. Cross-functional cooperation enables innovations that can be useful for both domains, such as progressive disclosure of security settings, interactive dashboards for privacy, and gaming security perception tools (Bakar et al., 2024).

Another area where interdependence is obvious is user reliability. Despite being a different framework across all domains, trust is the foundation of both UX and cybersecurity. From a UX perspective, trust is built through consistent, predictable, and satisfying interactions. From a cybersecurity perspective, trust is determined by robust defense, transparency, and accountability. Users must trust that their data is handled safely, that the platform works as expected, and that they will be notified immediately if something goes wrong. Violation of security can significantly damage your UX by eroding this trust (Chrusciak et al., 2025). Similarly, insufficient user interfaces lead to unintended data loading or violations of guidelines, as users overlook essential safety instructions that are misinterpreted or overlooked. Although users are often the last line of defense against phishing attacks, many systems cannot recognize suspicious activity. A well-designed UX helps reduce phishing risk by using recognizable domain names and specifying reliable sources, including warnings for unknown registrations or anomalous activities. At the same time, security mechanisms such as email checking, encrypted communications, and URL filtering work in the background to block or mark malicious content (Obisesan, 2024). If these elements are in harmony, users are less likely to become victims of deception and more frequently. These technologies often work with limited environments, minimal user input, or automated data collection, where traditional safety paradigms may not apply. Designing these contexts requires creative solutions that adjust safety with minimal user effort. For example, portable devices with proximity-based bases can use authentication or gesture recognition to reduce password dependency (Cosa, 2024). Smart-home devices can be protected through a centralized management interface that guides users to best practices without the need for technical knowledge. In such cases, user-friendliness is not a luxury but a need for effective security.

There is also a socio-technical aspect to this relationship. Users have different digital capabilities, cognitive skills, and security awareness. A common approach can alienate some users or make others vulnerable. Therefore, personalization and adaptability are essential. Educational interventions such as onboarding tutorials, just-in-time tips, and feedback mechanisms can improve security and usability by fostering well-configured, confident user behavior. The effects of this interdependence are profound for organizations. It is no longer sufficient to provide a secure system. These systems must also be usable to achieve widespread deployment and persistent commitment. Additionally, digital trusts that support customer loyalty and organizational calls are shaped by user experience and technical protection measures (Emma, 2025). Organizations that recognize the synergy of UX and cybersecurity and act on it are safe and suitable for creating digital environments and invitations. Users - Friendly and security are not naturally rejected. Instead, they strengthen each other when they are thoughtfully designed and implemented. The myths about their incompatibility are based on outdated design practices, a lack of interdisciplinary cooperation, and a narrow view of security as a purely technical challenge. In reality, good security is good, and vice versa. By implementing this paradigm, businesses can create adorable and integrated digital systems that remain safe and compliant and support the broader goals of sustainable digital transformation.

HUMAN-CENTERED DESIGN IN CYBERSECURITY

People-centric security design represents a change in how we think about protecting digital systems, recognizing that users are essential participants, not security obstacles. Traditional security models often treat users as the weakest link, constructing surrounding rigid systems and suspecting their actions will naturally match technical requirements. However, this approach often leads to frustration, avoidance, and ultimately system failure. This paradigm focuses on human-centric security by designing systems for fundamental human skills, needs, and limitations and embedding security to ensure that goals do not hinder users. At the heart of this approach are simple but powerful principles. Security must be used by design. If the user understands, trusts, and uses safety characteristics, their actions become an asset rather than a responsibility (Hosseini, 2024). The first is guarantees or clarity of what a user can or should do within the system. For example, a secure request or control should be intuitive and clearly state its purpose using familiar language and visual information. It is associated with feedback and is another essential principle that ensures that users receive direct and understandable answers to their actions. Users who enter a password incorrectly need to know exactly what went wrong. The password was too short, but did it contain undetected characters, or was it wrong? Clear feedback reduces assumptions and safe behavior, such as re-registration using correct login information instead of providing uncertain links.

Another fundamental principle is simple. Complexity is often confused with the strength of security design. However, users can interfere with or cause problems that undermine protection through complex security mechanisms. Human security seeks to simplify interactions without watering down effectiveness. This means that it is integrated into biometric authentication tools that reduce the steps required for secure registration and memory reliance (Saeed et al., 2024). Context awareness plays a key role that requires adaptation to the user's context, and it is essential to increase safety requirements only when the risk stage rises. For example, enrolling from a new location could lead to a secondary check step, but this may not be sufficient from a known device in your home. Large healthcare providers have had extensive incidents of frustrated clinicians with complex multi-stage authentication processes requiring rapid patient file access. The system required frequent passwords with strict formatting rules that were difficult to remember. As a result, many employees have written passwords on sticky notes and added them to computer monitors, causing extremely unsafe protocols aimed at effectively protecting sensitive data. Here, the system prioritizes theoretical security for the user and ultimately affects both (Emma, 2025).

Another meaningful example comes from the banking sector. The mobile banking app claimed complex alphanumeric passwords with each registration without storing biometrics or usernames (Affandi et al., 2025). Many users unhappy with the experience have simply guessed passwords or given up on the entire app. It has led some customers to switch to competitors that offer a friendly interface for more users. In this case, it is emphasized that UX can weaken inadequate security practices and reduce user trust and organizational risks regarding customer wear. For example, the State Advantage Portal had visually similar authentication screens on many phishing sites. Users used to this lack of visual security instructions could enter their login information on a malicious-looking website. When UX is not directed towards visual security standards, it undermines resilience to users' cyber threats. The approach to achieving this orientation is progressive disclosure, with security options or settings gradually appearing as needed rather than overwhelming the user first, this way, users can build familiarity and trust in basic features before handling more advanced configurations. For example, social media platforms can first arrange for users to enable two-factor authentication. At the same time, onboarding can provide detailed walkthroughs and context-sensitive help if users access security settings. This step-by-step approach promotes learning and commitment without intimidation.

USABILITY CHALLENGES IN SECURITY INTERFACES

Usability failures are critical to ensuring effective safety outcomes, particularly in authentication, access control, and data protection management. As digital systems become more demanding, the mechanisms by which users are protected are often more complicated, leading to tensions between user-friendliness and security. This voltage often appears in everyday interactions, registrations, approvals, and consent forms. Users need to control security measures that are unperceived, intrusive, or simply overwhelming. Ease of use in these areas irritates users and weakens the overall system integrity. This is because people bypass security features and make uncertain decisions due to confusion and fatigue. Passwords remain the dominant form of user authentication, but are the most problematic. In many cases, users must change it regularly and create complex passwords with a top letter and long strings with small letters, numbers, and special characters to avoid reusing it on their website. Concerning security, these requirements rarely meet human memory and human behavior (Komna & Mpungose, 2024). As a result, users will write down their passwords, use a qualified pattern, or rely on the same login information for multiple services. These coping strategies reduce the effectiveness of password security and show how strict security guidelines backfire when users are not considered. In a corporate environment, role-based access management can quickly become a maze. Due to the lack of clarity in default qualifications or rolling definitions, employees often receive too much or too little access. Employees without proper access either run a tedious approval process or seek an informal issue. B. Sharing login information or downloading data to personal devices (Hosseini, 2024). These actions introduce intentional and serious weaknesses. Conversely, excessive access to data leaks, internal misuse, or accidental exposures have been created, particularly if the user does not know the extent or sensitivity of information that the user has access to. In most social media, e-commerce, or mobile apps, data protection options buried in the menu layer are presented by splitting right-wing jargon or users into less secure standard settings. Often referred to as "dark patterns," this design pattern uses a limited understanding of user fatigue and prioritization of data collection or persecution. Users can agree to exercises they don't understand because the opt-out process is too difficult or time-consuming. The GDPR and similar regulations aim to mitigate this issue with clear disclosure and lighter opt-outs. However, enforcement and compliance are uneven, and many users are unaware of their rights or how they are effectively exercised. The cognitive burden required to constantly evaluate security applications, read data protection notes, and remind yourself of your login information is especially true when users participate in several platforms and devices throughout the day (Al-Janabi et al., 2024). Whether you trust the website, approve registration, or accept the cookie directive contributes to this intellectual burden. Ultimately, users can stop viewing, clicking warnings, or making claims most efficiently. In this tired state, they are susceptible to phishing, social engineering, and other attacks that exploit their low vigilance.

The problem is not limited to individual users. In a corporate setting, complex authentication protocols such as VPN access, two-factor authentication, and regular returns to password returns can lead to employee productivity and frustration. For example, many organizations implement strict access controls during relocations to long-distance tasks to protect sensitive data (Taherdoost, 2024). However, the system was often confused, making it difficult for employees to access basic tools. Registered agents' help desk tickets have been raised, and many employees have resorted to personal devices or uncertain communication channels to avoid these hurdles. It promotes security measures that organizations need to protect against accidental areas. Users expect a quick, seamless experience; anything that hinders this expectation can be blocked from purchasing. For example, suppose a customer is asked to check their identity several times by email or SMS during a single session. In that case, they can abandon the entire purchase. It affects income and reduces user trust in the platform (Bakar et al., 2024). These security steps are necessary to prevent fraud, but if integration into user travel is insufficient, it can be counterproductive. Mobile screens limit the information displayed, making sending clear data protection options or detailed permissions more difficult. As a result, many users unquestioningly allow access to contacts, locations, or microphone data for further development in the app.

Additionally, mobile operating systems often request permission in unclear or inadequately coordinated ways and require access to photos without explaining why they are currently needed. It leads to indiscriminate approval or flat-rate rejection. Both can affect app functionality and user security. Several companies have taken over single registration (SSO) and biometric authentication to simplify secure access without compromising protection. E-commerce platforms like Amazon integrate fraud awareness behind the scenes, allowing minimal friction between cash registers and, at the same time, a high level of security (Mick et al., 2024). In the mobile area, app developers are increasingly undertaking privacy and context-related authorization inquiries, and the principles of principles for using clear and friendly languages to lead user decisions. If the system is designed for users who recognize restrictions, contexts, and goals, security is an enabler, not a failure.

THE PSYCHOLOGY BEHIND SECURITY BEHAVIOUR

In a digital environment, user behavior is shaped by technical systems and psychological factors such as cognitive stress, trust, and risk awareness. When individuals navigate websites, applications, and digital interfaces, they must constantly process information, assess potential threats, and decide what is safe and available. The process can lead to cognitive stress, especially when security measures are complex or poorly designed. Cognitive burden refers to the total amount of mental effort in working memory. Cognitive burden increases when the security system is not intuitive, or the user is faced with a warning, warning, or decision point. It often means that users do not skip important security steps, reuse passwords, or ignore safety instructions from negligence, but reduce the effort caused by natural brain trends. Trust affects whether users release personal information, click on a link, or accept software updates (Runsewe et al., 2024). It is constructed through reliable visual or textual information, such as HTTPS indicators, data protection seals, clean, professional designs, consistent positive interactions, clear communication, and visual or textual information. Suppose the interface appears to be overcrowded, confusing, or suspicious. In that case, users will rather question the platform's legitimacy, even if the underlying system is safe. Conversely, overly sophisticated phishing websites use this association by mimicking trustworthy brands and aesthetics (Majeed et al., 2025). It indicates that trust is often visually and emotionally triggered and is not necessarily based on a technical understanding. Users can trust their website simply because they feel safe, regardless of risk level. This perception is often wrong, with a real risk. Users can underestimate the risk of clicking on malicious links or overestimate the risk of relatively harmless information. This separation is attributed to several psychological biases, including optimistic bias (not happening to me) and familiarity (a platform perceived as safe).

Suppose the security warnings are too frequent or too vague. In that case, the user will begin switching between "warning fatigue." Suppose even the intended users are constantly bombarded with decisions and warnings. In that case, they will be desensitized and begin to accept the results without understanding them. In cybersecurity, decision-making is rarely the result of pure logic (Al-Hajri et al., 2024). Instead, users rely on heuristic mental abbreviations to simplify complex decisions. For example, suppose a user sees a green padlock in the browser bar. In that case, the padlock only shows a secure connection rather than reliable content. However, you can assume that the site is completely secure. This heuristic leads to overcontrol for visual indications rather than a critical assessment of website legitimacy (Azevedo et al., 2024). Furthermore, the choice of options has a major impact on decision-making. Suppose your data protection options (experiences with activating a location) are actively framed. In that case, it's even more of a part, even if it means users will undermine privacy. In digital security, this can be used in framework campaigns concerning potential losses. It is not a software update to risk and non-potential benefits. Similarly, the standard setting is a strong nudge. Most users maintain a standard configuration, regardless of whether it is safest or most reasonable for their requirements. Therefore, data protection is an important aspect of user-centric security design by default. Suppose the default settings precede security, and the user needs to unsubscribe actively. In that case, the entire system becomes resistant to human error. Design elements such as color, typography, distance, feedback, and layout contribute to how users interpret and measure information. Pay attention to the visual hierarchy of important characteristics such as security settings and approval requirements. If this is presented in a hidden or confused way, the user can overlook it. The timing of the request is also important. Ask for permission for what is needed. For example, only if the user attempts to decide on a photo and decides on information more thoughtfully than asking in advance. A password-strength device that shows progress as users create stronger passwords and provides immediate positive enhancements. Context-related warnings explaining why certain actions in simple languages are dangerous are more effective than common error messages. The interface design also prevents dangerous operation with gentle friction. For example, users can make it a little more difficult without saving terms of use, reading terms and conditions, or scrolling through the user interface via data protection settings (Majeed et al., 2025). These misleading patterns manipulate cognitive distortions and encourage users to share more data, install unnecessary software, and accept less secure settings. Recognizing and regulating such patterns is important to maintain trust and ensure ethical design practices. The way people think, feel, and feel in respond to interface instructions, depending on interface instructions, determines the effectiveness of the most robust safety infrastructure. Designers, developers, and security experts must create systems that suit natural human behavior, reduce cognitive stress, build trust, and guide users to safer decisions. Using behavioral skills and user-centered design principles promotes safe behavior. It allows for the development of a digital environment that is seamlessly integrated into the user experience.

DESIGNING FOR USABLE SECURITY

Designing usable and secure digital security systems has become important in today's interconnected world. One of the most common components of a secure system is authentication. Assurance of authentication methods is effective, intuitive, and accessible to many users to build trust and protect sensitive information (Albarrak, 2024). Best practices for available authentication systems begin with a fundamental change in the design concerning the human-centered principles that consider how people behave and interact with the technology. Available authentication systems reduce friction without affecting security and consider memory limitations, behavioral patterns, and various technical contexts in which users operate. The most widespread method is still widespread, but passwords are due to memory loss and sensitivity to platform reuse, and phishing. A user-friendly and secure approach involves implementing multi-factor authentication (MFA) so as not to overwhelm the user. Biometrics, such as fingerprinting and facial recognition, provide a high level of security that requires minimal effort from users.

When using MFA, it is essential to provide many options, such as SMS code, Authenticator apps, hardware tokens, and more, to enable users to select the best method for their context and accessibility requirements (Chrusciak et al., 2025). Users often forget their login information or lose access to their authenticated devices. Additionally, if the recovery mechanism is not correctly designed, it can be a significant vulnerability. Knowledge-based questions, once typical for account recovery, are perceived as unstable as personal information is now available online. Instead, secure fallback options such as e-mail and phone number checks, one-time codes, or recovery keys should be implemented with clear instructions and minimal user confusion. The goal is to create a seamless way of making your system without introducing unnecessary risks (Tariq, 2025).

Feedback and transparency during the authentication process also improve user-friendliness. If the registration attempt fails because the password is incorrect, the login information has expired, or the user must be notified due to suspicious activity (Sinha, 2024). Ambiguous error messages can cause frustration and prevent resolution. Real-time feedback during password creation, such as the strength and suggestions of passwords for stronger alternatives, can help users improve security. The registration system must also switch on the secure password visibility feature and remember the user's preferences for future sessions (without affecting security). These factors are essential for compliance with regulatory compliance (such as GDPR and CCPA). However, it is even more essential to determine the criteria for trust between users and service providers. Data collection, storage, release, and usage information should be presented in a simple, daily language, with icons, infographic data, or extensible sections added to ensure that users can understand the content without being overwhelmed. Instead of putting all the terminology into a large document, designers can use multi-layered information that includes the essential information in advance in a link or dropdown for a more detailed explanation. This structure respects the user's time and decision-making ability and ensures transparency. Many systems require a declaration of consent to create an invoice. However, consent must be context-related, and you must remember or inform the user if a significant change in data usage occurs.

A declaration of consent means that the user not only has an actual choice but also understands the effect of this choice. It's not just about letting them know (Aldoseri et al., 2024). Clear notifications about data usage, warnings about access to third-party providers, and regular summaries of data interactions contribute to a sense of control and trust in the system. Inaccessible systems exclude large segments of the population. Suppose CAPTCHA or dyslexia users are not asking visually impaired users complex security questions. In that case, the system does not have secure access for everyone. Cybersecurity tools must be designed with various user needs, not as a subsequent thought. For example, a screen reader should be able to interpret the authentication interface and error messages (Ambore, 2024). Color contrast must meet minimum threshold values so that users can navigate with warnings and warnings with visual impairment. Alternate inputs, such as language and keyboard-only keyboard navigation, must be supported to record users who cannot use the mouse or touchscreen. Captcha Systems should provide audio alternatives or logic-based challenges that people with disabilities can access. According to the designer, users can interpret icons, colors, and labels differently based on their cultural background. Translation must go beyond merely being a language alternative. Local standards and legal frameworks must also be considered. You can dramatically improve access and reduce error rates between user groups by providing information in several languages, using commonly recognizable symbols, and including tutorials and guided experiences.

Security training and onboarding experience are other areas where accessibility plays a role. New users are not expected to understand sophisticated cybersecurity concepts intuitively. To fill knowledge gaps, the system must include contextual help, a glossary, short explanatory videos, or animations. This educational equipment should be accessible, providing capture, transcribing, and easy navigation (Munshi, 2024). The digital gap is extended when people complete essential services due to inaccessible authentication methods, disruption in data protection conditions, and inflexible interfaces. By taking over best practices to include authentication, clear and respectful data protection communications, and design, you get closer to a digital ecosystem where security is a common and seamless experience. The aim is not to align with security for user-friendly reasons but to increase both with thoughtful and inclusive designs that recognize the diversity of human experience.

MEASURING USABILITY AND SECURITY OUTCOMES

Evaluating orientations between user experience (UX) and cybersecurity requires a differentiated understanding of qualitative and quantitative metrics. Metrics in this area measure performance, security, and how users perceive and interact with security features (Al-kfairy et al., 2024). Traditional cybersecurity metrics such as the number of violations, response times, and sensitivity numbers are insufficient. When UX and security are combined, evaluations should also include how easily users can perform secure tasks, how often they make mistakes, and whether the interaction reflects an understanding of security protocols (Zabalawi et al., 2024). Usability metrics such as tasks, error frequency, task time, and user satisfaction ratings are important to determine whether a system's security measure interferes with or enhance user experience. For example, if your system offers multifactor authentication (MFA), but most users turn it off due to ease-of-use issues, the safe behavior rate will be low despite strong security measures. Similarly, users terminate processes such as centralizing their registration and transactions due to confusion in security procedures and indications of inconsistent UX security. Another obvious metric is the incidence of user issues. Write down your password, use a shared account, or bypass your consent settings. These behaviors reflect the gap between intended security design and actual user practice. By combining these metrics with direct user feedback via research, interviews, or usability testing, organizations can help with the fundamentals of numbers and improve security features accordingly. In contrast to traditional software testing, which focuses on error and performance, usability testing observes how realistic conditions interact with the system under realistic conditions. For safety-oriented usability tests, participants are asked to set up an account using secure login information, interpret data protection notes, or restore forgotten passwords. Traditional threat modeling identifies assets, potential threats, and system dusk (Asem et al., 2024). Suppose this process is carried out with the user. In that case, it also evaluates how human behavior can introduce or reduce these risks. For example, suppose your security process requires frequent changes to your password without allowing a password manager. In that case, the model should consider the risk of users using weaker, unmemorable passwords or insecure storage. This analysis can further enrich the inclusion of non-technical stakeholders in threat modeling workshops by revealing how different user staff interact with security controls under different circumstances. This approach helps ensure that security measures do not cause bottlenecks and frustration when used easily.

First, the platform used a traditional username and password registration system with normal forced password changes. Captcha had no options, which was poorly restored and designed for passwords. The system is theoretically protected, but causes important user frames. Customers' accounting inquiries were high, users were often reused in several services, and safety features such as two-factor authentication had very low adoption rates. In short, the system of the system did not match how the user liked it or could use it. They conducted usability tests on various user groups, performed barrier-free tests, and conducted behavioral threat modeling sessions. One of the most important changes was replacing CAPTCHA with an accessible option that allows password manager compatibility, integrating biometric registrations for mobile devices, and introducing a clear, step-by-step recovery process with multi-channel checks. If the risk increases (for example, from a new device or location), the system must be triggered only with context-conscious MFA. Registration failures were reduced by 45%, recovery requests decreased by 60%, and two-factor authentication acceptance increased to 72% of users. User satisfaction ratings related to the registration experience have increased significantly, with authentication-related customer service support tickets down by more than 50%. These quantifiable improvements have shown that user-friendliness and security are not in conflict but can enhance each other if intentionally designed. Users estimated the clarity of instructions, flexibility in choosing authentication methods, and transparency about how data is protected. This improved trust has had a downstream impact on customer loyalty and brand reputation, which is often overlooked in technical reviews but is extremely important to business success. Suppose the system is designed without considering cognitive burdens, user preferences, and skills (Alfityani et al., 2024). In that case, security features are probably not used, bypassed, or misunderstood. So, coordinating UX and cybersecurity is not just a design preference. It is a strategic need. Organizations investing in usability testing, user-based threat modeling, and evidence-based metrics are positioned better to create designed and safe systems.

ORGANIZATIONAL AND CULTURAL CONSIDERATIONS

Promoting a strong security culture within an organization requires more than providing advanced technology and enforcing strict protocols (Rajarathnam & Singh, 2024). There is a need for a change in mindset that integrates user-centric guidelines, continuing education, and organizational empathy. Security culture includes values, beliefs, and actions influencing people's perceptions of daily work and practices. When security is treated as a common responsibility embedded in a user-centric design, it is not a stressful obligation but a natural component of workplace behavior. User-centric guidelines are the basis of this shift. It is designed to enforce compliance and coordinate with the employee's actual needs and experience, reduce friction, and promote safe behavior through understanding rather than fear or coercion. Various roles, departments, and technical skills require a security approach created by tailors. For example, guidelines regulating HR teams' data access require differentiation between software engineers and customer service staff (Schneider, 2025). A common approach often leads to limiting caps that impact productivity and effectively undermine the security that is meant to protect the issue. Instead, user-centric guidelines aim for context-related relevance, practical enforcement, and accessibility in communication. It includes terminology to communicate essential points, precise language without visual information or infographics, and feedback mechanisms that allow employees to report friction points and suggest improvements. Including users in the guidelines development process through research, focus groups, or pilot programs promotes user challenges and challenges and cooperation.

The traditional annual security training module model - often filled with monotonous videos and general quiz questions - cannot evaluate users or their use behavior wisely. Effective programs for recognizing security employment must take on experimental scenario-based learning that combines emotionally and cognitively with users beyond passive information provision (Djatmiko et al., 2025). Suppose the training unit simulates realistic situations such as phishing attempts, suspicious file downloads, or inappropriate data exchange by users. In that case, the lessons are internalized with greater probability and used in the work environment. Interactive workshops, gaming learning platforms, role-specific micro-role modules, and just-in-time warnings can dramatically improve the storage and use of security knowledge. The safety threat develops quickly, just as quickly as users are prepared. Safety reminder bets to periodic workflows, such as e-mail client input request warnings that alert you to external links or fast guides integrated into intranet sites, enhance learning in context. Managers and managers play an essential role in modeling safe behavior and creating a support environment where users can ask questions and acknowledge errors. Security culture thrives when users are treated as being managed as defense collaborators. A common obstacle is the belief that security and user friendliness are naturally inconsistent.

Another barrier is the lack of organizational orientation or prioritization. In many agencies, security within a department or compliance department is separated from design, operation, or HR. This fragmentation leads to missed independent initiatives, inconsistent news, and potential synergy. Facilitating available security requires different cooperation and leadership commitments. Executive buy-ins are essential for allocating resources to iterative design processes, including usability testing, accessible training equipment, and security as a basic user requirement. If security is embedded in a broader user experience strategy, you receive visibility and legitimacy across your organization. Usability testing, guideline speech, and immersive training programs require preliminary investments (Obiseasan, 2024). Benefits such as reduced risk and improved compliance can be considered intangible or long-term. To improve this, businesses should pursue a risk-informed cost-benefit approach that quantifies the value of available security concerning reducing support costs, incidents, speed of mitigation times, and increasing employee satisfaction. When employees find security measures and intuitive guidelines they can manage, they find less time to look for bypassing support and control, freeing and reducing operational friction. Employees used to a particular workflow can hesitate to insert new security equipment, especially if the previous implementation is not burdened or communicated. Overcoming this resistance requires a transparent strategy to highlight the reasons behind the change and include pilot test users. Fast victory and positive feedback loops can help you develop and shape dynamics, such as presenting teams that successfully integrate new practices and celebrating milestones of security behavior. Without a channel where users can report, ask questions, and share experiences, organizations remain blind due to everyday obstacles and frustration undermining safe behavior. Establishing regular feedback loops through departmental digital research, internal forums, or security champions leads to a listening and continuous improvement culture. When users see feedback reflected in guidelines, training content, or system changes, it is more constructive than security efforts. Building systems that respect the reality of human behavior instead of supporting practices and are not restricted can help businesses promote an environment that is intuitive, accessible, and embedded in their daily operations. This human-oriented approach transforms security from friction points into common values, and users approve as participants and administrators of a secure digital future (Oladipo et al., 2024).

FUTURE TRENDS AND EMERGING TECHNOLOGIES

Artificial intelligence is revolutionizing security by shifting from a rigid, rule-based field to a dynamic, user-focused service. By analyzing various behavioral data, such as login times, device fingerprints, keystroke patterns, and navigation habits, machine-learning models create a profile that represents what is considered 'normal' for each person (Mitrovic & Thakur, 2024). When the profile shifts, the system discreetly adjusts its settings: it may request a second factor, reduce the session duration, or isolate a transaction for manual examination. When actions match what is expected, friction fades away and becomes less noticeable. The reciprocal relationship between risk signals and interface effort generates a personalized security experience: the more accurately the system identifies you, the fewer interruptions it imposes. Crucially, the AI must provide clear explanations for its decisions, using a simple banner that states, 'An additional verification is required due to you signing in from a new location.' It helps build trust and educates users about the importance of specific steps (Tariq, 2025).

Adaptive UX also creates opportunities for positive reinforcement. Subtle visual and tactile cues, such as a discreet green border or a gentle vibration, can indicate to users that the environment is secure, prompting them to continue following safe practices. Conversely, when the model detects a higher level of risk, it can escalate its warnings: begin with an inline suggestion to activate biometric unlock, then progress to a modal dialogue, and only, as a last resort, prevent the action. By combining these interventions, AI systems can manage cognitive load and maintain the smooth progression of work while ensuring security. In the background, reinforcement-learning techniques continuously evaluate small changes to the user interface, such as button placement, tone of copy, and MFA timing, and prioritize those that result in higher rates of secure behavior, transforming the interface into an ongoing experiment in usability and defense.

Voice and biometric interfaces enhance personalization by providing authentication methods that rely on the user's identity rather than their knowledge or possessions. Voice recognition on smart speakers, palm-vein scans at self-checkout counters, and gait recognition in access control systems offer quick and effortless experiences. When implemented thoughtfully, they alleviate password fatigue and assist individuals with limited dexterity or literacy. Despite their closeness, their relationship carries unique dangers. Biometric data is permanent. Once leaked, a fingerprint cannot be changed like a password. Spoofing attacks have become more advanced high-resolution 3-D masks, deep-faked voice samples, and adhesive fingerprints, and successful breaches erode trust more profoundly because they feel personal. The effectiveness of mitigation relies on the detection of liveliness, which can be achieved through monitoring blood flow, analyzing micro-expressions, or observing real-time vocal micro-shifts. Additionally, secure enclave storage ensures that raw biometric templates are never transferred outside the device.

From a user experience (UX) standpoint, openness is crucial. Users should be able to view the location of their biometric data and understand how it is utilized, ideally with an on-device interface that displays enrolled faces, fingerprints, or voiceprints and provides a convenient single-tap option for revoking access (Oladipo et al., 2024). Consent workflows should be detailed and specific, distinguishing between biometrics used for unlocking devices and those used for making payments and clearly outlining the advantages and disadvantages of each. Equally important: when a face scan fails due to low lighting or a hat, the system should gracefully transition to a PIN instead of locking out the user. Inclusive design necessitates adjustments to accommodate various skin tones, accents, and physical abilities while providing alternative options that respect privacy preferences.

Zero trust architecture transforms security assumptions by considering every internal or external request untrusted until verified otherwise. A simplistic implementation can feel like a slow and painful death for users, with numerous prompts and distractions. Adaptive UX based on continuous authentication softens that boundary. Rather than re-authenticating for each micro-service call, the system gathers contextual evidence, including device health scores, network provenance, and user behavior patterns over the past few minutes. The user moves through services without interruptions if the composite risk is low. However, the system activates additional checks to ensure safety if it increases significantly. The task for designers is to create a visual representation of this intangible boundary without overwhelming individuals. One promising pattern is the 'trust meter,' a discreet indicator that displays the current level of trust and allows users to click for more information, similar to how battery status metaphors are already familiar. Another is dynamic session mirrors: as you navigate to a sensitive dataset, the header subtly changes color or displays a shield icon, indicating that additional checks have been activated.

Blockchain solutions offer a new user experience. Their appeal of secure ledgers, decentralized identity, and self-control coincides with complexity: unique phrases, wallet addresses, fuel charges, and private keys. For the general public, these abstractions become usability barriers. Progressive disclosure once again proves beneficial: conceal the 24-word seed phrase behind a single ' secure your wallet' task, then guide users through step-by-step actions with clear explanations and spaced reminders. Social recovery schemes, where trusted contacts can reconstruct a lost key and replace catastrophic single-point failure with graduated risk, depend on clearly communicating responsibilities to the account holder and the guardians. Visual cues like transaction previews that show the amount being sent and names that make hex strings easier to understand help reduce errors like typing the wrong address.

In enterprise blockchain implementations, tracking supply chains and facilitating inter-bank transactions, the focus shifts to integrating workflows. Employees must sign transactions as part of routine tasks. Suppose the signing wallet sits in a separate app with unfamiliar jargon. In that case, they are likely to delegate credentials or skirt policy. Embedding sign-off buttons directly in the existing ERP interface, using single sign-on tokens mapped to hardware wallets or secure elements, and surfacing audit trails in natural language ('shipment 8243 certified at 14:03 GMT by Alice') aligns blockchain's cryptographic trust with everyday mental models. Latency, another blocker, is mitigated by design patterns like optimistic UI showing a provisional ' success' toast. At the same time, the transaction finalizes in the background, then reconciles state silently or through subtle alerts if confirmation fails.

When examining the advancements in AI-driven personalization, biometrics, zero trust, and blockchain, a common thread emerges: security cannot be a singular, impenetrable barrier. It should be adaptable, transparent, and compassionate. Interfaces serve as the means through which these architectures interact with human minds. Their effectiveness relies on understanding and simplicity. When the system adapts to the user, surfacing friction only when justified, speaking in the user's language, and offering clear paths to recover or opt out, security ceases to be a tax on cognitive bandwidth. It becomes a silent partner in getting things done.

RECOMMENDATIONS AND STRATEGIC IMPLICATIONS

Incorporating user experience (UX) into cybersecurity governance necessitates a change in organizational mindset, moving away from perceiving security as solely a technical matter and recognizing it as a complex socio-technical problem where human behavior, design, and policy converge. To guarantee systems' safety while being user-friendly, organizations must incorporate UX principles into their cybersecurity governance frameworks from the beginning. It implies engaging UX designers, behavioral specialists, and end users in designing and evaluating security controls, policies, and tools. Organizations should establish governance structures that require usability testing in addition to penetration testing, and risk assessments should consider both technical vulnerabilities and human factors, such as user error caused by complexity or confusion. A user-centric governance model views secure behavior as a result of carefully designed systems, effective communication, and user decision-making assistance.

To effectively integrate UX with cybersecurity, aligning it with the broader digital transformation objectives is crucial. As companies upgrade their systems, embrace cloud technologies, and implement AI-powered platforms, it is crucial to establish security measures that align with the speed and convenience of these advancements (Kumarasinghe, 2024). A strict security system that annoys users or hinders workflow will be ignored, resulting in shadow IT and data leakage. Integrating security into digital transformation involves creating policies and experiences that encourage secure innovation rather than hinder it. It encompasses prioritizing multi-factor authentication, configuring systems with built-in security measures that don't require specialized knowledge, and implementing access controls that adjust based on the specific context. This alignment helps achieve the objectives of operational efficiency, agility, and customer trust that are essential for digital transformation.

Policy and ethical considerations are of utmost importance in the development of systems that are both user-friendly and secure. From a policy standpoint, mandates should promote or necessitate usability in security-related procurement, system design, and compliance standards. Organizations should avoid punitive approaches that hold users accountable for errors while disregarding inadequate interface design. From an ethical standpoint, it is crucial to create systems that prioritize user autonomy, offer transparent consent options, and steer clear of manipulative tactics that encourage users to engage in risky actions. Ensuring transparency in data handling, providing clear explanations of security prompts, and offering the choice to opt out of invasive measures are crucial for maintaining trust. Ethical design necessitates inclusivity, ensuring that systems are accessible to individuals with disabilities, users with limited digital literacy, and individuals from diverse cultural backgrounds. Governance models must adapt to accommodate a comprehensive understanding of risk, considering technological safeguards and user-friendliness (Zipperle et al., 2024). Strategic alignment guarantees that security is a catalyst for digital advancement rather than an obstacle. Ethical and user-centric design forms the foundation of a digital environment that empowers individuals rather than burdening them with systems designed to safeguard their interests. By adopting this comprehensive approach, security outcomes are improved, user trust is strengthened, engagement is increased, and long-term digital resilience is achieved.

CONCLUSION

Integrating user experience (UX) and usability with cybersecurity is no longer optional, it is a fundamental requirement for achieving long-term digital transformation. In contrast, well-designed, intuitive interfaces can encourage secure behavior, foster trust, and alleviate cognitive load. Incorporating UX into cybersecurity governance guarantees that policies and technologies are designed to support users rather than impede them and align with broader digital objectives such as agility, inclusiveness, and resilience. By adopting a human-centered and ethical approach to security design, organizations can balance control and convenience, utilizing adaptive technologies and inclusive practices to protect assets while respecting user dignity. By viewing users as collaborators rather than burdens, organizations can establish secure digital ecosystems that are resilient and empowering, cultivating a culture of shared accountability and continuous progress.

REFERENCES

Affandi, N. A. M., Zahibi, M. F. H. M., Bakar, N. A., Hamidon, H., & Pauzi, N. M. U. M. (2025). Driving Digital Transformation in Healthcare: A Training Registration System for Efficiency and Data-Driven Decision Making. *Journal of Information and Knowledge Management, 15*(SI1).

Al-Hajri, A., Abdella, G. M., Al-Yafei, H., Aseel, S., & Hamouda, A. M. (2024). A systematic literature review of the digital transformation in the Arabian Gulf's oil and gas sector. *Sustainability (Basel), 16*(15), 6601. DOI: 10.3390/su16156601

Al-Janabi, S., Jabbar, H., & Syms, F. (2024). Cybersecurity Transformation: Cyber-Resilient IT Project Management Framework. *Digital, 4*(4).

Al-kfairy, M., Alomari, A., Al-Bashayreh, M. G., & Tubishat, M. (2024). Unveiling the metaverse: a survey of user experience, social dynamics, and technological interoperability. *Preprints.* https://www. preprints. org/manuscript/202402.0785/v1

Albarrak, A. M. (2024). Integration of Cybersecurity, Usability, and Human-Computer Interaction for Securing Energy Management Systems. *Sustainability (2071-1050), 16*(18).

Aldoseri, A., Al-Khalifa, K. N., & Hamouda, A. M. (2024). AI-powered innovation in digital transformation: Key pillars and industry impact. *Sustainability (Basel), 16*(5), 1790. DOI: 10.3390/su16051790

Alfityani, A., Alghadi, M. Y., Alnsour, I. R., Al-Smadi, R. W., Samroodh, M., & Al-Gasawneh, J. (2024). Financial Services Industry in Digital Era: Emerging Cyber Security and Sustainability Perspectives. *Calitatea, 25*(202), 134–142.

Ambore, S. M. (2024). *Cybersecurity for the unbanked: usable security heuristics for mobile financial services* (Doctoral dissertation, Bournemouth University).

Asem, A., Mohammad, A. A., & Ziyad, I. A. (2024). Navigating digital transformation in alignment with Vision 2030: A review of organizational strategies, innovations, and implications in Saudi Arabia. *Journal of Knowledge Learning and Science Technology ISSN: 2959-6386 (online), 3*(2), 21-29.

Azevedo, D., Ramelot, J., Legay, A., & Kieffer, S. (2024, June). With or Without U (sers): A Journey to Integrate UX Activities in Cybersecurity. In *International Conference on Human-Computer Interaction* (pp. 212-231). Cham: Springer Nature Switzerland. DOI: 10.1007/978-3-031-61379-1_14

Bakar, N. A. A., Mahmood, N. M. N., Nasrul, M. A., Ibrahim, R., & Yaa'cob, S. (2024). The Digital Transformation for UTMSPACE Educational Sustainability and Technology Innovation: An Enterprise Architecture Approach. In *Information and Communication Technology in Technical and Vocational Education and Training for Sustainable and Equal Opportunity: Education, Sustainability and Women's Empowerment* (pp. 3–17). Springer Nature Singapore. DOI: 10.1007/978-981-99-6909-8_1

Chrusciak, C. B., Szejka, A. L., & Junior, O. C. (2025). Integrating Digital Transformation with Human-Centric Factors Strategies to Enhance Organisational Process Performance: The HOPE Model. *Journal of Industrial Information Integration, 44*, 100785. DOI: 10.1016/j.jii.2025.100785

Cosa, M. (2024). Business digital transformation: Strategy adaptation, communication and future agenda. *Journal of Strategy and Management, 17*(2), 244–259. DOI: 10.1108/JSMA-09-2023-0233

Djatmiko, G. H., Sinaga, O., & Pawirosumarto, S. (2025). Digital transformation and social inclusion in public services: A qualitative analysis of e-government adoption for marginalized communities in sustainable governance. *Sustainability (Basel), 17*(7), 2908. DOI: 10.3390/su17072908

Emma, L. (2025). The Impact of Technology Acceptance Models on Business Innovation and Digital Transformation.

Hosseini, L. (2024). Driving Resilience Through Digital Transformation Strategies. *Digital Transformation and Administration Innovation, 2*(3), 1–6.

Komna, L., & Mpungose, S. (2024). Enhancing digital transformation strategies: a framework for SITA. *International Journal of Business Ecosystem & Strategy (2687-2293), 6*(4), 235-252.

Kumarasinghe, J. (2024). *Improving the B App to Improve Customer Experience and Operational Efficiency: From the Perspectives of User Engagement*. Functionality, and Security.

Majeed, M., Chaudhary, A., & Chadha, R. (Eds.). (2025). *Digital Transformation in the Customer Experience*. CRC Press.

Mick, M. M. A. P., Kovaleski, J. L., Mick, R. L., & Chiroli, D. M. D. G. (2024). Developing a sustainable digital transformation roadmap for SMEs: Integrating digital maturity and strategic alignment. *Sustainability (Basel), 16*(20), 8745. DOI: 10.3390/su16208745

Mitrovic, Z., & Thakur, C. (2024). *STRATEGIC INTEGRATION OF CYBERSECURITY: INSIGHTS FROM INFORMATION SYSTEMS MANAGEMENT VIEWPOINT*.

Munshi, D. (2024). Enhancing Digital Transformation Project Success through Design Thinking-Driven Agile Project Management.

Obisesan, S. M. (2024). Integrating Artificial Intelligence and Cybersecurity Frameworks: Challenges and Opportunities in E-commerce Cybersecurity Management. *SSRN* 5070108.

Oladipo, J. O., Okoye, C. C., Elufioye, O. A., Falaiye, T., & Nwankwo, E. E. (2024). Human factors in cybersecurity: Navigating the fintech landscape. *International Journal of Science and Research Archive*, *11*(1), 1959–1967. DOI: 10.30574/ijsra.2024.11.1.0258

Rajarathnam, S., & Singh, V. (2024, October). Systematic Literature Review of Cybersecurity and User Experience. In *2024 Cyber Awareness and Research Symposium (CARS)* (pp. 1-9). IEEE. DOI: 10.1109/CARS61786.2024.10778869

Runsewe, O., Akwawa, L. A., Folorunsho, S. O., & Osundare, O. S. (2024). Optimizing user interface and user experience in financial applications: A review of techniques and technologies. *World Journal of Advanced Research and Reviews*, *23*(3), 934–942. DOI: 10.30574/wjarr.2024.23.3.2633

Saeed, S., Gull, H., Aldossary, M. M., Altamimi, A. F., Alshahrani, M. S., Saqib, M., Zafar Iqbal, S., & Almuhaideb, A. M. (2024). Digital Transformation in Energy Sector: Cybersecurity Challenges and Implications. *Information (Basel)*, *15*(12), 764. DOI: 10.3390/info15120764

Schneider, G. B. C. (2025). The Importance of Cybersecurity in Digital Government Implementations. *COGNITIONIS Scientific Journal*, *8*(1), e585–e585. DOI: 10.38087/2595.8801.585

Sinha, M. (2024). Exploring the Role of Cybersecurity in Integrated Programs for Protecting and Improving Digital Platforms. *International IT Journal of Research, ISSN: 3007-6706, 2*(2), 190-197.

Taherdoost, H. (2024). *Digital transformation roadmap: From vision to execution*. CRC Press. DOI: 10.1201/9781003471226

Tariq, M. U. (2025). Innovative Mentoring Programs: Strategies for Success in Post-COVID-19 Education. In Putnam, J., VanValkenburgh Banks, J., & Brown, S. K. (Eds.), *Mentoring Students and Instructors for Retention and Success* (pp. 123–158). IGI Global Scientific Publishing., DOI: 10.4018/979-8-3693-7590-7.ch005

Tariq, M. U. (2025). AI-Driven Personalized Learning: Revolutionizing Student Engagement and Teacher Efficiency in Education 5.0. In Mobo, F. (Ed.), *AI and Emerging Technologies for Emergency Response and Smart Cities* (pp. 75–96). IGI Global Scientific Publishing., DOI: 10.4018/979-8-3693-9770-1.ch004

Tariq, M. U. (2025). Balancing Flexibility and Precarity: Ethical Implications and Sustainable Practices in Global Gig Economies. In Doon, R. (Ed.), *Sustainability and Adaptability of Gig Economies in Global Business* (pp. 323–346). IGI Global Scientific Publishing., DOI: 10.4018/979-8-3693-9385-7.ch012

Tariq, M. U. (2025). Harnessing the Power of GANs and Meta-Learning for Few-Shot Image Generation. In Simaiya, S., Lilhore, U., Sharma, Y., & Kumar, S. (Eds.), *Exploring Generative Adversarial Networks and Meta-Learning Synergies* (pp. 301–324). IGI Global Scientific Publishing., DOI: 10.4018/979-8-3693-7575-4.ch012

Tariq, M. U. (2025). Enhancing Cyber Resilience in Software Development: Integrating Secure Coding Practices and Cybersecurity Frameworks. In Shah, I., & Jhanjhi, N. (Eds.), *Navigating Cyber Threats and Cybersecurity in the Software Industry* (pp. 35–64). IGI Global Scientific Publishing., DOI: 10.4018/979-8-3693-6250-1.ch003

Zabalawi, I., Kordahji, H., & Aftimos, S. (2024). Digital Transformation in Universities: Strategic Framework, Implementation Tools, and Leadership. In *Higher Education in the Arab World: Digital Transformation* (pp. 145–210). Springer Nature Switzerland. DOI: 10.1007/978-3-031-70779-7_8

Zipperle, M., Becherer, M., Zhang, Y., Chang, E., Dillon, T., & Karduck, A. (2024). Enabling Digital Transformation with Sustainability Criteria through Resilient Cybersecurity: Challenges and Opportunities.

KEY TERMS AND DEFINITIONS

Usable Security: Security designed for efficient and easy user interaction.

Cognitive Load: The mental effort involved in processing information.

Human-centered Design: Design prioritizing users' requirements, contexts, and behaviors.

Compilation of References

2024. N. Y. P. (n.d.). Nearly half of employed people have fallen victim to cyberattack or scam. https://nypost.com/2024/09/26/lifestyle/nearly-half-of-employed-people-have-fallen-victim-to-cyberattack-or-scam/

A.Golitsyna & E.Sergina. (2015). Report on the sovereignty of the Russian internet.

Abdikhakimov I, (2024). "Preparing for a Quantum Future: Strategies for Strengthening International Data Privacy in the Face of Evolving Technologies". International Journal of Law and Policy.

Abdou, A. M. (2021). Good governance and COVID-19: The digital bureaucracy to response the pandemic (Singapore as a model). *Journal of Public Affairs*, *21*(4), e2656. DOI: 10.1002/pa.2656 PMID: 34230813

Abergos, V. J., & Medjek, F. (2024). A Risk Assessment Analysis to Enhance the Security of OT WAN with SD-WAN. *Journal of Cybersecurity and Privacy*, *4*(4), 910–937. DOI: 10.3390/jcp4040042

Abid, A., Cheikhrouhou, S., Kallel, S., & Jmaiel, M. (2022). NovidChain: Blockchain-based privacy-preserving platform for COVID-19 test/vaccine certificates. *Software, Practice & Experience*, *52*(12), 2551–2566. DOI: 10.1002/spe.2983 PMID: 34226768

Abushark, Y. B., Hassan, S., & Khan, A. I. (2025). Optimized Adaboost Support Vector Machine-Based Encryption for Securing IoT-Cloud Healthcare Data. *Sensors (Basel)*, *25*(3), 731. DOI: 10.3390/s25030731 PMID: 39943369

Acquisti, A., Brandimarte, L., & Loewenstein, G. (2020). Secrets and Likes: The Drive for Privacy and the Difficulty of Achieving It in the Digital Age. *Journal of Consumer Psychology*, *30*(4), 736–758. DOI: 10.1002/jcpy.1191

Adewumi, A., Ewim, S. E., & Sam-Bulya, N. J. (2024). Advancing business performance through data-driven process automation: A case study of digital transformation in the banking sector. *International Journal of Business and Management*. Advance online publication. DOI: 10.5296/ijbm.v12i1.23456

Adeyeri, A., & Abroshan, H. (2024). Geopolitical Ramifications of Cybersecurity Threats: State Responses and International Cooperations in the Digital Warfare Era. *Information (Basel)*, *15*(11), 682. DOI: 10.3390/info15110682

Adiba, F. I., Islam, T., Kaiser, M. S., Mahmud, M., & Rahman, M. A. (2020). Effect of corpora on classification of fake news using Naive Bayes classifier. *International Journal of Automation*.

Admass W S, Munaye Y Y, Diro A A, (2024). "Cyber security: State of the art, challenges and future directions". Cyber Security and Applications, 1-18. Doi: .DOI: 10.1016/j.csap.2023.100101

Affandi, N. A. M., Zahibi, M. F. H. M., Bakar, N. A., Hamidon, H., & Pauzi, N. M. U. M. (2025). Driving Digital Transformation in Healthcare: A Training Registration System for Efficiency and Data-Driven Decision Making. *Journal of Information and Knowledge Management*, *15*(SI1).

Afroz, S., Brennan, M., & Greenstadt, R. (2012). Detecting hoaxes, frauds, and deception in writing style online. In *2012 IEEE Symposium on Security and Privacy* (pp. 461–475). IEEE. DOI: 10.1109/SP.2012.34

Aggarwal, A., & Dhurkari, R. K. (2023). Association between stress and information security policy non-compliance behavior: A meta-analysis. *Computers & Security*, *124*, 102991. DOI: 10.1016/j.cose.2022.102991

Ahangama, S. (2023). Relating social media diffusion, Education level and cybersecurity protection mechanisms to e-participation initiatives: Insights from a cross-country analysis. *Information Systems Frontiers*, *25*(5), 1–17. DOI: 10.1007/s10796-023-10385-7 PMID: 37361893

Ahlers, D. (2006). News consumption and the new electronic media. *The Harvard International Journal of Press/Politics*, *11*(1), 29–52. DOI: 10.1177/1081180X05284317

Ahmad, K., Maabreh, M., Ghaly, M., Khan, K., Qadir, J., & Al-Fuqaha, A. (2022). Developing future human-centered smart cities: Critical analysis of smart city security, Data management, and Ethical challenges. *Computer Science Review*, *43*, 100452. DOI: 10.1016/j.cosrev.2021.100452

Ahmad, W., Rasool, A., Javed, A. R., Baker, T., & Jalil, Z. (2021). Cyber Security in IoT-Based Cloud Computing: A Comprehensive Survey. *Electronics (Basel), 11*(1), 16. DOI: 10.3390/electronics11010016

Ahmed, L. K., & Rashid, R. D. (2024). Advanced security: The application social media and their security. ITM Web Conf., 64, 1006. DOI: 10.1051/itmconf/20246401006

Ahmed, I., Zhang, Y., Jeon, G., & Lin, W. (2022). A blockchain-and artificial intelligence-enabled smart IoT framework for sustainable city. *Journal of Intelligent Information Systems, 60*(2), 267–279. DOI: 10.1007/s10844-021-00691-9

Ajao, O., Bhowmik, D., & Zargari, S. (2018). Fake news identification on Twitter with hybrid CNN and RNN models. In *Proceedings of the 9th International Conference on Social Media and Society*, Copenhagen, Denmark (pp. 226–230). DOI: 10.1145/3217804.3217917

Al Ihsan, R., & Sekti, B. A. (2024). Pentingnya Keamanan Data Dalam Era Digital: Refleksi Terhadap Serangan Hacker Pada Pusat Data Nasional Indonesia. *Prosiding SISFOTEK, 8*(1), 7–11.

Alam, M. S., Ahmed, S., Dhali, M., & Alam, S. S. (2025). Citizens' engagement with cybersecurity measures in Bangladesh: A cross-sectional study. *International Journal of Information Security, 24*(1), 4. DOI: 10.1007/s10207-024-00918-9

Albarrak, A. M. (2024). Integration of Cybersecurity, Usability, and Human-Computer Interaction for Securing Energy Management Systems. *Sustainability (2071-1050), 16*(18).

Al-Besher, A., & Kumar, K. (2022). Use of artificial intelligence to enhance e-government services. *Measurement. Sensors, 24*, 100484. DOI: 10.1016/j.measen.2022.100484

Albinali, H., & Azzedin, F. (2025). Replay attacks in RPL-based Internet of Things: Comparative and empirical study. *Computer Networks, 257*, 110996. DOI: 10.1016/j.comnet.2024.110996

AlDaajeh, S., Saleous, H., Alrabaee, S., & Barka, E. (2022). The role of national cybersecurity strategies on the improvement of cybersecurity education. *Computers & Electrical Engineering, 102*, 108134. DOI: 10.1016/j.compeleceng.2022.108134

Aldoseri, A., Al-Khalifa, K. N., & Hamouda, A. M. (2023). Re-thinking data strategy and integration for artificial intelligence: Concepts, opportunities, and challenges. *Applied Sciences (Basel, Switzerland), 13*(11), 1–24. DOI: 10.3390/app13127082

Aldoseri, A., Al-Khalifa, K. N., & Hamouda, A. M. (2024). AI-powered innovation in digital transformation: Key pillars and industry impact. *Sustainability (Basel), 16*(5), 1790. DOI: 10.3390/su16051790

Aldoseri, A., Al-Khalifa, K. N., & Hamouda, A. M. (2024). Methodological approach to assessing the current state of organizations for AI-Based digital transformation. *Applied System Innovation*, *7*(2), 31. DOI: 10.3390/asi7010014

Alfityani, A., Alghadi, M. Y., Alnsour, I. R., Al-Smadi, R. W., Samroodh, M., & Al-Gasawneh, J. (2024). Financial Services Industry in Digital Era: Emerging Cyber Security and Sustainability Perspectives. *Calitatea*, *25*(202), 134–142.

Al-Hajri, A., Abdella, G. M., Al-Yafei, H., Aseel, S., & Hamouda, A. M. (2024). A systematic literature review of the digital transformation in the Arabian Gulf's oil and gas sector. *Sustainability (Basel)*, *16*(15), 6601. DOI: 10.3390/su16156601

Alhanatleh, H., Khaddam, A., Abudabaseh, F., Alghizzawi, M., & Alzghoul, A. (2024). Enhancing the public value of mobile fintech services through cybersecurity awareness antecedents: A novel framework in Jordan. *Investment Management & Financial Innovations*, *21*(1), 417–430. DOI: 10.21511/imfi.21(1).2024.32

Alharbi, S., Attiah, A., & Alghazzawi, D. (2022). Integrating blockchain with artificial intelligence to secure IoT networks: Future trends. *Sustainability (Basel)*, *14*(11), 1–18. DOI: 10.3390/su142316002

Al-Hawamleh, A. M. (2024). Investigating the multifaceted dynamics of cybersecurity practices and their impact on the quality of e-government services: Evidence from the KSA. Digital Policy. *Regulation & Governance*, *26*(3), 317–336. DOI: 10.1108/DPRG-11-2023-0168

Alibaba. (2024). Alibaba security response centre.

Ali, R. F., Dominic, P. D. D., Ali, S. E. A., Rehman, M., & Sohail, A. (2021). Information Security Behavior and Information Security Policy Compliance: A Systematic Literature Review for Identifying the Transformation Process from Noncompliance to Compliance. *Applied Sciences (Basel, Switzerland)*, *11*(8), 3383. DOI: 10.3390/app11083383

Al-Janabi, S., Jabbar, H., & Syms, F. (2024). Cybersecurity Transformation: Cyber-Resilient IT Project Management Framework. *Digital, 4*(4).

Al-kfairy, M., Alomari, A., Al-Bashayreh, M. G., & Tubishat, M. (2024). Unveiling the metaverse: a survey of user experience, social dynamics, and technological interoperability. *Preprints*. https://www. preprints. org/manuscript/202402.0785/v1

Alkhalil, Z., Hewage, C., Nawaf, L., & Khan, I. (2021). Phishing Attacks: A Recent Comprehensive Study and a New Anatomy. *Frontiers of Computer Science*, *3*, 563060. DOI: 10.3389/fcomp.2021.563060

Alkhodair, S. A., Ding, S. H. H., Fung, B. C. M., & Liu, J. (2020). Detecting breaking news rumors of emerging topics in social media. *Information Processing & Management*, *57*(2), 102018. DOI: 10.1016/j.ipm.2019.02.016

Almeida, F. (2023). Challenges in the digital transformation of ports. *Businesses*, *3*(2), 147–157. DOI: 10.3390/businesses3040034

Almulihi, A. H., Alassery, F., Khan, A. I., & Shukla, S. (2022). Analyzing the Implications of Healthcare Data Breaches through Computational Technique. *Automation & Soft Computing*, *11*(2), 1–12. DOI: 10.32604/iasc.2022.023460

Alshaikh, M., Naseer, H., Ahmad, A., & Maynard, S. B. (2019). Toward sustainable behaviour change: an approach for cyber security education training and awareness.

Althobaiti, K., Jenkins, A. D. G., & Vaniea, K. (2021). A case study of phishing incident response in an educational organization. *Proceedings of the ACM on Human-Computer Interaction*, *5*(1), 1–27. DOI: 10.1145/3476079

Al-Zahrani, M. (2020). Integrating IS success model with cybersecurity factors for e-government implementation in the Kingdom of Saudi Arabia. *International Journal of Electrical and Computer Engineering*, *10*(5), 4937–4955. DOI: 10.11591/ijece.v10i5.pp4937-4955

Ambore, S. M. (2024). *Cybersecurity for the unbanked: usable security heuristics for mobile financial services* (Doctoral dissertation, Bournemouth University).

Amft, S., Höltervennhoff, S., Huaman, N., Krause, A., Simko, L., Acar, Y., & Fahl, S. (2023). "We've Disabled MFA for You": An Evaluation of the Security and Usability of Multi-Factor Authentication Recovery Deployments. In *CCS 2023 - Proceedings of the 2023 ACM SIGSAC Conference on Computer and Communications Security* (pp. 3138–3152). DOI: 10.1145/3576915.3623180

Aminah, S., & Saksono, H. (2021). Digital transformation of the government: A case study in Indonesia. Jurnal Komunikasi. *Malaysian Journal of Communication*, *37*(2), 272–288.

Anderson, J. (2022). *The Role of Identity and Access Management (IAM) in Securing Cloud Workloads*. ResearchGate.

Andrew, J., & Baker, M. (2021). The general data protection regulation in the age of surveillance capitalism. *Journal of Business Ethics, 168*(2), 257–272. DOI: 10.1007/s10551-019-04239-z

Anna, B., Dada, L., & Maria, K. (2017). Revizor: how does the system for controlling prohibited content work.

Antonakaki, D., Fragopoulou, P., & Ioannidis, S. (2021). A survey of Twitter research: Data model, graph structure, sentiment analysis and attacks. *Expert Systems with Applications, 164*, 114006. DOI: 10.1016/j.eswa.2020.114006

Aragani, V. M., Anumolu, V. R., & Selvakumar, P. (2025). Democratization in the Age of Algorithms: Navigating Opportunities and Challenges. In Wongmahesak, K., Wekke, I., Seftyono, C., & Nurdin, N. (Eds.), *Democracy and Democratization in the Age of AI* (pp. 39–56). IGI Global Scientific Publishing., DOI: 10.4018/979-8-3693-8749-8.ch003

Argaw, S. T., Troncoso-Pastoriza, J. R., Lacey, D., Florin, M.-V., Calcavecchia, F., Anderson, D., Burleson, W., Vogel, J.-M., O'Leary, C., Eshaya-Chauvin, B., & Flahault, A. (2020). Cybersecurity of Hospitals: Discussing the challenges and working towards mitigating the risks. *BMC Medical Informatics and Decision Making, 20*(1), 146. DOI: 10.1186/s12911-020-01161-7 PMID: 32620167

Ariffin, N. H. M., Iqbal, M. I. M., Yusoff, M., & Zulkefli, N. A. M. (2025). A Study on the Best Classification Method for an Intelligent Phishing Website Detection System. *Journal of Advanced Research in Applied Sciences and Engineering Technology, 48*(2), 197–210. DOI: 10.37934/araset.48.2.197210

Arigbabu A T, Olaniyi O O, Adigwe C S, (2024). "Data governance in AI-enabled healthcare systems: A case of the project nightingale". Asian Journal of Business Ethics.

Arshad, R., & Asghar, M. R. (2024). Characterisation and Quantification of User Privacy: Key Challenges, Regulations, and Future Directions. *IEEE Communications Surveys and Tutorials*, 1–1. DOI: 10.1109/COMST.2024.3519861

Arunthavanathan, R., Khan, F., Sajid, Z., Amin, M. T., Kota, K. R., & Kumar, S. (2025). Are the processing facilities safe and secured against cyber threats? *Reliability Engineering & System Safety, 260*, 111011. DOI: 10.1016/j.ress.2025.111011

Arzoglou, E., Kortesniemi, Y., Ruutu, S., & Elo, T. (2023). The role of privacy obstacles in privacy paradox: A system dynamics analysis. *Systems, 11*(4), 205. DOI: 10.3390/systems11040205

Asem, A., Mohammad, A. A., & Ziyad, I. A. (2024). Navigating digital transformation in alignment with Vision 2030: A review of organizational strategies, innovations, and implications in Saudi Arabia. *Journal of Knowledge Learning and Science Technology ISSN: 2959-6386 (online), 3*(2), 21-29.

Asiri, M., Saxena, N., Gjomemo, R., & Burnap, P. (2023). Understanding Indicators of Compromise against Cyber-attacks in Industrial Control Systems: A Security Perspective. *ACM Transactions on Cyber-Physical Systems, 7*(2), 1–33. DOI: 10.1145/3587255

Aslam, M., Abbasi, M. A. K., & Khalid, T. (2022). Getting Smarter about Smart Cities: Improving Data Security and Privacy through Compliance. *Sensors (Basel), 22*(23), 9338. DOI: 10.3390/s22239338 PMID: 36502039

Aslam, W., Hussain, A., Farhat, K., & Arif, I. (2020). Underlying Factors Influencing Consumers' Trust and Loyalty in E-commerce. *Business Perspectives and Research, 8*(2), 186–204. DOI: 10.1177/2278533719887451

Asr, F. T., & Taboada, M. (2019). Misinfotext: A collection of news articles, with false and true labels.

Atkins, S., & Lawson, C. (2021). An improvised patchwork: Success and failure in cybersecurity policy for critical infrastructure. *Public Administration Review, 81*(5), 847–861. DOI: 10.1111/puar.13322

Aung, Y. Y. M., Wong, D. C. S., & Ting, D. S. W. (2021). The promise of artificial intelligence: A review of the opportunities and challenges of artificial intelligence in healthcare. *British Medical Bulletin, 139*(1), 55–66. DOI: 10.1093/bmb/ldab016 PMID: 34405854

Avertium. (2023, Jul 18). An update on the pro-Russia threat actor, Killnet. https://www.avertium.com/resources/threat-reports/an-update-on-pro-russia-threat-actor-killnet

Aydin, I., Sevi, M., & Salur, M. U. (2018). Detection of fake Twitter accounts with machine learning algorithms. In *2018 International Conference on Artificial Intelligence and Data Processing (IDAP)* (pp. 1–4). DOI: 10.1109/IDAP.2018.8620830

Azad, M. A., Abdullah, S., Arshad, J., Lallie, H., & Ahmed, Y. H. (2024). Verify and trust: A multidimensional survey of zero-trust security in the age of IoT. *Internet of Things : Engineering Cyber Physical Human Systems, 27*, 101227. DOI: 10.1016/j.iot.2024.101227

Azevedo, D., Ramelot, J., Legay, A., & Kieffer, S. (2024, June). With or Without U (sers): A Journey to Integrate UX Activities in Cybersecurity. In *International Conference on Human-Computer Interaction* (pp. 212-231). Cham: Springer Nature Switzerland. DOI: 10.1007/978-3-031-61379-1_14

Bachura, E., Valecha, R., & Rao, H. R. (2022). The OPM data breach: An investigation of shared emotional reactions on Twitter. *Management Information Systems Quarterly*, *46*(2), 1–15. DOI: 10.25300/MISQ/2022/15596

Bakar, N. A. A., Mahmood, N. M. N., Nasrul, M. A., Ibrahim, R., & Yaa'cob, S. (2024). The Digital Transformation for UTMSPACE Educational Sustainability and Technology Innovation: An Enterprise Architecture Approach. In *Information and Communication Technology in Technical and Vocational Education and Training for Sustainable and Equal Opportunity: Education, Sustainability and Women's Empowerment* (pp. 3–17). Springer Nature Singapore. DOI: 10.1007/978-981-99-6909-8_1

Baranovskaya, S. (2017). Moscow's cyber-defence: How the Russian government plans to protect the country from the coming cyberwar.

Bécue, A., Praça, I., & Gama, J. (2021). Artificial intelligence, cyber-threats and Industry 4.0: Challenges and opportunities. *Artificial Intelligence Review*, *54*(2), 1517–1543. DOI: 10.1007/s10462-020-09942-2

Beigi, G., & Liu, H. (2020). A survey on privacy in social media. *ACM/IMS Transactions on Data Science*, *1*(1), 1–38. DOI: 10.1145/3343038

Bellantuono, N., Nuzzi, A., Pontrandolfo, P., & Scozzi, B. (2021). Digital transformation models for the I4.0 transition: Lessons from the change management literature. *Sustainability (Basel)*, *13*(11), 6231. DOI: 10.3390/su132312941

Bellare, M., Canetti, R., Krawczyk, H., & Krawczyk, H. (1996). Hash functions for message authentication. *Advances in Cryptology — CRYPTO '96*, 55–73. DOI: 10.1007/3-540-68697-5_6

Bellos, C., Stefanou, K., Tzallas, A., Stergios, G., & Tsipouras, M. (2025). Methods and Approaches for User Engagement and User Experience Analysis Based on Electroencephalography Recordings: A Systematic Review. *Electronics (Basel)*, *14*(2), 251. DOI: 10.3390/electronics14020251

Benjamin, L. B., & Adegbola, A. E. (2024). Digital transformation in SMEs: Identifying cybersecurity risks and developing effective mitigation strategies. *Global Journal of Management and Business Research*, *14*(2), 1–11.

Berdik, D., Otoum, S., Schmidt, N., Porter, D., & Jararweh, Y. (2021). A Survey on Blockchain for Information Systems Management and Security. *Information Processing & Management*, *58*(1), 102397. DOI: 10.1016/j.ipm.2020.102397

Bergengruen, V. (2022). How Telegram became the digital battlefield in Russia's invasion of Ukraine. TIME. https://time.com/6158437/telegram-russia-ukraine-information-war/.

Beuchelt, G. (2025). Information Technology Security Management. In *Computer and Information Security Handbook* (pp. 475–508). Elsevier., DOI: 10.1016/B978-0-443-13223-0.00027-8

Bezerra Sales Sarlet, G., & Piñeiro Rodriguez, D. (2023). Alternatives for an adequate structuring of the national data protection authority (ANPD) in its independent profile: Proposals to overcome the technological challenges in the age of digital governance. *International Cybersecurity Law Review*, *4*(2), 197–211. DOI: 10.1365/s43439-023-00081-2 PMID: 36819767

Bharadwaj, P., & Shao, Z. (2019). Misinformation detection with semantic features and text mining. *International Journal of Natural Language Computing*, *8*(3), 17–22. DOI: 10.5121/ijnlc.2019.8302

Bhuiyan, M. N., Rahman, M. M., Billah, M. M., & Saha, D. (2021). Internet of Things (IoT): A Review of Its Enabling Technologies in Healthcare Applications, Standards Protocols, Security, and Market Opportunities. *IEEE Internet of Things Journal*, *8*(13), 10474–10498. DOI: 10.1109/JIOT.2021.3062630

Bi.Zone. (2024). Bizone. Accessed: December 10, 2024.

Bikku, T., Biyyapu, N. S., Sekhar, J. C., Kumar, M. K., Nokerov, S. M., & Pratap, V. K. (2024). The social network dilemma: Safeguarding privacy and security in an online community. *International Journal of Safety and Security Engineering*, *14*(1), 125–133.. DOI: 10.18280/ijsse.140112

Birch, K., Cochrane, D. T., & Ward, C. (2021). Data as asset? The measurement, governance, and valuation of digital personal data by Big Tech. *Big Data & Society*, *8*(1), 1–16. DOI: 10.1177/20539517211017308

Bloomberg. (2023). What Huawei comeback says about US-China tech war.

Bokhari, S. A. A., & Myeong, S. (2023). The influence of artificial intelligence on e-Governance and cybersecurity in smart cities: A stakeholder's perspective. *IEEE Access : Practical Innovations, Open Solutions*, *11*, 69783–69797. DOI: 10.1109/ACCESS.2023.3293480

Boletskaya, X. (2019). Google began to remove sites banned in Russia from search.

Bonicalzi, S., De Caro, M., & Giovanola, B. (2023). Artificial Intelligence and Autonomy: On the Ethical Dimension of Recommender Systems. *Topoi*, *42*(3), 819–832. DOI: 10.1007/s11245-023-09922-5

Borisov, S. (2015). Territorial structure of GOSSOPKA.

Branigan, T. (2012). China's internet users temporarily blocked from foreign websites.

Breuer, A. (2012). The role of social media in mobilizing political protest: Evidence from the Tunisian revolution. • Browne, R. (219). Russia opens civil proceedings against Facebook and Twitter.

Bright, L. F., Lim, H. S., & Logan, K. (2021). "Should I Post or Ghost?": Examining how privacy concerns impact social media engagement in US consumers. *Psychology and Marketing*, *38*(10), 1712–1722. DOI: 10.1002/mar.21499

Brissaud, D., Sakao, T., Riel, A., & Erkoyuncu, J. A. (2022). Designing value-driven solutions: The evolution of industrial product-service systems. *CIRP Annals*, *71*(2), 553–575. DOI: 10.1016/j.cirp.2022.05.006

Brummette, J., DiStaso, M., Vafeiadis, M., & Messner, M. (2018). Read all about it: The politicization of 'fake news' on Twitter. *Journalism & Mass Communication Quarterly*, *95*(2), 497–517. DOI: 10.1177/1077699018769906

Budnitsky, S., & Jia, L. (2018). Branding internet sovereignty: Digital media and the Chinese–Russian cyberalliance. *European Journal of Cultural Studies*, *21*(5), 594–613. DOI: 10.1177/1367549417751151

Bu, F., Wang, N., Jiang, B., & Liang, H. (2020). "Privacy by Design" implementation: Information system engineers' perspective. *International Journal of Information Management*, *53*, 102124. DOI: 10.1016/j.ijinfomgt.2020.102124

Bukhari, S. D., & Irfan Zafar. (2025a). *Mass Media and Impact of Fake News on Supply Chains* (S. D. Bukhari & I. Zafar (eds.)). IGI Global. DOI: 10.4018/979-8-3373-2175-2

Bukhari, S. D., & Irfan Zafar. (2025b). *Supply Chain Disruptions and Impact on Global Inflation* (S. D. Bukhari & I. Zafar (eds.)). IGI Global. DOI: 10.4018/979-8-3373-1982-7

Buntain, C., & Golbeck, J. (2017). Automatically identifying fake news in popular Twitter threads. In *2017 IEEE International Conference on Smart Cloud (SmartCloud)* (pp. 208–215). New York, NY. DOI: 10.1109/SmartCloud.2017.40

Cain, J. A., & Imre, I. (2022). Everybody wants some: Collection and control of personal information, privacy concerns, and social media use. *New Media & Society*, *24*(12), 2705–2724. DOI: 10.1177/14614448211000327

Calder A, Watkins S, (2024). "IT governance: an international guide to data security and ISO 27001/ISO 27002".

Calzati, S. (2022). 'Data sovereignty' or 'Data colonialism'? Exploring the Chinese involvement in Africa's ICTs: A document review on Kenya. *Journal of Contemporary African Studies*, *40*(2), 270–285. DOI: 10.1080/02589001.2022.2027351

Carmichael, C. (2019). The cost of shutting down the internet.

Castro, D. (2013). *How much will Prism cost the US cloud computing industry*. The Information Technology & Innovation Foundation.

Cavoukian, A. (2021). *Privacy by design: The seven foundational principles*. IAPP Resource Center.

Cei & Chen. (2022). China's personal information protection law: A systematic and contextualized approach to understanding data protection. *International Data Privacy Law*, *12*(2), 75–88. DOI: 10.1093/idpl/ipac006

Cfr. (2023). Cyber operations tracker.

Chang, V., Golightly, L., Modesti, P., Xu, Q. A., Doan, L. M. T., Hall, K., Boddu, S., & Kobusińska, A. (2022). A Survey on Intrusion Detection Systems for Fog and Cloud Computing. *Future Internet*, *14*(3), 89. DOI: 10.3390/fi14030089

Chatfield, A. T., & Reddick, C. G. (2019). A framework for Internet of Things-enabled smart government: A case of IoT cybersecurity policies and use cases in US federal government. *Government Information Quarterly*, *36*(2), 346–357. DOI: 10.1016/j.giq.2018.09.007

Chaudhary, S., Gkioulos, V., & Katsikas, S. (2022). Developing metrics to assess the effectiveness of cybersecurity awareness program. *Journal of Cybersecurity*, *2*(2), 147–157. DOI: 10.1093/cybsec/tyac006

Chebakova, D., & Balashova, A. (2021). Russia tested the work of the Runet when disconnecting from the global network. *Online (Bergheim)*.

Cheimonidis, P., & Rantos, K. (2023). Dynamic Risk Assessment in Cybersecurity: A Systematic Literature Review. *Future Internet*, *15*(10), 324. DOI: 10.3390/fi15100324

Chen, T., Li, X., Yin, H., & Zhang, J. (2018). Call attention to rumors: Deep attention-based recurrent neural networks for early rumor detection. In *Lecture Notes in Computer Science* (pp. 40–52). Springer.

Chen, H.-T. (2018). Revisiting the privacy paradox on social media with an extended privacy calculus model: The effect of privacy concerns, privacy self-efficacy, and social capital on privacy management. *The American Behavioral Scientist, 62*(10), 1392–1412. DOI: 10.1177/0002764218792691

Chernenko, E. (2017). "Threats to information security are becoming ever more sophisticated and widespread."

Chhetri, T. R., Kurteva, A., DeLong, R. J., Hilscher, R., Korte, K., & Fensel, A. (2022). Data protection by design tool for automated GDPR compliance verification based on semantically modeled informed consent. *Sensors (Basel), 22*(11), 1–25. DOI: 10.3390/s22072763 PMID: 35408377

Chidukwani, A., Zander, S., & Koutsakis, P. (2022). A Survey on the Cyber Security of Small-to-Medium Businesses: Challenges, Research Focus and Recommendations. *IEEE Access : Practical Innovations, Open Solutions, 10*, 85701–85719. DOI: 10.1109/ACCESS.2022.3197899

Chodakowska, A., Kańduła, S., & Przybylska, J. (2022). Cybersecurity in the Local Government Sector in Poland: More Work Needs to be Done: More work needs to be done. Lex localis-journal of local self-government, 20(1), 161-192.

Chowdhary, K. (2020). Natural language processing. In *Fundamentals of Artificial Intelligence* (pp. 603–649). Springer. DOI: 10.1007/978-81-322-3972-7_19

Chowdhury, R. H. (2024). The evolution of business operations: Unleashing the potential of Artificial Intelligence, Machine Learning, and Blockchain. *World Journal of Advanced Research and Reviews, 10*(2), 1–13. DOI: 10.30574/wjarr.2024.10.2.0930

Chrusciak, C. B., Szejka, A. L., & Junior, O. C. (2025). Integrating Digital Transformation with Human-Centric Factors Strategies to Enhance Organisational Process Performance: The HOPE Model. *Journal of Industrial Information Integration, 44*, 100785. DOI: 10.1016/j.jii.2025.100785

CNCERT. (2014). China's cybersecurity landscape from the perspective of CNCERT/CC.

CNCERT. (2024). National computer network emergency response technical team/coordination centre of China.

Coalson, R. (2016). New Kremlin information-security doctrine calls for 'managing' internet in Russia.

Commissioner, I. P. (2004). British Columbia's Personal Information Protection Act.

Conroy, N. K., Rubin, V. L., & Chen, Y. (2015). Automatic deception detection: Methods for finding fake news. *Proceedings of the Association for Information Science and Technology*, *52*(1), 1–4. DOI: 10.1002/pra2.2015.145052010082

Cook, M. M. (2021). Bringing Down Big Data: A Call for Federal Data Privacy Legislation. *Oklahoma Law Review*, *74*, 733.

Cosa, M. (2024). Business digital transformation: Strategy adaptation, communication and future agenda. *Journal of Strategy and Management*, *17*(2), 244–259. DOI: 10.1108/JSMA-09-2023-0233

Cram, W. A., Proudfoot, J. G., & D'Arcy, J. (2021). When enough is enough: Investigating the antecedents and consequences of information security fatigue. *Information Systems Journal*, *31*(4), 521–549. DOI: 10.1111/isj.12319

Creemers, R., Triolo, P., and Webster, G. (2018). Section 2: Operations security for critical information infrastructure - Cybersecurity law of the People's Republic of China.

Cryptography World. (n.d.). *Algorithms*. https://www.cryptographyworld.com/algo.html

Culot, G., Nassimbeni, G., Podrecca, M., & Sartor, M. (2021). The ISO/IEC 27001 information security management standard: Literature review and theory-based research agenda. *The TQM Journal*, *33*(7), 76–105. DOI: 10.1108/TQM-09-2020-0202

Da Silva, C. D., Vieira, F., & Garcia, R. (2019). Can machines learn to detect fake news? A survey focused on social media. In *Proceedings of the 52nd Hawaii International Conference on System Sciences*. DOI: 10.24251/HICSS.2019.332

Daah, C., Qureshi, A., Awan, I., & Konur, S. (2024). Enhancing Zero Trust Models in the Financial Industry through Blockchain Integration: A Proposed Framework. *Electronics (Basel)*, *13*(5), 865. DOI: 10.3390/electronics13050865

Dahua-PSIRT. (2024). Dahua PSIRT.

Dash, B., Ansari, M. F., Sharma, P., & Ali, A. (2022). Threats and opportunities with AI-based cyber security intrusion detection: A review. *International Journal of Artificial Intelligence and Cybernetics*, *4*(2), 1–15. DOI: 10.5121/ijsea.2022.13502

DataEconomy. (2018). Regional data centres in China are only half-used admits government.

DataEconomy. (2019). Everything is bigger in China.

DataReportal. (2024). *Digital 2024: Global overview report*. https://datareportal.com/reports/digital-2024-global-overview-report

Datastar. (2024). Data star observatory.

Dawson, P. (2020). *Defending Assessment Security in a Digital World*. Routledge., DOI: 10.4324/9780429324178

DCD. (2015). Datacentredynamics, "Data moves to mother Russia."

de Souza, J. V., Gomes, J., de Souza Filho, F. M., de Oliveira Julio, A. M., & de Souza, J. F. (2020). A systematic mapping on automatic classification of fake news in social media. *Social Network Analysis and Mining*, *10*(1), 48. DOI: 10.1007/s13278-020-00659-2

Debnath, P., Deshmukh, S. M., Laroia, M., Selvakumar, P., Manjunath, T. C., & Bhattacharya, S. (2025). Challenges Faced by Countries in Renewable Energy Adoption. In Özsungur, F., Chaychi Semsari, M., & Küçük Bayraktar, H. (Eds.), *Geopolitical Landscapes of Renewable Energy and Urban Growth* (pp. 295–320). IGI Global Scientific Publishing., DOI: 10.4018/979-8-3693-8814-3.ch010

Dehghanpouri, H., Soltani, Z., & Rostamzadeh, R. (2020). The impact of trust, privacy and quality of service on the success of E-CRM: The mediating role of customer satisfaction. *Journal of Business and Industrial Marketing*, *35*(11), 1831–1847. DOI: 10.1108/JBIM-07-2019-0325

Demirkan, S., Demirkan, I., & McKee, A. (2020). Blockchain technology in the future of business cyber security and accounting. *Journal of Management Analytics*, *7*(2), 189–208. DOI: 10.1080/23270012.2020.1731721

Devara, J. S. M. (2024). Cloud, Ai, And Digital Transformation: A Winning Combination. *International Journal Of Computer Engineering And Technology*, *13*(2), 1–9.

Dev, M., & Saha, D. (2024). Does e-government development moderate the impact of female labor participation on national cybersecurity maturity? An empirical investigation. *Information and Computer Security*, *32*(1), 74–92. DOI: 10.1108/ICS-03-2023-0042

Dey, A., Rafi, R. Z., Parash, S. H., Arko, S. K., & Chakrabarty, A. (2018). Fake news pattern recognition using linguistic analysis. In *2018 Joint 7th International Conference on Informatics, Electronics & Vision (ICIEV)* and *2nd International Conference on Imaging, Vision & Pattern Recognition (icIVPR)* (pp. 305–309). DOI: 10.1109/ICIEV.2018.8641018

Di Minin, E., Fink, C., Hausmann, A., Kremer, J., & Kulkarni, R. (2021). How to address data privacy concerns when using social media data in conservation science. *Conservation Biology*, *35*(4), 1074–1084. DOI: 10.1111/cobi.13708 PMID: 33749044

Di Nocera, F., Tempestini, G., & Orsini, M. (2023). Usable Security: A Systematic Literature Review. *Information (Basel)*, *14*(12), 641. DOI: 10.3390/info14120641

Diamond, L. (2015). Liberation technology 1. In *In Search of Democracy* (pp. 132–146). Routledge. DOI: 10.4324/9781315685175-7

Díaz, A., Guerra, L., & Díaz, E. (2021). *"Digital transformation impact in security and privacy." Advances in Defense and Security*. Springer.

Díaz-Rodríguez, N., Del Ser, J., Coeckelbergh, M., López de Prado, M., Herrera-Viedma, E., & Herrera, F. (2023). Connecting the dots in trustworthy Artificial Intelligence: From AI principles, ethics, and key requirements to responsible AI systems and regulation. *Information Fusion*, *99*, 101896. DOI: 10.1016/j.inffus.2023.101896

DigiChina. (2018, June 29). Translation: Cybersecurity Law of the People's Republic of China (Effective June 1, 2017). https://digichina.stanford.edu/work/translation-cybersecurity-law-of-the-peoples-republic-of-china-effective-june-1-2017/.

Distler, V., Fassl, M., Habib, H., Krombholz, K., Lenzini, G., Lallemand, C., Cranor, L. F., & Koenig, V. (2021). A Systematic Literature Review of Empirical Methods and Risk Representation in Usable Privacy and Security Research. *ACM Transactions on Computer-Human Interaction*, *28*(6), 1–50. DOI: 10.1145/3469845

Dittrich, D. (n.d.). Network monitoring intrusion detection systems (IDS). University of Washington. http://staff.washington.edu/dittrich/misc/faqs/ids.faq

Djatmiko, G. H., Sinaga, O., & Pawirosumarto, S. (2025). Digital transformation and social inclusion in public services: A qualitative analysis of e-government adoption for marginalized communities in sustainable governance. *Sustainability (Basel)*, *17*(7), 2908. DOI: 10.3390/su17072908

Dordunoo, Lord. (2024). (pp. 283–348). Integrating Organizational and Social Network Theories to Mitigate Racial Bias in Facial Recognition Technology. DOI: 10.4018/979-8-3693-8562-3.ch009

Dubey, A., Saquib, Z., & Dwivedi, S. (2015, October). Electronic authentication for e-Government services—A survey. In 10th IET System Safety and Cyber-Security Conference 2015 (pp. 1-5). IET.

Dutta, P. K., Raj, P., Sundaravadivazhagan, B., & Selvan, C. P. (2024). *Artificial Intelligence Solutions for Cyber-Physical Systems*. Auerbach Publications., DOI: 10.1201/9781032694375

Dwivedi, Y. K., Hughes, L., Baabdullah, A. M., Ribeiro-Navarrete, S., Giannakis, M., Al-Debei, M. M., Dennehy, D., Metri, B., Buhalis, D., Cheung, C. M. K., Conboy, K., Doyle, R., Dubey, R., Dutot, V., Felix, R., Goyal, D. P., Gustafsson, A., Hinsch, C., Jebabli, I., & Wamba, S. F. (2022). Metaverse beyond the hype: Multidisciplinary perspectives on emerging challenges, opportunities, and agenda for research, practice and policy. *International Journal of Information Management*, *66*, 102542. DOI: 10.1016/j.ijinfomgt.2022.102542

Edwards, D. J. (2024). Security Awareness and Skills Training. In *Critical Security Controls for Effective Cyber Defense* (pp. 405–434). Apress., DOI: 10.1007/979-8-8688-0506-6_14

Elisa, N., Yang, L., Chao, F., & Cao, Y. (2023). A framework of blockchain-based secure and privacy-preserving E-government system. *Wireless Networks*, *29*(3), 1005–1015. DOI: 10.1007/s11276-018-1883-0

Elisa, N., Yang, L., Chao, F., Naik, N., & Boongoen, T. (2023). A Secure and Privacy-Preserving E-Government Framework Using Blockchain and Artificial Immunity. *IEEE Access : Practical Innovations, Open Solutions*, *11*, 8773–8789. DOI: 10.1109/ACCESS.2023.3239814

Elsafty, A., & Yehia, A. (2023). Digital Transformation Challenges for Government Sector. *Business and Management Studies*, *9*(1), 11. DOI: 10.11114/bms.v9i1.6160

Emma, L. (2025). The Impact of Technology Acceptance Models on Business Innovation and Digital Transformation.

Emon, M. M. H., Khan, T., Rahman, M. A., Hamid, A. B. A., & Yaakub, N. I. (2025). GreenTech Revolution: Navigating Challenges and Seizing Opportunities. In *AI and Green Technology Applications in Society* (pp. 63–90). IGI Global Scientific Publishing. DOI: 10.4018/979-8-3693-9879-1.ch003

Emon, M. M. H. (2025). The Mediating Role of Supply Chain Responsiveness in the Relationship Between Key Supply Chain Drivers and Performance: Evidence from the FMCG Industry. *Brazilian Journal of Operations & Production Management*, *22*(1), 2580. DOI: 10.14488/BJOPM.2580.2025

Emon, M. M. H., & Khan, T. (2024). A Systematic Literature Review on Sustainability Integration and Marketing Intelligence in the Era of Artificial Intelligence. *Review of Business and Economics Studies, 12*(4), 6–28. DOI: 10.26794/2308-944X-2024-12-4-6-28

Emon, M. M. H., & Khan, T. (2024). Unlocking Sustainability through Supply Chain Visibility: Insights from the Manufacturing Sector of Bangladesh. *Brazilian Journal of Operations & Production Management, 21*(4), 2194. DOI: 10.14488/BJOPM.2194.2024

Emon, M. M. H., & Khan, T. (2025). The mediating role of attitude towards the technology in shaping artificial intelligence usage among professionals. *Telematics and Informatics Reports, 17*, 100188. DOI: 10.1016/j.teler.2025.100188

Emon, M. M. H., & Khan, T. (2025b). The Role of Traditional Media in Crisis Amplification: How Mainstream Media Magnifies Fake News and Ethical Dilemmas in Supply Chain Crises. In *Mass Media and Impact of Fake News on Supply Chains* (pp. 59–90). IGI Global., DOI: 10.4018/979-8-3373-2175-2.ch003

Emon, M. M. H., & Khan, T. (2025c). The Rise of Circular Supply Chains: Recycling and Closed-Loop Systems Could Mitigate Inflationary Pressures. In *Supply Chain Disruptions and Impact on Global Inflation* (pp. 195–226). IGI Global., DOI: 10.4018/979-8-3373-1982-7.ch008

Emon, M. M. H., Khan, T., Rahman, M. A., & Siam, S. A. J. (2024). Factors Influencing the Usage of Artificial Intelligence among Bangladeshi Professionals: Mediating role of Attitude Towards the Technology. *2024 IEEE International Conference on Computing, Applications and Systems (COMPAS)*, 1–7. DOI: 10.1109/COMPAS60761.2024.10796110

Endtime. (2015). China presses for internet 'kill switch'.

Epifanova, A., and Dietrich, P. (2022). Russia's quest for digital sovereignty: Ambitions, realities, and its place in the world.

Epifanova, A. (2020). Deciphering Russia's sovereign internet law. *Online (Bergheim)*.

ERCHI, Z., and MIN, C. (2022). Five things to know about China's mega east-west data centre plan.

Espinosa, V. I., & Pino, A. (2025). E-Government as a development strategy: The case of Estonia. *International Journal of Public Administration, 48*(2), 86–99. DOI: 10.1080/01900692.2024.2316128

EU. (2016). General data protection regulation.

Eversec. (2024). Eversec - Hengan Jiaxin (Beijing) Technology Co. Ltd.

Ewdn. (2019). Apple provides details on compliance with Russian data-localization law.

Fahey, E. (2024). The evolution of EU–US cybersecurity law and policy: On drivers of convergence. *Journal of European Integration*, *46*(7), 1073–1088. DOI: 10.1080/07036337.2024.2411240

Fakeyede, O. G., Okeleke, P. A., & Hassan, A. O. (2023). Navigating data privacy through IT audits: GDPR, CCPA, and beyond. *Journal of Research*, *12*(3), 1–15. DOI: 10.1016/j.jr.2023.02.001

Farhad, M. A. (2024). Consumer data protection laws and their impact on business models in the tech industry. *Telecommunications Policy*, *48*(9), 102836. DOI: 10.1016/j.telpol.2024.102836

FBI. (2023). Russian interference in 2016 U.S. elections.

Ferrag, M. A., Maglaras, L., Moschoyiannis, S., & Janicke, H. (2020). Deep learning for cyber security intrusion detection: Approaches, datasets, and comparative study. *Journal of Information Security and Applications*, *50*, 102419. DOI: 10.1016/j.jisa.2019.102419

Fielding, N., and Cobain, I. (2011). Revealed: US spy operation that manipulates social media.

FinCERT. (2024). FinCERT.

FIRST. (2024). *Forum of Incident Response and Security Teams*. FIRST.

Forouzan, B. A. (2006). *Data communication and networking* (4th ed.). McGraw-Hill Education.

Fürstenau, D., Gersch, M., & Schreiter, S. (2023). Digital Therapeutics (DTx). *Business & Information Systems Engineering*, *65*(3), 349–360. DOI: 10.1007/s12599-023-00804-z

Gaie, C., & Karpiuk, M. (2024). The Provision of e-Services by Public Administration Bodies and Their Cybersecurity. In *Transforming Public Services—Combining Data and Algorithms to Fulfil Citizen's Expectations* (pp. 175–188). Springer Nature Switzerland. DOI: 10.1007/978-3-031-55575-6_7

García, A., Gómez García, S., Sanz Prieto, G., Moreno Guerrero, M., & Jiménez, A. J. (2020). The impact of term fake news on the scientific community: Scientific performance and mapping in Web of Science. *Social Sciences*, *9*(5).

García, A., Gómez García, S., Sanz Prieto, G., Moreno Guerrero, M., & Jiménez, A. J. (2020). The impact of the term misinformation on the scientific community: Scientific performance and mapping in Web of Science. *Social Sciences*, *9*(5), 1–18.

Garg, M., Wang, T., & Wilkin, C. L. (2025). Impact of reporting information security breaches, accounting quality, and the opportunistic disclosure of good news and bad news. *International Journal of Accounting Information Systems*, *56*, 100729. DOI: 10.1016/j.accinf.2025.100729

Gaur, L., Ujjan, R. M. A., & Hussain, M. (2022). The Influence of Deep Learning in Detecting Cyber Attacks on E-Government Applications. In *Cybersecurity Measures for E-Government Frameworks* (pp. 107–122). IGI Global. DOI: 10.4018/978-1-7998-9624-1.ch007

Gawer, A. (2022). Digital platforms and ecosystems: Remarks on the dominant organizational forms of the digital age. *Innovation (North Sydney, N.S.W.)*, *25*(1), 1–15. DOI: 10.1080/14479338.2021.1965888

Ghadge, N. (2024). Use of blockchain technology to strengthen identity and access management (IAM). *International Journal of Information Technology : an Official Journal of Bharati Vidyapeeth's Institute of Computer Applications and Management*, *16*(1), 1–15.

Ghayoomi, H., Laskey, K., Miller-Hooks, E., Hooks, C., & Tariverdi, M. (2021). Assessing resilience of hospitals to cyberattack. *Digital Health*, *7*, 20552076211059366. DOI: 10.1177/20552076211059366 PMID: 34868621

Ghelani, D. (2022). "Cyber security, cyber threats, implications and future perspectives: A Review." *Authorea Preprints*. Doi: DOI: 10.22541/au.166385207.73483369/v1

Ghobakhloo, M., & Iranmanesh, M. (2021). Digital transformation success under Industry 4.0: A strategic guideline for manufacturing SMEs. *Journal of Manufacturing Technology Management*, *32*(6), 1045–1066. DOI: 10.1108/JMTM-11-2020-0455

Gierlich-Joas, M., Hess, T., & Neuburger, R. (2020). More self-organization, more control—Or even both? Inverse transparency as a digital leadership concept. *Business Research*, *13*(3), 921–947. DOI: 10.1007/s40685-020-00130-0

Girgis, S., & Amer, E. (2022, May). A proposed ensemble voting model for misinformation detection. In *2022 2nd International Mobile, Intelligent, and Ubiquitous Computing Conference (MIUCC)* (pp. 316–322). IEEE.

Gogus, A., & Saygn, Y. (2019). Privacy perception and information technology utilization of high school students. *Heliyon*, *5*(5), e01614. DOI: 10.1016/j.heliyon.2019.e01614 PMID: 31193323

Golightly, L., Modesti, P., Garcia, R., & Chang, V. (2023). Securing distributed systems: A survey on access control techniques for cloud, blockchain, IoT and SDN. *Cyber Security and Applications*, *1*, 100015. DOI: 10.1016/j.csa.2023.100015

González-Granadillo, G., González-Zarzosa, S., & Diaz, R. (2021). Security information and event management (SIEM): Analysis, trends, and usage in critical infrastructures. *Sensors (Basel)*, *21*(14), 4759. DOI: 10.3390/s21144759 PMID: 34300500

Goodkind, N. (2023). Apple lost 200 billion dollars in two days after reports of iPhone ban in China.

Goodstats.id. (2023). Serangan Phishing di Indonesia Terus Meningkat. https://goodstats.id/article/serangan-phishing-di-indonesia-terus-meningkat-ini-statistiknya-U8VdY

Gov-cert. (2024). Gov CERT.

Government, A. (2014a). Personally controlled electronic health records act 2012.

Government, B. (2014b). Marco civil.

Government, C. (2019a). Personal information protection and electronic documents act (S.C. 2000, c. 5).

Government, K. (2011). Personal information protection act.

Government, R. (2014c). The Ministry of Communications, the FSB, and the Ministry of Defence conducted exercises to protect the Russian segment of the internet.

Government, R. (2015). Russian national security strategy.

Government, R. (2017a). Ministry of Telecommunications and Communications conducts exercises to improve information security, integrity, and stability of the functioning of the unified telecommunication network of the Russian Federation.

Government, R. (2019b). Amendments to the federal law on communications and the federal law on information, information technologies, and the protection of information.

Government, R. (2019c). Procedure for centralized management of a public communication network.

Government, V. (2013). Management, provision, and use of internet services and online information.

Government, M. (2010). *Laws of Malaysia, Act 709*. Personal Data Protection Act.

Government, R. (2017b). *Protection of critical information infrastructure*.

Granik, M., & Mesyura, V. (2017). Misinformation detection using naive Bayes classifier. In *2017 IEEE First Ukraine Conference on Electrical and Computer Engineering (UKRCON)*, Kiev. DOI: 10.1109/UKRCON.2017.8100379

Gray, C. M., Santos, C., Bielova, N., & Toth, M. (2021). "Dark patterns and the legal requirements of consent banners: An interaction criticism perspective". *Proceedings of the 2021 CHI Conference on Human Factors in Computing Systems*. DOI: 10.1145/3411764.3445779

Greenwal, G. and MacAskill, E. (2013). NSA Prism program taps into user data of Apple, Google, and others.

Grill, M., Sommestad, T., Karlzén, H., & Pousette, A. (2025). Training for improved information security culture: A longitudinal randomized controlled trial. *Information and Computer Security*. Advance online publication. DOI: 10.1108/ICS-08-2024-0189

Group-IB. (2023, Jul 26). Statement on the conviction of Ilya Sachkov. *Group-IB*. https://www.group-ib.com/media-center/press-releases/statement-on-the-conviction-of-ilya-sachkov/

Group-ib. (2024). CERT GIB.

Gruzd, A., & Hernández-García, Á. (2018). Privacy concerns and self-disclosure in private and public uses of social media. *Cyberpsychology, Behavior, and Social Networking*, *21*(7), 418–428. DOI: 10.1089/cyber.2017.0709 PMID: 29995525

Guay, R., & Birch, K. (2022). A comparative analysis of data governance: Socio-technical imaginaries of digital personal data in the USA and EU (2008–2016). *Big Data & Society*, *9*(2), 20539517221112925. DOI: 10.1177/20539517221112925

Gull, H., Alabbad, D. A., Saqib, M., Iqbal, S. Z., Nasir, T., Saeed, S., & Almuhaideb, A. M. (2023). E-commerce and cybersecurity challenges: Recent advances and future trends. Handbook of Research on Cybersecurity Issues and Challenges for Business and FinTech Applications, 91-111.

Gull, H., Saeed, S., Iqbal, S. Z., Bamarouf, Y. A., Alqahtani, M. A., Alabbad, D. A., Saqib, M., Al Qahtani, S. H., & Alamer, A. (2022). An empirical study of mobile commerce and customers security perception in Saudi Arabia. *Electronics (Basel), 11*(3), 293. DOI: 10.3390/electronics11030293

Gumzej, R. (2021). *Intelligent Logistics Systems for Smart Cities and Communities*. Springer International Publishing., DOI: 10.1007/978-3-030-81203-4

Gupta, I., Singh, A. K., Lee, C. N., & Buyya, R. (2022). Secure data storage and sharing techniques for data protection in cloud environments: A systematic review, analysis, and future directions. *IEEE Access : Practical Innovations, Open Solutions, 10*, 53111–53135. DOI: 10.1109/ACCESS.2022.3188110

Habbal, A., Ali, M. K., & Abuzaraida, M. A. (2024). Artificial Intelligence Trust, Risk and Security Management (AI TRiSM): Frameworks, applications, challenges and future research directions. *Expert Systems with Applications, 240*, 122442. DOI: 10.1016/j.eswa.2023.122442

Hakak, S., Alazab, M., Khan, S., Gadekallu, T. R., Maddikunta, P. K. R., & Khan, W. Z. (2021). An ensemble machine learning approach through effective feature extraction to classify fake news. *Future Generation Computer Systems, 117*, 47–58. DOI: 10.1016/j.future.2020.11.022

Hakimi M, Quchi M M, Fazil A W, (2024). "Human factors in cybersecurity: an in depth analysis of user centric studies." Jurnal Informatika Indonesia (JIM-ID), 7(1), 1-12.

Hakimi, M., Sazish, B., Rastagari, M. A., & Shahidzay, K. (2024). Artificial intelligence for social media safety and security: A systematic literature review. *Smjc, 1*(1), 10–21. DOI: 10.32996/smjc.2023.1.1.2x

Hale, B., van Bossuyt, D. L., Papakonstantinou, N., & O'Halloran, B. (2021). A zero-trust methodology for security of complex systems with machine learning components. In *Proceedings of the ASME Design Engineering Technical Conference* (Vol. 2). DOI: 10.1115/DETC2021-70442

Hamed, S. K., Ab Aziz, M. J., & Yaakub, M. R. (2023). Misinformation detection model on social media by leveraging sentiment analysis of news content and emotion analysis of users' comments. *Sensors (Basel), 23*(4), 1748. DOI: 10.3390/s23041748 PMID: 36850346

Han, H., Shiwakoti, R. K., Jarvis, R., Mordi, C., & Botchie, D. (2023). Accounting and auditing with blockchain technology and artificial Intelligence: A literature review. *International Journal of Accounting Information Systems*, *48*, 100598. DOI: 10.1016/j.accinf.2022.100598

Haque, A. K. M. B., Islam, A. K. M. N., Hyrynsalmi, S., Naqvi, B., & Smolander, K. (2021). GDPR compliant blockchains–a systematic literature review. *IEEE Access : Practical Innovations, Open Solutions*, *9*, 129494–129514. DOI: 10.1109/ACCESS.2021.3069877

Hassan, A. O., Ewuga, S. K., & Abdul, A. A. (2024). "Cybersecurity in banking: a global perspective with a focus on Nigerian practices." Science & IT Conference, 1-12. Doi: DOI: 10.2139/ssrn.4079155

Heawood, J. (2018). Pseudo-public political speech: Democratic implications of the Cambridge Analytica scandal. *Information Polity*, *23*(4), 429–434. DOI: 10.3233/IP-180009

Heckler, N., & Kim, Y. (2022). Crypto-Governance: The Ethical Implications of Blockchain in Public Service. *Public Integrity*, *24*(1), 66–81. DOI: 10.1080/10999922.2020.1848106

Heidari, A., Navimipour, N. J., & Unal, M. (2022). Applications of ML/DL in the management of smart cities and societies based on new trends in information technologies: A systematic literature review. *Sustainable Cities and Society*, *85*, 104089. DOI: 10.1016/j.scs.2022.104089

Hemamalini, V., Mishra, A. K., & Tyagi, A. K. (2024). Artificial intelligence–blockchain-enabled–internet of things-based cloud applications for next-generation society. *Journal of Software (Malden, MA)*. DOI: 10.1002/smr.2406

Henni, S. H., Maurud, S., Fuglerud, K. S., & Moen, A. (2022). The experiences, needs and barriers of people with impairments related to usability and accessibility of digital health solutions, levels of involvement in the design process and strategies for participatory and universal design: A scoping review. *BMC Public Health*, *22*(1), 35. DOI: 10.1186/s12889-021-12393-1 PMID: 34991540

Herath, G., Khanna, T. B. G., & Ahmed, M. (2022). Cybersecurity practices for social media users: A systematic literature review. *Journal of Cybersecurity and Privacy*, *2*(3), 436–455. DOI: 10.3390/jcp2010001

Hermansyah, M., Najib, A., Farida, A., Sacipto, R., & Rintyarna, B. S. (2023). Artificial intelligence and ethics: Building an artificial intelligence system that ensures privacy and social justice. *The International Journal of Science in Society*, *5*(1), 154–168. DOI: 10.54783/ijsoc.v5i1.644

Hielscher, J., Kluge, A., Menges, U., & Sasse, M. A. (2021). "Taking out the Trash": Why Security Behavior Change requires Intentional Forgetting. *New Security Paradigms Workshop*, 108–122. DOI: 10.1145/3498891.3498902

Hikvision. (2024). Hikvision Cyber Security Centre.

Hilowle, M., Yeoh, W., Grobler, M., Pye, G., & Jiang, F. (2024). Leveraging Human-Centric Cybersecurity to Improve Usage of National Digital Identity Systems in Australia. *Computer*, *57*(7), 87–98. DOI: 10.1109/MC.2024.3395523

Hinderks, A., Domínguez Mayo, F. J., Thomaschewski, J., & Escalona, M. J. (2022). Approaches to manage the user experience process in Agile software development: A systematic literature review. *Information and Software Technology*, *150*, 106957. DOI: 10.1016/j.infsof.2022.106957

Hoffman, I., & Cseh, K. B. (2020). E-administration, cybersecurity and municipalities–the challenges of cybersecurity issues for the municipalities in Hungary. *Cybersecurity and Law*, *2*(2), 199–211. DOI: 10.35467/cal/133999

Hopping, C. (2019). Huawei moves into Russian cloud market with third-party data centre support.

Hosseini, L. (2024). Driving Resilience Through Digital Transformation Strategies. *Digital Transformation and Administration Innovation*, *2*(3), 1–6.

How, M. L., & Cheah, S. M. (2023). Business Renaissance: Opportunities and challenges at the dawn of the Quantum Computing Era. *Businesses*, *3*(2), 1–18. DOI: 10.3390/businesses3040036

Hua, J., & Shaw, R. (2020). Coronavirus (COVID-19) "infodemic" and emerging issues through a data lens: The case of China. *International Journal of Environmental Research and Public Health*, *17*(7), 2309. DOI: 10.3390/ijerph17072309 PMID: 32235433

Huawei-PSIRT. (2024). Huawei Product Security Incident Response Team.

Huld, A. (2021). Critical information infrastructure - China's new cybersecurity regulations.

Hunton (2019). China issues draft regulation on cross-border transfer of personal information.

Hussain, A. A., & Al-Turjman, F. (2021). Artificial intelligence and blockchain: A review. *Journal of Telecommunications Technologies*, *19*(2), 123–135. DOI: 10.33118/jtt.2021.169730.1032

ICANN (2013). Montevideo statement on the future of internet cooperation.

Ige A B, Kupa E, Ilori O, (2024). "Best practices in cybersecurity for green building management systems: Protecting sustainable infrastructure from cyber threats." Journal of Science and Research Archive. Doi: .DOI: 10.48165/JSRA.2024.12423

Ihtesham, M., Tahir, S., Tahir, H., Hasan, A., Sultan, A., Saeed, S., & Rana, O. (2023). Privacy preserving and serverless homomorphic-based searchable encryption as a service (SEaaS). *IEEE Access : Practical Innovations, Open Solutions*, *11*, 115204–115218. DOI: 10.1109/ACCESS.2023.3324817

Imran, R., Alraja, M. N., & Khashab, B. (2023). Sustainable Performance and Green Innovation: Green Human Resources Management and Big Data as Antecedents. *IEEE Transactions on Engineering Management*, *70*(12), 4191–4206. DOI: 10.1109/TEM.2021.3114256

In4-CERT (2024). In4-CERT.

Investopedia. (n.d.). *Social media.* https://www.investopedia.com/terms/s/social-media.asp

Iparraguirre-Villanueva, O., Alvarez-Risco, A., Herrera Salazar, J. L., Beltozar-Clemente, S., Zapata-Paulini, J., Yáñez, J. A., & Cabanillas-Carbonell, M. (2023). The public health contribution of sentiment analysis of Monkeypox tweets to detect polarities using the CNN-LSTM model. *Vaccines*, *11*(2), 312. DOI: 10.3390/vaccines11020312 PMID: 36851190

Iqbal, Y., Tahir, S., Tahir, H., Khan, F., Saeed, S., Almuhaideb, A. M., & Syed, A. M. (2022). A novel homomorphic approach for preserving privacy of patient data in telemedicine. *Sensors (Basel)*, *22*(12), 4432. DOI: 10.3390/s22124432 PMID: 35746213

Iskandar, O., Yusuf, B., Mahmudjon, S., Azizbek, X., & Javohir, I. (2021). Analysis of existing standards for information security assessment. In *International Conference on Information Science and Communications Technologies: Applications, Trends and Opportunities, ICISCT 2021*. DOI: 10.1109/ICISCT52966.2021.9670428

ISL-CERT (2024). ISL-CERT.

Ismagilova, E., Hughes, L., Rana, N. P., & Dwivedi, Y. K. (2022). Security, Privacy and Risks Within Smart Cities: Literature Review and Development of a Smart City Interaction Framework. *Information Systems Frontiers*, *24*(2), 393–414. DOI: 10.1007/s10796-020-10044-1 PMID: 32837262

Issabayeva, S., Yesseniyazova, B., & Grega, M. (2019). Electronic Public Procurement: Process and Cybersecurity Issues. *NISPAcee Journal of Public Administration and Policy*, *12*(2), 61–79. DOI: 10.2478/nispa-2019-0014

ISW (2024). Russian offensive campaign assessment.

ITU (2019a). Global cybersecurity index.

ITU (2019b). Global cybersecurity index & cyber wellness profiles.

ITU (2019c). ITU statistics.

Jaeger, L., & Eckhardt, A. (2021). Eyes wide open: The role of situational information security awareness for security-related behaviour. *Information Systems Journal*, *31*(3), 429–472. DOI: 10.1111/isj.12317

Jafari, M., & Shaghaghi, Z. (2023). Navigating privacy concerns: Social Media users' perspectives on data sharing. *Aitechbesosci*, *1*(1), 20–26. DOI: 10.61838/kman.aitech.1.1.4

Jagannath, R. O., & Jain, A. K. (2024). Browser-in-the-middle attacks: A comprehensive analysis and countermeasures. *Security and Privacy*, *7*(5), e410. DOI: 10.1002/spy2.410

Jain, V., Kaliyar, R. K., Goswami, A., Narang, P., & Sharma, Y. (2021). AENeT: An attention-enabled neural architecture for misinformation detection using contextual features. *Neural Computing & Applications*, *34*(1), 1–12. PMID: 34305326

Jarvers, S., & Schachtner, C. (2024). Linking smart city projects to the internal e-government projects of municipalities in Germany: synergies and challenges. In *Proceedings of the Central and Eastern European eDem and eGov Days 2024* (pp. 61-69). DOI: 10.1145/3670243.3670261

Javaid, M., Haleem, A., Singh, R. P., & Suman, R. (2023). Towards insighting cybersecurity for healthcare domains: A comprehensive review of recent practices and trends. *Cyber Security and Applications*, *1*, 100016. DOI: 10.1016/j.csa.2023.100016

Jazeera, A. (2019). Zimbabwe imposes internet shutdown amid crackdown on protests. Al Jazeera. https://www.aljazeera.com/news/2019/1/18/zimbabwe-imposesinternet-shutdown-amid-crackdown-on-protests

Jet-CERT (2024). Jet-CERT.

Jha, R. K., & Jha, M. (2024). Optimizing E-Government Cybersecurity through Artificial Intelligence Integration. *Journal of Trends in Computer Science and Smart Technology*, *6*(1), 67–87. DOI: 10.36548/jtcsst.2024.1.005

Jimmy, F. (2021). *Emerging threats: The latest cybersecurity risks and the role of artificial intelligence in enhancing cybersecurity defenses*. Valley International Journal Digital Library., DOI: 10.47028/valley.ijdl.2021.02.001

Jin, H., & Xiao, J. (2022). Towards trustworthy blockchain systems in the era of "Internet of value": Development, challenges, and future trends. *Science China. Information Sciences*, *65*(5), 153101. DOI: 10.1007/s11432-020-3183-0

Jin, Z., Cao, J., Zhang, Y., Zhou, J., & Tian, Q. (2017). Novel visual and statistical image features for microblogs news verification. *IEEE Transactions on Multimedia*, *19*(3), 598–608. DOI: 10.1109/TMM.2016.2617078

Johri, A., & Kumar, S. (2023). Exploring customer awareness towards their cyber security in the Kingdom of Saudi Arabia: A study in the era of banking digital transformation. *Human Behavior and Emerging Technologies*, *5*(2), 147–157. DOI: 10.1155/2023/2103442

Jonas, D., Yusuf, N. A., & Zahra, A. R. A. (2023). *Enhancing security frameworks with artificial intelligence in cybersecurity*. International Transactions on Computer and Information Security., DOI: 10.33050/itee.v2i1.428

Jörke, M., Sefidgar, Y. S., Massachi, T., & Suh, J. (2023). "Pearl: A technology probe for machine-assisted reflection on personal data". *Proceedings of the 28th*. DOI: 10.1145/3581641.3584054

Jowarder, R. A., & Jahan, S. (2024). *Quantum computing in cyber security: Emerging threats, mitigation strategies, and future implications for data protection*. World Journal of Advanced Engineering and Technology.

Judijanto, L., & Hindarto, D. (2023). Edge of enterprise architecture in addressing cyber security threats and business risks. *Journal of Information and Computational Science*, *18*(1), 1–12. DOI: 10.33073/jics.v18i1.1849

Julakanti, S. R. KiranmayeeSattiraju NS, (2025). "Data Protection through Governance Frameworks." arXiv preprint arXiv, 1-12. Doi: /arXiv.2302.03985.DOI: 10.48550

Kaaniche, N., Laurent, M., & Belguith, S. (2020). Privacy enhancing technologies for solving the privacy-personalization paradox: Taxonomy and survey. *Journal of Network and Computer Applications*, *171*, 102807. DOI: 10.1016/j.jnca.2020.102807

Kafeero, S. (2021). Uganda cuts off internet ahead of election polls opening. Quartz Africa. https://qz.com/africa/1957137/uganda-cuts-off-internet-ahead-of-election-polls-opening

Kafi, M. A., & Akter, N. (2023). Securing financial information in the digital realm: Case studies in cybersecurity for accounting data protection. *American Journal of Trade and Policy*, *4*(2), 1–12. DOI: 10.18034/ajtp.v10i1.659

Kaggle. (2022). *Datasets.* https://www.kaggle.com/datasets

Kaliyar, R. K., Goswami, A., & Narang, P. (2021). DeepFakE: Improving misinformation detection using tensor decomposition-based deep neural network. *The Journal of Supercomputing*, *77*(2), 1015–1037. DOI: 10.1007/s11227-020-03294-y

Kandasamy, V., & Roseline, A. A. (2025). Harnessing advanced hybrid deep learning model for real-time detection and prevention of man-in-the-middle cyber attacks. *Scientific Reports*, *15*(1), 1697. DOI: 10.1038/s41598-025-85547-5 PMID: 39799192

Kania, E. (2019). Made in China 2025, explained.

Kania, E. B., & Costello, J. K. (2018). The strategic support force and the future of Chinese information operations. *The Cyber Defence Review*, *3*(1), 105–122.

Karimi, H., & Tang, J. (2019). Learning hierarchical discourse-level structure for misinformation detection. In *Proceedings of the 2019 Conference of the North American Chapter of the Association for Computational Linguistics*, Minneapolis, Minnesota.

Kaspersky (2024). Kaspersky Industrial Cybersecurity.

Kassen, M. (2022). Blockchain and e-government innovation: Automation of public information processes. *Information Systems*, *103*, 101862. DOI: 10.1016/j.is.2021.101862

Kaur, J., Hazrati Fard, S. M., Amiri-Zarandi, M., & Dara, R. (2022). Protecting farmers' data privacy and confidentiality: Recommendations and considerations. *Frontiers in Sustainable Food Systems*, *6*, 1–12. DOI: 10.3389/fsufs.2022.903230

Kaur, S., Kumar, P., & Kumaraguru, P. (2020). Automating misinformation detection system using multi-level voting model. *Soft Computing*, *24*(12), 9049–9069. DOI: 10.1007/s00500-019-04436-y

Kechagias, E. P., Chatzistelios, G., Papadopoulos, G. A., & Apostolou, P. (2022). Digital transformation of the maritime industry: A cybersecurity systemic approach. *International Journal of Critical Infrastructure Protection*, *37*, 100454. DOI: 10.1016/j.ijcip.2022.100526

Khan, T., & Hasan Emon, M. M. (2024). Determinants of AI Image Generator Adoption Among Marketing Agencies: The Mediating Effects of Perceived Usefulness. *2024 IEEE 3rd International Conference on Robotics, Automation, Artificial-Intelligence and Internet-of-Things (RAAICON)*, 177–182. DOI: 10.1109/RAAICON64172.2024.10928548

Khan, T., Emon, M. M. H., & Nath, A. (2024). Quantifying the Effects of AI-Driven Inventory Management on Operational Efficiency in Online Retail. *2024 27th International Conference on Computer and Information Technology (ICCIT)*, 2092–2097. DOI: 10.1109/ICCIT64611.2024.11021996

Khan, T., Emon, M. M. H., & Rahman, S. (2024). Marketing Strategy Innovation via AI Adoption: A Study on Bangladeshi SMEs in the Context of Industry 5.0. *2024 6th International Conference on Sustainable Technologies for Industry 5.0 (STI)*, 1–6. DOI: 10.1109/STI64222.2024.10951050

Khando, K., Gao, S., Islam, S. M., & Salman, A. (2021). Enhancing employees information security awareness in private and public organisations: A systematic literature review. *Computers & Security*, *106*, 102267. DOI: 10.1016/j.cose.2021.102267

Khan, R. A., Khan, S. U., Akbar, M. A., & Alzahrani, M. (2024). Security risks of global software development life cycle: Industry practitioner's perspective. *Journal of Software (Malden, MA)*, *36*(3), e2521. DOI: 10.1002/smr.2521

Khan, T., & Emon, M. M. H. (2024). Exploring the Potential of the Blue Economy: A Systematic Review of Strategies for Enhancing International Business in Bangladesh in the context of Indo-Pacific Region. *Review of Business and Economics Studies*, *12*(2), 55–73. DOI: 10.26794/2308-944X-2024-12-2-55-73

Khan, T., & Emon, M. M. H. (2025). Supply chain performance in the age of Industry 4.0: Evidence from manufacturing sector. *Brazilian Journal of Operations & Production Management*, *22*(1), 2434. DOI: 10.14488/BJOPM.2434.2025

Kickbusch, I., Piselli, D., Agrawal, A., Balicer, R., & Banner, O. (2021). "The Lancet and Financial Times Commission on governing health futures 2030: growing up in a digital world". The Lancet, 398(10298), 473-492. DOI: 10.1016/S0140-6736(21)00756-9

Kiran, J. S., Anusha, M., Kumar, A. V., & Kavya, M. (2016). Cryptography: The science of secure communication. *International Journal of Computer Science and Network Security*, *16*(6), 1–6.

Klyuev, V. (2018). Fake news filtering: Semantic approaches. In *2018 7th International Conference on Reliability, Infocom Technologies and Optimization (Trends and Future Directions) (ICRITO)*, Noida, India.

Kock, F., Berbekova, A., & Assaf, A. G. (2021). Understanding and managing the threat of common method bias: Detection, prevention and control. *Tourism Management*, *86*, 104330. DOI: 10.1016/j.tourman.2021.104330

Kodama, S. and Nikkei (2018). China's strict new cybersecurity law ensnares Japanese companies.

Kollar, A. M., & Katona, J. (2024). Enhancing Password Security: Analyzing Password Management Practices Among IT Students. In *CANDO-EPE 2024 - Proceedings: IEEE 7th International Conference and Workshop Obuda on Electrical and Power Engineering* (pp. 59–64). DOI: 10.1109/CANDO-EPE65072.2024.10772755

Kolomychenko, M. (2017). Introduced cyber military. Kommersant. https://www.kommersant.ru/doc/3187320

Komna, L., & Mpungose, S. (2024). Enhancing digital transformation strategies: a framework for SITA. *International Journal of Business Ecosystem & Strategy (2687-2293)*, *6*(4), 235-252.

Kremlin (2016a). Approved doctrine of information security of Russia.

Kremlin (2016b). Information security doctrine of the Russian Federation.

Kremlin (2022). Decree on measures to ensure technological independence and security of critical information infrastructure.

Kreutz, H., & Jahankhani, H. (2024). *Impact of Artificial Intelligence on Enterprise Information Security Management in the Context of ISO 27001 and 27002: A Tertiary Systematic Review and Comparative Analysis* (pp. 1–34). DOI: 10.1007/978-3-031-52272-7_1

Krishna, B., Krishnan, S., & Sebastian, M. P. (2025). Understanding the process of building institutional trust among digital payment users through national cybersecurity commitment trustworthiness cues: A critical realist perspective. *Information Technology & People*, *38*(2), 714–756. DOI: 10.1108/ITP-05-2023-0434

Kritika, E. (2025). A comprehensive literature review on ransomware detection using deep learning. *Cyber Security and Applications*, *3*, 100078. DOI: 10.1016/j.csa.2024.100078

Kucharski, A. (2016). Post-truth: Study epidemiology of fake news. *Nature*, *540*(7634), 525. DOI: 10.1038/540525a PMID: 30905947

Kulkarni, S. (2022). Expert Systems in Behavioral and Mental Healthcare: Applications of AI in Decision-Making and Consultancy. In *Big Data Analytics and Machine Intelligence in Biomedical and Health Informatics* (pp. 147–186). Wiley. DOI: 10.1002/9781119792376.ch6

Kumarasinghe, J. (2024). *Improving the B App to Improve Customer Experience and Operational Efficiency: From the Perspectives of User Engagement*. Functionality, and Security.

Kumari, R., & Ekbal, A. (2021). AMFB: Attention based multimodal Factorized Bilinear Pooling for multimodal misinformation detection. *Expert Systems with Applications*, *184*, 115412. DOI: 10.1016/j.eswa.2021.115412

Kumar, K., & Zolkipli, M. F. (2024). A Review on Identity and Access Management (IAM) for Digital Environment Security. *Borneo International Journal*, *7*(1), 1–12.

Kumar, R., Hamid, A. B. A., Inayah Binti Ya'akub, N., Nyamasvisva, T. E., & Tiwari, R. K. (2024). *AI and Green Technology Applications in Society (R. Kumar, A. B. Abdul Hamid, N. I. Binti Ya'akub* (Nyamasvisva, T. E., & Tiwari, R. K., Eds.). IGI Global., DOI: 10.4018/979-8-3693-9879-1

Kumar, S., & Mallipeddi, R. R. (2022). Impact of cybersecurity on operations and supply chain management: Emerging trends and future research directions. *Production and Operations Management*, *31*(4), 1470–1485. DOI: 10.1111/poms.13859

Kumar, V., Ashraf, A. R., & Nadeem, W. (2024). AI-powered marketing: What, where, and how? *International Journal of Information Management*, *77*, 102783. DOI: 10.1016/j.ijinfomgt.2024.102783

Kun, E. (2025). Searching for the appropriate legal basis for personal data processing for cybersecurity purposes under the NIS 2 Directive: Legal obligation and/or legitimate interest? *Computer Law & Security Review*, *56*, 106098. DOI: 10.1016/j.clsr.2024.106098

Kwok Choon, M. J. (2018). Revisiting the privacy paradox on social media: An analysis of privacy practices associated with Facebook and Twitter. *Canadian Journal of Communication*, *43*(2), 339–358. DOI: 10.22230/cjc.2018v43n2a3267

Labadie, C., & Legner, C. (2023). Building data management capabilities to address data protection regulations: Learnings from EU-GDPR. *Journal of Information Technology*, *38*(1), 16–44. DOI: 10.1177/02683962221141456

LaGrone, S. (2018). China has stolen vast amounts of navy submarine, missile data in multiple breaches from contractor's servers.

Lakshmanarao, A., Swathi, Y., & Kiran, T. S. R. (2019). An efficient misinformation detection system using machine learning. *International Journal of Innovative Technology and Exploring Engineering*, *8*(10), 3125–3129. DOI: 10.35940/ijitee.J9453.0881019

Lallie, H. S., Thompson, A., Titis, E., & Stephens, P. (2025). Analysing Cyber Attacks and Cyber Security Vulnerabilities in the University Sector. *Computers*, *14*(2), 49. DOI: 10.3390/computers14020049

LawBlog (2018). China's cybersecurity law - 2017.

Lazer, D. M. J., Baum, M. A., Benkler, Y., Berinsky, A. J., Greenhill, K. M., Menczer, F., Metzger, M. J., Nyhan, B., Pennycook, G., Rothschild, D., Schudson, M., Sloman, S. A., Sunstein, C. R., Thorson, E. A., Watts, D. J., & Zittrain, J. L. (2018). The science of fake news. *Science*, *359*(6380), 1094–1096. DOI: 10.1126/science.aao2998 PMID: 29590025

Ledford, H. (2020). How Facebook, Twitter and other data troves are revolutionizing social science. *Nature*, *582*(7812), 328–330. DOI: 10.1038/d41586-020-01747-1 PMID: 32555492

Leerssen, P. (2023). An end to shadow banning? Transparency rights in the Digital Services Act between content moderation and curation. *Computer Law & Security Review*, *48*, 105790. DOI: 10.1016/j.clsr.2023.105790

Lewallen, J. (2021). Emerging technologies and problem definition uncertainty: The case of cybersecurity. *Regulation & Governance*, *15*(2), 267–279. DOI: 10.1111/rego.12341

Liang, W., Yang, Y., Yang, C., Hu, Y., & Xie, S. (2022). PDPChain: A consortium blockchain-based privacy protection scheme for personal data. *IEEE Transactions on Industrial Informatics*, *18*(10), 7341–7350. DOI: 10.1109/TII.2022.3141409

Lindsey, N. (2019). New CNCERT report shows most cyber attacks on China originate from the United States.

Li, T. (2024). Analysis of personal privacy risks and protection countermeasures under the privacy paradox dimension. Transactions on Social Science. *Education and Humanities*, *11*, 509–515.

Liu, C., Zhu, T., Zhang, J., & Zhou, W. (2020). Privacy intelligence: A survey on image privacy in online social networks. *arXiv*. https://arxiv.org/abs/2007.07906

Liu, X., Ahmad, S. F., Anser, M. K., Ke, J., Irshad, M., Ul-Haq, J., & Abbas, S. (2022). Cyber security threats: A never-ending challenge for e-commerce. *Frontiers in Psychology, 2*, 1–12. DOI: 10.3389/fpsyg.2022.927398 PMID: 36337532

Li, Y., & Guo, H. (2022). Sustainable development of shared mobility in China in relation to the privacy paradox of users. *Journal of Advanced Transportation, 2022*, 1–11. DOI: 10.1155/2022/8538347

Li, Y., & Liu, Q. (2021). A comprehensive review study of cyber-attacks and cyber security; Emerging trends and recent developments. *Energy Reports, 7*, 8176–8186. DOI: 10.1016/j.egyr.2021.08.126

Lněnička, M., & Máchová, R. (2022). A theoretical framework to evaluate ICT disparities and digital divides: Challenges and implications for e-government development. *Review of Economic Perspectives, 22*(1), 25–51. DOI: 10.2478/revecp-2022-0002

Lobe, B., Morgan, D., & Hoffman, K. A. (2020). Qualitative Data Collection in an Era of Social Distancing. *International Journal of Qualitative Methods, 19*, 1609406920937875. DOI: 10.1177/1609406920937875

Long, Y. (2017). *Misinformation detection through multi-perspective speaker profiles*. Association for Computational Linguistics.

Lubua, E. W., & Pretorius, P. D. (2019, Jul). Cyber-security policy framework and procedural compliance in public organisations. In *Proceedings of the International Conference on Industrial Engineering and Operations Management* (pp. 1-13).

Luh, R., Eresheim, S., Tavolato, P., Petelin, T., Gmeiner, S., Holzinger, A., & Schrittwieser, S. (2025). Gamifying information security: Adversarial risk exploration for IT/OT infrastructures. *Computers & Security, 151*, 104287. DOI: 10.1016/j.cose.2024.104287

Luo, S., & Choi, T. M. (2022). E-commerce supply chains with considerations of cyber-security: Should governments play a role? *Production and Operations Management, 31*(5), 2107–2126. DOI: 10.1111/poms.13666

Luxmoore, M. (2019). Russia clarifies threats that would lead it to decouple Runet from the World Wide Web.

Lu, Y., Zhang, M. M., Yang, M. M., & Wang, Y. (2023). Sustainable human resource management practices, employee resilience, and employee outcomes: Toward common good values. *Human Resource Management, 62*(3), 331–353. DOI: 10.1002/hrm.22153

Lyngaas, S. (2024, Jul 15). US bans Russian cybersecurity firm Kaspersky Lab over espionage fears. *CNN*.https://edition.cnn.com/2024/07/15/tech/russian-firm-kaspersky-lab-ban/index.html

Mabunda, S. (2025). The South African and Senegalese Legislative Response to Malware-Facilitated Cybercrime. In *Advances in Information Security* (Vol. 91, pp. 233–249). DOI: 10.1007/978-3-031-66245-4_10

Ma, C. (2021). Smart city and cyber-security; technologies used, leading challenges and future recommendations. *Energy Reports*, *7*, 3359–3367. DOI: 10.1016/j.egyr.2021.08.124

Maglaras, L., Drivas, G., Chouliaras, N., Boiten, E., Lambrinoudakis, C., & Ioannidis, S. (2020, Nov). Cybersecurity in the Era of digital transformation: the case of Greece. In *2020 International Conference on Internet of Things and Intelligent Applications (ITIA)* (pp. 1-5). IEEE. DOI: 10.1109/ITIA50152.2020.9312297

Mahabub, A. (2020). A robust technique of misinformation detection using ensemble voting classifier and comparison with other classifiers. *SN Applied Sciences*, *2*(4), 525. DOI: 10.1007/s42452-020-2326-y

Mahadev Madgule, N. (2023). Vinayaka, Yeshwant M. Sonkhaskar, Dhiren Ramanbhai Patel, R. Karthikeyan, P. Selvakumar,(2023). Mechanical properties and microstructure of activated TIG welded similar joints of Inconel alloys by desirability approaches. *Materials Today: Proceedings*, *77*, 528–533. DOI: 10.1016/j.matpr.2022.12.250

Maharaj, M. S., & Munyoka, W. (2019). Privacy, security, trust, risk and optimism bias in e-government use: The case of two Southern African Development Community countries. *South African Journal of Information Management*, *21*(1), 1–9.

Majeed, M., Chaudhary, A., & Chadha, R. (Eds.). (2025). *Digital Transformation in the Customer Experience*. CRC Press.

Makatur, M. Y., Gultom, R. A., Wadjidi, A. F., & Dinisfusya'ban, D. (2025). Analysis of Electronic-Based Government Systems (SPBE) Using the Six-Ware Cyber Security Framework (SWCSF) in West Sumatra Province. *Formosa Journal of Multidisciplinary Research*, *4*(2), 899–912. DOI: 10.55927/fjmr.v4i2.67

Malatji, M., Marnewick, A. L., & Von Solms, S. (2022). Cybersecurity capabilities for critical infrastructure resilience. *Information and Computer Security*, *30*(2), 255–279. DOI: 10.1108/ICS-06-2021-0091

Malhotra, C., & Malhotra, U. (2024). Putting Interests of Digital Nagriks First: Digital Personal Data Protection (DPDP) Act 2023 of India. *The Indian Journal of Public Administration, 70*(3), 516–531. DOI: 10.1177/00195561241271575

Malik, S. Y., Hayat Mughal, Y., Azam, T., Cao, Y., Wan, Z., Zhu, H., & Thurasamy, R. (2021). Corporate Social Responsibility, Green Human Resources Management, and Sustainable Performance: Is Organizational Citizenship Behavior towards Environment the Missing Link? *Sustainability (Basel), 13*(3), 1044. DOI: 10.3390/su13031044

Malina, L., Dzurenda, P., Ricci, S., & Hajny, J. (2021). Post-quantum era privacy protection for intelligent infrastructures. *IEEE Transactions on Industrial Informatics, 17*(4), 2556–2565. DOI: 10.1109/TII.2020.3031478

Manoharan A, Sarker M, (2023). "Revolutionizing Cybersecurity: Unleashing the Power of Artificial Intelligence and Machine Learning for Next-Generation Threat Detection." Doi: .DOI: 10.56726/ijais/2023.123456

Mao, Z., & Zhu, Y. (2023). Tension between the safe flow of government data across organizational boundaries and fragmentations in secure collaboration: The Chinese e-government. *Aslib Journal of Information Management.*

Marabelli, M., Newell, S., & Handunge, V. (2021). The lifecycle of algorithmic decision-making systems: Organizational choices and ethical challenges. *The Journal of Strategic Information Systems, 30*(3), 101683. DOI: 10.1016/j.jsis.2021.101683

Marczak, B., Weaver, N., Dalek, J., Ensafi, R., Fifield, D., McKune, S., Rey, A., Scott-Railton, J., Deibert, R., & Paxson, V. (2015). An analysis of China's "Great Cannon". In *5th USENIX Workshop on Free and Open Communications on the Internet (FOCI 15).*

Masombuka, M., Grobler, M., & Duvenage, P. (2021, June). Cybersecurity and local Government: Imperative, Challenges and Priorities. In ECCWS 2021 20th European Conference on Cyber Warfare and Security (p. 285). Academic Conferences Inter Ltd.

Masur, P. K. (2023). Understanding the effects of conceptual and analytical choices on 'finding' the privacy paradox: A specification curve analysis of large-scale survey data. *Information Communication and Society, 26*(3), 584–602. DOI: 10.1080/1369118X.2021.1963460

Maurer, T., Skierka, I., Morgus, R., & Hohmann, M. (2015). Technological sovereignty: Missing the point? In 2015 7th International Conference on Cyber Conflict: Architectures in Cyberspace, pages 53–68. IEEE.

Mawgoud, A. A., Taha, M. H. N., Khalifa, N. E. M., & Loey, M. (2019, October). Cyber security risks in MENA region: threats, challenges and countermeasures. In *International conference on advanced intelligent systems and informatics* (pp. 912-921). Cham: Springer International Publishing.

Mayer, P., Zou, Y., Schaub, F., & Aviv, A. J. (2021). ""Now I'm a bit {angry:}" Individuals' Awareness, Perception, and Responses to Data Breaches that Affected Them". 30th USENIX Security Symposium.DOI: 10.5555/3477114.3477123

McKune, S., & Ahmed, S. (2018). The contestation and shaping of cyber norms through China's internet sovereignty agenda. *Online (Bergheim).*

Mejias, R. J., Greer, J. J., Greer, G. C., Shepherd, M. M., & Reyes, R. Y. (2025). A model for information security vulnerability awareness. *Computers & Security, 151*, 104305. DOI: 10.1016/j.cose.2024.104305

Meltzer, J. P. (2020). Cybersecurity, digital trade, and data flows: Re-thinking a role for international trade rules. Global Economy & Development WP, 132.

Mendhurwar, S., & Mishra, R. (2021). Integration of social and IoT technologies: Architectural framework for digital transformation and cyber security challenges. *Enterprise Information Systems, 15*(4), 432–451. DOI: 10.1080/17517575.2019.1600041

Meshcheryakov, V. (2013). Microelectronics illegally purchased in the USA can be used to create wiretapping technologies and to falsify negotiations in the interests of Russian special services.

Michtner, P., & Pinzolits, R. F. J. (2025). Web accessibility gaps in online video platforms: Video services ahead of the European Accessibility Act (EAA). *Universal Access in the Information Society.* Advance online publication. DOI: 10.1007/s10209-025-01219-1

Mick, M. M. A. P., Kovaleski, J. L., Mick, R. L., & Chiroli, D. M. D. G. (2024). Developing a sustainable digital transformation roadmap for SMEs: Integrating digital maturity and strategic alignment. *Sustainability (Basel), 16*(20), 8745. DOI: 10.3390/su16208745

Migliano, S. and Woodhams, S. (2023). List of websites blocked in Russia since Ukraine invasion.

Mijwil, M., Filali, Y., Aljanabi, M., Bounabi, M., & Al-Shahwani, H. (2023). The Purpose of Cybersecurity Governance in the Digital Transformation of Public Services and Protecting the Digital Environment. Mesopotamian journal of cybersecurity, 2023, 1-6.

Mijwil, M., Filali, Y., Aljanabi, M., & Bounabi, M. (2023). The purpose of cybersecurity governance in the digital transformation of public services and protecting the digital environment. *Journal of Cybersecurity*, 1–12. DOI: 10.1093/cybsec/tyac018

Mishra, S., Alowaidi, M. A., & Sharma, S. K. (2021). Impact of security standards and policies on the credibility of e-government. *Journal of Ambient Intelligence and Humanized Computing*, 1–12. DOI: 10.1007/s12652-020-02767-5

Misra, N. N., Dixit, Y., Al-Mallahi, A., Bhullar, M. S., Upadhyay, R., & Martynenko, A. (2022). IoT, Big Data, and Artificial Intelligence in Agriculture and Food Industry. *IEEE Internet of Things Journal, 9*(9), 6305–6324. DOI: 10.1109/JIOT.2020.2998584

Mitrovic, Z., & Thakur, C. (2024). *STRATEGIC INTEGRATION OF CYBERSECURITY: INSIGHTS FROM INFORMATION SYSTEMS MANAGEMENT VIEWPOINT.*

Mızrak, F. (2023). Integrating cybersecurity risk management into strategic management: A comprehensive literature review. *Research Journal of Business and Management, 10*(2), 1–15. DOI: 10.17261/Pressacademia.2023.1807

Mohamed, E. A. S., Osman, M. E., & Mohamed, B. A. (2024). The impact of artificial intelligence on social media content. *Journal of Social Sciences (New York, N. Y.), 20*(1), 12–16. DOI: 10.3844/jssp.2024.12.16

Mohbey, K. K., Meena, G., Kumar, S., & Lokesh, K. (2022). A CNN-LSTM-based hybrid deep learning approach to detect sentiment polarities on Monkeypox tweets. *arXiv preprint arXiv:2208.12019.*

Mok, C. (2022). *China and Russia want to rule the global internet.* Website.

Möller, D. P. F. (2023). *"Cybersecurity in digital transformation." Guide to Cybersecurity in Digital Transformation: Trends*. Springer., DOI: 10.1007/978-3-031-26845-8

Monti, F., Frasca, F., Eynard, D., Mannion, D., & Bronstein, M. M. (2019). Misinformation detection on social media using geometric deep learning. *arXiv preprint arXiv:1902.06673.*

Moşteanu, N. R. (2020). Challenges for organizational structure and design as a result of digitalization and cybersecurity. *The Business & Management Review, 11*(1), 278–286. DOI: 10.24052/BMR/V11NU01/ART-29

Mskagency (2018). NTSci: The maximum number of computer attacks on the Runet was recorded on the day of the election of the president of the Russian Federation.

Mueller, M. (2017). *Will the Internet Fragment?: Sovereignty, Globalization, and Cyberspace*. Wiley.

Munshi, D. (2024). Enhancing Digital Transformation Project Success through Design Thinking-Driven Agile Project Management.

Murdoch, B. (2021). Privacy and artificial intelligence: Challenges for protecting health information in a new era. *BMC Medical Ethics*, *22*(1), 1–11. DOI: 10.1186/s12910-021-00687-3 PMID: 34525993

Murikah, W., Nthenge, J. K., & Musyoka, F. M. (2024). Bias and ethics of AI systems applied in auditing - A systematic review. *Scientific African*, *25*, e02281. DOI: 10.1016/j.sciaf.2024.e02281

Nafrees, A. C. M., Sujah, A. M. A., & Mansoor, C. (2021). Smart Cities: Emerging technologies and Potential solutions to the Cyber security threads. *Computer Technologies and Information Security*, *1-5*, 220–228. Advance online publication. DOI: 10.1109/ICEECCOT52851.2021.9707994

Nair M M, Tyagi A K, (2023). "AI, IoT, blockchain, and cloud computing: The necessity of the future". Distributed Computing to Blockchain, 1-12. .DOI: 10.1016/B978-0-323-99243-5.00001-5

Nakashima, E. (2013). U.S. weapons system designs compromised by Chinese cyberspies.

Napoli, P. M. (2018). What if more speech is no longer the solution? First Amendment theory meets misinformation and the filter bubble. *Federal Communications Law Journal*, *70*, 55–104.

Naresh, A., & Krishna, P. V. (2021). An efficient approach for sentiment analysis using machine learning algorithm. *Evolutionary Intelligence*, *14*(2), 725–731. DOI: 10.1007/s12065-020-00429-1

Nasaw, D. (2009). Hackers breach defences of Joint Strike Fighter jet program. Accessed on July 20, 2023.

Naseer, A., Naseer, H., Ahmad, A., Maynard, S. B., & Siddiqui, A. M. (2023). Moving towards agile cybersecurity incident response: A case study exploring the enabling role of big data analytics-embedded dynamic capabilities. *Computers & Security*, *135*, 103525. DOI: 10.1016/j.cose.2023.103525

National Institute of Standards and Technology. (2001, November 26). *Announcing the Advanced Encryption Standard (AES) (FIPS PUB 197)*. U.S. Department of Commerce. https://nvlpubs.nist.gov/nistpubs/FIPS/NIST.FIPS.197.pdf

NATO (2011). Conceptual views on the activities of the armed forces of the Russian Federation in the information space.

Neelakrishnan, P. (2024). Data Security Fundamental Requirements. In *Autonomous Data Security* (pp. 1–39). Apress., DOI: 10.1007/979-8-8688-0838-8_1

Netim (2015).SU domain name.

News, B. C. (2022, Nov 26). US bans sale of Huawei, ZTE tech amid security fears. https://www.bbc.com/news/world-us-canada-63764450.

Newton, M. (2018). Russian data localization laws: Enriching "security" and the economy.

Ni, S. (2023). How do privacy concerns affect consumers' self-disclosure on social media? In Advances in Social Science, Education and Humanities Research (pp. 953–962). Atlantis Press SARL.

Ning, S., Han, W., Yuanshan, L., and Xuezi, D. (2019). Development of PRC regulations on cross-border data transfer.

Nkongolo, M. (2023). "Navigating the complex nexus: cybersecurity in political landscapes." arXiv preprint arXiv:2308.08005.

Nookhao, S., & Kiattisin, S. (2023). Achieving a successful e-government: Determinants of behavioral intention from Thai citizens' perspective. *Heliyon*, *9*(8), e18944. DOI: 10.1016/j.heliyon.2023.e18944 PMID: 37588601

Norris, D. F., Mateczun, L., Joshi, A., & Finin, T. (2019). Cyberattacks at the grass roots: American local governments and the need for high levels of cybersecurity. *Public Administration Review*, *79*(6), 895–904. DOI: 10.1111/puar.13028

Norris, D. F., Mateczun, L., Joshi, A., & Finin, T. (2021). Managing cybersecurity at the grassroots: Evidence from the first nationwide survey of local government cybersecurity. *Journal of Urban Affairs*, *43*(8), 1173–1195. DOI: 10.1080/07352166.2020.1727295

North-Samardzic, A. (2020). Biometric Technology and Ethics: Beyond Security Applications. *Journal of Business Ethics*, *167*(3), 433–450. DOI: 10.1007/s10551-019-04143-6

NTIA (2014). NTIA announces intent to transition key internet domain name functions.

Obisesan, S. M. (2024). Integrating Artificial Intelligence and Cybersecurity Frameworks: Challenges and Opportunities in E-commerce Cybersecurity Management. *SSRN* 5070108.

Oducado, R. M. F., Sales, M. R., Magarzo, A. J. P., Panes, P. M. A., & Lapastora, J. T. P. (2019). Perceptions and attitude on using social media responsibly: Toward social media literacy in nursing education. *Belitung Nursing Journal*, *5*(3), 116–122. DOI: 10.33546/bnj.789

Oladipo, J. O., Okoye, C. C., & Elufioye, O. A. (2024). Human factors in cybersecurity: Navigating the fintech landscape. *Journal of Science and Research*, *10*(2), 1–13.

Oladipo, J. O., Okoye, C. C., Elufioye, O. A., Falaiye, T., & Nwankwo, E. E. (2024). Human factors in cybersecurity: Navigating the fintech landscape. *International Journal of Science and Research Archive*, *11*(1), 1959–1967. DOI: 10.30574/ijsra.2024.11.1.0258

Olanrewaju, O. I. K., & Daramola, G. O. (2024). Transforming business models with ESG integration: A strategic framework for financial professionals. *World Journal of Advanced Research and Reviews*, *11*(2), 1–13. DOI: 10.30574/wjarr.2024.11.2.0930

Omotunde, H., & Ahmed, M. (2023). A comprehensive review of security measures in database systems: Assessing authentication, access control, and beyond. *Mesopotamian Journal of CyberSecurity*, *4*(1), 1–20.

OneTrust (2021). France announces strategy for cloud technology.

OneTrust. (2018). *Orders on CII officially published.*

Oni, S., Berepubo, K. A., Oni, A. A., & Joshua, S. (2019, Apr). E-government and the challenge of cybercrime in Nigeria. In 2019 Sixth International Conference on eDemocracy & eGovernment (ICEDEG) (pp. 137-142). IEEE.

Orehek, Š., & Petrič, G. (2021). A systematic review of scales for measuring information security culture. *Information and Computer Security*, *29*(1), 133–158. DOI: 10.1108/ICS-12-2019-0140

Oshikawa, R., Qian, J., & Wang, W. Y. (2018). A survey on Natural Language Processing for misinformation detection. *arXiv preprint arXiv:1811.00770.*

Ou, C. X., Zhang, X., Angelopoulos, S., Davison, R. M., & Janse, N. (2022). Security breaches and organization response strategy: Exploring consumers' threat and coping appraisals. *International Journal of Information Management*, *65*, 102498. DOI: 10.1016/j.ijinfomgt.2022.102498

Ovchinnikova, O., & Upadhyay, N. K. (2023). The Level of Cybersecurity of the BRICS Member Countries in International Ratings: Prospects for Cooperation. *BRICS Law Journal*, *10*(1), 7–34. DOI: 10.21684/2412-2343-2023-10-1-7-34

Oye, E., & Mitchell, N. (2022). "Future of Data Privacy Regulations Beyond CCPA". ResearchGate. DOI: 10.13140/RG.2.2.36055.75684

Paas, F., & van Merriënboer, J. J. G. (2020). Cognitive-Load Theory: Methods to Manage Working Memory Load in the Learning of Complex Tasks. *Current Directions in Psychological Science*, *29*(4), 394–398. DOI: 10.1177/0963721420922183

Padmaja, K., & Seshadri, R. (2021). Analytics on real time security attacks in healthcare, retail and banking applications in the cloud. *Evolutionary Intelligence*, *14*(2), 595–605. DOI: 10.1007/s12065-019-00337-z

Panakaduwa, C., Coates, P., & Munir, M. (2024). Identifying sustainable retrofit challenges of historical Buildings: A systematic review. *Energy and Building*, *313*, 114226. DOI: 10.1016/j.enbuild.2024.114226

Patel, V., Department of Computer Engineering Silver Oak College of Engineering & Technology, S. O. U. and D. D. J. A., Khara, D. S., & Tivari, G. D. (2024). Examining the integration of responsible AI principles in Social Media Marketing for Digital Health: A theoretical analysis. INTERANTIONAL JOURNAL OF SCIENTIFIC RESEARCH IN ENGINEERING AND, 08(07), 1–13.

Pathmabandu, C., Grundy, J., Chhetri, M. B., & Baig, Z. (2023). Privacy for IoT: Informed consent management in Smart Buildings. *Future Generation Computer Systems*, *145*, 367–383. DOI: 10.1016/j.future.2023.03.045

Pauletto, C. (2021). Options towards a global standard for the protection of individuals with regard to the processing of personal data. *Computer Law & Security Review*, *40*, 105433. DOI: 10.1016/j.clsr.2020.105433

Paul, M., Maglaras, L., Ferrag, M. A., & Almomani, I. (2023). Digitization of healthcare sector: A study on privacy and security concerns. *ICT Express*, *9*(1), 1–12. DOI: 10.1016/j.icte.2023.02.007

Pazhohan, H. (2023). *Global Data Protection Standards: A Comparative Analysis of GDPR and Other International Privacy Laws*. Legal Studies in Digital Age., DOI: 10.5206/lsda.2023.1.1

Pearson, J. and Bing, C. (2022). The cyber war between Ukraine and Russia: An overview.

Pérez-Rosas, V., Kleinberg, B., Lefevre, A., & Mihalcea, R. (2017). Automatic detection of fake news. *arXiv preprint arXiv:1708.07104*.

Perlroth, N. (2015). China is said to use powerful new weapon to censor internet.

Perunicic, K. (2023). Complete list of blocked websites in China.

Petrov, V. (2016). Rostec engaged in a response to cyber threats.

Phadke, A., Medrano, F. A., & Ustymenko, S. (2022, Feb). Applications of Blockchain in E-government. In *2022 International Symposium on Electrical, Electronics and Information Engineering (ISEEIE)* (pp. 157-164). IEEE. DOI: 10.1109/ISEEIE55684.2022.00035

Pieke, F. N. (2017). The Communist Party and social management in China. In *Critical Readings on Communist Party of China* (pp. 998–1018). BRILL. DOI: 10.1163/9789004302488_036

Pietras, E. (2019). Information security–its essence and threats. *Scientific Journal of the Military University of Land Forces*, *51*(1), (191), 25–34.

Pitt, D. C., Levine, N., & Yan, X. (1996). Touching stones to cross the river: Evolving telecommunication policy priorities in contemporary China. *Journal of Contemporary China*, *5*(13), 347–365. DOI: 10.1080/10670569608724259

Poehlmann, N., Caramancion, K. M., Tatar, I., Li, Y., Barati, M., & Merz, T. (2021). *The Organizational Cybersecurity Success Factors: An Exhaustive Literature Review* (pp. 377–395). DOI: 10.1007/978-3-030-71017-0_27

Pollini, A., Callari, T. C., Tedeschi, A., Ruscio, D., Save, L., Chiarugi, F., & Guerri, D. (2022). Leveraging human factors in cybersecurity: An integrated methodological approach. *Cognition Technology and Work*, *24*(2), 267–279. DOI: 10.1007/s10111-021-00683-y PMID: 34149309

Polyakova, E., Filonova, O., Chelovechkova, A., & Zmyzgova, T. (2021). Condition and prospects of legal regulation of the security of critical information infrastructure in Russia and in foreign countries. SHS Web of Conferences, 93(93): 02014–02014. DOI: 10.1051/shsconf/20219302014

Popescu, N., & Secrieru, S. (2018). *Hacks, Leaks, and Disruptions: Russian Cyber Strategies*. Publications Office.

Popkova, E. G., & Gulzat, K. (2020). Contradiction of the digital economy: public well-being vs. cyber threats. In Digital Economy: Complexity and Variety vs. Rationality 9 (pp. 112-124). Springer International Publishing.

Potthast, M., Kiesel, J., Reinartz, K., Bevendorff, J., & Stein, B. (2017). A stylometric inquiry into hyperpartisan and fake news. *arXiv preprint arXiv:1702.05638*.

Princewill, N., & Busari, S. (2021, June 4). Nigeria suspends Twitter's operations. CNN. https://edition.cnn.com/2021/06/04/africa/nigeria-suspends-twitter-operations-intl/index.html

Prodinger B, Neuhofer B, (2023). "Never-ending tourism: Tourism experience scenarios for 2030". ENTER22 e-Tourism Conference, 1-12.

Propp, K. (2023 Forthcoming). A US Perspective on Negotiating with the European Union. In Fahey, E. (Ed.), *Routledge International Handbook on Transatlantic Relations* (pp. 38–51). Routledge. DOI: 10.4324/9781003283911-5

Putro, P. A. W., Sensuse, D. I., & Wibowo, W. S. S. (2024). Framework for critical information infrastructure protection in smart government: A case study in Indonesia. *Information and Computer Security*, *32*(1), 112–129. DOI: 10.1108/ICS-03-2023-0031

QiAnXin (2024). Qi An Xin CERT.

Quach, S., Thaichon, P., Martin, K. D., Weaven, S., & Palmatier, R. W. (2022). Digital technologies: Tensions in privacy and data. *Journal of the Academy of Marketing Science*, *50*(6), 1299–1323. DOI: 10.1007/s11747-022-00845-y PMID: 35281634

Quinn, K., & Epstein, D. (2018, July). #MyPrivacy. *Proceedings of the 9th International Conference on Social and Society*.

Quishi (2017). In-depth implementation of General Secretary Xi Jinping's strategic thinking of network power, solidly promote network security and informationization.

Rachmad Y E, (2024). "The Future of Influencer Marketing: Evolution of Consumer Behavior in the Digital World".

Radoglou-Grammatikis, P., Sarigiannidis, P., Iturbe, E., Rios, E., Martinez, S., Sarigiannidis, A., Eftathopoulos, G., Spyridis, Y., Sesis, A., Vakakis, N., Tzovaras, D., Kafetzakis, E., Giannoulakis, I., Tzifas, M., Giannakoulias, A., Angelopoulos, M., & Ramos, F. (2021). SPEAR SIEM: A Security Information and Event Management system for the Smart Grid. *Computer Networks*, *193*, 108008. DOI: 10.1016/j.comnet.2021.108008

Rafiq, F., Awan, M. J., Yasin, A., Nobanee, H., Zain, A. M., & Bahaj, S. A. (2022). Privacy Prevention of Big Data Applications: A Systematic Literature Review. *SAGE Open*, *12*(2), 21582440221096445. DOI: 10.1177/21582440221096445

Rajarathnam, S., & Singh, V. (2024, October). Systematic Literature Review of Cybersecurity and User Experience. In *2024 Cyber Awareness and Research Symposium (CARS)* (pp. 1-9). IEEE. DOI: 10.1109/CARS61786.2024.10778869

Rajawat A S, Bedi P, Goyal S B, Shaw R N, (2022). "AI and blockchain for healthcare data security in smart cities". AI and IoT for Smart City, 1-12. .DOI: 10.1007/978-981-19-0743-1_1

Raju, V., Hannani, A., & Perumal, K. (2025). The Impact of Organizational Challenges and Technical Challenges on the Implementation of E-government Military Institutions in Netherlands. Spectrum Bizsctech Journal, 1(1).

Rakova, B., Yang, J., Cramer, H., & Chowdhury, R. (2021). Where Responsible AI meets Reality. *Proceedings of the ACM on Human-Computer Interaction, 5*(CSCW1), 1–23. DOI: 10.1145/3449081

Ramadhani, E. H., Suyitno, D., & Suryantoro, S. (2024, Feb). Information technology security assessment (ITSA) methodology for web-based E-government. In AIP Conference Proceedings (Vol. 2838, No. 1). AIP Publishing.

Ramakrishnan, T., Mohan Gift, M. D., Chitradevi, S., Jegan, R., & Subha Hency Jose, P. Nagaraja, Rajneesh Sharma H.N., Selvakumar P., Sintayehu Mekuria Hailegiorgis, (2022). "Study of Numerous Resins Used in Polymer Matrix Composite Materials", Advances in Materials Science and Engineering, vol. 2022, Article ID 1088926, 8 pages, 2022. DOI: 10.1155/2022/1088926

Ramos, J. (2003). Using tf-idf to determine word relevance in document queries. In *Proceedings of the First Instructional Conference on Machine Learning* (Vol. 242, pp. 29–48).

Ramzy, A. (2011). State stamps out small 'Jasmine' protests in China.

Rani S, Bhambri P, Kataria A, Khang A, Sivaraman A K, (2023). "Big Data, Cloud Computing and IoT: Tools and Applications."

Rashkin, H., Choi, E., Jang, J. Y., Volkova, S., & Choi, Y. (2017). Truth of varying shades: Analyzing language in misinformation and political fact-checking. In *Proceedings of the 2017 Conference on Empirical Methods in Natural Language Processing* (pp. 2931–2937). DOI: 10.18653/v1/D17-1317

Rawas, S. (2024). ChatGPT: Empowering lifelong learning in the digital age of higher education. *Education and Information Technologies*, *29*(6), 6895–6908. DOI: 10.1007/s10639-023-12114-8

Raynor, B. (2022). The shadow of sanctions: Reputational risk, financial reintegration, and the political economy of sanctions relief. *European Journal of International Relations*, *28*(3), 696–721. DOI: 10.1177/13540661221100540

Raza, M. A.Md. Asaad Raza. (2024). Cyber Security and Data Privacy in the Era of E-Governance. *Social Science Journal for Advanced Research*, *4*(1), 5–9. DOI: 10.54741/ssjar.4.1.2

Rbc.ru (2017). Duma toughens punishment for cyber attacks on critical infrastructure.

Rebouças Filho, W. L. (2025). The Role of Zero Trust Architecture in Modern Cybersecurity: Integration with IAM and Emerging Technologies. *Brazilian Journal of Development, 11*(1), e76836–e76836. DOI: 10.34117/bjdv11n1-060

Renaud, K., Orgeron, C., Warkentin, M., & French, P. E. (2020). Cyber security responsibilization: An evaluation of the intervention approaches adopted by the Five Eyes countries and China. *Public Administration Review, 80*(4), 577–589. DOI: 10.1111/puar.13210

Reud, M. (2016). *China and cyber: Attitudes, strategies, organization.* Tallinn Paper.

Reuters (2014). U.S. knocks plans for European communication network.

Reuters (2019). Russia thwarts U.S. cyber attacks on its infrastructure.

Reuters (2021). Russian law requires smart devices to come pre-installed with domestic software. Reuters.

Reuters (2024). U.S. imposes sanctions on Russia's AO Kaspersky Lab, executives over cyber risks. *Reuters.* https://www.reuters.com/technology/cybersecurity/us-imposes-sanctions-russias-ao-kaspersky-lab-executives-over-cyber-risks-2024-06-21/

RGRU. (2013). Decree of the president of the Russian Federation of January 15, 2013, N 31S, Moscow.

Riedel, B., Augenstein, I., Spithourakis, G. P., & Riedel, S. (2017). A simple but tough-to-beat baseline for the Fake News Challenge stance detection task. *arXiv [cs.CL].*

Riyanto, Y. E., & Zhang, J. (2020). Diminishing personal information privacy weakens image concerns. *PLoS One, 15*(4), e0232037. DOI: 10.1371/journal.pone.0232037 PMID: 32339179

Rizvi, M. (2023). Enhancing cybersecurity: The power of artificial intelligence in threat detection and prevention. *Journal of Advanced Engineering Research and Science, 10*(2), 1–9. DOI: 10.22161/ijaers.105.8

Robb, A. (2017). Anatomy of a fake news scandal. *Rolling Stone (San Francisco, Calif.), 1301*, 28–33.

Robinson, Sakurayuki, B., and Dawborn, D. (2012). Law no. 11 of 2008 on electronic information and transactions.

Ross, S. (2021). The 5 biggest Chinese software companies.

Rostec (2024). Rostec.

Roussi, A. (2022, Sep 9). Meet Killnet, Russia's hacking 'patriots' plaguing Europe. Politico. https://www.politico.eu/article/meet-killnet-russias-hacking-patriots-plaguing-europe/

RTS-CERT (2024). RTS-CERT.

RuCert (2024). RuCert.

Ruchansky, N., Seo, S., & Liu, Y. (2017). CSI: A hybrid deep model for misinformation detection. *arXiv preprint arXiv:1703.00956*, 797–806.

Runsewe, O., Akwawa, L. A., Folorunsho, S. O., & Osundare, O. S. (2024). Optimizing user interface and user experience in financial applications: A review of techniques and technologies. *World Journal of Advanced Research and Reviews*, *23*(3), 934–942. DOI: 10.30574/wjarr.2024.23.3.2633

Sabeeh, V., Zohdy, M., & Bashaireh, R. A. (2019). Enhancing the misinformation detection by applying effective feature selection based on semantic sources. In *International Conference on Computational Science and Computational Intelligence (CSCI)* (pp. 1365–1370).

Sacks, S. (2019). China's emerging cyber governance system.

Saeed, S., Azizi, N., Tahir, S., Ahmad, M., & Almuhaideb, A. M. (Eds.). (2024). Strengthening Industrial Cybersecurity to Protect Business Intelligence. IGI Global. 5. DOI: 10.4018/979-8-3693-0839-4

Saeed, S., Gull, H., Aldossary, M. M., Altamimi, A. F., Alshahrani, M. S., Saqib, M., ... & Almuhaideb, A. M. (2024). Digital Transformation in Energy Sector: Cybersecurity Challenges and Implications. Information, 15(12), 764. 4.

Saeed, S. (2023). A customer-centric view of E-commerce security and privacy. *Applied Sciences (Basel, Switzerland)*, *13*(2), 1020. DOI: 10.3390/app13021020

Saeed, S. (2023). Digital Workplaces and Information Security Behavior of Business Employees: An Empirical Study of Saudi Arabia. *Sustainability (Basel)*, *15*(7), 6019. DOI: 10.3390/su15076019

Saeed, S. (2024). Usable Privacy and Security in Mobile Applications: Perception of Mobile End Users in Saudi Arabia. *Big Data and Cognitive Computing*, *8*(11), 162. DOI: 10.3390/bdcc8110162

Saeed, S. (2025). Digital Transformation in Governmental Public Service Provision and Usable Security Perception in Saudi Arabia. *Information (Basel)*, *16*(3), 247. DOI: 10.3390/info16030247

Saeed, S., Altamimi, S. A., Alkayyal, N. A., Alshehri, E., & Alabbad, D. A. (2023). Digital transformation and cybersecurity challenges for businesses resilience: Issues and recommendations. *Sensors (Basel), 23*(3), 1–15. DOI: 10.3390/s23156666 PMID: 37571451

Saeed, S., & Amjad, A. (2013). Understanding Usability Issues of Pakistani University Websites. *Life Science Journal, 10*(6s), 479–482. https://www.lifesciencesite.com/lsj/life1006s/073_17605life1006s_479_482.pdf

Saeed, S., Bolívar, M. P. R., & Thurasamy, R. (2021). *Pandemic, lockdown, and digital transformation*. Springer International Publishing. DOI: 10.1007/978-3-030-86274-9

Saeed, S., Gull, H., Aldossary, M. M., Altamimi, A. F., Alshahrani, M. S., Saqib, M., Zafar Iqbal, S., & Almuhaideb, A. M. (2024a). Digital transformation in energy sector: Cybersecurity challenges and implications. *Information (Basel), 15*(12), 764. DOI: 10.3390/info15120764

Saeed, S., Suayyid, S. A., Al-Ghamdi, M. S., Al-Muhaisen, H., & Almuhaideb, A. M. (2023). A Systematic Literature Review on Cyber Threat Intelligence for Organizational Cybersecurity Resilience. *Sensors (Basel), 23*(16), 7273. DOI: 10.3390/s23167273 PMID: 37631808

Saeed, S., Wahab, F., Cheema, S. A., & Ashraf, S. (2013). Role of Usability in E-Government and E-Commerce Portals: An Empirical Study of Pakistan. *Life Science Journal, 10*(1s), 8–13.

Safitra, M. F., Lubis, M., & Fakhrurroja, H. (2023). Counterattacking cyber threats: A framework for the future of cybersecurity. *Sustainability (Basel), 15*(11), 8351. DOI: 10.3390/su151813369

Sahoo, S. R., & Gupta, B. B. (2021). Multiple features based approach for automatic misinformation detection on social networks using deep learning. *Applied Soft Computing, 100*, 106983. DOI: 10.1016/j.asoc.2020.106983

Saini, K., & Sehrawat, P. (2024). "Cybersecurity in Digital Transformation: Challenges and Solutions." *2024 Second International Conference*, 1-5. DOI: 10.1109/ICACCTech65084.2024.00079

Samadi, M., Mousavian, M., & Momtazi, S. (2021). Deep contextualized text representation and learning for misinformation detection. *Information Processing & Management, 58*(6), 102723. DOI: 10.1016/j.ipm.2021.102723

Samani, F. S., Zhang, H., & Stadler, R. (2019). Efficient learning on high-dimensional operational data. In *2019 15th International Conference on Network and Service Management (CNSM)*, Halifax, NS, Canada (pp. 1–9). DOI: 10.23919/CNSM46954.2019.9012741

Sandhu, A. K. (2021). Big data with cloud computing: Discussions and challenges. *Big Data Mining and Analytics*, *4*(2), 123–135. DOI: 10.26599/BDMA.2021.9020005

Sanjay (2017). Internet sovereignty.

Sarker, I. H. (2023). Machine Learning for Intelligent Data Analysis and Automation in Cybersecurity: Current and Future Prospects. *Annals of Data Science*, *10*(6), 1473–1498. DOI: 10.1007/s40745-022-00444-2

Sawan, A., & Thaher, T. (2021, Oct). Sentiment analysis model for fake news identification in Arabic tweets. In *2021 IEEE 15th International Conference on Application of Information and Communication Technologies (AICT)* (pp. 1–6). IEEE. DOI: 10.1109/AICT52784.2021.9620509

Schaberreiter, T., Röning, J., Quirchmayr, G., Kupfersberger, V., Wills, C., Bregonzio, M., & Spyros, A. (2022). A cybersecurity situational awareness and information-sharing solution for local public administrations based on advanced big data analysis: the CS-AWARE project. In *Challenges in Cybersecurity and privacy-the European research landscape* (pp. 149–180). River Publishers. DOI: 10.1201/9781003337492-8

Schia, N., & Gjesvik, L. (2017). *China's cyber sovereignty (policy brief)*. ResearchGate.

Schlackl, F., Link, N., & Hoehle, H. (2022). Antecedents and consequences of data breaches: A systematic review. *Information & Management*, *59*(3), 1–18. DOI: 10.1016/j.im.2022.103638

Schneider, G. B. C. (2025). The Importance of Cybersecurity in Digital Government Implementations. *COGNITIONIS Scientific Journal*, *8*(1), e585–e585. DOI: 10.38087/2595.8801.585

Seddari, N., Derhab, A., Belaoued, M., Halboob, W., Al-Muhtadi, J., & Bouras, A. (2022). A hybrid linguistic and knowledge-based analysis approach for misinformation detection on social media. *IEEE Access : Practical Innovations, Open Solutions*, *10*, 62097–62109. DOI: 10.1109/ACCESS.2022.3181184

Seddon, M. (2020). Telegram becomes a digital battleground in Russia's war on Ukraine. Financial Times. https://www.ft.com/content/b1e76905-29f2-4ac0-99e0-7af07cef280d

Segal, A. (2020). China's vision for cyber sovereignty and the global governance of cyberspace: An emerging China-centric order. China's Vision for a New World Order in Practice.

Selvakumar, P., Palanisamy, S. K., Cinthaikinian, S., Palanisamy, V., Mariappan, R., & Selvakumar, P. K. (2024). Biosensors and its diverse applications in healthcare systems. *Zeitschrift für Physikalische Chemie, 2024*. DOI: 10.1515/zpch-2023-0406

Serohina, S., Harashchuk, I., Murtishcheva, A., Poproshaieva, O., & Fomina, S. (2024). International Experience in Ensuring Cybersecurity in Local Self-Government Management as a Component of the National Security of Ukraine. *Pakistan Journal of Criminology*, *16*(2).

Shah, I. A. (2022). Cybersecurity Issues and Challenges for E-Government During COVID-19: A Review. Cybersecurity Measures for E-Government Frameworks, 187-222.

Shah, I. A., Wassan, S., & Usmani, M. H. (2022). E-Government Security and Privacy Issues: Challenges and Preventive Approaches. In Cybersecurity Measures for E-Government Frameworks (pp. 61-76). IGI Global.

Shahid, J., Ahmad, R., Kiani, A. K., Ahmad, T., Saeed, S., & Almuhaideb, A. M. (2022). Data protection and privacy of the internet of healthcare things (IoHTs). *Applied Sciences (Basel, Switzerland)*, *12*(11), 1–24. DOI: 10.3390/app12041927 PMID: 36330151

Shah, N. (2021). Digital infrastructure, liminality, and world-making via asia|(dis) information blackouts: Politics and practices of internet shutdowns. *International Journal of Communication*, *15*, 17.

Shandilya, S. K., Datta, A., Kartik, Y., & Nagar, A. (2024). *Navigating the Regulatory Landscape.*, DOI: 10.1007/978-3-031-53290-0_3

Shandler, R., & Gomez, M. A. (2023). The hidden threat of cyber-attacks–undermining public confidence in government. *Journal of Information Technology & Politics*, *20*(4), 359–374. DOI: 10.1080/19331681.2022.2112796

Shen, X. (2022). China's new cross-border data transfer law burdens firms with onerous paperwork.

Shende, A. D., Tekade, S. A., Deshmukh, A. A., Tembhurkar, S. P., & Selvakumar, P. (2025). Water Quality Monitoring and Control With AI. In Ruiz-Vanoye, J., & Díaz-Parra, O. (Eds.), *Smart Water Technology for Sustainable Management in Modern Cities* (pp. 51–80). IGI Global Scientific Publishing., DOI: 10.4018/979-8-3693-8074-1.ch003

Shen, F. (2014). *Great Firewall of China.*

Sherman, J. (2022). Russia's internet censor is also a surveillance machine.

Shibuya, Y., Hamm, A., & Cerratto Pargman, T. (2022). Mapping HCI research methods for studying social media interaction: A systematic literature review. *Computers in Human Behavior, 129*, 107131. DOI: 10.1016/j.chb.2021.107131

Shidong, Z. (2019). China offers five-year tax breaks to chip makers, software developers to bolster industry as trade war stretches to tech. Accessed on July 19, 2023.

Shinde, N., & Kulkarni, P. (2021). Cyber incident response and planning: A flexible approach. *Computer Fraud & Security, 2021*(1), 10–14. DOI: 10.1016/S1361-3723(21)00009-9

Shinde, R. D., Jathar, K. R., Pardeshi, A. D., & Thorat, S. A. (2023). Graphical Password Authentication Using Decentralized Single-Sign-On. *2023 World Conference on Communication & Computing (WCONF)*, 1–9. DOI: 10.1109/WCONF58270.2023.10235134

Shu, K., Wang, S., & Liu, H. (2017). Beyond news contents: The role of social context for misinformation detection. *arXiv preprint arXiv:1710.08998*, 312–320.

Shu, K., Bernard, H. R., & Liu, H. (2019). Studying fake news via network analysis: Detection and mitigation. In *Lecture Notes in Social Networks* (pp. 43–65). Springer.

Shu, K., Sliva, A., Wang, S., Tang, J., & Liu, H. (2017). Misinformation detection on social media: A data mining perspective. *SIGKDD Explorations, 19*(1), 22–36. DOI: 10.1145/3137597.3137600

Shu, K., Wang, S., & Liu, H. (2018). Understanding user profiles on social media for misinformation detection. In *2018 IEEE Conference on Multimedia Information Processing and Retrieval (MIPR)* (pp. 430–435). IEEE. DOI: 10.1109/MIPR.2018.00092

Siddiqui, Z. A., & Haroon, M. (2022). *"Application of artificial intelligence and machine learning in blockchain technology." Artificial Intelligence and Machine Learning for Blockchain*. Elsevier., DOI: 10.1016/B978-0-323-85575-5.00001-6

Sideri, K., & Prainsack, B. (2023). COVID-19 contact tracing apps and the governance of collective action: Social nudges, deliberation, and solidarity in Europe and beyond. *Policy Studies, 44*(1), 132–153. DOI: 10.1080/01442872.2022.2130884

Singh, C., Thakkar, R., & Warraich, J. (2023). IAM identity Access Management—Importance in maintaining security systems within organizations. *European Journal of Engineering and Technology, 11*(2), 1–12. DOI: 10.24018/ejeng.2023.8.4.3074

Singh, V., Dasgupta, R., Sonagra, D., Raman, K., & Ghosh, I. (2017). Automated misinformation detection using linguistic analysis and machine learning. In *International Conference on Social Computing, Behavioral-Cultural Modeling, Prediction and Behavior Representation*.

Sinha, M. (2024). Exploring the Role of Cybersecurity in Integrated Programs for Protecting and Improving Digital Platforms. *International IT Journal of Research, ISSN: 3007-6706, 2*(2), 190-197.

Sitalieva, A., Homyakova, V., Zheleznov, M., & Shorokhov, K. (2022). Analysis of the national program "Digital Economy of the Russian Federation". Available at *SSRN* 4256387. DOI: 10.2139/ssrn.4256387

Sivetc, L. (2021). Controlling free expression "by infrastructure" in the Russian internet: The consequences of Runet sovereignization. *First Monday*. DOI: 10.5210/fm.v26i5.11698

Smith, K. J., Dhillon, G., & Carter, L. (2021). User values and the development of a cybersecurity public policy for the IoT. *International Journal of Information Management, 56*, 102123. DOI: 10.1016/j.ijinfomgt.2020.102123

Solano, J., Camacho, L., Correa, A., Deiro, C., Vargas, J., & Ochoa, M. (2021). Combining behavioral biometrics and session context analytics to enhance risk-based static authentication in web applications. *International Journal of Information Security*, *20*(2), 181–197. DOI: 10.1007/s10207-020-00510-x

Soll, J. (2016). The long and brutal history of fake news. *Politico Magazine, 18*(12).

Sontan, A. D., & Samuel, S. V. (2024). The intersection of Artificial Intelligence and cybersecurity: Challenges and opportunities. *World Journal of Advanced Research and Reviews*, *12*(2), 1–13.

Sreenivasulu, A., & Manimozhi, T. Satheesh kumar P., Selvakumar P. and Singh P., (2022). "The Model of Smart Sensing Device For Sensitive Nanoclusters Modification in Sensing Properties," 2022 2nd International Conference on Advance Computing and Innovative Technologies in Engineering (ICACITE), Greater Noida, India, 2022, pp. 1043-1047, DOI: 10.1109/ICACITE53722.2022.9823846

Stadnik, I. (2019a). A closer look at the "sovereign Runet" law.

Stadnik, I. (2019b). Internet governance in Russia.

Stallings, W. (2011). *Cryptography and network security: Principles and practice* (5th ed.). Pearson.

Stanford (2014). Federal law No. 242-FZ. — Wilmap.

Staves, A., Anderson, T., Balderstone, H., Green, B., Gouglidis, A., & Hutchison, D. (2022). A cyber incident response and recovery framework to support operators of industrial control systems. *International Journal of Critical Infrastructure Protection, 37*, 100454. DOI: 10.1016/j.ijcip.2021.100505

Steele, C. (2014). The 10 most disturbing Snowden revelations.

Stevens, T. (2016). Breaching protocol: The threat of cyber espionage. *Jane's Intelligence Review (Coulsdon), 22*(3), 8–13.

Stewart, H. (2023). Digital transformation security challenges. *Journal of Computer Information Systems, 63*(2), 234–241. DOI: 10.1080/08874417.2021.1877063

Subramaniam, C., Johari, J., Mashi, M. S., & Mohamad, R. (2023). The influence of safety leadership on nurses' safety behavior: The mediating role of safety knowledge and motivation. *Journal of Safety Research, 84*, 117–128. DOI: 10.1016/j.jsr.2022.10.013 PMID: 36868640

Subramani, S., & Svn, S. K. (2025). Review of security methods based on classical cryptography and quantum cryptography. *Cybernetics and Systems, 56*(3), 302–320. DOI: 10.1080/01969722.2023.2166261

Sufi, F. K., & Alsulami, M. (2021). Automated Multidimensional Analysis of Global Events With Entity Detection, Sentiment Analysis and Anomaly Detection. *IEEE Access : Practical Innovations, Open Solutions, 9*, 152449–152460. DOI: 10.1109/ACCESS.2021.3127571

Sugumaran, K. M. D., Pandiyarajan V., Y. B S, Selvakumar P. and M. S, (2024). "Analysis of Electromyography Signals for Control of Mechanical Prosthesis using Machine Learning Techniques," 2024 2nd International Conference on Intelligent Data Communication Technologies and Internet of Things (IDCIoT), pp. 1059-1067, DOI: 10.1109/IDCIoT59759.2024.10467707

Sukharenko, A. (2019). Russian ITC security policy and cybercrime.

Suleski, T., Ahmed, M., Yang, W., & Wang, E. (2023). A review of multi-factor authentication in the Internet of Healthcare Things. *Digital Health, 9*, 20552076231177144. Advance online publication. DOI: 10.1177/20552076231177144 PMID: 37252257

Sundaram, A., & Radha, P. (2019). Social media security and privacy protection concerning youths: "How to be safe, secure and social". *International Journal of Business Innovation and Research, 18*(4), 453–471. DOI: 10.1504/IJBIR.2019.098761

Svärd, P. (2017). *Enterprise content management, records management and information culture amidst e-government development*. Chandos Publishing.

Swinhoe, D. (2021). Apple officially opens data centre in China.

Tacchini, E., Ballarin, G., Della Vedova, M. L., Moret, S., & de Alfaro, L. (2017). Some like it hoax: Automated misinformation detection in social networks. *arXiv preprint arXiv:1704.07506*.

TAdvisor (2019). Law "about security of critical information infrastructure of the Russian Federation".

TAdvisor (2022a). The Ministry of Digital Industry is preparing a mechanism to counter the sale of rights to Russian software abroad.

TAdvisor (2022b). Register of Russian programs.

Taherdoost, H. (2024). *Digital transformation roadmap: From vision to execution.* CRC Press. DOI: 10.1201/9781003471226

Tang, C. (2016a). In-depth analysis - Great Firewall of China.

Tang, C. (2016b). LinkedIn blocked by Roskomnadzor.

Tan, T. M., & Saraniemi, S. (2023). Trust in blockchain-enabled exchanges: Future directions in blockchain marketing. *Journal of the Academy of Marketing Science*, *51*(4), 914–939. DOI: 10.1007/s11747-022-00889-0

Tariq, M. U. (2025). AI-Driven Personalized Learning: Revolutionizing Student Engagement and Teacher Efficiency in Education 5.0. In Mobo, F. (Ed.), *AI and Emerging Technologies for Emergency Response and Smart Cities* (pp. 75–96). IGI Global Scientific Publishing., DOI: 10.4018/979-8-3693-9770-1.ch004

Tariq, M. U. (2025). Balancing Flexibility and Precarity: Ethical Implications and Sustainable Practices in Global Gig Economies. In Doon, R. (Ed.), *Sustainability and Adaptability of Gig Economies in Global Business* (pp. 323–346). IGI Global Scientific Publishing., DOI: 10.4018/979-8-3693-9385-7.ch012

Tariq, M. U. (2025). Enhancing Cyber Resilience in Software Development: Integrating Secure Coding Practices and Cybersecurity Frameworks. In Shah, I., & Jhanjhi, N. (Eds.), *Navigating Cyber Threats and Cybersecurity in the Software Industry* (pp. 35–64). IGI Global Scientific Publishing., DOI: 10.4018/979-8-3693-6250-1.ch003

Tariq, M. U. (2025). Harnessing the Power of GANs and Meta-Learning for Few-Shot Image Generation. In Simaiya, S., Lilhore, U., Sharma, Y., & Kumar, S. (Eds.), *Exploring Generative Adversarial Networks and Meta-Learning Synergies* (pp. 301–324). IGI Global Scientific Publishing., DOI: 10.4018/979-8-3693-7575-4.ch012

Tariq, M. U. (2025). Innovative Mentoring Programs: Strategies for Success in Post-COVID-19 Education. In Putnam, J., VanValkenburgh Banks, J., & Brown, S. K. (Eds.), *Mentoring Students and Instructors for Retention and Success* (pp. 123–158). IGI Global Scientific Publishing., DOI: 10.4018/979-8-3693-7590-7.ch005

Taufick, R. D. (2021). The underdeterrence, underperformance response to privacy, data protection laws. *Technology in Society*, *67*, 101752. DOI: 10.1016/j.techsoc.2021.101752

Tawalbeh, L., Muheidat, F., Tawalbeh, M., & Quwaider, M. (2020). IoT privacy and security: Challenges and solutions. *Applied Sciences (Basel, Switzerland)*, *10*(12), 4102. DOI: 10.3390/app10124102

Tayal, S., Gupta, N., Gupta, P., Goyal, D., & Goyal, M. (2017). A review paper on network security and cryptography. *Advances in Computational Sciences and Technology, 10*(5), 1337–1343. ISSN: 0973-6107

Teletrust (2019). IT security made in Germany.

Thomas, T. K. (2014). National security council proposes 3-pronged plan to protect internet users.

Thota, A., Tilak, P., Ahluwalia, S., & Lohia, N. (2018). Misinformation detection: A deep learning approach. *SMU Data Science Review*, 1(3).

Tian, X. (2025). Unraveling the dynamics of password manager adoption: A deeper dive into critical factors. *Information and Computer Security*, *33*(1), 117–139. DOI: 10.1108/ICS-09-2023-0156

Tian, X., Chen, L., & Zhang, X. (2022). The role of privacy fatigue in privacy paradox: A PSM and heterogeneity analysis. *Applied Sciences (Basel, Switzerland)*, *12*(19), 9702. DOI: 10.3390/app12199702

Tiezzi, S. (2015). China (finally) admits to hacking.

Tikanmäki, I., & Ruoslahti, H. (2024). Insights on Human Factors Enhancing Cybersecurity. *Information & Security*, *56*(2), 145–158.

Timan T, Mann Z, (2021). "Data protection in the era of artificial intelligence: trends, existing solutions and recommendations for privacy-preserving technologies." The Elements of Big Data Value: Foundations of, 1-15. Doi: .DOI: 10.1007/978-3-030-86835-8_1

Tor (2019). Tor: Pluggable transports.

Totonchi, A. (2023). E-government Challenges in Developing Countries: Development of Iraqi e-government. *Journal of Computing Research and Innovation, 8*(2), 200–214.

Tran-Dang, H., & Kim, D. S. (2021). The physical internet in the era of digital transformation: Perspectives and open issues. *IEEE Access : Practical Innovations, Open Solutions, 9*, 111537–111548. DOI: 10.1109/ACCESS.2021.3131562

Tsatsou, P. (2022). Vulnerable people's digital inclusion: Intersectionality patterns and associated lessons. *Information Communication and Society, 25*(10), 1475–1494. DOI: 10.1080/1369118X.2021.1873402

Tully, J., Selzer, J., Phillips, J. P., O'Connor, P., & Dameff, C. (2020). Healthcare Challenges in the Era of Cybersecurity. *Health Security, 18*(3), 228–231. DOI: 10.1089/hs.2019.0123 PMID: 32559153

Tursunbayeva, A., Pagliari, C., Di Lauro, S., & Antonelli, G. (2022). The ethics of people analytics: Risks, opportunities and recommendations. *Personnel Review, 51*(5), 1423–1443. DOI: 10.1108/PR-12-2019-0680

Twizeyimana, J. D., & Andersson, A. (2019). The public value of E-Government–A literature review. *Government Information Quarterly, 36*(2), 167–178. DOI: 10.1016/j.giq.2019.01.001

Tyagi, A. K., Abraham, A., Kaklauskas, A., Sreenath, N., Rekha, G., & Malik, S. (2022). *Security and Privacy-Preserving Techniques in Wireless Robotics*. CRC Press., DOI: 10.1201/9781003156406

Ullah, A., Anwar, S. M., Li, J., Nadeem, L., Mahmood, T., Rehman, A., & Saba, T. (2024). Smart cities: The role of Internet of Things and machine learning in realizing a data-centric smart environment. *Complex & Intelligent Systems, 10*(1), 1607–1637. DOI: 10.1007/s40747-023-01175-4

UN (2019). Social indicators.

Vaddadi, S. A., & Vallabhaneni, R. (2023). *Utilizing AI and machine learning in cybersecurity for sustainable development through enhanced threat detection and mitigation*. International Journal of Sustainable Development and Green Economics., DOI: 10.4018/IJSDGG.2023.010205

Van Tran, D., Van Nguyen, P., Nguyen, A. T. C., Vrontis, D., & Dinh, P. U. (2024). Exploring the influence of government social media on cybersecurity compliance: Employee attitudes, motivation and behaviors. *Journal of Asia Business Studies, 18*(1), 204–223. DOI: 10.1108/JABS-09-2023-0343

VanLeeuwen, C. A., Veletsianos, G., Johnson, N., & Belikov, O. (2021). Never-ending repetitiveness, sadness, loss, and "juggling with a blindfold on:" Lived experiences of Canadian college and university faculty members during the COVID-19 pandemic. *British Journal of Educational Technology, 52*(4), 1431–1446. DOI: 10.1111/bjet.13065 PMID: 34230673

Vasudev, R., Harini, N., & Neethu, M. R. (2023). Multi-Factor Authentication System With ID Card Credentials For Secure Transactions. In *2023 14th International Conference on Computing Communication and Networking Technologies, ICCCNT 2023*. DOI: 10.1109/ICCCNT56998.2023.10308252

Vedova, D., Tacchini, M. L., Moret, E., Ballarin, S., Dipierro, G., & De Alfaro, M. (2018). *Automatic online misinformation detection combining content and social signals.*

Verma, A., & Gurtoo, A. (2024). *Evaluating global data policies around non-personal data on social and public good.* Digital Policy, Regulation and Governance., DOI: 10.1108/DPRG-03-2023-0044

Verstraete, M., & Zarsky, T. (2021). Optimizing breach notification. *U. Ill. L. Rev., 2021*(3), 551–604.

Vijayakumar, G., Rajkumar, M., Rajiv Chandar, N., Selvakumar, P., & Duraisamy, R. (2024). Muniyandi Rajkumar, Rajiv Chandar N, Selvakumar P and Ramesh Duraisamy, (2024). Environmentally friendly TDS removal from waste water by electrochemical ion exchange batch-type recirculation (EIR) technique. *Environmental Science. Water Research & Technology, 10*(4), 826–835. DOI: 10.1039/D3EW00793F

Viljoen, S. (2021). A relational theory of data governance. *The Yale Law Journal, 130*(6), 1314–1344. DOI: 10.2307/26796823

Volberda, H. W., Khanagha, S., Baden-Fuller, C., Mihalache, O. R., & Birkinshaw, J. (2021). Strategizing in a digital world: Overcoming cognitive barriers, reconfiguring routines and introducing new organizational forms. *Long Range Planning, 54*(5), 102110. DOI: 10.1016/j.lrp.2021.102110

Vosoughi, S., Roy, D., & Aral, S. (2018). The spread of true and false news online. *Science, 359*(6380), 1146–1151. DOI: 10.1126/science.aap9559 PMID: 29590045

Voss, W. G. (2021). "The CCPA and the GDPR are not the same: why you should understand both". CPI Antitrust Chronicle. DOI: 10.2139/ssrn.3912121

Wagner, B. (2018). Understanding Internet shutdowns: A case study from Pakistan. *International Journal of Communication, 12*(1), 22.

Wairagade, A. (2025). Role of Identity and Access Management in Corporate Management. In *Corporate Management in the Digital Age* (pp. 397–424). IGI Global., DOI: 10.4018/979-8-3693-8412-1.ch014

Wang, W. Y. (2017). Liar, liar pants on fire: A new benchmark dataset for misinformation detection.

Wang, B., Zhou, H., Li, X., Yang, G., Zheng, P., Song, C., Yuan, Y., Wuest, T., Yang, H., & Wang, L. (2024). Human Digital Twin in the context of Industry 5.0. *Robotics and Computer-integrated Manufacturing*, *85*, 102626. DOI: 10.1016/j.rcim.2023.102626

Wang, S., Asif, M., Shahzad, M. F., & Ashfaq, M. (2024). Data privacy and cybersecurity challenges in the digital transformation of the banking sector. *Computers & Security*, *124*, 103134. DOI: 10.1016/j.cose.2024.104051

Wang, Z., Li, M., Lu, J., & Cheng, X. (2022). Business Innovation based on artificial intelligence and Blockchain technology. *Information Processing & Management*, *59*(1), 102759. DOI: 10.1016/j.ipm.2021.102759

Wang, Z., Zhu, H., & Sun, L. (2021). Social Engineering in Cybersecurity: Effect Mechanisms, Human Vulnerabilities and Attack Methods. *IEEE Access : Practical Innovations, Open Solutions*, *9*, 11895–11910. DOI: 10.1109/ACCESS.2021.3051633

Wan, S., Lin, H., Gan, W., & Chen, J. (2024). Web3: The next internet revolution. *IEEE Internet of Things Journal*, *11*(2), 1–14. DOI: 10.1109/JIOT.2023.3235512

Ward, A. (2019). New Senate Intelligence report shows "extensive" Russia 2016 election interference.

Wardhono, W. S., Priandani, N. D., Ananta, M. T., Brata, K. C., & Tolle, H. (2018). End-to-end privacy protection for Facebook mobile chat based on AES with multi-layered MD5. *Int. J. Interact. Mob. Technol.*, *12*(1), 160. DOI: 10.3991/ijim.v12i1.7472

Warkentin, M., & Orgeron, C. (2020). Using the security triad to assess blockchain technology in public sector applications. *International Journal of Information Management*, *52*, 102090. DOI: 10.1016/j.ijinfomgt.2020.102090

Watney, M. (2024). Privacy and personal information protection by social media companies in an AI era. *European Conference on Social Media*, 11(1), 266–272. DOI: 10.34190/ecsm.11.1.2089

WebproNews (2012). Does China have an internet kill switch? • Wei, Y. (2018). Chinese data localization law: Comprehensive but ambiguous.

Weickert, T. D., Joinson, A., & Craggs, B. (2023). Is cybersecurity research missing a trick? Integrating insights from the psychology of habit into research and practice. *Computers & Security, 128*, 103130. DOI: 10.1016/j.cose.2023.103130

Weth, C. V. D., Abdul, A., Fan, S., & Kankanhalli, M. (2020). Helping users tackle algorithmic threats on social media: A multimedia research agenda. *arXiv*. https://arxiv.org/abs/2012.05701

Whittaker, Z. (2021, September 29). Russian authorities arrest cybersecurity giant Group-IB's CEO on treason charges. *TechCrunch*.https://techcrunch.com/2021/09/29/russian-authorities-arrest-cybersecurity-giant-group-ibs-ceo-on-treason-charges/

Wilner, A. S., Luce, H., Ouellet, E., Williams, O., & Costa, N. (2021). From public health to cyber hygiene: Cybersecurity and Canada's healthcare sector. *International Journal (Toronto, Ont.), 76*(4), 522–543. DOI: 10.1177/00207020211067946

Wilson (2022). Digital sovereignty on paper: Russian ambitious laws conflict with its tech dependence. https://tinyurl.com/2tnakjr8.

Wilson, S. (2020). The pandemic, the acceleration of digital transformation and the impact on cyber security. *Computer Fraud & Security, 2020*(12), 13–15. DOI: 10.1016/S1361-3723(20)30128-7

Wong, J. (2016). *Almost all the traffic to fake news sites is from Facebook, new data show*. The Medium.

World, S. C. (2016, September 29). New NATO report claims China's cyber-space influence continues to grow. https://www.scworld.com/news/new-nato-report-claims-chinas-cyber-space-influence-continues-to-grow.

Wu, P. F. (2019). The privacy paradox in the context of online social networking: A self-identity perspective. *Journal of the Association for Information Science and Technology, 70*(3), 207–217. DOI: 10.1002/asi.24113

Wylde, V., Rawindaran, N., Lawrence, J., Balasubramanian, R., Prakash, E., Jayal, A., Khan, I., Hewage, C., & Platts, J. (2022). Cybersecurity, data privacy and blockchain: A review. *SN Computer Science, 3*(2), 1–14. DOI: 10.1007/s42979-022-01020-4 PMID: 35036930

Xinhua (2023). China spending on research and development hits 3 trln yuan in 2022.

Yang, Z., & Couts, A. (2025). A US TikTok ban could wipe out other ByteDance apps too. Wired. https://www.wired.com/story/bytedance-tiktok-ban-lemon8-capcut-gauthai-app-stores/

Yang, P., Xiong, N., & Ren, J. (2020). Data Security and Privacy Protection for Cloud Storage: A Survey. *IEEE Access : Practical Innovations, Open Solutions*, *8*, 131723–131740. DOI: 10.1109/ACCESS.2020.3009876

Yang, R., Chen, X., & Fu, S. (2023). Unlocking privacy paradox in social media from a configurational perspective. *Proceedings of the Association for Information Science and Technology*, *60*(1), 1197–1199. DOI: 10.1002/pra2.990

Yarovoy, T. S., Kozyrieva, O. V., Bielska, T. V., Zhuk, I. I., & Mokhova, I. L. (2020). The E-government development in ensuring the country financial and information security. Financial and credit activity problems of theory and practice, 2(33), 268-275.

Yeoh, W., Liu, M., Shore, M., & Jiang, F. (2023). Zero trust cybersecurity: Critical success factors and A maturity assessment framework. *Computers & Security*, *124*, 103159. DOI: 10.1016/j.cose.2023.103412

Yeoh, W., Wang, S., Popovič, A., & Chowdhury, N. H. (2022). A systematic synthesis of critical success factors for cybersecurity. *Computers & Security*, *122*, 102744. DOI: 10.1016/j.cose.2022.102724

Yerby, J., Koohang, A., & Paliszkiewicz, J. (2019). Social media privacy concerns and risk beliefs. *Online J. Appl. Knowl. Manag.*, *7*(1), 1–13. DOI: 10.36965/OJAKM.2019.7(1)1-13

Yeung, K., & Bygrave, L. A. (2022). Demystifying the modernized European data protection regime: Cross-disciplinary insights from legal and regulatory governance scholarship. *Regulation & Governance*, *16*(2), 257–275. DOI: 10.1111/rego.12401

Yu, L., Zhao, Y., & Chin, W. S. (2019). Extracting typhoon disaster information from VGI based on machine learning. *Journal of Marine Science and Engineering*, *7*(9), 318. DOI: 10.3390/jmse7090318

Zabalawi, I., Kordahji, H., & Aftimos, S. (2024). Digital Transformation in Universities: Strategic Framework, Implementation Tools, and Leadership. In *Higher Education in the Arab World: Digital Transformation* (pp. 145–210). Springer Nature Switzerland. DOI: 10.1007/978-3-031-70779-7_8

Zavolokina, L., Bauer-Hänsel, I., Hacker, J., & Schwabe, G. (2024). Organizing for value creation in blockchain information systems. *Information and Organization*, *34*(3), 100522. DOI: 10.1016/j.infoandorg.2024.100522

Zhang, M. and Judd, D. (2023). China says it hasn't issued any ban on Apple's iPhone — CNN Business.

Zhang, C., Gupta, A., Kauten, C., Deokar, A. V., & Qin, X. (2019). Detecting fake news for reducing misinformation risks using analytics approaches. *European Journal of Operational Research*, *279*(3), 1036–1052. DOI: 10.1016/j.ejor.2019.06.022

Zhang, Q., Sun, X., & Zhang, M. (2022). Data Matters: A Strategic Action Framework for Data Governance. *Information & Management*, *59*(4), 103642. DOI: 10.1016/j.im.2022.103642

Zhou, X., & Zafarani, R. (2018). A survey of fake news: Fundamental theories, detection methods, and opportunities. *arXiv preprint arXiv:1812.00315*, 1–40.

Zhou, L., Diro, A., Saini, A., Kaisar, S., & Hiep, P. C. (2024). Leveraging zero knowledge proofs for blockchain-based identity sharing: A survey of advancements, challenges and opportunities. *Journal of Information Security and Applications*, *80*, 103678. DOI: 10.1016/j.jisa.2023.103678

Zhu, G., Li, F., Yan, Y., & Guenis, H. (2024). Privacy paradox resolution in mHealth: The moderating effect of rationality degree. *Journal of Enterprise Information Management*, *37*(1), 55–75. DOI: 10.1108/JEIM-03-2023-0119

Zhukova, C. (2018). Russian software is disconnected from abroad.

Zimmermann, V., Schäfer, S., Dürmuth, M., & Marky, K. (2025). Authenticate as You Go: From Exploring Smart Home Authentication with Daily Objects to Authenticating with Primary Tasks. *ACM Transactions on Computer-Human Interaction*, *32*(2), 1–69. DOI: 10.1145/3702318

Zipperle, M., Becherer, M., Zhang, Y., Chang, E., Dillon, T., & Karduck, A. (2024). Enabling Digital Transformation with Sustainability Criteria through Resilient Cybersecurity: Challenges and Opportunities.

Zouai, M., Naidji, I., Tibermacine, A., & Aloui, A. (2024). The evolution of social media: Implications for privacy and personal data. *STUDIES IN ENGINEERING AND EXACT SCIENCES*, *5*(2), e6074. DOI: 10.54021/seesv5n2-050

ZTE-PSIRT (2024). ZTE PSIRT.

Żurawski, S., Ciekanowski, Z., Pauliuchuk, Y., & Ratter, E. (2025). The Impact of Supply Chain Security Management on the Functioning of Modern Organizations. *European Research Studies*, *28*(1), 44–56. DOI: 10.35808/ersj/3889

Zykov, V. (2017). A national internet filtering system will appear in Russia.

About the Contributors

Saqib Saeed received the B.Sc. degree (Hons.) in computer science from International Islamic University Islamabad, Pakistan, in 2001, the M.Sc. degree in software technology from the Stuttgart Technology University of Applied Sciences, Germany, in 2003, and the Ph.D. degree in information systems from the University of Siegen, Germany, in 2012. He is currently an Associate Professor with the Department of Computer Information Systems, Imam Abdulrahman Bin Faisal University, Dammam, Saudi Arabia. He is also a Certified Software Quality Engineer from the American Society of Quality. His research interests include human-centered computing, data visualization and analytics, software engineering, information systems management, and digital business transformation.

Shahzaib Tahir is an academician and a Serial Entrepreneur. He did his PostDoc and PhD in Information Engineering from City, University of London, UK and MS in Information Security from NUST. He enjoys doing research in the domains of Cloud Security, privacy-preserving techniques and applied cryptography. He is an HEC Approved PhD supervisor. He has published several research papers in journals/ conferences of repute and has been granted US and UK Patents in cloud security.

***

Muhammad Adnan has received his Master's Degree in Electrical Engineering from Fast National University Islamabad, and a Bachelor's Degree in Electronics Engineering from the International Islamic University Islamabad. His research interests include Embedded Systems, Machine Learning, Artificial Intelligence and Information Security.

Shaik Ahammad is a commerce lecturer in Kavitha Memorial Degree and PG College.

Muhammad Faisal Amjad is a senior member of the Institute of Electrical and Electronics Engineers (IEEE), an Associate Professor and the Head of Department of Information Security, National University of Sciences and Technology (NUST), Pakistan. He is a Director of National Cyber Security Auditing and Evaluation Lab (NCSAEL) and the Co-Founder and CEO of Lynx Information Security (Pvt) Ltd. Dr Faisal received his PhD degree in Computer Science from University of Central Florida USA in 2015. He has served as a Research Scientist at the University of Nevada Reno, USA. He has extensive experience of cyber security research as well as consultancy with the industry and government agencies. His current research focusses on the application of machine learning and game theoretic techniques in the domains of IoT and network security and malware analysis. He specializes in dynamic spectrum access and defense against security vulnerabilities in Cognitive Radio Networks as well as wireless sensor and ad hoc networks. Dr. Faisal is recipient of the prestigious Fulbright Fellowship under the Institute of International Education 2010, USA, President's Gold Medal for Top honors in Masters' program 2004 and NUST-MCS Best Researcher Award 2020.

Nilesh Anute is an Associate Professor at Sri Balaji University, Pune. With a strong academic background and extensive teaching experience, he specializes in areas such as marketing, strategic management, and business analytics. Dr. Anute is known for his dynamic teaching style and commitment to fostering industry-academia collaboration. He has contributed to various research publications and actively participates in academic conferences and seminars. His dedication to student development and academic excellence makes him a respected figure in the field of management education.

Pakalapati Arpitha is a Commerce lecturer in TGSWRDC(W), Vikarabad, Hyderabad, Telangana, India.

Sanaa Ashiq is currently serving as a Lecturer in the Department of Software Engineering at the National University of Modern Languages (NUML), Rawalpindi, Pakistan. She holds a Bachelor's degree in Information Technology and a Master's degree in Software Engineering. Areas of focus include software quality assurance, software engineering education, artificial intelligence, and cybersecurity. Responsible for teaching undergraduate courses, supervising final year projects, and contributing to curriculum development and academic research. She is committed to bridge the gap between theoretical foundations and practical applications in software engineering

Shiney Chib is a distinguished academician in the field of Management. She is currently serving as a faculty member in the Department of Management at Datta

Meghe Institute of Management Studies, located in Nagpur, Maharashtra. With her expertise and dedication, Dr. Chib contributes significantly to the academic and professional development of her students, while actively engaging in research and institutional activities.

Prashant Bhavarlal Chordiya is an Assistant Professor at Savitribai Phule Pune University, Pune. With a strong academic background and a passion for research and teaching, He has contributed significantly to his field through scholarly publications, participation in academic conferences, and student mentorship. Dr. Chordiya is known for his dedication to academic excellence and his commitment to fostering a dynamic learning environment.

Noor Aldossary holds a Master of Science in Information Systems and Data Analytics from Imam Abdulrahman Bin Faisal University and a Bachelor's degree in Management Information Systems from Jubail University College. She has professional experience in ERP systems, cybersecurity governance, and digital transformation. Noor completed a Tamheer training program at SABIC's Center of Excellence, where she contributed to AI tool testing, process improvement, and procurement system optimization. Her research interests include machine learning, data analytics, digital transformation, and business intelligence applications.

Md Mehedi Hasan Emon is a research practitioner in Business and Management, with specialized in Supply Chain Management, Digital Transformation, Marketing, Information Systems, and Educational Technology (Edutech). His work bridges a diverse range of domains including Artificial Intelligence in Business, Human-Computer Interaction, Cognitive Behaviour, E-commerce, and Smart Logistics. His research extensively explores the integration of emerging technologies in business ecosystems focusing on AI-driven innovation, behavioral responses to technology adoption, and digital marketing strategies. He has also contributed significantly to sustainability-focused fields such as GreenTech, Green Finance, Renewable Energy, and Blockchain-enabled financial innovation. Additionally, his work in Smart Cities and IoT adoption emphasizes the importance of user trust, security, and operational efficiency. Emon has authored numerous peer-reviewed publications on topics including AI adoption intention, supply chain visibility, digital learning acceptance, and crisis-resilient supply chains. Many of his studies adopt behavioral and cognitive perspectives to understand how professionals and consumers interact with technology highlighting the psychological and user-centric aspects of digital transformation. He has participated in several research initiatives funded by the University Grants Commission of Bangladesh and the European Union. His work aligns closely with the United Nations Sustainable Development Goals (SDGs), particularly in areas such as poverty reduction, access to quality education, clean and affordable energy, inclusive economic growth, sustainable industrialization, responsible consumption, climate resilience, and ocean sustainability. His work also reflects a commitment to reducing inequalities and fostering international partnerships for sustainable development. In addition to his research contributions, he serves as a peer reviewer for several high-impact academic journals and is widely recognized for promoting academic rigor and ethical scholarship. As a prolific author, he continues to shape the discourse on sustainability, innovation, and digital advancement through his research, writing, and knowledge dissemination.

G. Gopalakrishnan is a seasoned academic leader and the current Director of the Balaji Institute of Management and Human Resource Development (BIMHRD), under the aegis of Sri Balaji University, Pune. With a rich blend of academic and industry experience, Dr. Gopalakrishnan has played a pivotal role in shaping future leaders through innovative management education and holistic student development. His expertise spans across strategic management, human resources, and leadership development. Under his guidance, BIMHRD has consistently delivered academic excellence and industry-ready professionals.

K Deepthi Reddy received her M.Tech in Computer Science and Engineering from JNTUH, India and currently pursuing his Ph.D. in Informatics, Department of Computer Science and Engineering from SRM UNIVERSITY, India. she is currently working as an Sr.Assistant Professor in the Department of Computer Science and Engineering at CVR College of Engineering, Hyderabad, India. research interests are image processing deep learning programming and machine learning.

Jasbir Kaur is the Director of GNIMS Business School, Mumbai, where she leads academic and strategic initiatives with a vision to foster innovation, leadership, and industry-relevant education. With over two decades of experience in management education, Dr. Kaur is recognized for her expertise in organizational behavior, leadership development, and academic administration. Under her leadership, GNIMS has strengthened its industry collaborations, research culture, and student-centric learning approach. A passionate educator and thought leader, she continues to mentor future business professionals while contributing to the academic community through research and institutional development.

Shaheen Layaq is a Computer science Lecturer in Singareni Collierie's Women's Degree & PG College, Kothagudem, Telangana, India.

T.C. Manjunath was born on 6th February 1967. He did his BE from RV College of Engg. in 1989, ME in Robotics & Automation from LD College of

Engg. in 1992 with First Rank and PhD in Systems & Control Engg. from IIT Bombay in the year 2007. He is currently working as the Dean Research R D and as Professor in the Dept. of Computer Science & Engineering with specialization in IoT, Cyber Security & Blockchain Technology in Rajarajeswari College of Engineering, Bengaluru, Karnataka. He has completed B.E. Degree from R.V. College of Engg., M.E. Govt.'s LD College of Engg., Gujarat Univ., Ahmedabad in First Rank and Ph.D. in Systems and Control Engineering from the Indian Institute of Technology Bombay IIT Bombay He has got a teaching academic, research and administrative experience of more than 35+ years 10 years as Principal, 8 years as HoD rest as faculty and has published more than 1200+ research papers in various national & international journals and conferences, with 175+ patents, 25 book-chapters, 25 awards and also published 25 text books in various field of science, engineering and technology, completed projects worth Rs. 9 Crores till date apart from guiding 10 PhD scholars. He is a member of 30 Professional Society Chapters and is a fellow of IE, IETE, AMIEE and a chartered engineer. He got the best research scholar award in 2006 in IIT Bombay amongst all the research scholars of the institute. He has got 10 awards in academics and research activities.

Md. Mazid-Ul-Haque is working as an Assistant Professor in the Department of Computer Science at American International University- Bangladesh. He has completed both his Master of Science in Computer Science degree and Bachelor of Science in Computer Science and Engineering degree from American International University- Bangladesh. He did his HSC at Notre Dame College, Dhaka. Previously, he worked as a Lecturer and as an Instructor in the Department of Computer Science at American International University- Bangladesh. His research interests include ML, Wireless Communication, WSN, etc. He was born in Kushtia. He has a strong passion and dedication for teaching and research work. He believes in hard work and sincerity for achieving life goals. Apart from teaching, his hobbies include playing football, traveling, watching movies, and reading newspapers.

P. Selvakumar is currently an Associate Professor in the Department of Science and Humanities at Nehru Institute of Technology, Coimbatore, Tamil Nadu, India. Prior to joining Nehru Institute of Technology, he held positions as an Assistant Professor in the Department of Science and Humanities various engineering colleges in Coimbatore, Tamil Nadu, India, spanning from 2011 to 2023. Dr.P. Selvakumar's academic and research interests lie primarily in the field of phytochemistry. He has made significant contributions to his field, with an impressive record that includes 30 journal publications, 12 patents, and 20 conference papers. Additionally, he has organized 5 seminars and conferences, further demonstrating his commitment to academic and scientific exchange. Throughout his career, Dr. P.Selvakumar has been recognized for his dedication and excellence in teaching, having been honored with several awards, including the Best Teacher Awards. He holds a prominent position in the academic community, contributing actively to research.

Ravikumar is an experienced educator with 11+ years of teaching in Computer Science across India and overseas. Currently an Assistant Professor at Marwadi University, Rajkot, he specializes in Advanced Java, Machine Learning, Data Science, and AI. He holds a Mini MBA from the Swiss eLearning Institute (2015), an M.E. in Computer Science Engineering from VMRF University (2013), and a B.E. from Anna University (2010). Completed PhD at Amity University, Jaipur, he is dedicated to research, professional development, and advancing education through technology.

Imran Rashid did his B.E. in Electrical (Telecomm) Engineering from National University of Sciences and Technology, Pakistan, in 1999. He received his M.Sc. degree in Telecomm Engineering (Optical Communication) from D.T.U Denmark in 2004 and his Ph.D. in Mobile Communication from University of Manchester, UK in 2011. He has no of Cyber Security Certifications at his credit. Currently, he is working as Professor at MCS, National University of Sciences and Technology, Pakistan. His research interests are Mobile and Wireless Communication, MIMO Systems, Compressed Sensing for MIMO OFDM systems, Massive MIMO Systems, M2M for Mobile systems, Cognitive Radio Networks, Cyber Security and Information Assurance.

Aarthi S is a dedicated Assistant Professor in Computer Science with over six years of teaching experience. She is currently pursuing her Ph.D. at Marwadi University, Gujarat, and holds an M.Phil. and MCA from Bharathiar University, Tamil Nadu. Throughout her academic career, Aarthi has specialized in programming languages such as C++, Java, and C, and contributed to research in recommender systems and AI-related data privacy. She has published journal articles, contributed to book chapters, and actively participated in technical workshops. Known for her student mentorship and engagement in academic events, Aarthi remains committed to fostering innovation and excellence in computer science education.

Guru Basava Aradhya S is a seasoned academician with 17 years of experience in management education. He currently serves as the HoD & Professor at Dayananda Sagar Business Academy, Bangalore. He holds a Ph.D. in Management and has mentored five Ph.D. scholars. His expertise includes HR, marketing, and business analytics. A prolific researcher, he has published in SCOPUS, ABDC, and UGC CARE journals. He has organized numerous international conferences and contributed to NAAC and NBA accreditations. His industry collaborations include faculty exchange programs and consultancy projects. Passionate about academia, he actively fosters innovation, research, and student development.

Valisher Sapayev Odilbek Uglu working as Associate Professor at Department of General Professional Subjects, Mamun university, Khiva, Uzbekistan

Madeeha Saqib is currently a lecturer with the Department of Computer Information Systems, Imam Abdulrahman Bin Faisal University, Dammam, Saudi Arabia. Her research interests include technology management, organizational management, and organizational communication.

Binastya Anggara Sekti has been a Lecturer at the faculty of Computer Science, at Esa Unggul University, Jakarta since 2016 and is active in the Artificial Intelligence and Information Security Study Group. He is a graduate of Informatics Engineering from the Bandung Institute of Technology and achieved a Master's Degree from Trisakti University, Jakarta. Before as a Lecture, he was an IT practitioner at several companies in Jakarta for more than 25 years. Some of the projects that have been completed are building Data Centers at Internet Service Providers . He also finished many IT projects.

Sudarshan Seshanna B.A. (Hons.), St. Stephen's College, University of Delhi, Delhi; M.A., Jawaharlal Nehru University, New Delhi; M. Phil. and Ph. D., University of Geneva, Geneva, Switzerland; Dip. Int. Trade, Symbiosis Institute of Management Studies, Pune. Sudarshan Seshanna, Ph. D., is Professor in Marketing, CMS Business School, Jain University, Bangalore and teaches marketing at the postgraduate level. An alumnus of the St. Stephen's College, University of Delhi and University of Geneva, Switzerland, he has over 28 years of experience in teaching, research, consulting, and publishing with career stints in in leading business schools; National Council of Applied Economic Research, New Delhi; Encyclopedia Britannica, Gurgaon; and Oxford University Press, New Delhi. Sudarshan is a regular academic reviewer with the American Marketing Association, USA.

Mohit Sharma is a research scholar at the Institute of Management Studies and Research, Maharshi Dayanand University, Rohtak, Haryana, India. His research focuses on the dynamic relationship between brand image and purchase intentions, particularly in the context of brand extensions within the FMCG sector. Mohit actively engages in bibliometric research, analyzing publication trends and identifying research gaps in his area of interest. He has co-authored several scholarly works and continues to contribute to the academic community.

Anand Singh is working in the Department of Computer Engineering at Marwadi University, Rajkot, India.

Abduvali Sottarov is working in Department of Information Technology and Exact Sciences at Termez University of Economics and Service, Termez, Uzbekistan.

Hasan Tahir is an Assistant Professor and Head of Department Information Security at School of Electrical Engineering and Computer Science (SEECS), NUST. He holds a PhD in Information Security from the University of Essex UK. He obtained his BE in Software Engineering from Bahria University, Islamabad, Pakistan and MS in Software Engineering from College of E&ME, NUST. Dr Hasan was the recipient of the University of Essex Doctoral Scholarship award. He specializes in Computer Security and IoT. He actively researches applications of cryptography in one to one and group settings. His primary area of research is the use of Physically Unclonable Functions for securing group of devices. Dr Hasan Tahir teaches courses related to applied cryptography, cyber security, information security management, cloud computing security, software engineering, software requirements analysis and design. Dr Hasan has served as a committee member in many renowned IEEE conferences. He is a Senior Member of IEEE.

Muhammad Usman Tariq has more than 16+ year's experience in industry and academia. He has authored more than 200+ research articles, 110+ case studies, 150+ book chapters and several books other than 4 patents. He is founder and CEO of The Case HQ, a unique repository for courses, narrative and video case studies. He has been working as a consultant and trainer for industries representing six sigma, quality, health and safety, environmental systems, project management, and information security standards. His work has encompassed sectors in aviation, manufacturing, food, hospitality, education, finance, research, software and transportation. He has diverse and significant experience working with accreditation agencies of ABET, ACBSP, AACSB, WASC, CAA, EFQM and NCEAC. Additionally, Dr. Tariq has operational experience in incubators, research labs, government research projects, private sector startups, program creation and management at various industrial and academic levels. He is Certified Higher Education Teacher from Harvard University, USA, Certified Online Educator from HMBSU, Certified Six Sigma Master Black Belt and has been awarded PFHEA, SFSEDA, SMIEEE, and CMBE.

Qamar Yasmeen is a PhD in Biochemistry and currently serves as Associate Professor at Niazi Medical and Dental College. She has a strong academic and research background with a passion for teaching. She is actively involved in curriculum design and academic development. Her work reflects a commitment to scientific advancement and public awareness on social media.

Index

A

B

C

D

R

S

U